national
STATISTICS

UK2003

The Official Yearbook of the United Kingdom of
Great Britain and Northern Ireland

London: TSO

Contact points
We welcome readers' comments and suggestions on this publication:
e-mail   uk.yearbook@ons.gov.uk
telephone +44 (0)20 7533 5778
or write to the Editor, UK Yearbook,
Office for National Statistics, Room B5/02,
1 Drummond Gate, London SW1V 2QQ

For general enquiries, contact the National Statistics Public Enquiry Service:
e-mail: info@statistics.gov.uk
telephone: +44 (0)845 601 3034 (English)
             +44 (0)1633 813381 (Welsh)
             +44 (0)1633 812399 (Minicom)
fax: +44 (0)1633 652747
letters: National Statistics Public Enquiry
             Service
             Cardiff Road
             Newport
             NP10 8XG

You can also find National Statistics on the internet – go to **www.statistics.gov.uk**

This report is available on the web
www.statistics.gov.uk/yearbook

About the Office for National Statistics
The Office for National Statistics (ONS) is the government agency responsible for compiling, analysing and disseminating many of the United Kingdom's economic, social and demographic statistics, including the retail prices index, trade figures and labour market data, as well as the periodic census of the population and health statistics. It is also the agency that administers the statutory registration of births, marriages and deaths in England and Wales. The Director of ONS is the National Statistician and the Registrar General for England and Wales.

A National Statistics publication
National Statistics are produced to high professional standards set out in the National Statistics Code of Practice. They undergo regular quality assurance reviews to ensure they meet customer needs. They are produced free from any political interference.

Contents

Contributors

UK 2003 was researched, written and edited by a combination of in-house and freelance authors.

Authors Tajbee Ahmed
Carl Bird
Ben Bradford
Simon Burtenshaw
John Collis
David Gardener
Richard German
David Harper
Steve Howell
Henry Langley
Hannah McConnell
Oliver Metcalf
Shiva Satkunam
Conor Shipsey
Derek Tomlin
Anna Upson

Charts Adkins Design

Colour pages Guy Warren

Cover Andy Leach

Index Richard German

Maps Alistair Dent
Ray Martin

Picture research Frances Riddelle

Production Kate Myers
Sharon Adhikari
John Chrzczonowicz
Sunita Dedi
Joseph Goldstein

Proof readers Richard German
Rosemary Hamilton
Jane Howard
Jeff Probst

Typesetting Spire Origination, Norwich

Editors Carol Summerfield
Jill Barelli
Henry Langley
Penny Babb

Acknowledgements

UK 2003 has been compiled with the help of around 250 organisations, including many government departments and agencies. The editors would like to thank all the people from these organisations who have taken so much time and care to ensure that the book's high standards of accuracy have been maintained. Their contributions and comments have been extremely valuable.

Cover photographs
Stonehenge, Edinburgh and Giant's Causeway © britainonview.com
Cardiff Millennium Stadium © Duncan Miller/Photolibrary Wales

Preface

UK 2003 is the 54th edition of the annual reference book on the United Kingdom. Drawing on a wide range of official and other authoritative sources, it provides a factual and up-to-date overview of Great Britain and Northern Ireland, including the main aspects of government policy, how services are provided, and the organisations involved. Social, economic, cultural, environmental and foreign affairs are all covered. The Yearbook is a widely used work of reference, both in the United Kingdom and overseas, where it is an important element of the information service provided by British diplomatic posts.

This edition has been fully updated and revised. The photographs provide a record of events during the year, including the Queen's Golden Jubilee celebrations. The text indicates some of the ways the UK has changed during the reign. Fifty years ago – having established the NHS and overhauled the social security system – post-war governments were turning their attention to other issues such as the national housing shortage. Television was then in its infancy. Tower blocks, motorways and out-of-town shopping centres were still unknown in the UK.

The following decades have seen steadily improving living standards and a major expansion of higher education and international travel. Children born today will live about nine years longer than those born in 1952. Working lives and leisure activities have been transformed by technological change and the UK has become a multicultural society in which ownership of home and car are the norm rather than the exception.

Many of these changes are documented in this edition. There is also a reminder of some of the major scientific advances made in the UK over the half century.

Notes and definitions

1. The full title of the UK is 'the United Kingdom of Great Britain and Northern Ireland'. 'Great Britain' comprises England, Wales and Scotland.

2. Statistics in this book apply to the UK as a whole wherever possible. However, data are not always available on a comparable basis, so in some areas information has been given for one or more of the component parts of the UK. Geographical coverage is clearly indicated.

3. Every effort is made to ensure that the information given in UK 2003 is accurate at the time of going to press. The text is generally based on information available up to the end of August 2002. Data for the most recent year may be provisional or estimated.

4. The mid-2001 population estimates quoted in chapters 1–5 and 9 are based on the results of the 2001 Census. ONS is due to publish final revised mid-year estimates for 1982 to 2000 in early 2003. Other data – for example birth rates and death rates – will also be revised in due course to take account of the Census-based population estimates.

5. Figures given in tables and charts may not always sum to the totals shown because of rounding.

6. Information about particular companies has been taken from company reports and news releases, or from other publicly available sources. No information about individual companies has been taken from returns submitted in response to ONS statistical inquiries: these remain entirely confidential.

Symbols and conventions
1 billion means 1,000 million.

Financial and academic years are shown as 2001/02.

Data covering more than one year such as 1999, 2000 and 2001 are shown as 1999–2001.

In tables:
n/a means not available.
–   means zero or negligible (less than half the final digit shown)
.   means not applicable.

Units of measurement
Area
1 hectare (ha) = 10,000 sq metres = 2.4711 acres.
1 square kilometre = 100 hectares
= 0.3861 square miles.

Length
1 centimetre (cm) = 10 millimetres (mm)
= 0.3937 inches.
1 metre (m) = 1,000 millimetres = 3.2808 feet (ft).
1 kilometre (km) = 1,000 metres = 0.6214 miles.

Mass
1 kilogram (kg) = 2.2046 pounds (lb).
1 tonne (t) = 1,000 kilograms = 0.9842 long tons (UK).

Volume
1 litre (l) = 1.7598 UK pints = 0.2200 UK gallons.
1 cubic metre = 1,000 litres.

SI prefixes
hecto (h)	= 100	= 10^2
kilo (k)	= 1,000	= 10^3
mega (M)	= 1 million	= 10^6
giga (G)	= 1 billion	= 10^9
tera (T)	= 1 thousand billion	= 10^{12}

1 The United Kingdom

The United Kingdom of Great Britain and Northern Ireland (UK) was formed in 1801 and constitutes the greater part of the British Isles. The largest of the islands is Great Britain, which comprises England, Scotland and Wales. The next largest is Ireland, comprising Northern Ireland, which is part of the UK, and, in the south, the Irish Republic.

Western Scotland is fringed by the large island chains known as the Inner and Outer Hebrides, and to the north of the Scottish mainland are the Orkney and Shetland Islands. All these, along with the Isle of Wight, Anglesey and the Isles of Scilly, have administrative ties with the mainland, but the Isle of Man in the Irish Sea and the Channel Islands between Great Britain and France are largely self-governing, and are not part of the UK (see page 6).

Physical features
The UK has a varied geological structure giving rise to distinctive features in the landscape. The clays and sandstones of the south east produce the fertile soil characteristic of the farmland found in parts of East Anglia and the London Basin, while the chalk which underlies the gently rolling hills in Sussex and Kent is exposed as sheer cliffs on the coast at places such as Beachy Head and Dover.

Jurassic limestone stretches from Dorset and Devon to Yorkshire and includes the Cleveland Hills, Lincoln Edge, the Northampton Uplands and the Cotswolds. A typical feature of this type of landscape is that fields are separated not by hedges but by walls built, like many of the houses in the region, of local stone.

Carboniferous limestone lies further to the north and forms the Pennine Chain, popularly known as the 'backbone of England'. In the central Pennines there are extensive platforms of almost pure limestone, notably around Malham Tarn, where the rock is so porous that despite heavy rainfall there is virtually no surface water as the rain immediately soaks through to the subterranean caverns which predominate in the area.

The metamorphic rocks (old grits and slates) found in much of Wales, the Lake District and southern Scotland produce the austerely wild scenery, characteristic of these parts of the UK, while much of the Scottish Highlands and Outer Hebrides is formed of Britain's oldest rocks (ancient gneiss and schists), created up to 2,600 million years ago.

England
England is a country of mostly low hills and plains with a 3,200 km coastline cut into by bays, coves and estuaries. Upland regions in the north include the Pennine Chain, which splits northern England into western and eastern sectors. The north-west is the home of the Lake District, which includes the highest point in England, Scafell Pike at 978 m, while the north-east includes the rugged landscape of the Yorkshire moors.

Northern Ireland
Northern Ireland's north-eastern coast, at its nearest point, is separated from Scotland by a stretch of water – the North Channel – only 21 km wide. It has a 488 km border with the Irish Republic, forming the UK's only land boundary with another Member State of the European Union.

The landscape consists mainly of low hill country, although there are two significant mountain ranges: the Mournes, extending from South Down to Strangford Lough in the east, and the Sperrins, reaching through the north-western boundaries of Northern Ireland.

On the Antrim coast near Bushmills is the Giant's Causeway. At this World Heritage Site there are almost 40,000 massive basalt columns which formed around 60 million years ago when volcanic rock intruded into the surrounding chalk, cooled and slowly solidified into huge polygonal columns, mainly hexagonal. The longest columns are around 12 m high.

Lough Neagh is the largest freshwater lake in the British Isles and one of the largest in Europe, covering an area of 382 sq km.

Scotland

Scotland, the most northerly of the four parts of the United Kingdom, covers about one-third of the island of Great Britain. Bounded by England to the south, the Atlantic Ocean to the west and north, and the North Sea to the east, Scotland is a country with large areas of unspoilt and wild landscape, and many of the UK's mountains, including its highest peak, Ben Nevis (1,343 m).

The Scottish Lowlands and Borders are largely areas of gentle hills and woodland, contrasting dramatically with the rugged landscape of the Highlands in the north. A striking physical feature is Glen More, or the Great Glen, which cuts across the central Highlands from Fort William on the west coast for 97 km north-east to Inverness on the east coast. A string of lochs in deep narrow basins are set between steep-sided mountains that rise past forested foothills to high moors and remote rocky mountains.

Wales

Wales is a mountainous country on the western side of Great Britain. Around one-quarter of the land is above 305 m and in the north its highest peak, Snowdon (Yr Wyddfa), rises to 1,085 m. The Welsh coastline stretches for 1,180 km and consists of many bays, beaches, peninsulas and cliffs.

Climate

The climate in the United Kingdom is generally mild and temperate. Prevailing weather systems move in from the Atlantic, and the weather is mainly influenced by depressions and their associated fronts moving eastwards, punctuated by settled, fine, anticyclonic periods lasting from a few days to several weeks. The temperature rarely rises above 32°C (90°F) or falls below −10°C (14°F).

Rainfall is greatest in western and upland parts of the country, where the annual average exceeds 1,100 mm; the highest mountain areas receive more than 3,000 mm. Over much of lowland central England, annual rainfall ranges from 700 to 850 mm, although parts of East Anglia and the South East receive just 550 mm. Rain is fairly well

Physical geography of the UK

Area: 243,610 sq km, including inland water

Length and breadth: just under 1,000 km from the south coast to the extreme north of the Scottish mainland and just under 500 km across at the widest point

Highest mountain: Ben Nevis, in the Highlands of Scotland, 1,343 m

Longest river: the Severn, 322 km long, which rises in central Wales and flows through Shrewsbury, Worcester and Gloucester in England to the Bristol Channel

Largest lake: Lough Neagh, Northern Ireland, 382 sq km

Deepest lake: Loch Morar in the Highlands of Scotland, 310 m deep

Highest waterfall: Eas a'Chual Aluinn, from Glas Bheinn, also in the Highlands of Scotland, with a drop of 200 m

Deepest cave: Ogof Ffynnon Ddu, Powys, Wales, 308 m deep

Most northerly point on the British mainland: Dunnet Head, north-east Scotland

Most southerly point on the British mainland: Lizard Point, Cornwall, England

distributed throughout the year, with late winter/spring (February to March) the driest period and autumn/winter (October to January) the wettest. During May, June and July (the months of longest daylight) the mean daily duration of sunshine varies from five hours in northern Scotland to eight hours in the Isle of Wight. During the months of shortest daylight (November, December and January) sunshine is at a minimum, with an average of an hour a day in northern Scotland and two hours a day on the south coast of England.

Population

The population of the UK at mid-2001 was 58.8 million (see Table 1.1). Official projections, based on 2000 population estimates, suggest that the population will reach nearly 65 million by 2025.

Table 1.1 UK population, 2001

	England	Wales	Scotland	Northern Ireland	United Kingdom
Population (thousands)	49,181	2,903	5,064	1,689	58,837
population aged:					
under 5	5.9	5.8	5.5	6.8	5.9
5–15	14.2	14.5	13.7	16.7	14.2
16 to pension age[1]	61.5	59.7	62.2	61.0	61.4
above pension age[1]	18.4	20.1	18.6	15.5	18.4
Area (sq km)	130,433	20,778	78,822	13,576	243,610
Population density (people per sq km)	377	140	64	124	242
% population change 1981 to 2001	5.0	3.2	−2.2	9.5	4.4
Live births per 1,000 population (2000)	11.5	10.6	10.4	12.7	11.4
Deaths per 1,000 population (2000)	10.1	11.4	11.3	8.8	10.2

1 Pension age is 65 for males and 60 for females.
Source: Office for National Statistics, National Assembly for Wales, General Register Office for Scotland and Northern Ireland Statistics and Research Agency

Table 1.2 Key demographic statistics, EU Member States

	Population in 2001 (thousands)	% population change 1981 to 2001	Live births per 1,000 population in 2000	Deaths per 1,000 population in 2000
Austria	8,121	7.3	9.6	9.3
Belgium	10,263	4.1	11.2	10.2
Denmark	5,349	4.5	12.6	10.9
Finland	5,181	7.9	11.0	9.5
France	59,040	9.0	13.2	9.1
Germany	82,193	4.8	9.2	10.1
Greece	10,565	8.6	11.7	10.5
Irish Republic	3,781	9.8	14.4	8.2
Italy	57,884	2.4	9.4	9.7
Luxembourg	441	20.8	13.1	8.6
Netherlands	15,987	12.2	13.0	8.8
Portugal	10,243	4.0	11.8	10.3
Spain	40,122	6.3	9.9	9.3
Sweden	8,833	6.2	10.2	10.5
United Kingdom	58,837	4.4	11.4	10.2

Source: Office for National Statistics

The UK population was the third largest in the European Union (EU) in 2001 after Germany (82 million) and France (59 million) (see Table 1.2). Having been static in the 1970s, overall population has begun to grow again. The rate of increase is in line with some other EU countries, but significantly slower than the United States or Australia. The 2001 Census showed that for the first time there are more people over 60 than there are children.

Historical outline
(see Appendix B for a list of significant dates)

'Britain' derives from Greek and Latin names which probably stem from a Celtic original. Although in the prehistoric timescale the Celts were relatively late arrivals in the British Isles, only with them does Britain emerge into recorded history. The term 'Celtic' is often used rather generally to distinguish the early inhabitants of the British Isles from the later Anglo-Saxon invaders.

After two expeditions by Julius Caesar in 55 and 54 BC, contact between Britain and the Roman world grew, culminating in the Roman invasion of AD 43. Roman rule, which lasted till about 409, was gradually extended from south-east England to include Wales and, for a time, the lowlands of Scotland.

England

When the Romans finally withdrew from Britain, the lowland regions were invaded and settled by Angles, Saxons and Jutes (tribes from what is now north-western Germany). England takes its name from the first of these. To begin with, the Anglo-Saxon kingdoms were fairly small and numerous, but as time went on they formed themselves into fewer but larger areas of control. Eventually the southern kingdom of Wessex came to dominate, mainly because it played a leading role in resisting the Viking invasions of the 9th century. Athelstan (who reigned from 924 to 939) used the title of 'King of all Britain', and from 954 there was a single kingdom of England.

In 1066 the last successful invasion of England took place. Duke William of Normandy defeated the English at the Battle of Hastings and became King William I, known as 'William the Conqueror'. Many Normans and others from France came to settle; French became the language of the ruling classes for the next three centuries; and the legal and social structures were influenced by those in force across the Channel.

When Henry II, originally from Anjou, was king (1154–89), his 'Angevin empire' stretched from the river Tweed on the Scottish border, through much of France to the Pyrenees. However, almost all of the English Crown's possessions in France were finally lost during the late Middle Ages.

In 1215 a group of barons demanded a charter of liberties as a safeguard against the seemingly arbitrary behaviour of King John. The rebels captured London and the King agreed to negotiate. He eventually attached his seal to a document containing their demands and the resulting formal royal grant became known as the *Magna Carta*. Among other things, the charter promised that 'To no one will we sell, to no one deny or delay right or justice'. It established the important constitutional principle that the power of the king could be limited.

The Civil War that broke out in England in 1642, and which resulted in the capture and eventual execution of Charles I, brought about a lasting change in the balance of power between monarch and Parliament. A leading statesman at this time was Oliver Cromwell (1599–1658) who, as Lord Protector from late 1653 until his death, had supreme legislative and executive power in association with Parliament and the Council of State during the interregnum before Charles II ascended the throne, restoring the monarchy.

Parliamentary reform was a recurrent issue in the 18th and 19th centuries. The 1832 *Reform Act* began the process of dismantling the old parliamentary system and extending the franchise, while the *Reform Acts* of 1867 and 1884 gave the vote to a gradually wider section of the population. During the 20th century, the *Representation of the People Acts* took the process still further. In 1918, women over the age of 30 were enfranchised and in 1928 the *Equal Franchise Act* lowered the voting age for women to 21. Universal suffrage for all eligible people over 18 (see page 31) was granted in 1969.

Northern Ireland

Henry II of England invaded Ireland in 1169. He had been made the country's overlord by the English Pope Adrian IV, who wanted the Irish Church to be fully obedient to Rome. Although Anglo-Norman noblemen controlled part of the country during the Middle Ages, little direct authority came from England.

The Tudor monarchs tended to intervene in Ireland far more, and during the reign of Elizabeth I there were several attempts to deal with rebellion. The northern province of Ulster was particularly subject to unrest, but in 1607, after the rebel leaders had been defeated and had fled, Protestant immigrants went to settle there from Scotland and England.

The English civil wars (1642–51) coincided with further uprisings in Ireland, which Oliver Cromwell suppressed. More fighting took place after the overthrow of King James II, a Roman Catholic, in 1688. At the Battle of the Boyne (1690) the Protestant William of Orange (later King William III) defeated the forces of James II who was trying to regain the English throne from his power base in Ireland.

In 1782 the Government in London gave the Irish Parliament power to legislate on Irish affairs. This Parliament, however, represented only the Anglo-Irish minority. Following the unsuccessful rebellion of Wolfe Tone's United Irishmen movement in 1798, Great Britain took back control of Ireland under the 1800 *Act of Union*. The Irish Parliament was abolished in 1801 and Irish interests were represented by members sitting in both Houses of the Westminster Parliament.

The question of 'Home Rule' for Ireland remained one of the major issues of British politics. By 1910 the Liberal Government in London depended for its political survival on support from the Irish Parliamentary Party. The conflict deepened as some unionists and nationalists in Ireland formed private armies. In 1914 Home Rule was approved in the *Government of Ireland Act* but implementation was suspended because of the First World War.

In 1916 a nationalist uprising in Dublin was put down and its leaders executed. Two years later the nationalist Sinn Féin party won a large majority of the Irish seats in the General Election to the Westminster Parliament. Its members refused to attend the House of Commons and instead formed their own assembly – the Dáil Éireann – in Dublin and the Irish Republican Army (IRA) began operations against the British administration in 1919.

In 1920 a new *Government of Ireland Act* provided for separate Parliaments in Northern and Southern Ireland, subordinate to Westminster. The Act was implemented in Northern Ireland in 1921, giving six of the nine counties of the province of Ulster their own Parliament with powers to manage internal affairs. However, the Act proved unacceptable in the South and the 26 counties of Southern Ireland eventually left the UK in 1922.

From 1921 until 1972 Northern Ireland had its own Parliament in which the unionists, primarily representing the Protestant community, held a permanent majority and formed the regional government. The nationalist minority was effectively excluded from political office and influence.

In the late 1960s and early 1970s, the civil rights movement and reactions to it resulted in serious inter-communal rioting, leading to the British Army being sent in to help the police keep law and order in 1969.

In 1972, when terrorism and violence reached its peak, the British Government decided to take back direct responsibility for law and order. The Northern Ireland Unionist Government resigned in protest, the regional government was abolished and direct rule from Westminster began; this was to last until devolved powers were given back to a Northern Ireland Assembly in December 1999 (see page 14).

Scotland

Evidence of human settlement in what is now known as Scotland dates from around the third millennium BC. By the time the Romans invaded Britain, many tribes were living in the region, but despite a number of attempts to control them, Roman rule never permanently extended to most of Scotland. In the sixth century, the Scots, a Celtic people from Ireland, settled on the north-west coast of the island of Great Britain, giving their name to the present-day Scotland.

The kingdoms of England and Scotland were frequently at war during the Middle Ages. When King Edward I tried to impose direct English rule over Scotland in 1296, a revolt for independence broke out, which ended in 1328 when King Edward III recognised its leader, Robert the Bruce, as King Robert I of Scotland.

In 1603 Queen Elizabeth I of England, who never married and had no children of her own, was succeeded by her nearest heir, King James VI of Scotland. He became King James I of England and so united the English and Scottish crowns in one person.

In 1745 Charles Edward Stuart (also known as 'Bonnie Prince Charlie' or 'The Young Pretender') attempted to retake the British throne for the Stuarts. Landing in the Hebrides, he went on to Edinburgh, defeating government forces at Prestonpans. He advanced southwards into England, capturing Carlisle, but was turned back at Derby and eventually defeated at the Battle of Culloden, north-east of Inverness, in April 1746.

Politically, England and Scotland remained separate during the 17th century, apart from a period of union forced on them by Oliver Cromwell in the 1650s. It was not until 1707 that the English and Scottish Parliaments agreed on a single Parliament for Great Britain to sit at Westminster in London. Nearly 300 years later, in July 1999, devolution meant that power to administer Scottish affairs was returned to a new Scottish Parliament (see page 21).

Wales

Wales remained a Celtic stronghold ruled by sovereign princes under the influence of England after the Romans had left Britain. In 1282 King Edward I brought Wales under English rule and the castles he built in the north remain among the UK's finest historic monuments. Edward I's eldest son – later King Edward II – was born at Caernarfon in 1284 and was created the first English Prince of Wales in 1301. The eldest son of the reigning monarch continues to bear this title, Prince Charles being made Prince of Wales in 1969.

At the beginning of the 15th century, Welsh resentment of unjust English laws and administration, and widespread economic discontent, resulted in the nationalist leader Owain Glyndŵr heading an unsuccessful revolt against the English. From 1485 to 1603 the Tudor dynasty, which was of Welsh ancestry, ruled England and it was during this time that the *Acts of Union* (1536 and 1542) united England and Wales administratively, politically and legally.

This situation prevailed until July 1999, when devolution gave the National Assembly for Wales specific powers to make secondary legislation to meet distinctive Welsh needs (see page 27).

Channel Islands and Isle of Man

The Channel Islands (Jersey, Guernsey, Alderney and Sark being the largest in the group) were part of the Duchy of Normandy in the 10th and 11th centuries and remained subject to the English Crown after the loss of mainland Normandy to the French in 1204. The Isle of Man was under the nominal sovereignty of Norway until 1266, and eventually came under the direct administration of the British Crown in 1765, when it was bought for £70,000. Its parliament, Tynwald, was established more than 1,000 years ago and is the oldest legislature in continuous existence in the world.

Today these territories have their own legislative assemblies and systems of law, and their own taxation systems. The UK Government is responsible for their international relations and external defence.

The UK is one of the 15 Member States of the European Union (EU – see page 59) but the Channel Islands and Isle of Man are neither EU Member States in their own right nor part of the UK Member State. Broadly speaking, EU rules on the free movement of goods and the Common Agricultural Policy apply to the Islands, but not those on the free movement of services or persons. Islanders benefit from the provision for free movement of persons only if they have close ties with the UK.

Further reading

Annual Abstract of Statistics. Office for National Statistics. The Stationery Office.

Population Trends. Office for National Statistics. The Stationery Office.

Regional Trends. Office for National Statistics. The Stationery Office.

Social Trends. Office for National Statistics. The Stationery Office.

Websites

British Geological Survey
www.bgs.ac.uk

Environment Agency for England and Wales
www.environment-agency.gov.uk

The Met Office
www.metoffice.com

Office for National Statistics
www.statistics.gov.uk

Public Record Office
www.pro.gov.uk

2 England

Population

Nearly 84 per cent of the total population of the United Kingdom lives in England, mainly in the major cities and metropolitan areas in London and the South East, South and West Yorkshire, Greater Manchester and Merseyside, the West Midlands, and conurbations on the rivers Tyne, Wear and Tees. The population of England almost trebled between 1851 and the end of the 20th century. Table 2.1 shows that the South West, East and South East regions each grew by more than 10 per cent between 1981 and 2001.

England is by far the most densely populated part of the UK. In 2001 it had a population density of 377 people per sq km compared with Wales (140), Northern Ireland (124) and Scotland (64).

In contrast to Northern Ireland, Scotland and Wales, England has no separate elected national body exclusively responsible for its central administration (see chapters 3, 4 and 5). Instead a number of government departments look after England's day-to-day administrative affairs (see Appendix A) and there is a network of nine Government Offices for the Regions (GOs – see page 9). However, in the longer term, the Government is committed to providing for directly elected regional assemblies in those regions that want them (see page 10).

Representation at Westminster and in Europe

There are 529 English parliamentary constituencies represented in the House of Commons (see Table 2.2). Conservative support tends to be strongest in suburban and rural areas, and the party has a large number of parliamentary seats in the southern half of England. The Labour Party's key support comes mainly from the big cities and areas associated with heavy industry, but it currently holds many seats which had in the past been considered safe Conservative constituencies. The Liberal Democrats, who are traditionally strong in the South West, now have over a third (15) of their English seats in Greater London and the South East.

A Standing Committee on Regional Affairs was revived in April 2000. It consists of 13 Members sitting for constituencies in England and reflects party representation in the House. Any Member representing an English constituency may take part in its proceedings, but they may not make a motion, vote or be counted in the quorum. The committee considers issues specific to the English regions.

Structure of local government

In many areas of England a two-tier system of county and district councils is responsible for government at the local level. However, there are also a number of single-tier, or unitary, authorities – especially in the larger cities (see map on page 8). Some 'borough' or 'city' councils are unitary and others operate at the district level. Since July 2000 the strategic government of London has been the

Table 2.1 England population and population change, by region,[1] 2001

	Population (thousands)	Change in population 1981–2001 (%)
North East	2,517	−4.5
North West	6,732	−3.0
Yorkshire and the Humber	4,967	1.0
East Midlands	4,175	8.4
West Midlands	5,267	1.6
East	5,395	11.1
London	7,188	5.6
South East	8,007	10.5
South West	4,934	12.6
England	49,181	5.0

1 These are the areas covered by Government Offices – see map on page 8.
Source: Office for National Statistics

England: counties and unitary authorities

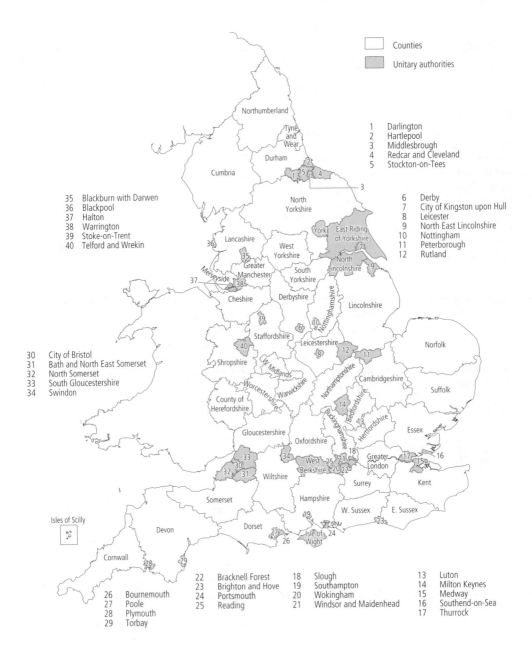

- Counties
- Unitary authorities

1 Darlington
2 Hartlepool
3 Middlesbrough
4 Redcar and Cleveland
5 Stockton-on-Tees

6 Derby
7 City of Kingston upon Hull
8 Leicester
9 North East Lincolnshire
10 Nottingham
11 Peterborough
12 Rutland

35 Blackburn with Darwen
36 Blackpool
37 Halton
38 Warrington
39 Stoke-on-Trent
40 Telford and Wrekin

30 City of Bristol
31 Bath and North East Somerset
32 North Somerset
33 South Gloucestershire
34 Swindon

22 Bracknell Forest
23 Brighton and Hove
24 Portsmouth
25 Reading

18 Slough
19 Southampton
20 Wokingham
21 Windsor and Maidenhead

13 Luton
14 Milton Keynes
15 Medway
16 Southend-on-Sea
17 Thurrock

26 Bournemouth
27 Poole
28 Plymouth
29 Torbay

Table 2.2 Electoral representation in England, July 2002

	UK Parliament (MPs)	European Parliament (MEPs)
Labour	322	24
Conservative	165	33
Liberal Democrats	41	9
UK Independence Party	–	3
Green Party	–	2
Others	1	–
Total seats	**529**	**71**

Source: House of Commons Information Office

responsibility of the Greater London Authority (see below).

Metropolitan county areas

The six metropolitan county areas in England – Tyne and Wear, West Midlands, Merseyside, Greater Manchester, West Yorkshire and South Yorkshire – have 36 district councils, but no county councils. The district councils are responsible for all services apart from those which have a statutory authority over areas wider than the individual boroughs and districts. For example, waste disposal (in certain areas); the fire services and civil defence; and public transport are run by joint authorities composed of elected councillors nominated by the borough or district councils.

Non-metropolitan counties

County councils in England are responsible for large-scale services in their areas such as transport, planning, highways, traffic regulation, education, consumer protection, refuse disposal, the fire service, libraries and the personal social services. They are each subdivided into a number of district councils which are responsible for more local matters like environmental health, housing, decisions on most local planning applications, and collection of household waste. Both tiers of local authority have powers to provide facilities such as museums, art galleries and parks; these arrangements depend on local agreement. In areas containing unitary authorities, the latter provide both county and district level functions.

Greater London

Greater London is made up of 32 boroughs and the City of London, each with a council

responsible for most services in its area. In May 2000 Londoners voted for a directly elected Mayor[1] for the capital, and a separately elected Assembly of 25 members. Subsequent elections will take place every four years. The Mayor and the London Assembly form the Greater London Authority (GLA), the first elected London-wide body since the Greater London Council (GLC) was abolished in 1986. The Mayor of London sets key strategies on a range of London-wide issues, such as transport, economic development, strategic and spatial development and the environment. The London Assembly scrutinises both the activities of the Mayor and issues of concern to Londoners.

In elections for London's Mayor, voters are required to mark both their first and second choices on their ballot papers. If, in the first round, no candidate receives more than 50 per cent of the total votes cast, the second choices for the two leading candidates are added to their initial scores to decide the overall winner. For the Assembly elections, London is divided into 14 constituencies whose members are elected using the 'first-past-the-post' system. A further 11 London-wide seats are allocated on a 'top-up' basis, whereby votes are counted across London and the seats shared among the political parties in proportion to the votes each party receives. In the May 2000 elections, the Labour Party won nine seats, the Conservatives also won nine, the Liberal Democrats four and the Green Party three. The Mayor stood as an Independent candidate.

Parishes

The smallest type of administrative area in England is the parish. These date from medieval times but have operated in their current form only since 1894. Modern parish councils (which may choose to call themselves town councils) have two main roles: to represent community views and to deliver local services. There are now around 9,500 parishes in England, including over 100 that have been created since the introduction of the Local Government and Rating Act 1997.

The regions of England

Nine Government Offices (GOs – see map on page 8) are responsible for the effective co-ordination of central government programmes at

---

1 The new arrangements do not affect the separate post of Lord Mayor of London (first established in 1191), whose role is restricted to the City of London.

Cities in England

City status is purely honorific and confers no additional powers or functions on the town. In December 2000 the Government announced that the Queen had decided to mark her Golden Jubilee by grants of city status to a suitably qualified town in each of the four countries of the United Kingdom. In March 2002, Preston was chosen to receive this honour in England.

Preston is the administrative capital of Lancashire. It is mentioned in the Domesday Book and was granted its first Charter in 1179 by King Henry II. The University of Central Lancashire, founded in 1828 as the Preston Institution for the Diffusion of Knowledge, is now one of the country's largest universities, while Preston North End Football Club, one of the founding members of the Football League in 1888, is home to the new National Football Museum which contains the FIFA Football Collection and other important footballing items.

The 50 English cities are:
Bath, Birmingham, Bradford, Brighton and Hove, Bristol, Cambridge, Canterbury, Carlisle, Chester, Chichester, Coventry, Derby, Durham, Ely, Exeter, Gloucester, Hereford, Kingston upon Hull, Lancaster, Leeds, Leicester, Lichfield, Lincoln, Liverpool, London, Manchester, Newcastle upon Tyne, Norwich, Nottingham, Oxford, Peterborough, Plymouth, Portsmouth, Preston, Ripon, Salford, Salisbury, Sheffield, Southampton, St Albans, Stoke-on-Trent, Sunderland, Truro, Wakefield, Wells, Westminster, Winchester, Wolverhampton, Worcester and York.

a regional level. They bring together the English regional services for nine departments – the Office of the Deputy Prime Minister, Department of Trade and Industry, Department for Education and Skills, Department for Work and Pensions, Department of Health, Department for Transport, Home Office, Department for Culture, Media and Sport and Department for Environment, Food & Rural Affairs – and work with regional partners, including local authorities and Regional Development Agencies (RDAs – see page 339).

In April 2000 the Government set up a Regional Co-ordination Unit in order to co-ordinate the delivery of regional initiatives, promote the use of GOs by Whitehall departments, and manage the shared functions of the GOs.

Voluntary regional chambers have also been established in each region. They provide a means through which the RDAs can consult on their proposals and give an account of their activities.

Proposals for devolution to the English regions

In May 2002 the Government published a White Paper *Your Region, Your Choice: Revitalising the English Regions*, which proposed the establishment of elected assemblies in regions that want them.

Such assemblies would be responsible for setting priorities, delivering regional strategies and allocating funding. Their functional responsibilities would cover economic development, skills and employment, spatial planning, housing, transport, environmental protection, tourism, culture, sport and public health.

Before any elected regional assembly is established, a referendum would be held and

A few distinctive facts about England

- English law comprises 'common law' (based on ancient custom and previous rulings in similar cases), 'statute law' (parliamentary and European Community legislation) and 'equity' (general principles of justice correcting or adding to common or statute law). Wales also uses English law, but devolution has meant that some legislation now applies differently in that part of the UK (see page 28).

- The Church of England broke away from the Roman Catholic Church during the Reformation in the early 16th century. The Sovereign is head of the Church of England and appoints its two archbishops and 42 diocesan bishops (see page 34).

- Despite its high population density and degree of urbanisation, England has a diverse natural environment with many unspoilt rural and coastal areas which are protected under the law (see chapter 19). The English landscape is distinct in character from many other parts of the UK, and several of its regions and counties have inspired great English writers, artists and musicians over the centuries; these include the Lake District (William Wordsworth, poet), Dorset (Thomas Hardy, novelist), Essex and Suffolk (John Constable, landscape painter) and Worcestershire (Edward Elgar, composer).

Physical features

Orkney Islands

Shetland Islands

Land over 400 metres
Land 100–399 metres
Land 0–99 metres
Peaks
Rivers
National borders

Cape Wrath
Dunnet Head
Lewis
Ben Hope
927 m
Morven
705 m
Clisham
799 m
Ben More
Assynt 998 m
Harris
Ben Dearg
1081 m
St Kilda
Skye
Ben Wyvis
1045 m
Moray Firth
Outer Hebrides
Inner Hebrides
Loch Ness
Cairn Gorm
1245 m
Cuillin Hills
1009 m
Carn Eige
1182 m
Ben Macdhui
1311 m
R. Dee
Loch Morar
Ben Nevis
1343 m
Lochnagar
1154 m
Grampians
Schiehallion
1081 m
Mull
Ben More
966 m
Ben Lawers
1014 m
Firth of Tay
Loch Lomond
Atlantic Ocean
Islay
R. Forth
Firth of Forth
SCOTLAND
Holy I.
Bute
R. Clyde
R. Tweed
NORTHERN IRELAND
Goat Fell
874 m
Arran
Southern Uplands
The Cheviot
816 m
North Sea
R. Foyle
Mountains of Antrim
Trostan
554 m
Sperrin Mountains
Merrick
843 m
R. Tyne
Sawel
683 m
Lough Neagh
Lower Lough Erne
R. Lagan
Strangford Lough
Cross Fell
893 m
Solway Firth
Cumbrian
Scafell Pikes
978 m
R. Tees
Upper Lough Erne
Mourne Mountains
Slieve Donard
852 m
Isle of Man
Snaefell
620 m
Mountains
Whernside
737 m
North Yorkshire Moors
454 m
Flamborough Head
Morecambe Bay
Yorkshire Wolds
REPUBLIC
Lough Ree
Irish Sea
R. Ribble
R. Wharfe
R. Ouse
R. Don
Spurn Head
OF
Anglesey
R. Aire
Lincolnshire Wolds
The Peak
636 m
R. Mersey
The Wash
IRELAND
Lough Derg
Cheshire Plain
R. Dee
R. Trent
The Fens
Snowdon
1085 m
R. Welland
The Broads
Cader Idris
892 m
ENGLAND
R. Nene
Cardigan Bay
Cambrian Mountains
Plynlimon
752 m
East Anglia
R. Ouse
Gog Magog Hills
Celtic Sea
St. George's Channel
WALES
Cleeve Cloud
330 m
Cotswolds
Chiltern Hills
R. Lea
North Foreland
Lundy I.
Bristol Channel
Brecon Beacons
886 m
R. Severn
R. Avon
Mendip Hills
Berkshire Downs
R. Thames
R. Kennet
North Downs
Strait of Dover
Hartland Point
Exmoor
Dunkery Beacon
520 m
Salisbury Plain
Hampshire Downs
The Weald
Beachy Head
High Willhays
621 m
R. Parrett
R. Exe
North Dorset Downs
South Downs
R. Wey
R. Medway
Brown Willy
419 m
Dartmoor
Bodmin Moor
Lyme Bay
Portland Bill
Isle of Wight
English Channel
Scilly Isles
Land's End
Lizard Point
Greenwich Meridian
0° longitude
0   40   80   120 km
0   20   40   60   80 miles
Channel Islands
FRANCE
R. Seine

September 2001: a memorial service is held at St Paul's Cathedral, London, for victims of the 11 September attacks on the United States.

March 2002: Lisburn, Northern Ireland (top) and Stirling, Scotland are two of the towns granted city status as part of the Queen's Golden Jubilee celebrations.

PHOTOGRAPHY SUPPLIED BY LISBURN CITY COUNCIL

STIRLING COUNCIL COMMUNICATIONS UNIT

August 2002: 'Britain in Bloom'.

Left: Llandudno in Wales achieved a Silver Award in the coastal resort category.

Centre: Perth, Scotland. Winner of the large town category.

Bottom left: Bournemouth, England. Muscliff gardening club was one of the community groups that helped Bournemouth win the large city category.

Bottom right: Waringstown in Northern Ireland achieved a Silver Award for the small country town category.

PERTH IN BLOOM

BOURNEMOUTH BOROUGH COUNCIL

a majority of those voting would need to be in favour of the proposal. The Government recognises that interest in elected regional assemblies varies across England, so referendums would be held only in regions where there was sufficient interest.

Elected regional assemblies would be based on the existing administrative boundaries used by the GOs and RDAs. They would have between 25 and 35 members, including a leader and a cabinet of up to six members chosen by, and wholly accountable to, the full assembly. The voting system would be the Additional Member System of proportional representation (see page 22) which is used for the Scottish Parliament and the Welsh Assembly. This would ensure that the overall composition of an assembly broadly reflected the votes cast for the different parties.

Most of an assembly's money would come through a single government grant, with the assembly deciding how it should use this to address key regional priorities. Using figures for 2001/02, an assembly in the North East, for example, would be responsible for around £350 million and would influence decisions on how another £500 million would be spent. Additional funds would be raised through the council tax, collected on behalf of the assembly by the local authorities in the region as part of their existing arrangements.

The Government intends to introduce a Bill to provide for referendums and associated local government reviews when parliamentary time allows, with the aim of enabling the first referendum to be held during the current Parliament. Once at least one region has voted for an elected assembly, legislation would be introduced to provide for an assembly to be set up. The Government envisages having the first regional assembly established and operating early in the next Parliament.

Economic performance

Economic performance varies considerably between and within the nine English regions. For example, Inner London has had the highest level of gross domestic product (GDP) per head in the European Union (EU) for a number of years, but it also contains some of the worst pockets of deprivation in the UK. Under the Objective 1 status for EU funding that came into force in January 2000 (see page 340), three areas of

The English language

Modern English derives primarily from one of the dialects of Old English (or Anglo-Saxon), itself made up of several Western Germanic dialects brought to Britain in the early fifth century. However, it has been very greatly influenced by other languages, particularly Latin and, following the Norman conquest, by French – the language of court, government and the nobility for many years after 1066. The re-emergence of English was marked by events such as the Statute of Pleading in 1362, which laid down that English was to replace French as the language of law. The 14th century saw the first major English literature since Anglo-Saxon days, with works such as *Piers Plowman* by William Langland and the *Canterbury Tales* by Geoffrey Chaucer.

English is one of the most widely used languages in the world. Estimates suggest that around 310 million people speak it as their first language, with a similar number speaking it as a second language. It is the official language of air traffic control and maritime communications; the leading language of science, technology, computing and commerce; and a major medium of education, publishing and international negotiation.

Because of today's accessibility of oral communication (via the telephone, television, radio and cinema), the language is changing faster than it did in the past. New words from many sources are constantly being adopted and words which become popular with the public are repeated again and again in different circumstances by thousands of people, quickly adding to their meaning and sometimes changing it.

British English has borrowed much from other English-speaking countries, particularly the United States, but many words and phrases have also entered the language from Commonwealth countries, notably Australia and those in the Caribbean.

England – Merseyside, South Yorkshire, and Cornwall and the Isles of Scilly – qualified for funding from 2000 to 2006. According to the latest figures, household disposable income per head in 1999 was above the England average in London (by 19 per cent) and in the South East and East (both by 8 per cent), and the same three regions had the highest gross weekly earnings for full-time employees in 2000. The North East had the lowest household disposable income and GDP per head in 1999, as well as the lowest average weekly earnings in 2000.

Further reading

Regional Trends (annual publication), Office for National Statistics. The Stationery Office.

Social Trends (annual publication), Office for National Statistics. The Stationery Office.

Economic Trends (monthly publication), Office for National Statistics. The Stationery Office.

Your Region, Your Choice: Revitalising the English Regions. Cm 5511. The Stationery Office, 2002.

Websites

Department of Trade and Industry
www.dti.gov.uk

Greater London Authority
www.london.gov.uk

Local Government Association
www.lga.gov.uk

Lord Chancellor's Department
www.lcd.gov.uk

Office for National Statistics
www.statistics.gov.uk

Office of the Deputy Prime Minister
www.odpm.gov.uk

The Official On-line Guide to England
www.travelengland.org.uk

United Kingdom Parliament
www.parliament.uk

www.

3 Northern Ireland

Population

About half of Northern Ireland's 1.7 million population live in the eastern coastal region, at the centre of which is the capital, Belfast. The population has increased by 5 per cent in the past ten years. Within Northern Ireland, the population density in 2001 was highest in the district council area of Belfast at 2,528 people per sq km and lowest in Moyle at only 32 people per sq km. Around 36 per cent of the population was aged under 25 in 2001, a higher proportion than in any other region of the United Kingdom. In the late 1990s the Northern Ireland Continuous Household Survey (CHS) reported that 54 per cent of the Northern Irish population regarded themselves as Protestants and 42 per cent as Roman Catholics.

Cities in Northern Ireland

There are now five cities in Northern Ireland: Armagh, Belfast, Lisburn, Londonderry and Newry. Unlike the other parts of the UK, where only one town was granted city status to mark the Queen's Golden Jubilee in 2002 (see chapters 2, 4 and 5), in Northern Ireland both Lisburn and Newry were honoured.

- Lisburn became the home of French Huguenots in the 17th century who nurtured the growing linen industry and the town quickly became a major linen producer. Today the focus has changed to the manufacturing of synthetic fabrics but the city remains an important centre for commerce and industry.

- Newry is notable for having the first inland waterway in the British Isles, which contributed greatly to the town's prosperity in the 19th century. The canal had 14 locks and provided a means to export goods (mainly linen and stone). Today Newry is a busy city benefiting from its close proximity to the border with the Irish Republic.

Table 3.1 Northern Ireland population, by Board[1] and District, 2001

	Population (thousands)	Change in population 1981–2001 (%)
Eastern	667	4.0
Ards	73	26.6
Belfast	277	−12.4
Castlereagh	67	9.2
Down	64	19.3
Lisburn	109	27.9
North Down	77	14.4
Northern	428	13.7
Antrim	49	5.9
Ballymena	59	6.9
Ballymoney	27	17.5
Carrickfergus	38	31.4
Coleraine	56	20.4
Cookstown	33	15.2
Larne	31	5.9
Magherafelt	40	21.9
Moyle	16	10.4
Newtonabbey	80	10.6
Southern	312	13.8
Armagh	54	10.4
Banbridge	42	38.1
Craigavon	81	10.1
Dungannon	48	8.9
Newry and Mourne	87	12.8
Western	282	12.5
Derry	105	16.8
Fermanagh	58	10.7
Limavady	33	19.5
Omagh	48	7.4
Strabane	38	5.3
Northern Ireland	**1,689**	**9.5**

1 Health and Social Services Board areas.
Source: Office for National Statistics and Northern Ireland Statistics and Research Agency

Northern Ireland: districts

Cf	Carrickfergus
Cr	Castlereagh
ND	North Down
Nta	Newtownabbey

Representation at Westminster

For UK Government General Elections, Northern Ireland is divided into 18 single-seat constituencies and there is a simple 'first-past-the-post' electoral system. Although there are 18 MPs elected to represent Northern Ireland in the House of Commons, the four Sinn Féin party members have not taken their seats. Since December 2001, however, they have had access to facilities at Westminster.

Following devolution (see below), the Secretary of State for Northern Ireland – a member of the UK Cabinet whose main function is to ensure that the devolution settlement works satisfactorily – remains responsible for Northern Ireland Office matters not devolved to the Northern Ireland Assembly. These include policing, security policy, prisons and criminal justice.

The Westminster Parliament also has a Northern Ireland Grand Committee to consider Bills at the second and third reading stages, take oral questions and ministerial statements, and debate matters relating specifically to Northern Ireland. It includes all sitting Northern Ireland MPs and up to 25 others as nominated by the committee of selection.

In 1994 the Northern Ireland Affairs Select Committee was established to examine the expenditure, policy and administration of the Northern Ireland Office. The Committee has the power to send for people, papers and records, and has investigated areas such as employment, electricity prices, education, BSE and the security forces in Northern Ireland.

Northern Ireland Assembly and Executive

The first elections to the Northern Ireland Assembly were held in June 1998 using the single transferable vote system of proportional representation. The 18 constituencies are the

Table 3.2 Northern Ireland electoral representation

House of Commons (June 2001 General Election)		Northern Ireland Assembly (as at July 2002)	
Party	Seats	Party	Seats
Ulster Unionist	6	Ulster Unionist	27
Social Democratic and Labour	3	Social Democratic and Labour	24
Democratic Unionist	5	Democratic Unionist	21
Sinn Féin[1]	4	Sinn Féin	18
		Alliance	6
		Northern Ireland Unionist	3
		United Unionist Assembly	3
		Progressive Unionist	2
		NI Women's Coalition	2
		United Kingdom Unionist	1
		Independent Unionist	1
Total	**18**		**108**

1 The Sinn Féin members have not taken their seats in the Westminster Parliament.

same as those for the UK Parliament, but each returns six MLAs (Members of the Legislative Assembly), giving the Assembly a total of 108 members.

At its first meeting in July 1998, the Assembly elected, on a cross-community basis, a First Minister and a Deputy First Minister and appointed ten ministers with responsibility for each of the Northern Ireland departments (see Appendix A), which together form the Executive. These 12 ministers make up the Executive Committee, which meets to discuss and agree on those issues which cut across the responsibilities of two or more ministers. Its role is to prioritise executive business and recommend a common position where necessary.

Powers and responsibilities

Power to run most of Northern Ireland's domestic affairs was fully devolved by the Westminster Parliament to the Northern Ireland Assembly and its Executive Committee of Ministers in December 1999. The Assembly meets in Parliament Buildings at Stormont, Belfast, and is the prime source of authority for all devolved responsibilities. It has full legislative and executive powers within this framework, which means it can make laws and take decisions on all the functions of the Northern Ireland departments.

The Executive's main function is to plan each year, and review as necessary, a programme of government with an agreed budget. This is subject to approval by the Assembly, after scrutiny in Assembly Committees, on a cross-community basis. MLAs can be on more than one Assembly Committee.

The Assembly has ten Statutory Committees. Membership of Committees is in broad proportion to party strengths in the Assembly to ensure that the opportunity of Committee places is available to all Members. Each Committee has a scrutiny, policy development and consultation role in relation to its department and a role in the initiation of legislation.

A 60-member Civic Forum, whose chairperson is appointed by the First Minister and Deputy First Minister, represents the business, trade union, voluntary and other sectors of the Northern Ireland community. It acts as a consultative mechanism on social, economic and cultural matters.

Representation in Europe

Northern Ireland forms a single, multi-seat constituency to elect three of the 87 UK representatives to the European Parliament (MEPs) every five years. As with local and Assembly elections, the single transferable vote form of proportional representation is used.

Structure of local government

Northern Ireland is divided into 26 local government districts, each forming a single-tier local authority. They are responsible for refuse collection, leisure and recreation facilities,

Countdown to devolution

Direct rule from Westminster (imposed in 1972) was never intended to be permanent. Over the years, successive British and Irish Governments have worked closely together to try to bring lasting peace to Northern Ireland, recognising the need for new political arrangements acceptable to both sides of the community. The key events leading up to the establishment of the Northern Ireland Assembly were:

- 1985: an Anglo-Irish Agreement provided a new basis for relations between the UK and the Irish Republic, creating an Intergovernmental Conference in which to discuss issues of mutual interest, such as improved cross-border co-operation and security.

- 1993: the Downing Street Declaration set out the British and Irish Governments' views on how a future settlement might be achieved and restated that any constitutional change would require the consent of a majority of people in Northern Ireland.

- 1997: a new UK Government (elected in May) confirmed its intention of making the talks process as inclusive as possible and maintained that any agreement reached would have to have the broad support of the parties representing each of the main communities.

- 1998 (April): multi-party talks held in Belfast concluded with the Belfast (Good Friday) Agreement. Legislation was passed at Westminster authorising a referendum on the settlement in Northern Ireland and permitting elections to a new Northern Ireland Assembly. The Irish Parliament also considered the Agreement and passed legislation authorising a concurrent referendum in the Irish Republic.

- 1998 (May): referendums were held in both parts of Ireland, and the Agreement received a clear endorsement. Northern Ireland voted 71.1 per cent in favour and 28.8 per cent against, while in the Irish Republic the result was 94.3 per cent and 5.6 per cent respectively.

- 1998 (June): a new Northern Ireland Assembly of 108 members was elected.

- 1999: power was devolved to the Assembly and its Executive Committee of Ministers under the *Northern Ireland Act 1998.* At the same time a number of institutions set up to assist intergovernmental dialogue became fully functional (see page 17).

building control, cemeteries and tourist amenities, and nominate locally elected representatives to sit as members of the various statutory bodies dealing with, for example, education, libraries and healthcare. Local authorities in Northern Ireland also have a consultative role in matters such as planning, roads and housing, and offer leadership and support in local economic development.

Finance

Unlike the other parts of the United Kingdom, local authorities in Northern Ireland are not financed through a council tax. Instead they continue to raise revenue to help fund the services they provide by levying a domestic rate on homes and a business rate on commercial property.

In 2002/03 net revenue expenditure for local authorities in Northern Ireland is estimated at £313 million: £261 million is financed from district rates, £47 million financed by general grant and £5 million from the reserves.

Security policy

The Government remains committed to ensuring that the security forces in Northern Ireland have available the powers they need to counter the terrorist threat.

The system of separate and temporary legislation for Northern Ireland and Great Britain has now been replaced by permanent UK-wide anti-terrorist legislation contained in the *Terrorism Act 2000* and the *Anti-Terrorism Crime and Security Act 2001* (see page 188).

Reform of policing

An independent Commission on Policing, set up under the terms of the Belfast (Good Friday) Agreement, carried out an extensive review of policing in Northern Ireland. Its report – *A New Beginning: Policing in Northern Ireland* (the Patten Report) – was published in September 1999 and made recommendations which led to the *Police (Northern Ireland) Act 2000.*

Intergovernmental dialogue

Under the 1998 Belfast (Good Friday) Agreement, a number of new institutions were set up to facilitate intergovernmental dialogue between Northern Ireland, the Irish Republic and the UK Government. They came into operation at the same time as power was devolved to the Northern Ireland Assembly in December 1999.

- The North/South Ministerial Council is a forum for those with executive responsibilities in Northern Ireland and the Irish Government. The Council meets on a regular basis to develop consultation, co-operation and action on an all-island and cross-border basis.

- The North/South Implementation Bodies, established by international agreement between the British and Irish Governments, implement the policies agreed by ministers in the North/South Ministerial Council. They deal with waterways, food safety, trade and business development, special European Union programmes, marine matters, and language.

- The British-Irish Council aims to promote and develop good relationships among all the peoples of the United Kingdom and Ireland. It has representatives from the British and Irish Governments, the devolved institutions in Northern Ireland, Scotland and Wales, and others from the Channel Islands and the Isle of Man.

- The British-Irish Intergovernmental Conference's role is to promote bilateral co-operation on matters of mutual interest between the two governments.

Provisions contained in the Act have:

- enhanced the police service's accountability through a new Policing Board to be made up of ten members of the Northern Ireland Assembly and nine independent members;

- given the Board powers to call for reports and initiate inquiries, and require it to monitor and assess police performance;

- provided for the establishment of new district policing partnerships aimed at improving local accountability;

- introduced measures to redress the religious imbalance in the police service between Protestants and Catholics. The first group of recruits trained specifically for the new police service graduated in April 2002;

- changed the name of the RUC to the 'Police Service of Northern Ireland (incorporating the Royal Ulster Constabulary)'. For operational purposes, the service is called the 'Police Service of Northern Ireland'; and

- established a Commissioner to oversee the implementation of changes.

The *Police (Northern Ireland) Act 1998* set up the office of a Police Ombudsman to provide an independent means of impartially investigating complaints against police officers in Northern Ireland. When it is perceived to be in the public interest, the Police Ombudsman can also react to incidents, even if no individual complaint has been made.

Review of criminal justice

In parallel with the work of the Commission on Policing, the Government carried out a review of the criminal justice system in Northern Ireland in which political parties, interested bodies, organisations and individuals were consulted. Its recommendations, published in March 2000, were subject to further consultation which ended the following September and in November 2001 the draft Justice (Northern Ireland) Bill was published.

Having consulted further on the measures in the draft, the Government introduced the Justice (Northern Ireland) Bill in the House of Commons in December 2001 and it received Royal Assent in July 2002. The *Justice (Northern Ireland) Act 2002* contains provisions to:

- amend the law relating to the judiciary and courts in Northern Ireland, including provision for the creation of a Judicial Appointments Commission and for the removal of judges, changes to eligibility criteria, a new oath and provisions to make the Lord Chief Justice head of the judiciary in Northern Ireland;

- provide for the appointment of the Attorney General for Northern Ireland after devolution of responsibility for justice matters to the

Northern Ireland Assembly (scheduled for May 2003) and establish a public prosecution service;

■ establish a Chief Inspector of Criminal Justice and a Northern Ireland Law Commission;

■ set out the aims of the youth justice system and make other provisions dealing with this system, including extending it to 17 year olds;

■ provide for the disclosure of information about the release of offenders in Northern Ireland to victims of crime and to confer on victims the right to make representations in relation to the temporary release of offenders; and

■ provide for measures in relation to community safety.

Economy

Northern Ireland accounts for 2.2 per cent of UK gross domestic product (GDP). GDP rose from £9.3 billion in 1989 to £17.0 billion in 1999 (at current prices), an increase of 82 per cent. In 1999 GDP per head in Northern Ireland was 77.5 per cent of the UK average, an increase from 74.7 per cent in 1989. Between 1989 and 1999 real GDP per head increased by 20.8 per cent in Northern Ireland, compared with 16.5 per cent for the UK as a whole.

Some comparisons between the Northern Irish and UK economies

■ Manufacturing industry accounted for some 19.0 per cent of Northern Ireland's GDP in 1998, compared with 20.3 per cent for the UK as a whole at that time.

■ Agriculture, forestry and fishing accounted for 4.0 per cent of Northern Ireland's GDP in 1998, compared with 1.3 per cent for the UK.

■ In 2001, 60.2 per cent of export trade was to the EU, slightly higher than the UK average of 58.9 per cent. Trade from the EU accounted for nearly 42 per cent of imports, lower than the UK average of 49 per cent.

Northern Ireland's economic development strategy was reviewed following the Enterprise, Trade and Investment Committee's consideration

Human rights and equality

The European Convention on Human Rights became part of Northern Ireland domestic law when the *Human Rights Act 1998* (see page 183) came into effect throughout the UK in October 2000.

A commitment to protect human rights and promote equality was central to the Belfast (Good Friday) Agreement. The subsequent *Northern Ireland Act 1998* not only placed a statutory duty of equality on all public authorities but also established the following bodies with specific responsibilities for fostering equal opportunities and good community relations:

■ *The Northern Ireland Human Rights Commission* – to give advice to the Government and the Northern Ireland Assembly on human rights issues, particularly on any need for legislation to protect human rights.

■ *The Equality Commission for Northern Ireland* – to be responsible for fair employment, equal opportunities, racial equality, disability issues and enforcing the statutory duty of equality on public authorities.

■ *The Parades Commission* – to help implement the *Public Processions (Northern Ireland) Act 1998*, the purpose of which is to regulate public processions in Northern Ireland. The Commission imposed some form of restriction on 152 contentious parades in the year to 31 March 2002 out of a total of 3,301 notified parades. The majority of parades each year are organised by the Protestant/Unionist community and most take place during the six months from around Easter to the end of September.

■ *The Victims Commission* – whose 1998 report *We Will Remember Them* led the Government to appoint a minister for victims and establish a Victims Liaison Unit in the Northern Ireland Office. Since then, the Government has committed more than £18 million to support victims of inter-community unrest in Northern Ireland.

of the 'Strategy 2010' report, published in March 1999. Strategy 2010 emphasised the need for economic change and made over 60 recommendations for developing the economy over the following ten years, one of which was the establishment of an Economic Development Forum (EDF). The EDF is a partnership body that provides a formal mechanism through which a wide range of key organisations can advise ministers in Northern Ireland on issues relating to the development and future competitiveness of the Northern Ireland economy. Membership of the forum comprises central government, local government and the major social partners.

The EDF's first publication – *Working Together for a Stronger Economy* – was launched in June 2002 and sets out seven key strategic priorities to be addressed if the Northern Ireland economy is to be significantly strengthened by the year 2010.

A few distinctive facts about Northern Ireland

- Estimates from the 1991 Census suggest that around 142,000 people in Northern Ireland had some ability to use Irish as a means of communication, either orally or in writing.

- Unlike most other areas of the UK, Northern Ireland's secondary education retains a largely selective system with pupils going to grammar schools or secondary intermediate schools according to academic ability, although there are proposals to change this arrangement (see page 105). Since 1998 education authorities have a statutory duty to promote Irish-medium education.

- Northern Ireland has some excellent facilities for the arts. The Waterfront Hall in Belfast is an entertainment venue and convention centre and home to the Ulster Concert Orchestra, while the Odyssey Centre on the east bank of the river Lagan includes a science centre, IMAX film theatre, indoor arena, entertainment pavilion and piazzas (see chapter 16).

- Gaelic Athletic Association (GAA) footballers, hurlers and camogie players from northern counties are often involved in all-Ireland championships in these traditional Irish sports (see chapter 18).

- A fifth of the total area in Northern Ireland is designated as an Area of Outstanding Natural Beauty and just under a sixth is Green Belt land (see chapter 19).

A new research, development and innovation strategy, due to be published in March 2003, will lead to increased emphasis on the promotion of innovation and creativity within the Northern Ireland economy.

The public expenditure allocation within the Northern Ireland Executive's responsibility for 2002/03 is £6.9 billion.

Economic assistance

The Berlin EU summit at the end of March 1999 agreed a Special Programme for Northern Ireland in support of peace, worth about £366 million between the years 2000 and 2004. It also confirmed the renewal for three years of EU support of approximately £10 million a year for the International Fund for Ireland, set up in 1986 by the British and Irish Governments to encourage cross-border co-operation in business enterprise, tourism, community relations, urban development, agriculture and rural development. Donors include the United States, Canada, Australia, New Zealand and the European Union. The total resources available to the fund to date amount to £431 million.

Further reading

Northern Ireland Office Departmental Report 2002: The Government's Expenditure Plans 2002–03 to 2003–04. Cm 5432. The Stationery Office, 2002.

Northern Ireland Yearbook 2002: A Comprehensive Reference Guide to the Political, Economic and Social Life of Northern Ireland. Lagan Consulting 2001. Distributed by The Stationery Office.

Websites

Northern Ireland Assembly
www.niassembly.gov.uk

Northern Ireland Executive
www.northernireland.gov.uk

Northern Ireland Office
www.nio.gov.uk

Northern Ireland Tourist Board
www.discovernorthernireland.com

www.

4 Scotland

Population

Scotland's population has changed relatively little in the last 50 years. In June 2001 the estimated population was 5.1 million (see Table 4.1), compared with 5.2 million in 1971 and 5.1 million in 1951. The population density is the lowest in the UK, averaging 64 people per sq km in 2001. Within Scotland, the population density was highest in Glasgow City at 3,298 people per sq km and lowest in the Highland council area at only 8 people per sq km. Three-quarters of the population live in the central lowlands where two of Scotland's largest cities are situated: the capital, Edinburgh (population 449,000) in the east and Glasgow (population 579,000) in the west.

Representation at Westminster

Of the 659 seats in the UK Parliament at Westminster, 72 currently represent constituencies

Cities in Scotland

The granting of city status is a 'reserved matter' on which UK Government ministers advise the Sovereign. However, any comments which the devolved administrations may wish to make are taken into account in deciding which towns should be honoured in this way.

In March 2002 Stirling was one of five towns in the UK granted city status to mark the Queen's Golden Jubilee (see also chapters 2, 3 and 5). Its roots were established over 800 years ago when it was one of the most important settlements in Scotland, occupying a position which allowed it to control the lowest crossing point of the River Forth. One of the most significant events in its history is the Battle of Stirling Bridge which was fought and won by William Wallace in 1297 against an occupying English army.

The other Scottish cities are Aberdeen, Dundee, Edinburgh, Glasgow and Inverness.

Table 4.1 Scotland population and population change, 2001

	Population (thousands)	Change in population 1981–2001 (%)
Aberdeen City	212	−0.3
Aberdeenshire	227	20.1
Angus	108	2.6
Argyll and Bute	91	0.4
Clackmannanshire	48	−0.3
Dumfries and Galloway	148	1.6
Dundee City	145	−14.2
East Ayrshire	120	−5.5
East Dumbartonshire	108	−1.3
East Lothian	90	11.7
East Renfrewshire	89	11.4
Edinburgh, City of	449	0.7
Eilean Siar[1]	26	−16.2
Falkirk	145	0.1
Fife	350	2.4
Glasgow City	579	−18.8
Highland	209	7.2
Inverclyde	84	−16.8
Midlothian	81	−3.1
Moray	87	4.2
North Ayrshire	136	−1.1
North Lanarkshire	321	−6.0
Orkney Islands	19	0.2
Perth and Kinross	135	10.7
Renfrewshire	173	−6.6
Scottish Borders	107	5.6
Shetland Islands	22	−16.7
South Ayrshire	112	−0.9
South Lanarkshire	302	−2.5
Stirling	86	7.4
West Dumbartonshire	93	−11.8
West Lothian	159	14.2
Scotland	**5,064**	**−2.2**

1 Formerly Western Isles.
Source: Office for National Statistics and General Register Office for Scotland

Scotland: council areas

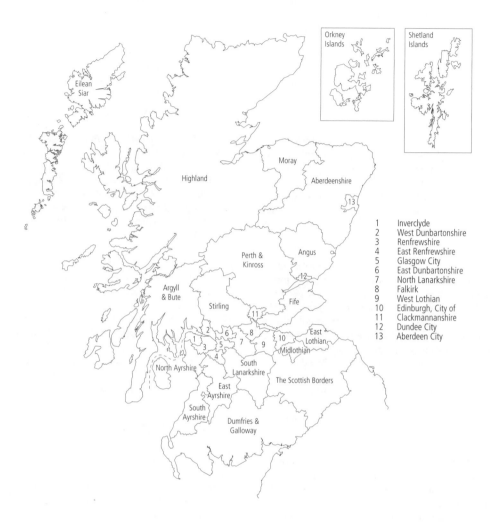

1	Inverclyde
2	West Dunbartonshire
3	Renfrewshire
4	East Renfrewshire
5	Glasgow City
6	East Dunbartonshire
7	North Lanarkshire
8	Falkirk
9	West Lothian
10	Edinburgh, City of
11	Clackmannanshire
12	Dundee City
13	Aberdeen City

in Scotland. The *Scotland Act 1998*, which set up the Scottish Parliament and Executive (see below), removed the statutory minimum of 71 Scottish seats, and required the Boundary Commission for Scotland to determine the level of Scottish representation by applying the same electoral quota as in England. The Boundary Commission published its provisional recommendations of new boundaries for Westminster constituencies in Scotland in February 2002, recommending that there should be 59 Scottish seats at the Westminster Parliament. The Commission is due to make its final review report between December 2002 and December 2006.

The House of Commons Scottish Grand Committee comprises all MPs in Scottish constituencies and may be convened anywhere in Scotland as well as at Westminster. Its business can include questions tabled for oral answer, ministerial statements, and other debates that are referred to it, including those on statutory instruments.

The Scottish Parliament and Scottish Executive

In a referendum held in September 1997, 74 per cent of those who voted endorsed the UK Government's proposals to set up a Scottish Parliament and Executive to administer Scottish affairs. On a second question – whether to give the new Parliament tax-varying powers – 64 per cent were in favour. Legislation was introduced in the Westminster Parliament in December 1997 and the following November the *Scotland Act 1998* passed into law.

Elections to the first Scottish Parliament for almost 300 years were held in May 1999, and it met for the first time in July of that year. Unlike the Westminster Parliament, the Scottish Parliament does not have a second chamber to revise legislation which comes before it. Detailed scrutiny of Bills is carried out in committees or by taking evidence from outside experts. The House of Lords no longer considers Scottish legislation on devolved matters (although it remains the final court of appeal in hearing civil cases arising from the Scottish courts – see chapter 14).

The Scottish Parliament's 129 members (MSPs) are elected for a fixed four-year term. The Additional Member System of proportional representation is used in Scottish Parliamentary elections, giving each voter two votes: one for a constituency MSP and one 'regional' vote for a registered political party or an individual independent candidate. There are 73 single-member constituency seats and 56 seats representing eight regions (based on the European parliamentary constituencies), with each region returning seven members. These MSPs are allocated so that each party's overall share of seats in the Parliament reflects its share of the regional vote.

The Labour Party, which has traditionally done well in elections in Scotland, is the largest single party (see Table 4.2), with 55 MSPs. It has 52 of the 73 constituency seats, including nearly all those in central Scotland. The Scottish National Party is the second largest party, with 34 MSPs. Most of its seats come from the 'top-up' PR system, as do 18 of the Conservative Party's 19, making the latter the third largest party in the Parliament. The Conservatives won their first constituency seat in a by-election in March 2000, taking it from the Labour Party.

The Secretary of State for Scotland has a seat in the UK Cabinet and is responsible for representing Scottish interests within the Government through the Scotland Office.

The Scottish Executive – the administrative arm of government in Scotland – has responsibility for all

---

Responsibilities

The Scottish Parliament is responsible for health; education and training; local government; housing; economic development; many aspects of home affairs and civil and criminal law; transport; the environment; agriculture, fisheries and forestry; and sport, culture and the arts. In these areas, the Scottish Parliament is able to amend or repeal existing Acts of the UK Parliament and to pass new legislation of its own.

Responsibility for a number of other issues, including overseas affairs, defence and national security, overall economic and monetary policy, energy, employment legislation and social security, anti-discrimination, asylum and immigration, remains with the UK Government and Parliament as 'reserved' matters under Schedule 5 of the *Scotland Act 1998*.

---

public bodies whose functions and services have been devolved to it, and is accountable to the Scottish Parliament for them.

The Parliament currently meets at the General Assembly Hall in Edinburgh. A new Parliament building is being built at Holyrood, at the lower end of the Royal Mile, where the previous Scottish Parliament met in Parliament House from 1640 to 1707. It is due for completion in autumn 2003.

The First Minister, normally the leader of the party with most support in the Parliament, heads the Scottish Executive. Since the first elections, the Executive has been run by a partnership between Labour and the Liberal Democrats, with the latter having two seats in the Cabinet of the Scottish Parliament, including that of Deputy First Minister. There are 11 Cabinet positions in all. (See Appendix A for addresses and functions of Scottish Executive departments.)

Finance

The Scottish Executive's budget for 2003/04 is £22.8 billion. The majority of the funding for the Scottish Parliament comes from the UK Parliament's block grant through the Secretary of State for Scotland's Office, but other sources of revenue include non-domestic rate income. The Scottish Parliament is solely responsible for the allocation of the total Scottish budget.

The Scottish Parliament has the power to increase or decrease the basic rate of income tax in

Table 4.2 Electoral representation in Scotland, July 2002

	Scottish Parliament			Westminster Parliament (MPs)	European Parliament (MEPs)
	Constituency MSPs	Additional MSPs	Total MSPs		
Labour	52	3	55	56[1]	3
Scottish National Party	7	27	34	5	2
Conservative	1	18	19	1	2
Liberal Democrats	12	5	17	10	1
Independent	1	1	2	–	–
Scottish Socialist Party	–	1	1	–	–
Green	–	1	1	–	–
Total seats	**73**	**56**	**129**	**72**	**8**

1 Including the Speaker of the House of Commons.
Source: Scottish Executive

Scotland – currently 22 pence in the pound – by a maximum of 3 pence. The Scottish Executive has made a commitment not to make use of this power for the lifetime of the current Parliament. A person is liable to pay income tax if he or she is a UK resident for tax purposes and either spends 50 per cent or more of the tax year in Scotland or has his or her only or principal home there.

Representation in Europe

Scotland elects eight of the UK's 87 members (MEPs) to the European Parliament and in 1999 opened an office in Brussels specifically aimed at helping to promote Scotland's interests within the European Union.

Structure of local government

Scotland's 32 single-tier councils are responsible for the full range of local government services, including education, social work, police and fire services, roads, public transport, local planning, urban development, housing, libraries, leisure and recreation. They are not compelled to provide these services themselves: if they choose, they may buy them in from other authorities or the private sector.

A few distinctive facts about Scotland

- Scottish Gaelic, a Celtic language related to Irish, was introduced into Scotland in about AD 500. Today it is spoken by an estimated 70,000 people mostly living along the north-west coast and in the Hebrides. The Scottish Executive is providing over £13.0 million to support Gaelic in 2002/03. Broadcasting is the largest single area, accounting for £8.5 million.

- Education in Scotland is structured differently from other parts of the UK, with significant differences in the school curriculum and a separate system of public examinations (see chapter 10).

- The Scottish legal system (see chapter 14) differs in many respects from that of England. During the 16th century, certain aspects of medieval church law and much of the Roman, or civil, law as developed by the jurists of Holland and France was brought together to form the basis of Scots law. The 1707 Treaty of Union allowed Scotland to keep Scots law, its own courts and its legal profession. The prosecution, prison and police services are also separate from those in England and Wales.

- Scotland has a rich cultural heritage, which invigorates its tradional arts scene and its contemporary culture, particularly in terms of music and the performing arts. There are also several major collections of the fine and applied arts, such as the National Gallery of Scotland and the Scottish National Gallery of Modern Art in Edinburgh, and the Burrell Collection in Glasgow. In July 2001 a Museum of Scottish Country Life was opened at Kittochside near East Kilbride, the first major national museum in the west of Scotland (see chapter 16).

Although local authorities are independent and manage their own day-to-day business, the First Minister has powers to oversee their work in areas such as finance, town and country planning, transport and housing.

Six of the eight police and fire brigades cover the area of more than one local authority and are administered by joint boards appointed by the authorities in their areas. These boards appoint their own Chief Constables and Firemasters who are responsible for day-to-day operations.

'Community Planning' is a key theme in the forthcoming Local Government in Scotland Bill. In practical terms, it would create a framework for local authorities, other public and private bodies, the voluntary sector and the local community aimed at improving service delivery and providing a means of linking national and local priorities.

Community councils

Scotland also has around 1,200 community councils. They are similar to parishes in England and as such are non-political, broadly-based organisations through which communities can speak and act on issues they have identified locally. Although they have no statutory powers, they do have a right to be consulted on local planning issues.

Economy

Extraction of offshore oil and gas, growth in services and, more recently, developments in high-technology industries (such as chemicals, electronic engineering and information technology) have taken the place of the traditional Scottish industries of coal mining, steel production and shipbuilding. Manufacturing still remains important, however, and Scotland's manufacturing exports in 2001 were valued at £18.7 billion.

Some key features of the Scottish economy

- *Electronics:* Scotland has one of the biggest concentrations of the electronics industry in Western Europe. Electrical and instrument engineering exports were worth £11.0 billion in 2001, accounting for 58 per cent of Scotland's manufactured exports.

- *Financial services:* Financial services are one of Scotland's most important industries, responsible for contributing at least £11 billion to the economy. Scotland is the sixth largest equity management centre in Europe and fifteenth in the world. Ten of Scotland's top 20 companies are in the financial services sector, including Scotland's largest company by capital value. Scotland now commands 70 per cent of the UK financial services market outside London. Direct employment in financial services in Scotland is now close to 100,000 with a similar number of people in supporting economic activity, accounting for more than 10 per cent of the Scottish working population.

- *Fishing:* Fishing remains significant, particularly in the north-east and in the Highlands and Islands. In 2001, landings into Scotland accounted for 66 per cent by weight and over 60 per cent by value of landings by UK vessels into the UK. Fish farming, particularly of salmon, has grown in importance;

Scotland produces the largest amount of farmed salmon in the EU.

- *Forestry:* Scotland accounts for just under half of the UK's timber production. In the last ten years there has been significant international and local investment in wood-based panel production and in pulp and paper processing.

- *Oil and gas:* Offshore oil and gas production has made a significant contribution to the UK economy in the last 30 years. Many of the UK's 118 offshore oilfields are to the east of the Isles of Shetland and Orkney or off the east coast of the mainland.

- *Tourism:* Tourism is a major source of revenue and industries supporting tourism provide about 200,000 jobs. In 2001 expenditure by tourists was valued at £4.1 billion and there were around 19.1 million tourist trips, including those originating in Scotland.

- *Whisky:* Whisky production continues to be important to Scotland. In 2001 the value of drinks exports, dominated by whisky, was estimated at £2.3 billion. There are 90 whisky distilleries in Scotland, most of them in the north-east.

Scottish Enterprise and Highlands and Islands Enterprise (see page 339) manage domestic support for industry and commerce, while Scottish Development International (formerly known as Locate in Scotland), a joint operation between the Scottish Executive and Scottish Enterprise, encourages inward investment. In 2001/02, 59 inward investment projects were recorded, which are expected to lead to investment of £271 million and the creation or safeguarding of nearly 6,400 jobs.

Further reading

The Scottish Budget: Annual Expenditure Report of the Scottish Executive. Scottish Executive, 2002.

Scotland Office Departmental Report 2002: The Government's Expenditure Plans 2002–03 to 2003–04. Cm 5430. The Stationery Office, 2002.

Websites

Convention of Scottish Local Authorties
www.cosla.gov.uk

Scotland Office
www.scottishsecretary.gov.uk

Scottish Development International
www.lis.org.uk

Scottish Executive
www.scotland.gov.uk

The Scottish Parliament
www.scottish.parliament.uk

Scottish Tourist Board
www.visitscotland.com

5 Wales

Population

Wales (Cymru in Welsh) has a population of just over 2.9 million, about two-thirds of whom live in the southern valleys and the lower-lying coastal areas. Cardiff, the capital, grew in the 19th century as a coal exporting port, and the two other large ports of Swansea and Newport also depended for their prosperity on the surrounding mining and metal production during the Industrial Revolution. They are still among the most densely populated areas today. The population has grown by 89,700 (3 per cent) in the past 20 years, with Ceredigion (23.1 per cent) seeing the greatest population growth, while both Blaenau Gwent and Merthyr Tydfil lost 7.5 per cent of their populations.

The highest population density in 2001 was in the unitary authority area of Cardiff with 2,176 people per sq km, and the lowest was in Powys with only 24 people per sq km.

Cities in Wales

Throughout the UK, city status cannot be claimed by a town fulfilling certain criteria. Instead, those known to be interested in the honour are invited to apply by way of competition held from time to time. Each application is considered on its merits and the commonly held belief that the place chosen has to have a cathedral is not true.

There are five cities in Wales. Cardiff was made a city in 1905, while Swansea was honoured with city status in 1969 to mark the investiture of the Prince of Wales. The others are Bangor, St David's and the latest, marking the Queen's Golden Jubilee in 2002, Newport.

Newport has been the gateway to Wales since it was the Roman town of Caerleon. Once famous for steelmaking, it is now a centre of high technology industry. In 2010 the city will host the Ryder Cup golf tournament at the Celtic Manor Resort and Hotel.

Representation at Westminster

As part of the UK, Wales returns 40 Members of Parliament (MPs). In July 2002 there were 34

Table 5.1 Wales population and population change, 2001

	Population (thousands)	Change in population 1981–2001 (%)
Blaenau Gwent	70	−7.5
Bridgend (Pen-y-bont ar Ogwr)[1]	129	2.0
Caerphilly (Caerffili)	170	−1.3
Cardiff (Caerdydd)	305	6.4
Carmarthenshire (Sir Gaerfyrddin)	174	5.2
Ceredigion (Sir Ceredigion)	75	23.1
Conwy	110	10.9
Denbighshire (Sir Ddinbych)	93	7.4
Flintshire (Sir y Fflint)	149	7.2
Gwynedd	117	4.4
Isle of Anglesey (Sir Ynys Môn)	67	−2.0
Merthyr Tydfil (Merthyr Tudful)	56	−7.5
Monmouthshire (Sir Fynwy)	85	11.0
Neath Port Talbot (Castell-nedd Port Talbot)	134	−5.8
Newport (Casnewydd)	137	3.5
Pembrokeshire (Sir Benfro)	113	5.2
Powys	126	12.6
Rhondda, Cynon, Taff (Rhondda, Cynon, Taf)	232	−2.7
Swansea (Abertawe)	223	−2.7
Torfaen (Tor-faen)	91	0.3
The Vale of Glamorgan (Bro Morgannwg)	119	5.4
Wrexham (Wrecsam)	129	7.8
Wales (Cymru)	2,903	3.2

1 Welsh-language local authority names are given in parenthesis if there are differences between the English and Welsh names.
Source: Office for National Statistics and National Assembly for Wales

Wales: unitary authorities

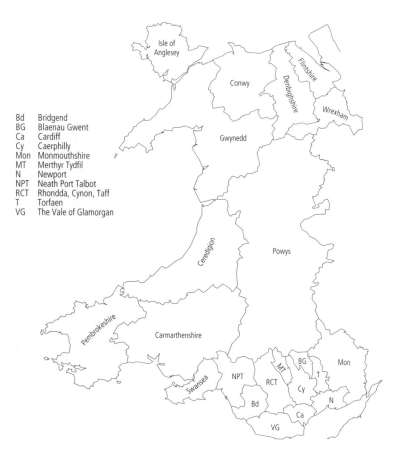

Bd   Bridgend
BG   Blaenau Gwent
Ca   Cardiff
Cy   Caerphilly
Mon   Monmouthshire
MT   Merthyr Tydfil
N   Newport
NPT   Neath Port Talbot
RCT   Rhondda, Cynon, Taff
T   Torfaen
VG   The Vale of Glamorgan

Labour, four Plaid Cymru – The Party of Wales and two Liberal Democrats.

The House of Commons Welsh Grand Committee comprises all MPs in Welsh constituencies and up to five others who may be added from time to time. Its role is to consider Bills referred to it at second reading stage, questions tabled for oral answer, ministerial statements, and other matters relating exclusively to Wales.

Following devolution (see below), the UK Government retains responsibility in Wales for certain matters including foreign affairs, defence, taxation, overall economic policy, crime, justice and prisons, human rights and anti-discrimination issues, social security and broadcasting. The office of Secretary of State for Wales continues with the post holder keeping a seat in the UK Cabinet. He or she is responsible for promoting the devolution settlement, bringing forward primary legislation, bidding for the Assembly's budget and ensuring that Welsh interests are properly represented and considered within the UK Government.

National Assembly for Wales and Welsh Assembly Government

In 1997 the Welsh people narrowly endorsed government proposals to devolve certain powers and responsibilities to a National Assembly. Of those who voted, 50.3 per cent were in favour. The *Government of Wales Act 1998* laid down the necessary statutory framework to establish the National Assembly for Wales, which held its first elections in May 1999 and began functioning as a devolved administration two months later.

In February 2002 the National Assembly voted to make clear the difference in roles between

Table 5.2 Electoral representation in Wales, July 2002

	National Assembly (AMs)			UK Parliament (MPs)	European Parliament (MEPs)
	Constituency seats	Regional seats	Total seats		
Labour	27	1	28	34	2
Plaid Cymru – The Party of Wales	9	8	17	4	2
Conservative	1	8[1]	9	–	1
Liberal Democrats	3	3	6	2	–
Total seats	**40**	**20**	**60**	**40**	**5**

1 One of the Conservative members is not currently a member of the Welsh Conservative Group.
Source: Welsh Assembly Government

ministers and the Assembly as a whole. The Welsh Assembly Government develops and implements policy. It is accountable to the National Assembly and is primarily located in Cathays Park, Cardiff. The National Assembly for Wales debates and approves legislation and holds the Assembly Government to account. Its debating chamber and members are located at Cardiff Bay.

Electors have two votes in Assembly elections: one for their local constituency and one for their electoral region. The Assembly comprises 60 members (AMs): 40 from local constituencies (with the same boundaries as those for Welsh seats in the House of Commons) and 20 regional members. The Assembly is elected by the Additional Member System of proportional representation.

The Labour Party has traditionally had strong support in Wales. It has the largest number of seats in the Assembly (see Table 5.2), although it does not have an overall majority. Since October 2000 it has run the Assembly in partnership with the Liberal Democrats.

The First Minister, who heads the Assembly, is supported by a Cabinet of eight ministers in charge of: economic development; finance, local government and communities; education and lifelong learning; health and social services; culture, sport and the Welsh language ; rural development and Wales abroad; environment; and open government.

The Assembly is also responsible for over 50 public bodies. These include the Welsh Development Agency, with a budget of £202 million in 2002/03 and total expenditure of some £380 million; the Higher Education Funding

Powers of the Welsh Assembly

The National Assembly for Wales only has powers to make secondary legislation (see page 40) which it uses to meet distinctive Welsh needs. Primary legislation on Welsh affairs continues to be made in the UK Parliament at Westminster.

Within Wales, the Assembly has power to develop and put into practice policies in the following areas: agriculture, forestry, fisheries and food; ancient monuments and historic buildings; culture; economic development; education and training; the environment; health and health services; highways; housing; industry; local government; social services; sport and recreation; tourism; town and country planning; transport; water and flood defence; and the Welsh language.

Council for Wales (with planned gross expenditure in 2002/03 of £321 million); the Sports Council for Wales, with projected gross expenditure of £21 million (£10 million in grant in aid from the Welsh Assembly Government and £11 million in Lottery funding for sport) and the Welsh Language Board (with a budget of £7.3 million in 2002/03).

The Secretary of State for Wales is voted the Welsh Budget by the UK Parliament which he must then pass on to the Assembly, after keeping back enough to run his own office. The Assembly's budget for 2002/03 is £10.5 billion and for 2003/04, £11.2 billion.

Representation in Europe

Five representatives from Wales sit as Members of the European Parliament (MEPs) in Brussels: currently two Labour, two Plaid Cymru – The Party of Wales and one Conservative. Elections to

A few distinctive facts about Wales

- Welsh literature has a long tradition and is one of the oldest in Europe. Music is also very important to the Welsh people and Wales is particularly well-known for its choral singing. Special festivals, known as eisteddfodau, encourage both Welsh literature and music (see chapter 16).

- The media in Wales include several Welsh and English language newspapers, local radio stations and the television broadcaster, Sianel Pedwar Cymru (S4C – see chapter 17).

- Among many sporting activities, there is particular interest in rugby union, which has come to be regarded as the Welsh national game. Soccer is also very popular in Wales, and the Football Association Cup Finals of May 2001 and 2002 were held at the Millennium Stadium in Cardiff (see chapter 18).

- About one-quarter of the land in Wales is designated as a National Park or Area of Outstanding Natural Beauty. The three National Parks are Snowdonia, the Brecon Beacons and the Pembrokeshire Coast. In addition, Wales has over 1,000 Sites of Special Scientific Interest and a number of internationally important nature conservation sites (see chapter 19).

the European Parliament are by proportional representation. Wales forms a single constituency.

An office in Brussels aims to promote Welsh interests within the EU and works in close co-operation with the UK Representative Office (UKREP).

Structure of local government

The 22 Welsh unitary authorities (see map on page 27) have collective responsibility for spending over a third of the National Assembly's budget. The Assembly sets the policy framework and makes the secondary legislation within which local government operates. It also has a responsibility to ensure that local decision-making reflects the requirements of the law and, where appropriate, priorities fixed by the Assembly. Whole council elections are held every fourth year, with the next due in 2004.

The unitary authorities in Wales are responsible for schools; social services; local environmental services; housing; local roads; emergency planning; libraries; museums and art galleries; and economic development. Separate authorities are responsible for the police and fire services.

The National Assembly has set up a Partnership Council to advise it on the various functions of local government. It comprises locally elected representatives – including those from the National Parks, police and fire authorities, and community councils (see below) – and selected members of the Assembly. It also assists the Assembly in preparing guidance and advice to local councils.

Communities and community councils

Welsh unitary authorities are subdivided into a number of smaller areas called 'communities'. There are around 1,000 such communities, about 750 of which have community councils with similar powers and functions to parish councils in England (see page 9).

The Welsh language

- Welsh is a Celtic language whose nearest cousins are Cornish and Breton. The language as spoken today is descended directly from Early Welsh which emerged as a distinct tongue as early as the sixth century.

- Estimates suggest that 20 per cent of the population over the age of three in private households are able to speak Welsh. In much of the rural north and west, Welsh remains the first language. It is widely used for official purposes, and is treated equally with English in the work of the National Assembly.

- The National Assembly encourages Welsh-medium education in its schools. Since September 2000, Welsh has been taught – as a first or second language – to all pupils between the ages of 5 and 16, and other subjects are taught in Welsh to primary and secondary schoolchildren in about 500 schools (see chapter 10).

Economy

The Welsh economy, which traditionally relied on coal and steel, experienced some major changes during the 20th century. In recent years, Wales has

Some key features of the Welsh economy

- Although there has been a decline in the steel industry over recent years, it still remains important to the Welsh economy, with crude steel production in Wales at around 4.7 million tonnes in 2001, accounting for 35 per cent of UK steel output.

- Manufacturing accounts for 27 per cent of gross domestic product (GDP) in Wales, compared with 19 per cent in the UK as a whole.

- In the service sector, tourism and leisure services are significant – estimates indicate that about 12.8 million tourist trips were made to Wales from the UK and overseas in 2001.

- A key feature of the economy has been the volume of investment from overseas companies and from elsewhere in the UK. Since 1983, over 2,000 inward investment projects have been recorded in Wales, bringing in a total of £14.3 billion and promising the creation and safeguarding of over 227,000 jobs. Overseas-owned manufacturing companies in Wales employ more than 74,000 people.

attracted a more varied range of manufacturing industries, including many at the forefront of technology, and a growing number involved in e-commerce. Inward investment has also become an important factor in the Welsh economy, and cultural industries are now a rapidly growing contributor.

The Welsh Development Agency (WDA – see page 340) has broad functions and powers, so that it is well placed to contribute to economic regeneration across the whole of Wales.

Further reading

Wales Office Departmental Report 2002: The Government's Expenditure Plans 2002–03 to 2003–04. Cm 5431. The Stationery Office, 2002.

Websites

National Assembly for Wales and Welsh Assembly Government
www.wales.gov.uk

Wales Office
www.walesoffice.gov.uk

Wales Tourist Board
www.visitwales.com

6 Government

The United Kingdom is a parliamentary democracy, based on universal suffrage. It is also a constitutional monarchy in which ministers of the Crown govern in the name of the Sovereign, who is both Head of State and Head of the Government. There is no 'written constitution' as such; instead, the relationship between the State and the people relies on statute law, common law and conventions.[1]

The *UK Parliament* makes primary legislation (other than for matters devolved to the Scottish Parliament and the Northern Ireland Assembly – see chapters 3 and 4) and is the highest authority in the land. It continues to have the supreme authority for government and law-making in the UK as a whole (see page 33). The *executive* comprises the Government (members of the Cabinet and other ministers responsible for policies); government departments and agencies; local authorities; public corporations; independent regulatory bodies; and certain other organisations subject to ministerial control. The *judiciary* (see chapter 14) determines common law and interprets statutes.

In her role as Monarch, the Queen is head of the executive and plays an integral part in the legislature. She heads the judiciary and is both the commander-in-chief of all the armed forces of the Crown and 'supreme governor' of the established Church of England.

Following devolution (see chapters 3, 4 and 5), the responsibilities of the Secretaries of State for

Scotland, Wales and Northern Ireland changed considerably, although they retain their positions in the UK Cabinet. They ensure that the 'reserved interests' (see pages 22 and 33) of the countries they represent are properly considered in central government and they lead the presentation of government policy in their parts of the UK. They are also responsible for safeguarding and promoting the devolution settlements of their respective countries.

Parliamentary electoral system

For electoral purposes the UK is divided into 659 constituencies, each of which returns one member to the House of Commons. To ensure that constituency electorates are kept roughly equal, four permanent Parliamentary Boundary Commissions, one each for England, Wales, Scotland and Northern Ireland, have kept constituency size under review. After 2005, when the Boundary Commissions for England, for Wales and for Scotland are due to report on their latest reviews, all four Commissions will be absorbed into the independent Electoral Commission – see page 55.

Voters

British citizens, and citizens of other Commonwealth countries and the Irish Republic resident in the UK, may vote in parliamentary elections provided that they are:

- aged 18 or over;

- included in the register of electors for the constituency; and

- not subject to any legal incapacity to vote.

---

1 Conventions are rules and practices which are not legally enforceable but which are regarded as indispensable to the working of government.

People not entitled to vote include members of the House of Lords, foreign nationals resident in the UK (other than Commonwealth citizens or citizens of the Irish Republic), some patients detained under mental health legislation, sentenced prisoners and people convicted within the previous five years of corrupt or illegal election practices. Members of the armed forces, Crown servants and staff of the British Council employed overseas (together with their wives or husbands if accompanying them) may be registered at an address in the constituency where they would live if not serving abroad. British citizens living abroad may apply to register as electors for a period of up to 15 years after they have left the UK.

Voting procedures

Each elector may cast one vote, and usually does so in person at a polling station. However, measures aimed at modernising voting and registration procedures for UK elections were introduced under the *Representation of the People Act 2000* and implemented for the first time in the General Election held in June 2001. Provisions in the Act include:

- the right for electors to cast their vote by post if they find that method more convenient;

- a rolling register, updated monthly, to enable voters to register at any time of the year;

- improved access and facilities for disabled voters; and

- easier registration for homeless people, those in mental institutions, and unconvicted or remand prisoners.

Voting is not compulsory in the UK and the simple majority system is used for Westminster elections. Candidates are elected if they have more votes than any of the other candidates (although not necessarily an absolute majority over all other candidates).

Candidates

British citizens, and resident citizens of other Commonwealth countries and the Irish Republic, may stand for election as Members of Parliament (MPs) provided that they are aged 21 or over and are not disqualified. Disqualified people include undischarged bankrupts; those sentenced to more than one year's imprisonment; members of the

Table 6.1 General Election results by party, June 2001

	MPs elected	% share of UK vote
Labour	412[1]	40.7
Conservative	166	31.7
Liberal Democrats	52	18.3
Scottish National	5	1.8
Plaid Cymru – The Party of Wales	4	0.7
Ulster Unionist	6	0.8
Democratic Unionist	5	0.7
Social Democratic and Labour	3	0.6
Sinn Féin[2]	4	0.7
Speaker	1	0.1
Others	1	0.1

1 One Labour MP subsequently changed parties and now sits as a Liberal Democrat.
2 The Sinn Féin Members have not taken their seats.
Source: House of Commons

House of Lords; and holders of certain offices listed in the *House of Commons Disqualification Act 1975*.

A candidate's nomination for election must be proposed and seconded by two electors registered as voters in the constituency and signed by eight other electors. Candidates do not have to be backed by a political party. A candidate must also deposit £500, which is returned if he or she receives 5 per cent or more of the votes cast.

The maximum sum a candidate may spend on a General Election campaign is £5,483 plus 4.6 pence for each elector in a borough constituency, or 6.2 pence for each elector in a county constituency. A higher limit of £100,000 has been set for by-elections because they are often seen as tests of national opinion in the period between General Elections. All election expenses, apart from the candidate's personal expenses, are subject to these statutory maxima. A candidate is also entitled to send one election communication to each voter free of postal charges.

Parliament

Origins

Medieval kings had to meet all royal expenses, private and public, out of their own income. If extra resources were needed for an emergency, such as going to war, the Sovereign would seek help from his barons in the Great Council – a gathering of leading men which met several times a year. During the 13th century several English kings found their own private revenue, together with aid from the barons, insufficient to meet the expenses of government. They therefore called not only their land-owning barons to the Great Council but also representatives of counties, cities and towns, mainly to get them to agree to additional taxation. In this way the Great Council came to include those who were summoned *by name* (who, broadly speaking, were later to form the House of Lords) and those who were *representatives of communities* – the Commons. These two groups, together with the Sovereign, became known as 'Parliament' – a term meaning a meeting for *parley* or discussion.

Originally the King's legislation needed only the agreement of his councillors, but, starting with the right of individuals to present petitions, the Commons was eventually allowed to appeal to the Crown on behalf of groups of people. During the 15th century they won the right to take part in the process of giving their requests – or 'Bills' – the form of law.

Powers

There are three parts of Parliament – the elected House of Commons, the appointed House of Lords and the Sovereign. They meet together only on occasions of symbolic significance such as the State Opening of Parliament, when the Commons is summoned by the Sovereign to the House of Lords. The agreement of all three is normally needed to pass laws, but that of the Sovereign is given as a matter of course.

Parliament at Westminster can legislate for the UK as a whole and has powers to legislate for any parts of it separately. However, by convention it will not normally legislate on devolved matters in Scotland and Northern Ireland without the agreement of the Scottish Parliament and the Northern Ireland Assembly respectively. Under the Acts of Parliament which set up these administrations, the Westminster Parliament still has UK-wide responsibility in a number of areas, including defence, foreign affairs, economic and monetary policy, social security, employment, and equal opportunities.

In the Channel Islands and the Isle of Man, which are Crown dependencies and not part of the UK

(see also page 6), legislation on domestic matters normally takes the form of laws enacted by Island legislatures. However, UK laws are sometimes extended to the Islands, with their agreement, for example in matters such as immigration and broadcasting.

As there are no legal restraints imposed by a written constitution, Parliament may legislate as it pleases, as long as the UK meets its obligations as a member of the European Union (see page 59). It can make or change law, and overturn established conventions or turn them into law. It can even legislate to prolong its own life beyond the normal period without consulting the electorate.

In practice, however, Parliament does not assert itself in this way. Its members work within the common law and normally act according to precedent. The House of Commons is directly responsible to the electorate, and, during the 20th century, the House of Lords increasingly recognised the supremacy of the elected chamber.

Functions

The main functions of Parliament are:

- to pass laws;

- to provide (by voting for taxation) the means of carrying on the work of government;

- to scrutinise government policy and administration, including proposals for expenditure; and

- to debate the major issues of the day.

In performing these, Parliament helps to bring the relevant facts and issues to the attention of the electorate. By custom, Parliament is also informed before important international treaties and agreements are ratified. The making of treaties is, however, a royal prerogative carried out on the advice of the Government and does not need parliamentary approval.

Meetings

A Parliament has a maximum duration of five years, but not all Parliaments serve their full five-year term. The maximum life has been prolonged by legislation only in rare circumstances, such as the two World Wars. The Sovereign dissolves Parliament and calls for a General Election on the advice of the Prime Minister.

The life of a Westminster Parliament is divided into sessions. Each usually lasts for one year – normally beginning and ending in October or November. There are 'adjournments' (when the House does not sit) at night, at weekends, at Christmas, Easter and the late Spring Bank Holiday, and during a long summer break usually starting in late July. The average number of 'sitting days' in a session is about 148 in the House of Commons and about 152 in the House of Lords.[2] At the start of each session the Sovereign's speech to Parliament outlines the Government's policies and proposed legislative programme. Each session is ended by the Sovereign dismissing it – called 'prorogation'. Parliament then 'stands prorogued' for a few days until the new session begins. Prorogation brings to an end nearly all parliamentary business: in particular, public Bills which have not been passed by the end of the session are lost, unless the Opposition has agreed they may be carried over.

House of Commons

The House of Commons consists of 659 elected MPs. In July 2002 there were 118 women MPs and 12 MPs who had declared that they were of minority ethnic origin. Of the 659 seats, 529 represent constituencies in England, 40 in Wales, 72 in Scotland, and 18 in Northern Ireland.

After a Parliament has been dissolved, and a General Election has been held, the Sovereign summons a new Parliament. When an MP dies, resigns[3] or is made a member of the House of Lords, a by-election takes place. Members are paid an annual salary of £55,118 (from April 2002) and provided with up to £72,310 for staff salaries and £18,234 for incidental expenses. (For ministers' salaries see page 45). All MPs are entitled to travel allowances and London members may claim a supplement for the higher cost of living in the capital. MPs from other parts of the UK may receive allowances for subsistence and for a second home near Westminster.

Officers of the House of Commons

The chief officer of the House of Commons is the Speaker, elected by MPs to preside over the House. Other officers include the Chairman of Ways and Means and two deputy chairmen, who may all act as Deputy Speakers. They are elected by the House as nominees of the Government, but may come from the Opposition as well as the government party. The House of Commons Commission, a statutory body chaired by the Speaker, is responsible for the administration of the House.

Permanent officers (who are not MPs) include the Clerk of the House of Commons – the principal adviser to the Speaker on the House's privileges and procedures. The Clerk's other responsibilities relate to the conduct of the business of the House and its committees. The Clerk is also accounting officer for the House. The Serjeant at Arms, who waits upon the Speaker, carries out certain orders of the House. He is also the official housekeeper of the Commons' part of the Palace of Westminster and is responsible for security.

House of Lords

Current composition

The House of Lords consists of the Lords Spiritual and the Lords Temporal. The Lords Spiritual are the Archbishops of Canterbury and York, the Bishops of London, Durham and Winchester, and the 21 next most senior bishops of the Church of England. The Lords Temporal consist of:

- hereditary peers;

- life peers created to help carry out the judicial duties of the House (up to 12 Lords of Appeal in Ordinary or 'Law Lords' and a number of other Lords of Appeal);[4] and

- all other life peers.

The number of peers eligible to sit at July 2002 is shown in Table 6.2 (see page 35), which also shows how the three main political parties were represented. Crossbenchers, many of whom have specialist knowledge and expertise, do not vote with a political party. There were 116 women peers at July 2002.

2 Taken over the last seven sessions. This includes two 'short' sessions in the election years of 1997 (1996–97, 79 days) and 2001 (2000–01, 83 days) and the 'long' session in 1997–98 (228 days).

3 By tradition, an MP who wishes to resign from the House can do so only by applying for office as Crown Steward or Bailiff of the Chiltern Hundreds, or Steward of the Manor of Northstead. These positions disqualify the holder from membership of the House of Commons.

4 The House of Lords is the final court of appeal for civil cases in the UK and for criminal cases in England, Wales and Northern Ireland (see chapter 14).

Table 6.2 Composition of the House of Lords at July 2002

	Hereditary	Life
Lords Spiritual		26
Lords Temporal		
Conservative	49	170
Labour	4	187
Liberal Democrat	5	60
Crossbenchers[1]	32	147
Other	0	8
Total Lords Temporal	90	572

1 Includes Law Lords.
Source: House of Lords

Members of the House of Lords receive no salary for their parliamentary work, but they can claim for expenses incurred in attending the House (for which there are maximum daily rates) and for certain travelling expenses. Average daily attendance is about 369 members.

Reform
In its first term of office, the Government announced that it wanted the House of Lords to be more representative of British society at the start of the 21st century. As a first step, it passed legislation in November 1999 to reduce the number of hereditary peers from over 750 to 92.

In May 2000 the House of Lords Appointments Commission was set up to make recommendations on the appointment of non-political peers to be chosen from public nominees. The Commission invited nominations in September 2000 and in April 2001 the Queen announced her intention to give non-political life peerages to the 15 people recommended. They were selected from a total of 3,166 applications on the basis that they would bring considerable experience and authority to the House of Lords, adding to the range of expertise available in a number of areas, including science, social policy, housing, employment, education, business and international affairs.

After winning its second consecutive term of office in June 2001, the Government announced its intention to consult and then introduce legislation to implement the next phase of House of Lords reform. A White Paper (*The House of Lords – Completing the Reform*) was published in November 2001. In May 2002 the Lord Chancellor announced that the Government was inviting the House of Commons and the House of Lords to establish a Joint Committee to take the reform forward.

The Joint Committee has been asked to prepare a report on options for the ultimate composition and powers of the House of Lords once a complete reform has been accomplished. These options, which include a fully nominated and fully elected House, and any intermediate options, will be presented to both Houses and put to a free vote. The Committee has also been asked to recommend a transition strategy for the reform process.

Officers of the House of Lords
The House is presided over by the Lord Chancellor (see page 45), who sits on the woolsack[5] and acts as Speaker of the House. If the Lord Chancellor is not present, a nominated deputy takes his place.

As Clerk of the House of Lords, the Clerk of the Parliaments is responsible for the records of proceedings of the House of Lords and for the text of Acts of the UK Parliament. He is the accounting officer for the House, and is in charge of its administrative staff, known as the Parliament Office. The Gentleman Usher of the Black Rod, usually known simply as 'Black Rod', is responsible for security, accommodation and services in the House of Lords' part of the Palace of Westminster.

Parliamentary privilege
To ensure that Parliament can carry out its duties without hindrance, certain rights and immunities apply collectively to each House and its staff, and individually to each Member. These include freedom of speech; first call on the attendance of Members, who are therefore free from arrest in civil actions and excused from serving on juries, or being forced to attend court as witnesses; and the right of access to the Crown, which is a collective privilege of the House. Further privileges include the rights of the House to control its own proceedings (so that it is able, for instance, to keep out 'strangers'[6] if it wishes); to decide upon legal disqualifications for

5 The woolsack is a seat in the form of a large cushion stuffed with wool from several Commonwealth countries; it is a tradition dating from the medieval period, when wool was the chief source of the country's wealth.

6 All those who are not members or officials of either House.

membership and to declare a seat vacant on such grounds; and to punish for breach of its privileges and for contempt. Parliament has the right to punish anybody, inside or outside the House, who commits a breach of privilege – that is, offends against the rights of the House.

Parliamentary procedure

Parliamentary procedure is largely based on precedent and is set down by each House in a code of practice known as its 'Standing Orders'. The debating system is similar in both Houses. Every subject starts off as a proposal or 'motion' by a member. After debate, in which each member (except the person putting forward the motion) may speak only once, the motion may be withdrawn: if it is not, the Speaker or Chairman 'puts the question' whether to agree to the motion or not. The question may be decided without voting, or by a simple majority vote. The main difference between the two Houses is that in the House of Lords the Lord Chancellor or the deputising Chairman do not control procedure; instead such matters are decided by the general feeling of the House, which is sometimes interpreted by its Leader.

In the Commons the Speaker has full authority to enforce the rules of the House and must uphold procedure and protect minority rights. The Speaker may or may not allow a motion to end discussion so that a matter may be put to the vote, and has powers to stop irrelevant and repetitious contributions in debate. In cases of serious disorder the Speaker can adjourn or suspend the sitting. The Speaker may order members who have broken the rules of behaviour of the House to leave the Chamber, or may suspend them for a number of days.

The Speaker supervises voting in the Commons and announces the final result. If there is a tie, the Speaker gives a casting vote (usually to keep the situation as it is), without expressing an opinion on the merits of the question. Voting procedure in the House of Lords is broadly similar. The Lord Chancellor may vote, but does not have a casting vote.

Public access to parliamentary proceedings

Proceedings of both Houses are normally public and may be broadcast on television and radio, either live or, more usually, in recorded or edited form. Complete coverage is available on cable and satellite television and a pilot project to 'webcast'

parliamentary debates on the Internet began in January 2002. The minutes, speeches and parliamentary questions (see page 37) are transcribed in *Hansard*, the Official Report, and are also published daily on the Parliament website.

Select committees

Select committees are appointed for a particular task, generally one of enquiry, investigation and scrutiny. They report their conclusions and recommendations to the House as a whole; in many cases they invite a response from the Government, which is also reported to the House. A select committee may be appointed for a Parliament, or for a session, or for as long as it takes to complete its task. Each committee is constituted on a basis which is in approximate proportion to party strength in the House.

In their examination of government policies, expenditure and administration, select committees may question ministers, civil servants, interested bodies and individuals. Through hearings and published reports, they bring before Parliament and the public an extensive amount of fact and informed opinion on many issues, and build up considerable expertise in their subjects of inquiry.

Fifteen committees have been set up by the House of Commons to examine aspects of public policy, expenditure and administration across the main government departments and their associated public bodies. The Foreign Affairs Select Committee, for example, 'shadows' the work of the Foreign & Commonwealth Office. Other regular Commons select committees include those on Public Accounts and on Standards and Privileges, and there are 'domestic' select committees covering the internal workings of Parliament.

Each House has a select committee to keep it informed of EU developments, and to enable it to scrutinise and debate EU policies and proposals, while three Commons standing committees debate specific European legislative proposals.

In the House of Lords, besides the Appeal and Appellate Committees in which most of the House's judicial work is carried out, there are select committees – working in the same manner as House of Commons committees – on the European Union, Science and Technology, the Constitution, and Economic Affairs. From time to time other committees may also be set up to

Examination of government policy

In addition to the scrutiny by select committees, both Houses offer a number of other opportunities for the Opposition and the Government's own backbenchers to examine policy. In the House of Commons, these include:

- *Question Time:* for 55 minutes on Monday, Tuesday, Wednesday and Thursday, ministers answer MPs' questions. Prime Minister's Question Time takes place for half an hour every Wednesday when the House is sitting. Parliamentary Questions are one means of finding out about the Government's intentions. They are also a way of raising complaints brought to MPs' notice by constituents. MPs may also put questions to ministers for written answer; the questions and answers are published in *Hansard*. There are about 40,000 questions every year.

- *Adjournment debates:* MPs use motions for the adjournment of the House to raise constituency cases or matters of public concern. There is a half-hour adjournment period at the end of the business of the day, and opportunities for several adjournment debates on Wednesday mornings. Westminster Hall is also widely used for adjournment debates.

- *Emergency debates:* an MP wishing to discuss a 'specific and important matter that should have urgent consideration' may, at the end of Question Time, ask for an adjournment of the House. On the very few occasions when this action is successful, the matter is debated for three hours in what is known as an emergency debate, usually on the following day.

- *Early day motions (EDMs):* backbench MPs may express their views on particular issues in this way. A number of EDMs are tabled each sitting day; they are very rarely debated but can be useful in measuring the amount of support for the topic by the number of MPs who add their signatures to the EDM.

- *Opposition days:* on 20 days in each session (sometimes divided into half-days) opposition parties choose the business to be discussed. Of these days, 17 are allocated to the Leader of the Opposition and three to the second largest opposition party.

- *Expenditure debates:* the details of proposed government expenditure are debated on three days in each session.

- *Procedural opportunities:* criticism of the Government may also occur during the debate on the Queen's Speech at the beginning of each session, on motions of censure for which the Government provides time, and in debates on the Government's legislative and other proposals.

- *Motions of no confidence:* as a final act of parliamentary control, the House of Commons may force the Government to resign by passing a resolution of 'no confidence'. The Government must also resign if the House rejects a proposal which the Government considers so vital to its policy that it has declared it a 'matter of confidence' or if the House refuses to vote the money required for the public service.

consider particular issues (or, sometimes, a particular Bill), and 'domestic' committees – as in the Commons – cover the internal workings of the House.

Control of finances

The UK Parliament (and in particular the House of Commons) has the responsibility of overseeing revenue generation and public expenditure. It has to be sure that the sums granted on each area of spending are used only for the purposes intended. No payment out of the central government's public funds can be made, and no taxation or loans authorised, except by Act of Parliament. However, limited interim payments can be made from the Contingencies Fund.

The Finance Act is the most important piece of annual legislation. It authorises the raising of revenue and is based on the Chancellor of the Exchequer's Budget statement (see page 335). Scrutiny of public expenditure is carried out by House of Commons select committees (see page 36).

The law-making process in the UK Parliament

Statute law consists of Acts of Parliament (primary legislation) and delegated or secondary legislation (usually in the form of statutory instruments) made by ministers under powers given to them by an Act (see page 40). While the *interpretation* of the law is refined constantly in the courts (see chapter 14), *changes* to statute law can only be made by Parliament. (Since devolution, the Scottish Parliament and the Northern Ireland Assembly can also make primary legislation on devolved matters – see pages 22 and 15.)

Draft laws take the form of parliamentary Bills. Proposals for legislation affecting the powers of particular bodies (such as individual local authorities) or the rights of individuals (such as certain plans relating to railways, roads and harbours) are known as Private Bills, and are subject to a special form of parliamentary procedure. Bills which change the general law and make up the more significant part of the parliamentary legislative process are called Public Bills.

Public Bills can be introduced into either House, by a government minister or any MP or peer. Most Public Bills which become Acts of Parliament are introduced by a government minister and are known as 'Government Bills'. Bills introduced by other MPs or peers are known as 'Private Members' Bills (see box on page 40). Government Bills are generally accompanied by Explanatory Notes, written by the Department which is promoting the Bill and updated if it is enacted. The notes are not passed or endorsed by Parliament. The purpose is to provide background information and to make it easier for the reader to understand what the Bill is seeking to achieve.

The main Bills forming the Government's legislative programme are announced in the Queen's Speech at the State Opening of Parliament, which usually takes place in November or shortly after a General Election, and the Bills themselves are introduced into one or other of the Houses over the following weeks.

Before a Government Bill is drafted, there may be consultation with professional bodies, voluntary organisations and others with an interest, including pressure groups looking to promote specific causes. 'White Papers', which are government statements of policy, often contain proposals for changes in the law; these may be debated in Parliament before a Bill is introduced. As part of the process of modernising procedures, some Bills are now published in draft for pre-

legislative scrutiny before beginning their passage through Parliament. The aim is to allow more input from backbenchers and other interested parties at an early stage, helping to save time and reducing the number of amendments made during the legislative process. The Government may also publish consultation papers, sometimes called 'Green Papers', setting out proposals which are still taking shape and inviting comments from the public.

Passage of Government Bills

Public Bills must normally be passed by both Houses (see Figure 6.3 on page 39). Bills relating mainly to financial matters are almost always introduced in the Commons.

Committees of the Whole House

Either House may vote to turn itself into a 'Committee of the Whole House' in order to consider Bills in detail after their second reading. This allows unrestricted discussion: the general rule that an MP or peer may speak only once on each motion does not apply in committee.

Standing committees

House of Commons standing committees debate and consider Public Bills at the committee stage. The committee examines the Bill clause by clause, and may amend it before reporting back to the House. Ordinary standing committees do not have names but are called simply Standing Committee A, B, C and so on; a new set of members is appointed to them to consider each Bill. Each committee has between 16 and 50 members, with a party balance reflecting as far as possible that in the House as a whole. In the Lords, various sorts of committees on Bills may be used (such as Grand Committees and Select Committees – see page 36) instead of, or as well as, a Committee of the Whole House.

In the Commons the House may vote to limit the time available for consideration of a Bill. This is done by passing a 'timetable' motion proposed by the Government, commonly known as a 'guillotine'.

When a Bill has passed through all its parliamentary stages, it is sent to the Queen for Royal Assent, after which it becomes an Act of Parliament. The Royal Assent has not been refused since 1707. In the 2000–01 session 21 Public Bills were enacted.

Figure 6.3 How legislation is made in the UK

House of Commons

Introduction and First Reading

- Lets MPs know that a piece of new legislation is coming up for consideration
- The Bill's title is read out in the House and it is ordered to be printed

Second Reading

- Explains the main purpose of the Bill
- There is a wide-ranging debate on the general policy and principles of the proposed legislation

Committee Stage

- The Bill is examined clause by clause
- Usually takes place in standing committee, although it may occasionally come before a Committee of the Whole House
- MPs may suggest changes by way of amendments

Report Stage

- Gives the whole House an opportunity to reconsider the Bill in its latest form

Third Reading

- House considers the complete Bill as amended
- Only minor amendments can be made

House of Lords

First Reading

- There is no debate: the Bill is ordered to be printed

Second Reading

- The debate has the same purpose as its counterpart in the Commons
- Points that proved contentious in the Commons are likely to be raised again in the Lords

Bill as amended passes to the House of Lords

Committee Stage

- A Committee of the Whole House enables all Members of the Lords to participate and suggest amendments

Report Stage

- Gives another opportunity to look at the amended Bill as a whole
- Often further amendments are made and there is a debate on matters unresolved in committee

Third Reading

- Reviews the Bill in its final form
- Only minor amendments can be made

Commons' consideration of Lords' amendments

- The Commons normally accepts most of the Lords' amendments to non-controversial Bills
- Bills with contentious amendments pass back and forth between the Houses until agreement is reached
- If no agreement can be reached, the Bill can be reintroduced in the next session and would not then need the agreement of the Lords. This happens very rarely

Royal Assent

- The final stage of the legislative process and the point at which the Bill becomes an Act of Parliament

Private Members' Bills

Early in each session backbench members of the Commons ballot for the chance to introduce a Bill on one of the Fridays when such Bills have precedence over government business. The first 20 members whose names are drawn win this privilege, but it does not guarantee that their Bills will pass into law. Members may also present a Bill on any day without debate, while on most Tuesdays and Wednesdays when the Commons is sitting MPs may introduce a Bill under the 'ten minute rule', which gives an opportunity for a brief speech by the member proposing the Bill and one by a member opposing it.

In most sessions some Private Members' Bills become law (although there were none in the 2000–01 session). They do not often require public expenditure, but if they do they cannot go forward to committee stage unless the Government decides to provide the necessary money. Peers may introduce Private Members' Bills in the House of Lords at any time. A Private Member's Bill passed by one House will not proceed in the other unless taken up by a member of that House.

Private Bills

Private Bills are promoted by people or organisations outside Parliament (often local authorities) to give them special legal powers. They go through a similar process to Public Bills, but most of the work is done in committee, where procedures follow a semi-judicial pattern.

Hybrid Bills

Hybrid Bills are Public Bills which may affect private rights, for example, the Channel Tunnel Rail Link Bill, which was passed in 1996. As with Private Bills, there are special arrangements for the passage of Hybrid Bills through Parliament which allow those affected to put their case.

Limitations on the power of the Lords

The main legislative function of the House of Lords is to act as a revising chamber, complementing but not rivalling the elected House of Commons. As a result, it has some limitations on its powers. Under the provisions of the Parliament Acts of 1911 and 1949, the powers of the Lords in relation to 'money Bills' are very restricted. Bills authorising taxation or national expenditure are passed without amendment as a formality. A Bill dealing only with taxation or

expenditure must become law within one month of being sent to the Lords, whether or not the Lords agree to it, unless the Commons direct otherwise.

The Parliament Acts also make it possible for a Bill to be passed by the Commons without the consent of the Lords in certain, though very rare, circumstances. The Lords do not usually prevent Bills from being enacted which the Commons are keen to pass, although they will often amend and return them for further consideration. If no agreement is reached between the two Houses on a non-financial Commons Bill, the Lords can delay the Bill for a period which, in practice, amounts to at least 13 months. Following this, the Bill may be presented to the Queen for Royal Assent, provided it has been passed in the current session and previous session by the Commons. There is one important exception: any Bill to lengthen the life of a Parliament needs the full assent of both Houses.

Secondary legislation

To reduce unnecessary pressure on parliamentary time, primary legislation often gives ministers or other authorities the power to make detailed rules and regulations under an Act by means of secondary or 'delegated' legislation (usually in the form of 'statutory instruments' or 'SIs'). Such powers are normally delegated only to authorities directly accountable to Parliament or to the devolved legislatures, so that the risk of undermining the authority of the UK Parliament is kept to a minimum. Acts which allow for delegated legislation usually give Parliament the opportunity to agree ('affirmative procedure') or disagree ('negative procedure') with any resulting SIs, while some also require that organisations affected must be consulted before rules and orders can be made.

A joint committee of both Houses reports on the technical propriety of these SIs. In order to save time on the floor of the House, the Commons uses standing committees to debate the merits of instruments (unless they are simply laid before the House or subject to negative resolution); actual decisions are taken by the House as a whole. In the Lords, debates on SIs take place on the floor of the House, which (in contrast to primary legislation) does have the power of veto. The House of Lords has appointed a delegated powers scrutiny committee which examines the appropriateness of the powers to make secondary legislation in Bills.

Joint committees

Joint committees, with a membership drawn from both Houses, are appointed in each session to deal with Consolidation Bills[7] and SIs (see page 40). The two Houses may also agree to set up joint select committees on other subjects, such as the Joint Committee on the Reform of the House of Lords (see page 35) and on Human Rights.

The Monarchy

The Monarchy is the oldest institution of government. The Queen's title in the UK is 'Elizabeth the Second, by the Grace of God of the United Kingdom of Great Britain and Northern Ireland and of Her other Realms and Territories Queen, Head of the Commonwealth, Defender of the Faith'. In the Channel Islands and the Isle of Man she is represented by a Lieutenant-Governor.

In addition to being queen of the United Kingdom, the Queen is also Head of State of 15 other realms[8] and Head of the Commonwealth. In each country where she is Head of State, she is represented by a Governor-General, appointed by her on the advice of the ministers of the country concerned and independent of the UK Government.

In the Overseas Territories (see page 66) the Queen is usually represented by governors who are responsible to the UK Government for the administration of the countries in which they serve.

Succession, accession and coronation

The title to the Crown derives partly from statute and partly from common law rules of descent. Despite interruptions in the direct line of succession, inheritance has always been how the Monarchy has passed down the generations, with sons of the Sovereign coming before daughters in succeeding to the throne. When a daughter does succeed, she becomes Queen Regnant, and has the same powers as a king. The 'consort' of a king takes her husband's rank and style, becoming Queen. No special rank or privileges are given to the husband of a Queen Regnant.

7   A Consolidation Bill brings together several existing Acts into one, with the aim of simplifying the statutes.

8   Antigua and Barbuda; Australia; the Bahamas; Barbados; Belize; Canada; Grenada; Jamaica; New Zealand; Papua New Guinea; St Kitts and Nevis; St Lucia; St Vincent and the Grenadines; Solomon Islands; and Tuvalu.

Facts and figures from the current reign
In June 2002 the Queen celebrated her Golden Jubilee. Here are some statistics gathered from her 50 years on the throne:

- the Queen is the fifth longest serving British monarch – only Victoria, George III, Henry III and Edward III have reigned for 50 years or more;

- she is the 40th monarch since William the Conqueror ruled England;

- she has conferred over 380,000 honours and awards, personally held more than 450 investitures and received around 3 million items of correspondence;

- over the course of the reign, well over 1 million people have attended garden parties at Buckingham Palace in London or the Palace of Holyroodhouse in Edinburgh;

- she has given Royal Assent to more than 3,100 Acts of Parliament;

- she has given regular Tuesday evening audiences to ten Prime Ministers;

- in 50 years the Queen has undertaken 251 official visits to 128 different countries ranging in size from the Cocos Islands (area 14 sq km, population 655) to the People's Republic of China (area 9.6 million sq km, population 1.25 billion). By the end of 2002 she will have visited Canada 20 times, Australia 14 times, New Zealand ten times and Jamaica six times;

- she has sent almost 100,000 telegrams to people aged 100 and more than 280,000 telegrams to couples celebrating their 60th wedding anniversaries in the UK and the Commonwealth;

- she has given 88 State banquets and launched 17 ships (including the *Queen Elizabeth 2* in September 1967); and

- she has sat for over 120 portraits during her reign, the most recent being painted in 2001 by Lucian Freud.

Under the Act of Settlement of 1700, only Protestant descendants of Princess Sophia, the Electress of Hanover (a granddaughter of James I

Figure 6.4 Principal members of the Royal Family from the reign of Queen Victoria to July 2002

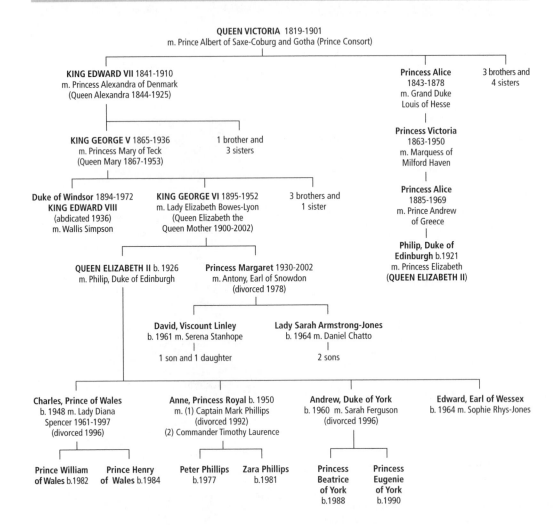

QUEEN VICTORIA 1819-1901
m. Prince Albert of Saxe-Coburg and Gotha (Prince Consort)

KING EDWARD VII 1841-1910
m. Princess Alexandra of Denmark
(Queen Alexandra 1844-1925)

Princess Alice
1843-1878
m. Grand Duke
Louis of Hesse

3 brothers and
4 sisters

KING GEORGE V 1865-1936
m. Princess Mary of Teck
(Queen Mary 1867-1953)

1 brother and
3 sisters

Princess Victoria
1863-1950
m. Marquess of
Milford Haven

Duke of Windsor 1894-1972
KING EDWARD VIII
(abdicated 1936)
m. Wallis Simpson

KING GEORGE VI 1895-1952
m. Lady Elizabeth Bowes-Lyon
(Queen Elizabeth the
Queen Mother 1900-2002)

3 brothers and
1 sister

Princess Alice
1885-1969
m. Prince Andrew
of Greece

QUEEN ELIZABETH II b. 1926
m. Philip, Duke of Edinburgh

Princess Margaret 1930-2002
m. Antony, Earl of Snowdon
(divorced 1978)

Philip, Duke of
Edinburgh b.1921
m. Princess Elizabeth
(QUEEN ELIZABETH II)

David, Viscount Linley
b. 1961 m. Serena Stanhope

Lady Sarah Armstrong-Jones
b. 1964 m. Daniel Chatto

1 son and 1 daughter

2 sons

Charles, Prince of Wales
b. 1948 m. Lady Diana
Spencer 1961-1997
(divorced 1996)

Anne, Princess Royal b. 1950
m. (1) Captain Mark Phillips
(divorced 1992)
(2) Commander Timothy Laurence

Andrew, Duke of York
b. 1960 m. Sarah Ferguson
(divorced 1996)

Edward, Earl of Wessex
b. 1964 m. Sophie Rhys-Jones

Prince William
of Wales b.1982

Prince Henry
of Wales b.1984

Peter Phillips
b.1977

Zara Phillips
b.1981

Princess
Beatrice
of York
b.1988

Princess
Eugenie
of York
b.1990

of England and VI of Scotland), are eligible to succeed. The order of succession to the throne (see also page 44) can be altered only by common consent of the countries of the Commonwealth of which the Monarch is Sovereign.

The Sovereign succeeds to the throne as soon as his or her predecessor dies: there is no interval without a ruler. He or she is at once proclaimed at an Accession Council, to which all members of the Privy Council (see page 44) are called. Members of the House of Lords, the Lord Mayor, Aldermen and other leading citizens of the City of London are also invited.

The coronation follows the accession. The ceremony takes place at Westminster Abbey in London in the presence of representatives of both Houses of Parliament and all the major public organisations in the UK. The Prime Ministers and leading members of the Commonwealth nations and representatives of other countries also attend.

Royal income, expenditure and business activity

Public funds (known as the 'Civil List') and government departments together meet the costs of the Queen's official duties. In June 2002 an annual report of Civil List expenditure was

February–August 2002: the Queen makes a Golden Jubilee tour of Australia, Jamaica and New Zealand, and visits 70 cities in the UK.

Montego Bay, Jamaica.

PA

Portree, Isle of Sky.

PA

Bangor, North Wales.

PA

Scunthorpe, Lincolnshire.

PA

3-4 June 2002: Golden Jubilee celebrations in London.

PA

PA

PA

Above left: Brian May, standing on the roof of Buckingham Palace, plays the National Anthem at the start of the Jubilee pop concert.

Above right: Concorde and the Red Arrows, part of a formation flight over The Mall.

Left: the Queen and Prince Philip meet members of a youth theatre group.

Opposite

Above left: fireworks seen from The Mall.

Above right: the Queen travels in the Gold State Coach on her way to a thanksgiving service at St Paul's Cathedral.

Bottom: fireworks over Buckingham Palace.

REUTERS

PA

PA

3 June 2002: Golden Jubilee celebrations at home and abroad.

Scientists from the British Antarctic Survey celebrate in temperatures close to -20^0 C. The beacon is one of many lit in the UK and abroad, a reminder of events at the last Golden Jubilee (that of Queen Victoria).

REUTERS

Afghanistan: British soldiers serving with the International Security Assistance Force (ISAF).

REUTERS / CAREN FIROUZ

Greater Manchester.   PA

Glasgow.   PA

February 2002: Five stamps are issued to commemorate the 50th anniversary of the Queen's accession to the throne.

April 2002: members of the public pay their respects to Queen Elizabeth the Queen Mother as her coffin lies in state at Westminster Hall.

The European Union

Member countries
Candidate countries

Finland
Estonia
Latvia
Lithuania
Sweden
Poland
Slovakia
Hungary
Czech Republic
Austria
Slovenia
Denmark
Germany
Netherlands
Belgium
Luxembourg
France
Italy
United Kingdom
Ireland
Spain
Portugal
Romania
Bulgaria
Turkey
Greece
Cyprus
Malta

The Commonwealth

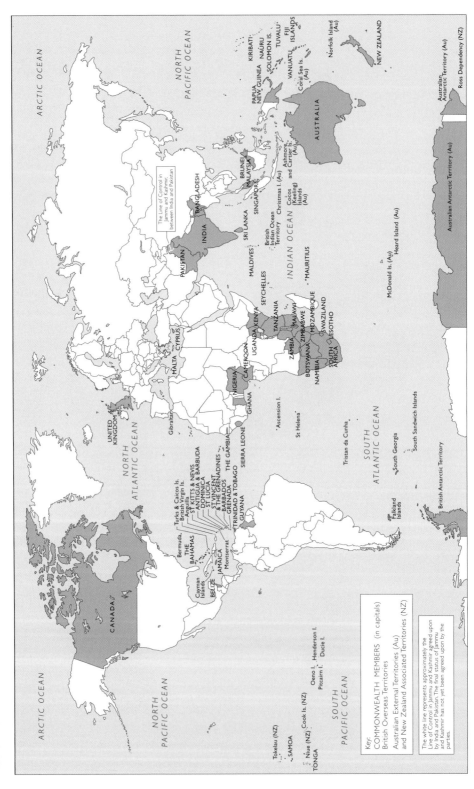

ARCTIC OCEAN

NORTH
PACIFIC OCEAN

Tokelau (NZ)
SAMOA
Niue (NZ) Cook Is. (NZ)
TONGA

SOUTH
PACIFIC OCEAN

Key:
COMMONWEALTH MEMBERS (in capitals)
British Overseas Territories
Australian External Territories (Au)
and New Zealand Associated Territories (NZ)

The white line represents approximately the
Line of Control in Jammu and Kashmir agreed upon
by India and Pakistan. The final status of Jammu
and Kashmir has not yet been agreed upon by the
parties.

CANADA

Oeno I. Henderson I.
Pitcairn I. Ducie I.

Bermuda
Cayman Islands
THE BAHAMAS
Turks & Caicos Is.
British Virgin Is.
Anguilla
ST KITTS & NEVIS
ANTIGUA & BARBUDA
DOMINICA
ST LUCIA
ST VINCENT
& THE GRENADINES
BARBADOS
GRENADA
TRINIDAD & TOBAGO
JAMAICA
BELIZE
Montserrat
GUYANA

NORTH
ATLANTIC OCEAN

UNITED
KINGDOM

Gibraltar

MALTA
CYPRUS

Ascension I.

St Helena

Tristan da Cunha

Falkland
Islands

South Georgia

South Sandwich Islands

SOUTH
ATLANTIC OCEAN

British Antarctic Territory

NORTH
PACIFIC OCEAN

The Line of Control in
Jammu and Kashmir,
between India and Pakistan

PAKISTAN

INDIA

SRI LANKA

MALDIVES

SEYCHELLES

NIGERIA
CAMEROON
GHANA
THE GAMBIA
SIERRA LEONE

UGANDA KENYA
TANZANIA
ZAMBIA
ZIMBABWE
BOTSWANA
NAMIBIA
SOUTH
AFRICA
SWAZILAND
LESOTHO
MALAWI
MOZAMBIQUE

INDIAN OCEAN

British
Indian Ocean
Territory

MAURITIUS

Christmas I. (Au)

Cocos
(Keeling)
Islands
(Au)

BANGLADESH

BRUNEI
MALAYSIA
SINGAPORE

Ashmore
and Cartier Is.
(Au)

AUSTRALIA

PAPUA
NEW GUINEA
SOLOMON IS.

KIRIBATI
NAURU
TUVALU

VANUATU
FIJI
ISLANDS

Coral Sea Is.
(Au)

Norfolk Island (Au)

NEW ZEALAND

McDonald Is. (Au)
Heard Island (Au)

Australian Antarctic Territory (Au)

Australian
Antarctic Territory (Au)

Ross Dependency (NZ)

ARCTIC OCEAN

published for the first time as part of the Royal Household's commitment to openness and accountability in its use of public money. The Civil List Report is more detailed than the ten-yearly Royal Trustees Report (see below), with more information about Royal Household operations, performance indicators and future developments.

In July 2000 a Royal Trustees' Report recommended that Civil List payments should remain at the 1991 level of £7.9 million a year for a further ten years from 2001. About three-quarters of the Queen's Civil List provision is needed to meet the cost of staff. Under the Civil List, the Duke of Edinburgh receives an annual parliamentary allowance of £359,000 (which the Queen reimburses) to enable him to carry out his public duties. In return for the Civil List and other financial support, the Queen surrenders the income from the Crown Estate (£148 million in 2001/02) and other hereditary revenues to the nation. The Prince of Wales does not receive a parliamentary allowance since he is entitled to the annual net revenues of the Duchy of Cornwall.

In 2001/02 the Queen's total expenditure as Head of State was £35.3 million, of which £15.5 million was spent on the upkeep of the royal palaces, £4.9 million on royal travel, and £643,000 on communications and information services.

The Queen's private expenditure as Sovereign comes from the Privy Purse, which is financed mainly from the revenues of the Duchy of Lancaster;[9] her expenditure as a private individual is met from her own personal resources.

Since 1993 the Queen has voluntarily paid income tax on all personal income and on that part of the Privy Purse income which is used for private purposes. She also pays tax on any realised capital gains on her private investments and on the private proportion of assets in the Privy Purse. In line with this, the Prince of Wales pays tax on the income from the Duchy of Cornwall so far as it is used for private purposes.

In July 2001 the Lord Chamberlain, the most senior member of the Queen's Household,

published revised guidelines setting out how members of the Royal Family could pursue careers, including those in business, in a way which would avoid allegations that they were exploiting their royal status. Before a member of the Royal Family takes on a new business activity, he or she must consult the Lord Chamberlain, who would be expected to advise against accepting an invitation to an engagement which could not be kept entirely separate from any aspects of the business activities of the member of the Royal Family concerned.

The Monarch's role in government

As a result of a long process of change during which the Monarchy's absolute power has been gradually reduced, custom now dictates that the Queen usually follows ministerial advice. Within this framework she performs a range of important duties, such as summoning, proroguing (see page 34) and dissolving Parliament; and giving Royal Assent to legislation passed by the UK or Scottish Parliament or by the Northern Ireland Assembly. The Queen formally appoints important office holders, including the Prime Minister and other government ministers (see page 44), judges, officers in the armed forces, governors, diplomats, bishops and some other senior clergy of the Church of England. In instances where people have been wrongly convicted of crimes, she is involved in pardoning them. She also confers peerages, knighthoods and other honours.[10] In international affairs the Queen, as Head of State, has the power to declare war and make peace, to recognise foreign states, to conclude treaties and to take over or give up territory.

The Queen holds Privy Council meetings (see page 44), gives audiences to her ministers and officials in the UK and overseas, receives accounts of Cabinet decisions, reads dispatches and signs state papers. She is consulted on many aspects of national life, and must show complete impartiality.

The law states that a regent has to be appointed to perform the royal functions if the monarch is totally incapacitated. The regency follows the line of succession, provided that the person concerned has reached the age of 18. The first eight members

---

9 The Duchy of Lancaster is a landed estate which has been held in trust for the Sovereign since 1399. It is kept quite apart from his or her other possessions and is separately administered by the Chancellor of the Duchy of Lancaster.

10 Although most honours are conferred by the Queen on the advice of the Prime Minister, a few are granted by her personally – the Order of the Garter, the Order of the Thistle, the Order of Merit and the Royal Victorian Order.

of the Royal Family in order of succession to the Throne are: The Prince of Wales, Prince William of Wales, Prince Henry of Wales, The Duke of York, Princess Beatrice of York, Princess Eugenie of York, The Earl of Wessex, and the Princess Royal.

The Privy Council

The Privy Council was formerly the chief source of executive power in the State, but as the system of Cabinet government developed in the 18th century, the Cabinet took on much of its role. Today the Privy Council is the main way in which ministers advise the Queen on the approval of Orders in Council (such as those granting Royal Charters or enacting subordinate legislation) or on the issue of royal proclamations (such as the summoning or dissolving of Parliament).

In August 2002 there were 474 Privy Counsellors, whose appointments are for life. The Privy Council consists of all members of the Cabinet, other senior politicians, senior judges and some individuals from the Commonwealth. It is only members of the government of the day, however, who play any part in its policy work. The Prime Minister recommends membership of the Privy Council to the Sovereign.

Committees of the Privy Council

There are a number of Privy Council committees (of which the Cabinet is technically one), normally comprising ministers with the relevant policy interest, such as those dealing with legislation from the Channel Islands and the Isle of Man. Except for the Judicial Committee, membership is confined to members of the administration of the day.

The Judicial Committee of the Privy Council is the final court of appeal from courts in UK Overseas Territories and those Commonwealth countries which decided to keep this method of appeal after their independence. In addition, the Committee hears appeals from the Channel Islands and the Isle of Man, and (until the end of 2002) from the disciplinary and health committees of the medical and associated professions. It is the court of final appeal for determining devolution issues (that is, issues as to the limits of the powers and functions of the executive and legislative authorities in Scotland, Northern Ireland and Wales). It also has a limited jurisdiction to hear certain ecclesiastical appeals. Members of the Judicial Committee include the

Lord Chancellor, the Lords of Appeal in Ordinary, other Privy Counsellors who hold or have held high judicial office and certain judges from the Commonwealth.

Her Majesty's Government

Her Majesty's Government consists of those ministers responsible for the conduct of national affairs. The Queen alone appoints the Prime Minister, and all other ministers are appointed by her on the Prime Minister's recommendation. Most ministers are members of the Commons, although the Government is also fully represented by ministers in the Lords. The Lord Chancellor (see page 45) is always a member of the House of Lords.

The composition of governments can vary both in the number of ministers and in the titles of some offices. New ministerial offices may be created, others may be abolished, and functions may be transferred from one minister to another.

Prime Minister

The Prime Minister is also, by tradition, First Lord of the Treasury and Minister for the Civil Service. The Prime Minister's unique position of authority comes from majority support in the House of Commons and from the power to appoint and dismiss ministers. By modern convention, the Prime Minister always sits in the Commons.

The Prime Minister presides over the Cabinet (see page 46), is responsible for allocating functions among ministers and, at regular meetings with the Queen, informs her of the general business of the Government.

The Prime Minister's other responsibilities include recommending a number of appointments to the Queen. These include Church of England archbishops, bishops and certain deans and some 200 other clergy in Crown 'livings'; senior judges, such as the Lord Chief Justice; Privy Counsellors; and Lords Lieutenant. He also recommends certain civil appointments, such as Lord High Commissioner to the General Assembly of the Church of Scotland (after consultation with the First Minister of the Scottish Parliament), The Poet Laureate, The Constable of the Tower of London, and some university posts; and appointments to several public boards and institutions, such as the BBC (British Broadcasting

Corporation), as well as various royal and statutory commissions.

The Prime Minister's Office supports him in his role as head of government. This includes providing policy advice, tracking the delivery of government commitments and initiatives, and ensuring effective communications to Parliament, the media and the public. Following the 2001 General Election, several new units – including the Delivery Unit, the Forward Strategy Unit and the Office of Public Services Reform – have been set up within the Cabinet Office to assist the Prime Minister in these tasks.

Deputy Prime Minister

In May 2002 the Prime Minister announced that the Office of the Deputy Prime Minister (ODPM) would be separated from the Cabinet Office (see page 46) and established as a central government department in its own right, taking responsibility for policy areas from both the old Department for Transport, Local Government and the Regions (DTLR) and the Cabinet Office.

The Deputy Prime Minister is First Secretary of State, deputising for the Prime Minister in his responsibilities in the UK and abroad and chairing seven Cabinet Committees and sub-committees. He will be taking forward the White Papers on regional governance – *Your Region, Your Choice: Revitalising the English Regions* (see page 10) – and urban policy – *Our Towns and Cities: The Future* (see page 307).

The ODPM oversees the work of the Social Exclusion Unit and has responsibility for the Regional Co-ordination Unit and the Government Offices for the Regions (GOs – see page 9). It also assists the Deputy Prime Minister in his role in support of the Prime Minister on issues such as Northern Ireland and climate change. Its new responsibilities include: regional policy; local government; local government finance; planning; housing; urban policy; the Neighbourhood Renewal Unit; and the Fire Service.

Departmental ministers

Ministers in charge of government departments are usually in the Cabinet; they are known as 'Secretary of State' or may have a special title, as in the case of the Chancellor of the Exchequer.

Non-departmental ministers

The holders of various traditional offices, namely the President of the Council, the Chancellor of the Duchy of Lancaster, the Lord Privy Seal, the Paymaster General and, from time to time, Ministers without Portfolio, may have few or no departmental duties. They are therefore available to carry out any duties the Prime Minister may wish to give them. In the present administration, for example, the President of the Council is Leader of the House of Commons, and the Chancellor of the Duchy of Lancaster is Minister for the Cabinet Office.

Lord Chancellor and law officers

The Lord Chancellor holds a special position, as both a minister with departmental functions and the head of the judiciary (see page 197). The three Law Officers of the Crown advising the UK Government are the Attorney General and the Solicitor General (for England and Wales) and the Advocate General for Scotland.

Other ministers

Ministers of State are middle-ranking ministers. They normally have specific responsibilities, and are sometimes given titles which reflect these functions, for example, 'Minister for Housing and Planning' or 'Minister for E-Commerce and Competitiveness'.

The most junior ministers are Parliamentary Under-Secretaries of State (or, where the senior minister is not a Secretary of State, simply Parliamentary Secretaries). They may be given responsibility, directly under the departmental minister, for specific aspects of the department's work.

Ministerial salaries

The salaries of ministers in the House of Commons (from April 2002) range from £82,624 a year for junior ministers to £124,979 for Cabinet ministers (inclusive of their parliamentary salaries – see page 34). The Prime Minister receives a salary of £171,554 and the Lord Chancellor £180,045.

Ministerial salaries in the House of Lords (as at April 2002) range from £64,485 for junior ministers to £94,826 for Cabinet ministers.

The Leader of the Opposition in the Commons receives a salary of £119,159 (inclusive of his parliamentary salary); two Opposition whips in the Commons and the Opposition Leader and Chief Whip in the Lords also receive additional salaries.

Ministerial responsibility

Ministerial responsibility refers both to the collective responsibility for government policy and actions which ministers share, and to ministers' individual responsibility for the work of their own departments.

Collective responsibility means that all ministers unanimously support government policy once it has been settled. The policy of departmental ministers must agree with the policy of the Government as a whole. Once the Government has decided its policy on a particular matter, each minister is expected to support it or resign. On rare occasions, ministers are allowed free votes in Parliament on important issues of principle or conscience.

Ministers are individually accountable for the work of their departments and agencies, and have a duty to Parliament to answer for their policies, decisions and actions.

Departmental ministers normally decide all matters within their responsibility. However, many issues cut across departmental boundaries and need the agreement of more than one minister. The full Cabinet or a Cabinet Committee considers proposals where the issue is one which raises major policy concerns, is likely to lead to significant public comment or criticism, or where the departmental ministers concerned have been unable to agree.

On taking up office ministers resign directorships in private and public companies, and must ensure that there is no conflict between their public duties and private interests. Detailed guidance on handling ministers' financial interests is set out in a ministerial code.

The Cabinet

About 20 ministers (the number can vary) chosen by the Prime Minister sit in the Cabinet; these may include both departmental and non-departmental ministers. The Cabinet balances ministers' individual duties with their collective responsibility as members of the Government and takes the final decisions on all government policy.

Cabinet meetings

The Cabinet meets in private and its business is confidential, although after 30 years Cabinet papers usually become available for inspection in the Public Record Office at Kew, Surrey.

Normally the Cabinet meets weekly when Parliament is sitting, and less often when it is not. Cabinet Committees take some of the pressure off the full Cabinet by settling issues among smaller groups of people or at a lower level, or at least by clarifying them and defining points of disagreement. Committees let those ministers most closely concerned come to decisions in a way which ensures that the Government as a whole can accept full responsibility for them. This delegated responsibility means that Cabinet Committee decisions have the same formal status as those taken by the full Cabinet.

Cabinet Committees include those dealing with defence and overseas policy, economic policy, home and social affairs, the environment, and local government. The membership and terms of reference of all ministerial Cabinet Committees are published. Where appropriate, the Secretary of the Cabinet and other senior Cabinet Office officials go to meetings of the Cabinet and its Committees.

The Cabinet Office

In June 2002 the Cabinet Secretary designate announced that, with the agreement of the Prime Minister, he would restructure the Cabinet Office on taking up office in September. The restructured Cabinet Office would focus its work on four key objectives:

- to support the Prime Minister in leading the Government;

- to support the Government in transacting its business;

- to lead and support Civil Service reform and the delivery of better public service programmes; and

- to co-ordinate national security and intelligence (see page 82).

The Cabinet Secretary is a senior civil servant who reports directly to the Prime Minister. Since 1983, he has also had the role of Head of the Home Civil Service.

The party political system

The party system, which has existed in one form or another since the 18th century, depends upon

The Lobby

As press adviser to the Prime Minister, the Prime Minister's Official Spokesman (PMOS) and other staff in the Prime Minister's Press Office have direct contact with the parliamentary press through regular meetings with the Lobby correspondents. The Lobby correspondents are a group of political journalists with the special privilege of access to the Lobby of the House of Commons, where they can talk privately to government ministers and other members of the House. The PMOS is the accepted channel through which information about parliamentary business is passed to the media.

In May 2002 the Prime Minister's Office put forward proposals to change the Lobby system by opening up the morning briefings to others, including the foreign press, once new, larger premises could be found. Under the proposed new system, Cabinet members, ministers and senior officials would be able to brief the media directly, in addition to the PMOS or his deputy.

there being organised political groups, each of which presents its policies to the electorate for approval. In practice, most candidates in elections, and almost all winning candidates, belong to one of the main parties. A system of voluntary registration for political parties in the UK was introduced in 1998.

For the last 150 years Britain has had a predominantly two-party system. Since 1945 either the Conservative Party, whose origins go back to the 18th century, or the Labour Party, which emerged in the last decade of the 19th century, has held power, each having won eight General Elections. The Liberal Democrats were formed in 1988 when the Liberal Party, which also traced its origins to the 18th century, merged with the Social Democratic Party, formed in 1981. Other parties include two national parties, Plaid Cymru – The Party of Wales (founded in 1925) and the Scottish National Party (founded in 1934). Northern Ireland has a number of parties. They include the Ulster Unionists, formed in the early part of the 20th century; the Democratic Unionists, founded in 1971 by a group which broke away from the Ulster Unionists; the Social Democratic and Labour Party, founded in 1970; and Sinn Féin, which is the political wing of the IRA (see page 5).

The party which wins most seats (although not necessarily the most votes) at a General Election,

or which has the support of a majority of members in the House of Commons, usually becomes the Government. By tradition, the Sovereign invites the leader of that party to form a government. About 100 members of the governing party in the House of Commons and the House of Lords receive ministerial appointments (including appointment to the Cabinet – see page 46) on the advice of the Prime Minister. The largest minority party becomes the official Opposition, with its own leader and 'shadow cabinet'.

The party system in Parliament

Leaders of the Government and Opposition sit opposite one another on the front benches in the debating chamber of the House of Commons, with their supporters ('the backbenchers') sitting behind them. There are similar seating arrangements for the parties in the House of Lords, but many peers do not wish to be associated with any political party, and therefore choose to sit on the 'crossbenches'.

The effectiveness of the party system in Parliament relies to a large extent on the relationship between the Government and the Opposition parties. Depending on the relative strengths of the parties in the House of Commons, the Opposition may try to overthrow the Government by defeating it on a 'matter of confidence' vote. In general, however, the Opposition aims to contribute to the formulation of policy and legislation by constructive criticism; to oppose government proposals with which it disagrees; to table amendments to Government Bills; and to put forward its own policies in order to improve its chances of winning the next General Election.

The Government Chief Whips in the Commons and the Lords, in consultation with their Opposition counterparts, arrange the scheduling of government business; they do so under the direction of the Prime Minister and the Leaders of the two Houses. Collectively, the Chief Whips are often referred to as 'the usual channels' when the question of finding time for a particular item of business is being discussed.

The Chief Whips and their assistants, who are usually chosen by the party leaders, manage their parliamentary parties. Their duties include keeping members informed of forthcoming parliamentary business, maintaining the party's voting strength by ensuring members attend important debates, and passing on to the party leadership the opinions of backbench members.

Unofficial party committees

The Parliamentary Labour Party comprises all members of the party in both Houses. When the Labour Party is in office, a parliamentary committee, half of whose members are elected and half of whom are government representatives, acts as a channel of communication between the Government and its backbenchers in both Houses. When the party is in opposition, the Parliamentary Labour Party is organised under the direction of an elected parliamentary committee, which acts as the 'shadow cabinet'.

The Conservative and Unionist Members' Committee (the 1922 Committee) consists of the backbench membership of the party in the House of Commons. When the Conservative Party is in office, ministers attend its meetings by invitation and not by right. When the party is in opposition, the whole membership of the parliamentary party may attend meetings. The leader appoints a consultative committee, which acts as the party's 'shadow cabinet'.

Financial controls over parties

The *Political Parties, Elections and Referendums Act 2000* contained provisions to make party funding more open, control spending on elections and ensure the fair conduct of referendums. Under the financial provisions in the Act:

- political parties may only accept donations of over £200 from 'permissible donors' – individuals on the UK electoral register, registered companies incorporated in the EU which do business in the UK, registered political parties and trade unions;

- all donations of over £5,000 to a political party's central organisation must be reported to the Electoral Commission (see page 55) on a quarterly basis – weekly during a General Election campaign;

- all donations of over £1,000 to accounting units, such as a constituency association, must be reported to the Electoral Commission;

- individual MPs and other people elected to office, including MEPs (see page 57), members of the devolved assemblies of Wales

and Northern Ireland and the Scottish Parliament, members of local authorities and the Mayor of London, are subject to similar controls on the source of donations and have to report to the Electoral Commission any donations over £1,000;

- a cap on campaign spending by political parties applies before a General Election. A party has an allowance of £30,000 for each constituency contested; and

- third parties at elections (such as trade unions) are also subject to expenditure limits set at 5 per cent of the maximum for political parties.

Government departments

The main role of government departments and their agencies is to implement government policy and advise ministers. They are staffed by politically impartial civil servants and generally receive their funding from money provided by Parliament. They often work alongside local authorities, non-departmental public bodies, and other government-sponsored organisations.

The structure and functions of departments are sometimes reorganised if there are major changes in government policy. A change of government, however, does not necessarily affect the functions of departments.

The work of some departments (for instance, the Ministry of Defence) covers the UK as a whole. Other departments, such as the Department for Work and Pensions, cover England, Wales and Scotland, but not Northern Ireland. Others again, such as the Department for Education and Skills, are mainly concerned with affairs in England and Wales. (For responsibilities associated with the devolved administrations, see chapters 3, 4 and 5.)

Most departments are headed by ministers. However, some are non-ministerial departments headed by a permanent office holder and ministers with other duties are accountable for them to Parliament. For example, the Secretary of State for Education and Skills accounts to Parliament for the work of the Office for Standards in Education (OFSTED). OFSTED is headed by HM Chief Inspector of Schools in

England, who is largely independent of the Secretary of State.

The functions of the main government departments and agencies are set out in Appendix A, pages 477–487.

Non-departmental public bodies

A non-departmental public body (NDPB, sometimes known as a 'quango') is a national or regional public body, working independently of ministers to whom they are accountable. There are two main types of NDPB:

- *Executive NDPBs* are those with executive, administrative, commercial or regulatory functions. They carry out set functions within a government framework but the degree of operational independence varies. Examples include the Arts Council of England, the Environment Agency and the Health and Safety Executive.

- *Advisory NDPBs* are those set up by ministers to advise them and their departments on particular matters. Examples include the Committee on Standards in Public Life and the Low Pay Commission. Some Royal Commissions are also classified as advisory NDPBs.

There are currently over 1,000 NDPBs in the UK. A list of all NDPBs is held centrally by the Cabinet Office and is issued annually in the publication *Public Bodies*. An electronic directory is available via the Cabinet Office website.

The Civil Service

The constitutional and practical role of the Civil Service in Great Britain is to help the Government of the United Kingdom, the Scottish Executive and the National Assembly for Wales formulate their policies, carry out decisions and administer public services for which they are responsible. A separate Northern Ireland Civil Service was created in 1921 to serve the local administration. Its present role is to support the Northern Ireland Executive in the administration of public services for which it has responsibility.

Civil servants are servants of the Crown; in effect this means the Government of the United Kingdom, the Scottish Executive and the National

Assembly for Wales. Executive powers are generally exercised by ministers of the Crown who are in turn answerable to the appropriate Parliament or Assembly. The Civil Service as such has no separate constitutional personality or responsibility. The duty of the individual civil servant is first and foremost to the minister in charge of the department in which he or she is serving. A change of minister, for whatever reason, does not involve a change of staff.

Cabinet ministers may each appoint a maximum of two special advisers. The Prime Minister approves all appointments and they are paid for from public funds. There are about 80 such advisers in the present administration. Their appointments come to an end when the Government's term of office finishes, or when the appointing minister leaves the Government or moves to another appointment.

The Civil Service Code, introduced in 1996, is a concise statement of the role and responsibilities of civil servants. It was revised in 1999 to take account of devolution. The Code includes an independent line of appeal to the Civil Service Commissioners (see page 50) on alleged breaches of the Code.

At June 2001 civil servants constituted about 2 per cent of the working population in employment, and about 10 per cent of all public sector employees. The number of permanent civil servants (on a full-time equivalent basis), including those in the Diplomatic Service (see page 50) fell from 751,000 in 1976 to 482,700 in April 2001. These figures include the Senior Civil Service, which in April 2001 comprised around 3,850 (non-industrial) of the most senior managers and policy advisers. Part-time working has increased over recent years with 13.8 per cent of civil servants (on a headcount basis) working part time at April 2001.

In April 2001 about half of all civil servants (full-time equivalent) provided services direct to the public. These included paying benefits and pensions, running employment services, staffing prisons, issuing driving licences, and providing services to industry and agriculture. Around one in five were employed in the Ministry of Defence and its agencies. The rest were divided between central administrative and policy duties; support services; and services that were largely financially self-supporting, for instance, those provided by the Royal Mint. About four-fifths of civil servants (full-time equivalent) worked outside London.

Civil Service Commissioners

The Civil Service Commissioners are responsible for ensuring that recruitment to the Civil Service should be on merit and based on fair and open competition. The Commissioners, who are independent of government, produce a mandatory recruitment code and audit the recruitment policies and practices of departments and agencies to ensure that they comply. They also approve appointments through external recruitment to the Senior Civil Service, and hear and determine appeals in cases of concern about propriety and conscience under the Civil Service Code.

The Diplomatic Service

The Diplomatic Service, a separate service of some 5,200 people, provides staff for the Foreign & Commonwealth Office (FCO – see page 68) in London and at British diplomatic missions abroad. Terms and conditions of service are comparable, but take into account the special demands of the Diplomatic Service, particularly the requirement to serve abroad. UK civil servants, members of the armed forces and individuals from the private sector may also serve in the FCO and at overseas posts on loan or attachment.

Northern Ireland

The Northern Ireland Civil Service (NICS) is modelled on its counterpart in Great Britain, and has its own Civil Service Commission. There were about 26,500 permanent non-industrial civil servants in the NICS at 31 March 2002. There is a degree of mobility between the NICS and the Civil Service in Great Britain.

Equality and diversity

The Civil Service aims to create a culture in which the different skills, experience and expertise that individuals bring are valued and used. Its equal opportunities policy states that there must be no unfair discrimination on the basis of age, disability, gender, marital status, sexual orientation, race, colour, nationality, ethnic or national origin or (in Northern Ireland) community background. The Civil Service is committed to achieving greater diversity, particularly at senior levels, where women, people from ethnic minorities and those with disabilities are under-represented.

In April 2001, 50.5 per cent of civil servants were female; minority ethnic representation was 6.0 per cent; and at least 3.1 per cent of staff employed were disabled. Progress is monitored and reported on regularly by the Cabinet Office.

Central management

As Minister for the Civil Service, the Prime Minister is responsible for central co-ordination and management of the Civil Service. He is supported by the Head of the Home Civil Service who chairs the Civil Service Management Board. (The function of official Head of the Home Civil Service is combined with that of the Cabinet Secretary – see page 46.) The Cabinet Office oversees the central framework for management of the Civil Service. Day-to-day responsibility for a wide range of terms and conditions has been delegated to departments and agencies, and to the Scottish Executive and the National Assembly for Wales.

Executive agencies

Executive agencies were introduced to deliver government services more efficiently and effectively within available resources. They are part of the Civil Service but, under the terms of individual framework documents and subject to overall budgets agreed with their parent department and/or the Treasury, they have delegated authority to employ their own staff and organise service provision in ways best suited to meet customer needs. Agencies are headed by chief executives who are personally responsible for day-to-day operations. They are normally directly accountable to the responsible minister, who in turn is accountable to Parliament. Abolition, privatisation, contracting-out, merger or rationalisation of a given government function are all options considered on their merits before an agency is set up. Certain changes to the way agencies will operate in the future, including how they will be reviewed, have been set out in a policy review report – *Better Government Services: Executive Agencies in the 21st Century* – published in July 2002.

Local government

Powers

Local authorities work within the powers laid down under various Acts of Parliament. Their functions are far-reaching. Some are mandatory, which means that the authority must do what is required by law; others are discretionary, allowing an authority to provide services if it wishes. In certain cases, ministers have powers to secure uniformity in standards in order to safeguard public health or to protect the rights of individual citizens. Where local authorities exceed their statutory powers, they are regarded as acting outside the law and can be challenged in court.

The main link between local authorities and central government in England is the Office of the Deputy Prime Minister. However, other departments, such as the Department for Education and Skills, the Department for Work and Pensions, the Department of Health and the Home Office, are also concerned with various local government functions.

In Scotland, Wales and Northern Ireland local authorities now deal mainly with the devolved Parliament and Assemblies. The structure of local government in each country of the UK is described in chapters 2–5.

Employees

About 2 million people (on a full-time equivalent basis) are employed by local authorities in the UK. These include school teachers, the police, firefighters (see below) and other non-manual and manual workers. Education is the largest locally provided service, with 0.9 million full-time equivalent jobs. Councils are individually responsible, within certain legislative requirements, for deciding the structure of their workforces.

Every part of the UK is covered by a local authority fire service. Each of the 59 fire authorities must by law provide a firefighting service and maintain a brigade to meet all normal requirements. Each fire authority appoints a Chief Fire Officer (or Firemaster in Scotland) who has day-to-day control of operations. The fire services in England and Wales employ around 56,400 staff and spend about £1.6 billion each year. In Scotland nearly 12,000 people are employed in fire brigades (including uniformed, non-uniformed and volunteer personnel) and forecast current expenditure on the service in 2002/03 is £212 million.

Elections

Local authorities consist of elected councillors who are paid a basic allowance but may be entitled to additional allowances and expenses for attending meetings or taking on special responsibilities.

The procedure for local government voting is broadly similar to that for elections to the UK Parliament, except that proportional representation is used in Northern Ireland. Eligibility rules for voters are also similar to those for UK parliamentary elections, except that citizens of other Member States of the EU may vote. To stand for election, candidates must either be registered as an elector or have some other close connection within the electoral area of their candidature, such as their principal place of employment.

Whole council elections are held every four years in all county councils in England, borough councils in London, and about two-thirds of non-metropolitan district councils. In all other district councils (including the metropolitan districts) one-third of the councillors are elected in each of the three years when county council elections are not held. However, a few non-metropolitan district councils will soon hold biennial elections with half of the councillors elected every two years. Whole council elections are every fourth year in Scotland, Wales and Northern Ireland.

At present, counties in England are divided into electoral areas called 'divisions' that can only return one member. However, provisions in the *Local Government Act 2000* will, if they come into force, allow them to have multi-member county divisions. Districts in England and Northern Ireland are divided into 'wards' and Welsh unitary authorities into electoral 'divisions'. Wards in metropolitan districts return three councillors. Wards in London boroughs and non-metropolitan authorities return between one and three councillors. In Scotland the unitary councils are divided into wards, each returning one councillor.

The electoral arrangements of local authorities in England are kept under review by the Boundary Committee for England, established in April 2002 as a statutory committee of the Electoral Commission (see page 55). Periodic electoral reviews of local authorities are undertaken in Scotland by the Local Government Boundary Commission for Scotland.

Provision of local services

The duty of Best Value requires local authorities to deliver services by the most economic, efficient and effective means available to meet the requirements of local communities; and to make arrangements to secure continuous

Electronic and postal voting in local elections

As part of the Government's commitment to make voting easier and modernise the electoral process (see page 32), 30 councils were given approval to run electoral pilots in the 2002 English local and mayoral elections. These included all-postal ballots, voting electronically using mobile phone text messaging and voting online via the Internet:

- in South Tyneside, where all-postal voting was used, turnout was 55 per cent compared with 27 per cent in the previous local election; and

- St Albans announced the first e-voting and counting results of the local elections just four minutes after the close of the poll. In the two wards piloting e-democracy over half those voting did so online (26.5 per cent) or by telephone (23.9 per cent).

The Electoral Commission undertook a full evaluation of these electoral pilots and published its report in August 2002. The evaluation will be used in deciding a further pilot programme for 2003.

Local authorities in Scotland can apply to Scottish Ministers for approval to run similar pilots at local by-elections. The first, an all-postal ballot, took place in Stirling Council in April 2002 where the turnout was 63 per cent, an increase of 20 per cent over the previous by-election. These pilots are also being evaluated by the Electoral Commission.

improvements. They have to review all their functions; monitor their performance against national and local indicators; and publish an annual performance plan which is subject to audit.

In June 2002 the Government published for consultation a draft Local Government Bill, aimed at paving the way for substantial new freedoms for councils to help them improve services, including public transport and care for those most in need and creating safer and cleaner communities. The draft Bill includes provisions which would, when enacted, give councils:

- freedom to borrow to pay for major projects, such as new buildings and infrastructure;

- powers to set up schemes with businesses to improve their area;

- new provisions on council tax (see page 357), including the introduction of a fixed ten-year cycle of revaluations;

- greater power to charge for discretionary services; and

- business rate relief for properties with rateable values of under £8,000.

Internal organisation

Some districts have the ceremonial title of borough, or city, both granted by royal authority. Traditionally, their councillors choose a Mayor (in Scotland a Provost) to act as presiding officer and perform ceremonial duties. In the City of London and certain other large cities, he or she is known as the Lord Mayor. In Scotland the presiding officer of the council of the four longest established cities – Aberdeen, Dundee, Edinburgh and Glasgow – is called the Lord Provost.

The *Local Government Act 2000* required local authorities in England and Wales to implement

Table 6.5 English local election results by party, May 2002

Party	Councils		Seats	
	Total	Net change	Total	Net change
Labour	63	−8	2,402	−339
Conservative	42	9	2,006	238
Liberal Democrats	15	2	1,262	44
Independent	0	0	136	−79
Others	2	2	101	2
No overall control	52	−5	.	.

Source: BBC News website

new decision-taking structures, including the option of a directly elected mayor (see below). In most authorities the arrangements are based on one of three executive frameworks: a mayor and cabinet; a council leader and cabinet; or a mayor and council manager. Within these options local authorities have considerable flexibility to work under a constitution which reflects local circumstances. Small shire district councils with a population of fewer than 85,000 have, in addition to executive arrangements, the choice of reforming their existing committee system. The majority of English and Welsh local authorities have opted for a style of executive where the leader of the cabinet is chosen by other councillors.

Directly elected mayors

Provisions in the *Local Government Act 2000* required councils in England and Wales to hold binding referendums if, following consultation, local people indicated that they wanted to directly elect a mayor under the new executive arrangements the Act put in place. Although the Government has powers to direct a local authority to hold a referendum in certain circumstances, in June 2002 it announced that it would not intervene in cases where it did not agree with the judgement made by a council following consultation.

In the May 2002 English local elections, there were seven elections for an executive mayor (Watford, Hartlepool, North Tyneside, Doncaster, Middlesbrough and the London boroughs of Lewisham and Newham) and five referendums on adopting the framework in which a council's mayor is elected by the public. Bedford, Mansfield, Oxford, Stoke-on-Trent and the London Borough of Hackney will be holding mayoral elections in October 2002. The Stoke-on-Trent election will result in the first occasion where a directly elected mayor will be supported by a council manager. A further two local authorities (Corby and the London Borough of Ealing) will be holding mayoral referendums in October and December 2002 respectively.

Decision-making and scrutiny

All new decision-making structures are required to incorporate rigorous arrangements for review and scrutiny of councils' policies and the decisions they make. Some decisions, such as the acceptance of policies and the budget, are reserved for the full council, but most of those relating to the

implementation of policy are for the executive. The executive is also responsible for preparing the policies and budget to propose to the council. Decisions may be taken by the executive collectively, by individual members of the executive, by committees of the executive or by officers of the authority. The executive is also able to delegate decision-making to area committees and to enter into partnership arrangements with other authorities.

The new arrangements are designed to ensure that people know who in the council is responsible for taking decisions, how they can make their input into decision-making and how to hold decision-makers to account.

Public access

The public (including the press) is admitted to meetings of the executive when key decisions are being discussed. They also have access to agendas, reports and minutes of meetings and certain background papers. In addition, local authorities must publish a forward plan setting out the decisions which will be taken over the coming months. Local authorities may exclude the public from meetings and withhold papers only in limited circumstances.

Local authority finance

Local government expenditure accounts for about 25 per cent of public spending. In 2001/02 expenditure by local authorities in the UK was about £98.8 billion. Current expenditure amounted to £84.7 billion; capital expenditure, net of capital receipts, was £7.2 billion; and debt interest £3.1 billion. Local government capital expenditure is financed primarily by borrowing within limits set by central government and from capital receipts from the disposal of land and buildings.

Local authorities in Great Britain raise revenue through the council tax (see chapter 23), which meets about 25 per cent of their revenue expenditure. Their spending is, however, financed primarily by grants from central government or the devolved administrations and by the redistribution of revenue within each country from their national non-domestic rate, a property tax levied on businesses and other non-domestic properties.

District councils in Northern Ireland continue to raise revenue through the levying of a domestic rate and a business rate.

Financial safeguards

Local councils' annual accounts must be audited by independent auditors appointed by the Audit Commission in England and Wales, or in Scotland by the Accounts Commission for Scotland. In Northern Ireland the chief local government auditor carries out this role. Local electors have a right to inspect the accounts to be audited. They may also ask questions and lodge objections with the auditor.

Standards and accountability in government

A number of safeguards are in place to ensure the probity of individuals in carrying out their public duties.

Committee on Standards in Public Life

The Committee on Standards in Public Life (now known as the Wicks Committee) was originally set up in 1994 under Lord Nolan. Its role is to examine the standards of conduct of all holders of public office, including arrangements relating to financial and commercial activities, and make recommendations as to any changes necessary to ensure the highest standards of propriety in public life.

The Committee has published seven reports. The first, in 1995, led to the appointment of a Parliamentary Commissioner for Standards (see below) and a Commissioner for Public Appointments (see page 55). Other reports have resulted in:

- changes in the ethical framework for local government, including the establishment in 2001 of a new Standards Board for England (*www.standardsboard.co.uk*);

- a new regulatory regime for political party funding in the UK, overseen by an independent Electoral Commission, (see page 55);

- new rules governing the conduct and discipline of MPs and strengthened guidance on lobbying;

- the introduction of new Codes of Conduct for government ministers and special advisers; and

- the mandatory registration of all peers' relevant financial interests and a short code of conduct for members of the House of Lords.

In December 2001 the Committee announced an inquiry into the regulation of MPs' standards of conduct. Written and oral submissions were considered during May and June 2002 and the Committee expects to publish its conclusions and recommendations in autumn 2002.

The Committee announced a further inquiry – *Defining the Boundaries within the Executive: Ministers, Special Advisers and the Permanent Civil Service* – in February 2002 and published a consultation paper to launch the process the following month. The key issues to be considered are:

- what special advisers do;

- how they relate to permanent civil servants;

- how effective are the codes of conduct governing the work of special advisers and other civil servants;

- the role of the Civil Service Commissioners; and

- the need for a Civil Service Act.

Public hearings began in June 2002 and a report (the Committee's ninth) is expected to be published towards the end of 2002.

Parliamentary Commissioner for Standards

The post of Parliamentary Commissioner for Standards was created in 1995, following recommendations of the Committee on Standards in Public Life. The Commissioner, who is independent of government, can advise MPs on matters of standards, and hold initial investigations into complaints about alleged breaches of the rules by Members. The Commissioner reports to the House of Commons Select Committee on Standards and Privileges.

Financial interests of MPs and Members of the House of Lords

The Commons has a public register of MPs' financial (and some non-financial) interests. Members with a financial interest must declare it when speaking in the House or in Committee and must indicate it when giving notice of a question or motion. They must also disclose any relevant financial interest in other proceedings of the House and in dealings with other Members, ministers or civil servants. The House of Lords has its own register on similar lines to that for MPs, based on a Code of Conduct which came into force in April 2002.

Commissioner for Public Appointments
The Commissioner for Public Appointments is independent of government and is responsible for monitoring, regulating and auditing ministerial appointments to a range of public bodies including non-departmental public bodies (NDPBs – see page 49), public corporations, nationalised industries, National Health Service Trusts and utility regulators. Departments are required to follow the Commissioner's Code of Practice which covers the seven principles to be applied to these appointments – ministerial responsibility, merit, independent scrutiny, equal opportunities, probity, openness and transparency, and proportionality.

Complaints

Parliamentary Commissioner for Administration
The Parliamentary Commissioner for Administration – more usually known as the Parliamentary Ombudsman – investigates complaints from members of the public (referred to him by MPs) alleging that they have been unfairly treated through maladministration. The Ombudsman is independent of government and reports to a select committee of the House of Commons. The Ombudsman's area of authority covers central government departments and agencies, and a large number of NDPBs. He cannot investigate complaints about government policy, the content of legislation or relations with other countries.

In making investigations, the Ombudsman has access to all departmental papers, and has powers to call before him those from whom he wishes to take evidence. When an investigation is completed, he sends a report with his findings to the MP who referred the complaint (with a copy for the complainant). When a complaint is upheld, the Ombudsman normally recommends that the department or other body makes some kind of compensation (which might be financial in appropriate cases). There is no appeal against the Ombudsman's decision.

The Ombudsman received 2,139 new complaints in 2001/02, an increase of 24 per cent over the previous year and the highest number ever

received. A total of 1,988 cases were concluded during the year: of these, 781 complaints were resolved informally and 195 statutory investigations were completed. The Department for Work and Pensions received the largest number of complaints against a single department, accounting for 32 per cent of the total received.

Separate arrangements apply for complaints about the Scottish Executive, the National Assembly for Wales, the Northern Ireland Assembly and devolved public bodies. Complaints to the Scottish Parliamentary Commissioner for Administration are referred through Members of the Scottish Parliament; complaints to the Welsh Administration Ombudsman can be made direct.

Local government complaints system
Local authorities are encouraged to settle complaints through internal mechanisms, and members of the public often ask their own councillor for help in this. Local authorities must also appoint a monitoring officer, whose duties include ensuring that the local authority acts lawfully when carrying out its business.

Complaints against inefficient or badly managed local government may be investigated by independent Commissions for Local Administration, often known as 'the Local Ombudsman service'. There are Local Government Ombudsmen in England and Wales; the functions of the Local Government Ombudsman in Scotland are to be taken over by the new Scottish Public Services Ombudsman. A report is issued on each complaint fully investigated and, if injustice is found, the Local Ombudsman normally proposes a solution. The council must consider the report and reply to it.

In Northern Ireland a Commissioner for Complaints deals with complaints alleging injustices suffered as a result of maladministration by district councils and certain other public bodies.

Electoral Commission
An independent Electoral Commission was set up under the *Political Parties, Elections and Referendums Act 2000* (see also page 48) to supervise the financial restrictions on parties, oversee referendums and have broad responsibility for electoral law. From April 2002 it took over the functions of the Local Government Boundary Commission for England and in due course it will

also take over the functions of the four Parliamentary Boundary Commissions. At the discretion of Scottish Ministers and the National Assembly for Wales respectively it could also take over the functions of the Local Government Boundary Commissions for Scotland and for Wales (see page 51).

Modernising government

The Government has taken a number of measures as part of its long-term programme to modernise and improve public services. These include:

- drawing up Public Service Agreements (PSAs) with government departments (see page 350) to set a clear framework of policy objectives and resource allocation, and provide a way of measuring and monitoring effectiveness;

- measures aimed at improving the quality of public services and making them more responsive, including schemes like Charter Mark (see below);

- the establishment of the Prime Minister's Delivery Unit to drive improvements in health, education, crime reduction and transport, and the creation of the Centre for Management and Policy Studies to improve policy-making, draw on external experience and strengthen the skills of civil servants;

- making all government services available electronically by 2005. By the end of 2001, 54 per cent of public services were online with over 73 per cent planned to be available by the end of 2002; and

- a reform programme to create a more open, diverse and professional Civil Service.

Freedom of information

The *Freedom of Information Act 2000* provides for a statutory right of access to recorded information held across the public sector, including Parliament, government departments, local authorities, health trusts, doctors' surgeries, publicly funded museums and other organisations.

The main features of the Act are:

- a right of wide general access to information, subject to clearly defined exemptions and conditions;

- a requirement to consider discretionary disclosure in the public interest even when an exemption applies;

- a duty to publish information; and

- powers of enforcement through an independent Information Commissioner and an Information Tribunal.

The Information Commissioner is also responsible for promoting the rules for the processing of personal information set out in the *Data Protection Act 1998*.

National Statistics

National Statistics, the UK's independent national statistical service, was set up in June 2000. It aims to provide an accurate, up-to-date, comprehensive and meaningful picture of the UK economy and society to support the formulation and monitoring of economic and social policies by government at all levels. In line with the Government's commitment to greater openness and accessibility of publicly held information, all its online data are available free of charge.

Charter Mark

A key objective of the Government's plans is to improve the delivery of public services with more emphasis on the consumer. The Charter Mark scheme aims to help public service organisations become more focused on the needs of users. The scheme applies to all public services, at both national and local level. It sets out clear standards of service, ensures consultation with users, and has an easy-to-use complaints procedure.

Pressure groups

Pressure groups are informal organisations which aim to influence the decision-making of Parliament and Government, to the benefit of their members and the causes they support. The range of issues pressure groups cover is very wide: from politics and consumer affairs to religion and the environment. Some have over 1 million members; others only a few. Some bring pressure to bear on a number of different issues; others are concerned with a single subject. Some have come to play a recognised role in the way the UK is governed; others attempt to influence through radical protest. Frequently national newspapers will take up the cause of a pressure group and help campaign on its behalf.

Ministers have a duty to give fair consideration and due weight to informed and impartial advice from civil servants, so pressure groups often try to guide the views of civil servants and in this way influence the briefing they give to ministers. Members of pressure groups often have direct expertise and an awareness of what is practicable, and can therefore offer useful advice to the Government in forming policy or drafting legislation. The contacts between civil servants and pressure group representatives may be relatively informal – by letter, telephone or e-mail – or more formal, through involvement in working parties or by giving evidence to committees of inquiry.

Many pressure groups employ full-time parliamentary workers or liaison officers, whose job is to develop contacts with MPs and peers sympathetic to their cause, and to brief them when issues affecting the group are raised in Parliament.

The UK in the European Union

As a Member State of the European Union, the UK is bound by the various types of European Community (EC) legislation and wider policies based on a series of treaties since the 1950s (see chapter 7). Almost all UK government departments are involved in EU-wide business, and European legislation is an increasingly important element of government.

The Community enacts legislation which is binding on the national governments of the 15 Member States or, in certain circumstances, on individuals and companies within those states. UK government ministers take part in the discussions and decision-making, and the final decision is taken collectively by all the Member States.

The UK Representative Office (UKREP), based in Brussels, conducts most of the negotiations on behalf of the UK Government. Following UK devolution, offices to promote the interests of Scotland and Wales within the EU opened in Brussels in 1999 and 2000 respectively. Both work in close co-operation with UKREP.

Council of the European Union
This is the main decision-making body. Member States are represented by the ministers appropriate to the subject under discussion. When, for instance, education matters are being discussed,

the UK's Secretary of State for Education and Skills attends with his or her European counterparts. The Presidency of the Council changes at six-monthly intervals and rotates in turn among the 15 Member States of the Union.

In some cases Council decisions must be unanimous; in others taken by qualified majority voting (a qualified majority being the number of votes required for a decision to be adopted) with votes weighted according to a country's population – currently ten each for Germany, France, the United Kingdom and Italy; eight for Spain; five each for Belgium, Greece, the Netherlands and Portugal; four each for Austria and Sweden; three each for Denmark, Finland and the Irish Republic; and two for Luxembourg. The threshold for the qualified majority is set at 62 votes out of 87.

European Council
This usually meets twice a year and comprises the Heads of State or Government (accompanied by their foreign ministers), the President of the European Commission and one other Commissioner. The Council defines general political guidelines.

European Commission
This is the executive body. It implements the Council's decisions, initiates legislation and ensures that Member States put it into effect. Each of the 20 Commissioners, who are drawn from all Member States (there are two from the UK), is responsible for a specific policy area, for example, education, transport or agriculture. The Commissioners are entirely independent of their countries, and serve the EU as a whole.

European Parliament
This plays an increasingly important role in the legislative process. There are 626 directly elected members (MEPs), including 87 from the UK. The Parliament is consulted about major decisions and has substantial shared power with the Council of the European Union over the EC budget (see page 60). In areas of legislation, its role varies between *consultation*, where it can influence but does not have the final say in the content of legislation; *co-operation and assent* procedures, where its influence is greater; and *co-decision* (introduced by the Maastricht Treaty and extended in the Amsterdam Treaty – see page 59), where a proposal requires the agreement of both the Council and the European Parliament. The Parliament meets in full session in Strasbourg for

Table 6.6 European Parliament elections, June 1999

United Kingdom	Number of MEPs
Conservative	36
Labour	29
Liberal Democrats	10
UK Independence Party	3
Green	2
Plaid Cymru – The Party of Wales	2
Scottish National Party	2
Democratic Unionist Party	1
Ulster Unionist Party	1
Social Democratic and Labour Party	1
Total	**87**

Source: House of Commons

about one week every month, although its committee work normally takes place in Brussels.

Elections to the European Parliament take place every five years, most recently in June 1999. In the UK, these were held under a proportional representation system,[11] bringing the country into line with the other Member States.

EC legislation

Some EC legislation is issued jointly by the Council of the European Union and the European Parliament, some by the Council and some by the Commission under delegated powers. It consists of Regulations, Directives and Decisions.

- *Regulations* are directly applicable in all Member States, and have the force of law without the need for implementing further measures;

- *Directives* are equally binding as to the result to be achieved but allow each Member State to choose the form and method of implementation; and

- *Decisions*, like Regulations, do not normally need national implementing legislation. They

11 The regional list system is used for England, Scotland and Wales, under which an elector may cast his or her vote for a party list of candidates. England is divided into nine regions while Scotland and Wales each constitute one region. These 11 regions each return between four and 11 MEPs, depending on the size of the electorate of each region. Northern Ireland, which also constitutes one region, continues to use the single transferable vote system to return its three MEPs.

are binding on those to whom they are addressed.

Other EU institutions

Each Member State provides one of the judges to serve in the European Court of Justice, which is the final authority on all aspects of Community law. Its rulings must be applied by Member States, and fines can be imposed on those failing to do so. The Court is assisted by a Court of First Instance, which handles certain cases brought by individuals and companies. The UK is also represented on the *Court of Auditors*, which examines Community revenue and expenditure, to see that it is legally received and spent.

Further reading

Cabinet Office Annual Report 2002. Cm 5429. The Stationery Office, 2002.

Department for Transport, Local Government and the Regions Annual Report 2002. Cm 5405. The Stationery Office, 2002.

Websites

The British Monarchy
www.royal.gov.uk

Cabinet Office
www.cabinet-office.gov.uk

Central government
www.ukonline.gov.uk

National Assembly for Wales
www.wales.gov.uk

National Statistics
www.statistics.gov.uk

Northern Ireland Executive
www.northernireland.gov.uk

Office of the Deputy Prime Minister
www.odpm.gov.uk

Prime Minister's Office
www.number-10.gov.uk

Scottish Executive
www.scotland.gov.uk

United Kingdom Parliament
www.parliament.uk

7 International relations

The United Kingdom has global foreign policy interests. It is a member of the European Union (EU), United Nations (UN), North Atlantic Treaty Organisation (NATO), Group of Eight (G8) and Organisation for Security and Co-operation in Europe (OSCE). It has close relationships with a large number of countries through the Commonwealth and with the United States.

European Union

The UK is a Member State of the EU, which promotes co-ordinated social and economic progress among its members, common foreign and security positions, police and judicial co-operation in criminal matters, and European citizenship. The EU's principal institutions and its legislative processes are described on pages 57–8.

Treaties
The structure and operation of the EU are governed by a series of treaties. The objectives of the 1957 Rome Treaty establishing the European Community (which the UK joined in 1973) were the creation of a common internal, or single, market (see page 60), including the elimination of customs duties between Member States, free movement of goods, people, services and capital, and the elimination of distortions in competition within this market. These aims were reaffirmed by the 1986 Single European Act, which incorporated measures to complete the single market. Under the Rome Treaty, the European Commission speaks on behalf of the UK and the other Member States in international trade negotiations.

The 1992 Maastricht Treaty amended the Rome Treaty and made other new commitments, including moves towards economic and monetary union (see page 60). It established the European

Union, which comprises the European Community and intergovernmental arrangements for a Common Foreign and Security Policy (CFSP – see pages 60–1) and for increased co-operation on justice and home affairs policy issues (see page 61). It also enshrined the principle of subsidiarity under which, in areas where the Community and Member States share competence, action should be taken at European level only if its objectives cannot be achieved by Member States acting alone and can be better achieved by the Community. In addition, the Treaty introduced the concept of EU citizenship as a supplement to national citizenship.

The Amsterdam Treaty, in force from 1999, provides for the further protection and extension of citizen's rights; integration of the 'social chapter' (previously a separate protocol to the Maastricht Treaty) into the treaty framework following its adoption by the UK; new mechanisms to improve the operation of the CFSP; and an increase in the areas subject to co-decision between the Council of Ministers and European Parliament, and simplification of the co-decision procedure.

The Nice Treaty, which was signed in February 2001 but is yet to enter into force, would introduce changes to the EU's institutional machinery in preparation for enlargement (see page 61). From 2005 the number of votes for each EU country in the Council of the European Union would be altered to take account of prospective new members, the total number rising from the 87 votes for the current 15 Member States up to 345 votes for 27 Member States. The UK, Germany, France and Italy would each have 29 votes. The total needed for a qualified majority (see page 57) would increase from 62 to 255, and for a blocking minority from 26 to 91, in an EU of 27 Member

States. Qualified majority voting would be extended to 35 more areas, including trade in some services, aspects of asylum and immigration policy, and regulation of the European Court of Justice. From 2005 the European Commission would be composed of one member from each country, up to 27.

Any amendments to the Treaties must be agreed unanimously and must then be ratified by each Member State according to its own constitutional procedures. In the UK, Treaty ratifications must be approved by Parliament before they can come into force.

Policies

The Community budget and broader EU policies are described below. Policies affecting more specific UK sectors – for example, the Common Agricultural Policy – appear in the appropriate chapters.

European Community budget

The Community's revenue consists of levies on agricultural imports from non-member countries, customs duties, a proportion of value added tax (VAT) receipts and contributions from Member States based on gross national product (GNP). Increasingly, more revenue is being raised from contributions linked to GNP and less from VAT receipts and customs payments. The UK continues to receive an annual budget rebate, which has been in place since 1984.

Single market

The single European market, providing for the free movement of people, goods, services and capital within the EU, came into effect in 1993 (see also page 366). It covers, among other benefits, the removal of customs barriers, the liberalisation of capital movements, the opening of public procurement markets and the mutual recognition of professional qualifications. Under the European Economic Area (EEA) Agreement, which came into force in 1994, most of the EU single market measures have been extended to Iceland, Norway and Liechtenstein.

Economic and monetary union

The Maastricht Treaty envisaged the achievement of economic and monetary union in stages, culminating in the adoption on 1 January 1999 of a single currency (the euro). In 1998 a meeting of EU Heads of State and Government agreed that 11 of the 15 EU Member States (excluding the

UK, Denmark, Greece and Sweden) would take part in the single currency from its launch date. It also agreed the establishment of the European Central Bank (ECB).

On 1 January 1999 conversion rates between currencies of qualifying countries and the euro were legally fixed. The euro became the legal currency in those countries and the ECB assumed responsibility for formulating the monetary policy of the euro area. Since no euro banknotes or coins would be available until 1 January 2002, national currencies continued to exist in parallel with the euro, and national banknotes and coins were used for all cash transactions. Greece, having earlier failed the economic convergence criteria, joined the euro area on 1 January 2001. On 1 January 2002 euro notes and coins were introduced officially. By 1 March 2002 all remaining national banknotes and coins in the 12 Member States making up the euro area ceased to be legal tender. See page 334 for the UK Government's economic tests for joining the single currency.

Regional and infrastructure development

The economic and social imbalances within the EU are considerable, and will become more evident with further enlargement. To address these, there are four Structural Funds promoting economic advancement in underdeveloped regions and supporting the conversion of areas facing structural difficulties (see also page 340). Infrastructure projects and schemes to promote development and diversification of industry are financed by the European Regional Development Fund. The European Social Fund supports human resource and equal opportunities schemes and training measures for the unemployed and young people. The Guidance Section of the European Agricultural Guidance and Guarantee Fund supports agricultural restructuring and some rural development activities. The Financial Instrument for Fisheries Guidance promotes the modernisation of the fishing industry. The UK will receive over £10 billion from the Structural Funds in 2000–06. A Cohesion Fund, set up under the Maastricht Treaty, provides financial help to reduce disparities between EU members' economies. Only Spain, Portugal, Greece and the Irish Republic were in receipt of such funding in 2002.

Common Foreign and Security Policy

The intergovernmental CFSP, introduced under the Maastricht Treaty, provides for Member States to agree unanimously common policies and/or joint actions on a wide range of international issues, in the belief that when they are able to speak with one voice on international affairs they carry more weight than any single Member State could alone. The Amsterdam Treaty preserves the principle that all policy should be decided by unanimity, but states that decisions implementing common strategies, which are themselves agreed by unanimity, will be by qualified majority voting. A Member State may prevent a vote being taken by qualified majority voting for 'important and stated reasons of national policy'. In addition, qualified majority voting does not apply to decisions having military or defence implications. A Member State may abstain and stand aside from an EU decision/action when its interests are not affected.

In 1998 the UK and France launched an initiative to strengthen the EU's capacity to respond to crises, on the basis that, if the Union is to play a coherent and effective political role, this needs to be underpinned by a credible European military capability. In support of this initiative, the European Council in 1999 agreed to develop by 2003 the capability, drawing on forces from Member States, to deploy up to 60,000 ground troops, with naval and air support as appropriate. These forces would be able to deal with the full range of military and civilian crisis management tasks. At the maximum scale of operation, the UK could contribute up to 12,500 ground troops, 18 warships and 72 combat aircraft. Collective defence remains the responsibility of NATO, which will also continue to have a major role in crisis management (see also page 79).

Justice and home affairs
The Maastricht Treaty established intergovernmental arrangements for increased co-operation among EU states on justice and home affairs issues. These issues include visa, asylum, immigration and other policies related to free movement of people; and police, customs and judicial co-operation in criminal matters (including co-operation through EUROPOL – see page 76). This is a growing aspect of EU work and, since the Amsterdam Treaty came into force, has both Community-based and intergovernmental-based areas of co-operation. A protocol annexed to the Amsterdam Treaty recognises the UK's right to exercise its own frontier controls.

Enlargement
A key policy objective of the EU is to enlarge the Union, to include those European nations sharing its democratic values and aims, and which are functioning market economies, able to compete in the EU and to take on the obligations of membership. In 1998 an accession process with the applicant states was launched, and formal negotiations started with Poland, Hungary, Slovenia, Estonia, Cyprus and the Czech Republic. Then, in 1999, the EU agreed to invite six other countries – Bulgaria, Latvia, Lithuania, Malta, Romania and Slovakia – to open accession negotiations (which were launched in February 2000), and also confirmed Turkey's candidature for membership. Up to ten new members are likely to accede in time to take part in the 2004 elections to the European Parliament.

In 1999 the European Council agreed the EU's budgetary arrangements for the period 2000–06, including making financial provision for the first new Member States to join the Union in that period. Upon its entry into force, the Treaty of Nice (see page 59) would provide for the institutional changes necessary for enlargement.

A Convention on the Future of Europe was instigated by the European Council at its summit at Laeken, Belgium, in December 2001 to prepare for the next intergovernmental conference in 2004 on the future direction of the EU. Inaugurated in February 2002, the year-long Convention is considering how to make the EU more democratic, effective and transparent. In the context of planned enlargement, its agenda amounts to a fundamental re-examination of the Union's institutional architecture. The Convention involves members of national parliaments and the European Parliament, as well as representatives of EU Member State governments, the European Commission and applicant countries.

Other international organisations

United Nations
The UK is a founder member of the UN and one of the five permanent members of the Security Council, along with China, France, Russia and the United States. It supports the purposes and principles of the UN Charter, including the maintenance of international peace and security,

the development of friendly relations among nations, the achievement of international co-operation on economic, social, cultural and humanitarian issues, and the protection of human rights and fundamental freedoms. The UK is the fifth largest contributor to the UN regular budget and to peacekeeping operations, and one of the biggest voluntary contributors to UN funds, programmes and agencies. In order to enhance the UN's effectiveness, the UK is advocating modernisation of the organisation, including reform of the Security Council's composition. The UK is also committed to the reinforcement of the UN's role in preventing and resolving conflicts around the world.

Commonwealth

There are 54 members of the Commonwealth,[1] including the UK (see map). It is a voluntary association of independent states, nearly all of which were once British territories. The organisation promotes democracy, the rule of law, good governance and human rights, as well as economic and social development. Comprising nearly one-third of the world's countries, it represents a combined population of 1.7 billion people.

The Queen is Head of the Commonwealth and is Head of State in the UK and 15 other member countries (see page 41). The Commonwealth Secretariat, based in London, is the main intergovernmental agency of the Commonwealth. It helps host governments to organise Commonwealth Heads of Government Meetings (CHOGM – which take place every two years), ministerial meetings and other conferences. It administers assistance programmes agreed at these meetings, including the Commonwealth Fund for Technical Co-operation, which provides expertise, advisory services and training to Commonwealth developing countries.

Following the 11 September terrorist attacks in the United States, the Heads of Government Meeting was postponed from Brisbane in October 2001 to Coolum, Australia, in March 2002.

---

1 Pakistan and Zimbabwe are suspended from the councils of the Commonwealth. Pakistan was suspended in October 1999 following a military coup. Zimbabwe was suspended for a year in March 2002 following international criticism of the conduct of presidential elections. Fiji's suspension, imposed in 2000, has been lifted.

North Atlantic Treaty Organisation

Membership of NATO is central to UK defence policy (see page 79). NATO's stated functions are to:

- help provide security and stability in the Euro-Atlantic area;

- provide a transatlantic forum for Member States to consult on issues of common concern;

- deter and defend against any threat to the territory of any NATO member state;

- contribute to crisis management and conflict prevention on a case-by-case basis; and

- promote partnership, co-operation and dialogue with other countries in the Euro-Atlantic area.

Each of the 19 Member States – Belgium, Canada, the Czech Republic, Denmark, France, Germany, Greece, Hungary, Iceland, Italy, Luxembourg, the Netherlands, Norway, Poland, Portugal, Spain, Turkey, the United Kingdom and the United States – has a permanent representative at NATO headquarters in Brussels. The main decision-taking body is the North Atlantic Council. It meets at least twice a year at foreign minister level, and weekly at the level of permanent representatives. Defence ministers also meet at least twice a year.

Group of Eight

The UK is one of the Group of Eight (G8) leading industrialised countries. The other members are Canada, France, Germany, Italy, Japan, Russia (included as a full member from 1998, although the other countries continue to function as the G7 for some discussions) and the United States. The G8 is an informal group with no secretariat. Its presidency rotates each year among the members, the key meeting being an annual summit of Heads of Government. Originally formed in 1975 (as the G7) to discuss economic issues, the G8 agenda now includes a wide range of foreign affairs and international issues such as terrorism, nuclear safety, the environment, UN reform and development assistance. Heads of State or Government agree a communiqué issued at the end of summits. The G8 summit meeting in June 2002 was hosted by the Canadian Government in

Kananaskis, Alberta. It focused in particular on increased aid to Africa on a partnership basis (see also page 66).

Organisation for Security and Co-operation in Europe

The UK is a member of the OSCE, a regional security organisation whose 55 participating states are from Europe, Central Asia and North America. All decisions are taken by consensus. The OSCE is based in Vienna, where the UK has a permanent delegation. The main areas of work are:

- early warning and prevention of potential conflicts through field missions and diplomacy and the work of the OSCE High Commissioner on National Minorities;

- observing elections and providing advice on human rights, democracy and law, and media;

- post-conflict rehabilitation, including civil society development; and

- promoting security through arms control and military confidence-building.

Council of Europe

The UK is a founding member of the Council of Europe, which is open to any European state accepting parliamentary democracy, the rule of the law and fundamental human rights. There are 44 full Member States. One of the Council's main achievements is the European Convention on Human Rights (see page 70).

Other international bodies

The UK belongs to many other international bodies, including the International Monetary Fund (IMF), which regulates the international financial system and provides credit for member countries facing balance-of-payments difficulties; the World Bank, which provides loans to finance economic and social projects in developing countries; the Organisation for Economic Co-operation and Development (OECD), which promotes economic growth, support for less developed countries and worldwide trade expansion; and the World Trade Organisation (WTO – see page 366). Other organisations to which Britain belongs or extends support include the regional development banks in Africa, the Caribbean, Latin America and Asia, and the European Bank for Reconstruction and Development.

Regional relations

Central and Eastern Europe and Central Asia

European security

In 1990 the UK and its NATO allies, together with former adversaries in the Warsaw Pact Communist bloc, set up the North Atlantic Co-operation Council to promote understanding. In 1994 NATO invited the non-Alliance states in Central and Eastern Europe and Central Asia to join a Partnership for Peace programme, a form of association which enlists the Partners' assistance in peacekeeping operations. The Euro-Atlantic Partnership Council was set up in 1997 to develop closer political and military links between NATO countries and non-members.

The UK played a significant role in negotiations leading to a NATO-Ukraine partnership charter, signed in 1997, and the accession to NATO in 1999 of the Czech Republic, Hungary and Poland. Mechanisms for a permanent relationship between NATO and Russia, established in a Founding Act in 1997, have been extended by the creation in May 2002 of a NATO-Russia Council (see also page 79). The Council will provide a framework for partnership and co-operation, with the aim of taking joint decisions and actions.

Economic help

The UK and other Western countries continue to help deal with the economic problems following the fall of Communism, and to promote the development of market economies. The IMF provides support for stabilisation programmes and the World Bank finance for structural reform to nearly all countries in the region. This is further bolstered by the European Bank for Reconstruction and Development's investments and its role in attracting additional private investment. The EU's PHARE scheme is primarily devoted to aiding Central European countries in the process of reform and development of their infrastructure. Countries of the former Soviet Union (excluding Estonia, Latvia and Lithuania) and Mongolia receive help through a parallel programme (TACIS), which concentrates on democratisation, financial services, transport, energy (including nuclear safety) and public administration reform. The Community Assistance for Association, Democratisation and Stabilisation (CARDS) programme is focused on countries in the Western Balkans.

Association and co-operation agreements

The EU has strengthened relations with Bulgaria, the Czech Republic, Estonia, Hungary, Latvia, Lithuania, Poland, Romania, Slovakia and Slovenia by signing Europe (Association) Agreements with them. The agreements provide an institutional framework to support the process of integration, and anticipate accession of these countries to the EU when they are able to assume the obligations of membership (see page 61).

EU Partnership and Co-operation Agreements are in force with Russia, Ukraine, Moldova, Kazakhstan, Kyrgyzstan, Georgia, Armenia, Azerbaijan and Uzbekistan. Similar agreements have been signed with Belarus and Turkmenistan. Trade and Co-operation Agreements with Albania and Macedonia are also in force. The purpose of these agreements is to reduce trade barriers, develop wide-ranging co-operation and increase political dialogue.

The EU is promoting closer links through Stabilisation and Association Agreements (SAA) with states in south-eastern Europe, provided that they meet the EU's conditions on democracy, electoral and media reform, and respect for human rights. The first SAA, with Macedonia, was signed in April 2001. Croatia signed its SAA in October 2001.

Middle East

Arab–Israeli peace process

The UK supported the breakthrough in the Middle East peace process in 1993, when Israel and the Palestine Liberation Organisation (PLO) agreed to mutual recognition and signed a declaration on interim self-government for the Palestinians in Israeli-held territories occupied since 1967. The first stage of the declaration was implemented in 1994, when the Palestinians adopted self-government in the Gaza Strip and the Jericho area. A peace treaty between Israel and Jordan was also signed in that year. The UK has continued to encourage peace talks between Israel, Syria and Lebanon.

In 1995 Israel and the PLO reached an agreement providing for a phased Israeli troop withdrawal from occupied Palestinian areas of the West Bank and for elections to a new Palestinian Council with legislative and executive powers. The UK took part in the EU-coordinated observation of the Palestinian elections in 1996.

Subsequent progress in the process has been far from smooth, with frequent disruptions over political and security concerns. Since September 2000 there has been a serious and continuing escalation of violence between Israelis and Palestinians, which increasingly has involved Palestinian suicide bomb attacks on Israeli civilians and Israeli military incursions and reprisals in Palestinian-administered territory. The UK Government has pressed for an end to the violence and for a resumption of political engagement, believing that a solution to the crisis will not be reached if it is seen purely as a security or military question. The Government maintains its conviction that a lasting resolution must both protect Israel's security and provide a just exchange of land for peace; and, with its EU partners, has reaffirmed the Palestinian right to self-determination including the option of statehood.

Iraq

The UK condemned Iraq's invasion of Kuwait in 1990 and supported all UN Security Council resolutions designed to force Iraqi withdrawal and restore international legality. Because of Iraq's failure to withdraw, its forces were expelled in 1991 by an international coalition led by the United States, the UK, France and Saudi Arabia, acting under a UN mandate.

UN sanctions against Iraq have remained in force (although with substantial humanitarian exemptions), because Iraq has failed to comply with the relevant Security Council resolutions, particularly those relating to the supervision of the elimination of its weapons of mass destruction. British initiatives at the UN led, in 1996, to the establishment of an oil-for-food programme for Iraq and, in 1999, to the lifting of the ceiling on Iraq's oil exports and an expansion of the humanitarian programme. In May 2002 the Security Council adopted a new resolution revising the sanctions arrangements. While maintaining strict, targeted controls on military and 'dual-use' equipment (having a legitimate civil use as well as a potential military application), the system allows Iraq to freely import civilian goods. Nevertheless, the UK Government remains concerned about Iraq's breach of outstanding UN obligations and seeks the disarmament of the Iraqi regime. The UK Parliament was recalled on 24 September 2002 to discuss the issue of Iraq and its weapons of mass destruction. On the same day the Government published a 50-page dossier detailing

Iraq's breach of UN resolutions and its attempts to rebuild illegal weaponry.

In order to protect the Shia minority in southern Iraq and the Kurdish population in the north against attacks by Iraqi forces, UK and US warplanes continue to patrol 'no-fly' zones over southern and northern Iraq, established after the war in 1991.

Mediterranean

The UK and other EU Member States are developing, on the basis of the Barcelona Declaration of 1995, closer links with 12 Mediterranean partners (Morocco, Algeria, Tunisia, Egypt, Syria, Lebanon, Jordan, Israel, the Palestinian Authority, Turkey, Cyprus and Malta) with the aim of promoting peace and prosperity in the region. Libya has also been invited to sign up to the Declaration. Euro-Mediterranean Association Agreements covering political dialogue, free trade and co-operation in a number of areas are in force with Tunisia, Morocco and Israel, as well as an Interim Agreement with the Palestine Liberation Organisation. An Association Agreement with Jordan is in the process of ratification and another with Egypt awaits signature. Turkey, Cyprus and Malta have long-standing Association Agreements with the EU.

Asia-Pacific region

The UK has well-established relations with Japan, China, the Republic of Korea, many South East Asian nations, Australia and New Zealand, and has defence links with some countries in the region. It is a member, with Malaysia, Singapore, Australia and New Zealand, of the Five Power Defence Arrangements, which celebrated their 30th anniversary in November 2001. British commercial activity has developed through increased trade and investment, and through the setting up of business councils, joint commissions or industrial co-operation agreements. The UK is also taking advantage of increased opportunities for English language teaching, co-operation in science and technology, and educational exchanges.

The Asia-Europe Meeting (ASEM) process was inaugurated in 1996. ASEM is intended to foster closer economic and political ties between EU countries and Brunei, China, Indonesia, Japan, the Republic of Korea, Malaysia, Singapore, the Philippines, Thailand and Vietnam. The fourth ASEM took place in Copenhagen, Denmark, in September 2002.

The UK and its EU and G8 partners continue to encourage India and Pakistan to join international nuclear non-proliferation regimes (see page 74). This became of increasing concern during 2002 as bilateral tensions over terrorism and the disputed territory of Kashmir have brought the two regional powers to the brink of war, with potent international implications. The UK Government has played a significant role in the co-ordinated diplomatic efforts of the international community to defuse the crisis.

In 1998 the UK rejoined the South Pacific Commission, having withdrawn in 1995. The Commission provides technical advice and assistance to its Pacific Island members, with which the UK has long-standing and Commonwealth ties. See page 367 for trading relations between the EU and the 76 African, Caribbean and Pacific (ACP) countries.

Hong Kong

In 1997 the UK returned Hong Kong to Chinese sovereignty under the provisions of the 1984 Sino-British Joint Declaration, which guarantees that Hong Kong's way of life, including its rights and freedoms, will remain unchanged for 50 years from the handover. The UK continues to have responsibilities towards Hong Kong and the 3.5 million British passport holders living there. The territory is the UK's second largest export market in Asia.

The Americas

The UK Government considers that the close transatlantic links between the UK, the United States and Canada remain essential to guarantee the security and prosperity of Europe and North America.

The UK and the US co-operate closely on nuclear, defence and intelligence matters. As founding members of NATO, the UK and US are deeply involved in Western defence arrangements and, as permanent members of the UN Security Council, work closely together on major international issues. In addition, there are important economic links. The UK and US are each other's biggest source of inward investment, and the US is the UK's largest single trading partner. More than 5,000 US companies are based in the UK, and almost 10,000 across the EU as a whole. Over 3 million jobs on each side of the Atlantic depend on this investment. EU-US summit meetings are held twice a year.

Strong political and economic links are maintained with Canada, with which the UK shares membership of the Commonwealth, NATO and other key international organisations. EU-Canada summit meetings take place twice a year. The UK is the second largest investor in Canada (after the US) and Canada is the fifth largest investor in the UK.

Important British connections with Latin America date from the early 19th century. Greater democracy and freer market economies have enabled the UK to strengthen its modern links with the region, and it is now one of the largest investors after the United States. UK exports to Latin America are worth £2.5 billion a year. An increasingly important part of the UK's relationship with Latin America takes place through the EU. The first summit of EU, Latin American and Caribbean Heads of State and Government was held in Rio de Janeiro, Brazil, in 1999. The second took place in Madrid, Spain, in May 2002, when a trade agreement was signed between the EU and Chile (the EU's only other such agreement in Latin America being with Mexico). The EU is the largest provider of developmental assistance to Latin America, and the region is the largest per capita recipient of EU aid in the world.

The first UK/Caribbean Forum, held in 1998 in Nassau, Bahamas, marked the beginning of a new longer-term process of co-operation between the UK and the countries of the region. The second meeting was hosted by the UK Government in London in 2000, and the third was held in Georgetown, Guyana, in April 2002. See page 367 for trading relations between the EU and the 76 African, Caribbean and Pacific (ACP) countries.

Africa

British aims in Africa are to promote peace and security, prosperity and democracy. The UK Prime Minister declared African development a policy priority for his administration's second term in office. The UK is giving political and practical support to efforts to prevent or end African conflicts; promoting trade, reducing debt and supporting development for lasting prosperity; and supporting African governments, organisations and individuals espousing the principles of democracy, accountability, the rule of law and human rights. The UK Government has welcomed the New Partnership for Africa's Development (NEPAD), an African-led strategy (endorsed in

July 2001 by the Organisation of African Unity) for sustainable growth and development. In support of NEPAD, the G8 countries (see page 62) adopted a development assistance action plan at their summit in Canada in June 2002.

Since the abolition of apartheid and the election of the first African National Congress government in 1994, South Africa's relations with the UK have broadened into areas ranging from development assistance to military advice, and from sporting links to scientific co-operation. There has also been a steady flow of state and ministerial visits to and from South Africa. The UK is South Africa's largest single trading partner, and largest foreign investor. A trade, development and co-operation agreement between the EU and South Africa was signed in 1999, providing for the creation of a free trade area and for further substantial development assistance from the EU.

See page 367 for trading relations between the EU and the 76 African, Caribbean and Pacific (ACP) countries.

Overseas Territories

The UK's Overseas Territories (OTs) have a combined population of about 190,000. The territories are listed on page 67. Most have considerable self-government, with their own legislatures. Governors appointed by the Queen are responsible for external affairs, internal security, defence and international financial services. Most domestic matters are delegated to locally elected governments and legislatures. The British Indian Ocean Territory, the British Antarctic Territory, and South Georgia and the South Sandwich Islands have non-resident Commissioners, not Governors. None of the Territories has expressed a desire for independence from the UK.

The UK aims to provide the OTs with security and political stability, ensure efficient and honest government, and support their economic and social advancement. The Overseas Territories Economic Diversification Fund was established in 2001 to help the OTs to develop a sustainable economic future. Offshore financial service industries are of major importance in several of the Territories. The UK Government's policy is to ensure that international standards of regulation are met and that effective steps are taken to combat financial crime and regulatory abuse.

The Overseas Territories at a glance

Anguilla (capital: The Valley)
Area: 96 sq km (Sombrero, 5 sq km).
Population: 11,560 (2001).
Economy: tourism, offshore banking, fishing and farming.
History: British territory since 1650.

Bermuda (capital: Hamilton)
Area: 53 sq km.
Population: 63,000 (2000).
Economy: financial services and tourism.
History: first British settlers in 1609–12. Government passed
to the Crown in 1684.
UN World Heritage Site: town of St George and related
fortifications (from 2000).

British Antarctic Territory
Area: 1.7 million sq km.
Population: two permanent British Antarctic Survey stations
are staffed by 40 people in winter and 150 in summer.
Scientists from other Antarctic Treaty nations have bases in
the Territory.
History: the British claim to the Territory dates back to 1908.
The UK is one of 44 signatories to the 1961 Antarctic Treaty,
which states that the continent should be used for peaceful
purposes only.

British Indian Ocean Territory
Area: 54,400 sq km of ocean, including the Chagos
Archipelago land area.
Economy: Territory used for defence purposes by the UK and
United States.
History: archipelago ceded to Britain by France under the
1814 Treaty of Paris.

British Virgin Islands (capital: Road Town)
Area: 153 sq km.
Population: 20,650 (2001).
Economy: tourism and financial services.
History: discovered in 1493 by Columbus and annexed by
Britain in 1672.

Cayman Islands (capital: George Town)
Area: 259 sq km.
Population: 40,790 (1999).
Economy: tourism and financial services.
History: the 1670 Treaty of Madrid recognised Britain's claim
to the islands.

Falkland Islands (capital: Stanley)
Area: 12,173 sq km.
Permanent population: 2,913 (2001), plus military garrison.
Economy: fishery management and wool sales.
History: first known landing in 1690 by British naval captain,
John Strong. Under British administration since 1833, except
for brief Argentine occupation in 1982.

Gibraltar
Area: 6.5 sq km.
Population: 28,230 (2001).
Economy: financial services, tourism and port services.
History: ceded to Britain in 1713 under the Treaty of Utrecht.

Montserrat (capital: Plymouth, although destroyed by
volcanic activity which has rendered the south of the island
an exclusion zone)
Area: 102 sq km.
Population: 4,500 (2002).
Economy: agriculture, construction and fishing.
History: colonised by English and Irish settlers in 1632.

Pitcairn, Ducie, Henderson and Oeno (capital: Adamstown)
Area: 36 sq km.
Population: 45 (2001).
Economy: fishing, agriculture and postage stamp sales.
History: occupied by mutineers from the British ship *Bounty*
in 1790; annexed as a British colony in 1838.
UN World Heritage Site: Henderson Island (from 1988).

St Helena (capital: Jamestown)
Area: 122 sq km.
Population: 5,000 (1998).
Economy: fishing and agriculture.
History: taken over in 1659 by the British East India
Company.

Ascension Island (St Helena Dependency)
Area: 88 sq km.
Population: 1,050 (1999).
Economy: communications and military base.
History: the British garrison dates from Napoleon's exile on
St Helena after 1815.

Tristan da Cunha (St Helena Dependency)
Area: 98 sq km.
Population: 284 (2002).
Economy: fishing.
History: occupied by a British garrison in 1816.
UN World Heritage Site: Gough Island Wildlife Reserve (from
1995).

South Georgia and the South Sandwich Islands
No indigenous population. First landing by Captain Cook in
1775. British Antarctic Survey research stations at King
Edward Point and Bird Island.

Turks and Caicos Islands (capital: Cockburn Town)
Area: about 500 sq km.
Population: 19,350 (2000).
Economy: tourism, financial services and fishing.
History: Europeans from Bermuda first occupied the islands
from about 1678, then planters from southern states of
America settled after the American War of Independence in
the late 18th century.

New citizenship provisions under the *British Overseas Territories Act 2002* came into effect on 21 May 2002. From that date all existing OT citizens (with the exception of those deriving their citizenship from a connection with the British Sovereign Base Areas of Cyprus) automatically became British citizens with the right of abode in the UK.[2]

An OT Department within the Foreign & Commonwealth Office (FCO – see below) provides a single focus and direct point of contact with the UK Government, although Gibraltar, because of its EU status, is dealt with primarily by the FCO's European Departments. The Department for International Development (DFID – see page 71) also has an OT Department, which administers development assistance to Anguilla, the British Virgin Islands, Montserrat, the Turks and Caicos Islands, St Helena (and Tristan da Cunha) and Pitcairn. An OT Consultative Council, comprising the Chief Minister or equivalent from each territory and British ministers (and chaired by the relevant FCO minister), convenes annual meetings in September.

Falkland Islands

The Falkland Islands are the subject of a territorial claim by Argentina. The UK Government does not accept the Argentine claim and is committed to defending the Islanders' right to live under a government of their own choice. This right of self-determination is enshrined in the United Nations Charter and is embodied in the 1985 Falkland Islands Constitution. Nevertheless, the UK and Argentina maintain good bilateral relations and co-operate on practical issues of common interest affecting the South Atlantic, such as conservation of fish stocks and surveying of the continental shelf.

Gibraltar

Having been captured by British-Dutch forces in 1704, Gibraltar was ceded by Spain to Britain in perpetuity under the 1713 Treaty of Utrecht. However, Spain has long sought its return. The UK stands by its commitment, set out in the preamble to the 1969 Gibraltar Constitution, that it will not enter into arrangements under which the people of Gibraltar would pass under the

sovereignty of another state against their freely and democratically expressed wishes.

Gibraltar has an elected House of Assembly, and responsibility for a range of 'defined domestic matters' is devolved to elected local ministers. The Territory is within the EU, as part of the United Kingdom Member State, although it is outside the common customs system and does not participate in the Common Agricultural or Fisheries Policies or the EU's value added tax arrangements. The people of Gibraltar have been declared UK nationals for EU purposes.

Administration of foreign policy

Foreign & Commonwealth Office

The FCO is in charge of foreign policy. It is headed by the Foreign and Commonwealth Secretary, who is responsible for the work of the department and the Diplomatic Service (see page 50). Diplomatic, consular and commercial relations are maintained with about 190 countries, and the UK has over 230 diplomatic posts worldwide. British diplomatic missions also employ nearly 8,000 locally engaged staff. Staff overseas deal with political, commercial and economic work; entry clearance to the UK and consular work; aid administration; and information and other activities, such as culture, science and technology.

The FCO's executive agency, Wiston House Conference Centre in West Sussex, contributes to the solution of international problems by organising conferences in the UK, attended by politicians, business people, academics and other professionals from all over the world.

An important function of the FCO is to promote understanding of British foreign policies and to project an up-to-date image of the UK worldwide, beyond the sphere of government-to-government diplomacy. Key elements of FCO-funded public diplomacy work include:

- publications, television and radio programmes, and the FCO and Planet Britain websites (*www.fco.gov.uk* and *www.planet-britain.org*);

- scholarship schemes for overseas students (see page 121) and programmes for influential foreign visitors;

---

2 Many British Overseas Territories citizens from Gibraltar and the Falkland Islands already possessed British citizenship under previous legislation applying to those Territories.

- the BBC World Service (see page 234);

- the British Council (see below);

- the London Radio Service and British Satellite News, used extensively by overseas radio and television broadcasters to supplement their news coverage;

- International Press Section, the FCO's specialist link with foreign journalists, both visiting and based in the UK; and

- the London Press Service, which supplies material for publication overseas.

In 2000 the FCO, British Council, Design Council, British Trade International (see page 368) and British Tourist Authority established the Britain Abroad Task Force to co-ordinate the projection of a modern image of the UK overseas.

Other departments

Several other government departments are closely involved with foreign policy issues. The DFID is responsible for promoting poverty reduction overseas. It is also responsible for the UK's relations with the World Bank and international organisations concerned with development. The Ministry of Defence maintains military liaison with the UK's NATO and other allies and has defence relationships around the world. The Department of Trade and Industry (DTI) has an important influence on international trade policy and commercial relations with other countries, including EU Member States. The joint work of the FCO and DTI in support of British trade and investment overseas is co-ordinated through British Trade International. HM Treasury is involved in British international economic policy and is responsible for the UK's relations with the International Monetary Fund.

British Council

The British Council is the UK's principal agency for educational and cultural relations overseas. Operating in 109 countries, its work includes teaching English; promoting British education and training; running information centres; supporting good governance and human rights; and encouraging appreciation of British science, arts, literature and design.

It is financed partly by a grant from the FCO and partly by income from revenue-earning activities, such as English language teaching and the administration of examinations. Some of the programmes organised by the Council as part of the British aid programme receive funding from the DFID.

In 2000/01 the Council issued nearly 8 million books and videos to 350,000 British Council library members, and dealt with almost 2 million enquiries in its libraries and information centres. It also organised more than 1,500 science events in over 60 countries; managed or supported 3,000 arts events worldwide; administered 700,000 professional and academic examinations; helped 13,000 young people take part in exchange projects; and supported over 4,000 trainers and trainees for vocational projects across Europe.

Educational exchanges

The British Council recruits teachers for work overseas, organises short overseas visits by British experts, encourages cultural exchange visits, and organises academic interchange between British universities and colleges and those in other countries. Its Central Bureau for International Education and Training aims to raise standards in UK education and training through international partnership and exchange. The Bureau is the UK national agency for many EU education and training programmes. It also hosts the Secretariat of the UK National Commission for UNESCO (UN Educational, Scientific and Cultural Organisation), inaugurated in 2001.

Human rights

The UK Government has stated its commitment to working for improvements in human rights standards across the world and, in September 2002, published its fifth annual human rights report describing the activities and initiatives pursued during the previous year (from July 2001 to July 2002). The Human Rights Project Fund, launched in 1998, provides direct financial assistance for grass-roots human rights projects around the world.

International conventions

United Nations

Universal respect for human rights is an obligation under the UN Charter. Expressions of concern about human rights do not, therefore, constitute interference in the internal affairs of another state.

The UK Government supports the Universal Declaration of Human Rights, which was adopted by the UN General Assembly in 1948. Since this is not a legally binding document, the General Assembly adopted two international covenants on human rights in 1966, placing legal obligations on those states ratifying or acceding to them. The covenants came into force in 1976, the UK ratifying both in the same year. One covenant deals with economic, social and cultural rights and the other with civil and political rights. Other international instruments to which the UK is a party include those on:

- the elimination of racial discrimination;

- the elimination of all forms of discrimination against women;

- the rights of the child;

- torture and other cruel, inhuman or degrading treatment or punishment;

- the prevention of genocide;

- the abolition of slavery; and

- the status of refugees.

Council of Europe
The UK is also bound by the Council of Europe's Convention for the Protection of Human Rights and Fundamental Freedoms (ECHR), which covers areas such as:

- the right to life, liberty and a fair trial;

- the right to marry and have a family;

- freedom of thought, conscience and religion;

- freedom of expression, including freedom of the press;

- freedom of peaceful assembly and association;

- the right to have a sentence reviewed by a higher tribunal; and

- the prohibition of torture and inhuman or degrading treatment.

The rights and obligations of the ECHR were enshrined in UK law upon the implementation of the *Human Rights Act 1998* in 2000 (see page 183).

Organisation for Security and Co-operation in Europe
The OSCE's Office for Democratic Institutions and Human Rights (in Warsaw) promotes participating states' adherence to commitments on human rights, democracy and the rule of law, and takes a lead in monitoring elections within the OSCE area. The Office provides a forum for exchanges of experts on the building of democratic institutions and the holding of elections in participating states. It also provides expertise and training on human rights, constitutional and legal matters, and promotes practical measures to strengthen civil administration.

International Criminal Court
The UK has supported the establishment of an International Criminal Court to try cases of genocide, crimes against humanity and war crimes. The Government signed the Court's Statute in 1998 and ratification took place in October 2001. Over 60 other states have also ratified the Statute (although not the United States, which does not recognise its jurisdiction), enabling the Court to come into existence on 1 July 2002. Based in The Hague in the Netherlands, its powers are not retrospective.

Development co-operation

The UK's development aid policy is focused on its commitment to internationally agreed development targets – Millennium Development Goals – such as halving the proportion of people living in extreme poverty and providing universal access to primary education and improved healthcare by 2015. The UK Government believes that globalisation – involving, for example, increased flows of goods, services, capital and trade – offer poor countries opportunities to access knowledge and technology, new trade and investment if they can be brought into the global economy.

In 2000 the Government published a White Paper, *Eliminating World Poverty: Making Globalisation Work for the Poor*, setting out its strategy to bring sustainable benefits to those living in extreme poverty. This includes working for fair trade and international agreements to promote financial stability and foreign investment in poor countries, supporting worldwide environmental initiatives and assisting countries that are introducing economic and social policies while protecting human rights.

In 2001/02 total Department for International Development expenditure was £2.91 billion (see charts on page 72): £1.51 billion on bilateral aid, £1.31 billion on multilateral aid and £88 million on administration. Official development assistance is planned to rise from 0.26 per cent of gross national income in 1997 to 0.33 per cent in 2003/04, when the projected budget of the DFID is planned to be £3.7 billion. Further rises announced in 2002 will take the budget to £4.6 billion by 2005/06. UK Official development assistance is expected to increase to 0.4 per cent of gross national income, reflecting the Government's continued commitment to make progress towards meeting the United Nations target of 0.7 per cent. The Government is committed to increasing annual bilateral aid to Africa to £1 billion by 2006.

Poverty reduction

The DFID considers that growth, equity and security are the three central requirements to achieve poverty reduction. Growth depends on national market-based policies, supported by the people, which will promote investment and deliver effective macroeconomic management. This, in turn, requires both a continuing commitment by governments to economic reform and liberalisation, and the establishment of strong governance and institutions. Equity is also fundamental if people are to be able to participate in growth using their own assets and capabilities and to have access to education, health, information, transport and financial services. Measures to redistribute income and assets can also generate growth. Increased security against physical and economic vulnerability is essential in any poverty reduction programme. The UK is shifting its assistance from individual projects to direct support to governments implementing agreed poverty reduction strategies and better financial management.

Debt relief

The heavy burden of servicing debt reduces the ability of the poorest countries to tackle poverty effectively. The UK is focusing on accelerating the

implementation of the revised 1999 Heavily Indebted Poor Countries (HIPC) debt initiative, which is designed to deliver wider and faster relief to countries committed to poverty reduction. The UK goes further than required under the HIPC initiative and writes off 100 per cent of debt from HIPC countries once they qualify for relief. The Government is also providing full debt relief on the remaining ECGD (Export Credits Guarantee Department) debt – about £2 billion – for countries that qualify for the HIPC initiative.

Good governance and human rights

The quality of governance has a major impact on economic growth and the effectiveness of services. The DFID is focusing on issues such as democratic accountability (bringing poor people into the democratic process); fundamental freedoms (including rights to education, health and an adequate livelihood); combating child labour; tackling corruption and money laundering; better revenue and public finance management; access to basic services; and personal safety and security in the community with access to justice.

Women's empowerment

An estimated 70 per cent of the world's poor are female. Eliminating gender discrimination and supporting measures to improve women's equality are crucial to reducing poverty and upholding human rights. A priority in DFID assistance is the promotion of equal access to education for all girls and boys.

Health

Three of the eight Millennium Development Goals involve health: the reduction of child mortality, the improvement in maternal health and the fight against diseases (including HIV, tuberculosis, and malaria). The impact of these major diseases on the poor is an important obstacle to social and economic development. The UK has worked with the G8 countries, developing countries and the UN to establish a Global Health Fund to increase access to effective treatments against these diseases. Operational since December 2001, the Fund has received pledges of some US$2 billion over five years, including US$200 million from the UK.

Since 1997 the DFID has committed around £1.5 billion to improving basic healthcare in developing countries. The improvement of poor people's access to healthcare and to new and

Figure 7.1 DFID Programme 2001/02: bilateral aid programme by aid type

Total: £1.5 billion

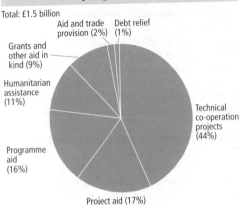

Source: Department for International Development

Figure 7.3 DFID Programme 2001/02: multilateral aid programme by recipient agency

Total: £1.3 billion

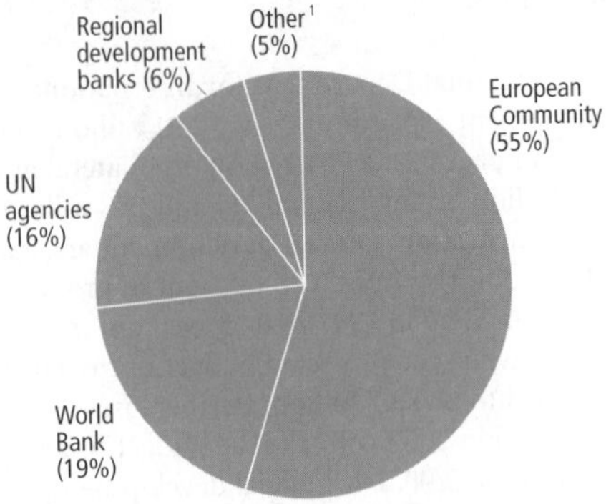

1 Includes Global Environmental Assistance (2%), International Monetary Fund (1%) and other agencies.
Source: Department for International Development

Figure 7.2 DFID Programme 2001/02: bilateral aid programme by region

Total: £1.3 billion[1]

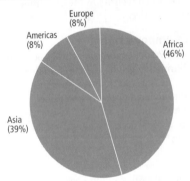

1 Excludes funding for global projects and for the Pacific region. The Pacific region accounts for less than 1 per cent of funding.
Source: Department for International Development

existing drugs and vaccines needs substantial investment (including from the private sector) in health service infrastructure and financial and human resources.

Education

Education is a fundamental right and the key to economic and social development. More than 120 million children around the world do not go to school and one child in five drops out before completing five years of basic education. One in five adults is illiterate, two-thirds of them women. DFID resources are focused on basic and primary education.

The UK is working with other governments to develop well-integrated and sustainable education systems, helping them to provide high-quality primary education. Literacy skills (such as reading, writing and numeracy) are an integral part of many aid programmes. They give access to information on, for example, health, education and the market economy, and provide a vital link to greater opportunities for improving people's livelihoods and their human rights.

The environment

Maintaining and improving the environment are crucial to the elimination of poverty. The DFID's main priority is to promote better environmental management, reverse environmental degradation, and reduce poor people's vulnerability to the effects of global environmental trends (particularly climate change).

Conflict and natural disasters

Conflict and natural disasters are major barriers to reducing poverty. Many of the 40 poorest countries are either in the middle of armed conflict or have only recently emerged from such conflict. The DFID's objectives are to reduce the tensions that lead to conflict, limit the means of waging warfare and provide the early humanitarian assistance and support needed for long-term reconstruction. The UK has contributed £60 million in aid towards the humanitarian emergency and reconstruction of

Afghanistan (see also page 75), and is also providing critical support in helping to re-establish stability in Sierra Leone.

The DFID's humanitarian assistance is targeted to improving the quality and speed of the response to a disaster; promoting effective recovery and early transition from emergency assistance to rehabilitation and reconstruction; and helping countries to reduce their vulnerability to natural, environmental and industrial disasters. The DFID is also continuing its commitment to strengthen the response of the multilateral institutions to humanitarian relief and crisis management.

During 2000/01 the UK responded to a number of natural disasters, including flooding in Mozambique and earthquakes in India and El Salvador. It also funded winter relief for Serbia and assistance for refugees in West Africa, Sudan, Indonesia and the Middle East.

Peacekeeping and security

The UN is the principal body responsible for the maintenance of international peace and security. At the end of May 2002 there were some 45,100 military personnel and civilian police from 87 nations serving in 15 peacekeeping operations around the world. The UK provides civilian police, military observers and troops for a range of UN missions and NATO deployments.

Cyprus
The UK has a contingent of about 390 troops in the UN Force in Cyprus, established in 1964 to help prevent the recurrence of fighting between Greek and Turkish Cypriots. Since the hostilities of 1974, when Turkish forces occupied the northern part of the island, the Force has been responsible for monitoring the ceasefire and for control of a buffer zone between the two communities.

Iraq/Kuwait
In 1991 UN Security Council Resolution 687 established a demilitarised zone extending 10 km into Iraq and 5 km into Kuwait to deter violations of the boundary and to observe hostile or potentially hostile actions. The UK, with the other permanent members of the Security Council, contributes 11 personnel to the UN Iraq/Kuwait observer mission.

Sierra Leone
In May 2000 there was a serious deterioration in the security situation in war-torn Sierra Leone as members of the UN peacekeeping mission were taken hostage by rebel forces. In response, the UK Government rapidly deployed forces to the capital, Freetown, to evacuate UK citizens and secure the airport to allow the arrival of UN reinforcements. Having achieved these aims, the British force was withdrawn and British training teams were deployed from June 2000 to help establish new, accountable Sierra Leone armed forces and a police force. Over 9,000 soldiers have since been trained and equipped by the UK, which has continued to help the Government of Sierra Leone and UN forces to regain control over the whole country and stage the peaceful elections held in May 2002.

Bosnia and Herzegovina
The UK supports the consolidation of a peaceful, multi-ethnic and democratic Bosnia and Herzegovina, and is helping to implement the 1995 Dayton/Paris Peace Agreement. The Stabilisation Force (SFOR) comprises troops from NATO nations and other contributing countries. The UK contributes some 1,850 troops to SFOR and around 80 British police officers to the UN International Police Task Force in Bosnia.

While ensuring continuing compliance with the military requirements of the Dayton Agreement, SFOR also provides support to the main organisations responsible for its civil aspects, including the Office of the High Representative, the International Police Task Force, the UN High Commissioner for Refugees, the OSCE and the UN Mission in Bosnia and Herzegovina.

The UK is helping the International Criminal Tribunal in The Hague, which was set up to try those indicted for war crimes in the former Yugoslavia. British forces have been at the forefront of SFOR's efforts to detain those indicted for war crimes. As well as contributing to the funding of the Tribunal, the UK provides staff, information and forensic science expertise.

Kosovo
Kosovo continues to be governed by a UN interim civilian administration (UNMIK), which was set up in the war-ravaged province of the Federal Republic of Yugoslavia under a UN Security Council resolution in 1999. The UK provides

some 200 civilian police, along with specialist officers, local government administrators and judicial experts to UNMIK, which is helping to establish self-government in the province. The UK maintains its commitment to the Kosovo Force (KFOR), contributing some 2,500 personnel to KFOR operations.

Macedonia

NATO forces were deployed to Macedonia in August 2001 following months of internal conflict between ethnic Albanian insurgents, led by the National Liberation Army (NLA), and Macedonian armed forces. The purpose of the 30-day NATO operation, including some 2,000 British personnel, was to collect weapons volunteered by the NLA following a framework agreement for a political settlement between Albanian and Macedonian leaders. A new NATO task force, to which the UK contributes 35 personnel, was subsequently deployed to ensure the security of international monitors overseeing the progress of the political process and the return of police to the former areas of conflict.

Arms control

Because of the global reach of modern weapons, the UK has a clear national interest in preventing proliferation of weapons of mass destruction and promoting international control. In addition, the attacks in the United States on 11 September 2001 have reinforced the need to prevent terrorists from obtaining such weapons.

Weapons of mass destruction

Nuclear weapons

The main instrument for controlling nuclear weapons is the Treaty on the Non-Proliferation of Nuclear Weapons (NPT), which entered into force in 1970 and to which the UK Government remains committed. The UK helped secure its indefinite extension in 1995, and played an active role in the sixth review conference in 2000 (where, for the first time since 1985, all participants agreed a final document which reviewed progress on nuclear non-proliferation and disarmament over the previous five years, and set out an agenda for the next five).

The UK was also involved in the negotiations on the Comprehensive Test Ban Treaty (CTBT), which it signed in 1996 and ratified in 1998. The

CTBT, with its permanent verification system, will come into force upon ratification by the remaining 13 of 44 named states. The UK Government is also pressing for the negotiation of a treaty banning the future production of fissile material for use in nuclear weapons.

The UK welcomed the signing of the Treaty of Moscow (Strategic Offensive Reductions Treaty) by the United States and Russia in May 2002, which will reduce their respective strategic nuclear warheads by two-thirds by 2012. Nevertheless, while large nuclear arsenals and the risks of proliferation remain, the Government considers that the UK's minimum nuclear deterrent (see page 82) remains a necessary and continuing element of the UK's security.

Biological weapons

The 1972 Biological and Toxic Weapons Convention provides for a worldwide ban on such weapons, but there are no effective compliance mechanisms. The UK continues to look for ways of strengthening the Convention.

Chemical weapons

The 1993 Chemical Weapons Convention, which came into force in 1997, provides for a worldwide ban on these weapons. The Organisation for the Prohibition of Chemical Weapons is responsible for verification. All the necessary British legislation is in place to license the production, possession and use of the most toxic chemicals and to implement the Convention's trade controls.

Conventional armed forces

The UK continues to work with its NATO partners and other European countries to develop and improve agreements to enhance stability in Europe in the light of the changed security environment. The main agreements reached are:

- the Conventional Armed Forces in Europe (CFE) Treaty (signed originally in 1990 and adapted at an OSCE summit in 1999), which limits the numbers of heavy weapons in the countries of NATO and the former Warsaw Pact, and includes a verification regime. The CFE Treaty is widely regarded as a linchpin of European security;

- the Vienna Document, developed under the auspices of the OSCE, which is a politically binding agreement on the promotion of stability and openness on military matters in Europe; revised in 1999, it contains confidence- and security-building measures, and verification arrangements; and

- the 1992 Open Skies Treaty, which provides for the overflight and photography of the entire territory of the 27 participating states to monitor their military capabilities and activities. The Treaty entered into force on 1 January 2002.

The UN Register of Conventional Arms, which came into effect in 1992, is intended to allow greater transparency in international transfers of conventional arms and to help identify excessive arms build-ups in any one country or region.

Landmines

The UK signed the Ottawa Convention banning the use, production, trade, transfer and stockpiling of anti-personnel landmines in 1997. The Convention, which Britain ratified in 1998, entered into force on 1 March 1999. The UK destroyed its stockpile of anti-personnel mines by October 1999. It has a programme to support humanitarian demining activities, which is focused on helping affected countries develop the capacity to clear landmines and on improving the co-ordination of international demining resources.

Export controls

The UK is a founding member of all the international export control regimes which govern the export of conventional arms, technology associated with weapons of mass destruction, missiles, and 'dual-use' goods.

In 1997 the UK Government issued new criteria for assessing licence applications for arms exports, one of which is that licences will not be granted if there is a clearly identifiable risk that weapons might be used for internal repression or international aggression. At the same time it banned the export of certain items for which there is clear evidence of use for torture or other abuses; it also declared its commitment to preventing British companies from manufacturing, selling or procuring such equipment and to pressing for a global ban. In 1998 EU Member States agreed on a Code of Conduct on Arms Exports, setting similar common standards to which all EU members would adhere.

International terrorism

The UK Government is committed to eliminating terrorism as a force in international affairs. It regards acts of terrorism as unacceptable in all circumstances and opposes concessions to any terrorist demands. It works bilaterally with other

Afghanistan

Usama Bin Laden's Al Qaida terrorist network was responsible for the seizure and crashing of civil airliners in New York, Washington and Pennsylvania on 11 September 2001. Al Qaida operated training camps in Afghanistan and Bin Laden was sheltered by the Taliban regime. Following the Taliban's refusal to hand over Bin Laden, the US-led coalition began military action in Afghanistan on 7 October 2001. The UK was involved from the outset, initially launching cruise missiles against terrorist training camps and providing other naval and air support to the coalition. In November a small force was also deployed to help secure and maintain the airbase at Bagram, near the Afghan capital of Kabul.

By December 2001 the Taliban regime had collapsed. It was replaced by the Afghan Interim Authority, created out of an Afghan-led peace process (initiated at a meeting in Bonn, Germany) designed to rebuild the country. To support the new government the UN also authorised the dispatch of a 5,000-strong International Security Assistance Force (ISAF) to Kabul to help stabilise the city. The UK led the ISAF for its first six months and at one point had some 2,100 troops serving with the force. Eighteen other countries also contributed forces, while the United States provided a liaison team. In June 2002 command of ISAF was transferred to Turkey and it was announced that the British contingent would be scaled down to about 400. Also in June, the *Loya Jirga* (grand council) of representatives from across Afghanistan met in Kabul to choose the future government of the country.

Despite this progress, pockets of the Al Qaida and Taliban remained active in Afghanistan. A 1,700-strong British commando battle group was deployed to Afghanistan at the request of the US to undertake offensive operations from April 2002. On the completion of its operations, it began a phased withdrawal in July. However, the UK is retaining a significant air, naval and ground force presence in Afghanistan and the region.

like-minded governments and multilaterally through the UN, EU, G8 and other international and regional organisations to promote action against terrorist groups and to foster closer international co-ordination against terrorism. The UK Government has stepped up assistance to those countries that lack the means to tackle terrorism themselves and is committed to challenging the political, social and economic conditions that are exploited by terrorists. The UK has ratified all 12 United Nations terrorism conventions, the most recent – the International Convention for the Suppression of Financing of Terrorism – in February 2001, upon the entry into force of the *Terrorism Act 2000*.

Campaign against international terrorism

The UK has played a leading part in the global response to the 11 September 2001 terrorist attacks in the United States, in which around 60 British people are thought to have died. The unanimity of the international community in its condemnation of the attacks was unprecedented, and the UN Security Council mandated action to suppress terrorism worldwide. The UK, which chairs the UN Counter Terrorism Committee, has been a leading member of the coalition against international terrorism. The British Government published a report on 9 September 2002 to update Parliament on progress in the campaign against terrorism, detailing actions taken by the Government in the UK and overseas in the year following the attacks in the United States.

International crime

The UK supports international efforts to combat illegal drugs, working with producer and transit countries, especially those where drug production and trafficking represent a direct threat to the UK. Over 60 drug liaison officers are stationed in UK missions in key countries, in co-operation with the host authorities. Working with its EU partners, the UK is helping Latin American, Caribbean and Central Asian states to stem the transit of drugs across their territories. It also participated in the negotiation of the EU drugs strategy for 2000–04,

which was endorsed by the European Council in 1999. The UK Government contributed £7.3 million to anti-drugs assistance overseas in 2001/02 and this will increase to over £10 million in 2002/03. The UK is involved in the United Nations drug control structure, and is one of the largest contributors to the UN International Drug Control Programme. Diplomatic efforts are backed up by the UK's overseas drugs assistance programme.

The UK also contributes to international efforts to counter financial crime, for example through its membership of the Financial Action Task Force against money laundering, and through its support for regional anti-money laundering groups.

Together with its EU partners, the UK is confronting serious and organised international crime through, for example, the European Police Office (EUROPOL) which supports investigations and operations conducted by national law enforcement agencies. EU Member States also belong to the International Criminal Police Organisation (INTERPOL). UK liaison with INTERPOL is provided by the National Criminal Intelligence Service (see page 196).

The UK participated in the negotiation of the UN Convention Against Transnational Crime, and three protocols covering the smuggling of migrants, trafficking in human beings and illegal firearms. The Convention was signed by 120 states, including the UK, in 2000.

Further reading

Foreign & Commonwealth Office Departmental Report 2002: The Government's Expenditure Plans 2002–03 to 2003–04. Cm 5413. The Stationery Office, 2002.

Department for International Development Departmental Report 2002: The Government's Expenditure Plans 2002–03 to 2003–04. Cm 5414. The Stationery Office, 2002.

Human Rights Annual Report 2002. Foreign & Commonwealth Office, 2002.

Websites

Foreign & Commonwealth Office
www.fco.gov.uk

Department for International Development
www.dfid.gov.uk

Ministry of Defence
www.mod.uk

British Council
www.britcoun.org

United Nations
www.un.org

Commonwealth
www.thecommonwealth.org

Organisation for Security and Co-operation in Europe
www.osce.org

Council of Europe
www.coe.int

www.

8 Defence

UK security

Defence policy

The purpose of the Ministry of Defence and the armed forces is to defend the United Kingdom (UK), its Overseas Territories, and its people and interests, and to act as a force for good by strengthening international peace and security.

The defence of the UK, as well as its economic and other wider interests, is linked with the security of Europe. The primary means of ensuring that security is the North Atlantic Treaty Organisation (NATO), of which the UK is a founder member and to which most of its armed forces are assigned. The Government is involved in the development of European military capabilities to strengthen Europe's contribution to NATO and to allow the European Union (EU) to conduct crisis management operations where NATO as a whole chooses not to be engaged (see page 79). The armed forces also contribute to the peacetime security of the UK and its Overseas Territories, and assist in humanitarian and peacetime operations worldwide.

The 1998 Strategic Defence Review (SDR) is the foundation of the country's defence policy and of plans for reshaping and modernising the services for this century. The SDR concluded that, although there was no direct military threat to the UK or its Overseas Territories following the conclusion of the Cold War, there were new threats such as the proliferation of nuclear, chemical and biological weapons, organised crime, and the break-up of the old communist states with attendant ethnic and religious conflict.

The SDR laid out a force structure in which the armed services would be able to respond to a major international crisis. This might involve operations of a similar scale and duration to the

Gulf War, or of more extended overseas deployment on a lesser scale (such as in Bosnia and Kosovo), while retaining the ability to mount a second, substantial deployment (up to a combat brigade with supporting naval and air forces).

War on terrorism: Afghanistan

Britain is one of a coalition of more than 20 nations which have been contributing troops, equipment and logistical support to the 5,000-strong International Security Assistance Force (ISAF), in order to assist the new Afghan Interim Authority in bringing security and stability in Kabul. Britain has also provided troops to the United States in operations against Al Qaida terrorists in Afghanistan. (See page 75 for the Government's policy on terrorism.)

The number of UK forces on operations in Afghanistan varied over time according to the situation on the ground. Between October 2001 and July 2002, UK forces at their peak included:

- an amphibious force including the helicopter carrier HMS *Ocean*, two frigates and a nuclear-powered submarine armed with Tomahawk land-attack missiles;

- some 2,100 troops in the ISAF;

- an infantry battlegroup of 1,700 troops built around 45 Commando, Royal Marines, and RAF helicopters assisting US-led forces in offensive operations; and

- RAF reconnaissance, refuelling and Hercules transport aircraft.

The 45 Commando group was withdrawn in summer 2002, while the British contribution to the ISAF was reduced to 400 personnel.

The growth and type of missions undertaken by UK forces since the SDR assessment point to the likelihood of the armed services conducting smaller, but frequent assignments – often simultaneous and sometimes prolonged, and some at short notice. In response to the attacks upon the United States in September 2001, an update to the SDR, *The New Chapter*, was issued in July 2002, highlighting the need to ensure that the right forces, concepts and capabilities were in place to deal with the new threats.

The strategy outlined in the SDR is also designed to reinforce the UK's contribution to international peace and security through NATO and the EU, and through other international organisations such as the United Nations (UN – see page 61) and the Organisation for Security and Co-operation in Europe (OSCE – see page 63).

North Atlantic Treaty Organisation

Membership of NATO is the cornerstone of British defence policy, and most of the UK's forces are assigned to it. The Alliance embodies the transatlantic relationship that links North America and Europe in a unique defence and security partnership. The number of members was increased to 19 with the accession of the Czech Republic, Hungary and Poland in 1999. The Alliance remains open to new members willing and able to assume the obligations and responsibilities of membership. Ten countries (Albania, Bulgaria, Croatia, Estonia, Latvia, Lithuania, Macedonia, Romania, Slovakia and Slovenia) are preparing for membership. NATO is expected to issue new invitations to some of these countries to join the Alliance at the Prague summit in November 2002.

NATO is adapting to the changed security environment in Europe. This includes a fundamental transformation in the Alliance's relationship with Russia after 11 September 2001. A summit meeting in May 2002 established a NATO-Russia Council to provide NATO allies and Russia with a mechanism for consultation, consensus-building, co-operation and joint action on a wide range of security issues of common interest, including terrorism, crisis management and non-proliferation.

Following the 1999 NATO summit, measures were put in place to increase the ability of the

Euro-Atlantic Partnership Council countries to operate effectively in NATO-led crisis management operations (see also page 63). These include greater involvement of the 27 non-NATO 'Partnership for Peace' states in the political consultation and decision-making process and in operational planning and command arrangements. NATO is also committed to the development of its relationship with Ukraine, following a consultation and co-operation agreement signed in 1997.

NATO is undertaking internal restructuring, including a major review of the military command structure and the implementation of the Combined Joint Task Force concept to ensure that it remains an effective military alliance able to meet the challenges of the post-11 September world. At the 1999 summit the allies launched an initiative to improve its military capabilities that will lead to increased effectiveness of Alliance operations. NATO is also reassessing its defence policy in the aftermath of the terrorist attacks on the United States. NATO foreign ministers agreed at Reykjavik in May 2002 that NATO forces should be usable wherever they are needed to counter the new threats of terrorism and weapons of mass destruction.

European security and defence

While NATO is the primary means of ensuring UK and European security and defence, operations such as in Bosnia and Kosovo (see page 73) have led the EU countries to initiate a programme designed to improve their military capabilities to enable the EU to undertake crisis management operations where NATO is not engaged. This programme will also help to ensure that the European countries contribute more effectively to the Alliance. At the Helsinki European Council in 1999, EU Member States committed themselves to the goal of modernising their armed forces so that by 2003 they would be able to deploy collectively up to 60,000 personnel, together with appropriate air and naval elements, within 60 days. This force would be used to carry out humanitarian, rescue, peacekeeping and peacemaking tasks, and would be sustainable for at least a year. The UK contribution to an individual operation could be up to 12,500 ground troops, 18 warships and 72 combat aircraft. A crucial priority in achieving this objective is the setting up of permanent arrangements for consultation and co-operation with NATO and for drawing on NATO planning and other capabilities. Collective defence remains the responsibility of NATO, which will also continue to have a major role in crisis management.

Defence tasks

The UK and its Overseas Territories
The armed forces are responsible for safeguarding Britain's territory, airspace and territorial waters. They also provide for the security and reinforcement of the Overseas Territories and support to the civil authorities in both the UK and the Overseas Territories.

Maritime defence
The Royal Navy aims to patrol, police and defend the UK's territorial waters and ensure the protection of its rights and interests in the surrounding seas (including offshore oil and gas reserves), and of British interests around the world. The maintenance of a 24-hour, year-round presence in waters around the British Isles provides reassurance to merchant ships and other mariners, as well as security of the seas. In addition, threats to British flagged ships overseas remain a national responsibility, particularly in view of the continuing global terrorist danger. The Royal Air Force (RAF) also contributes to maritime requirements, for instance through the Nimrod force, which provides air surveillance of surface vessels and submarines.

Land defence
The British Army aims to provide, through either the deployment of the whole or appropriate elements of its available forces, the capability to defend the UK and its Overseas Territories. In addition, the Army is committed to such tasks as giving military aid to peace support and humanitarian operations, responding to regional conflict outside the NATO area and contributing forces to counter a strategic attack on NATO.

Air defence
Air defence of the UK and the surrounding seas is maintained by a system of layered defences. Continuous radar cover is provided by the Air Surveillance and Control System (ASACS) supplemented by the NATO Airborne Early Warning Force, to which the RAF contributes six aircraft. The RAF also provides five squadrons of

Tornado F3 air defence aircraft, supported by tanker aircraft and, in wartime, an additional F3 squadron. Royal Navy air defence destroyers can also be linked to the ASACS, providing radar and electronic warfare coverage and surface-to-air missiles. Ground-launched Rapier missiles defend the main RAF bases. Naval aircraft also contribute to British air defence.

Overseas garrisons
The UK maintains garrisons in Gibraltar, the Sovereign Base Areas of Cyprus, the Falkland Islands and Brunei. Gibraltar contains support, logistic, communications and training facilities in the western Mediterranean, while Cyprus provides basing facilities in the eastern Mediterranean. The garrison on the Falkland Islands is a tangible demonstration of the Government's commitment to uphold the right of the islanders to determine their own future (see page 68). The garrison in Brunei is maintained at the request of the Brunei Government. In addition, a jungle warfare-training unit is maintained in Belize.

Northern Ireland
The armed forces provide support to the police in Northern Ireland (see page 16) in maintaining law and order and countering terrorism. The number of units deployed at any one time is dependent on the prevailing security situation. The Royal Navy patrols territorial waters around Northern Ireland and its inland waterways in order to deter and intercept the movement of terrorist weapons. The Royal Marines provide troops to meet Navy and Army commitments, while the RAF provides elements of the RAF Regiment and Chinook, Wessex and Puma helicopters.

Other tasks
Other tasks include the provision of:

- military aid to other government departments, for example support during the foot-and-mouth outbreak and carrying out fishery protection duties;

- military aid to the civil power, such as assisting the police in response to terrorist threats and in helping in the fight against drugs;

- military aid to the civil community, including during floods; and

- military search and rescue.

Britain in NATO

Maritime forces

Most Royal Navy ships are committed to NATO. Permanent contributions are made to NATO's Standing Naval Forces in the Atlantic and the Mediterranean, and to NATO's Rapid Reaction Forces. The UK also contributes to NATO's Maritime Augmentation Forces, which are held at the lowest state of readiness and in peacetime comprise ships mainly in routine refit or maintenance.

The main components of the fleet available to NATO are:

- three aircraft carriers operating Joint Force Harrier aircraft and Sea King or Merlin anti-submarine helicopters;

- 32 destroyers and frigates, and 22 mine counter-measure vessels;

- 12 nuclear-powered attack submarines; and

- amphibious forces, including a commando brigade of the Royal Marines, and a helicopter carrier.

Land forces

The multinational HQ of the Allied Command Europe Rapid Reaction Corps (ARRC) and its supporting forces is the key land component of NATO's Rapid Reaction Forces. Capable of deploying at short notice up to four NATO divisions, the HQ ARRC is commanded by a British general. The UK provides two of the ten divisions available to the Corps – an armoured division of three armoured brigades stationed in Germany, and a division of three mechanised brigades based in Britain. Up to 55,000 British troops may be assigned to HQ ARRC for operations. An air-mobile brigade, assigned to one of the Corps' multinational divisions, is also sited in the UK.

Air forces

The RAF contributes to NATO's Immediate and Rapid Reaction Forces and its main defence forces. Around 100 aircraft and 40 helicopters are allocated to them. Tornado F3, Harrier and Jaguar aircraft, and Rapier surface-to-air missiles form part of the Supreme Allied Commander Europe's Immediate Reaction Force, while Harrier, Jaguar and Tornado GR1/4 aircraft provide offensive support and tactical reconnaissance for the Rapid Reaction Force. Chinook and Puma helicopters, as part of the Joint Helicopter Command, supply troop airlift facilities for the ARRC or other deployed land forces. The RAF provides Nimrod maritime patrol aircraft, and search and rescue helicopters. In addition, the RAF is the main European provider of air-to-air refuelling and strategic airlift, and contributes to the NATO airborne early warning and control component.

Wider security interests

Military tasks to promote the UK's wider security interests may be undertaken by British forces working within NATO, assisting the United Nations, in coalition with allies, or acting alone. Contingents are deployed on UN operations in Cyprus, Georgia, Bosnia, Kosovo, Macedonia, Sierra Leone, the Democratic Republic of Congo and on the Iraq/Kuwait border. Over Iraq (see pages 64–5), Tornado GR1/4s and Jaguars, supported by VC-10s, are policing the no-fly zones to ensure that Iraq does not resume repression of minorities and that it does not threaten its neighbours. The Royal Navy is deployed to the Gulf to enforce UN sanctions against Iraq. A large British force was deployed in Afghanistan to provide stability in Kabul, and to assist the US in operations against terrorist elements (see page 75).

The number of operations against trafficking in illicit drugs has increased in recent years, for example in the Caribbean, where a Royal Navy destroyer or frigate works closely with the authorities of the United States, the Overseas Territories and the Regional Security System to combat drug trafficking. The ship on station, HMS Newcastle, seized £42 million worth of drugs in an operation carried out in July 2002.

In recent years, British forces have taken part in international evacuation or humanitarian relief operations in Rwanda, Somalia, Angola, Eritrea, the Democratic Republic of Congo, Sierra Leone, Mozambique, East Timor, the Caribbean and Central America.

Defence diplomacy is the use of defence assets to build and promote stability and assist in the development of democratically accountable armed forces. British service personnel and civilians working in defence are involved in a range of non-operational activities including:

- help in verifying arms control agreements (see pages 74–5);

- outreach programmes of bilateral assistance and co-operation with other countries in areas such as English language training, defence management, and modernisation and reform of armed forces; and

- training of some 4,000 military and civilian students from over 100 countries each year at UK defence establishments.

UK intelligence and security services

The UK has three intelligence and security services: the Secret Intelligence Service (SIS), the Security Service and the Government Communications Headquarters (GCHQ). The SIS and the GCHQ are responsible to the Foreign and Commonwealth Secretary, and the Security Service is responsible to the Home Secretary. The planned budget for these agencies in 2002/03 is £893 million. The main role of the SIS is the production of secret intelligence in issues regarding Britain's vital interests in the fields of security, defence, foreign and economic policies. The Security Service (also known as 'MI5') is responsible for the protection of Britain against threats to national security, primarily from terrorism and espionage. GCHQ carries out signals intelligence to support national security, military operations and law enforcement, and also helps secure government communications and key systems supporting the UK's national infrastructure. The Ministry of Defence has its own Defence Intelligence Staff, which provide intelligence analyses, assessments, advice and strategic warnings to the Ministry of Defence, the armed forces and government.

Nuclear forces

Although the four Trident submarines are retained as the ultimate guarantee of national security, the UK and other members of NATO have radically reduced their reliance on nuclear weapons. The UK continues to support mutual, balanced and verifiable reductions in the number of nuclear weapons worldwide (see page 74). When the UK Government is satisfied that sufficient progress has been made to allow the inclusion of British nuclear weapons in multilateral negotiations without endangering UK security interests, the Government will do so.

As a result of an examination of Britain's deterrence requirements, the Government concluded that fewer than 200 operationally available nuclear warheads were needed – a reduction of one-third. Therefore, the UK now has only one Trident submarine on patrol at a time. It carries a reduced load of up to 48 warheads compared with the previous maximum of 96. The submarine's missiles are not targeted and it is normally at several days' 'notice to fire'.

Strategic Defence Review implementation

Over two-thirds of the SDR measures have been implemented, which has increased the armed forces' capabilities. Progress towards the more flexible and rapidly deployable expeditionary forces also continues, with improvements in:

- strategic transport capabilities by leasing four C17 aircraft pending the introduction of 25 multinational A400M aircraft, by ordering six roll-on, roll-off ferries in a Private Finance Initiative (see page 350), and placing contracts for four new landing ships;

- tactical mobility through combining airborne and airmobile forces with the new Apache attack helicopter to form a highly capable air manoeuvre formation (16 Air Mobile Brigade) trained and equipped for long-range operations;

- new long-range and strike 'smart' weapons; and

- measures against chemical, biological, radiological and nuclear warfare threats, including the setting up of a joint nuclear, chemical and biological defence regiment.

The strike capability is also being improved. Replacement aircraft carriers will enter service from 2012, and will be able to carry the Royal Navy and RAF Future Joint Combat Aircraft (planned to be the Joint Strike Aircraft), which will also operate from land. Two other replacement vessels, the amphibious assault ships *Albion* and *Bulwark*, are scheduled to enter service in 2003 and 2004.

Other SDR initiatives to co-ordinate service activities more closely have been completed. These include the establishment of:

- the Joint Rapid Reaction Force, a more easily deployed and better supported force that includes 50 warships and support vessels, four army brigades and 100 aircraft, elements of which have been operating successfully in Kosovo, East Timor and Sierra Leone;

- an additional brigade, 12 Mechanised Brigade, created from the Army's armoured and mechanised formations;

- the Joint Helicopter Command of tri-service force of some 350 attack, troop-carrying and heavy lift helicopters;

- the Joint Force Harrier, an interim offensive command of Royal Navy and RAF Harrier aircraft;

- the Defence Logistics Organisation (DLO), which provides a more streamlined logistic service to the front line; and

- the Joint Doctrine and Concepts Centre for the development of defence doctrine.

In addition, the Territorial Army (see page 85) has been reorganised. Its units and individuals are more integrated into the regular army, concentrating on specialist roles such as communications, equipment maintenance, logistics and medical support.

Defence equipment

Modern equipment is essential if one of the key aims of Britain's force restructuring programme is to be achieved, namely that of increasing the flexibility and mobility of its armed forces.

Improvements for the Royal Navy equipment programme include:

- the Astute-class attack submarines;

- two new aircraft carriers; and

- the Type 45 destroyer, which will deploy an anti-air missile system developed with France and Italy.

The Army front line is being strengthened by:

- the introduction of the Challenger 2 tank;

- Apache attack helicopters equipped with new anti-tank missiles; and

- improved Rapier and new Starstreak air defence missiles.

Improvements for the RAF include:

- the upgrading of the Tornado GR1 fleet to GR4 standard (nearing completion);

- the introduction of the Eurofighter Typhoon combat aircraft;

- new Nimrod maritime patrol and attack aircraft;

- the introduction of EH101 and Chinook support helicopters and improved Hercules aircraft; and

- the replacement of the Joint Force Harriers with aircraft operating from the new aircraft carriers and from land.

Defence procurement
Some £10 billion is spent each year on military equipment. Responsibility for this budget lies with the Defence Procurement Agency and Defence Logistics Organisation. All defence acquisition projects are run on a 'smart' acquisition procedure. When assessing options, consideration is given to the initial costs of a project and to the cost of support throughout its service life. Competition for contracts takes place wherever possible. Once a contract is awarded, integrated teams, including representatives from industry, control the project throughout its life. Equipment is acquired incrementally, with the basic equipment entering into service quickly and then being upgraded as technology improves. The involvement of the private sector through public-private partnerships (see page 350) is a major element of procurement strategy. Under this policy, capital investment with a value of some £1.8 billion is being undertaken.

International procurement collaboration
The UK is a member of NATO's Conference of National Armaments Directors, which promotes equipment collaboration between NATO nations. It is also a founder member of OCCAR, an armament co-operation organisation formed with France, Germany and Italy for managing joint

procurement activities. Current collaborative programmes in which the UK participates include:

- development of the Eurofighter Typhoon (with Germany, Italy and Spain);

- a maritime anti-air missile system (France and Italy);

- a 'beyond visual' anti-air missile system (France, Italy, Spain, Germany and Sweden);

- the EH101 helicopter (Italy);

- a multi-role armoured vehicle (France and Germany);

- the large transport Airbus A400M aircraft (Belgium, France, Germany, Italy, Spain and Turkey); and

- the Joint Strike Fighter (US).

The armed forces

Commissioned ranks

Commissions, either by promotion from the ranks or by direct entry based on educational and other qualifications, are granted for short, medium and long terms. All three services have schemes for school, university and college sponsorships.

Commissioned ranks receive initial training at the Britannia Royal Naval College, Dartmouth; the Commando Training Centre, Lympstone (Devon); the Royal Military Academy, Sandhurst; or the Royal Air Force College, Cranwell. This is followed by specialist training, which may include degree courses at service establishments or universities. Courses of higher training for officers, designed to emphasise the joint approach to the tactical and operational levels of conflict, are provided at the Joint Services Command and Staff College at Shrivenham (Wiltshire).

Non-commissioned ranks

Engagements for non-commissioned ranks vary widely in length and terms of service. Subject to a minimum period, entrants may leave at any time, giving 18 months' notice (12 months for certain engagements). Discharge may also be granted on compassionate or medical grounds.

In addition to their basic training, non-commissioned personnel receive supplementary

specialist training throughout their careers. Study for educational qualifications is encouraged, and service trade and technical training leads to nationally recognised qualifications. New vocational training and educational initiatives have been set up to improve recruitment and retention. The Army Foundation College offers a 42-week course combining military training and the opportunity to acquire national qualifications. The course is intended to attract high-quality recruits who will go on to fill senior posts in front-line roles.

Reserve Forces

The Reserve Forces serve alongside the regular forces and are integral to the ability to expand the services in times of crises. For example, under the current commitment, around 10 per cent of UK forces in Bosnia are reservists at any one time. In particular, reserves can provide skills and units not available or required in peacetime. The reserves include former members of the regular armed forces liable for service in an emergency (regular reserve) and volunteer reserves, recruited directly from the civilian community – the Royal Naval Reserve, the Royal Marines Reserve, the Territorial Army and the Reserve Air Forces (which comprise the Royal Auxiliary Air Force and the Royal Air Force Reserve).

To support the regular forces, the reserves – both individuals and formed units – need to be fully integrated into regular formations and readily available for service, where necessary through selective compulsory call-out during situations short of a direct threat to the UK. Reserves are also liable for service in peace support operations. Training for this role is given at the Reserve Training Mobilisation Centre at Chilwell near Nottingham. Under the SDR, Royal Naval and RAF volunteer reserve numbers will increase, and,

Table 8.1 Strength of service and civilian personnel, April 2002

Royal Navy	42,400
Army	114,800
RAF	53,300
Regular reserves	224,600
Volunteer reserves	36,400
Civilians	103,400
UK-based	89,300
Locally based	14,100

Source: Defence Analytical Services Agency

while the strength of the TA has been reduced from 56,000 to 41,200, it is more closely integrated with the Regular Army, with greater emphasis on combat support. In the light of the terrorist attack on the United States, the Government is considering the creation of a reaction force of some 6,000 personnel formed from the volunteer reserves to provide at short notice support and assistance to the police and other civil authorities in UK in the event of an impending or actual terrorist incident.

Administration

The defence budget

The defence budget for 2002/03 is £29.4 billion, rising to £30.9 billion in 2003/04, £31.8 billion in 2004/05 and £32.8 billion in 2005/06. The Ministry of Defence believes that this growth in defence spending – the largest sustained real increase for 20 years – will provide necessary investment in the armed forces' capabilities and structures to deal with extra priorities as outlined in *The New Chapter* in the SDR, including the demands of the war on terrorism.

Defence management

The Ministry of Defence is both a Department of State and the highest-level military headquarters. The Secretary of State for Defence is responsible for the formulation and conduct of defence policy and for providing the means by which it is conducted. Three junior ministers support the Secretary of State and have responsibilities for operational, policy and service personnel issues; defence equipment development, acquisition and defence exports; and veterans, civilian personnel, environmental and regulatory matters respectively.

Ministers are assisted by the Chief of the Defence Staff (CDS) and the Permanent Secretary. The CDS is the head of the armed forces and the principal military adviser to the Secretary of State and the Government. The Permanent Secretary is the Government's principal civilian adviser on defence and has primary responsibility for policy, finance and administration of the department.

A large proportion of the Ministry of Defence's support activities is undertaken by defence agencies (see page 480), such as the Defence Procurement Agency.

Further reading

The Strategic Defence Review: Modern Forces for the Modern World. Cm 3999. Ministry of Defence. The Stationery Office, 1998.

Defence Policy 2001. Ministry of Defence. The Stationery Office, 2001.

The Future Strategic Context for Defence. Ministry of Defence. The Stationery Office, 2001.

The Government's Expenditure Plans 2001–2002 to 2003–2004 and Main Estimates 2001–2002. Cm 5401. Ministry of Defence. The Stationery Office, 2002.

The Strategic Defence Review: A New Chapter. Cm 5566. Ministry of Defence. The Stationery Office, 2002.

Websites

British Army
www.army.mod.uk

MI5
www.mi5.gov.uk

Ministry of Defence
www.mod.uk

NATO
www.nato.int

Royal Air Force
www.raf.mod.uk

Royal Navy
www.royalnavy.mod.uk

WWW.

9 The social framework

The population of the UK has grown and changed significantly since the Queen came to the throne in 1952. Increased life expectancy and lower fertility rates have produced an older population, while immigration has led to ethnic diversity. Living arrangements and relationships have changed. More people are living alone, cohabitation before marriage is now commonplace and there has been a rise in births outside marriage. Many more women are participating in the labour market, although they still do most of the housework and childcare. Living standards are much higher, but there remain concerns about the relative deprivation of some people and communities.

Population

The population of the United Kingdom was estimated to be 58.8 million in mid-2001. This estimate, which is based on results from the 2001 Census, indicates that the population is approximately 1 million smaller than was suggested by the estimates for mid-2000. It is very difficult to get accurate information about people leaving the country and this is thought to have caused most of the discrepancy. Over the last 20 years more people have emigrated than was previously thought, causing the population to grow a little more slowly than expected. Population projections, based on the previous mid-2000 estimates, suggested that the population of the UK might increase to nearly 65 million by 2025 and peak at almost 66 million in 2040 before beginning a gradual decline.

Age and gender

The UK has an ageing population. Lower fertility rates and lower mortality rates have both contributed to this. In 2001 there were 10.8 million people over state pension age, and 11.9 million children aged under 16.

More boys are born each year than girls, and in 1981 men outnumbered women until around the age of 48. Above this age there were increasingly more women than men. Results from the 2001 Census indicate that women now outnumber men from the age of 22. By age 90 and over there are three times as many women as men. This reflects the longer life expectancy of women. In 2001 projected average life expectancy at birth in the

Then and now – population

According to the 1951 Census, there were an estimated 50.2 million people in the UK. Since then the population has increased by 17 per cent. This compares with an average growth for the EU of 23 per cent.

Some 8.3 million people were living in Greater London in 1951. By the early 1990s this had fallen to 6.9 million, but the population of the capital has been increasing again and reached 7.2 million in 2001.

Over the last 50 years there has been a gradual increase in the proportion of people over state pension age and a fall in the proportion of working age. In 1951, 14 per cent of the population were over state pension age and 63 per cent were of working age. By 2001, 18 per cent of the population were over state pension age and 61 per cent were of working age.

	1951	Per cent 2001
Under 16	24	20
Working age	63	61
Over state pension age	14	18

The ageing of the population is particularly evident when the number of people aged 85 and over is considered. In 1951 there were 0.2 million people in this age group. This had grown to 1.1 million by 2001.

Figure 9.1 Births[1] and deaths, UK

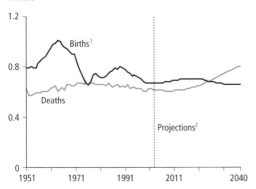

Millions

1 Data from 1981 exclude the non-residents of Northern Ireland.
2 2000-based.
Source: Office for National Statistics, Government Actuary's Department, General Register Office for Scotland and Northern Ireland Statistics and Research Agency

UK was 76 years for males and 80 years for females.

Births and deaths

There were 669,000 live births in the UK in 2001, representing 11.2 per 1,000 population. There has

Then and now – births and deaths
Babies born in 2001 in the UK can expect to live an average of nine years longer than their 1951 counterparts. Infant mortality rates (deaths of infants under one year old per 1,000 live births) fell by over 80 per cent between 1951 and 2001.

Infant mortality
1950–1952 (annual average)
- boys – 34 deaths per 1,000 live births

- girls – 26 deaths per 1,000 live births

2001
- boys – 6 deaths per 1,000 live births

- girls – 5 deaths per 1,000 live births

Adult mortality
Over the same period the death rate for men aged 55–64 fell by 54 per cent, from 23.2 per 1,000 in 1951 to 10.6 per 1,000 in 2001. Among women of the same age it fell by 49 per cent, from 12.9 to 6.6 per 1,000 women.

The 2001 Census
The 2001 Census was held on 29 April 2001 and is estimated to have had a response rate of 94 per cent in England and Wales. The first results – the population on Census Day for each local authority area by age and sex – were published at the end of September 2002. The population of the UK on Census Day 2001 was **58,789,194**.

The release of more detailed results will start in February 2003. Census reports and linked publications will be available on the National Statistics website and many will be part of the Neighbourhood Statistics service (see page 98).

been a gradual reduction in the number of births since 1990, when the figure was 798,000. In the last 50 years the highest number of births in any year was in 1964, when there were over 1 million.

Over 604,000 deaths were registered in the UK in 2001, a crude death rate of 10.1 per 1,000 population. Despite population growth over the last century the number of deaths has remained relatively constant, due to large declines in mortality rates. Rising standards of living and developments in medical technology and practice help to explain these declines. Death rates are higher for males than females in all age groups, explaining some of the gender imbalance among the older population.

Households and families

The number of households in Great Britain rose by 50 per cent between 1961 and 2002, from 16.3 million to 24.4 million. Many more people now live alone: in spring 2002, 29 per cent of households in Great Britain consisted of just one adult, compared with 11 per cent in 1961 (see Table 9.2). Most of the increase in one-person households since 1981 is attributable to people below pension age.

Despite the growth in the number of people living alone, most households (57 per cent) are still based on couples, although the proportion has fallen from 74 per cent in 1961. These couple households, however, are now less likely to contain dependent children than in 1961 or 1981.

Lone parents with dependent children now account for 6 per cent of households, compared with 2 per cent in 1961. Lone parents have increasingly become householders in their own

Table 9.2 Households by type of household and family, Great Britain[1]

	1961	1981	Per cent 2002
One person			
Under state pension age	4	8	15
Over state pension age	7	14	14
Two or more unrelated adults	5	5	3
One-family households[2]			
Couple with:			
No children	26	26	29
1–2 dependent children[3]	30	25	19
3 or more dependent children[3]	8	6	4
Non-dependent children only	10	8	6
Lone parent with:			
Dependent children[3]	2	5	6
Non-dependent children only	4	4	3
Multi-family households	3	1	1
All households (millions)	**16.3**	**20.2**	**24.4**

1 Census data for 1961 and 1981; Labour Force Survey data at spring 2002.
2 Other individuals who were not family members may also be included.
3 May also include non-dependent children.
Source: Census of Population, Labour Force Survey, Office for National Statistics

Figure 9.3 Marriages and divorces, UK

Thousands

1 For both partners.
2 Includes annulments. Divorces data are for Great Britain only from 1950 to 1970.
3 For one or both partners.
Source: Office for National Statistics, General Register Office for Scotland and Northern Ireland Statistics and Research Agency

right: 40 years ago it would have been more common for them to live with relatives.

Cohabitation, marriage and divorce

Patterns of partnership formation have also changed. Most people still get married at some stage, but the proportions who cohabit or live outside a relationship have increased. It was estimated that there were just over 1.5 million cohabiting couples in England and Wales in 1996; this number is projected to double by 2021. Figures for Great Britain show that around 12 per cent of adults aged 16 to 59 were cohabiting with their partner in 2000/01. This was most likely among men aged 25 to 34 and women aged 20 to 29. Cohabitation has become increasingly common before marriage, although 14 per cent of adults aged 16 to 59 reported at least one cohabiting union that did not lead to marriage.

In 2000 there were 306,000 marriages in the UK, a slight increase on the previous year's figure of 301,000. Of the marriages that took place in 2000, 180,000 were first marriages for both partners, almost half the number in 1950. First marriages accounted for 81 per cent of all marriages in 1950 but only 59 per cent in 2000.

Around 155,000 divorces were granted in the UK in 2000 – 14 per cent fewer than in 1993 (see Figure 9.3). The divorce rate in England and Wales peaked at 14.2 per 1,000 married people in 1993, but has since fallen. The rate in 2000 was 12.7 per 1,000 married people, the lowest since 1984.

Family formation

There were 766,000 conceptions in England and Wales in 2000, a fall of 1 per cent from 1999.

Registering vital events

Births, marriages and deaths in England and Wales have been registered since 1837. The White Paper *Civil Registration: Vital Change*, published by the Government in January 2002, outlines plans to modernise and improve the civil registration service. These would:

- enable people to register births and deaths online, by telephone or in person at any register office;

- provide couples with more choice of where and when to marry. It is currently possible to marry in places approved by the relevant local authority, such as hotels and stately homes. In future, there would be standards and guidance on suitable places for marriage ceremonies to take place. These standards would cover accessibility, health and safety, and maintain the seemly and dignified nature of the ceremony. The new proposals would also remove time restrictions; currently weddings can only take place between 8 am and 6 pm;

- provide for new services, such as naming ceremonies and reaffirmation of marriage vows; and

- create a central database of registrations of births, marriages and deaths.

Similar proposals are being implemented in Scotland.

Almost 80 per cent of these led to a maternity (a live or still birth).

The UK fertility rate in 2000 was 55 live births per 1,000 women of childbearing age, a fall of 40 per cent since 1961. Since the 1970s fertility rates have been below the level needed for the long-term natural replacement of the population. In England and Wales women giving birth are now on average three years older than those in the early 1970s – in 2001 the mean age of women at birth was 29.2 years, compared with 26.2 in 1972. In addition, the proportion of women remaining childless has risen. Sixteen per cent of women born in 1924 were still childless by the age of 45. It is projected that over 20 per cent of women born in or after 1965 will remain childless.

Then and now – families

Britain 1952: An Official Handbook reported on falling family sizes in comparison to Victorian Britain. It was estimated that in the 1950s the average number of children per family was 2.2. Couples married in the mid-Victorian era had, on average, five or six children. The decline was most marked among those in the professional classes. Average completed family size was expected to continue declining and eventually to level off for women born after 1970 at 1.8 children per woman.

Most children are born to married couples, but an increasing proportion of births occur outside marriage. Forty per cent of all births in the UK in 2001 occurred outside marriage, around four times the proportion in 1971. Most of this growth is accounted for by the increase in births to cohabiting couples. Eighty-two per cent of births outside marriage in England and Wales in 2001 were jointly registered by both parents. Over three-quarters of these parents were living at the same address. Teenage mothers are more likely to give birth outside marriage – in England and Wales 89 per cent of births to women under 20 were outside marriage. Twenty-six per cent of births to teenage mothers were registered by the mother alone, compared with only 4 per cent of births to women in their late thirties or early forties.

Migration

Population movements occur both within the UK and internationally. During the second half of the 20th century there was an internal movement of population from the coal, shipbuilding and steel industry areas in the north of England, Scotland and Wales to the south of England and the Midlands where the light industries and service industries are based. Over the same period, immigration from Commonwealth countries and more recently by people seeking asylum increased the cultural and religious diversity of the UK population (see also chapter 15).

Internal migration

During the year to mid-2001, Wales and Scotland gained 8,000 and 3,000 people respectively from migration within the UK. England experienced a net loss of 11,000 people, while the net change in Northern Ireland was negligible. At a regional level, the greatest fall in population occurred in

Table 9.4 Inter-regional movements within the United Kingdom, mid-2000 to mid-2001

Thousands

	Origin				
	England	Wales	Scotland	Northern Ireland	Total for rest of UK
Destination					
England	.	50	47	9	106
Wales	57	.	2	0	59
Scotland	51	2	.	2	55
Northern Ireland	9	–	3	.	12
Total for rest of UK	117	52	51	11	.

Source: Office for National Statistics, General Register Office for Scotland, Northern Ireland Statistics and Research Agency

Table 9.5 Acceptances for settlement in the United Kingdom, by region of origin

Thousands

	1997	1998	1999	2000	2001
Asia	25.6	30.1	40.1	47.5	43.3
Africa	13.2	16.1	27.0	44.5	31.4
Europe[1]	7.7	7.6	16.0	15.1	13.8
Americas	7.8	10.8	8.5	11.5	11.9
Oceania	3.1	3.7	4.1	4.9	5.5
Other[2]	1.3	1.5	1.4	1.6	0.9
All regions	**58.7**	**69.8**	**97.1**	**125.1**	**106.8**

1 Includes European Economic Area (EEA) countries – EEA nationals are not obliged to seek settlement and the figures relate only to those who chose to do so.
2 Mainly British overseas citizens and those whose nationality was unknown.
Source: Home Office

London where 69,000 more people moved to other regions of the UK than moved into London. Nearly two-fifths of people leaving London for elsewhere in the UK moved into the neighbouring South East region. The South West experienced the highest net gain of all the regions due to internal migration (almost 30,000 people).

Young adults are the most mobile age group. Many people in their twenties leave their parental home to study, seek employment or set up their own home. In 2001, London experienced the largest net increase of people aged 16 to 24, of 19,000. The West Midlands experienced the biggest net loss of people in this age group (over 4,000). London also experienced the largest net losses among all the other age groups, particularly those aged 35 to 44. The South West, East and South East experienced the highest net gains in this age group.

International migration

In the last 20 years net inward migration has become an increasingly important factor in population growth. Almost three-quarters of the UK population increase between 1999 and 2000 was due to international migration. In 2000 an estimated 183,000 more people migrated to the UK than emigrated from the UK, almost double the figure for 1997.

Immigration into the UK is largely governed by the *Immigration Act 1971*. Rules made under this Act set out the requirements to be met by those who are subject to immigration control and seek entry to, or leave to remain in, the UK. The 1971 Act has been amended by subsequent legislation, including the *Immigration and Asylum Act 1999*.

In April 2002 the Government introduced a Nationality, Immigration and Asylum Bill setting out measures to reform the existing system. These measures would:

- require naturalisation applicants to demonstrate knowledge of the English language and life in the UK;

- introduce a citizenship ceremony, including a citizenship pledge (see page 92);

- create a system of accommodation centres for asylum seekers, with new arrangements for detention, temporary release and removal; and

- tackle fraud, including a 14-year penalty for people-trafficking or for facilitating illegal entry to the UK.

In 2001, 106,800 people were accepted for settlement, 18,300 fewer than in 2000 (see Table 9.5). Asia, which accounted for 40 per cent of total acceptances in 2001, was the leading region, followed by Africa and then Europe.

Under the Immigration Rules, nationals of certain countries must obtain a visa before they can enter the UK. Other nationals, subject to immigration control, require entry clearance when coming to work or settle in the UK. Visas and other entry clearances are normally obtained from the nearest

---

Highly skilled migrant programme
Under this programme, skilled individuals who are not British citizens can apply to come to the UK to seek work. Applications are assessed on a points-based system in the following areas:

- educational qualifications;

- work experience;

- past earnings;

- achievement in a chosen field; and

- a special category for overseas doctors wishing to work as general practitioners in the UK.

Successful applicants are granted leave to enter the UK for one year, following which further leave may be granted depending on the individual's employment status.

British diplomatic post in a person's home country. Nationals of the European Economic Area (EEA) – EU Member States and Norway, Iceland and Liechtenstein – are not subject to substantive immigration control. They may work in the UK without restriction. Provided they are working or able to support themselves financially, EEA nationals have a right to reside in the UK.

Asylum

The UK has a tradition of giving asylum to those in need of protection, and is a signatory to the 1951 United Nations Convention, and its 1967 Protocol relating to the Status of Refugees. These provide that lawful residents who have been granted refugee status should enjoy treatment at least as favourable as that accorded to the indigenous population.

In the late 1980s applications for asylum (based on the principal applicant) started to rise sharply from around 4,000 a year in 1985 to 1988, to 44,800 in 1991, and reached a record 80,300 in 2000. There were 71,400 applications in 2001, an 11 per cent drop on the 2000 level. The main nationalities applying for asylum in the UK in 2001 were:

- Afghanistan (9,000 applicants);

- Iraq (6,700 applicants);

- Somalia (6,500 applicants);

- Sri Lanka (5,500 applicants); and

- Turkey (3,700 applicants).

In the first six months of 2002 applications for asylum averaged 6,655 a month. This was 15 per cent higher than in the same period a year earlier.

An estimated 119,000 initial asylum decisions were made in 2001, a 9 per cent rise on the number in 2000 and more than three-and-a-half times the number in 1999, reflecting a drop in the backlog of cases. In 2001, 10 per cent of these decisions were grants of asylum, compared with 12 per cent in 2000. A further 17 per cent of decisions in 2001 were grants of exceptional leave to remain and 73 per cent of applicants were refused. Many failed asylum seekers appeal against their refusal decision. Independent adjudicators determined 43,400 appeals in 2001, more than double the number in 2000. Of these, 8,200 (19 per cent) were successful.

Since April 2000 the National Asylum Support Service has been responsible for the provision of support for those asylum seekers who are destitute. Support is provided until the asylum claim is finally decided. Those granted refugee status or exceptional leave to remain on humanitarian grounds are entitled to claim public funds.

Until April 2002 support for people seeking asylum took the form of vouchers. This system has now been amended and the vouchers replaced with cash benefits; a single adult aged 25 or over receives approximately £38 a week. Accommodation may also be provided to destitute asylum seekers. This is on a 'no choice' basis at one of a number of centres throughout the UK. Prior to July 2002 asylum seekers could apply for the right to work after six months if their asylum application was still outstanding; if they found work the cash benefits were stopped. A reduction in the time taken to make initial asylum decisions meant that this concession was rarely used and it has now been abolished. Children of compulsory school age in families seeking asylum are entitled to attend school, and all asylum seekers and their dependants are eligible to receive free healthcare.

Legal advice for asylum seekers is available from immigration law advisers and firms of solicitors contracted to provide immigration services under the Community Legal Services Fund (formerly the Legal Aid scheme). They provide advice on the initial claim and any appeal.

Citizenship

Under the *British Nationality Act 1981*, there are three forms of citizenship:

- British citizenship for people closely connected with the UK, the Channel Islands or the Isle of Man;

- British Dependent Territories citizenship, for people connected with the dependent territories (now commonly referred to as 'Overseas Territories' – see page 66); and

- British Overseas citizenship, for those citizens of the UK and Colonies without connections with either the UK or dependent territories.

British citizens have the right to live permanently in the UK and are free to leave and re-enter the country at any time. British citizenship is acquired

---

Economic effects of migration

In February 2002 the Home Office published research on the impact of migrants to the UK on the public purse. The main findings of the report were:

- In 1999/2000 migrants made a net fiscal contribution to the Exchequer estimated at £2.5 billion, paying an estimated £31.2 billion in taxes and receiving £28.8 billion in benefits and services.

- Migrants who are highly qualified and fluent in English do better financially than those with fewer skills.

- Migration brings wider benefits, both economic – through the skills and experience of the individuals concerned who may, for example, set up new businesses creating new jobs – and social, through cultural diversity.

---

automatically at birth by a child born in the UK if his or her mother (or father, if legitimate) is a British citizen or settled in the UK. British citizenship may also be acquired by registration or naturalisation. Among those entitled to apply for registration are British Dependent Territories and British Overseas citizens, children born in the UK who did not automatically acquire British citizenship at birth, and stateless people. Naturalisation is at the Home Secretary's discretion and there are a number of residential and other requirements. Details can be found via the Home Office website by following the link to the Immigration and Nationality Directorate.

Citizenship oath and pledge

The Nationality, Immigration and Asylum Bill includes a proposed citizenship oath for people becoming British citizens:

'I, [name], swear by Almighty God that, on becoming a British citizen, I will be faithful and bear true allegiance to Her Majesty Queen Elizabeth the Second, Her Heirs and Successors according to the law.'

Proposed citizenship pledge:
'I will give my loyalty to the United Kingdom and respect its rights and freedoms. I will uphold its democratic values. I will observe its laws faithfully and fulfil my duties and obligations as a British citizen.'

Entitlement cards

In July 2002 the Home Office published a consultation paper to assess public opinion on entitlement cards. These cards would be used as proof of identity for people who are legally resident in the UK. Entitlement cards may be useful in combating identity fraud, which the Cabinet Office has estimated costs the UK economy more than £1.3 billion a year, and illegal immigration. This consultation will last for six months and aims to consider the different types of card that could be introduced, the information they may hold, and issues of cost, effectiveness and the risk of abuse.

Figure 9.6 Grants of British citizenship in the United Kingdom in 2001, by previous nationality

Total: 90,295

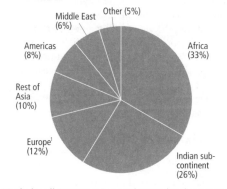

1 Includes all European Economic Area (EEA) countries.
Source: Home Office

In 2001, 90,300 people were granted British citizenship in the UK, compared with 82,200 in 2000. Of the applications in 2001, 9,500 were refused, 2,700 more than in 2000. One in three successful applications were from citizens of countries in Africa, with the Indian subcontinent accounting for 26 per cent and Europe about 12 per cent (see Figure 9.6). Residence in the UK continued to be the most frequent basis on which people were granted British citizenship in 2001, amounting to 40 per cent of the total, while marriage to a British citizen accounted for 30 per cent.

Ethnicity and identity

For centuries people from overseas have settled in the UK, either to escape political or religious persecution or in search of better economic opportunities. Irish people have a long history of migration and many Jewish refugees arrived towards the end of the 19th century and in the 1930s. Substantial immigration from the Caribbean and the Indian subcontinent dates principally from the 1950s and 1960s, when the Government encouraged immigration to tackle labour shortages. Many people of south Asian descent also entered the UK from Kenya, Malawi and Uganda in the 1960s and 1970s.

The Labour Force Survey estimated that over the period 2001–02 around 4.5 million people in Great Britain (8 per cent) described themselves as belonging to an ethnic group other than 'White'. In general, minority ethnic groups tend to have a younger age profile than the White population, reflecting past immigration and fertility patterns.

In 2001–02, 97 per cent of people from minority ethnic groups in the UK lived in England, with relatively small numbers in Scotland, Wales and Northern Ireland. Thirty-eight per cent of the total minority ethnic population lived in Greater London, where they comprised 28 per cent of the population. However, the extent to which individual ethnic groups were concentrated in London varied considerably; for example, 76 per cent of people of Black African origin lived in the capital compared with 20 per cent of people of Pakistani origin.

The classification of ethnic groups

The recommended classification of ethnic groups for National Statistics data sources has been changed to bring it in line with the 2001 Census.

There are two levels to this classification. The first level is a broad classification into five groups: White; Mixed; Asian or Asian British; Black or Black British; and Chinese or other ethnic background. The second level is a more detailed classification: for example, the Asian or Asian British group is subdivided into Indian; Pakistani; Bangladeshi; and other Asian background.

Further details can be found on the National Statistics website at:
www.statistics.gov.uk/themes/compendia_reference/ key_reports.asp

Table 9.7 Population by ethnic group, 2001–02,[1] Great Britain

	Per cent	Number of people (millions)
White	92.2	53.0
Asian or Asian British		
Indian	1.7	1.0
Pakistani	1.2	0.7
Bangladeshi	0.5	0.3
Other Asian background	0.5	0.3
All Asian groups	4.0	2.3
Black or Black British		
Caribbean	1.0	0.6
African	0.9	0.5
Other Black background	0.2	0.1
All Black groups	2.1	1.2
Mixed	0.9	0.5
Chinese	0.3	0.2
Other ethnic groups	0.5	0.3
All ethnic groups[2]	100.0	57.5

1 Population living in private households. Four-quarter average: spring 2001 to winter 2001/02.
2 Includes those who did not state their ethnic group.
Source: Labour Force Survey, Office for National Statistics

Outside London there were relatively high concentrations of people of Indian origin in Leicester, Wolverhampton and Birmingham, and of Pakistani origin in Birmingham, Greater Manchester and West Yorkshire.

Race equality issues

Many people from minority ethnic groups are concentrated in the inner cities of the UK, a number of which have problems of deprivation and social disadvantage. Unemployment rates for some minority groups are well above the national average (see page 124).

However there are some wide variations between ethnic groups. For example, people of Indian ethnic origin are more likely to own their own homes than either White people or people from other minority ethnic groups; 81 per cent were owner occupiers over the period 1998–2001 in England, compared with 34 per cent of people of Bangladeshi origin. Young people of Indian origin are also more likely than White people or those from other minority ethnic groups to achieve five

or more GCSE grades A* to C. In 2000, in England and Wales, 60 per cent of 16 year old school pupils of Indian origin achieved these grades, compared with 50 per cent of White pupils and 29 per cent of those from both the Pakistani and Bangladeshi groups.

The percentage of people from minority ethnic groups in professional and managerial positions is increasing. Over 25 per cent of men of Indian origin were employed at this level in 2000; this is very similar to the percentage of White men. Twelve MPs from minority ethnic groups were elected in July 2001 and in May 2002 a Black cabinet minister was appointed for the first time.

The Home Office has overall responsibility in the Government for policy and legislation on racial equality. Extra resources may be channelled into specific projects, for example, to provide specialist teachers for children needing English language tuition. The Government also promotes equal opportunities through training programmes, for example through projects for unemployed people who need training in English as an additional language. The Northern Ireland Executive has set up a unit to promote equal opportunities and good relations between people of different ethnic backgrounds.

Race relations legislation

In Great Britain the *Race Relations Act 1976*, as amended by the *Race Relations (Amendment) Act 2000*, makes it unlawful for anybody to discriminate on grounds of race, colour, nationality (including citizenship), or ethnic or national origins (referred to as 'racial grounds'). The *Race Relations Act 1976* applies to employment, training, education and the

Community cohesion

Following disturbances over the summer of 2001 in a number of towns and cities in the north of England, including Oldham and Bradford, the Home Office published an official report identifying the problems common to these communities. These included poverty and deprivation, and a failure to understand people from different backgrounds, religions or cultures. The report made a number of recommendations and proposed that there should be an honest and open national debate in order to develop shared principles on the rights and responsibilities of citizenship.

provision of goods and services. Legislation along similar lines was introduced in Northern Ireland in 1977.

The *Race Relations (Amendment) Act* extended the scope of the 1976 Act to cover the way public authorities carry out all their functions. The Act now gives certain listed public authorities a statutory general duty to work to eliminate unlawful discrimination and promote equal opportunities and good relations between people of different racial groups. Most of the listed authorities also have specific duties to fulfil, including publishing a race equality scheme to explain how they will meet the general and specific duties. There are also specific duties to monitor staff and applicants for jobs, promotion and training, by ethnic group. The Commission for Racial Equality (CRE) (see below) enforces the specific duties. It published a statutory code of practice in May 2002 to help public authorities to meet the new duties.

The *Crime and Disorder Act 1998* created racially aggravated versions of a number of existing offences in England and Wales, including assault, criminal damage and harassment. These racially aggravated offences carry a higher maximum penalty. Other provisions in criminal law prohibit incitement to racial hatred and the publication or dissemination of material that is likely to incite racial hatred.

Commission for Racial Equality

The CRE was set up under the *Race Relations Act 1976*, with the duty to tackle racial discrimination and promote equal opportunities and good race relations in Great Britain. In 2001 around 10,000 people contacted the CRE for advice and 1,200 made formal applications for assistance. The Commission has the power to investigate unlawful discriminatory practices and to issue non-discrimination notices, requiring such practices to stop. It also has an important role in promoting racial equality and funds research. In Northern Ireland equivalent responsibilities rest with the Equality Commission for Northern Ireland, whose remit covers other types of unlawful discrimination.

In 2001/02 the CRE supported the work of 95 racial equality councils in Great Britain. These are voluntary bodies, jointly funded by the CRE and local authorities to promote good race relations locally.

Equal opportunities

Employment and income

The economic and domestic lives of women have changed considerably over time, and women have taken an increasingly important role in the labour market. In 1971, 56 per cent of women of working age, compared with 91 per cent of men, were economically active in the UK. By spring 2002 the rate for women had increased to 73 per cent of women of working age, while the rate for men had declined to 84 per cent. The number of women in the UK labour force increased from 10 million in 1971 to nearly 13 million in spring 2002.

In spring 2002, almost 70 per cent of women were in employment. The likelihood of being in employment varied considerably according to whether or not they had dependent children. Employment rates were lowest for those with a child under the age of five, at 53 per cent.

There is still a gap between male and female earnings, although this has been declining (see Figure 9.8). Female full-time employees earned around 82 per cent of the male hourly rate in 2001. The average individual total weekly income[1] of men was higher than that of women in all age bands in 2000/01. Among women those aged 25 to 29 had the highest average income, whereas income peaked in the 35 to 44 age group for men. Overall, women's weekly income was only 49 per cent of that of men.

These gender differences in income are largely due to differences in working hours and occupation. Women tend to work shorter hours than men and are more likely to work part time. They are also more likely to take career breaks. Pay rates are considerably lower in sectors dominated by women. In spring 2002 women employees outnumbered men in administrative and secretarial occupations by nearly four to one, and more than twice as many men were managers and senior officials (see page 127).

Despite women's increasing participation in the labour market they still do the majority of the housework and childcare. Recent ONS research looked at time spent on these activities and

---

1 Total income is gross income plus tax credits.

Figure 9.8 Ratio of women's to men's earnings, Great Britain[1]

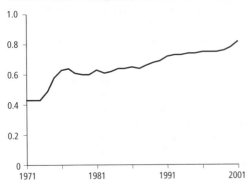

1 Average hourly earnings excluding overtime for adults whose pay for the survey pay period was not affected by absence.
Source: New Earnings Survey, Office for National Statistics

estimated the time spent on passive care[2] of adults and children. Fifty-nine per cent of all the time spent on housework and care of others in the UK was done by women. The type of household work undertaken by women and men also differed; women spent more time preparing meals and washing and ironing clothes, while men were more likely to undertake DIY and gardening.

Equal opportunities policy

There are two Ministers for Women, supported by the Women and Equality Unit (WEU) in the Department of Trade and Industry. They are responsible for a wide range of gender equality issues in Government, including issues of sexual orientation. The WEU's projects include:

- aiming to increase women's participation in the labour market, including developing policies which support flexible working and are family friendly;

- aiming to reduce the gender pay gap;

- reviewing the existing equality legislation on gender, race, age, beliefs, sexual orientation and disability; and

- aiming to reduce domestic violence.

2 This refers to time when an adult is not interacting directly with a child or helping another adult, but they are still responsible or 'on call'.

The Scottish Executive has established an Equality Unit to take forward its work in this area. The Northern Ireland Executive has set up a Gender Policy Unit to promote equality between men and women, people of different sexual orientation, people with and without dependants and people of different marital status.

Equal opportunities legislation

The *Sex Discrimination Act 1975*, which applies in Great Britain, makes discrimination between men and women unlawful in employment, education, training and the provision of housing, goods, facilities and services. Discrimination in employment against married people and discriminatory job recruitment advertisements are also unlawful. Under the *Equal Pay Act 1970*, women and men are entitled to equal pay when doing work that is the same, or broadly similar, work which is rated as equivalent, or work which is of equal value. Parallel legislation on sex discrimination and equal pay applies in Northern Ireland.

The Equal Opportunities Commission (EOC), set up under the 1975 Act in Great Britain, is an independent statutory body which has the powers to:

- work towards the elimination of discrimination on the grounds of sex or marriage;

- promote equality of opportunity between women and men;

- review, and propose amendments to, the *Sex Discrimination Act* and the *Equal Pay Act*; and

- provide legal advice and assistance to individuals who have been discriminated against.

The Equality Commission for Northern Ireland tackles discrimination and promotes gender equality in Northern Ireland. The remit of this Commission also includes race, religious and political beliefs, age, marital status, sexual orientation, disability and people with dependants.

The Government is currently reviewing the possibility of merging the Equal Opportunities Commission, the Commission for Racial Equality and the Disability Rights Commission to form a single equality body in Great Britain, responsible for the promotion of equality in relation to sex, race, disability, sexual orientation, religion and age. Changes are unlikely to take place before the next General Election.

Disability Rights Commission

The Disability Rights Commission (DRC) was established in 2000 in Great Britain following the *Disability Rights Commission Act 1999*. It is an independent body with statutory duties to provide information and advice to disabled people and employers on their rights and duties under the *Disability Discrimination Act 1995*. It gives employers guidance on how to meet these duties and undertakes formal investigations into unlawful discrimination. The DRC promotes equal opportunities for disabled people and advises the Government on the working of the disability legislation.

Under the *Disability Rights Commission Act*, businesses have a duty to make reasonable adjustments to the way they provide services to the public, changing their policies, practices and procedures where reasonable. From 2004 service providers will have to take reasonable steps to remove, alter or provide reasonable means of avoiding physical features that make it impossible or unreasonably difficult for disabled people to use their services. A Code of Practice on the rights of access that businesses and services must afford disabled people was issued by the DRC in May 2002. The code also provides practical guidance and information.

Living standards

The trend in the UK's standard of living, using gross domestic product (GDP) per head at constant market prices as an indicator, has generally been one of steady growth over the last 50 years. Since 1995 the annual rate of growth has been in a relatively narrow range, from 1.9 per cent to 3.1 per cent.

Real household disposable income (the total resources available to households after deductions) more than quadrupled between 1951 and 2001. There was a rise of 6.5 per cent in 2001, which was above the long-term annual average rise of 3.1 per cent between 1991 and 2001 and the strongest rise since 1978.

The wealth of the household sector[3] in the UK, net of any loans outstanding, including those on the purchase of assets such as housing, has shown strong growth in recent years. It rose in real terms by an average of 4.6 per cent a year between 1987 and 2000, although there was a fall in 2001. In terms of value, at the end of 2001 the household sector's net worth totalled £4,573 billion: £2,562 billion of non-financial assets, of which residential dwellings accounted for 83 per cent, and £2,011 billion of financial assets. During 2001 the value of residential dwellings (excluding housing association properties) rose by 8 per cent, in contrast to household net financial wealth which fell by 16 per cent, reflecting the effect of weak equity markets (see page 462) on holdings of shares, life assurance and pension funds.

Although there have been substantial long-term improvements in the standard of living, there remain concerns about the relative deprivation of some people and communities. The distribution of income and wealth is uneven. For example, the latest available figures show that:

- the average original income of the top fifth of households in 2000/01 of £55,700 was 18 times the average of the bottom fifth, £3,100. Benefits and, to a lesser extent, taxes reduce this inequality so that the ratio for final income is four to one;

- in 2000/01, 17 per cent of the population of Great Britain lived in households with low income,[4] before housing costs are taken into account, although this has fallen since the peak of 21 per cent in 1992. Lone parents, pensioners and children are more likely to live in a low-income household than people of working age who do not have children; and

- the most wealthy 10 per cent of the population of the UK owned 54 per cent of marketable wealth in 2000, or 72 per cent of marketable wealth excluding the value of dwellings.

---

3 Including non-profit institutions serving households.

4 Low income is defined as below 60 per cent of the median equivalised household disposable income – a measure in which household disposable income is adjusted to take account of the size and composition of the household.

Social exclusion

Social exclusion is a term used to describe individuals or areas suffering from a combination of linked problems, such as unemployment, lack of skills, low incomes, poor housing, high crime, bad health and family breakdown.

The Social Exclusion Unit (SEU), based in the Office of the Deputy Prime Minister, was set up in 1997 to reduce social exclusion in England by working with government departments and external organisations. It also liaises with the Scottish, Welsh and Northern Ireland administrations, which have their own strategies for tackling social exclusion. The SEU is currently working on projects looking at young runaways, children in care and education, transport and social exclusion, and reducing re-offending by ex-prisoners. Previously published reports have led to new policies to tackle, for example, truancy, rough sleeping, teenage pregnancy and neighbourhood renewal.

Neighbourhood renewal

The Neighbourhood Renewal Unit (NRU), based in the Office of the Deputy Prime Minister, was set up in April 2001 to implement government strategies to tackle unemployment, poor educational achievement, poor health, inadequate housing and crime in England's most deprived communities. The NRU aims to narrow the gap between deprived areas and the rest of the country, so that within 10 to 20 years no one should be seriously disadvantaged by where he or she lives. The Scottish Executive and the Welsh Assembly Government have established similar initiatives. These programmes focus on the most deprived communities in their parts of the UK and try to ensure that these communities play a role in their own regeneration.

These problems in unemployment, educational achievement, health, housing and crime are also

Neighbourhood Statistics

Neighbourhood Statistics (*www.statistics.gov.uk/neighbourhood*) was created as part of the National Strategy for Neighbourhood Renewal. In partnership with many government departments, it provides a web-based statistical service to supply information to tackle local issues of deprivation. The core of this information resource will be the 2001 Census, expanded by other data held across the public sector.

being monitored through the Government's sustainable development strategy (see page 268), using quality of life indicators linked to each of these aspects of poverty and social exclusion.

Social participation

There are over 500,000 voluntary and community groups across the UK, ranging from national and international bodies to small local groups. An increasing number of public services are delivered by voluntary organisations on behalf of the Government. The 2002 Spending Review (see page 350) allocated £125 million for the creation of a new investment fund to help voluntary and community organisations in their public service work.

In September 2002 the Treasury completed a review of the role of this sector in the delivery of public services. This review recommended a number of ways in which the Government could work more effectively with these organisations, for example by:

- involving voluntary and community organisations in the planning, as well as delivery, of services;

- moving to a more stable funding relationship and ensuring that the sector is equipped to work effectively in partnership with government; and

- ensuring that the cost of contracts for services reflects the full cost of delivery.

The Government's voluntary and community policies will be implemented by the Active Community Unit at the Home Office.

Volunteering

Many voluntary and community organisations are involved in activities that improve the quality of life in the local community, working in areas as diverse as social welfare, education, sport, heritage, the environment and the arts.

Thirty-nine per cent of adults in England and Wales interviewed in the Home Office's 2001 Citizenship Survey had formally volunteered (giving unpaid help to a group or organisation) in the previous 12 months. A quarter of adults did

Table 9.9 Participation in voluntary activities within the last 12 months, by level of deprivation[1] of home area, England, 2001

	Informal volunteering	Per cent Formal volunteering
1 Least deprived areas	71	47
2	71	41
3	66	39
4	66	36
5 Most deprived areas	63	31
All respondents (number)	9,429	9,431

1 In accordance with the former Department of the Environment, Transport and the Regions' Index of Multiple Deprivation.
Source: Citizenship Survey, Home Office

this at least once a month. These volunteers were most likely to have raised money (22 per cent of respondents) or organised or helped at an activity or event (21 per cent). Sixty-seven per cent of adults had volunteered informally (giving unpaid help to an individual who was not a family member) in the previous 12 months. A third did this at least once a month. Informal volunteers were most likely to have given someone advice (31 per cent) or have looked after their property or pets while they were away (28 per cent).

People living in the least deprived areas of England were most likely to volunteer, formally or informally, while those living in the most deprived areas were least likely to volunteer (see Table 9.9). Almost half of people living in the least deprived areas formally volunteered compared with under a third from the most deprived areas.

The Government is keen to encourage links between the statutory, voluntary and community sectors. The Youth Service is a partnership between local government and voluntary organisations concerned with the informal personal and social education of young people aged 11 to 25 (5 to 25 in Northern Ireland). Local authorities manage their own youth centres and clubs and provide most of the public support for local and regional organisations.

Charities
The Charity Commission is the statutory organisation responsible for the registration,

regulation and support of organisations that are charitable under the law of England and Wales. It does not make grants, but advises trustees about administrative matters and has a statutory responsibility to ensure that charities make effective use of their resources.

In 2001/02, over 9,400 applications were received for registration from organisations, of which 5,200 were accepted and placed on the Public Register of Charities. There were approximately 186,000 registered charities in England and Wales at the end of March 2002. Many other charitable organisations are not required to register, for example some churches and schools. Charities elsewhere in the UK are not required to register with a government organisation, but do need to seek recognition of their charitable status with the Inland Revenue, for tax purposes.

To become a registered charity in England and Wales an organisation must have purposes that are exclusively philanthropic, such as:

- the relief of financial hardship;

- the advancement of education;

- the advancement of religion; or

- other charitable purposes for the benefit of the community, such as the promotion of urban and rural regeneration or the relief of unemployment.

The Charity Commission has the power to investigate and supervise charities, including measures to protect both charities and donors from fraudulent fund-raisers. One of the Commission's duties is to investigate allegations of fraud or dishonesty and evaluate them for cause for concern; 1,300 evaluations were carried out in 2001/02. Such evaluations can lead to formal inquiries: over 200 of these were completed during the same period.

Funding
At the end of March 2002, the total annual income of all registered charities in England and Wales was estimated at £27.8 billion. Approximately 6 per cent of registered charities receive nearly 90 per cent of the total annual income recorded, while around 63 per cent have an income of £10,000 or less a year and account for less than 1 per cent of the annual total. In 2000/01 the average weekly donation made to charity was £1.80 per household in the UK.

Table 9.10 Income and expenditure of the top[1] fund-raising charities, United Kingdom, 1999/2000

	Voluntary income	Total income	£ million Total expenditure
Imperial Cancer Research Fund[2]	111	136	122
National Trust	106	192	171
Royal Opera House, Covent Garden	105	134	41
Oxfam	101	158	152
British Heart Foundation	89	101	116
Cancer Research Campaign[2]	87	98	97
Royal National Lifeboat Institution	82	100	94
Salvation Army	70	95	76
National Society for the Prevention of Cruelty to Children	65	78	75
Macmillan Cancer Relief	59	65	62

1 Ranked by voluntary income.
2 These organisations have since merged to form Cancer Research UK.
Source: Charities Aid Foundation

Voluntary organisations may receive income from several sources, including:

- central and local government grants;

- contributions from individuals, businesses and trusts;

- earnings from commercial activities and investments; and

- fees from central and local government for services provided on a contractual basis.

The introduction of the National Lottery (see page 263) in 1994 has given charities and voluntary organisations substantial funding for projects across a range of activities. Another valuable source of revenue for charities is through tax relief and tax exemptions. The Gift Aid scheme provides tax relief on one-off and regular cash donations of any amount, while under the Payroll Giving scheme employees and those drawing a company pension can make tax-free donations from their earnings. In 2001/02, over 0.5 million PAYE employees gave in this manner, giving over £72.5 million, almost double the amount two years earlier. In addition, gifts of listed stocks and shares, and gifts of land and property can now be offset against income for tax purposes.

The Charities Aid Foundation (CAF) is a registered charity that works to increase resources for the voluntary sector in the UK and overseas. As well as providing services that are both charitable and financial, CAF undertakes a comprehensive programme of research and is a leading source of information on the voluntary sector.

Further reading

Asylum Statistics, United Kingdom. Home Office.

Better Communities in Scotland: Closing the Gap. Scottish Executive, 2002. The Stationery Office.

Building Cohesive Communities: A Report of the Ministerial Group on Public Order and Community Cohesion. Home Office, 2002.

Family Spending. Office for National Statistics. The Stationery Office.

Households Below Average Income. Department for Work and Pensions.

International Migration. Office for National Statistics. The Stationery Office.

Living in Britain: Results from the General Household Survey. Office for National Statistics. The Stationery Office.

The migrant population in the UK: Fiscal effects. Home Office, 2002.

Population Trends. Office for National Statistics. The Stationery Office.

Preventing Social Exclusion. Social Exclusion Unit, 2001.

Race Equality in Public Services. Home Office, 2001.

Social Focus on Men. Office for National Statistics. The Stationery Office, 2001.

Social Trends. Office for National Statistics. The Stationery Office.

Tackling Racial Equality: International Comparisons. Home Office, 2002.

Websites

Charities Aid Foundation
www.cafonline.org

Charity Commission
www.charitycommission.gov.uk

Commission for Racial Equality
www.cre.gov.uk

Department for Work and Pensions
www.dwp.gov.uk

Disability Rights Commission
www.drc.org.uk

Equality Commission for Northern Ireland
www.equalityni.org

Equal Opportunities Commission
www.eoc.org.uk

Government Actuary's Department
www.gad.gov.uk

Home Office
www.homeoffice.gov.uk

National Youth Agency
www.nya.org.uk

Neighbourhood Renewal Unit
www.neighbourhood.gov.uk

Neighbourhood Statistics
www.statistics.gov.uk/neighbourhood

Office for National Statistics
www.statistics.gov.uk

Social Exclusion Unit
www.socialexclusionunit.gov.uk

Women and Equality Unit
www.womenandequalityunit.gov.uk

10 Education and training

Parents are required by law to see that their children receive full-time education between the ages of 5 and 16 in Great Britain and between 4 and 16 in Northern Ireland. About 70 per cent of young people in the United Kingdom choose to stay in full-time education after this age, either in school or further education colleges. Around 8 per cent of 16 year olds in Great Britain are on government training programmes. About a third of all young people enter universities or other institutions of higher education.

Increasing emphasis is being placed on lifelong learning as a way of creating skills and improving employment prospects in a changing labour market. If people are to move more frequently between jobs and careers they will need to be able to change and update their qualifications and skills.

Pre-school children

Pre-school education is expanding considerably in order to ensure that all children begin school with a basic foundation in literacy and numeracy. The proportion of three and four year olds enrolled in UK schools rose from 23 per cent in 1971/72 to 63 per cent in 2001/02 (see Figure 10.1). In 2001/02 a further 30 per cent were enrolled in non-education settings, such as playgroups, in the private and voluntary sectors.

Childcare
It is recognised that there is a need for good quality affordable childcare for working parents. To meet this need childcare strategies have been implemented across the United Kingdom.

In England, since 1998, all four year olds have been guaranteed a free, part-time early education place if their parents want one. In 2002, 70 per cent of three year olds had a place and the aim is to provide a place for all of this age group by September 2004.

The Welsh Assembly Government is committed to expanding provision for three year olds. The Scottish Executive has set a number of targets, which include making a nursery place available to every three year old by autumn 2002, training more childcare workers and expanding provision outside schools.

In Northern Ireland the aim is to provide a year of pre-school education for every child whose parents wish them to have one by March 2003. A phased expansion programme has already increased free provision from 45 per cent in 1997/98 to 85 per cent in 2001/02.

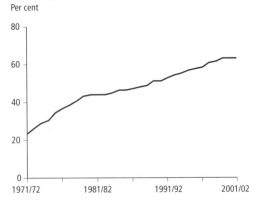

Figure 10.1 Children under five[1] in schools as a percentage of all children aged three and four, UK

Per cent

1 Pupils aged three and four at 31 December each year. The figure for 2001/02 includes 2000/01 data for Wales and Scotland.
Source: Department for Education and Skills, National Assembly for Wales, Scottish Executive and Northern Ireland Department of Education

Sure Start

In the UK Sure Start projects aim to improve the health and well-being of families and children before and from birth. They are concentrated in areas where a high proportion of children live in poverty. Locally based programmes work with parents and children to try to improve children's life chances through better access to family support, advice on nurturing, health services and early learning. Good practice learned from local programmes is disseminated to others involved in providing services for young children.

In England the aim is to establish 500 local programmes by 2004, covering 400,000 children. By July 2002, 522 programmes had been announced, 300 of which were under way. In Wales there are programmes in all 22 local authority areas. Northern Ireland had 23 projects by March 2001. Scotland has implemented Sure Start differently and funds all 32 local authorities to work in partnership with health services and voluntary organisations. Sure Start Scotland was implemented in 1999 and by 2000/01 over 15,000 additional children had received support, as had over 6,000 parents.

Integrated early education and childcare services

The distinction between early education and childcare is becoming less significant with the growth of extended or full day, integrated services which best fit the shape of parents' lives. In England the Government has decided to bring together the responsibility for Sure Start, childcare and early years within one inter-departmental unit, and establish children's centres at the heart of some of the most disadvantaged communities (see page 148). It expects that by 2006 up to 650,000 children will be covered by children's centre services.

Schools

About 94 per cent of pupils in the UK receive free education from public funds, while 6 per cent attend independent fee paying schools.

State schools

In England and Wales state schools are classified into three broad categories. Community schools consist mainly of schools that were traditionally owned and funded by Local Education Authorities

(LEAs). Foundation schools include many of the former grant maintained schools. Voluntary schools are divided into controlled and aided, of which many are connected to a particular religious faith. LEAs are responsible for employing staff and for admission arrangements in controlled schools and the governing body performs this role in aided schools. In England in 2001, in the primary and secondary sectors, there were 13,642 community schools, 854 foundation schools and 7,059 voluntary schools. These categories include state specialist and special schools. There are 1,851 state primary and secondary schools in Wales (excluding special schools).

In Scotland, there are 2,845 state schools managed by local authorities, nine grant aided schools, and one self-governing school.

In Northern Ireland all schools must be open to all religions. In practice, however, most Protestant children attend one of the 641 controlled schools, managed by education and library boards, while most Catholic children attend one of the 540 voluntary maintained schools. There are, in addition 54 voluntary grammar schools (which tend to be Catholic or non-denominational in character). The 46 integrated schools aim to educate Catholic and Protestant children together; these schools are controlled or grant maintained. The Government has a statutory duty to encourage integrated education as a way of breaking down sectarian barriers. Publicly financed schools can apply to become integrated, following a majority vote by parents.

Table 10.2 Number of schools by type in the UK, 2001/02

Type of school	Number
State nursery	3,214
State primary	22,798
State secondary	4,306
of which specialist schools	685
Non-maintained (including independent) schools	2,403
Special schools[1]	1,480
Pupil referral units	337
All schools	**34,538**

1 Catering for children with special educational needs (see page 104).
  The great majority of special schools are publicly maintained.
Source: Department for Education and Skills, National Assembly for Wales, Scottish Executive and Northern Ireland Department of Education

Independent schools

Independent schools are not funded by the state and obtain most of their finances from fees paid by parents. Some of the larger independent boarding schools are known as 'public schools'. In 2001/02 there were 2,156 independent schools in England, 56 in Wales, 122 in Scotland and 25 in Northern Ireland. Independent schools providing full-time education for five or more pupils of compulsory school age are required to register with the appropriate government department and are subject to inspection.

The Independent Schools Council (ISC) represents the seven independent schools' associations in the United Kingdom and has overall responsibility for the Independent Schools Inspectorate (ISI). In England and Wales the ISI inspects schools in the ISC every five or six years, using criteria approved by OFSTED and Estyn (see page 120) and the Government. Independent schools have to pass an inspection to qualify for membership of an association within ISC. All other independent schools are inspected by the relevant national inspectorates.

In England, the Independent/State School Partnership (ISSP) Scheme, set up in 1997, aims to encourage the sharing of experience and good practice. The fifth round of ISSP included a package of £778,000 which will fund 32 new projects in 2002/03. In 2002/03, as well as general projects, the scheme is funding projects which specifically focus on citizenship and on music, and projects aimed at gifted and talented pupils.

Specialist schools

The Government wishes to increase the number of specialist schools in the belief that this will raise standards and promote diversity in secondary education. Specialist schools meet the full national curriculum requirements (see page 105), but focus on a chosen specialism. Any maintained secondary school in England can apply to be designated as a specialist school in one of the following subject areas: technology, languages, sports, arts, science, engineering, business and enterprise, or mathematics and computing. Schools can also combine two specialisms. The Government has set a target to increase the number of specialist schools from 685 in 2001/02 to 2,000 by 2006.

Special educational needs

A child is said to have special educational needs (SEN) if he or she has significantly greater

Table 10.3 Number of pupils by school type in the UK, 2001/02[1]

Type of school	Thousands
State nursery[2]	149
State primary	5,246
State secondary	3,948
Non-maintained schools	633
Special schools[3]	112
Pupil referral units	10
All schools	**10,100**

1 Figures based on head counts.
2 Nursery classes within primary schools are included in primary schools.
3 Includes maintained and non-maintained sectors.
Source: Department for Education and Skills, National Assembly for Wales, Scottish Executive and Northern Ireland Department of Education

difficulty in learning than other children of the same age, or a disability which makes it difficult to use normal educational facilities. Each SEN child has the right to receive a broad and balanced education. State schools must publish information for parents about their SEN policy. In England, a new SEN Code of Practice came into force in January 2002. It includes new rights and duties introduced by the *Special Educational Needs and Disability Act 2001* and associated regulations. In December 2001 a SEN Code of Practice for Wales was published and came into effect in April 2002. In Northern Ireland legislation similar to the 2001 Act will be introduced following consultation.

In the UK in 2000/01 approximately 1.9 million pupils were identified as having special educational needs. If an education authority or board believes that it should determine the education for an SEN child, it must draw up a formal statement of the child's special needs and the action it intends to meet them. About 300,800 children with SEN have these statements (called Record of Needs in Scotland). Parents have a right of appeal if they disagree with decisions about their child. Over 60 per cent of SEN pupils with statements are educated in mainstream schools while most of the others are educated in special schools.

Secondary schools

In 2001/02 around 88 per cent of the 3.3 million state secondary pupils in England and all 212,000 pupils in Wales attended comprehensive schools.

These largely take pupils without reference to ability or aptitude, providing a wide range of secondary education for all or most of the children in a district.

Scottish state secondary education is also non-selective, without reference to ability or aptitude. In 2001/02, 96 per cent of pupils attended state secondary schools and 4 per cent (17,635) independent schools.

Secondary education in Northern Ireland is organised largely on selective lines, with grammar schools admitting pupils on the basis of '11-plus' tests in English, mathematics and science. In 2001/02, 62,743 pupils attended grammar schools (40 per cent of secondary pupils), of whom 9,247 were being educated in integrated schools. The Burns Report, a review of post-primary education in Northern Ireland, was published in October 2001. The main proposal was for the abolition of the 11-plus and the ending of academic selection, which has been part of the education system in Northern Ireland since 1947. Following public consultation, the minister for education intends to bring forward proposals for change in post-primary education arrangements in autumn 2002.

Raising standards

City Technology Colleges
There are 15 City Technology Colleges situated in urban areas across England. They are state-funded independent schools run by private sponsors, operating outside the normal local government framework. They provide free education for 11 to 16 year olds in inner city areas with a curriculum focusing on science and technology.

City Academies
City Academies are publicly funded independent schools in England. They replace schools in challenging circumstances or are set up as part of a wider school reorganisation or where there is an unmet demand for school places. Sponsors from the private and voluntary sectors, church and other faith groups help to set up and run these schools. They provide free education to secondary age pupils of all abilities, including provision for children with special educational needs. Academies aim to offer a broad and balanced curriculum, including a specialism. By the end of

July 2002 there were 22 partnerships working to establish academies. The first three opened in September 2002. The *Education Act 2002* (see page 118) extends the City Academy model into rural areas, and allows for all-age, primary and sixth form Academies. The Government intends to set up at least 33 Academies in England by 2006.

Other initiatives
Excellence in Cities (EiC) tackles educational problems facing children in English cities. Local partnerships implement the EiC programme and focus on the needs and aspirations of individual pupils and their parents. The programme includes about 1,000 secondary schools and one-third of all secondary age pupils, and some 1,000 primary schools.

The Beacon Schools initiative is intended to raise standards by sharing and spreading good practice. The initiative is supporting schools in the most under-achieving areas. By September 2002 there were 1,150 Beacon Schools in England of which 451 were in EiC areas.

Education Action Zones have been formed in deprived areas in order to help raise educational standards. Zones are built around groups of about 15 to 25 schools. An action forum runs each zone. In 2002 there were 2,109 schools with 765,909 pupils participating in 175 zones.

International comparisons
The Organisation for Economic Co-operation and Development's (OECD – see page 63) Programme for International Student Assessment assesses the ability of 15 year olds to apply knowledge and skills in three broad areas: reading, mathematics and science. The OECD mean scores for each area were set at 500. The mean scores for the UK in 2000 were significantly higher than for the OECD as a whole (see Table 10.4). Within the EU, Finland was the top performing country in all areas; the UK was second for mathematics and science and third for reading.

Curriculum

All state schools in the UK must provide religious education, but parents have the right to withdraw their children from these classes. In Northern Ireland the main churches have approved a core syllabus for religious education, which must be taught in all grant-aided schools.

Table 10.4 Mean scores of 15 year olds, by EU[1] country, 2000

	Reading	Mathematics	Science
Austria	507	515	519
Belgium	507	520	496
Denmark	497	514	481
Finland	546	536	538
France	505	517	500
Germany	484	490	487
Greece	474	447	461
Irish Republic	527	503	513
Italy	487	457	478
Luxembourg	441	446	443
Portugal	470	454	459
Spain	493	476	491
Sweden	516	510	512
United Kingdom	523	529	532

1 The response rate of schools in the Netherlands was too low to allow accurate estimates.
Source: OECD

All state secondary schools in the UK are required to provide sex education for all pupils, including education about HIV/AIDS and other sexually transmitted diseases.

England, Wales and Northern Ireland

Children follow the National Curriculum in England and Wales and the Northern Ireland Curriculum in Northern Ireland. The curricula contain programmes of study for age groups split into key stages (see Table 10.5). These stages outline what pupils should be taught and set out expected standards of performance. There are four key stages covering the ages of compulsory schooling. Key stages 1 and 2 are studied in primary schools, and stages 3 and 4 in secondary school.

Subjects such as drama, dance and classical languages are optional. It is intended that over time every primary school child should have the opportunity to learn to play a musical instrument and explore one of a range of sports.

Scotland

There is no statutory national curriculum in Scotland. There are five national priorities in education set out under the following headings:

- achievement and attainment;

- framework for learning;

Table 10.5 Organisation of compulsory school years

	Pupil ages	Year group	Attainment expected in final year of the group[1]
England and Wales			
Key stage 1	5–7	1–2	Level 2
Key stage 2	7–11	3–6	Level 4
Key stage 3	11–14	7–9	Level 5/6
Key stage 4	14–16	10–11	GCSE
Northern Ireland			
Key stage 1	4/5–8	1–4	Level 2
Key stage 2	8–11	5–7	Level 3/4
Key stage 3	11–14	8–10	Level 5/6
Key stage 4	14–16	11–12	GCSE
Scotland			
(Curriculum	5–7	P1–P3	Level A
following	7–8	P3–P4	Level B
national	8–10	P4–P6	Level C
guidelines from	10–11	P6–P7	Level D
ages 5 to 14)	11–13	P7–S2	Level E
NQ[2]	14–15	S3–S4	Standard Grade

1 For more details see pages 107 and 108.
2 Standard Grades are now part of the National Qualifications (NQ) framework in Scotland. They are broadly equivalent to GCSEs.

Table 10.6 Compulsory subjects at key stages

	England	Wales[1]	Northern Ireland[2]
All key stages			
English	•	•	•
Welsh/Irish		•	•
Mathematics	•	•	•
Science	•	•	•
Physical education	•	•	•
Design and	•	•	•
Information and communications technology (ICT)	•		
Cross curricula themes			•
Key stages 1 to 3			
History	•	•	•
Geography	•	•	•
Art and design	•	•	•
Music	•	•	•
Key stages 3 and 4			
Citizenship	•		
Modern foreign language	•	•	•
Cross curricula themes			•
Humanities			•

1 Design and technology is technology, which includes information and communications technology (ICT). Art and design is art. A language is optional at key stage 4.
2 Irish is taken in Irish speaking schools. Science includes science and technology at key stages 1 and 2. Design and technology is taken at key stages 3 and 4 only. Cross curricula themes include cultural heritage, education for mutual understanding, health education and ICT at stages 1 to 4 and economic awareness and careers education at stages 3 and 4. At key stage 4 pupils must choose a humanities subject.

- inclusion and equality;

- values and citizenship; and

- learning for life.

The content and management of the curriculum are the responsibility of educational authorities and individual headteachers. National guidelines for pupils aged 5 to 14 set out the ground to be covered and the way pupils' learning should be assessed and reported.

There are curriculum guidelines for languages, mathematics, ICT, environmental studies, expressive arts, religious and moral education, health education, and personal and social development. Pupils can study a modern European language during the last two years of primary education.

There are 59 units in primary schools where education takes place through the Gaelic language.

There are some other schools where Gaelic can be learned as a second language.

Attainment

In 2001, at key stage 1 over 80 per cent of both boys and girls in England achieved the expected level in English. By key stage 3 this had fallen to 57 per cent and 73 per cent respectively. The proportion of boys in England, Wales and Northern Ireland reaching the required standard for English was lower than for girls at all key stages, particularly stages 2 and 3. This was also true of Welsh in Wales. Similar proportions of boys and girls reached the expected level in tests for mathematics and science at all key stages. The proportion of pupils achieving the expected level generally reduced with age for both sexes.

Scotland

The percentage of pupils attaining target levels increased between 1999/2000 and 2000/01 for most local authorities, across all subjects. As in the rest of the UK, the proportions of pupils achieving the expected level was lower in the older age groups.

Assessment

England and Wales

Pupils are assessed formally at the ages of 7, 11 and 14 by their teachers and/or by national tests in the core subjects of English, mathematics and science. In Wales there is no statutory national testing at age 7. At age 14, pupils are also assessed in other subjects.

Northern Ireland

Pupils are formally assessed at the ages of 8, 11 and 14. The requirements are broadly similar to those in England and Wales. Pupils at key stages 1 and 2 are assessed in English and mathematics, and also in science at key stage 3. Assessment takes the form of teacher assessment and (at key stage 3) tasks or tests.

Scotland

Progression is measured by attainment of five levels, based on the expectation of the performance of the majority of pupils at certain ages between 5 and 14 (see Table 10.5). Pupils are assessed by their teachers and by tests in reading, writing and mathematics which are selected and administered from a national catalogue. Tests can take place at any time during the school year and at any age.

Table 10.7 Percentage of pupils attaining target levels in each subject, Scotland, 2000/01

	P3	P6	S2
Mathematics	94.9	78.0	51.2
Reading	87.2	82.9	56.4
Writing	82.8	71.3	45.9

Source: Scottish Executive

Qualifications

In England, Wales and Northern Ireland the General Certificate of Secondary Education (GCSE) is the main examination at the end of key stage 4. GCSEs are generally taken at age 16 and are graded A* to G. In Scotland students study for the Scottish Certificate of Education

Figure 10.8 Pupils obtaining GCSE or equivalent[1] qualifications, UK, 2000/01

Per cent[2]

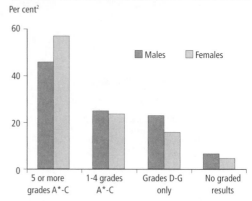

1 See text for explanation of Scottish qualifications.
2 Percentage of pupils aged 15 at the start of the academic year, or in year S4 in Scotland, who obtained the grade shown.
Source: Department for Education and Skills, National Assembly for Wales, Scottish Executive and Northern Ireland Department of Education

(SCE)/National Qualifications (NQ) at Standard Grade and are examined at the age of 16. These qualifications are awarded on a scale of 1 to 7.

In 2000/01, 51 per cent of pupils in the United Kingdom gained five or more GCSE grades A* to C or equivalent, compared with 45 per cent in 1995/96.

In order to expand vocational opportunities in England in line with the 14–19 consultation exercise (see page 109), new GCSEs in vocational subjects were introduced in September 2002 and are designed to replace the General National Vocational Qualification (GNVQ) Part One. Northern Ireland also introduced vocational GCSEs at this time. They are available in eight subjects: Applied Art and Design; Applied Business; Engineering; Health and Social Care; Applied ICT; Leisure and Tourism; Manufacturing; and Applied Science. In Scotland the General Scottish Vocational Qualification (GSVQ) is the equivalent.

In England, Wales and Northern Ireland the General Certificate of Education Advanced (GCE A) Level is usually taken at the age of 18 after two years of full-time study. The Advanced Subsidiary (AS) qualification is equivalent to 50 per cent of an A level and is designed to encourage the take-

The Welsh Baccalaureate qualification

Wales is piloting a new broader post-16 qualification, the Welsh Baccalaureate. The pilot project will incorporate existing qualifications and will have a common core curriculum, including Key Skills, Wales, Europe and the World (including a language module), Work-related Education and Personal and Social Education. The development of the qualification and the pilot project is managed by the Welsh Joint Education Committee. There are 19 pilot centres (schools and further education colleges), with the first students due to start in September 2003.

Figure 10.9 Achievement at GCE A level[1] or equivalent, UK

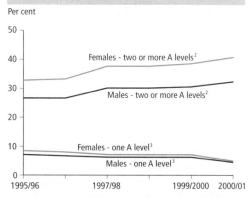

Per cent

Females - two or more A levels[2]

Males - two or more A levels[2]

Females - one A level[3]

Males - one A level[3]

1995/96   1997/98   1999/2000   2000/01

1 As a percentage of those aged 18 (17 in Scotland). Two AS levels count as one A level pass. Includes pupils from schools and further education colleges.
2 Or three or more highers.
3 Or one or two highers. Includes those with 1.5 A levels.
Source: Department for Education and Skills, National Assembly for Wales, Scottish Executive and Northern Ireland Department of Education

up of more subjects. The GCE A and AS levels are graded A to E.

In Scotland, National Qualifications courses were phased in from 1999/2000. NQs consist of five main levels of award: Access (subdivided into three levels); Intermediate 1; Intermediate 2; Higher; and Advanced Higher. These courses are mainly studied as post-16 qualifications though, under arrangements for curricular flexibility, some students may study NQs in addition to, or in place of, Standard Grades.

GCE A/AS levels and GCSEs (or NQs in Scotland) can also be taken in a school sixth form or in further education institutions.

In 2000/01, 36 per cent of young people in schools and further education in the United Kingdom achieved two or more GCE A levels or equivalent, compared with 30 per cent in 1995/96 (see Figure 10.9). Female pupils obtained better results than males. By contrast in 1965/66, 9 per cent of female and 13 per cent of male school leavers had at least two GCE A levels or equivalent.

All GCSE, GCE and other qualifications offered to pupils in state schools must be approved by the appropriate minister. Specifications and assessment procedures must comply with national guidelines and be accredited by the Qualifications and Curriculum Authority (QCA) in England, by its Welsh counterpart, Qualifications, Curriculum and Assessment Authority for Wales/Awdurdod Cymwysterau, Cwricwlwm ac Asesu Cymru (ACCAC), or the Northern Ireland Council for Curriculum, Examinations and Assessment (CCEA). These independent government agencies

New proposals for 14 to 19 year olds in England

The Government published a Green Paper in February 2002. Proposals include: a wide range of high-quality vocational and academic options in school, college and the workplace; reform of the 14–16 curriculum; more use of both accelerated and slower paced learning; and more collaborative work between schools, colleges, training providers and employers. The Green Paper also suggests an award to recognise the breadth and depth of student achievement by the age of 19.

are responsible for ensuring that the curriculum and qualifications are of high quality, coherent and flexible. NQs in Scotland are managed by the Scottish Qualifications Authority (SQA).

All secondary schools in England and Wales, and primary and secondary schools in Northern Ireland, provide leavers with a Record of Achievement setting out their attainments, including public examinations and National Curriculum assessment results. The Record is not compulsory in Scotland.

Careers

All young people in full-time education are entitled to career information, advice and guidance.

In England the Connexions Service is the support service for 13 to 19 year olds. It provides integrated advice, guidance and access to personal development opportunities and aims to help young people make a smooth transition to adulthood and working life. The service co-ordinates careers, youth and other statutory and voluntary services for young people. It is delivered at a local level through Connexions Partnerships, by a network of personal advisers based in a variety of settings, including schools and colleges.

The Learning and Skills Council (LSC – see page 111) is responsible for developing education business links in England. The aim is to ensure that all young people have high-quality work experience during their time at school in order to help raise standards of achievement, develop key skills and prepare them more effectively for adult and working life.

Careers Wales works with schools and colleges to deliver information, advice and guidance to all age groups. It also works with schools and employers to facilitate work experience placements and opportunities to learn about business and enterprise. It provides additional help to those most at risk of failing to realise their potential.

In Northern Ireland careers education is a cross-curricular theme in secondary schools. Business links to provide work experience for young people are fostered through the Northern Ireland Business Education Partnership, which supports a network of local partnerships and five area partnerships aligned to the five education and library boards.

Careers Scotland commenced work in April 2002. It offers a careers advisory service to all ages. Like Careers Wales, it has a particular focus on supporting vulnerable young people.

Young people and adults

Further education
After compulsory education is finished, young people can choose to stay on at school, attend college or take part in work-based learning. About 70 per cent of 16 year olds continue in full-time education in school sixth forms, sixth form colleges or further education colleges. Students

Table 10.10 Students[1] in further and higher education, by type of course and sex, UK

	Males	Thousands Females
1999/2000		
Further education[2]		
Full-time	518	518
Part-time	1,251	1,764
All further education	**1,769**	**2,282**
2000/01		
Higher education[3]		
Undergraduate		
Full-time	511	602
Part-time	228	320
Postgraduate		
Full-time	82	81
Part-time	118	124
All higher education	**940**	**1,128**

1 Home and overseas students.
2 Excludes adult education centres.
3 Includes Open University.
Source: Department for Education and Skills, National Assembly for Wales, Scottish Executive and Northern Ireland Department of Education

Centres of Vocational Excellence (CoVEs) aim to provide the skills needed by employers across a wide range of occupations. The LSC (see page 111), which is implementing the programme across England, aims to develop a network of at least 150 CoVEs by the end of March 2004. CoVEs are mainly based in further education colleges, but the programme has been extended to develop centres in other organisations such as private or voluntary training providers. In 2002, there were 85 CoVEs in further education colleges and five non college based centres.

may continue to study for examinations (such as the GCE A level) leading to higher education, professional training or vocational qualifications. They can also take non-examination courses.

Further education colleges
People over the age of 16 can take courses in further education colleges with a choice of academic and vocational provision. Many colleges offer government-sponsored training

programmes. Most students attend part-time, either by day release, block release from employment or during the evenings. The sector has strong ties with commerce and industry and can play an important role in promoting economic development and social inclusion.

Student support

Support for further education students in England includes a subsidy towards course fees for 16 to 18 year olds, fee remission for those aged 19 or over on low incomes and a discretionary access fund (£92 million in 2002/03) to help meet the costs of books, equipment, travel and fees. The Child Care Support Fund (£30 million in 2002/03) provides discretionary childcare support for students.

The Further Education Funding Council for Wales and the Scottish Further Education Funding Council provide help for eligible students in further education. In 2002/03 the Welsh Assembly Government introduced Assembly Learning Grants, for which further education students are eligible (depending upon age, income and course of study).

In Northern Ireland the Executive provides funding and support through the Further Education Funding Formula. Funding is also provided to colleges and students through a number of special budgets, which are designed to widen access, increase participation, address skills shortages and enhance the role of the sector in supporting economic development.

National Vocational Qualifications (NVQs)

NVQs, equivalent to Scottish Vocational Qualifications (SVQs), are awards which recognise work-related skills and knowledge in areas such as business, engineering and health and social care. They are based on national standards developed by employer-led bodies, approved across the UK, and accredited by the regulatory bodies (which also accredit academic qualifications outside higher education).

Types of vocational qualification

NVQs or SVQs are awarded at five levels. Vocational GCSEs and Vocational A levels are an alternative to GCSEs and GCE A levels in England, Wales and Northern Ireland (see also page 108). NQs in Scotland include vocational subjects alongside traditional academic ones. Other vocational qualifications include, for example, a BTec Higher National Diploma or a City and Guilds Craft award (see page 115).

Vocational and academic comparability

Vocational and academic qualifications are broadly comparable at the following levels:

- an NVQ or SVQ level 5 is equivalent to a Higher Degree;

- an NVQ or SVQ level 4 is equivalent to a First Degree, an HND or HNC, a BTec Higher Diploma, an RSA Higher Diploma, a nursing qualification or other higher education;

- an NVQ or SVQ level 3 is equivalent to two GCE A levels, an RSA advanced diploma, a City and Guilds advanced craft, an OND, ONC or a BTec National Diploma; and

- an NVQ or SVQ level 2 is equivalent to five GCSEs at grades A* to C, an RSA diploma, a City and Guilds craft or a BTec first or general diploma.

NVQs or SVQs are achieved through assessment and training. Assessment is normally through on-the-job observation and questioning. These qualifications are available for almost all occupations, covering general, industrial and commercial sectors.

Learning and Skills Council

In England, the Learning and Skills Council is responsible for planning and funding post-16 learning, up to but not including higher education. Its remit includes further education, work-based training, and adult and community learning. It is now also responsible for funding LEAs for their school sixth form provision. The LSC is a single unitary body and operates through a national office and 47 local arms, known as local LSCs. The Council has a statutory duty to encourage participation in learning and works with employers and others to promote workforce development.

National Council for Education and Training for Wales

The National Council has a similar remit to the LSC. It is responsible for post-16 education and training, with the exception of higher education. There are 21 local voluntary partnerships (Community Consortia for Education and Training) linking LEAs, schools, colleges, voluntary organisations, private training

Then and now
In 1952 there were 17 universities in England, 1 in Wales, 4 in Scotland and 2 in Northern Ireland. In 2002 the figures were 72, 2, 14 and 2 respectively. A number of new universities were endowed in the 1960s and 1970s. The number of universities increased considerably after 1992, when polytechnics were given degree awarding powers and were allowed to call themselves universities as a result of the *Further and Higher Education Act 1992*. In 2000/01 there were just over 2 million students in full- or part-time higher education, compared with around 222,000 in the mid-1950s.

providers, employers and trade unions. The National Council and the Higher Education Funding Council for Wales operate together under the name Education and Learning Wales (ELWa).

Higher education

Around 30 per cent of young people in England and Wales, 40 per cent in Scotland and 45 per cent in Northern Ireland take degree and other advanced courses in universities and other colleges. An increasing number of mature students also study for these qualifications.

Universities and higher education colleges

There are 90 university institutions in the UK, including the Open University. This figure does not include the constituent colleges of the universities of London and Wales, both of which have a federal structure. The UK's universities enjoy academic freedom, appoint their own staff, admit students and award their own degrees. The universities of Oxford and Cambridge date from the 13th century and the Scottish universities of St Andrews, Glasgow and Aberdeen from the 15th century. The University of Edinburgh was established in the 16th century. All the other universities were founded in the 19th and 20th centuries.

In addition, there are 64 higher education colleges which have different backgrounds and purposes. Some are very specialised, such as art and design, teacher education and agriculture colleges, while others are multi-disciplinary. Some award their own degrees and qualifications, while in others these are validated by a university or national body.

Applications for full-time first degrees and HND courses are usually made through the Universities

and Colleges Admission Service (UCAS). In 2001 nearly 360,000 applications were accepted to higher education through UCAS. Around 28,000 students were accepted as deferred entrants – nearly double the figure for 1994 and accounting for nearly 8 per cent of accepted applications.

Students at university in England, Wales and Northern Ireland usually spend three years of study, leading to a Bachelor's degree, such as a Bachelor of Arts (BA) or Bachelor of Science (BSc). There are some four-year courses, especially for those studying languages, and medical and veterinary courses normally require five or six years. A full-time first degree in Scotland (where students usually start a year earlier) generally takes four years for Honours and three years for the broad-based Ordinary degree.

In 2001 some 265,300 students gained a first degree in the UK compared with 232,200 in 1995. 32,600 graduated with a first degree in business and administration in 2001, by far the highest category.

Some students go on to do postgraduate studies. These usually lead to a Masters degree, such as a Master of Arts (MA) or Master of Science (MSc), or to a doctorate (PhD). A Masters degree usually lasts one year full-time or two years part-time. A PhD usually lasts three years full-time or six years part-time. The Government also launched the 'New Route PhD' in 2001 in response to the changes in knowledge and skills demanded of PhD graduates. It lasts four years and combines a specific research project with a coherent programme of formal coursework and professional skills development.

Applications for postgraduate study are processed separately by each institution and are made directly to the university.

The Open University

The Open University (OU) is a non-residential university offering 377 degree and other courses for adult students who wish to study in their own time. Teaching is through a combination of printed texts, correspondence tuition, television broadcasts, audio/video cassettes and, for some courses, short residential schools. Some 160,000 of its 218,400 students study online from home and many OU learning resources are delivered on interactive CD-ROM or computer software. There is a network of local tutorial centres for contact with part-time tutors and fellow students.

Distance learning

With the growth of the Internet, many UK universities and colleges now offer study through distance learning. This usually means learning at home or work, with no need to visit the learning centre. Distance learning courses are available at many levels, including degree and postgraduate qualifications. The Department for Education and Skills (DfES) offers advice on which institutions are recognised as having degree awarding powers and recommends that a check is made before applying for an online course.

UK eUniversities Worldwide is a public-private initiative. The venture will aim to provide an e-learning platform to deliver high-quality education, principally via the Internet. The first courses will be available in January 2003.

Students do not need any formal academic qualifications to register for most courses.

The OU's first degrees are the BA (Open) and the BSc (Open), which are awarded on a system of points for each course completed. Either degree can be awarded with honours. The OU offers honours degrees in named subject areas and an MEng degree to enable students to achieve the highest professional status of Chartered Engineer. There are a number of certificates and diplomas. Higher degrees are also available.

Finance

In 2000/01 LEAs and central government spent £6 billion on higher education in the United Kingdom. Government finance is distributed to higher education institutions by higher education funding councils in England, Wales and Scotland, and in Northern Ireland by the Department for Employment and Learning. The private University of Buckingham does not receive public funds.

Institutions also charge tuition fees, which are partly funded by students. In addition, they provide paid training, research or consultancy for commercial firms. Many establishments have endowments or receive grants from foundations and benefactors.

Student support

Support for full-time higher education students in England and Wales is provided in several ways.

The maximum student contribution towards tuition fees in 2002/03 is £1,100, but the amount actually paid depends on student and family income. Half of students do not pay any fees. Student loans are the main form of help for students in meeting living costs. The maximum loan in 2002/03 for full-time students living away from home was £3,905 (£4,815 for those in London). Loans are repaid on the basis of income after the student has completed his/her course, and only when he or she starts earning over £10,000 a year.

Student support in Scotland

In 2001 the Scottish Executive introduced a new support scheme for full-time higher education. Student loans and supplementary grants are still the main source of help with living costs. The main feature of the new system is that young students from low income families are entitled to have up to £2,000 of their annual loan entitlement replaced by a non-repayable bursary. Most graduates who start courses from 2001/02 are required to make a one-off payment to the Graduate Endowment, of £2,000, when they complete their course and start earning over £10,000 a year (mature students, lone parents and students with a disability are exempt). Since 2000/01 tuition fees have not been payable by eligible full-time Scottish-domiciled students or EU students studying in Scotland.

Support is also available for part-time students on low incomes. Eligible applicants who wish to pursue a course of part-time study can obtain help towards the cost of tuition fees, and also a one-off loan payment of £500 per academic year.

For both full- and part-time study, extra, non-repayable help is available to those with disabilities or dependants, and to some of those entering higher education from low income families. Help may also be available from higher education institutions for those who get into financial difficulties as students.

In 2002/03 the Welsh Assembly Government introduced a scheme of means-tested Assembly Learning Grants. This provides grants for poorer students from Wales wherever they study in the UK.

In Northern Ireland support for higher education students generally operates on a similar basis to

England and Wales. However, from September 2002 means-tested bursaries of up to £1,500 became available to low-income families.

Postgraduate support

Most postgraduates have to pay a significant contribution towards tuition fees. The average fee for a one-year Masters programme is £2,805, although the figure varies with the programme of study and the institution. Some postgraduates receive an award from a public body, some support themselves through a mixture of public and private finance, and others receive funding through scholarships and bursaries. Most public funding is provided by the Research Councils (see chapter 25, page 379), the Arts and Humanities Research Board, the Students Awards Agency for Scotland and the Department for Employment and Learning in Northern Ireland. Employers may offer support by paying for all or part of the tuition fees and/or other costs such as examination fees and books, and by allowing paid leave for study.

Adult education

Education for adults is carried out in a wide range of locations, including LEAs' own premises, local community centres, libraries, museums, schools and both adult and further education colleges. Overall, about half of LEAs provide Adult and Community Learning through direct delivery; the other half are through contracts with other providers, predominately community schools and colleges. The duty to secure such education rests with the LSC in England and the National Council for Education and Training for Wales (see page 111). Adult education in Scotland is a statutory duty of education authorities and is generally known as community learning or community education. In Northern Ireland it is provided by the further education sector, supplemented by the work of a range of non-statutory providers. General adult education courses include languages, physical education/sport/fitness and practical craft skills, such as embroidery or woodwork.

The National Institute of Adult Continuing Education and the Basic Skills Agency jointly manage the Adult and Community Learning Fund on behalf of the DfES. The Fund supports innovative learning opportunities and aims to encourage people who have been reluctant to participate in learning and who may be disadvantaged as a result.

Literacy and numeracy

The Adult Basic Skills Strategy Unit, based in the DfES, is responsible for the implementation of 'Skills for Life', the national strategy for improving adult literacy and numeracy. Around 7 million adults in England have literacy levels below level 1 (equivalent to GCSE grades D–G) or what is expected of 11 year olds, and even more have a problem with numeracy. Skills for Life was launched in March 2001. The strategy caters for the literacy, language (English for Speakers of Other Languages – ESOL) and numeracy needs of all post-16 learners, including those with learning difficulties or disabilities. From pre-entry level up to and including level 2 (equivalent to GCSE grades A*–C), it provides free tuition for learners.

The Scottish Executive Enterprise and Lifelong Learning Department is responsible for improving adult literacy and numeracy in Scotland. A National Training Project was set up in 2001 and is part of Communities Scotland, which is the lead agency for improving adult literacy and numeracy. In Northern Ireland a framework and consultation paper on Adult Literacy was launched in July 2002. It aims to tackle low levels of literacy and numeracy.

Training and learning programmes

Several programmes are available to help increase work-related skills. These are offered as alternatives to academic education for 16 to 19 year olds or as part of an existing employee's training. The Government has several initiatives to help young people train for work and achieve NVQs, such as the New Deal and Modern Apprenticeships. See chapter 11 for more information on these initiatives and other work-related training.

Modern Apprenticeships (MAs)

MAs provide structured learning programmes for young people which combine work-based training with off-the-job learning. MAs are available throughout the UK. They offer a chance to train in an industry as well as the educational qualifications of an NVQ or SVQ to level 3 and in some cases above. The quality of MAs is being improved through technical certificates that develop knowledge and understanding, and through an Apprenticeship diploma or equivalent. Every young person with the necessary aptitude and ability will be entitled to an MA and there will be better access from an MA to higher education.

More than 80 sectors of business and industry already offer MAs, ranging from accountancy to sport. Each industry has its own guidance on entry requirements.

BTecs and City and Guilds qualifications
Business and Technology Education Council (BTec) and City and Guilds qualifications can be studied for in business and finance, leisure and tourism, engineering, and catering. In order to take a BTec National, which takes two years to complete, students usually need four GCSEs at grades A*–C. For the BTec Higher Nationals, the requirement is usually a BTec National or one GCE A level.

Other training schemes
Other workplace training includes:

- the right for 16 and 17 year old employees with few, if any, qualifications to reasonable paid time off work to study or train for an approved qualification at NVQ level 2 or equivalent;

- career development loans to help people pay for vocational education or learning in Great Britain. Loans of between £300 and £8,000 are provided through major banks; interest payments on the loan during training and one month after training are funded by the Government. They help to pay for courses lasting up to two years and, if relevant, for up to one year's practical work experience where it forms part of the course. Since the scheme began in 1988, over 169,000 loans have been made with an average value of £3,462. In 2001/02, around 16,000 loans were taken out;

- Small Firms Training Loans, which help firms with 50 or fewer permanent employees to meet a range of vocational training related expenses, including training consultancy. Loans of between £500 and £125,000 are available through high street banks and repayments can be deferred for between six and 12 months. Since the scheme began in 1994, nearly £4.1 million has been lent to 621 small firms. In 2001, £298,705 was lent and 37 small firms took up loans; and

- work-based learning for adults, open to those aged 25 and over who have been unemployed for six months or longer.

In Wales, SkillBuild, targeted at those young people who are most at risk in the labour market, aims to develop social skills, literacy, numeracy, ICT and other skills. A new programme – the Modern Skills Diploma for Adults – was introduced in April 2001 to provide high-level (level 3 and above) skills training for people aged over 25, including those in employment. In the first year of operation over 700 people joined the programme. The Welsh Assembly Government, in collaboration with ELWa, is developing a new series of 'all age' work-based programmes for introduction in April 2004.

In Scotland all young people aged between 16 and 17 are entitled to training under the government-funded Skillseekers scheme. Its key elements are:

- training leading to a recognised qualification, up to SVQ level 3;

- an individual training plan; and

- employer involvement.

Around 78 per cent of Skillseekers are in paid employment, with the remainder on work placements and in receipt of a training allowance.

A network of Local Enterprise Companies is responsible for the delivery of the Scottish Executive's national training programmes. They run under contract to two non-departmental public bodies: Scottish Enterprise and Highlands and Islands Enterprise.

In Northern Ireland the Jobskills Programme is available to all 16 to 17 year olds. It provides training to NVQ level 2 with progress routes to NVQ level 3 through Modern Apprenticeship arrangements.

Learning initiatives

Sector Skills Councils
From April 2002 a new Sector Skills Council (SSC) network, replacing National Training Organisations, has been established by the Sector Skills Development Agency. SSCs are independent UK-wide organisations developed by groups of employers in industry and business sectors. They bring together employers, trade unions and professional bodies working with government to develop the skills that UK business needs.

New Technology Institutes
In May 2002 the locations of 18 New Technology Institutes (NTIs) were announced. The NTIs will

include higher education institutions, further education colleges, and private sector partners, and provide training in advanced technology skills both to businesses and students. The Higher Education Funding Council for England is working in partnership with the LSC to establish the institutes by autumn 2002. All the NTIs should be fully operational by 2004/05.

learndirect

The online network, learndirect, provides learning opportunities to people at home, in the workplace and at over 1,760 centres throughout England, Wales and Northern Ireland. Its primary objective is to stimulate demand for lifelong learning among adults and small and medium-sized enterprises, and to increase the availability of high quality learning through the use of ICT. There is a learndirect telephone helpline and a learndirect website (*www.learndirect.co.uk*). Learndirect Scotland now has 300 learning centres. The network underpins 6,000 UK online centres, which aim to reduce the gap between those who have access to ICT and those who do not.

Individual Learning Accounts

In September 2000 the Government and the devolved administrations launched a programme to help people plan and pay towards the cost of their learning. Qualifying applicants were able to receive funding through Individual Learning Accounts (ILAs). Over 2.6 million accounts were opened and some 8,910 organisations registered as learning providers. The programme was suspended in 2001 following allegations that a small minority of providers had been involved in potential fraud and theft from ILAs. Replacement schemes are under consideration.

Information and communications technology

The National Grid for Learning (NGfL) is a government initiative to help learners and educators in the UK benefit from ICT. Launched in 1998, its aim is to increase and widen access to learning opportunities in both formal and informal environments, such as schools, colleges, libraries, homes and workplaces. The NGfL involves the development of educational material, a programme for the delivery of ICT infrastructure, and training to develop good ICT practice.

By 2002, 96 per cent of primary schools in the UK and 99 per cent of secondary schools were connected to the Internet. Computer to pupil ratios were about 1:12 and 1:7 respectively. Over

96 per cent of eligible teachers have registered for ICT teacher training through the New Opportunities Fund and over 99 per cent of schools have now signed up for the training.

The British Educational Communications and Technology Agency is the Government's lead agency on the use of ICT in education and manages the NGfL in England and Wales. Learning and Teaching Scotland and the Northern Ireland Network for Education manage the NGfL in their respective areas.

Teachers and other staff

In 2000/01 the average UK pupil to teacher ratios for state nursery, primary and secondary schools were 26.5, 22.3 and 16.5 respectively. In the younger age groups the work of qualified teachers is more likely to be supplemented by teaching assistants (see page 117).

England and Wales

New teachers in state primary and secondary schools must be graduates and hold Qualified Teacher Status (QTS). There are two main ways of achieving this: by taking a Bachelor of Education degree (four years) at a university or college of higher education; or by taking a one-year Post Graduate Certificate in Education (PGCE) course leading to QTS. A third route into the profession allows undergraduates on traditional academic

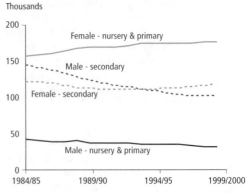

Figure 10.11 Full-time nursery and primary and secondary school teachers,[1] UK

Thousands

1 Qualified teachers only. As at 31 March of each year.
Source: Department for Education and Skills, National Assembly for Wales, Scottish Executive and Northern Ireland Department of Education

degree courses to take education modules and so gain part of a teacher education qualification.

Other programmes, available in England only, offer the opportunity for people aged 24 and over to earn a salary while following a teacher training programme in a school. These programmes are particularly suitable for overseas-trained teachers who do not hold QTS, mature career changers, school support staff and people who have had previous teaching experience.

All teachers working in state schools must be registered with the General Teaching Council for England or Wales. These are teachers' professional bodies which, among other things, have the power to strike a teacher from the register on grounds of professional misconduct or incompetence.

Figure 10.11 shows the number of teachers in maintained schools in recent years.

Northern Ireland

All entrants to teaching in grant-aided schools are graduates and hold an approved teaching qualification. Initial teacher training is integrated with induction and early in-service training, the latter covering a period of three years. The General Teaching Council in Northern Ireland, which has similar duties to those in England and Wales, is due to hold its first full meeting of elected and appointed members in October 2002. As with the rest of the UK, the main teacher training courses are the Bachelor of Education degree and the PGCE. The education and library boards have a statutory duty to provide curricular support services and in-service training.

Scotland

All teachers in education authority schools must be registered with the General Teaching Council for Scotland. The Council gives advice to the Scottish Executive on teacher supply and the professional suitability of teacher training courses. It is also responsible for disciplinary procedures under which a teacher guilty of professional misconduct may be removed temporarily or permanently from the register.

Teacher qualification procedures are similar to those in England and Wales, including the Bachelor of Education degree and the PGCE. There is also a combined degree, sometimes known as a concurrent degree. All pre-service courses are validated by a higher education institution accredited by the Council and approved by the Scottish Executive. The Education Inspectorate has powers to inspect teacher education and training.

Teaching assistants

The term teaching assistant refers to those whose primary role is either to assist the teacher in the classroom, or to provide support for individual pupils. There are no nationally set qualifications for this role, although some local authorities have their own requirements. National Occupational Standards for teaching assistants have been published and NVQs (levels 2 and 3) based on the standards are being developed.

Headteachers

In England the National College for School Leadership (NCSL) was launched in 2000. The college is responsible for the three national headship training programmes: the National Professional Qualification for Headship (NPQH) for aspiring headteachers; the Leadership and Management Programme for New Headteachers; and the Leadership Programme for Serving Headteachers. The DfES and the NCSL recently consulted on proposals to make the NPQH mandatory for all those seeking their first headship post from April 2004.

Wales and Northern Ireland have their own versions of the NPQH, adapted to suit their respective school systems. The Scottish Executive announced in December 2001 its intention to make the Scottish Standard for Headship mandatory in Scotland from August 2005. At present, the only route to gaining the Standard is through the Scottish Qualification for Headship.

Teacher recruitment and retention

The purpose of the Teacher Training Agency is to raise standards in schools in England by attracting able and committed people to teaching and by improving the quality of teacher training. Government measures to tackle teacher recruitment and retention issues include:

- an increase (from 1,500 to 2,000) in the number of flexible training places for people wanting to train while still working;

- a £4,000 'golden hello' for those who train in and then go on to teach in subjects in which there are shortages of teachers; and

- proposals to pay off, over time, the student loans of newly qualified teachers in shortage subjects, such as mathematics, science, English, modern languages and technology.

Allied professions

A range of other professions are involved in education and training. Examples are given below.

Childcare

There are a range of relevant qualifications for those working in this sector. For example, in nursery work, trainees under supervision work towards a level 2 qualification on the National Qualifications Framework in Early Years Education, Childcare and Playwork. On-the-job progression can then be made to level 3.

Careers advisers

In England and Wales fully qualified advisers are required to hold a relevant qualification at NVQ or SVQ level 4 or equivalent. In England advisers must also complete specific Connexions training: there are four main programmes.

Further and higher education

There were 55,000 full-time further education lecturers and 76,000 full-time higher education lecturers in the UK in 1999/2000. With the exception of Northern Ireland, professional teaching qualifications are not essential in this sector, although prospects tend to be better for those who have them. In Northern Ireland a Postgraduate Certificate in Further and Higher Education is required if an approved teaching qualification is not already held.

Administration and management

State schools in England and Wales are maintained by local government education authorities. With a few exceptions, this is also the position in Scotland. In Northern Ireland five education and library boards fund all controlled and maintained schools and the Department of Education funds voluntary grammar and grant-maintained integrated schools. Further education colleges in the UK are controlled by autonomous governing bodies, with representation from businesses and the local community. Universities and higher education colleges are legally independent corporate institutions with individual governing bodies.

Education Act 2002

Key provisions of the *Education Act 2002*, which covers England and Wales, include:

- opportunities for schools and LEAs to experiment with new ways of raising standards;

- more autonomy for schools that perform well, in order to encourage innovation;

- a more flexible curriculum allowing tailoring of provision to individual needs;

- powers for schools to offer community facilities, form companies, and decide upon models of school governance that suit them best;

- measures to support a more flexible framework for the staffing of schools;

- enhanced provisions to tackle under-performance; and

- greater transparency for school finance.

A number of central government departments are responsible for education policy:

- the Department for Education and Skills (DfES) in England;

- the Welsh Assembly Government Training and Education Department;

- the Scottish Executive Education Department (primary and secondary education) and the Scottish Executive Enterprise and Lifelong Learning Department; and

- the Department of Education and the Department for Employment and Learning in the Northern Ireland Executive.

The education service in Great Britain is financed in the same way as other local government services (see chapter 6, page 53), with education authorities funding schools largely on the basis of pupil numbers. Specific central government grants are made to LEAs in Great Britain in order to improve school performance in literacy, numeracy and ICT. The Government also allocates some resources directly to schools for them to use as they wish. The costs of education and library

2002 Spending Review

Under the 2002 Spending Review (see page 350), published in July 2002, a record increase in education spending is envisaged in the UK over the next three years with spending forecast to rise to 5.6 per cent of GDP by 2005/06. For example in England the Review set out that:

- spending will rise by an average of 6 per cent a year in real terms over the next three years, to £57.8 billion in 2005/06;

- payments directly to schools will be at least £165,000 for a typical secondary school, and £50,000 for a primary school: increases of £50,000 and £10,000 respectively; and

- from September 2004, Education Maintenance Allowances of up to £30 a week, will be available to 16–19 year olds, depending on parental income, with additional bonuses for attendance and achievement.

Further investment will also be made in childcare and early years learning, further education, improving the basic skills of adults, and expanding Modern Apprenticeships and work-related qualifications.

boards are met directly by the Northern Ireland Executive.

School management

England and Wales

All state schools work in partnership with, and receive recurrent funding from, LEAs, while managing 85 per cent of their budgets and staffing. They are run by governing bodies, comprising parents, school staff, LEA and local community representation.

LEAs and school governing bodies responsible for pupil admissions are expected to take part in local discussions with headteachers, churches and others, in order to co-ordinate admission arrangements, taking account of statutory codes of practice. Any disagreements on school organisation or admissions in England are referred to an independent adjudicator; those regarding religious or denominational admission criteria are referred to the Secretary of State for

Education and Skills. In Wales the Assembly Government decides all cases of disagreement.

Admission authorities are not allowed to introduce selection by ability, unless it is for sixth form admission or is designed to ensure that pupils of all abilities are admitted and that no one level of ability is over- or under-represented. Where existing partial selection by ability is challenged, the Adjudicator (in Wales the Assembly Government) decides whether it should continue.

In England there are 164 designated grammar schools which select pupils on ability. Local parents are allowed to petition for a ballot and (if sufficient numbers locally wish it) to vote on whether to keep these selective admission arrangements.

Scotland

Nearly all Scottish schools are education authority schools financed by the authorities and central government. The headteacher is responsible for decision-making on at least 80 per cent of school-level expenditure.

In May 2000, 83 per cent of eligible education authority schools had a school board consisting of elected parents and teachers and members co-opted from the local community. In addition to promoting contact between parents, school and community, they are involved in procedures to appoint senior staff and to determine the community use of school premises. They may also take on further executive functions by delegation from their education authority.

Nine grant-aided schools, one primary, one secondary, and seven for children with special educational needs, are run by boards of managers who receive government grants.

Northern Ireland

Boards of governors are responsible for the management of individual schools and include elected parents and teachers among their members. Virtually all schools have delegated budgets under which school governors determine spending priorities.

Rights of parents

England and Wales

Parents have a statutory right to information about schools and to express a preference for a school for their child. There is an appeal system if their choice is not met. Parents must be given a copy of the annual report from the school governors, which includes summaries of the school's results in National Curriculum assessment tests, public examinations, vocational qualifications (if applicable) and rates of pupil absence.

Parents must be given a written annual report on their child's achievements in all subjects, including results of tests and examinations. Arrangements must also be made for the discussion of reports with teachers.

Parents are also entitled to see or be provided with a copy of their child's pupil record within 15 school days of making a written request. Unless there is a court order preventing it, all parents have a right to participate in decisions about their child's education.

Home/school agreements set out the responsibilities of schools, pupils and parents and are a statutory requirement for all maintained schools.

Scotland
Parents have a statutory right to express their choice of school and the education authority must meet this request except in certain circumstances set out in law. Information is published on school costs, examination results, pupil attendance or absence, 5–14 attainment targets and results, and the destinations of school leavers. Schools are required to provide parents with information about their children's attainment in each subject, pupil attainment targets and teachers' comments on their progress.

Northern Ireland
The system of reporting to parents is broadly similar to that in England and Wales, except that no annual performance tables on a school-by-school basis are published.

Educational standards

England and Wales
The Office for Standards in Education (OFSTED) in England and the Office of Her Majesty's Chief Inspector in Wales (Estyn) aim to improve the quality and standards of education through independent inspection and advice.

Schools are inspected at least once in six years, but more often where weaknesses have been identified in an earlier inspection. They must produce an action plan to address the key issues raised in the inspection report. A school failing to provide an acceptable standard of education is deemed to need Special Measures and remains subject to regular monitoring visits by inspectors.

The *Education Act 2002* allows for earlier and wider intervention in weak and failing schools. The Act introduced new powers to replace a governing body with an interim executive board if the governing body is part of the problem. LEAs will also be expected to invite external partners to help turn round weak and failing schools. These could be successful schools, other LEAs, other educational establishments, voluntary, faith or private bodies.

In April 2001 OFSTED acquired responsibility for inspecting all 16 to 19 education and training in sixth form and further education colleges, which it carries out with the Adult Learning Inspectorate. From September 2001 OFSTED also became responsible for the regulation of all early years childcare providers.

The Adult Learning Inspectorate performs the same function as OFSTED for post-19 provision in colleges and for work-based learning and LEA-secured adult and community learning. Estyn already has responsibility for these areas as well as adult education and work-based training.

Scotland
Her Majesty's Inspectorate of Education began operating as an executive agency of the Scottish Executive in April 2001. It inspects, reviews and reports on state and independent schools, further education colleges and the education functions of local authorities. Reports are published and are usually followed up within two years.

Northern Ireland
The Education and Training Inspectorate monitors, inspects and reports on standards of education and training provided by schools, colleges and other grant-aided organisations, and provides information and policy advice to the Department of Education, the Department of Culture, Arts and Leisure, and the Department for Employment and Learning.

International links

Large numbers of people from other countries come to the UK to study, and many British people work and train overseas. The British Council (see chapter 7) encourages links between educational institutions in the UK and developing countries.

European Union schemes

Exchange of students is promoted by the EU's Socrates-Erasmus programme which provides grants enabling university students from the EU, Norway, Iceland, Liechtenstein, and all the Associated Countries in Central and Eastern Europe, as well as Cyprus and Malta, to study in other states (Turkey is expected to participate in 2003). All academic subjects are covered, the study period normally lasting between three and 12 months. About 9,000 UK students take part each year. Since it began in 1987 more than 1 million students have participated in the programme, of whom almost 120,000 were from the UK.

No UK students on Erasmus exchanges who come under the student support arrangements and who go abroad for a full academic year (nine months or more) have to pay any tuition fee contribution, regardless of family income. In addition to any student support entitlements, Erasmus students may also be eligible for an Erasmus grant that contributes towards the extra costs arising from studying abroad.

The Socrates programme also supports partnerships between schools, language learning, mobility opportunities for educational staff and a range of multinational projects, including open and distance learning and adult education. Competence in another European language is supported in all activities.

The Leonardo da Vinci programme supports vocational training policies and practices through

The Commonwealth Education Fund
This fund was launched in 2002 to mark the Queen's Golden Jubilee year. It aims to highlight the need for universal primary education in the Commonwealth and to raise children's awareness of development issues. Actionaid, Oxfam and Save the Children administer the fund. The Government has announced a grant of £10 million to the fund over the years to December 2005, and will match contributions by businesses and others. There are estimated to be 75 million children in the Commonwealth who do not complete a basic education.

multinational pilot projects, placements and exchanges, and research projects. The Youth Programme supports youth exchanges and volunteering activities. It gives young people from the age of 15 upwards the chance to broaden their horizons and develop their sense of initiative through projects at home or abroad.

Overseas students and teachers in the UK

In 1999/2000 there were 114,600 overseas students in further education institutions in the UK; and in higher education in 2000/01 there were 229,900. Most of them pay fees covering the full costs of their courses. Nationals of other EU states generally pay the lower level of fees applicable to British home students.

In order to teach in maintained schools in England, it is generally necessary to hold QTS (see page 116) and be registered with a General Teaching Council. Regulations do not allow for the automatic recognition of teaching qualifications gained abroad unless the teacher is a national of the EEA (see page 60). Other nationals can be appointed under certain circumstances through the Overseas Trained Teachers programme. Some 6,000 UK work permits were issued to teachers in 2001.

Government scholarship schemes

The Government makes provision for foreign students to study in the UK through its Chevening programme and other scholarship schemes. In 2001 about 4,000 students from overseas received awards from scholarship schemes funded in part by the Foreign & Commonwealth Office (FCO), and other government departments. These are the Chevening programme, Commonwealth Scholarships and Fellowships Plan, Department for International Development Shared Scholarships, Marshall Scholarships, and North Atlantic Fellowships. The FCO is also increasing the number of scholarships jointly funded with British or foreign commercial firms, and with academic and other institutions.

Other schemes

The Overseas Research Students Award Scheme, funded by the higher education funding councils, provides help for overseas full-time postgraduate students with outstanding research potential. In addition, most British universities and colleges offer bursaries and scholarships for which graduates of any nationality are eligible. Other public and private scholarships are available to students from overseas and to British students who want to study in other countries.

The Teachers' International Development Programme aims to provide teachers with opportunities for international study visits or exchanges which will enable them to experience good practice, develop international educational links with other schools, carry out research and share information with a network of other participants. Around 3,900 teachers have participated in the programme since its launch in May 2000.

Further reading

Choice and Excellence – A Vision for Post 14 Education. Department for Education and Skills, 2002.

Education and Skills: Delivering results – A Strategy to 2006. Department for Education and Skills, 2001.

Education and Training Statistics for the United Kingdom. Department for Education and Skills. Annual.

Education for the 21st Century – Post Primary Review. Department of Education, Northern Ireland, 2001

The Government's Expenditure Plans 2002–03 to 2004–05. Department for Education and Skills and Office for Standards in Education. The Stationery Office, 2002.

The Learning Country – A Comprehensive Education and Lifelong Learning Programme to 2010 in Wales. National Assembly for Wales, 2001.

Plan for Wales 2001. National Assembly for Wales, 2001.

Schools: Achieving Success. Department for Education and Skills. The Stationery Office, 2001.

Websites

Department for Education and Skills
www.dfes.gov.uk

Scottish Executive
www.scotland.gov.uk

National Assembly for Wales/Welsh Assembly Government
www.wales.gov.uk

Department of Education (NI)
www.deni.gov.uk/index.html

Department for Employment and Learning (NI)
www.delni.gov.uk

11 The labour market

For almost a decade, the number of people employed in the United Kingdom labour market has been growing, and now exceeds 28 million. Both full-time and part-time employment have risen. The increase has been predominantly in the service sector, in which over three-quarters of employees now work. At the same time unemployment has fallen considerably since the last peak at the end of 1992 and in 2001 reached its lowest level since the introduction of the International Labour Organisation (ILO) measure of unemployment in 1984. Since spring 2001, however, unemployment has been increasing slightly.

Patterns of employment

The Labour Force Survey (LFS)[1] carried out by the Office for National Statistics shows that, on a seasonally adjusted basis, over 30 million people aged 16 and over were economically active in the UK in spring (March to May) 2002, comprising 28.5 million in employment and 1.6 million ILO unemployed (see Table 11.1). The economic activity rate was 63.5 per cent for all persons aged 16 and over and 78.9 per cent for those of working age (men aged 16 to 64 and women aged 16 to 59). Among the working age group, some 7.8 million people were economically inactive, of whom 5.5 million people did not want a job and 2.3 million people wanted a job but were either not seeking work or not available to start work.

The number of people aged 16 and over in employment[2] in the UK rose by 179,000 in the year to spring 2002 to 28.5 million: some 15.7

Measures of unemployment
The ILO measure of unemployment is based on LFS estimates of the number of people without a job who are seeking work. It refers to the number available to start work within two weeks who have either looked for work in the previous four weeks or are waiting to start a job they have already obtained. It is based on internationally agreed definitions and is the official measure of unemployment in the UK.

An alternative measure is the claimant count. This is a count of the number of people claiming unemployment-related benefits.

Economic activity
The labour market can be divided into two groups: the economically active and inactive. The economically active are defined as those who are either in employment (employee, self-employed, unpaid family worker or on a government-supported training programme) or unemployed and actively seeking work. The economically inactive are people who are not in work, but who do not satisfy all the criteria for ILO unemployment; it includes those in retirement and those not actively seeking work.

million men and 12.8 million women. This represented an increase of 0.6 per cent during the year: 1.1 per cent for women and 0.3 per cent for men. The employment rate among those of working age was 74.7 per cent, close to the previous high achieved in 1990 (see Figure 11.2).

One of the main long-term trends in the labour market is the increased participation of women in employment. In spring 2002, nearly 70 per cent of working age women were in employment, compared with 47 per cent in 1959 (the year for which estimates are first available). Among many reasons for their greater involvement is that more women delay having children until their thirties

1 All LFS data quoted are based on pre-2001 Census totals and will be subject to revision.
2 There are two main measures of employment: the number of people in employment and the number of jobs; they differ because one person can have more than one job.

Table 11.1 Employment in the UK, spring 2002

Thousands, seasonally adjusted

	Males	Females	Total
All aged 16 and over	23,229	24,117	47,346
Total economically active	16,629	13,454	30,083
of whom:			
In employment	15,674	12,837	28,511
ILO unemployed[1]	955	617	1,572
Economic activity rate (%)[2]	*84.1*	*73.0*	*78.9*
Employment rate (%)	*67.5*	*53.2*	*60.2*
ILO unemployment rate (%)	*5.7*	*4.6*	*5.2*

1 International Labour Organisation definition of unemployment.
2 For men aged 16 to 64 and women aged 16 to 59.
Source: Labour Force Survey, Office for National Statistics

and are then more likely to return to work afterwards, making use of a range of childcare options. Other reasons include the increasing levels of educational attainment among women and changing social attitudes to women working.

Older workers

There were 6.0 million people aged between 50 and state pension age in employment in spring 2002, representing 21 per cent of all employed people. Their employment rate was unchanged from the previous year at 68 per cent, as was their

Figure 11.2 Working age employment rates,[1] UK, 1959–2001

Per cent

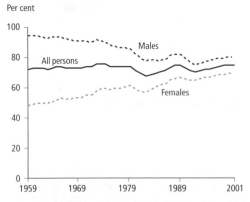

1 At summer each year. From 1959 to 1971, males aged 15 to 64 and females aged 15 to 59; from 1972 onwards males aged 16 to 64 and females aged 16 to 59.
Source: Department for Work and Pensions

economic inactivity rate (30 per cent). The economic inactivity rate among men aged 50 to 64 increased from 23 per cent in 1984 to peak at 29 per cent in 1995 and has since declined to 27 per cent from 1999 to 2002. In contrast, the rate for women aged 50 to 59 declined from 41 per cent to 33 per cent between 1984 and 2002.

In spring 2002, 15 per cent of the ILO unemployed were over 50, of whom 36 per cent had been unemployed for more than 12 months, a decrease of 4 percentage points since spring 2001. For details on the New Deal 50 Plus for this age group see page 131.

Age Positive website

The Government has launched an Age Positive website (*www.agepositive.gov.uk*) to promote the Code of Practice on Age Diversity in Employment. The code highlights the business benefits of an age-diverse workforce and sets the standard for non-ageist approaches to recruitment, selection, training, promotion, redundancy and retirement. The website includes good practice guides with case studies illustrating how organisations have tackled some of the issues.

Over 90 per cent of people above retirement age were economically inactive in spring 2002, but 886,000 of them were in employment, an increase of 9 per cent on the previous year.

Young people

The economic activity of 16–19 year olds is closely linked to their participation in full-time education (FTE). Of those not in FTE in spring 2002, 85 per cent were economically active, of whom 18 per cent were ILO unemployed. For those in FTE, 44 per cent were economically active.

There has been an increase in youth ILO unemployment, with 406,000 people aged 18 to 24 unemployed in spring 2002, 5 per cent higher than a year earlier. However, the number who had been out of work for more than a year fell by 19 per cent, suggesting that long-term unemployment among younger people continues to fall.

Ethnicity and the labour market

In spring 2002 there were estimated to be 3.1 million people aged 16 and over from minority ethnic groups in the UK, of whom 1.7 million were in employment. The working age employment rate for all minority ethnic groups was 58.3 per cent, compared with 75.8 per cent for the White group. There were differences between the employment rates of people from different minority ethnic groups, ranging from 67.0 per cent and 65.3 per cent for those from the Indian and Black Caribbean groups to 47.0 per cent and 35.5 per cent for those from the Pakistani and Bangladeshi groups. These figures are affected by the comparatively low employment rates of women of Pakistani and Bangladeshi origin (27.9 per cent and 17.7 per cent respectively), compared with 71.2 per cent for White women and 64.0 per cent for Black Caribbean women.

In spring 2002 the ILO unemployment rate for all minority ethnic groups was 10.7 per cent, more than double the rate for the White group (4.7 per cent). There were wide variations between minority ethnic groups: for example, 24.2 per cent for those from the Bangladeshi group; 14.6 per cent for those from the Black African group and 6.2 per cent for those from the Indian group. The overall ILO unemployment rate among women from minority ethnic groups was 9.7 per cent, compared with 11.4 per cent for men.

Disability and the labour market

In spring 2002 there were 7 million people of working age with long-term disabilities (using the LFS definition) in the UK, of whom just over half were economically active. The rates of ILO unemployment among disabled people were higher than for those not long-term disabled (8.6 per cent compared with 4.7 per cent). Among the economically inactive, those with disabilities were more likely to want a job than those without a disability. For details on the New Deal for Disabled People see page 131.

> **Then and now**
> The workforce has grown by about a fifth over the last 50 years. However, while the number of men in employment has barely risen, the female workforce has grown by two-thirds. As a result, almost half of the workforce is now female, compared with around a third in 1952.

Households with no one in work

The number of workless households (among households where at least one adult was of working age) was 3.1 million in spring 2002, an increase of 70,000 since spring 2001 but 138,000

fewer than five years earlier. This represented a rate of worklessness of 16.4 per cent in spring 2002, compared with 17.9 per cent in 1997.

Unemployment

The trend in the unemployment rate was steadily downward from 1993 to spring 2001. However, the latest estimates point to a slight increase. The UK ILO unemployment rate in spring 2002 was 5.2 per cent, an increase of 0.3 percentage points since the same period in 2001. The new rate represents nearly 1.6 million ILO unemployed people (see Table 11.1) and compares with the EU average of 7.6 per cent and the G7 group of nations average of 6.5 per cent. Within the UK, the rate fell by 0.8 percentage points in Northern Ireland (to 5.4 per cent), and rose by 1.0 percentage points (to 6.9 per cent) in Scotland. Within England, London and the North East had the highest ILO unemployment rates, at 6.9 per cent. In addition, there can be significant variations in unemployment rates within regions.

In recent years there have been substantial falls in long-term unemployment. In spring 2002 some 343,000 people aged 16 and over had been ILO unemployed for a year or more, of whom 183,000 had been out of work for two years or more. These figures represent falls of 10 per cent and 16 per cent respectively since spring 2001.

In April 2002 the claimant count was 951,600, representing 3.2 per cent of the total UK workforce. Around two-thirds had been claiming benefits for less than six months and 44 per cent for less than 13 weeks.

Redundancies

Redundancy levels in the UK have remained roughly constant since the statistical series began in 1995. In spring 2002, 201,000 people were made redundant, representing a redundancy rate of 8.1 per 1,000 employees. Redundancy rates were highest in manufacturing and transport, and lowest in the public administration, education and health sectors.

Working patterns

Over the past decade, three-quarters of those in employment have been permanent full-time workers. In spring 2002 there were 21.4 million people in full-time employment, an increase of nearly 2 million since 1993 (see Table 11.3). Significant numbers of people have alternative

Economic inactivity

In spring 2002, there were 7.8 million economically inactive people of working age in the UK, of whom 2.3 million wanted a job but were either not seeking work or were not available to start work. Sickness and disability are the major reasons for economic inactivity among men. Looking after the family or home is the most common reason for inactivity among women – 44 per cent of women who wanted a job gave this as their main reason for inactivity. Government policy is aimed at helping those who are currently inactive to make the transition towards activity, primarily through the New Deal programme (see page 131) and the introduction of Jobcentre Plus (see page 130).

employment patterns, such as part-time working and second and temporary jobs.

Part-time work

There were over 7 million people in part-time work in the UK in spring 2002 (see Table 11.3), of whom 80 per cent were women. Over the past decade the number of people working part time has increased by over 1 million, but as a proportion of all those in employment it has remained at around 25 per cent. People work part time for a variety of reasons. In spring 2002 nearly 75 per cent did not want a full-time job while 8 per cent were working part time because they could not find full-time work, a

proportion which has steadily decreased over the past decade.

Secondary and temporary work

Just under 1.2 million people had a second job in spring 2002, a small decrease over the year. About 1.6 million people (6 per cent of all employees) were engaged in temporary jobs in spring 2002, 8 per cent fewer than in spring 2001. Temporary employment is lower in the UK than in most other EU countries. Of temporary employees in spring 2002, a quarter worked in a temporary job because they could not find a permanent one and almost a third because they preferred to do so.

Overseas workers

More temporary overseas workers would be able to come to the UK under plans announced by the Home Office in May 2002. The Government is consulting on expanding two existing foreign workers schemes – the Working Holidaymakers Scheme (WHS) and the Seasonal Agricultural Workers Scheme – to meet recruitment difficulties and demand for short-term and seasonal workers. The Government wants to encourage young people from all Commonwealth countries to take part and is proposing a number of changes aimed at increasing participation, such as increasing the upper age limit and relaxing the restrictions on the type and amount of work holidaymakers can do during their stay.

Table 11.3 Employment status of the UK workforce[1]

Thousands

	1998	1999	2000	2001	2002
Employees	23,657	24,119	24,622	24,889	25,060
Self-employed	3,290	3,232	3,178	3,193	3,249
Unpaid family workers	102	102	110	98	96
Government-supported training and employment programmes	178	159	144	151	105
Employment	**27,227**	**27,611**	**28,053**	**28,332**	**28,511**
of whom:					
Full-time workers	20,473	20,761	21,083	21,293	21,400
Part-time workers	6,755	6,850	6,970	7,038	7,111
Workers with a second job	1,190	1,282	1,191	1,185	1,151
Temporary workers	1,745	1,712	1,727	1,728	1,588

1 Spring figures, seasonally adjusted.
Source: Labour Force Survey, Office for National Statistics

Self-employment

In spring 2002, 3.2 million people (three-quarters of whom were men) were self-employed in the UK. This represented 11 per cent of those in employment, a small increase since spring 2001. Agriculture and fishing, and construction had the highest proportions of self-employed people, while relatively few of those engaged in manufacturing and public administration were self-employed.

Homeworking

Homeworking (defined as those who work mainly in their own home) is growing, but remains at a low level. In winter 2001/02, the LFS estimated that there were 650,000 people working as homeworkers in their main job, representing 2.3 per cent of all people in employment. Of these, 54 per cent worked part time and 63 per cent were women. Those in personal services were most likely to be homeworkers, and almost three-quarters of these were women working in childcare-related occupations.

Occupations

There has been a long-term growth in managerial and professional occupations and a decline in skilled trades, elementary occupations[3] and process, plant and machine operatives.

The patterns of occupations followed by men and women are quite different (Table 11.4). Nearly a quarter of women employees are in administrative and secretarial work, while men are most likely to be employed as managers and senior officials or in skilled trades. Only the professional and associated occupations, and elementary occupations, are followed by similar proportions of men and women.

Employment by sector

The major long-term trend in employment by sector in the UK has been a big increase in employment in service industries (see Table 11.5). Between March 1982 and March 2002 the number of workforce jobs in service industries increased from 17 million to 23 million, a rise of 38 per cent, compared with a rise in the total number of jobs of 16 per cent. Growth in finance and business services was particularly strong, up by 91 per cent in this period, although there were falls in the year to March 2002.

3 Occupations involving mainly routine tasks which do not require formal qualifications, but usually have a period of formal on-the-job training.

Table 11.4 Employment by gender[1] and occupation, UK, spring 2002[2]

	Percentages	
	Males	Females
Managers and senior officials	18	10
Professional occupations	12	10
Associate professional and technical	14	14
Administrative and secretarial	5	23
Skilled trades	20	2
Personal service	2	13
Sales and customer service	4	12
Process, plant and machine operatives	13	3
Elementary occupations	12	13
All employees[3] (million)	15.6	12.8

1 Males aged 16 to 64, females aged 16 to 59.
2 Not seasonally adjusted.
3 Includes a few people who did not state their occupation. Percentages are based on totals which exclude this group.
Source: Labour Force Survey, Office for National Statistics

In recent years most other sectors have experienced falling levels of employment, particularly the traditional manufacturing industries, such as steel, shipbuilding and textiles. Between 1982 and 2002 the total number of manufacturing jobs declined by 33 per cent. Agriculture and fishing have also declined, and in the year to March 2002 jobs in the sector fell by 3.9 per cent. The biggest long-term decline though has been in energy and water with a reduction of 70 per cent between 1982 and 2002, reflecting, among other things, a large fall in jobs in the coal industry.

Workforce skills

In its Green Paper *Towards Full Employment in a Modern Society* (see page 129), published in 2001, the Government outlined three goals in its strategy to help raise employability and productivity in the UK through the development of skills:

- to ensure that young people have the skills and rounded education to progress in employment and that adults can acquire the skills needed to get, keep and progress in decent jobs;

- to provide the technical and higher level skills needed by employers to improve business

Table 11.5 Workforce jobs by industry, UK, March 2002[1]

	Workforce jobs (thousands)	Per cent of workforce jobs	Per cent change 1982–2002
Agriculture and fishing	455	2	−28
Energy and water	192	1	−70
Manufacturing	3,959	13	−33
Construction	1,975	7	12
Services	22,917	78	38
Distribution, hotels and restaurants	6,754	23	24
Transport and communication	1,761	6	10
Finance and business services	5,692	19	91
Public administration, education and health	6,963	24	28
Other services	1,748	6	57
All jobs	**29,499**	*100*	16

1 Seasonally adjusted.
Source: Office for National Statistics

performance and raise productivity, and a system in which people are able to change and improve as jobs change; and

■ to ensure, in consultation with employers and the network of Sector Skills Councils (see page 115), that the skills people acquire are those which are needed in the labour market as well as for their personal development.

According to the LFS, in spring 2002 an estimated 3.9 million employees of working age received job-related training, representing 16 per cent of all employees.

England
The Learning and Skills Council (LSC) was set up in April 2001, with an annual budget of £7.4 billion, to replace the Training and Enterprise Councils and the Further Education Funding Council. Its key objectives include increasing engagement of employers in workforce development, maximising the achievement and participation in education and training of young people, and increasing the demand for learning by adults. One of its early tasks is to develop a measure to assess the participation of employers in the provision of education and training for post-16 year olds.

Scotland
Two organisations, Scottish Enterprise and Highlands and Islands Enterprise (HIE), deliver a

similar programme to the LSC in Scotland. Scottish Enterprise was set up in 1991 with a remit that includes highlighting the importance of developing skills, primarily through Local Enterprise Companies. The HIE lists among its key objectives improving the operation of the labour market and assisting in the development of the training and learning infrastructure.

Wales
The National Council for Education and Training for Wales and the Higher Education Funding Council for Wales are responsible for all post-16 education and training in Wales. This includes the delivery of training for adults and developing strategies for reducing the proportion of adults with no qualifications. Together these organisations are known as Education and Learning Wales (ELWa).

Northern Ireland
The Department for Employment and Learning (DEL) of the Northern Ireland Executive is responsible for higher and further education, employment, skill development and lifelong learning. The department's Learning and Skills Advisory Board was formed in January 2002 to advise on the business development of education, training and employment services.

Changes in skill requirements
The Skills in England Survey 2001 for the Department for Education and Skills (DfES)

highlighted a growth in jobs that require higher level skills, and a subsequent decline in those requiring lower level skills. The fastest growing occupational groups are professional occupations, such as information technology (IT) and software professionals, scientists and teachers; associate professional and technical occupations (such as nurses, police and estate agents); and personal service occupations (such as care assistants, travel agents and sports/leisure staff). According to the survey, there is an increasing need for specific technical skills as well as a greater demand for basic and generic skills (including verbal, numerical, planning and communication skills).

The Learning and Training at Work 2001 survey for the DfES (see Figure 11.6) found that IT is the most common course offered by employers and that training is also given in the generic skills identified by the Skills in England Survey. Overall, 88 per cent of employers had provided some job-related training to their employees in the previous 12 months.

The demand for different types of skill varies across regions and this is reflected in the organisational structure of skills management organisations, such as the LSC and Scottish Enterprise. Both organisations have a network of local learning and skills councils whose remit is to reflect the needs of the local economy. For information on attainment of qualifications, see chapter 10, page 108.

Investors in People

Investors in People (IiP) is the National Standard which sets a level of good practice for improving an organisation's performance through its people. It is designed to improve business performance by linking the training and development of employees to an organisation's business objectives. Reported benefits include increased productivity, higher profits, lower rates of absenteeism and improved morale. Investors in People UK, which is responsible for the promotion, quality assurance and development of the Standard, has carried out an extensive review to simplify the Standard and make it more accessible, especially for small firms. IiP celebrated its tenth anniversary in autumn 2001, by which time 25,595 organisations in the UK had been recognised as Investors in People. Almost 6 million employees work in recognised organisations, covering just over a fifth of the UK workforce.

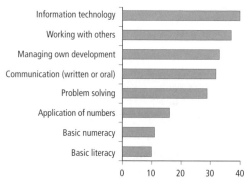

Figure 11.6 Proportion of employers offering learning opportunities, England, 2001

Per cent

Source: *Learning and Training at Work Survey*, IFF Research Ltd for the Department for Education and Skills

Labour market policy

The Government's strategy for ensuring employment opportunity for all was set out in its Green Paper, *Towards Full Employment in a Modern Society*, published in 2001. It is based on:

- helping people to move from welfare to work, through extending the series of New Deals (see page 131);

- easing the transition to work by removing barriers to working and ensuring that people are financially secure when moving from welfare to work;

- making paid work more attractive, through promoting incentives to work and reforming the tax and benefits system (see chapters 23 and 12); and

- securing progression in work through lifelong learning, in order to ensure that people are well trained and able to adapt to changing economic circumstances.

New Deal

The Government's welfare-to-work programme is delivered throughout the UK primarily through a number of 'New Deal' programmes, targeted at specific groups (see page 131).

In 2002/03 the provision for expenditure on New Deals includes £354 million for young people, £302 million for the 25 plus programme, £142 million for lone parents and £58 million for disabled people.

Welfare-to-Work

In February 2002 the DWP announced a series of measures to help people into work, including:

- *Step Up* – a £40 million programme, from April 2002, to provide guaranteed jobs in areas of high unemployment;

- *Progress2work* – a £40 million programme helping drug misusers find employment;

- *Adviser Discretion Fund* – which gives New Deal advisers access to up to £300 per jobseeker to help with the practical aspects of starting work, including buying clothes for interviews, travel to interviews and to work, and necessary equipment; and

- *Ambition Programmes* – industry-specific training and recruitment programmes in sectors such as IT, retailing and construction.

Existing programmes include:

- *Employment Zones* – these have been piloted as an alternative for the New Deal 25 plus client group in 15 areas where there are high concentrations of unemployment. Introduced in April 2000, new approaches in these areas include the use of personal job accounts, which allow for a more flexible use of available funds.

- *Action Teams for Jobs* – Action teams in 63 areas in Great Britain aim to remove the barriers to employment faced by jobless people and, by working with employers, to move them into suitable vacancies. The teams look at innovative ways of achieving their aim, and lessons learned are incorporated in the main Jobcentre Plus services. The Budget in April 2002 provided £15 million a year to support transport schemes where travel is a barrier to work.

Recruitment and job finding

There are a variety of ways in which people look for work in the UK. According to the LFS, in winter 2001/02, more than half of all employees found out about the vacancy for their current job by hearing from someone who worked there or by replying to an advertisement.

Jobcentre Plus

In April 2002 parts of the Benefits Agency and Employment Service in Great Britain were replaced by the Jobcentre Plus network (*www.jobcentreplus.gov.uk*), which provides help in finding jobs and pays benefits to people of working age. It has responsibility for running local offices formerly managed by the Employment Service and the Benefits Agency, including Jobcentres and social security offices. A similar programme to combine jobcentre and social security offices is under way in Northern Ireland. The new offices are known as 'Jobs and Benefits'.

In 17 areas in Great Britain Jobcentre Plus 'pathfinder' offices are already offering a fully integrated work and benefit service and there are plans to open further Jobcentre Plus offices from October 2002. The Department for Work and Pensions expects 225 new pathfinder offices to be opened by mid-2003. However, it will take several years to integrate the entire local office network of Jobcentres and Benefits Agency offices fully. During this time, services will continue to be provided in local social security offices and Jobcentres, which will be part of the Jobcentre Plus network.

All Jobcentre Plus vacancies are now available over the Internet, on one of the largest job banks in the world. Vacancies are also available through electronic touch-screen kiosks, known as 'Jobpoints', which are replacing traditional vacancy display boards in Jobcentres. Employers with a vacancy can now use the Employer Direct service, which provides a single national telephone number for employers to have their vacancies advertised on the Internet and on all Jobpoint terminals.

Advisory services

Most customers who make a claim for a working age benefit have to take part in a meeting with a personal adviser, for example to discuss help to find work or support such as training or childcare.

New Deal programme

Young people
- Aimed at 18 to 24 year olds who have been unemployed and claiming jobseeker's allowance (JSA) for six months.
- Begins with a period of advice and guidance, called 'the gateway'.
- After the gateway a young person must choose one of a number of options, including a job (with a subsidised salary), self-employment, training or placement with a voluntary organisation.
- All options include an element of education and training.

25 plus
- A compulsory programme for people aged 25 and over who have been claiming JSA for 18 months or more. Earlier admittance is also available for certain groups, such as homeless people, ex-offenders, recovering addicts and refugees.
- A gateway period of up to four months, with weekly interviews and job search support from a personal adviser.
- An intensive period of 13 weeks, for those aged 25–49, where individuals choose a mix of activities, including subsidised employment, work-focused training, work placements and self-employment support.
- A follow-up period of up to 13 weeks of regular interviews with personal advisers.

50 plus
- A voluntary programme for those aged over 50 who have been claiming work-related benefits for six months or more.
- Offers personal advice, job search help, a tax-free credit of £60 a week for up to a year for those going into full-time work and £40 for part-time work.

- An in-work training grant of up to £1,500 over two years.

Lone parents
- Compulsory meeting with a personal adviser to discuss work issues and give advice on in-work benefits.
- Participation in the scheme is voluntary, after the initial interview.
- Participation in a work trial (if appropriate).
- Help with the costs of approved training or education courses.
- Help with costs incurred while training, such as travel expenses and registered childcare costs.

Disabled people
- Delivered by a range of organisations called Job Brokers, tasked with helping sick and disabled people into work.
- Job Brokers advise about job search and training, and offer support when the jobseeker starts work.
- People with disabilities are eligible for inclusion in all New Deal activities without a qualifying period.

Partners
- Designed for the partners of people claiming a range of work- and sickness-related benefits, with the aim of reducing the number of workless households.
- Offers help with job search activities, training opportunities, and a short course to refresh or boost existing skills before starting a job, or help and support with setting up a new business.

If the individual is claiming benefits other than jobseeker's allowance (JSA) (see chapter 12, page 153), it is his or her decision whether or not to look for work.

Jobcentre Plus advisers see all jobseekers when a claim is made for JSA to assess their eligibility and to provide advice about jobs, training and self-employment opportunities. To receive the allowance, each unemployed person has to complete a Jobseeker's Agreement, which sets out his or her availability for work, the types of job for which he or she is looking, and the steps which, if taken, offer the best chance of securing work. Jobseekers are required to attend a job search review each fortnight and periodic intensive advisory interviews to assess their situation and see what additional help, if any, is needed and, if appropriate, to revise the Jobseeker's Agreement.

A modular approach to job search courses is being developed, which takes more account of individual needs and local conditions. Other programmes include Jobclubs (offering guidance on jobseeking, interview skills and other practical assistance), Jobplan workshops (a five-day programme of individual assessment) and work trial, where jobseekers spend up to 15 days in an actual vacancy.

Employment agencies

There are many private employment agencies, including several large firms with significant branch networks. The law governing the conduct of employment agencies is less restrictive in the UK than in many other EU countries, but agencies must comply with legislation which establishes a framework of minimum standards designed to protect agency users, both workers and hirers.

The Recruitment and Employment Confederation is the association for the private recruitment and staffing industry in the UK. It has a membership of over 6,000 recruitment agencies and over 8,000 recruitment consultants. All members must abide by a code of good recruitment practice.

Pay and conditions

Earnings

According to the New Earnings Survey, average gross weekly earnings for all employees in Great Britain were £356 in April 2001. This represented

a 5.3 per cent increase since April 2000. Weekly earnings for full-time adult workers whose pay was not affected by absence were £444, an increase of 5.9 per cent since April 2000.

Average hourly pay for full-time male adult employees whose pay was not affected by absence was £11.97 in April 2001, compared with £9.76 for female employees. The pay gap between men and women has been narrowing in recent years (see page 95).

Average gross weekly earnings for full-time employees ranged from £381 in the North East to £594 in London.

According to the New Earnings Survey, the average gross weekly pay of treasurers and company financial managers was six times that of those working as retail cash desk and check-out operators (see Table 11.7). The weekly pay of the former increased by 11.4 per cent in the year to April 2001 and the latter by 5.4 per cent.

Table 11.7 Highest and lowest paid occupations,[1] Great Britain, April 2001

Average gross weekly pay (£)

Highest paid	
Treasurers and company financial managers	1,180
Aircraft flight deck officers	1,126
Medical practitioners	1,097
Underwriters, claims assessors, brokers, investment analysts	909
Management consultants, business analysts	886
Lowest paid	
Counterhands, catering assistants	204
Petrol pump forecourt attendants	204
Bar staff	199
Kitchen porters, hands	197
Retail cash desk and check-out operators	195

1 Full-time employees on adult rates, whose pay was unaffected by absence. Certain occupations have been excluded due to the small size of the sample.
Source: New Earnings Survey, 2001, Office for National Statistics

National minimum wage

The statutory national minimum wage (NMW) took effect from 1 April 1999. Minimum wage rates, from 1 October 2002, are:

- £4.20 an hour for those aged 22 or above; and

- £3.60 an hour for workers aged 18 to 21, and for those aged 22 or over receiving accredited training in the first six months of a new job with a new employer.

Almost all workers who are 18 or over are covered by the NMW – there are no exemptions for casual workers, agency workers, part-time workers, overseas workers or workers in small businesses. The only workers to whom it does not apply are the self-employed, people under 18 years of age, prisoners, voluntary workers, members of the armed forces, family members of the employer living in the employer's home, and unrelated people living in their employer's home who are treated as part of the family (for example, au pairs). Apprentices and trainees are exempted for the first year of their training.

The NMW is enforced through a combination of measures. For example:

- employers are required to keep NMW records;

- Inland Revenue Compliance Officers investigate all complaints about non-payment of the NMW, visit other employers thought to be likely to pay below the minimum wage, and take enforcement action where necessary; and

- individuals can take action through an employment tribunal or civil court.

The Department of Trade and Industry (DTI) and Inland Revenue work to publicise employer obligations and employee rights, principally through direct advertising, the DTI employment rights website (*www.tiger.gov.uk*) and the NMW helpline.

Fringe benefits

Fringe benefits are used by many employers to provide additional rewards to their employees. They include schemes to encourage financial participation by employees in their companies, pension schemes, medical insurance, subsidised meals, company cars and childcare schemes.

Many companies have adopted employee share schemes, known as share incentive plans, where employees receive free shares or options to buy

shares at a discount from their employer without paying income tax. A new all-employee share ownership plan was introduced in 2000, allowing employees to buy shares from their pre-tax salary and to receive free shares, with tax incentives for longer-term shareholding.

Hours of work

In spring 2002 the average weekly hours worked by full-time workers in the UK in their main job was 38 hours: 40 hours for men and 34 hours for women. For part-time workers the average was 16 hours.

Hours worked tend to be longest in agriculture, energy and water, and transport and communications, and shortest in public administration, education and health. The differences between industries also reflect the mix of part-time and full-time workers, as well as any difference in the standard working week. Self-employed people work, on average, longer hours than full-time employees.

Regulations implementing two EC Directives on working time and on young workers (in relation to rest and health assessments for adolescents) came into force in the UK in 1998. They apply to full-time, part-time and temporary workers, although workers in certain sectors – including transport, sea fishing, other work at sea, and doctors in training – are currently exempt. They provide for:

- a maximum working week of 48 hours (on average), although individual workers can choose to work longer;

- a minimum of four weeks' annual paid leave;

- minimum daily, weekly and in-work rest periods;

- a limit for night workers of an average eight hours' work in a 24-hour period; and

- a right for night workers to receive free health assessments.

There are specific provisions for adolescent workers in respect of the entitlement to rest and health assessments. Specific working time and night work limits are planned to come into force later in 2002.

Industrial relations

Individual employment rights

Employment protection legislation provides a number of safeguards for employees. For example, most employees have a right to a written statement setting out details of the main conditions, including pay, hours of work and holidays.

Employees with at least two years of continuous employment with their employer are entitled to lump sum redundancy payments if their jobs cease to exist and their employers cannot offer suitable alternative work.[4]

Minimum periods of notice are laid down for both employers and employees. Most employees who believe they have been unfairly dismissed have the right to complain to an employment tribunal (see page 135), subject to the general qualifying period of one year's continuous service. If the complaint is upheld, the tribunal may make an order for re-employment or award compensation.

Legislation prohibits discrimination, in employment, training and related matters, on grounds of sex or marital status, disability, or race, nationality (including citizenship) or ethnic or national origin (see pages 94–5). The disability discrimination legislation applies to employers with 15 or more employees. In Northern Ireland discrimination in employment, training and related matters on grounds of religious belief or political opinion is also unlawful. Legislation is currently being introduced to implement the EC Article 13 Employment Directive, which will extend protection against discrimination in employment and training to cover sexual orientation and religion by 2003 and age by 2006.

The purpose of the *Equal Pay Act 1970* is to eliminate pay discrimination between women and men, when doing work that is the same or broadly similar, work which is rated as equivalent, or work which is of equal value.

The Disability Rights Commission, the Equal Opportunities Commission and the Commission for Racial Equality have powers to investigate cases of discrimination at work in Great Britain. The Equality Commission in Northern Ireland has similar powers.

All pregnant employees have the right to statutory maternity leave with their non-wage contractual benefits maintained, and to protection against detriment and dismissal because of pregnancy. Statutory maternity pay is payable by an employer for up to 18 weeks to women with at least six months' service with that employer (see chapter 12, page 147).

Employment Act 2002

The main areas covered by this Act are paternity and adoption leave and pay, maternity leave and pay, flexible working for parents of young children, employment tribunal reform and dispute resolution in the workplace. It includes provisions for:

- six months paid, and a further six months unpaid, maternity leave for mothers;

- two weeks paid paternity leave for fathers;

- six months paid, and six months unpaid, leave for working adoptive parents;

- reforms of the employment tribunals system, including provision for cost recovery for management time in vexatious cases;

- requirements on employers to provide statutory grievance procedures at the workplace to help resolve disputes;

- requirements on employees, in most cases, to begin these procedures before taking a complaint to a tribunal;

- changes to the way tribunals calculate awards, to take into account whether the procedures have been used; and

- rights to time off for trade union learning representatives.

An Employment Bill making similar provision for maternity, paternity and adoption leave and pay in Northern Ireland is currently before the Northern Ireland Assembly.

---

4 The statutory redundancy payment is calculated according to a formula based on a person's age, the number of years of continuous service up to a maximum of 20 years and his or her weekly pay up to the current maximum of £250 per week. However, many employers pay more than the statutory amount.

Employment tribunals

Employment tribunals in Great Britain have jurisdiction over complaints covering a range of employment rights, including unfair dismissal, redundancy pay, equal pay, and sex and race discrimination. New tribunal regulations, including provisions designed to deter cases with weak claims and defences, took effect in July 2001. Further reforms will be brought about by the *Employment Act 2002* when the provisions in Part Two of the Act are brought into force. Tribunals received over 112,000 applications in 2001/02. Northern Ireland has a separate tribunal system.

Labour disputes

In the past 20 years there has been a substantial decline in working days lost through labour disputes. In the year to March 2002 there were 165 stoppages of work arising from labour disputes in the UK, and 584,400 working days were lost as a result. Stoppages over working conditions accounted for 43 per cent of days lost, compared with 34 per cent due to disputes over pay. During this period 51 per cent of working days lost were in the public administration and defence sector, with the next highest sector being transport, storage and communication, at 17 per cent.

Trade unions and employers' organisations

Trade unions

Trade unions have members in nearly all occupations. As well as negotiating pay and other terms and conditions of employment with employers, they provide benefits and services, such as educational facilities, financial services, legal advice and aid in work-related cases.

In autumn 2001 there were 7.6 million trade union members in the UK according to the Labour Force Survey, a reduction of 30,000 since 2000.[5] The proportion of employees who are union members was 29.1 per cent (compared with 32.3 per cent in 1995), and the proportion among those in employment was 26.8 per cent (29.0 per cent in 1995).

Trade union membership is more prevalent among older employees, those with long service and those in the public sector. By occupation, union membership is highest among professionals, nearly half of whom were trade union members in 2001. The long-term decline in membership has been particularly noticeable where membership has traditionally been high – among male employees, manual workers and those in production industries. Public administration has the highest density of union members, around 60 per cent of all employees. Sectors with relatively few union members include agriculture, forestry and fishing, hotels and restaurants, and wholesale and retail trade.

The largest union in the United Kingdom is the public service union UNISON which has around 1.3 million members. Other unions with membership over 500,000 are:

- Amicus – a new union formed in January 2002 by the merger of the Amalgamated Engineering and Electrical Union and the Manufacturing, Science and Finance union;

- the Transport and General Workers Union; and

- the GMB – a general union with members in a wide range of industries.

At the end of March 2002 there were 199 trade unions on the list maintained by the Certification Officer, who, among other duties, is responsible for certifying the independence of trade unions. Entry on the list is voluntary but to be eligible a trade union must show that it consists wholly or mainly of workers and that its principal purposes include the regulation of relations between workers and employers or between workers and employers' associations. A further 20 unions were known to the Certification Officer.

Trades Union Congress

The national body of the trade union movement in England and Wales is the Trades Union Congress (TUC), founded in 1868. In autumn 2001 its affiliated membership comprised 71 trade unions, which together represented some 6.7 million people.

---

5 There are two main sources of information on trade union membership: the ONS Labour Force Survey and data provided by trade unions to the Certification Office. Differences in coverage can result in different estimates. For example, the Certification Officer's figure for trade union membership in 2000/01 was 7.8 million, compared with the Labour Force Survey figure in autumn 2001 of 7.6 million members among those in employment.

There are six TUC regional councils for England and a Wales Trades Union Council. The TUC annual Congress meets in September to discuss matters of concern to trade unionists. A General Council represents the TUC between annual meetings.

In Scotland there is a separate national body, the Scottish Trades Union Congress, to which UK unions usually affiliate their Scottish branches. Nearly all trade unions in Northern Ireland are represented by the Northern Ireland Committee of the Irish Congress of Trade Unions (ICTU). Most trade unionists in Northern Ireland are members of unions affiliated to the ICTU, while the majority also belong to unions based in Great Britain, which are affiliated to the TUC.

The TUC participates in international trade union activity, through its affiliation to the International Confederation of Free Trade Unions and the European Trade Union Confederation. It also nominates the British workers' delegation to the annual International Labour Conference.

The TUC initiated the TUC Partnership Institute in 2001 to provide an advisory and training service to help unions and employers establish partnerships at work.

Trade union and industrial relations law
Among the legal requirements governing trade unions are:

- All individuals have the right not to be dismissed or refused employment (or the services of an employment agency) because of membership or non-membership of a trade union.

- Where a union is recognised by an employer for collective bargaining purposes, union officials are entitled to paid time off for undertaking certain trade union duties and training. The employer is also obliged to disclose information to the union for collective bargaining purposes.

- A trade union must elect every member of its governing body, its general secretary and its president. Elections must be held at least every five years and be carried out by a secret postal ballot under independent scrutiny.

- If a trade union wishes to set up a political fund, its members must first agree in a secret

ballot a resolution adopting those political objectives as an aim of the union. The union must also ballot its members every ten years to maintain the fund. Union members have a statutory right to opt out of contributing to the fund.

- For a union to have the benefit of statutory immunity when organising industrial action, the action must be wholly or mainly due to a trade dispute between workers and their own employer. Industrial action must not involve workers who have no dispute with their own employer (so-called 'secondary' action) or involve unlawful forms of picketing. Before calling for industrial action, a trade union must obtain the support of its members in a secret postal ballot.

Employers' organisations
Many employers in the UK are members of employers' organisations, some of which are wholly concerned with labour matters, while others are also trade associations concerned with commercial matters in general. Employers' organisations are usually established on an industry basis rather than a product basis, for example, the Engineering Employers' Federation. A few are purely local in character or deal with a sector of an industry or, for example, with small businesses; most are national and are concerned with the whole of an industry. At the end of March 2002, there were 94 employers' associations on the list maintained by the Certification Officer and a further 90 were known to the Certification Officer.

Most national organisations belong to the CBI (see page 345), which represents around 200,000 businesses.

ACAS
The Advisory, Conciliation and Arbitration Service (ACAS) is an independent statutory body with a general duty of promoting the improvement of industrial relations. ACAS aims to operate through the voluntary co-operation of employers, employees and, where appropriate, their representatives. Its main functions are collective conciliation; provision of arbitration and mediation; advisory mediation services for preventing disputes and improving industrial relations through the joint involvement of employers and employees; and the provision of a

public enquiry service. ACAS also conciliates in disputes on individual employment rights, and in April 2001 introduced a new voluntary arbitration system for resolving unfair dismissal claims. The overall number of complaints was 105,304 in 2000/01. In 2000/01 there were a total of 17,657 complaints of discrimination on the grounds of sex, race or disability, compared with 14,543 in 1999/2000. Over 70 per cent of all cases handled by ACAS were settled at the conciliation stage or were withdrawn and did not reach a tribunal.

In Northern Ireland the Labour Relations Agency, an independent statutory body, provides services similar to those provided by ACAS in Great Britain.

Health and safety at work

There has been a long-term decline in injuries to employees in the UK, partly reflecting a change in industrial structure away from the traditional heavy industries, which tend to have higher risks. In Great Britain in 2001/02 there were 249 deaths of employees and the self-employed from injuries at work, which represented a fatal injury rate of almost one per 100,000 workers. Falls from a height, being struck by a moving/flying object and being struck by a moving vehicle continue to be the three most common kinds of accident, accounting for 27 per cent, 17 per cent and 16 per cent of fatal injuries respectively.

The principal legislation in this area is the *Health and Safety at Work etc. Act 1974*. It imposes general duties on everyone concerned with work activities, including employers, the self-employed, employees, and manufacturers and suppliers of materials for use at work. Associated Acts and regulations deal with particular hazards and types of work. Employers with five or more staff must prepare a written statement of their health and safety policy and bring it to the attention of their staff.

The Department for Work and Pensions has lead responsibility for the sponsorship of the Health and Safety Commission and Health and Safety Executive. Other government departments have specific health and safety responsibilities, for example, the Department of Trade and Industry for civil nuclear matters and the Department for Transport for rail passenger safety.

Northern Ireland
The regulatory regime for health and safety at work in Northern Ireland broadly mirrors that of Great Britain. The principal legislation is contained in the Health and Safety at Work (Northern Ireland) Order 1978 as amended by the Health and Safety at Work (Amendment) (Northern Ireland) Order 1998. The Health and Safety Executive for Northern Ireland has primary responsibility for enforcing legislation. In 2001/02 there were nine fatal accidents in the workplace.

Health and Safety Commission
The Health and Safety Commission (HSC) has responsibility for developing policy on health and safety at work in Great Britain, including proposals for new or revised regulations and approved codes of practice. Recent work has concentrated on a simpler and more effective system of regulation.

The HSC has advisory committees covering subjects such as toxic substances, genetic modification and the safety of nuclear installations. There are also several industry advisory committees, each covering a specific sector of industry.

Health and Safety Executive
The Health and Safety Executive (HSE) is the primary instrument for carrying out the HSC's policies and has day-to-day responsibility for enforcing health and safety law.

In premises such as offices, shops, warehouses, restaurants and hotels, legislation is enforced by inspectors appointed by local authorities, working under guidance from the HSE.

> The HSE issued 11,058 enforcement notices in 2000/01, compared with 11,340 in 1999/2000. About 70 per cent of these notices were issued in the manufacturing and construction industries.

The HSE's Technology Division provides technical advice on industrial health and safety matters. The Health and Safety Laboratory (HSL), an agency of the HSE, aims to ensure that risks to health and safety from work activities are properly controlled. This involves HSL in two main areas: operational support through incident investigations and studies of workplace situations; and longer-term work on analysis and resolution of occupational health and safety problems.

Further reading

Labour Market Trends. Office for National Statistics. Monthly.

Labour Market Bulletin. Northern Ireland Department for Employment and Learning. Annual.

Towards Full Employment in a Modern Society. Department for Education and Employment, HM Treasury and the Department of Social Security. Cm 5084. The Stationery Office, 2001.

Annual reports

Advisory, Conciliation and Arbitration Service. ACAS.

Certification Officer. Certification Office for Trade Unions and Employers' Associations.

Health and Safety Commission. HSC.

Websites

Department for Employment and Learning (Northern Ireland)
www.delni.gov.uk

Department for Work and Pensions
www.dwp.gov.uk

Department of Trade and Industry
www.dti.gov.uk

Health and Safety Executive
www.hse.gov.uk

Learning and Skills Council
www.lsc.gov.uk

Office for National Statistics
www.statistics.gov.uk

Trades Union Congress
www.tuc.org.uk

WWW.

12 Social protection

Social protection refers to support provided by central government, local authorities and private bodies (such as voluntary organisations) related to certain needs or stages of the life cycle. Help may be provided to children and families; older people and survivors (such as widows); those who are physically disabled or sensorily impaired; people with learning disabilities or mental health problems; and low earners and the unemployed. Social protection by central government and local authorities is principally provided through the social security system and personal social services.

The social security system is designed to secure a basic standard of living for people in financial need. It provides income during periods of inability to earn (including periods of sickness and unemployment), pensions for retired people, financial help for low-income families and assistance with costs arising from disablement. The provision of these benefits is administered by the Department for Work and Pensions (DWP) in Great Britain and the Social Security Agency of the Department for Social Development in Northern Ireland. Tax credits are administered by the Inland Revenue.

Since April 2002 the DWP has administered benefits and provided advice principally through the Jobcentre Plus network and the Pension Service, which replaced elements of the Benefits Agency and the Employment Service (see page 130).

Personal social services refers to the assessment for and provision of practical help and support for older people, people with disabilities, vulnerable children and young people, those with mental health problems or learning disabilities, and their families and carers. Major services include

residential, day care, short-break and domiciliary services (provided for people needing support to live in their own homes). In certain circumstances, direct cash payments may be made to enable individuals to obtain relevant services for themselves.

In Great Britain, these services are predominantly provided by local authorities with social services responsibilities and by the voluntary and not-for-profit sectors. The social services departments of local authorities are responsible for ensuring the direct provision or commissioning of services and ensuring that people receive a high-quality service, regardless of the provider. In Northern Ireland services are provided by Health and Social Services (HSS) Trusts.

Central government is responsible for establishing national policies, issuing guidance and overseeing standards. There are plans, subject to parliamentary approval, for establishing a new body to be called the Commission for Social Care Inspection, which will inspect all aspects of personal social services.

Various voluntary and charitable organisations also offer care, assistance and support to vulnerable members of society. Examples include the Anchor Trust, which provides retirement housing, residential and home care services to older people, and Barnardo's, which aims to enable children to address problems like abuse, homelessness and poverty, and to tackle the challenges of disability. Citizens Advice Bureaux (see page 476) offer free, confidential, impartial and independent advice on many social issues including benefits, housing, debt, legal matters, employment, and immigration. They also use evidence from this work to try to influence policies and improve services.

Expenditure

Average social protection expenditure per head within the EU was € 5,793 in 1999. UK expenditure per head was just above this average, at € 5,872 (see Figure 12.1). These figures include government expenditure on social security and personal social services, sick pay paid by employers, and payments made from occupational and personal pension schemes. They are expressed in purchasing power parities (which take account of the general level of prices within each country) in order to allow direct comparisons. Different levels of expenditure therefore reflect differences in social protection systems, demographic structures, unemployment rates and other social, institutional and economic factors.

Social security is the largest single area of UK government spending. Spending on social security benefits, including tax credits, was £110 billion in 2001/02. Figure 12.2 shows how social security benefits expenditure (excluding tax credits) is distributed between different kinds of recipients within Great Britain. In the 2002 Budget it was announced that resources for social security benefits and tax credits in the UK would increase to £136 billion in 2005/06.

General taxation provides over half the income for the social security programme, employers'

National Insurance contributions (NICs) around a quarter and employees' NICs about a fifth.

In 2000/01 gross expenditure on personal social services by local authorities was £13 billion in England. Expenditure on older people accounted for 46 per cent of the total and children accounted for 22 per cent (see Figure 12.4). In Scotland expenditure on social work services was £1.6 billion. Local authorities in Wales spent £681 million.

In the 2002 Budget the Chancellor of the Exchequer announced that resources for personal social services in England would grow by 6 per cent a year in real terms over the next three years, and that spending on the National Health Service (NHS) would rise by 7.4 per cent a year for five years (see page 167).

The social security system

Benefits

Social security benefits can be grouped into three types:

- *means-tested,* available to people whose income and savings are below certain levels;

Figure 12.1 Expenditure[1] on social protection in the EU, 1999

€ per head

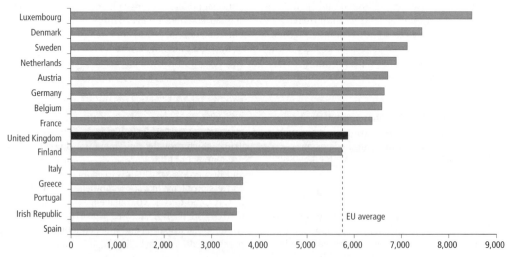

1 Before deduction of tax, where applicable. Tax credits are generally excluded. Figures are Purchasing Power
   Parities per inhabitant.
Source: Eurostat

Figure 12.2 Social security benefits expenditure, by recipient group, Great Britain, 2001/02

Total: £108.3 billion

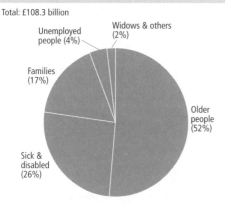

1 Excludes tax credits.
Source: Department for Work and Pensions

- *contributory,* paid to people who have made the required contributions to the *National Insurance Fund* (see below); and

- benefits which are neither means-tested nor contributory (mainly paid to cover extra costs, for example of disability, or paid universally, for example Child Benefit).

Most benefits are increased annually in line with percentage increases in retail prices. The main benefits (payable weekly) are described on pages 142 and 152. Table 12.3 gives the numbers of recipients of key benefits and tax credits.

Table 12.3 Numbers receiving selected social security benefits/tax credits in Great Britain, 2000

	Thousands
Retirement Pension	10,991
Child Benefit	7,108
Council Tax Benefit	4,731
Housing Benefit	3,952
Income Support	3,811
Disability Living Allowance	2,131
Incapacity Benefit	1,504
Attendance Allowance	1,250
Working Families' Tax Credit	1,195
Jobseeker's Allowance	973

Source: Department for Work and Pensions

Beveridge Report

The 60th anniversary of the publication of the *Social and Allied Services Report* (usually called the 'Beveridge Report', after its author) occurred in 2002. The report led to a complete overhaul of the social security system.

Large-scale unemployment in the 1930s had exposed the weaknesses of piecemeal provision. The report recommended a comprehensive system of National Insurance, to be topped up where necessary by national assistance and voluntary insurance. Benefit rates would be raised and cover extended to a wider range of people and risks. This 'social security' system would:

- replace earnings when they were lost or interrupted by unemployment, sickness or accident;

- provide for retirement after a certain age;

- provide against loss of support by the death of another person; and

- meet the cost of events such as birth, death or marriage.

The report recommended a flat rate of subsistence benefit – everyone would receive the same regardless of previous earnings. Similarly, there would be a flat rate of contribution, regardless of earnings or of the assumed degree of risk for particular individuals or forms of employment. This security was designed to provide the minimum income needed for subsistence. It left room for additional voluntary insurance, but did not assume it.

The post-war Government adopted many of the Beveridge Report's recommendations and it represents a key milestone in the development of social protection within the UK.

National Insurance contributions (NICs)

With the exception of a small National Health Service allocation, all National Insurance contributions are paid into the National Insurance Fund. All contributory benefits and their administrative costs are paid out of the Fund.

Entitlement to many benefits, for example Retirement Pension, Incapacity Benefit and

Selected key benefits and tax credits (at April 2002)

The basic *State Retirement Pension* is a taxable weekly benefit payable, if the contribution conditions have been met, to women from the age of 60 and men from the age of 65 (from 2020, the state pension age for both men and women will be 65). The basic pension is £75.50 for a single person and £120.70 for a married couple – lower rates apply for those who have not paid full contributions. It is not possible for people in work to choose to contract out of the basic scheme. There is an additional state pension scheme (see page 145), although many people contract out of this and belong instead to occupational schemes (run by employers), or personal pension plans (see page 145).

A *non-contributory retirement pension* of £45.20 a week is payable to people who are over 80 years of age, satisfy certain residence conditions and receive little or no state pension. People whose pensions do not give them enough to live on may be entitled to the Minimum Income Guarantee (see below).

Child Benefit is a tax-free, universal, non-contributory payment of £15.75 a week for the eldest qualifying child and £10.55 for each other child. It is not affected by income or savings and is payable for children up to the age of 16, and for those up to 19 who continue in full-time, non-advanced education.

Income Support is payable to certain people aged 16 or over who are not required to be available for work, and whose savings are below £8,000 (£12,000 for people aged over 60 and £16,000 for people in residential care or a nursing home). Those eligible include lone parents, pensioners, carers, and long-term sick and disabled people. Income Support is based on circumstances, including age and whether the claimant is single, a lone parent or has a partner.

The current rates are £32.50 for a person aged 16–17, £42.70 for someone aged 18–24 and £53.95 a week for people aged 25 or over. Couples aged 18 or over receive £84.65. There are additional allowances for dependent children and premium payments for those with extra expenses, for example, people with disabled children.

Minimum Income Guarantee is a benefit for those aged 60 or over. It tops up a person's income to £98.15 a week for a single person or £149.80 for a couple. The top-up may be higher for people with disabilities, carers or for those with dependent children.

Working Families' Tax Credit (WFTC) gives working families with children additional financial help. It is administered by the Inland Revenue and either paid directly or through workers' pay packets. Families (couples or lone parents) on low or middle incomes are eligible if they:

- have one or more children;

- work at least 16 hours a week;

- are resident and entitled to work in the UK; and

- have savings of £8,000 or less.

WFTC is made up of:

- basic credit – £62.50 per week;

- credit for working over 30 hours per week – £11.65; and

- tax credit for each child of £26.45 (aged up to 15 years) and £27.20 (aged 16 to 18).

contributory Jobseeker's Allowance, is dependent upon the payment of NICs. Employers, employees and self-employed people are all liable to pay contributions once their earnings exceed a certain amount. Where an employer operates an occupational pension scheme, the employee and his or her employer pay a reduced rate of contribution. The current NIC rates are set out on the Inland Revenue website (*www.inlandrevenue.gov.uk/rates*). In general, self-employed people make smaller payments and receive fewer benefits.

In the 2002 Budget the Chancellor of the Exchequer announced that there would be an increase in the rates of NICs from April 2003. This will be an additional 1 per cent contribution by employers, employees and the self-employed on all earnings above £89 per week.

Social care providers

Providers of care range from families, friends and volunteers to large statutory, voluntary and private

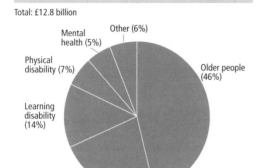

Figure 12.4 Local authority personal social services expenditure,[1] England, 2000/01

Total: £12.8 billion

- Other (6%)
- Mental health (5%)
- Physical disability (7%)
- Learning disability (14%)
- Older people (46%)
- Children (22%)

1 All figures include overhead costs.
Source: Department of Health

sector organisations. In England and Wales, the *Care Standards Act 2000*, and, in Scotland the *Regulation of Care (Scotland) Act 2001* established independent bodies to inspect and regulate social care services. Their remit includes a wide range of care services such as care homes and children's homes, private hospitals and clinics. The National Care Standards Commission (NCSC), the Scottish Commission for the Regulation of Care and the Care Standards Inspectorate for Wales all took over their regulatory powers in April 2002.

Informal carers

Much of the care given to older people and disabled people comes from families, volunteers and self-help groups. In 2000 one in six adults in Britain was caring for a sick, disabled or elderly person, and nearly one in ten was the main support for the person being looked after. Around 7 million adults in 5 million homes were providing care to their relatives or friends. Women were more likely to be carers than men (18 per cent compared with 14 per cent).

Invalid Care Allowance (ICA) is paid to full-time carers who are:

- aged 16 or over and under 65; and

- spending at least 35 hours a week looking after someone who is getting Attendance

Allowance, Disability Living Allowance at the middle or highest rate for personal care or Constant Attendance Allowance.

The rate in April 2002 was £42.45 a week. For every complete tax year it is received, this is counted as a contribution to the *State Second Pension* (see page 145). ICA is not paid if the carer is earning above £75 a week.

The *Carers and Disabled Children Act 2000*, implemented in England and Wales from 2001, provides carers with the right to have their need for services assessed by the local authority, and for the local authority to provide services direct to carers. The Act also extends the power of local authorities to offer direct payments to carers.

The *Community Care and Health (Scotland) Act 2002* (see page 147) entitles carers to have their ability to provide care assessed independently of the needs of the person receiving care. The Act also provides carers in Scotland with the right to have their views taken into account when any assessment of needs is carried out.

Local authorities

Local authority social services departments provide a wide range of support and services to children and their families, older people and those with learning disabilities, physical disabilities or mental health needs. This includes the assessment of needs, the provision of help, such as meals on wheels and home help, and the running of day centres and residential homes. Efforts are made in the provision of services to promote independence and choice, and to help disabled people live as independently as possible. A new framework for delivering housing support services, the Supporting People Programme, will begin in England and Wales in 2003 (see page 293).

In September 2001 social services departments in England employed 211,300 staff (full-time equivalent). This was 3 per cent fewer than in September 2000 and 10 per cent fewer than in September 1996. These reductions mainly reflect the transfer of some children's posts to education directorates and the greater use of the private sector for residential care and home care (see Table 12.5). In Scotland total numbers of staff were 34,700 for October 2001. This was 1.5 per cent higher than October 2000. In Wales there were 18,675 full-time equivalent staff in social service departments in September 2001, a 3 per cent increase since September 2000.

The *Care Standards Act 2000* established separate bodies in England and Wales to regulate the social care workforce. The General Social Care Council in England and the Care Council for Wales have responsibility for promoting high standards of conduct and training for social care workers by agreeing and issuing statutory codes of practice, setting up a register of social care workers, dealing with matters of conduct, and regulating and supporting social work education and training. The Scottish equivalent, the Scottish Social Services Council, was set up by the *Regulation of Care (Scotland) Act 2001*. The Council became operational in 2001.

Residential and nursing homes

Care homes provide a range of care for people who cannot manage at home. Residents who need regular and frequent care from a registered nurse are cared for in homes which are registered to provide nursing care. Most care homes are run by the independent sector. Residents' care and accommodation is funded in a number of ways: by the NHS where the person's primary need is for

Social services star ratings
In May 2002 the Social Services Inspectorate published the first-ever star ratings for local councils in England. Each council's performance across all social services was rated on a scale of zero to three stars. The ratings are intended to improve public information about the current performance of services. Eight councils (5 per cent) achieved a three-star rating, 50 (33 per cent) were awarded two stars and 82 (55 per cent) got a one-star rating. Ten councils (7 per cent) received a no-star rating.

healthcare, by local authority social services, or by the individual themselves following a means test. The elements covered by the means test vary in England, Scotland and Wales (see page 147).

Older people

People aged 65 and over represent the fastest growing section of the community (see chapter 9). About 52 per cent (£55.8 billion) of social security benefit expenditure in Great Britain is on older people (see Figure 12.2).

Table 12.5 Places available in residential care homes in England, by sector

	1996	1997	1998	1999	2000	Thousands 2001
Public sector[1]						
Older people	57.3	51.5	49.9	46.9	42.6	39.2
People with physical or sensory or learning disabilities	10.6	9.2	9.3	8.4	8.4	7.5
People with mental health problems[2]	4.7	4.9	4.5	3.5	4.1	3.9
Other people	0.1	0.2	0.2	0.2	0.3	0.2
All places in the public sector	72.7	65.8	64.0	59.0	55.5	50.9
Independent sector[3]						
Older people	185.3	190.2	196.9	197.5	197.8	197.6
People with physical or sensory or learning disabilities	41.0	46.9	48.7	50.7	53.7	52.9
People with mental health problems[2]	21.2	32.0	34.2	33.8	35.9	36.2
Other people	2.7	3.2	4.1	3.1	3.0	3.7
All places in the independent sector	250.3	272.3	283.9	285.0	290.4	290.3

1 Places in local authority residential care homes.
2 Figures include residential beds for older mentally infirm people.
3 Figures relate to residential places in private, voluntary, small (fewer than four places) and dual registered homes.
Source: Department of Health

Pensions

Additional state pension

It is possible to build up an additional state pension based on National Insurance contributions and earnings. Until recently this was known as the *State Earnings-Related Pension Scheme (SERPS)*, but on 6 April 2002 the *State Second Pension* was introduced to reform SERPS. Any SERPS entitlement that has already been built up is protected, both for those who have already retired and for those who have not yet reached pensionable age.

The State Second Pension provides a more generous additional state pension for low and moderate earners, and for certain carers and people with a long-term illness or disability who have not been able to make contributions. According to the Pension Service, around 18 million people will benefit from the reforms.

Occupational pensions

In 2000/01, according to the DWP's Family Resources Survey, 56 per cent of employees and 43 per cent of the self-employed were contributing to either an occupational or a personal pension scheme or both. About 10.3 million employees in the UK are acquiring rights to occupational pensions.

An occupational pension scheme is an arrangement employers make to provide pensions for their employees when they retire. These schemes may also provide a tax-free lump sum on retirement, and benefits for the dependants of an employee if he or she dies. Many employers provide occupational pension schemes and contribute more to them than the employee does. Two-thirds of large private sector employers (those with 20 or more employees) offer some form of pension provision. All employers with five or more employees are required to provide their employees with access to a stakeholder pension scheme (see below) if they do not provide access to an occupational scheme or to a personal pension with an employer contribution of at least 3 per cent.

There are two main types of occupational pension scheme:

Final salary schemes, which offer a predetermined level of pension benefit, expressed as a fixed proportion of the employee's final salary for every complete year as a scheme member. The scheme gives the member the option to convert part of the pension to a tax-free lump sum or may specifically provide a separate tax-free lump sum; and

Money purchase schemes, in which the contributions of the employer and the employee are invested. The size of the fund depends on the amount of these contributions and the performance of the investment. When an employee retires or leaves the scheme, he or she can receive a proportion of the fund as a tax-free lump sum, while the remainder must be used to purchase an annuity. An annuity is an arrangement by which a life assurance company pays a regular income, usually for life, in return for a lump-sum premium.

All pension rights built up after 6 April 1997 using final salary or money purchase schemes are protected against inflation.

Since 6 April 2001 members of occupational pension schemes have also been able to take out a personal pension or a stakeholder pension (see below) to build up extra pension provided they meet certain conditions. The main condition is that earnings from all employment do not exceed £30,000 a year.

Personal pensions

Personal pensions provide another way of making regular savings for retirement. Financial services companies, such as insurance companies, banks, investment companies and building societies, offer these plans and employers may make contributions in addition to those of employees. The money in the fund is invested to provide a pension when the owner retires.

Stakeholder pensions are a form of personal pension introduced by the Government in April 2001 to provide a pension option for people who do not have access to a good occupational or personal pension. Regulations provide that transfers can be made without charge from one stakeholder pension to another arrangement (including a different stakeholder) and for people to vary the amount that they contribute to the scheme. The annual administration charge must not exceed 1 per cent of fund value.

According to the Association of British Insurers, over 815,000 stakeholder pensions were sold between 6 April 2001 and 1 April 2002. Of these, around 100,000 were used to contract out of the additional state pension.

Regulation

The Occupational Pensions Regulatory Authority (OPRA) is the regulator of pension arrangements offered by employers and the registrar for occupational and personal pension schemes in the UK. It ensures that pension schemes comply with the *Pensions Act 1995* and the Pensions (Northern Ireland) Order 1995, which aimed to make pensions more secure. OPRA's Pension Schemes Registry maintains a register of all UK tax-approved occupational and personal pension schemes with two or more members, and offers a service for tracing pension schemes when people have lost touch (*www.opra.gov.uk/registry/regmenu.shtml*).

The Pensions Ombudsman deals with complaints of maladministration against occupational and personal pension schemes and adjudicates on disputes. The Office of the Pensions Advisory Service (OPAS) gives help and advice to people who have problems with their pensions.

The Pension Service

In April 2002 the Department for Work and Pensions set up new arrangements to improve the service received by pensioners and those who are planning for their retirement. The Pension Service works out and pays the amount of State Retirement Pension and Minimum Income Guarantee to which people are entitled. It also offers advice, and works in partnership with local organisations to help deliver related services.

Pension review

An independent review by Alan Pickering, published in July 2002, made a number of far-reaching recommendations for the simplification of pension legislation, including a new Pensions Act which would repeal or consolidate existing legislation on private pensions. The Government will consider the report, a related report on the commercial savings market (see page 461) and a forthcoming Inland Revenue report on the tax rules regarding pensions, and produce a set of proposals for pension reform. It has announced its intention to issue a Green Paper with these proposals in autumn 2002.

Other financial support

In addition to the *State Pension* (see page 142), people aged 60 or over are eligible for other benefits.

A *Winter Fuel Payment* of £200 is available to people aged 60 and over. It provides help towards the extra costs of keeping warm in winter. A *Cold Weather Payment* is also available to those on Minimum Income Guarantee (see page 142). This helps towards extra heating costs when there is a spell of cold weather in the claimant's area. Both payments are paid automatically. Free NHS prescriptions and eye tests are provided to those aged 60 or over. People on Minimum Income Guarantee can also get free NHS dental treatment, wigs and fabric supports, vouchers towards the cost of glasses or contact lenses, and refunds of necessary travel costs to hospitals for NHS treatment (including check-ups). Pensioners aged 75 and over can claim a free television licence.

In Great Britain men and women aged 60 or over and a range of people with disabilities are entitled to a minimum of half fare travel on public transport. Local authorities may provide more generous concessions and some offer free travel.

In April 2002 free bus travel was introduced across the whole of Wales, entitling all women over 60, men over 65 and registered disabled people to free transport on local buses. The Northern Ireland Concessionary Fares Scheme currently offers free travel on all public transport in Northern Ireland to men and women aged 65 or over, those who are registered blind and those in receipt of a war disabled pension. The Northern Ireland Scheme is currently under review, with the aim of considering how it could be extended to more groups of people.

Care services for older people

In England spending by local authorities on older people amounted to £5.9 billion in 2000/01, 46 per cent of total local authority spending on personal social services. The largest single category of expenditure is for 'residential provision', which accounts for 61 per cent of all expenditure on older people. A third of this residential provision is accounted for by nursing home placements and just under two-thirds by residential care home placements. In Wales £284 million was spent by local authorities on older people. Residential provision accounted for 52 per cent of this expenditure.

Community Care and Health (Scotland) Act 2002
Among other things, this Act:

- provides for free personal care for older people and nursing care for all who need it from July 2002;

- allows people to make top-up payments if they wish to enter more expensive accommodation than that which the local authority would normally pay for (they may also defer these payments until their home is sold after death); and

- expands access to direct payments for non-residential service users, giving people the ability to purchase their own services.

Over the past few years there has been a fall in the number of residential places provided for older people in England by the public sector and an increase in independent sector provision (see Table 12.5). In 1996 the public sector in England provided 24 per cent of places for older people, but this fell to 17 per cent by 2001.

Wherever possible, services are designed to help older people live at home. These services may include advice and help given by social workers, domestic help, the provision of meals in the home, sitters-in, night attendants and laundry services, as well as direct payments, day centres, lunch clubs and recreational facilities.

Following publication of *Improving Health in Wales – A Plan for the NHS with its Partners* and the introduction of the *Health and Social Care Act 2001*, the Welsh Assembly Government implemented a policy to ensure that the services of a registered nurse are free of charge in all care settings. Funding has been set at a level of £100 a week per individual self-funder who is assessed as needing nursing care.

Families and children

Financial support
Pregnant employees have the right to take a minimum of 18 weeks' maternity leave. Most receive *Statutory Maternity Pay* directly from their employer. It is paid for a maximum of 18 weeks to any woman who has been working for the same employer for 26 weeks and who earns on average at least £75 a week. Most women receive at least

90 per cent of their average weekly earnings for the first six weeks and a flat rate of £75 a week for the remaining 12 weeks.

Women who are not eligible for Statutory Maternity Pay because, for example, they are self-employed or have recently changed jobs or left their job, may qualify for a weekly *Maternity Allowance*, which is payable for up to 18 weeks at a standard rate of £75.

From April 2003 Statutory Maternity Pay and Maternity Allowance will be extended to 26 weeks and the flat rate after the first six weeks will be increased to £100 per week (or 90 per cent of average weekly earnings if this is less). Ordinary maternity leave will also be extended from 18 weeks to 26 weeks and additional (unpaid) maternity leave will be extended to a further 26 weeks – giving most mothers the possibility of up to one year off in total.

Fathers will have a new right to two weeks of paid paternity leave, which can usually be taken within two months of the child's birth. *Statutory Paternity Pay* will be at the same standard rate as Statutory Maternity Pay – £100 per week (or 90 per cent of average weekly earnings if this is less) from April 2003.

People who adopt a child after April 2003 may be eligible to new rights to time off work. Those eligible will be able to take 26 weeks of paid adoption leave followed by a further 26 weeks of additional (unpaid) leave. This will give adoptive parents the same length of leave – a total of one year – as mothers on maternity leave. *Statutory Adoption Pay* will be at the same standard rate as Statutory Maternity Pay – £100 per week (or 90 per cent of average weekly earnings if this is less) from April 2003.

At the same time, the Government will be introducing a right for parents of children aged under six or of disabled children aged under 18 to request flexible working patterns. Their employers will have a duty to consider these requests seriously.

Subject to certain qualifying requirements, both mothers and fathers are entitled to 13 weeks unpaid parental leave, up until the child's fifth birthday (18 weeks until the child's 18th birthday for disabled children).

Families who receive a low-income benefit or tax credit may be able to get a *Sure Start Maternity Grant* of £300 to help with the cost of buying things for the new baby.

The main social security benefit for children is Child Benefit. Additional financial help to families is available through the Working Families' Tax Credit (see page 142).

The introduction of a *Child Tax Credit* to provide a single system of income-related support for families with children was announced in the 2002 Budget. It will begin in April 2003 and will bring together the support for children currently provided through the Working Families' and Disabled Person's Tax Credits, the Children's Tax Credit, Income Support and Jobseeker's Allowance.

It was also announced in the Budget that personal mentors would be introduced to help lone parents into work. Eligibility for *Childcare Tax Credit* would be extended.

Other support for families and children

Local authorities in England and Wales and Health and Social Services Trusts in Northern Ireland are required to safeguard and promote the welfare of any children in need and, so far as is consistent with that, to promote the upbringing of children by their parents, by providing a range of services to meet their assessed needs. The services which may be provided include advice, guidance, counselling, help in the home and family centres. Help can be provided to the immediate family of the child in need or to any other member of the family, if it is done with a view to safeguarding and promoting the child's welfare. Local authorities can provide these services directly or arrange them through another agency such as a voluntary organisation. They are also required to publicise the help available to families in need.

Local authorities also help people fleeing domestic violence, often working with specialist voluntary organisations that provide refuges where women and children receive short-term accommodation and support pending a more permanent solution.

In July 2002 the Government announced a combined £1.5 billion budget by 2005/06 for Sure Start,[1] Early Years and Childcare in England. It also announced the creation of a single

interdepartmental unit, which has the following tasks:

- to establish children's centres in disadvantaged areas, combining childcare with early education, family support, health services, and training and employment advice. Children's centres will build on existing programmes like Sure Start, neighbourhood nurseries and early excellence centres;

- to support the existing and planned 522 Sure Start programmes, nine pilots and 50 Mini Sure Starts in rural areas and pockets of deprivation;

- to create a further 250,000 new childcare places by 2006, in addition to the existing target of new places for 1.6 million children by 2004; and

- to ensure parents are better informed about childcare opportunities.

Day care for children

Day care facilities are provided for young children by childminders, voluntary agencies, private nurseries and local authorities. In 2001 in England and Wales there were 318,000 childminder places for children under eight, 297,000 day nursery places, 161,000 out-of-school clubs, and 354,000 playgroup and pre-school places. Northern Ireland has 20,000 funded playgroup and pre-school places and around 40,000 registered childcare places.

According to the 2001 Childcare Workforce Survey, published by the Department for Education and Skills in April 2002:

- there were 274,520 professionals working in the childcare sector in England, an increase of 21 per cent since 1998;

- the number of providers of childcare rose, with an increase in the number of nursery schools from 5,500 to 7,800, and in out-of school providers from 2,640 to 4,900; and

- two-thirds of childminders had completed an approved pre-registration course.

In Scotland there were 2,079 nursery schools and 2,249 out-of-school providers of day care in 2001. The Early Education and Childcare Workforce

---

1 The Sure Start Programme (see also page 103) supports local projects for families with children under four years of age.

Survey estimated that in April/May 2000 there were 32,000 people working in the childcare sector in Scotland.

In September 2001 the Office for Standards in Education (OFSTED) (see page 120) took over responsibility from local authorities for the regulation of day care providers for children in England. The newly formed Early Years Directorate of OFSTED now registers and inspects nurseries, playgroups and pre-schools, crèches, out-of-school care and childminders for children up to the age of eight. Childcare Inspectors inspect the suitability of premises, the suitability of the people who will be with the children, and the welfare and development of the children.

In Scotland, local authority responsibility for regulation of day care providers for children transferred to the new Scottish Commission for the Regulation of Care in April 2002. New national care standards for early education and childcare up to the age of 16 have been published, and HM Inspectorate of Education and the Scottish Commission for the Regulation of Care are developing an inspection regime to be used in conjunction with these standards and other key documents. Local HSS Trusts in Northern Ireland are responsible for the regulation of day care providers. Regulation covers provision for children up to the age of 12.

Child Support Agency

The function of the Child Support Agency (*www.csa.gov.uk*) is to ensure that parents who live apart meet their financial responsibilities to their children. It:

- assesses claims for child support maintenance;

- traces and contacts non-resident parents;

- helps conclude paternity disputes when a man denies he is a child's father; and

- collects and passes on maintenance payments to the parent who is caring for the child, taking action to make the non-resident parent pay if necessary.

Assessments for child support maintenance are made using a formula which takes into account each parent's income and makes allowance for essential outgoings.

Child protection

Child protection is the joint concern of a number of different agencies and professions. Local authority area child protection committees determine how the different agencies should co-operate to help protect children from abuse and neglect in their area.

In England and Wales a child may be brought before a family proceedings court if he or she is suffering, or is likely to suffer, significant harm. The court can commit children to the care of the local authority under a care order or a supervision order. Certain pre-conditions have to be satisfied to justify such an order. These are that significant harm, or likelihood of harm, is attributable to a lack of reasonable parental care or because the child is beyond parental control. However, an order is made only if the court is also satisfied that this will positively contribute to the child's well-being and be in his or her best interests. All courts have to treat the welfare of children as the paramount consideration when reaching any decision about their upbringing. There is a general principle that, wherever possible, children should remain at home with their families.

Victoria Climbié and Kennedy McFarlane

Two recent cases have caused concern about various aspects of the child protection system. Eight year old Victoria Climbié died of hypothermia in London in February 2000. Her great-aunt, to whom her parents had entrusted her care, and her great-aunt's boyfriend were convicted of her murder in 2001. During the trial it became apparent that, despite being brought to the attention of social workers, doctors and the police, Victoria had not been protected from several months of abuse and neglect. An independent public inquiry is looking at the role played by these agencies in order to make recommendations to prevent such a tragedy happening again. The final report of the inquiry is expected towards the end of 2002.

In Scotland a review of child protection was announced in March 2001, following the death of three year old Kennedy McFarlane who died after being hit by her mother's boyfriend. An independent inquiry concluded that her death could have been prevented if action had been taken following concerns raised from repeated referrals and hospital admissions. An audit of child protection processes across Scotland will be carried out to assess the consistency and quality of practice of the agencies involved.

In Scotland, children who have committed offences or are in need of care and protection may be brought before a Children's Hearing, which can impose a supervision requirement on a child. In some cases, the supervision requirement will have a condition attached to it that the child must live away from home, either with foster parents, in a children's home or at a special residence where the Hearing believes the child will receive the right help or supervision. Supervision requirements are reviewed at least once a year until ended by a Children's Hearing.

Local authority social services help children who are considered to be at risk of abuse and hold a central register of such children. There were around 30,000 children on child protection registers in England, Wales and Northern Ireland at 31 March 2001.

Fostering and children's homes

When a child is made the subject of a care order, the local authority has legal responsibility for the child. Although it consults with the child's parents about where the child should live, the local authority makes the final decision. Children can also be accommodated by a local authority through a voluntary agreement with their parents. In the year ending 31 March 2001 there were some 38,400 children in foster care and 6,800 in children's homes in England (see Table 12.6).

Local authorities and HSS Trusts in Northern Ireland must also provide accommodation for children who have no parent or guardian, who have been abandoned, or whose parents are unable to provide for them. They have a duty to ensure that the welfare of children being looked after away from home is properly safeguarded. This includes protecting their health, providing for their education and ensuring contact with their families. They are as far as possible expected to work in partnership with the parents of children who are in their care.

The *Children Leaving Care Act 2000* came into force in England and Wales in October 2001. It is intended to ensure that young people who leave care continue to receive the support they need to make the most of their life chances. Young people aged 16 and 17 who qualify under the Act will have a written plan (called a Pathway Plan) agreed with their responsible authority (and with the parents where possible) and will be allocated a personal adviser.

Table 12.6 Children looked after by local authorities[1] by type of accommodation, England, 2001

	Number
Foster placements	38,400
With parents	6,900
Children's homes and hostels[2]	6,800
Placed for adoption	3,400
Living independently or in residential employment	1,200
Residential schools	1,100
Other	1,200
Total	**58,900**

1 Excludes children looked after under an agreed series of short-term placements.
2 Includes local authority, voluntary sector and private children's homes and secure units.
Source: Department of Health

Younger children are placed wherever possible with foster carers, sometimes as a short-term measure (for example when parents are temporarily unable to look after their child because of illness in the family) or, if necessary, in the longer-term. Children's homes can be run by local authorities, or by private or voluntary organisations such as Barnardo's.

Under the *Care Standards Act 2000* (see page 144), all children's homes are required to register with the NCSC or its equivalent bodies in Scotland and Wales. The Commission is responsible for inspecting all children's homes to assess the quality of care provided.

Adoption

There were 5,036 adoption orders in England and Wales in 2001. An adoption order gives parental responsibility for a child to the adoptive parent(s). Under the *Adoption Act 1976*, adoption orders can be granted to applicants by the High Court, County Courts and Magistrates' Courts.

In August 2001 the National Adoption Standards for England were published. These standards are intended to ensure that children, prospective adopters, adoptive parents and birth families receive a consistent and high-quality adoption service no matter where they live. Adoption standards for Scotland were published in March 2002 and will come into force in 2003. Draft standards and guidance for Wales were issued in 2001 and standards for Northern Ireland will be issued at a later date.

Adoption and Children Bill

The Adoption and Children Bill is intended to replace the *Adoption Act 1976* and modernise the existing legal framework for domestic and inter-country adoption. The aim is to improve the adoption service and promote greater use of adoption. Among its provisions are measures to:

- align adoption law with the *Children Act 1989* so as to make the child's welfare the paramount consideration in all decisions to do with adoption;

- introduce a new duty on local authorities to provide an adoption support service and a right for people affected by adoption to request and receive an assessment of their needs for such a service;

- allow unmarried couples to adopt together – at present only married couples and single people are legally allowed to adopt children;

- reduce delays by providing legal support for the Adoption Register to suggest matches between children and approved adopters and through measures requiring courts to draw up timetables for adoption;

- provide for a more consistent approach to the way in which people can gain access to information held in adoption agency records, so that the release of identifying information about adopted people and birth families happens in a proper manner and takes account of their views wherever possible; and

- improve the legal controls on inter-country adoption, and the legal controls on arranging adoptions and advertising children for adoption.

The majority of provisions in the Bill relate to England and Wales only, but some provisions also extend to Scotland and/or Northern Ireland.

The Adoption Register for England and Wales holds information on children waiting to be adopted and approved adoptive families waiting to adopt. The aim is to tackle delays in finding suitable adoptive families where a local family cannot be found, or the child needs to move away from the area.

People with a sickness or disability

The Disability Rights Commission (DRC), established in Great Britain in April 2000, aims to eliminate discrimination against disabled people, promote equal opportunities, encourage good practice and advise the Government on the operation of the *Disability Discrimination Act 1995* (see page 97). The Equality Commission (see page 96) has a similar role in Northern Ireland.

Under the Act, service providers have a duty to make reasonable adjustment to the way they provide services to the public, changing their policies, practices and procedures where reasonable. From 2004 service providers will have to take reasonable steps to remove, alter or provide reasonable means of avoiding physical features which make it impossible or unreasonably difficult for disabled people to use their service. A Code of Practice on the rights of access that businesses and services must afford disabled people was issued by the DRC in May 2002. The Code also provides practical guidance and information.

From April 2002 new rules apply to people who want to do paid work while getting Incapacity Benefit, Severe Disablement Allowance (see page 152), Housing Benefit, Council Tax Benefit (see page 154) or Income Support (see page 142), because of illness or disability. The new arrangements allow claimants to try some paid work without the need for prior approval from a doctor.

Care services for people with physical disabilities

Over the past decade there has been increasing emphasis on the provision of support services that enable disabled people to live independently in the community whenever possible.

Local authority social services departments and HSS Trusts in Northern Ireland help with social rehabilitation and adjustment to disability. They are required to identify the number of disabled people in their area and to provide and publicise services. These may include advice on personal and social problems arising from disability, as well as occupational, educational, social and recreational facilities, either at day centres or elsewhere.

Main benefits available to sick and disabled people (at April 2002)

Employers are responsible for paying *Statutory Sick Pay* to employees up to a maximum of 28 weeks. There is a single rate of Statutory Sick Pay (£63.25 a week) for all qualifying employees provided their average gross weekly earnings are at least £75.

Incapacity Benefit is for people out of work, who have an incapacity or disability that means it would not be reasonable to expect them to find work. Entitlement begins when entitlement to Statutory Sick Pay ends or, for those who do not qualify for Statutory Sick Pay, from the fourth day of sickness. Payments, which depend on age and the length of illness, range from £53.50 to £70.95 a week. Older claimants may receive extra benefits.

Severe Disablement Allowance is a tax-free benefit for people who have not been able to work for at least 28 weeks because of illness or disability but who cannot get Incapacity Benefit because they have not paid enough NICs. The benefit is £42.85 a week, plus additions of up to £14.90 depending on the person's age when he or she became incapable of work. Additions for adult dependants and for children may also be paid. In April 2001 this Allowance was abolished for new claims. People under 20, or 25 if they were in education or training before reaching 20, may now be able to receive Incapacity Benefit without having to satisfy the contribution conditions.

Disabled Person's Tax Credit is an allowance for people who are working but who have an illness or disability that puts them at a disadvantage in getting a job. Claimants must be 16 or over, working on average 16 hours a week or more and be restricted in the type of work, number of hours or amount they can earn because of illness or disability. Savings over £3,000 affect the amount that can be claimed, and those with savings over £16,000 are not entitled to the credit.

Disability Living Allowance is a non-contributory tax-free benefit to help severely disabled people aged under 65 with extra costs incurred as a result of disability. Entitlement is measured in terms of personal care and/or mobility needs. There are two components: a care component which has three weekly rates – £56.25, £37.65 and £14.90 – and a mobility component with two weekly rates, of £39.30 and £14.90. It is payable to those aged three or over who have severe difficulty walking, or aged five or over who need help getting around.

Attendance Allowance (AA) is paid to people who need help to look after themselves. It is paid if a person becomes ill or disabled on or after his or her 65th birthday and needs help for at least six months. There are different rates depending on whether the claimant needs care during the day, during the night, or both, and on the extent of the disability. However, AA is not affected by savings or income under normal circumstances. AA ranges from £37.65 to £56.25 a week depending on circumstances.

Industrial Injuries Disablement Benefit is a benefit for people who have been disabled by an accident at work or through a prescribed disease caused by a particular type of employment. It is usually paid after a qualifying period of 15 weeks if a person is at least 14 per cent or more physically or mentally disabled. The rate is between £14.07 and £70.35 a week depending on the level of disablement

People with disabilities may also be eligible for *cold weather payments* (see page 142). People injured as part of activity in the armed forces may be entitled to *War Disablement Pension* (WDP) (see page 155).

Other services provided may include adaptations to homes (such as ramps for wheelchairs, stairlifts and ground-floor toilets), the delivery of cooked meals, support with personal care at home and direct payments with which disabled people can purchase support to meet their assessed need. Local authorities and voluntary organisations may provide severely disabled people with residential accommodation, either on a permanent basis or temporarily in order to relieve their existing carers. Special housing may be available for those able to look after themselves. Some authorities provide free or subsidised travel for disabled people on public transport, and they are encouraged to provide special means of access to public buildings.

Care services for people with learning disabilities

The Government encourages the development of local services for people with learning disabilities and their families through co-operation between health authorities, local authorities, education and training services, and voluntary and other organisations.

Local authority social services departments and HSS Trusts in Northern Ireland are the leading statutory agencies for planning and arranging such services. They provide or arrange short-term care, support for families in their own homes, residential accommodation and support for various types of activity outside the home. People with learning disabilities may also be able to receive direct payments from local authorities to let them buy for themselves the support that they have been assessed as needing. The main aim is to ensure that, as far as possible, they can lead full lives in the community. They form the largest group for local authority-funded day centre places and the second largest group in residential care. The National Health Service provides specialist services when the ordinary primary care services cannot meet healthcare needs. Residential care is provided for those with severe or profound disabilities whose needs can effectively be met only by the NHS.

People with a mental health problem

Government policy aims to ensure that people with mental health problems should have access to all the services they need as locally as possible. Under the Care Programme Approach in England, each service user should receive an assessment leading to the formulation of an agreed care plan. A care co-ordinator is appointed to keep in contact with the service user, and review his or her care plan regularly in the light of the individual's changing needs. The separate Welsh Mental Health Strategy employs many of the same principles in delivering services in Wales.

In Scotland, mental health is a clinical priority for the NHS and each NHS board works with its local authority care partners, with users of mental health services and with their carers in order to develop joint strategies and provide local and comprehensive mental health services. These plans are expected to conform with the Framework for Mental Health Services and to comply with standards set by the Clinical Standards Board for Scotland. Northern Ireland has an integrated health and social services structure allowing a multi-disciplinary approach to care management.

Arrangements made by social services authorities for providing care in the community include direct payments, day centres, social centres and residential care. Social workers are increasingly being integrated with mental health staff in community mental health teams under single management. These teams include assertive outreach, crisis resolution, home treatment and early intervention teams. Assertive outreach is a way of managing the care of severely mentally ill people in the community by visiting service users at home and liaising with other services such as the GP or social services. Help is usually provided to find housing, secure an adequate income, and sustain basic daily living – shopping, cooking, and washing. Social workers help patients and their families with problems caused by mental illness. In certain circumstances they can apply for a person with a mental disorder to be compulsorily admitted to and detained in hospital. There are safeguards for patients to ensure that the law is used appropriately.

Unemployed people

Jobseeker's Allowance (JSA) is a benefit for unemployed people seeking work. Claimants must be capable of, available for, and actively seeking work. They must normally be at least 18 years of age and under pension age. JSA can be either contribution-based or income-based:

- *Contribution-based JSA* is available to those who have paid enough NICs. They are entitled to a personal JSA for up to six months (£53.95 a week for a person aged 25 or over), regardless of any savings or partner's income.

- *Income-based JSA:* those on a low income are entitled to an income-based JSA, payable for as long as the jobseeker requires support and continues to satisfy the qualifying conditions. The amount a claimant receives comprises an age-related personal allowance (£53.95 a week for a single person aged 25 or over), plus other allowances. Income-based JSA's benefit rates are determined by circumstances on a basis similar to Income Support (see page 142).

Recipients of JSA and people aged under 60 who receive Income Support can benefit from a *Back to Work Bonus*. The aim of this scheme is to encourage people to keep in touch with the labour market by undertaking small amounts of work while claiming benefit. It allows people to accrue a tax-free lump sum of between £5 and £1,000 if working part-time while in receipt of Income Support or JSA. There are a number of other financial benefits for unemployed people to help them back into employment, including various *New Deals* (see chapter 11).

A pilot scheme for extending eligibility for the *New Deal 25 plus* to jobseekers who have been out of work for 18 months in the previous three years was also announced in the 2002 Budget.

People on low incomes

People on low incomes can claim *Income Support* (see page 142) or, for those over 60, Minimum Income Guarantee. Other benefits for which unemployed people and those on low incomes may be eligible include exemption from NHS charges, vouchers towards the cost of spectacles, publicly funded legal help and free school meals for their children. People on low incomes, pensioners, widows, widowers and long-term sick people on Incapacity Benefit may be eligible for extra help to meet the cost of VAT (value added tax) on their fuel bills.

Housing Benefit is an income-related, tax-free benefit which helps people on low incomes meet the cost of rented accommodation. The amount paid depends on personal circumstances, income, savings, rent and whether other people are sharing the home. It also normally depends on the general level of rents for properties with the same number of rooms in the locality. Most single people under 25 years old who are not lone parents and who are renting privately have their Housing Benefit limited to the average cost of a single non-self-contained room (that is, with shared use of kitchen and toilet facilities) in the locality.

Council Tax Benefit helps people to meet their council tax payments (the tax set by local councils to help pay for services – see page 357). The scheme offers help to those claiming Income Support and income-based JSA and others with low incomes. In Northern Ireland, where council tax was not introduced, Housing Benefit helps with the cost of rent and/or rates.

It was announced in the Budget 2002 that a new *Working Tax Credit* would be introduced from April 2003. It will integrate the support currently available for adults under the Working Families' and Disabled Person's Tax Credits. The Working Tax Credit is designed to help tackle poor work incentives and persistent poverty among working people and extend in-work support to people on low incomes without children or a disability.

The *Social Fund* provides payments, in the form of loans or grants, to people on low incomes to help with expenses which are difficult to meet out of regular income. These payments can be:

- *budgeting loans* for intermittent expenses;

- *community care grants* to help, for example, people resettle into the community from care, or to remain in the community, to ease exceptional pressure on families, to set up home as part of a planned resettlement programme or to meet certain travel expenses; and

- *crisis loans* to help people in an emergency or as a result of a disaster where there is serious risk to health or safety.

Budgeting loans and community care grants are available only to people who are receiving social security benefits and some tax credits.

The Social Fund can also provide payments to help people with the costs of maternity or funerals, or to help older people with heating during very cold weather.

Widows and widowers

A new system of bereavement benefits for men and women was introduced in April 2001. However, it does not affect men or women who were already receiving benefits under the previous scheme as long as they continue to qualify under the rules.

Bereavement Payment is a one-off payment to widows under the age of 60, and widowers under the age of 65 – or those over 60/65 whose spouses were not entitled to a basic State Retirement Pension when they died. It is payable as long as their spouses paid a minimum number of National Insurance contributions.

Widowed Parent's Allowance is a regular payment for widows or widowers bringing up children. It is based on the late spouse's NICs and continues while the children are still dependent. *Bereavement Allowance* is a regular payment, also based on the late spouse's NICs, which is payable for 52 weeks.

A number of charities and voluntary organisations advise and support people who have been bereaved. In 2001 a consortium of some of the leading bodies published a set of national standards for bereavement care. This work will be taken forward by a new body, the Bereavement Care Standards: UK Council, the aim of which will be to promote and share good practice in this area.

War pensioners

In April 2002 the War Pensions Agency was renamed the Veterans Agency (VA). It is part of the Ministry of Defence (MoD) and provides advice and help with new and ongoing claims for war disablement pensions and war widows/widowers pensions. The Agency also provides a single point of contact within the MoD to obtain information or advice on a diverse range of veterans' issues, such as service records, medals, military graves and welfare issues.

The War Pensioners' Welfare Service (WPWS), through working closely with ex-Service organisations and other statutory and voluntary organisations, provides a comprehensive advice and support service for all war pensioners and war widows/widowers living in the UK and the Irish Republic.

There are approximately 280,000 beneficiaries of *War Disability* and *Widows' Pensions*, of whom 22,000 live outside the UK. The majority are Second World War veterans, but there are also small numbers of First World War veterans, ex-National Servicemen and those disabled in recent conflicts such as Northern Ireland, the Falklands, Bosnia and the Gulf War. War Disablement Pension is payable to ex-members of the armed forces as a result of disability due to service. War Widows'/Widowers' Pension is payable to widows/widowers of ex-members of the armed forces where death is due to or hastened by service. War Disablement Pension can also be claimed by civilians, merchant seamen and members of the Polish forces under British command, although special conditions apply in these cases.

The Royal British Legion is a UK charity for those who have served in the UK armed forces and their dependants. It provides financial, social and emotional support, such as advice about benefits or grants for the purchase of household appliances.

Asylum seekers

Asylum seekers receive limited cash benefits and may qualify for other services (see page 92). Psychological treatment is available for victims of torture.

In April 2002 the Government introduced the Nationality, Immigration and Asylum Bill (see page 93), which includes measures to reform the asylum system.

Arrangements with other countries

As part of the European Union's efforts to promote the free movement of labour, regulations provide for equality of treatment and the protection of benefit rights for people who move between Member States. The regulations also cover retired pensioners and other beneficiaries who have been employed, or self-employed, as well as dependants. Benefits covered include Child Benefit and those for sickness, maternity, unemployment, retirement, invalidity, accidents at work and occupational diseases.

The UK has reciprocal social security agreements with a number of other countries which also provide cover for some national insurance benefits and family benefits.

Further reading

Department for Work and Pensions Departmental Report: The Government's Expenditure Plans 2002–03 to 2003–04. Cm 5424. The Stationery Office, 2002.

Department of Health Departmental Report. The Government's Expenditure Plans 2002/2003 to 2003/2004. Cm 5403. The Stationery Office, 2002.

Valuing People: A New Strategy for Learning Disability for the 21st Century. Cm 5086. The Stationery Office, 2001.

Websites

Child Support Agency
www.csa.gov.uk

Citizens Advice Bureau
www.adviceguide.org.uk

Department for Social Development, Northern Ireland
www.dsdni.gov.uk

Department for Work and Pensions
www.dwp.gov.uk

Department of Health
www.doh.gov.uk

Department of Health, Social Services and Public Safety (Northern Ireland)
www.dhsspsni.gov.uk

Inland Revenue
www.inlandrevenue.gov.uk

National Assembly for Wales
www.wales.gov.uk

National Care Standards Commission
www.carestandards.org.uk

Occupational Pensions Regulatory Authority
www.opra.gov.uk

Pension Guide
www.pensionguide.gov.uk

Pensions Ombudsman
www.pensions-ombudsman.org.uk

Scottish Commission for the Regulation of Care
www.carecommission.com

Scottish Executive
www.scotland.gov.uk

Social Security Agency (Northern Ireland)
www.ssani.gov.uk

Veterans Agency
www.veteransagency.mod.uk

13 Health

The state of public health

Current government healthcare strategies throughout the United Kingdom aim to reduce avoidable ill health with particular emphasis on cancer, heart disease and mental illness. Sedentary lifestyles, obesity, smoking, and excessive consumption of alcohol have been identified as significant factors contributing to avoidable ill health in the UK.

Life expectancy

The increase in life expectancy is one of the most striking indications of how the nation's health improved during the 20th century. Improvements in the population's nutrition and housing, and advances in medicine and technology led to the prevention or successful treatment of many diseases which were commonplace, and often fatal, less than 100 years earlier.

Since the middle of the 19th century the expectation of life at birth for both females and males has almost doubled. Neither males nor females born in England and Wales in 1841 had an average life expectancy from birth much beyond 40, mainly because of high infant and child mortality. By 1998–2000 life expectancy at birth for females in the United Kingdom had risen to 80, and for males to just over 75 years. The local authority with the highest life expectancy at birth for males was East Dorset at 79.0 years, while Westminster (London) had the highest life expectancy at birth for females at 83.5 years. Glasgow City had the lowest life expectancy at birth for both males and females, at 68.7 and 75.7 years respectively.

Cancer

Cancer is a disease that affects mainly older people, with two-thirds of cases occurring in those aged over 65. As average life expectancy in the United Kingdom has risen, the population at risk of cancer has grown. About a third of people will be diagnosed with cancer during their lifetime and about a quarter will die from the disease. There are over 200 different types of cancer but the four major types – lung, colorectal, breast and prostate – account for over half of all cases diagnosed.

The incidence of all the major cancers (apart from breast cancer and malignant melanoma of the skin) is higher among males than females in all parts of the UK. The rates for all types of cancer combined is highest in Scotland and lowest in England, for both males and females, although the difference is more marked among males.

Lung cancer is the most common cancer diagnosed in men and the third most common in women, with the most significant risk factor being smoking. Although about twice as many men as women die from lung cancer, there has been a notable contrast in the trends of age-standardised[1] death rates since the 1970s. By 2000 there were 61 deaths per 100,000 men, compared with 111 per 100,000 in 1974. Among women, lung cancer deaths rose from 18 per 100,000 in 1971 to 31 per 100,000 in 1988, since when there have been around 30 deaths per 100,000 each year.

Colorectal cancer is the third most commonly diagnosed cancer in the United Kingdom in men and the second for women. Deaths from this form of cancer have been gradually declining, from 34 per 100,000 men and 26 per 100,000 women in 1971 to 25 and 15 deaths per 100,000 respectively in 2000.

---

1 Age-standardised incidence rates enable comparisons to be made over time (and between the genders) which are independent of changes in the age structure of the population.

The recorded incidence of breast and prostate cancer has risen considerably, partly because increased awareness and screening have led to earlier diagnosis. Breast cancer is the most common cancer diagnosed in women. Between 1986 and 2000 the death rate in the United Kingdom fell by 26 per cent to 31 deaths per 100,000. For prostate cancer, the slight fall in the death rate since the early 1990s was preceded by a 51 per cent rise between 1971 and 1992. Prostate cancer is the second most common cancer among men.

Circulatory disease

The United Kingdom has one of the highest premature death rates from circulatory disease (which includes heart disease and strokes) in Europe. In 1998 for those aged under 65, the rate for the United Kingdom was almost twice the rate in France, the country with the lowest death rate (see Figure 13.1). A number of risk factors have been identified, including drinking alcohol, smoking, obesity and lack of regular exercise.

In 2000 coronary heart disease (CHD) killed around 156,000 people in the United Kingdom. Death rates from CHD are higher in Scotland, Northern Ireland and northern England than they are in southern England.

Diabetes

Diabetes is a condition that can result in potentially debilitating complications and increases the risk of developing other illnesses. It affects around 1.3 million people in the United Kingdom. If not properly managed, diabetes can result in a range of long-term complications, such as heart disease, stroke, kidney disease, blindness, and foot problems that may lead to amputation.

Figures for 1994 to 1998 showed that prevalence rates for people with insulin treated diabetes in England and Wales increased steadily with age and peaked in the 65 to 74 year old age group. Prevalence rates for people with non-insulin treated diabetes increased markedly from the age of 55, with a peak in the 75 to 84 year old age group, reflecting the high proportion of late onset cases.

Asthma

Asthma is a disease of the lungs in which the airways are unusually sensitive to a wide range of stimuli, including inhaled irritants and allergens. The National Asthma Campaign's 2001 UK Asthma Audit estimated that 5.1 million people in the United Kingdom (1 in 8 children and 1 in 13 adults) were being treated for asthma. Research

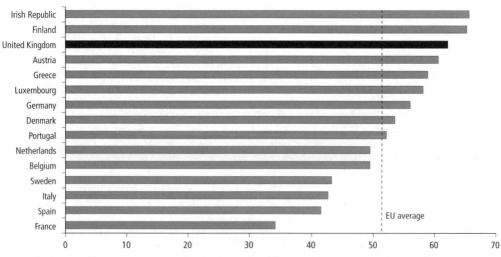

Figure 13.1 EU premature death rates from circulatory diseases, 1998[1]

Rates per 100,000 population[2]

1 Data are for 1998, except for Germany and Italy, which are for 1997, and Denmark and Belgium, which are for 1996.
2 Death rates for those aged under 65 standardised to the European standard population.
Source: Eurostat

into the causes and distribution of asthma has indicated that some of the main factors leading to recent increases are infections and allergens, these being far more significant than air pollution.

Infectious diseases

Trends in infectious diseases have changed considerably over the last 30 years. There has been a significant decline in the types of infectious diseases that children tend to suffer. For example, between 1971 and 2000, the number of cases of measles notified in the United Kingdom declined from 155,000 to 3,000. There has been a similar trend in cases of whooping cough, with 900 cases in 2000, compared with peaks of 71,000 in 1978 and 1982.

Immunisation

The decline in the occurrence of measles can be mainly attributed to the number of children receiving vaccination. The uptake of the measles vaccine rose from 50 per cent in the mid-1970s to 80 per cent in 1988, the year in which the combined measles, mumps and rubella (MMR) vaccine was introduced. Since then the number of notifications of measles has fallen dramatically.

Current government immunisation targets are for 95 per cent of children to be immunised by the age of two against diphtheria, tetanus, polio, whooping cough, Haemophilus influenzae b (Hib), meningitis C and measles, mumps and rubella. In the light of public concerns about the safety of the MMR vaccine, coverage in 2000/01 fell to 88 per cent, the lowest level since 1990.

In 1999 the United Kingdom was the first country in the world to introduce immunisation against Group C meningococcal disease, which had been progressively rising throughout the 1990s. Between 1998 and 2001 there was a decline of over 90 per cent in the number of cases and deaths.

Tuberculosis

In the 40 years to 1987 notifications of tuberculosis (TB) in England and Wales fell considerably, from around 51,700 in 1947 to around 5,700 in 1987. However, over the next 14 years they increased by 26 per cent, so that in 2001 there were around 7,200 notifications. The rise has been particularly noticeable in London and among young men.

Sexually transmitted diseases

Infections that can be sexually transmitted have been increasing in recent years. The Public Health Laboratory Service (PHLS) reported that by June 2001, 46,100 cases of Human Immunodeficiency Virus (HIV) had been diagnosed in the United Kingdom. In recent years the way in which those with HIV contracted the infection has changed (see Figure 13.2). In the late 1990s the number of diagnoses of infections acquired through sex between men and women overtook those due to sex between men. In 2001 around 4,400 people were diagnosed with HIV, over half of whom contracted the virus through heterosexual sex, more than double the proportion ten years earlier. Over 80 per cent of these heterosexually acquired infections in 2001 were estimated to have occurred abroad, with over 1,500 attributed to infection in Africa.

Figure 13.2 HIV infections,[1] by year of diagnosis and route of transmission, UK

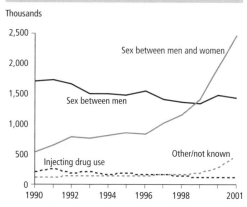

Thousands

1 The number of diagnoses recorded, particularly for recent years, will rise as further reports are received. Those where the probable route of infection was not known, particularly for recent years, will fall as follow-up continues.
Source: Public Health Laboratory Service

Recent trends for other sexually transmitted infections diagnosed in the United Kingdom also show increases. Between 1995 and 2000 the number of cases among people aged 19 and under more than doubled. In 2001 genital chlamydia infection became the most common sexually transmitted infection diagnosed in genito-urinary medicine clinics with a total of just over 71,000 cases. Diagnosis of uncomplicated gonorrhoea was the second most common infection. Between

2000 and 2001, cases in males rose by 8 per cent to 15,900, and in females cases rose by 6 per cent to 6,785. During this period diagnosis of primary and secondary syphilis showed the largest relative increases, rising by 144 per cent in males to 614 cases, and by 36 per cent in females to 102 cases.

Mental health

Mental health problems are a major cause of ill health. In 2000/01 there were 2.0 million attendances at NHS outpatient facilities for psychiatric specialties in England, 285,000 of which were new attendances. In 2001/02 mental health drugs dispensed in the community in England cost £531 million, representing 8 per cent of the net ingredient cost of all prescription medicines dispensed.

Research carried out by the Office for National Statistics in 1999 found that about 10 per cent of children and adolescents aged 5 to 15 years have some form of mental disorder. The proportion was greater among boys than girls and in those families without a working parent. A survey carried out by the ONS in 2000 found that one in six adults aged 16 to 74 living in private households in Great Britain had a neurotic disorder, such as depression, anxiety or a phobia.

Substance misuse

Alcohol

The consumption of alcohol in excessive amounts can lead to ill health and an increased likelihood of problems such as high blood pressure, cancer and cirrhosis of the liver. The current Department of Health advice on alcohol is that consumption of between three and four units[2] a day for men and two to three units a day for women should not lead to significant health risks. Consistently drinking more is not advised because of the progressive health risks. In the United Kingdom 39 per cent of men and 23 per cent of women had exceeded the recommended amount of alcohol on their heaviest drinking day in the week prior to being interviewed during 2000/01.

A survey commissioned by the Department of Health in 2001 found that, while the proportion of children aged 11 to 15 in England who reported

having a drink in the previous week had increased slightly since 1990 (but was still around a quarter), the amount of alcohol consumed per drinker had doubled. In 2001, among those who drank, the average number of units consumed during a week was 10.6 for boys and 8.9 for girls, compared with 5.7 and 4.7 units respectively in 1990.

Smoking

More cancer deaths in the United Kingdom can be attributed to smoking tobacco than to any other single risk factor. Over the past 30 years, the reduction in lung cancer deaths can be closely linked to the fall in the proportion of the population who smoke. In 1974, 51 per cent of men and 41 per cent of women in Great Britain reported that they were regular cigarette smokers. By 2000/01 these proportions had fallen to 29 per cent of men and 25 per cent of women.

The prevalence of smoking varies by social class. For both men and women, the proportion of smokers is higher among those in the manual socio-economic groups than among those in the non-manual groups. In 2000/01, while only 15 per cent of male professionals and 13 per cent of female professionals smoked, 39 per cent of unskilled males and 34 per cent of unskilled females did so.

Similar trends are shown in women who smoke during pregnancy. In 2000, 8 per cent of women in higher occupations reported smoking throughout pregnancy, compared with 29 per cent from the lower occupations.

Drugs

Findings from the 2000 British Crime Survey (see page 184) indicate that 9 per cent of 16 to 24 year olds in England and Wales had used Class A drugs[3] in the previous 12 months, and 5 per cent had done so during the previous month. The most commonly used illegal drug in 2000 among both young men and women was cannabis, which had been used by 29 per cent of men and 23 per cent of women aged 16 to 24 in the previous year. Some drug use also occurs among those under the age of 16. According to a survey in 2001, 20 per cent of 11 to 15 year old children in England had used one or more illegal drugs in the previous year. Cannabis was again the most commonly used drug taken by 13 per cent of this age group.

---

2 A unit of alcohol is 8 grams by weight or 10 millilitres (ml) by volume of pure alcohol. This is the amount contained in half a pint of ordinary strength beer or lager, a single measure of pub spirits (25 ml), one glass of ordinary wine and a small pub measure of sherry or other fortified wine.

3 Heroin, cocaine (both cocaine powder and 'crack'), ecstasy, magic mushrooms, LSD and unprescribed use of methadone.

Then and now – the health of the nation

UK	1952	2002[1]
Infant mortality rate per		
1,000 live births[2]	28.8	4.7
Life expectancy at birth		
males	66.7	75.7
females	71.8	80.4

Great Britain	1952	1999
Mortality rates per million population		
infections	775	85
respiratory	1,939	998
cancers	4,148	3,505
circulatory	7,766	3,296

1 2000-based projections.
2 Deaths within one year of birth.
Source: Office for National Statistics

The number of deaths due to drug-related poisoning in England and Wales rose from around 2,300 in 1993 to almost 3,000 in 2000, an increase of about one-third. The increase was far higher for males than females (50 per cent compared with 3 per cent). Deaths from paracetamol overdose have declined following 1998 legislation which limited the maximum amount of paracetamol allowed in a pack, although more research is needed to ascertain whether the decline is related to the legislation. In 2000 the number of deaths involving heroin or morphine rose to over 900, a fivefold increase on the 1993 figure.

Diet and nutrition

Since the early 1970s there have been marked changes in the British diet. One feature has been the long-term rise in consumption of poultry, while that of red meat (such as beef and veal) has fallen. Consumption of fresh fruit has increased since 1970, while consumption of fresh green vegetables was lower in 2000 than in 1970. In addition, the use of convenience food – both frozen and ready meals – has increased.

Despite these changes, the British diet is still noticeably different from that in other countries such as those in the Mediterranean, being relatively low in fruit, vegetables and fish. Health considerations appear to have been influencing some aspects of diet in recent years, such as the fall in sales of red meat and the rise in consumption of low-fat spreads. Nevertheless, 21 per cent of men and women aged 16 and over in England were classified as obese in 2000.

The Department of Health recommends that a healthy diet should include at least five portions of a variety of fruit and vegetables a day. During 2001 the Department of Health piloted five local 'five a day' community projects and the lessons learned have been incorporated into an evidence-based handbook to support the delivery of new local 'five a day' initiatives.

Following successful pilots in 2000 and 2001, the National School Fruit Scheme is being expanded region by region. By the end of 2002 over 500,000 children aged four to six will be receiving free fruit each school day. By 2004 the scheme will be available across the whole of England.

The Scottish Diet Action Plan – *Eating for Health* – provides the framework for wide-ranging action to tackle Scotland's poor health, with a particular focus on children and young people. The most recent initiatives in this area include fruit for infants, breakfast clubs, and school fruit and salad bars.

The National Health Service

The National Health Service (NHS) was created in 1948 to provide healthcare for the UK's resident population, based on need, not the ability to pay. It is made up of a wide range of health professionals, support workers and organisations.

The NHS is funded by the taxpayer and is accountable to Parliament. All taxpayers, employers and employees contribute to the cost, so that members of the community who do not require healthcare help to pay for those who do. Most forms of treatment are provided free, but others may incur a charge, such as prescription drugs and sight tests.

In England the NHS is managed by the Department of Health, which is responsible for developing and implementing policies and overall regulation and inspection of health services. The Welsh Assembly Government, the Scottish Executive Health Department and the Department of Health, Social Services and Public Safety in Northern Ireland have similar responsibilities for health provision in their respective countries.

NHS Direct

In 1998 NHS Direct, a nurse-led telephone helpline, was launched in England. NHS Direct aims to provide people at home with fast and

In a typical week:

- more than 800,000 people are treated in NHS hospital outpatient clinics;

- 700,000 visit an NHS dentist for a check-up;

- NHS district nurses make more than 700,000 visits;

- over 10,000 babies are delivered by the NHS;

- NHS chiropodists inspect over 150,000 pairs of feet;

- NHS ambulances make over 50,000 emergency journeys;

- pharmacists dispense approximately 10 million items on NHS prescriptions; and

- NHS surgeons perform around 1,200 hip operations, 3,000 heart operations and 1,050 kidney operations.

convenient access to health information and advice. The service helps people to be better able to care for themselves and their families, when it is appropriate to do so, and to direct them to the most appropriate level of care when they need professional help. During 2001/02 NHS Direct handled around 5 million calls.

Wales has a similar service, NHS Direct Wales, which offers advice in both English and Welsh. In Scotland, a new service – NHS 24 – was launched in May 2002 (see page 166). NHS Direct Online (*www.nhsdirect.nhs.uk*), an Internet extension of the telephone-based services, receives around 230,000 visitors a month. The website features an electronic version of the NHS Direct self-help guide, an encyclopedia of over 450 health topics and an interactive enquiry service for health information. During 2001/02 the Department of Health piloted four schemes exploring the potential for using digital television as another means of providing people with home access to health information and services. Results from the pilot schemes are being evaluated.

Health Action Zones

There are 26 Health Action Zones (HAZs) in deprived areas of England, including inner city, rural and ex-coalfield communities. A further ten

associated HAZs have been established in south-east England. The zones are local partnerships between the health service, local councils, voluntary groups and local businesses, and receive government funding. Their aim is to make measurable improvements in the health of local people and in the quality of treatment and care. Working closely with the Department of Health, the participants co-operate to tackle inequalities and deliver better services and healthcare. They focus on areas such as programmes to stop smoking, children's and young people's health, mental health, CHD and cancer, older people's health, and the health of minority ethnic groups. HAZs play an important role in the development of Local Strategic Partnerships (LSPs) and the NHS modernisation agenda.

Four HAZs have been established in Northern Ireland and an initiative to encourage local healthcare partnerships has been launched in Scotland. The Scottish Executive is also seeking to reduce health inequalities via Social Inclusion Partnerships.

Electronic initiatives

The NHS is making increasing use of new technology in patient care and is undertaking a major information technology (IT) development programme. This is focusing on improving the IT infrastructure and developing electronic national services for prescribing, patient records and booking appointments.

In England, a six-month evaluation of electronic prescription pilot schemes began in June 2002. Preliminary conclusions will be reported to the Department of Health by the end of 2002, with a final report due in spring 2003. Following evaluation, the aim is that there will be electronic transmission of half of all prescriptions throughout England by the end of 2005.

NHSnet is a range of voice and data services used by the NHS, covering radio, telephone and computer-based communications. Health authorities and trusts are connected to NHSnet, as are a number of major NHS suppliers and all GPs in Scotland. By April 2002 every GP practice in England was connected to NHSnet and able to send and receive e-mails.

NHSnet will support the longer-term goal of providing an electronic booking system and introducing electronic health records to replace the paper-based records. The Government has said that by 2005 every patient in England will be able to access his or her own electronic health record – a summary of key personal and health data about the patient. NHSnet will also give doctors secure access to patients' records in an emergency when they are away from home. An equivalent scheme, HPSSnet, has been set up in Northern Ireland by Northern Ireland Health and Personal Social Services (HPSS).

NHS Plus

NHS Plus was established in November 2001 as a national network providing occupational health services to the private sector, in particular focusing on small and medium-size businesses. Services provided by NHS Plus include workplace risk assessment, health surveillance, medical advice on sickness absence and retirements, stress counselling and drug and alcohol screening. Over 115 NHS Trusts have signed up to provide this service.

England

In July 2000 the Government set out in its NHS Plan, a ten-year programme of reform and investment for healthcare in England, aimed at improving clinical performance and health service productivity. Many of the Plan's legislative proposals were implemented through the *Health and Social Care Act 2001*. The NHS Plan includes a number of targets for the NHS to achieve by 2004. Among these are:

- patients to be able to see a general practitioner within 48 hours;

- hospital consultants to deliver approximately 4 million outpatient consultations a year, working additionally in primary care and community settings;

- GPs to be able to refer patients to around 1,000 'specialist' GPs instead of referring them to hospital; and

- waiting time in accident and emergency departments in hospitals to fall to 1 hour 15 minutes on average.

Targets to be met by the NHS by the end of 2005 include:

- the replacement of waiting lists for appointments and admission by booking systems;

- a reduction in the maximum waiting time for a routine outpatient appointment from six to three months; and

- a reduction in the maximum waiting time for inpatient treatment from 18 to 6 months.

Fundamental to the programme of reform is the way in which the NHS will be structured, and the roles and responsibilities of the organisations within it. The *NHS Reform and Health Care Professions Act 2002* includes provisions which will:

- devolve power over NHS resources to doctors and nurses, allocating NHS resources directly to Primary Care Trusts (PCTs) (see page 164). By 2004, 75 per cent of NHS spending will be directly controlled by doctors and nurses in local communities;

- strengthen the independence of the Commission for Health Improvement (CHI), which provides independent advice to the NHS on developing and improving the quality of NHS services, by giving it new powers to designate failing health services as in need of special measures. The CHI would in future assess and publish star ratings for NHS organisations;

- establish a Commission for Patient and Public Involvement in Health, to encourage public participation on hospital trusts and PCTs and ensure that public consultations are effective and inclusive throughout the NHS; and

- create a Council for the Regulation of Health Care Professionals, to oversee the activities of the various regulatory bodies of the healthcare professions, including the General Medical Council.

Strategic Health Authorities

In April 2002 the 95 former English Health Authorities were abolished and 28 larger and more strategic Health Authorities were established. The *NHS Reform and Health Care Professions Act 2002* provided for these to be called Strategic Health Authorities (StHAs) from October 2002. The StHAs, with typical populations of between 1.5 and 2.4 million (see Figure 13.3), have taken on some of the Department of Health's operational functions. They are responsible for creating, in consultation with stakeholders, a framework for local health services, building capacity, supporting performance improvement and managing the performance of PCTs and of NHS Trusts in their areas. The Department of Health continues to have responsibility for policy development and overall regulation and inspection of the NHS. The Department has established four directorates of health and social care to oversee the development of the NHS and provide a link between NHS organisations and the Government. The Department's eight regional offices are being disbanded.

Primary Care Trusts

The structural reorganisation established 302 local PCTs across England, replacing the 481 Primary Care Groups and taking over many of the responsibilities of the former 95 Health Authorities. PCTs are groups of between 50 and 100 GP practices and healthcare professionals. They are responsible for deciding which health services the local population needs and ensuring the provision of these services.

Appropriate provision of all other services, including hospitals, dentists, mental health services, Walk-in Centres, NHS Direct (see page 161), patient transport (including accident and emergency), population screening, pharmacies and opticians, is also the responsibility of PCTs. In addition, they develop health improvement programmes and ensure that local NHS organisations work effectively with local authorities and social services.

Health Improvement and Modernisation Plans

Health Improvement and Modernisation Plans (HIMPs) are three-year strategic plans for local health organisations. They focus on priorities for health improvement and reducing health inequalities, and aim to modernise health service planning and delivery. From October 2002 each PCT will be required to lead the development of an HIMP, ensuring the involvement from the outset of local organisations, including NHS Trusts, local authorities, the voluntary sector and local communities.

Care Trusts

Care Trusts are NHS bodies that work in both health and social care and can be established where NHS organisations and local authorities agree to work together. A Care Trust is usually set up where it is felt that closer integration between health and social care is needed or would be beneficial at a local level. Four Care Trusts were set

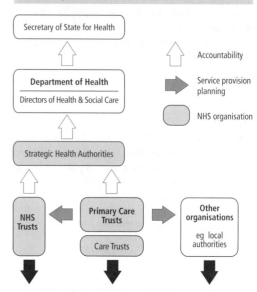

Figure 13.3 NHS structure in England from April 2002

Source: Department of Health

up in April 2002 and six more should be established by April 2003.

NHS Trusts

NHS trusts are the organisations responsible for running most NHS hospitals. There are currently 273 NHS Trusts in England. Although the statutory functions of the Trusts were not changed following the NHS reorganisation, they are now overseen by the StHAs.

NHS Walk-in Centres

NHS Walk-in Centres are a network of nurse-led centres – where no appointment is necessary – offering quick access to a range of services, including healthcare advice and information, and treatment for minor ailments and injuries. They are intended to complement GP surgeries and help reduce pressure on GPs. By the end of 2001, 42 NHS Walk-in Centres had opened in England.

National Institute for Clinical Excellence

The National Institute for Clinical Excellence (NICE) was established in 1999 to develop national standards for best practice in clinical care within the NHS in England and Wales. This includes drawing up guidelines based on clinical and cost effectiveness and ensuring that they apply to all parts of the NHS. The Institute's membership is drawn from the health professions, the NHS, academics, health economists and patients. It appraises new drugs and technologies, and produces clinical guidelines.

In March 2002 the Department of Health consulted on how topics are selected for appraisal by NICE, with the main objective of making it easier for interested parties to put topics forward. Among the drugs referred to NICE for appraisal in its work programme, starting in April 2003 is the use of cannabis derivatives for the treatment of various conditions, including management of pain relief in multiple sclerosis.

Health education
Responsibility for health education lies with separate NHS authorities working alongside the national health departments. The Health Development Agency (HDA) works to improve the health of people and communities in England, and in particular to reduce health inequalities. In partnership with others, it gathers evidence of what works, advises on standards and develops the skills of all those working to improve health.

In March 2002 Health Promotion England, which had run national campaigns on a number of subjects, including childhood immunisation, drugs, alcohol and sexual health, was closed. Its core functions were transferred to the Department of Health.

Wales
In Wales, the operation of the NHS is the responsibility of the Welsh Assembly Government. Its ten-year health programme – *Improving Health in Wales – A Plan for the NHS with its Partners –* was published in 2001. Effective partnership working is an important theme of the Welsh Plan. At a national level, a Health and Well-being Partnership Council has been established, chaired by the Health and Social Services Minister. The Council brings together key personnel from the NHS, local government, the voluntary and independent sectors, staff and professional groups, and patients' representatives, to ensure the direction and leadership of the agenda for health and well-being. The council is supported by a network of similar partnerships at a local level.

The Assembly Government has the power to make changes to the structure of the NHS in Wales

through secondary or 'delegated' legislation (see page 40). Through this means specific Welsh clauses were introduced in the *NHS Reform and Health Care Professions Act 2002*. In relation to Wales, the Act provided for the creation of 22 Local Health Boards (LHBs), to replace the existing five Health Authorities in Wales on 31 March 2003. The new structure will result in changes at two levels:

- at a local level, Local Health Groups will be developed into the new LHBs and their role strengthened, and they will take on new responsibilities for commissioning and delivering healthcare in their localities; and

- at a national level, the Assembly Government will hold both LHBs and NHS Trusts fully accountable for the services they provide and commission.

The Act also placed a duty on each LHB and local authority in Wales to formulate and implement a 'health and well-being' strategy for the population in the area. This will include agreeing joint investment priorities and co-operation with other organisations, such as NHS Trusts, Community Health Councils, voluntary bodies and local businesses.

Since devolution, the Welsh Assembly Government also has some control over the finances of the NHS in Wales. In February 2001 it announced additional investment, so that by 2003/04 the health budget is planned to be £3.6 billion, an increase of £1 billion on 1999/2000. The health budget for 2001/02 was £3.1 billion. Much of this new investment is being directed towards tackling the priorities outlined in *Improving Health in Wales*: coronary heart disease, cancer services, mental health services, intensive care, primary and community care, children's services and local priorities in Health Improvement Programmes. Other areas targeted are integrated working methods to address waiting lists and waiting times, pressures on admissions, human resource development for the NHS workforce, and the establishment of a new Inequalities in Health Fund.

Scotland
The Scottish Executive Health Department is responsible both for the executive leadership of

NHSScotland and for the development and implementation of health and community care policy.

Prior to devolution in 1999, healthcare in Scotland was already distinct from healthcare in England and Wales in many ways. In December 2000 the Scottish Executive Health Department published the Scottish Health Plan – *Our National Health: A plan for action, a plan for change* – which described its priorities. These are to:

- improve Scotland's health, and narrow the health gap between rich and poor;

- set national standards of care to be delivered locally across Scotland;

- improve patient access to health services;

- give patients and communities a voice in the running of the NHS;

- provide better care for the young, and for older people;

- reduce coronary heart disease, cancer and poor mental health; and

- change the ways in which the NHS works with its staff so as to improve care and standards.

To achieve these aims, the Executive's core spending on health is planned to rise from £6.2 billion in 2002/03 to £6.7 billion in 2003/04 – this represents approximately a third of the devolved Scottish budget. In addition, a new way of sharing NHS funds across Scotland is now in place to address relative healthcare needs, including those caused by deprivation and by geographical remoteness.

In September 2001 the decision-making powers of the 15 Health Boards and 28 NHS Trusts were brought together in 15 new unified NHS Boards, each of which is responsible for all NHS services in its area. The introduction of the new NHS Boards aims to unify local health services and ensure that national clinical and service standards are delivered in all parts of Scotland. The Boards are required to show how they are involving the public, and how this has affected the provision of services. Local Health Councils also provide a voice for the local public in each area. The Scottish Executive intends to announce further reform of NHSScotland early in 2003.

The 15 NHS Boards and 32 local authorities work together to strengthen the localised focus of health provision, and every local authority has a seat on its principal NHS Board. Acute services and primary care continue to be delivered through NHS Trusts, and the Island Boards remain as integrated structures with no separate Trusts. Other NHS bodies, such as the Scottish Ambulance Service, the Health Education Board for Scotland and the Clinical Standards Board for Scotland, provide services on a national basis. The Scottish Executive is investing £14 million in improving NHSScotland's ability to communicate and work with patients. One such initiative is the Patients' Project, a systematic assessment of patient information which aims to disseminate best practice and to act as a national source of patient information and advice.

The Scottish Health Plan includes the same clinical priorities as the NHS Plan for England: CHD, cancer and poor mental health. In July 2001 the Scottish Executive published *Cancer in Scotland: Action for Change*, a comprehensive cancer plan for Scotland. In November 2001 the Minister for Health and Community Care announced an extra £40 million investment for improving cancer care, and set out the first annual investment plan prepared by the regional cancer advisory groups in partnership with local NHS Boards and Trusts and the Scottish Cancer Group. In spring 2002 the Scottish CHD Task Force published a *CHD and Stroke Strategy for Scotland*.

The Executive sponsors the work of a number of organisations and initiatives aimed at improving the quality of healthcare provided in Scotland. These include the Clinical Standards Board for Scotland, the Health Technology Board for Scotland, the Scottish Needs Assessment Programme and the Scottish Medicines Consortium. The Clinical Standards Board is responsible for developing and running a national system of quality assurance in health care for the NHS in Scotland. The Health Technology Board is a single source of national advice on the most clinically and cost-effective health technologies, playing a similar role to NICE in England and Wales (see page 164).

In May 2002 NHS 24 was launched in Scotland. This is a nurse-led telephone advice service similar to NHS Direct in England (see page 161). The first call centre covers the Grampian region. The service will be fully operational across Scotland by the end of 2004. There are also plans to introduce an NHS 24 online service.

Northern Ireland

The Department of Health, Social Services and Public Safety (DHSSPS) is responsible for the development and implementation of health and community care policy in Northern Ireland. In March 2002 it published a public health strategy, *Investing for Health*. This focuses on the key objectives of preventing ill health and reducing health inequalities among different groups in the population. In order to meet these objectives, the strategy recognises the importance of working alongside other departments with responsibilities for housing, the environment and education. By 2010 it aims to:

■ increase life expectancy by at least three years for men and two years for women;

■ halve the gap in average life expectancy between those living in the fifth most deprived wards and the population as a whole; and

■ reduce by a fifth the gap in the proportion of people with a long-standing illness in the lowest and the highest socio-economic groups.

Northern Ireland's equivalent bodies to health authorities are the four health and social services boards. They are responsible for identifying the healthcare needs of people in their area, securing hospital and community health services, providing primary care services, and administering contracts. The boards have a major role to play in the implementation of *Investing for Health*. They are responsible for establishing an 'Investing for Health Partnership', reflecting the main public, voluntary and community interests in their area. They are also responsible for producing 'Health and Well-being Investment Plans'.

The Health Promotion Agency plays a key role in identifying needs and in developing and implementing programmes designed to promote health and prevent ill health. It co-ordinates regional health promotion activities throughout Northern Ireland, undertakes public education campaigns, evaluates and disseminates research findings, provides training and works with the wider health and personal social services and

other bodies in helping to implement the Government's public health policies.

One of the wider impacts of the Belfast (Good Friday) Agreement in 1999 (see page 17) was the setting up of bodies for cross-border co-operation between Northern Ireland and the Irish Republic. Co-operation on health matters was identified as an area suitable for consideration by the North/South Ministerial Council. Joint Working Groups have been set up in five areas: accident and emergency services, emergency planning, high technology equipment, cancer research and health promotion. These groups are looking in detail at where co-operation can yield the greatest benefit for people in both Northern Ireland and the Irish Republic. Joint ventures have included the production of an all-Ireland cancer incidence report, a folic acid advertising campaign, promotion of physical fitness, and training and research initiatives.

The Food Safety Promotion Board is involved in supporting North/South scientific co-operation, and promoting links between institutions working in the field of food safety, such as laboratories, food safety enforcement agencies and research bodies.

Finance

The NHS is financed mainly through general taxation, along with an element of National Insurance contributions (see chapter 12) paid by employed people, their employers and self-employed people. In 2001/02 an estimated 78 per cent of the NHS was financed through general taxation, with 12 per cent from National Insurance contributions and 10 per cent from charges and other receipts.

In the April 2002 Budget, the Chancellor of the Exchequer announced increases in National Insurance contributions from April 2003 to provide extra funding for the NHS. As a result, spending on the NHS will increase from £68.1 billion in 2002/03 to £109.4 billion in 2007/08. This will result in the proportion of the UK's GDP spent on health services increasing from 7.7 per cent to 9.4 per cent over this five-year period. Government spending plans for the next three financial years are set out in Table 13.4.

The extra funding is to be allocated mainly to training new health professionals and to a

Table 13.4 Government expenditure plans for the NHS

	Total expenditure	£billion of which capital investment
2002/03	68.1	2.8
2003/04	74.9	3.5
2004/05	82.2	4.1

1 Figures relate to total UK expenditure and capital investment as announced by the Chancellor of the Exchequer in the April 2002 Budget.
Source: HM Treasury

programme for modernising NHS infrastructure and information technology. Following the Budget, the Health Secretary published *Delivering the NHS Plan – next steps on investment; next steps on reform*, a five-year investment plan for the NHS. It sets targets, due to be achieved by 2008, of:

- 15,000 more GPs and consultants;

- 30,000 more scientists and therapists;

- 35,000 more nurses, midwives and health visitors; and

- waiting times for operations to fall from a maximum 15 months in 2002 to six months by 2005 and three months by 2008.

Some NHS funding is raised from other, non-government, sources. For example, some hospitals increase revenue by taking private patients, who pay the full cost of their accommodation and treatment. Hospitals can also use private finance for NHS capital projects, under the Private Finance Initiative (PFI), which aims to promote commercial partnership between the public and private sectors (see page 350). This involves new NHS facilities being designed, built, maintained and owned by the private sector, which then leases them back to the NHS. The NHS retains control of key planning and clinical decisions.

Less than a third of hospitals now pre-date the formation of the NHS in 1948. While much has been done to improve existing hospital buildings, the largest building programme in the history of the NHS is currently in progress, including several major PFI schemes. Altogether over 100 new hospital schemes are planned between 2000 and 2010.

Review of NHS resources

A review commissioned by the Chancellor of the Exchequer to examine future health trends and the resources required over the next two decades was published in April 2002. The Wanless Report – *Securing our Future Health: Taking a Long-Term View* – included the following recommendations:

- the proportion of gross domestic product (GDP) spent on health to rise from 7.7 per cent in 2002 to 12.5 per cent by 2022;

- NHS spending to increase by 7.7 per cent a year over the next five years, to £96 billion by 2007;

- a one-third increase in the number of nurses and two-thirds increase in the number of doctors;

- a maximum two-week waiting time for hospital appointments by 2022;

- a doubling of spending on information technology;

- a major increase in the new hospitals building programme;

- the introduction of charges for non-clinical services; and

- greater co-operation between the NHS and the private sector.

The Government accepts the conclusions of the review and has decided to allocate additional spending to the NHS (see page 167).

Charges

Around 587 million prescription items, worth around £6.1 billion, were dispensed in the community in England in 2001. The proportion of items provided free of charge was 85 per cent. The following groups are exempt from prescription charges: people aged 60 and over; children under 16 and full-time students under 19; women who are pregnant or have given birth in the previous 12 months; and people with certain medical conditions. In addition, people who receive (or whose partners receive) certain social security benefits (see chapter 12), or who otherwise qualify on low income grounds, do not have to pay prescription charges. There are charges for most types of NHS dental treatment, including examinations. However, the following people are entitled to free treatment: women who begin a course of treatment while pregnant or within 12 months of having a baby; children under 18; full-time students under 19; and adults on low incomes or receiving the same benefits or tax credits as for free prescriptions.

Free NHS sight tests are available for people aged 60 and over, children, full-time students under the age of 19, adults on low incomes or receiving the same benefits or tax credits as for free prescriptions, and people who have, or are at particular risk of, eye disease. Around 10.5 million sight tests were paid for by health authorities in England and Wales in the year to 31 March 2002.

Fraud prevention

The NHS Counter Fraud Service was set up in 1998 to counter all fraud and corruption in the Department of Health and NHS, with a specific priority on the Family Health Services. In 2000/01 losses to pharmaceutical and dental patient fraud in England were estimated at £99 million, a 37 per cent decrease on the 1999/2000 figure of £157 million. A system requiring patients to provide evidence that they are exempt from NHS charges has played a significant part in reducing fraud since it was introduced in 1999. Dentists and opticians are also now using a similar approach.

NHS workforce

The NHS is one of the largest employers in the world. In 2000 there were the equivalent of just over a million full-time direct care employees in NHS hospital and community health services in the United Kingdom (see Table 13.5).

Doctors and dentists

Only people on the medical or dentists' registers may practise as doctors or dentists in the NHS. University medical and dental schools are responsible for undergraduate teaching, and the NHS provides hospital and community facilities for training.

Full registration as a doctor requires five or six years' training in a medical school, in a hospital and in the community, with a further year's hospital experience. The regulating body for the

Great Ormond Street Hospital for Children 150th anniversary

Great Ormond Street Hospital is a specialist centre for the treatment of sick children, and was the first in the United Kingdom to offer inpatient care to children only. It has pioneered research into bone marrow transplant operations and the development of new drugs for epilepsy, arthritis and HIV.

Key dates in its history:

- 1852: Dr Charles West opens the hospital with just ten beds;

- 1875: the first purpose-built hospital building was completed;

- 1895: hospital's medical school established;

- 1929: J M Barrie, the author of *Peter Pan* donates the rights of the play to the hospital;

- 1946: Institute of Child Health (an international centre of research into childhood diseases) founded;

- 1966: new Institute of Child Health building opens;

- 1987: Wishing Well Appeal launched to raise money for new hospital building;

- 1994: Variety Club Building opens, funded by the Wishing Well Appeal;

- 2001: Gene therapy laboratory opens and clinical trials of gene therapy begin; and

- 2002: 150th anniversary.

The hospital:

- treats over 22,000 inpatients and 77,000 outpatients each year;

- performs 10,600 scheduled and 2,365 unscheduled operations a year;

- has 315 doctors, 900 registered nurses and healthcare assistants, and 135 allied medical professionals;

- provides overnight accommodation for 1,000 parents a week; and

- performs between 550 and 600 child heart operations each year.

Table 13.5 NHS workforce,[1] United Kingdom, September 2000

	England	Scotland	Wales	Northern Ireland	United Kingdom
Medical and dental staff	n/a	n/a	n/a	n/a	76,575
Nursing, midwifery and health visitors[2]	346,176	51,228	24,314	14,910	436,628
Other non-medical staff	393,223	47,819	27,467	22,248	490,757
All staff	n/a	n/a	n/a	n/a	**1,003,960**

1 Figures on a full-time equivalent basis rounded to the nearest whole number.
2 Excludes learners and agency staff.
Source: Department of Health, National Assembly for Wales, NHSScotland and Department of Health, Social Services and Public Safety, Northern Ireland

medical profession in the United Kingdom is the General Medical Council (GMC), and the main professional association is the British Medical Association. As a result of high-profile cases, such as that of Harold Shipman,[4] clinical governance has become an increasing concern.

In April 2002 it became obligatory for all GPs, excluding locums and assistants, to be appraised by a fellow GP, who will undergo training for the role. The appraisal system will also play an important role in five-yearly revalidation for doctors, which is due to be introduced by the GMC. The National Clinical Assessment Authority (NCAA) was established in April 2001. It provides a rapid objective assessment of a doctor's performance where necessary and advice about the handling of local cases.

For a dentist, five years' training at a dental school and satisfactory completion of one year's mandatory vocational training are required before permission is granted to work as a principal in the General Dental Services of the NHS. All general dental practitioners are paid by a combination of capitation fees for children registered with the practice, continuing care payments for adults registered, and a prescribed scale of fees for individual treatments. The regulating body for the dental profession in the United Kingdom is the General Dental Council, and the main professional association is the British Dental Association.

Nurses, midwives and health visitors

The majority of nursing students undertake the pre-registration Diploma in Higher Education programme, which emphasises health promotion as well as care of the sick and enables students to work either in hospitals or in the community. The programme lasts three years and consists of periods of university study combined with practical experience in hospital and in the community.

In 2000 the first nurse consultant posts were introduced. The NHS Plan committed the Government to establishing 1,000 such posts by 2004, and by June 2002 over 750 posts had been approved. The positions combine specialist practice with leadership, consultancy, education and research responsibilities.

In April 2001 the first 'modern matron' posts were created. Every hospital will have matrons, each in overall charge of a group of wards. They will help ensure high standards of care, set and monitor standards for cleaning and catering, and have authority to take action where these are not met. The Government's target is to have 2,000 matrons on wards by 2004. By April 2002, 1,895 appointments had already been made.

Midwifery education programmes for registered general/adult nurses take 18 months, while the direct entry programme lasts three years. Health visitors and district nurses are registered adult nurses who have a further specialist qualification and care for clients in the community.

The Nursing and Midwifery Council (NMC) is responsible for regulating and registering nurses, midwives and health visitors throughout the United Kingdom. In April 2002 it formally

4 In January 2000, a Manchester GP, Harold Shipman, was convicted of murdering 15 elderly patients. An ongoing public inquiry was established by Parliament in January 2001, with public hearings into individual cases beginning in June 2001.

replaced the United Kingdom Central Council for Nursing, Midwifery and Health Visiting and the four National Boards for England, Wales, Scotland and Northern Ireland. Its key responsibilities are to:

- maintain a UK register of qualified nurses, midwives and health visitors;

- set standards for education, practice and conduct;

- provide advice to nurses, midwives and health visitors; and

- consider allegations of professional misconduct or unfitness to practice due to ill health.

Pharmacists

Only people on the register of pharmaceutical chemists may practise as pharmacists. Registration requires four years' training in a school of pharmacy, followed by one year's practical experience in a community or hospital pharmacy approved for training by regulatory bodies for the profession – the Royal Pharmaceutical Society of Great Britain or the Pharmaceutical Society of Northern Ireland.

Community pharmacists are paid professional fees for dispensing NHS prescriptions, as well as being reimbursed for the cost of the drugs and appliances concerned. In April 2002 the Government outlined proposals for extending prescribing powers to pharmacists and nurses. This would mean that after diagnosis patients may no longer need to revisit their doctors for repeat prescriptions on items such as inhalers and hormone replacement therapy. Like nurses, pharmacists will need to undergo training to become supplementary prescribers. It is envisaged that the first training programmes for pharmacists will be in place by late spring 2003.

Opticians

The General Optical Council regulates the professions of optometrists (ophthalmic opticians) and dispensing opticians. Only registered ophthalmic opticians may test sight. Their training takes four years, including a year of practical experience under supervision. Dispensing opticians take a two-year full-time course with a year's practical experience, or follow a part-time day-release or distance learning course while employed with an optician.

Other health professions

The Health Professions Council (HPC) was established in April 2002 as a new UK-wide regulatory body responsible for setting and monitoring the standards of professional training, performance and conduct of 12 healthcare professions: arts therapists, chiropodists, clinical scientists, dietitians, medical laboratory technicians, occupational therapists, orthoptists, paramedics, physiotherapists, prosthetists and orthotists, radiographers, and speech and language therapists. The HPC replaced the Council for Professions Supplementary to Medicine and its 12 professional boards.

Recruitment

The NHS is seeking to attract more recruits to train as nurses, midwives and allied health professionals, such as physiotherapists and occupational therapists. Between September 1999 and September 2001 an extra 20,740 nurses joined the NHS. The NHS is also seeking to attract former staff under the 'Return to Practice' initiative. By September 2002 over 11,900 nurses, midwives and health visitors had returned to the NHS since February 1999. Affordable staff accommodation has also been prioritised. In September 2001 the Starter Home Initiative was launched (see page 296). This scheme provides key public workers with equity loans and shared ownership arrangements. By 2004 it is expected that around 5,000 NHS staff will have benefited from the scheme.

The NHS is also recruiting from abroad, and in 2000 set a target of recruiting 1,000 doctors and 2,000 nurses from abroad by March 2005, particularly from countries where there are surpluses of suitably qualified staff.

International Fellowship Scheme for the NHS

In February 2002 the Government launched a scheme, which by 2005 aims to attract up to 450 expert heart and lung surgeons, histopathologists, psychiatrists, radiologists and other top specialists from abroad. The fellowships will last for up to two years and allow the selected specialists opportunities to take part in clinical research and teaching, and study visits to hospitals at the forefront of their field.

Services for children, women and men

Children

Important activities in promoting the health of children include:

- prevention of childhood accidents;

- immunisation and vaccination (see page 159);

- screening and health surveillance; and

- health education on diet and exercise.

Babies and pre-school children

A comprehensive programme of health surveillance, provided for pre-school children (under five years of age), is run by community health services and GPs, who receive an annual payment for every child registered on the programme (in Scotland this is carried out by the Community Paediatric Service, which may be based in the primary care or acute services trust).

Health visitors have a central role in health promotion, in identifying the healthcare needs of under-fives and helping to ensure access to the services necessary to meet those needs. They visit new-born babies at home between 10 and 14 days after birth. Later checks take place usually at:

- six to eight weeks (with a physical examination by a health visitor, GP or clinic doctor);

- six to nine months (including hearing and sight assessments);

- 18 months to two years; and

- pre-school at three to four-and-a-half years.

New hearing tests for babies in the first few days of life were launched in 20 English pilot areas in autumn 2001. The new scheme, Universal Neonatal Hearing Screening, is intended to replace the current Infant Distraction Test, normally performed at seven to eight months.

School health services

Children attending state schools have access to the school health service, and are usually registered with a GP and a dentist. In addition to providing health advice to children and young people, the service assists teachers with pupils who have medical needs.

School nurses check hearing, sight, speech and weight, and administer vaccinations including Bacillus of Calmette and Guerin (BCG), diphtheria, tetanus and polio boosters. They are also involved in health education, counselling and sex education.

Child guidance and child psychiatric services provide help and advice to families and children with psychological or emotional problems. In recent years efforts have been made to improve co-operation between community-based child health services and local authority education and social services for children. This is particularly important in the prevention of child abuse and for the health and welfare of children being looked after by local authorities (see page 149).

Children's National Service Framework

In 2001 the Secretary of State for Health announced the development of a new Children's National Service Framework (NSF) in England. This will be aimed at developing new national

---

Public inquiry into children's heart surgery at Bristol Royal Infirmary

The Bristol Royal Infirmary inquiry was set up in 1998 to investigate the deaths of 29 babies undergoing heart surgery at the hospital in the late 1980s and early 1990s. The report of the public inquiry was published in July 2001. Its recommendations include the:

- appointment of a national director for children's services to lead the development of children's healthcare;

- introduction of appraisal and revalidation for all healthcare professionals;

- implementation of national standards of clinical and hospital care;

- creation of an independent monitoring service to identify good and failing hospitals; and

- more openness about clinical performance, allowing patients to access information about the relative performance of hospitals, services and consultants.

standards across the NHS and social services. Six external working groups have been established to help develop the framework, each focusing on different issues. The standards will aim to ensure better access and smoother progression in the provision of services for children, from initial contact with the NHS, via a GP surgery or NHS hospital, through to social services support.

Child and Adolescent Mental Health Services (CAMHS)

In 1998, 24 CAMHS projects were set up. They will receive £4 million annual funding from the Department of Health until March 2004. The services are a partnership between health and local authorities and aim to provide early intervention to prevent serious mental health or behavioural difficulties. They also provide innovative services for young people often excluded from mainstream services.

Women

Women have particular health needs related to pregnancy and certain forms of cancer.

Screening

Screening programmes are in operation for breast cancer and cervical cancer. At present, under the United Kingdom's breast cancer screening programme, every woman aged between 50 and 64 is invited for mammography (breast X-ray) every three years by computerised call-up and recall systems. This facility is to be extended to women aged 65 to 70 by 2004 in England. In Scotland, the extension to women aged 65 to 70 will begin in 2003/04 and be implemented over a three-year round of screening. In addition, all women over the age of 64 can refer themselves for screening. In England, 1.3 million women of all ages were screened and 8,345 cases of cancer were diagnosed in 2000/01. In Scotland 120,000 women were screened with 847 cases of cancer diagnosed.

National policy for cervical screening is that women should be screened every three to five years (three-and-a-half to five-and-a-half years in Scotland) so as to detect indications of the long developmental stage which may proceed to invasive cancer. The programme invites women aged 20 to 64 (20 to 60 in Scotland) for screening. However, since many women are not invited immediately when they reach their 20th birthday, the age group 25 to 64 is used to give a more accurate estimate of coverage of the target

population in England. By the end of March 2001, 83 per cent of women aged 25 to 64 had been screened at least once in the previous five years in England, 87 per cent in Scotland, 81 per cent in Wales and 70 per cent in Northern Ireland.

Maternity

Nearly all births take place in hospital, although there was a slight increase during the 1990s in the popularity of home births. These accounted for around 2 per cent of births in England and Wales in 2000, compared with around 1 per cent during the 1980s. Home births in Scotland remain relatively constant at under 1 per cent.

A woman is entitled to care throughout pregnancy, birth and the postnatal period. Care may be provided by a midwife, a community-based GP, a hospital-based obstetrician, or a combination of these. Special preventive services are provided under the NHS to safeguard the health of pregnant women and mothers with young children. Services include free dental treatment; health education; and vaccination and immunisation of children against certain infectious diseases (see page 159).

There is a welfare food scheme for mothers on low income, providing formula feed and vitamins free of charge. The NHS Plan envisages that the scheme will be reformed by 2004 to improve access to a healthy diet for children in poverty. As part of the drive to tackle health inequalities, breastfeeding is encouraged by the Infant Feeding Initiative in England and the Scottish Breastfeeding Group and the National Breastfeeding Adviser in Scotland.

In England, *The Pregnancy Book*, a complete guide to a healthy pregnancy, labour and giving birth as well as life with a new baby, and *Birth to Five*, a guide to the early stages of development, nutrition, weaning and common childhood ailments, are both made available to all first-time mothers free of charge. The Scottish equivalent is *Ready, Steady, Baby!*, produced by the Health Education Board for Scotland. New mothers also receive a Personal Child Health Record. This helps parents to keep a record of immunisation, tests, birth details and health checks.

In 2001 the Scottish Executive published the national *Framework for Maternity Services in Scotland*, designed to ensure choices for women and their families while recognising the need for clinical safety. It sets out a basis against which each NHS Trust and NHS Board should judge its own service provision, and covers key aspects of maternity care, the organisation of maternity services, and women's and parents' information needs. In England, the Children's NSF (see page 172) will include standards for maternity services, with an extra £100 million being invested to fund capital improvements to modernise the facilities in maternity units, as well as separate additional investment to provide 2,000 extra midwives by 2005.

Teenage pregnancy

The Social Exclusion Unit's report on teenage pregnancy, published in 1999, set out a national strategy for England to halve the rate of under 18 conceptions by 2010, with an interim reduction of 15 per cent by 2004. It also aims to increase the participation of teenage parents in education and work to 60 per cent by 2010. To ensure delivery of the national strategy aims, every top-tier local authority area has a ten-year local teenage pregnancy strategy and detailed three-year action plan. Between 1999 and 2000 the conception rate for women aged under 18 in England and Wales declined from 45.0 to 43.8 per 1,000.

Abortion

Under the *Abortion Act 1967*, as amended, a time limit of 24 weeks applies to the largest category of abortion – risk to the physical or mental health of the pregnant woman – and also to abortion because of a similar risk to any existing children of her family. There are three categories in which no time limit applies: to prevent grave permanent injury to the physical or mental health of the woman; where there is a substantial risk of serious foetal handicap; or where continuing the pregnancy would involve a risk to the life of the pregnant woman greater than if the pregnancy were terminated. The Act does not apply in Northern Ireland.

Between 2000 and 2001 the number of legal abortions performed on women resident in England and Wales rose by 0.5 per cent to 186,000. The overall age-standardised rate remained at 17 abortions per 1,000 women aged between 15 and 44.

Men

Men, particularly younger men, tend to use primary care services less than women. A 1998 Department of Health Survey showed that 69 per cent of men aged 18 to 24 in England had visited their GP in the preceding 12 months, compared with 90 per cent of women in the same age group.

Lower life expectancy (see page 157) is the most significant indication of the health inequalities that exist between men and women. The two main reasons for this are that men tend to have less healthy lifestyles in terms of diet and higher alcohol and drug intake, and are involved in more accidents. They also risk later diagnosis and treatment because they do not consult a doctor as quickly as women when a problem arises.

To address the health inequalities that exist between men and women, Health Action Zones (see page 162), Health Improvement and Modernisation Plans (HIMPs) (see page 164) and Healthy Living Centres are developing programmes to improve men's health. The Health Development Agency (see page 165) has also commissioned research into young men's health activities.

The NHS Cancer Plan set out the Government's intention to introduce prostate cancer screening when screening and treatment techniques have developed sufficiently. In the meantime, a prostate cancer risk management programme has been launched. One element of this is a project for prostate specific antigen (PSA) testing.

Hospital and specialist services

District general hospitals offer a broad spectrum of clinical specialities, supported by a range of other services, such as anaesthetics, pathology and radiology. Almost all have facilities for the admission of emergency patients, either through accident and emergency departments or as direct referrals from GPs. Treatments are provided for inpatients, day cases, outpatients and patients who attend wards for treatment such as dialysis.

Some hospitals also provide specialist services covering more than one region or district, for example for heart and liver transplants and rare eye and bone cancers. There are also specialist hospitals, such as the Hospital for Sick Children at Great Ormond Street (see page 169), Moorfields Eye Hospital, and the National Hospital for Neurology and Neurosurgery, all in London. These hospitals combine specialist treatment facilities with the training of medical and other students, and international research.

Organ transplants

United Kingdom Transplant (a special health authority of the NHS) provides a 24-hour support service to all transplant units in the UK and the Irish Republic for the matching and allocation of organs for transplant. In many cases transplants are multi-organ.

In the UK during 2001, 1,743 kidney transplants were performed, and at the end of that year there were 6,223 patients waiting for this operation. At the end of 2001 there were seven designated thoracic transplant centres in England, and one in Scotland. During that year, 166 heart, 93 lung, and 32 heart/lung transplants were performed. There are six designated liver transplant units in England and one in Scotland. In 2001, 675 liver transplants were performed.

People who are willing to donate their organs after death carry a donor card. The NHS Organ Donor Register contained around 9 million names at December 2001. The Government aims to have 16 million people registered by 2010. In February 2001 the Department of Health published a draft action plan for consultation, *Organs and Tissue Transplantation – A plan for the future*. This looks at ways of improving transplant services and increasing organ donation. In Scotland the Scottish Transplant Group published a report in July 2002 making recommendations for increasing organ donation rates.

Blood services

Blood services are run by the National Blood Services in England and north Wales, the Welsh Blood Service, the Scottish National Blood Transfusion Service and the Northern Ireland Blood Transfusion Agency. The United Kingdom is self-sufficient in blood components.

Over 3 million donations are made each year by voluntary unpaid donors in the UK. These are turned into many different life-saving components and products for patients. Red cells, platelets and other components with a limited 'life' are prepared at blood centres, while the production of plasma products is undertaken at the Bio Products Laboratory in Elstree (Hertfordshire) and the Protein Fractionation Centre in Edinburgh.

Each of the four national blood services co-ordinates programmes for donor recruitment, retention and education, and donor sessions are organised regionally, in towns and workplaces. Donors are aged between 17 and 70. Blood centres are responsible for blood collection, screening, processing and supplying hospital blood banks. They also provide laboratory, clinical, research, teaching and specialist advisory services and facilities. These blood centres are subject to nationally co-ordinated quality audit programmes, through the Medicines Control Agency (see page 179).

Ambulance and patient transport services

NHS emergency ambulances are available free to the public through the 999 telephone system for medical emergencies and accidents, as well as for doctors' urgent calls. Rapid response services, in which paramedics use cars and motorcycles to reach emergency cases, have been introduced in a number of areas, particularly major cities with areas of high traffic density. Helicopter ambulances, provided through local charities, serve many parts of the country and an integrated NHS-funded air ambulance service is available throughout Scotland. In England, between 2000/01 and 2001/02 the number of emergency calls to the NHS rose by 7 per cent to 3.8 million and the number of emergency patient journeys grew by 6 per cent to 3.1 million.

Non-emergency patient transport services are free to NHS patients considered by their doctor, dentist or midwife to be medically unfit to travel by other means. In many areas the ambulance service organises volunteer drivers to provide a hospital car service for non-urgent patients. Patients on low incomes may be eligible for reimbursement of costs of travelling to hospital.

Hospices

Hospice (or palliative) care is a special type of care for people whose illness may no longer be curable, enabling them to achieve the best possible quality of life during the final stages. It was first developed in the United Kingdom in 1967 by voluntary hospices. Most care continues to be provided by them, but is also increasingly provided within NHS palliative care units, and by hospitals and community palliative care teams. The care may be provided in a variety of settings: at home (with support from specially trained staff), in a hospice or palliative care unit, in hospital or at a hospice day centre.

Palliative care focuses on controlling pain and other distressing symptoms, and on providing psychological support to patients, their families and friends, both during the illness and into bereavement. Palliative care services mostly help people with cancer, although patients with other life-threatening illnesses, such as AIDS, motor neurone disease and heart failure, are also cared for. Currently 22 specialist hospice inpatient units provide respite care for children from birth to 16 years of age. Palliative care networks for children are being established across the country to co-ordinate how and where services are provided. In Scotland there is currently one children's hospice. A second is being built and will be operational by April 2004.

The National Council for Hospices and Specialist Palliative Care Services brings together voluntary and health service providers in England, Wales and Northern Ireland, in order to provide a co-ordinated view of the service. Its Scottish counterpart is the Scottish Partnership for Palliative Care.

Additional funding for palliative care services

In March 2002 the Government launched a £70 million programme of palliative care services for adults and children in England. Funds of £48 million for children's palliative care and £22 million for adult services were made available though the New Opportunities Fund, which uses money from the National Lottery to support good causes. Palliative care providers, including Primary Care Trusts, social services and voluntary sector organisations, are able to apply for funding and will be informed of the outcome in January 2003.

Sexual health

The Government's public health strategy aims to ensure the provision of effective sexual health services. Free contraceptive advice and treatment are available from GPs, family planning clinics and tailored services for young people. Clinics are able to provide condoms and other contraceptives free of charge. The Department of Health has developed a national sexual health and HIV strategy to bring together current initiatives in these areas, including work on chlamydia, the incidence of which has been increasing (see page 159). The Scottish Executive is also developing plans for a sexual health strategy. The Welsh

Assembly Government's *Strategic Framework for Promoting Sexual Health*, launched in 2000, is now being implemented. Local sexual health strategies are in place, and a two-year HIV prevention campaign targeted at homosexual men has been commissioned.

Alcohol

Part of the funds allocated for health promotion in England is for promoting the Government's sensible drinking guidelines (see page 160), and equivalent bodies are similarly funded in other parts of Britain. 'Drinkline' provides confidential telephone advice about alcohol problems and services in England and Wales. Treatment and rehabilitation within the NHS includes inpatient and outpatient services in general and psychiatric hospitals and some specialised alcohol treatment units.

There is also close co-operation between statutory and voluntary organisations. In England, Alcohol Concern plays a prominent role in improving services for problem drinkers and their families, increasing public awareness of alcohol misuse, and improving training for professional and voluntary workers. The Scottish Council on Alcohol has a similar function in Scotland.

In January 2002 the Scottish Executive published a *Plan for Action on Alcohol Misuse*. A national campaign involving television advertisements was launched, aimed at raising public awareness of the health risks associated with excessive drinking.

In Northern Ireland, a Regional Drug Strategy Co-ordinator was appointed in 2001 to take forward the Drug Strategy and the Strategy for Reducing Alcohol Related Harm.

Tobacco

The NHS Plan envisages an expansion in smoking cessation services for those smokers who need extra help to give up. Since April 2001 nicotine replacement therapy (NRT) has been available on prescription from GPs. NRT can provide the body with nicotine in decreasing doses until the craving can be coped with. This complements buproprion which was made available on NHS prescription on its launch in 2000. Both of these treatments were endorsed by the NICE (see page 164) in April 2002.

Drugs

The misuse of drugs, such as heroin, cocaine and amphetamines, is a serious social and health

Smoking cessation services

NHS smoking cessation services are now available across England. The services offer information, counselling and motivational support to smokers wanting to stop. They have received funding of £76 million over four years, including £23 million in 2002/03. The target for 2002/03 is for 100,000 smokers to have quit at the four-week follow-up stage. In 2001/02 around 119,800 smokers had successfully quit.

problem (see page 160). In response, the Government launched its ten-year anti-drugs strategy *Tackling Drugs to Build a Better Britain* in 1998. The strategy acknowledged the link between drug misuse and social conditions and problems; signalled a change in spending priorities in order to stop the problem happening, rather than reacting to it when it does; and developed targets for reducing drug misuse based on evidence and experience. The UK strategy sets out four key aims:

- encouraging young people to resist taking drugs in the first place;

- helping communities to protect themselves from drug-related anti-social and criminal behaviour;

- providing treatment to help people overcome their drug addiction; and

- tackling the availability of drugs.

Government targets for 2008 are to:

- reduce the use of Class A drugs and the frequent use of illicit drugs by those under the age of 25, especially among the most vulnerable;

- double the number of drug misusers in treatment;

- reduce the level of re-offending by drug misusing offenders; and

- reduce the availability of the most dangerous drugs, such as heroin and cocaine, on the streets.

Within the overall UK strategy, there are separate detailed strategies for Wales, Scotland and Northern Ireland. The Welsh Assembly's anti-

drugs strategy was published in May 2000 in *Tackling Substance Misuse in Wales: a Partnership Approach*. Scotland's drugs strategy is set out in *Tackling Drugs in Scotland – Action in Partnership*, published in 1999, and in the Scottish Executive's *Drug Action Plan*, published in May 2000. The strategy for Northern Ireland is set out in *Drug Strategy for Northern Ireland*, published in 1999.

A feature of the UK drug strategy is the close link between the agreed national policy and the programmes delivered at a local level by Drug Action Teams (DATs).[5] In England there are currently 150 DATs, composed of all those involved in drugs issues at a local level (for example PCTs, the social and probation services, and the police). They agree a local strategy that applies the national policy to the particular conditions in their area, and report annually to the Home Office on the progress achieved.

Medical standards

Standards of care

NHS Charters

In 2001 a new *NHS Charter for England – Your Guide to the NHS* – replaced the Patient's Charter. It provides information on how patients can access appropriate services to meet their healthcare needs, sets out a series of standards for each stage in the patient's care, and lists improvements patients can expect in the future. In Wales, a Health and Social Care Charter was launched in 2001, backed up with local charters at local health group level. A revised Charter for NHSScotland is planned

NHS complaints system

Under the current NHS complaints system, complaints should be resolved speedily at local level, but if the complainant remains dissatisfied with the local response he or she can request an independent review. Where such an investigation takes place, a report setting out suggestions and recommendations is produced. Complainants who remain dissatisfied, or whose request for a panel investigation is turned down, can refer their complaint to the Health Service Commissioner.

---

5 These comprise DATs in England and Scotland, Drug and Alcohol Action Teams (DAATs) in Wales, and Drug and Alcohol Co-ordination Teams (DCTs) in Northern Ireland. The arrangements in Scotland are mixed, including DATs, DAATs, and some teams which also have responsibility for smokers.

In 2000/01, 95,994 written complaints were made about hospital and community health services in England, and 44,442 complaints (covering general medical and dental services and family health services administration) were made about family health services. In Scotland in 1999/2000 there were 7,027 written complaints about hospital and community health services and 2,581 about family health services.

Health Service Commissioners

England, Wales and Scotland have Health Service Commissioners. They are responsible for investigating complaints from members of the public about health service bodies which have not been dealt with to their satisfaction by the body concerned. The English and Welsh posts are at present held by one person (with a staff of about 250), who is also Parliamentary Commissioner for Administration (the Ombudsman – see page 55). As Health Service Commissioner, he reports annually to Parliament and to the Welsh Assembly Government.

The Health Service Commissioner for Scotland is also the parliamentary and housing commissioner, and reports to the Scottish Parliament. In Northern Ireland complaints about health and social services bodies are investigated by the Commissioner for Complaints.

Health Service Commissioners can investigate complaints that a person has suffered hardship or injustice as a result of a failure in a service provided by a health service body; complaints of a failure to provide a service to which the patient was entitled; maladministration by an NHS authority; or action by health professionals arising from the exercise of clinical judgement.

National Service Frameworks

National Service Frameworks (NSFs) have been introduced in England to raise quality and reduce variations in service within the NHS. By mid-2002 there were NSFs for cancer, paediatric intensive care, mental health, coronary heart disease and older people. NSFs for diabetes and for children's services (see page 172) are being developed, and NSFs for renal services and long-term conditions (with a particular focus on neurological conditions) will follow.

In Scotland, the *Scottish Diabetes Framework* was published in April 2002. A Scottish Diabetes Group has been established to support and monitor its implementation.

Performance and safety

Inspection and regulation

The Bristol Royal Infirmary Inquiry (2002) (see page 172) recommended that the number of bodies inspecting and regulating health and social care should be rationalised and that the regulation of the public and private health sectors should be brought together. In line with these recommendations, the Government proposes to establish by 2004 the Commission for Healthcare Audit and Inspection (CHAI). The CHAI will have complete independence from the Department of Health to investigate the performance of all NHS organisations and private hospitals in England and Wales. Separate arrangements will continue in Scotland (see page 166).

CHAI will bring together the financial monitoring work of the Audit Commission within the NHS, the work of the Commission for Health Improvement (see page 163) and the private healthcare role of the National Care Standards Commission (see page 181). Following assessments, the CHAI will publish star ratings for all NHS organisations and be able to recommend special measures where there are persistent problems. It will also publish an annual report to Parliament on national progress on health care and how resources have been used.

NHS Foundation Trusts

In May 2002 proposals to establish free-standing NHS Foundation Trusts were announced. Hospitals attaining a three-star rating in the Department of Health's annual performance tables will be eligible to apply. The new trusts will no longer come under the direction of the Health Secretary and will be able to make independent decisions on investment and staff pay. They will also be able to retain the proceeds from land sales to invest in new services. The first trusts should start operating in shadow form in July 2003 and, subject to legislation, will become fully operational from April 2004.

Medical equipment

The Medical Devices Agency is responsible for safeguarding the interests of patients and users by ensuring that medical devices and equipment meet appropriate standards of safety, quality and performance, and that they comply with relevant

EC Directives. Medical devices cover all products, except medicines, used in healthcare. The range of products is very wide and includes contact lenses, heart valves, hospital beds, radiotherapy machines, surgical instruments, wheelchairs and walking frames.

Medicines

Only medicines that have been granted a marketing authorisation issued by the European Agency for the Evaluation of Medicinal Products or the Medicines Control Agency (MCA) may be supplied to the public. Marketing authorisations are issued following scientific assessment on the basis of safety, quality and effectiveness.

The MCA's Enforcement Group has responsibility for enforcing medicines legislation in England, and does so in Scotland and Wales on behalf of the Scottish Parliament and Welsh Assembly Government. The Enforcement Group investigates any illegal activities involving medicines and their availability, manufacture, import, sale and supply.

In April 2003 the Medicines and Healthcare products Regulatory Agency (MHRA) will be established, replacing the MDA and MCA. The single agency will be responsible for the regulation of both medicines and healthcare products.

Food safety

Under the *Food Safety Act 1990*, it is illegal to sell or supply food that is unfit for human consumption or falsely or misleadingly labelled. The Act covers a broad range of commercial activities related to food production, the sources from which it is derived, such as crops and animals, and articles which come into contact with food. There are also more detailed regulations, which apply to all types of food and drink and their ingredients. Local authorities are responsible for enforcing food law in two main areas: trading standards officers deal with the labelling of food, its composition and most cases of chemical contamination; and environmental health officers deal with hygiene, cases of microbiological contamination of foods, and food which is found to be unfit for human consumption.

The Food Standards Agency (FSA), which began operating in 2000, is responsible for all aspects of food safety and standards in the UK. The Agency has set a target to reduce foodborne disease (see box) and is seeking new ways to help disadvantaged consumers improve their diets. It also sets and audits standards for the enforcement of food law by local authorities.

National Food Hygiene Campaign

In February 2002, the FSA launched a £20 million five-year national campaign to reduce food poisoning by 20 per cent by 2006. In order to tackle inadequate hygiene standards in catering businesses, the campaign is initially targeted at the 370,000 catering businesses in the UK, before being extended to consumers and food safety in the home at a later date. Information on how to improve standards has been sent to businesses and employees have been reached by television, radio and press advertising.

Research

The Medical Research Council (MRC) (see also chapter 25) supports medical research in the United Kingdom by providing funding for research programmes and infrastructure, and by investing in training and employment, both in universities and in its own research centres. The MRC receives an annual grant from the Office of Science and Technology (OST – part of the Department of Trade and Industry). In 2001/02 the MRC received a grant of £345 million and realised a further £71 million from external sources, such as joint-funding initiatives and commercial funds.

The MRC advises the Government on matters relating to medical research, and co-operates with health departments throughout the UK, the NHS and other government departments concerned with biomedical and health service research. It also works closely with other research councils, medical research charities, industry and consumers, to identify and respond to current and future health needs.

Human fertilisation and embryology

The world's first 'test-tube baby' was born in the UK in 1978, as a result of the technique of *in vitro* fertilisation. The social, ethical and legal implications were examined by a committee of inquiry and led eventually to the passage of the *Human Fertilisation and Embryology Act 1990*. The Human Fertilisation and Embryology Authority (HFEA) licenses and inspects centres providing certain infertility treatments, undertaking human embryo research or storing gametes or embryos.

Since it was established in 1913, the MRC has been responsible for many significant medical discoveries and achievements. In the past ten years these have included:

- the production of artificial haemoglobin (1992);

- the discovery of the gene for Huntingdon's disease (1993);

- a new combination drug therapy for AIDS sufferers (1995);

- the discovery of a new treatment for malaria (1996);

- the development of 'DNA chip' technology (1997);

- the determination of the molecular structure of cells' 'energy engine' (1999); and

- research into the cellular manufacture of proteins and how this is disrupted in bacteria by antibiotics (2001).

The HFEA maintains a code of practice giving guidance to licensed centres and reports annually to Parliament.

In 2001 Parliament approved regulations made under the 1990 Act to extend the purposes for which research on human embryos could be permitted. The decision allowed scientists to seek approval from the HFEA to extract embryonic stem cells for research aimed at increasing knowledge about serious disease and applying such knowledge to the development of treatments. The first two licence applications made under the 2001 regulations were approved in February 2002 and involved research into Parkinson's Disease and pancreatic disease. To support research in this area, the MRC is to establish a UK stem cell bank which will provide researchers with adult foetal and embryonic stem cell lines.

Cancer Research UK
Cancer Research UK was established in February 2002 through the merger of the Cancer Research Campaign and the Imperial Cancer Research Fund to create the largest volunteer-funded cancer research organisation in the world. It has 3,000 scientists and an annual scientific budget of more than £175 million, raised almost entirely through public donations.

Health arrangements with other countries

The member states of the European Economic Area (EEA – see page 60) have special health arrangements under which EEA nationals resident in a member state are entitled to receive emergency treatment, either free or at a reduced cost, during visits to other EEA countries. These arrangements also now apply in Switzerland. Treatment is provided, in most cases, on production of a valid Form E111 which people in the United Kingdom normally obtain from a post office before travelling. There are also arrangements for people who go to another EEA country specifically for medical care, or who require continuing treatment for a pre-existing condition.

Unless they are in an exempted category (for instance those persons engaging in employment, taking up permanent residence or seeking asylum in the UK), visitors to the United Kingdom are generally expected to pay for all non-emergency treatment. The United Kingdom also has a number of separate bilateral agreements with some other countries, such as Australia and New Zealand.

NHS patients travelling abroad for treatment
Following the rulings of the European Court of Justice in July 2001, the Secretary of State for Health announced that treatment for patients in the EEA is one of the options open to NHS bodies seeking to increase the number of patients treated and reduce waiting times. Between January and April 2002, 190 patients from south-east England were treated in France and Germany in a pilot scheme. Draft guidance for the NHS has been issued and commissioning arrangements have been set up to assist NHS bodies wishing to refer patients to other countries in the EEA.

Health provision outside the NHS

Private healthcare
As an alternative to the NHS, people are entitled to pay for their own health and social care, by joining a private healthcare organisation. In addition, there is the option of private medical insurance, which, depending on the premium paid, will cover people's healthcare in times of need. In 2000, 6.9 million people in the United Kingdom were covered by private medical

insurance, more than three times the number in 1971 (2.1 million). The overall cost of claims to private medical insurers rose by 5.5 per cent between 1999 and 2000 to £1,934 million.

Regulation of the private healthcare sector is now primarily undertaken by the National Care Standards Commission (NCSC). This is an independent public body set up under the *Care Standards Act 2000* to regulate social care (see chapter 12) and private and voluntary health care services in England, in institutions such as care homes, children's homes, private hospitals and private clinics. The NCSC will assume its registration and inspection responsibilities in January 2003. This role had previously been the responsibility of local authority and health authority inspection units. The NCSC will carry out regular inspections of services and will have the power to ensure that standards meet national minima. In Wales, these functions are being performed by the Care Standards Inspectorate for Wales, a new division within the Welsh Assembly Government.

Partnerships
The Government is beginning to work formally in partnership with the private sector. In 2000 the Department of Health signed an agreement with the independent healthcare sector (which comprises the private and voluntary sectors), under which English health authorities are able to bring private sector providers into the planning of local healthcare on a systematic and long-term basis. The agreement covers care, workforce planning and service planning. It involves the NHS using the private sector's spare capacity; transfer of patients between the two sectors; exchange of information; and joint working on preventive and rehabilitation services.

Complementary and alternative medicine
There is a growing interest in complementary and alternative medicine (CAM). In November 2000 the House of Lords Select Committee on Science and Technology reported its findings on CAM, and in March 2001 the Government published its response. The Government agreed that acupuncture and herbal medicine were early candidates for regulation on a statutory basis, and that others, such as chiropractic, homeopathy and osteopathy, might also be regulated in due course. Information on CAM is now available through NHS Direct Online.

Further reading
The NHS Plan: A plan for investment, a plan for reform. Cm 4818. The Stationery Office, 2000.

Securing Our Future Health: Taking a Long-Term View. The Stationery Office, 2002.

Department of Health Departmental Report. The Government's Expenditure Plans 2002/2003 to 2003/2004. Cm 5403. The Stationery Office, 2002.

Improving Health in Wales – A Plan for the NHS with its Partners. Welsh Assembly Government, 2001.

Our National Health: A plan for action, a plan for change. Scottish Executive Health Department, 2000.

Investing for Health. Department of Health, Social Services and Public Safety, Northern Ireland, 2000.

Statistical publications
Cancer Trends in England and Wales 1950–1999. Series SMPS No 66. Office for National Statistics. The Stationery Office, 2001.

Geographic Variations in Health. Series DS No 16. Office for National Statistics. The Stationery Office, 2001.

Health Statistics Quarterly. Office for National Statistics. The Stationery Office.

Health and Personal Social Services Statistics for England. Department of Health. The Stationery Office.

Scottish Health Statistics. Information and Statistics Division, NHSScotland.

Health Statistics Wales. National Assembly for Wales.

On the State of the Public Health. The Annual Report of the Chief Medical Officer of the Department of Health. The Stationery Office.

Health in Scotland. The Annual Report of the Chief Medical Officer on the State of Scotland's Health. Scottish Executive.

Welsh Health: Annual Report of the Chief Medical Officer. National Assembly for Wales.

Websites

Department of Health
www.doh.gov.uk

Welsh Assembly Government
www.wales.gov.uk

Scottish Executive Health Department
www.scotland.gov.uk

NHSScotland, Information and Statistics Division
www.show.scot.nhs.uk/isd

Department of Health, Social Services and Public Safety, Northern Ireland
www.dhsspsni.gov.uk

Human Fertilisation and Embryology Authority
www.hfea.gov.uk

National Care Standards Commission
www.carestandards.org.uk

Public Health Laboratory Service
www.phls.co.uk

14 Crime and justice

Between 1996 and 2000, crime recorded by the police in England and Wales fell by 8 per cent, compared with a 1 per cent rise in all EU Member States. Survey evidence (see page 184) also suggests that crime in England and Wales was declining during this period. Since 2000/01, however, crimes recorded by the police have increased, while survey evidence indicates that the number of crimes has been relatively stable.

The UK has three legal systems (operating in England and Wales, Scotland and Northern Ireland) and three systems of criminal justice. Unlike many countries, there is no single criminal or penal code that sets out the principles on which the justice system operates, but there is emphasis on the independence of both prosecuting authorities and the judiciary.

Civil law is concerned primarily with regulating disputes between individuals or corporate bodies and requires a case to be proved on the balance of probabilities, rather than the 'beyond reasonable doubt' standard that is applied in criminal cases. In both criminal and civil cases, the courts make their decisions on an adversarial rather than an inquisitorial basis.

Statutes passed by the Westminster or Scottish Parliaments are the ultimate source of law, but there is also a legal duty to comply with European Community law, and courts in the UK are obliged to apply the latter in cases where the two conflict.

A statute may confer power on a minister, local authority or other executive body to make delegated legislation (see page 40).

In all three legal systems many areas of law have developed over the centuries through the decisions of the courts. Consistency is achieved because the decisions of higher courts are binding on those lower down the hierarchy. The House of Lords is the ultimate appeal court in the UK, except for Scottish criminal cases.

EC law, which applies in the UK as a member of the European Union (see page 59), is derived from the EC treaties, from the Community legislation adopted under them, and from the decisions of the European Court of Justice. That court has the highest authority, under the Treaty of Rome, to decide points of EC law. Where a point arises before a British court, it may refer the point of law to the Court of Justice for it to decide. Sometimes a court is obliged to make a reference to the European Court.

The European Convention on Human Rights was incorporated into UK law under the *Human Rights Act 1998*. This covers, among other things, the right to a fair trial, to freedom of thought and expression, and to respect for family and private life. All public authorities, including the courts, must act compatibly with these rights. The rights in the Convention do not take precedence over an Act of Parliament. Where they conflict, the higher courts may make a declaration of incompatibility and Parliament then decides what action to take.

Crime

There are two main measures of the scale of crime in the UK: the recording of crimes by the police; and surveys of victims, such as the British Crime Survey (BCS) – covering England and Wales – and the Scottish Crime Survey. It is difficult to compare or combine crime statistics from England and Wales, Northern Ireland and Scotland because of the different legal systems (see pages 200 to 205). Most of the information below therefore relates to England and Wales.

Recorded crime

In England and Wales the term 'recorded crime' refers to notifiable offences recorded by the police according to rules set down by the Home Office. Recorded crime includes a wide range of offences from homicide to minor theft and criminal damage, but does not include most of the 'summary' offences (such as motoring offences) that are dealt with by magistrates. Changes in recording practice since 1998 have made it difficult to compare trends over time (see box).

Overall recorded crime totalled 5.5 million offences in the year to 31 March 2002, representing an increase of 7 per cent over the previous 12 months. The overall detection rate was 23 per cent.

Table 14.1 Crimes recorded by the police in England and Wales for the year ended March 2002

	Thousands
Violence against the person	650
Sexual offences	41
Burglary	762
Robbery	121
Theft and handling stolen goods	2,267
Fraud and forgery	317
Criminal damage	1,064
Drug offences	186
Theft of and from a vehicle	983
Total	**5,527**

Source: Home Office

In Scotland 421,093 crimes were recorded by the police in 2001, a decrease of just under 0.5 per cent compared with 2000. The overall clear-up rate was 45 per cent. (In Scotland crimes detected are referred to as crimes cleared up.)

Recorded crime in Northern Ireland in 2001/02 totalled 140,000 offences. This was an increase of 17 per cent over the previous year. The overall clear-up rate was 20 per cent.

How crime is recorded

Home Office counting rules for recorded crime in England and Wales have been revised over the years, both to promote greater consistency between police forces and to ensure a more victim-oriented approach. In 1998 a 'one crime per victim' rule was introduced, which means, for example, that if an offender wounds three people in the course of one incident, three crimes are recorded. Since 2000, the police have been changing their systems to record the allegations of victims unless there is credible evidence that a crime has *not* taken place. In April 2002, a new National Crime Recording Service (NCRS) formalised these changes across England and Wales.

Detection or clear-up rates
Under the counting rules, a crime is 'detected' or 'cleared up' if a suspect has been identified and interviewed and there is sufficient evidence to bring a charge. There does not have to be a prosecution: for example, the offender may accept a caution or ask for the crime to be taken into consideration by the court, or the victim may not wish to give evidence.

Crime surveys

Unlike crime data recorded by the police, the British Crime Survey is restricted to crimes against people aged 16 or over who are living in private households at the time of the interview, and does not include some types of crime (for example, fraud, murder and so-called victimless crimes). In other ways the BCS is more comprehensive, however, because it asks respondents whether they have experienced certain personal and household crimes in the preceding year, regardless of whether or not they reported the incident to the police. On the basis of answers given, it is estimated that there were 13 million incidents of crime in England and Wales in 2001/02 (see Figure 14.2). The chances of being a victim of crime over the course of a year have remained stable at just below 28 per cent, around the lowest level since the BCS began in 1981.

The survey also covers such issues as whether the respondents are concerned or worried about crime. Individuals from Black and Asian groups have consistently shown higher levels of concern about crime than individuals from other ethnic groups and women of all ages and ethnic groups were more likely to be concerned than men.

Figure 14.2 British Crime Survey offences,[1] England and Wales

Millions

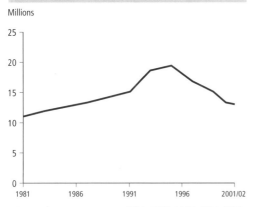

1 Data refer to survey years 1981, 1983, 1987, 1991, 1993, 1995, 1997, 1999, 2000 and 2001/02.
Source: British Crime Survey, Home Office

The 2000 Scottish Crime Survey estimated that around 843,000 crimes were committed against individuals and private households in Scotland during 1999. This was 13 per cent fewer than the number (estimated in the 1996 survey) of 969,000 crimes in 1995.

Offenders

Analysis of the latest available statistics for England and Wales (see Table 14.3) indicates that:

- more than four times as many males as females were found guilty of or cautioned for an offence. This ratio is much higher for some categories of crime (such as burglary and sexual offences);

- 37 per cent of male offenders and 60 per cent of female offenders were found guilty of, or cautioned for, theft-related offences, the most commonly committed offence; and

- the combined conviction and caution rate was much higher for those aged 16 to 24 than for other age groups.

Young offenders – then and now
Attitudes to crime have changed considerably over the last 50 years. Then some of the increases in juvenile delinquency were attributed to a 'failure to recognise and treat early enough children who are of sub-normal intelligence or who develop unstable, anti-social characters'; along with 'the temptation offered by the display in shops of goods which attract children'. Nowadays, research into causes of crime is more likely to identify poor parenting and the quality of a young person's home life as contributory factors in youth criminality.

Current issues of concern

An aim of the Home Office and the devolved administrations is to reduce crime and the fear of crime. As well as tackling the overall level of crime, particular concern is being paid to issues such as drug misuse and the threat of terrorism.

Crime reduction

A wide range of measures are being taken to try to reduce the overall level of crime. For example, there are 376 Crime and Disorder Reduction Partnerships in England and Wales bringing together the police, local authorities and other relevant agencies, such as youth offending teams, drug action teams, the courts and the prison service and others, in order to develop local strategies. The partnerships are monitored by ten crime reduction directors.

The Home Office has funded a range of initiatives under its Crime Reduction Programme over a three-year period from 1999. Over £340 million has already been allocated to around 1,470 projects, including closed circuit television surveillance systems in public areas such as housing estates, shopping centres, railway stations and car parks. The initiatives have been aimed at reducing crime and gathering evidence on what works in tackling crime and its causes. A website (*www.crimereduction.gov.uk*) has been developed with the aim of helping practitioners around the country and abroad. A number of toolkits can be found on the website.

Table 14.3 Offenders in England and Wales found guilty of, or cautioned for, indictable[1] offences, 2000

Rates per 10,000 population

	10–15	16–24	25–34	35 and over	All aged 10 and over (thousands)
Males					
Theft and handling stolen goods	113	205	89	16	142.1
Drug offences	14	143	53	8	76.5
Violence against the person	29	68	28	7	47.1
Burglary	32	53	16	2	31.0
Criminal damage	13	17	6	1	12.0
Robbery	6	11	2	–	5.9
Sexual offences	3	4	2	2	5.2
Other indictable offences	11	96	52	11	66.4
All indictable offences	**221**	**597**	**250**	**47**	**386.2**
Females					
Theft and handling stolen goods	65	72	30	6	53.5
Drug offences	2	15	8	1	9.3
Violence against the person	9	11	5	1	8.1
Burglary	3	3	1	–	1.8
Criminal damage	2	2	1	–	1.4
Robbery	1	1	–	–	0.6
Sexual offences	–	–	–	–	0.1
Other indictable offences	3	20	12	2	14.3
All indictable offences	**85**	**123**	**57**	**11**	**88.9**

1 Indictable offences are the more serious, non-summary offences (see page 189).
Source: Home Office

Within the Scottish Executive Justice Department, the Crime Prevention Unit has responsibility for developing crime prevention, community safety and domestic abuse policy on behalf of Scottish Executive ministers. All 32 local councils in Scotland have formed community safety partnerships. The Scottish Executive has formed a Scottish Forum on Community Safety.

Street crime

The Street Crime Initiative was launched in April 2002 with the aim of targeting recent increases in street crime. Street crime, defined as robbery, snatch theft, carjacking and gun-related crime, is concentrated in a relatively small number of mainly urban areas. The Initiative is running in ten police force areas, which in 2001/02 accounted for 83 per cent of street crime. Several government departments are involved as well as the police, courts and the Crown Prosecution Service (see page 189). Among the measures included are:

- the nomination of specialist street crime courts in the relevant police force areas, allowing street crime cases a speedier progress through the criminal justice system; and providing separate facilities and support to victims and witnesses;

- the provision of video identification equipment to enable more video identification parades to replace 'live' parades, reducing potential delays; and

- enabling lawyers and other professionals within the criminal justice system to form a dedicated investigation and prosecution service.

Elements of the initiative aimed at crime prevention are:

- funding from the Department for Education

and Skills (DfES) for truancy sweeps, for provision of full-time education for excluded pupils, and for new or expanded learning support units; and

- the provision, within 24 hours of their arrest or release from custody, of drug treatment services for street crime offenders with drug problems.

Drug misuse

The UK drugs strategy, introduced to co-ordinate the fight against illegal drugs, focuses on Class A drugs[1] which cause the most harm. It has four main aims:

- helping young people resist drug misuse in order to achieve their full potential in society;

- enabling people to overcome drug problems through treatment;

- protecting communities from drug-related anti-social and criminal behaviour; and

- reducing the supply of illegal drugs on the streets.

Scotland has its own drugs strategy within the UK framework and has also introduced national standards for drugs services. In an effort to reduce the availability of drugs in Scotland and to target organised drug crime, the Scottish Drug Enforcement Agency was launched in June 2000.

The *Crime and Disorder Act 1998* introduced drug treatment and testing orders, targeted at persistent offenders (aged 16 and over) who show a willingness to co-operate with treatment and are before the court for an offence that is sufficiently serious to attract a community sentence as a penalty. While subject to the drug treatment and testing order, offenders are closely supervised and follow an individually tailored treatment programme for several hours a day for the first 13 weeks of the order. After 13 weeks have elapsed, time spent under supervision may subsequently be reduced. There are also mandatory testing and court review requirements through which offenders' progress can

be effectively monitored. Drug treatment and testing order pilots ran from October 1998 to March 2000 in three areas and were managed by the relevant local probation services (see page 198). After evaluation of the pilot scheme, the orders were introduced in England and Wales in October 2000 and are being introduced on a phased basis in Scotland, where the use of drug courts is also being piloted. By April 2002 over 6,000 orders had been made in England and Wales.

The Drugs Prevention Advisory Service (DPAS) promotes community-based drugs prevention at local, regional and national level. DPAS teams have been established in each of the nine Government Regions in England.

Under provisions in the *Criminal Justice and Court Services Act 2000*, the drug testing of offenders will be extended across the criminal justice process in England and Wales. These provide for testing:

- of persons (for specified Class A drugs) in police detention after charge;

- of offenders under probation supervision through a new drug abstinence order; and

- as a condition of release on licence or notice of supervision.

The initial programme for the testing of offenders will run until 2004.

Drug misuse in England and Wales costs society up to £17.4 billion a year, according to recent research. Problem drug users – mainly hardcore heroin and cocaine addicts – account for 99 per cent of the bill, each costing the State a minimum of £10,400 a year. In 2001 the Government announced a programme to tackle drugs and drug-related crime in communities – *Communities Against Drugs* – and channelled over £200 million to Crime and Disorder Reduction Partnerships and drug action teams with the aim of tackling local drugs markets and cutting drug-related crime.

The Government intends to reclassify cannabis across the UK from Class B to Class C under the *Misuse of Drugs Act 1971*. As a result, the maximum penalty for the possession of cannabis will fall from five years to two years' imprisonment. Simultaneously, the Government also intends to increase the maximum penalty for supplying Class C drugs from 5 to 14 years' imprisonment. This means that, on reclassification,

---

1 The *Misuse of Drugs Act 1971* classifies drugs according to a scientific assessment of their harmfulness. The most dangerous drugs are Class A drugs, such as heroin and cocaine. Class B drugs include amphetamine and Class C drugs include steroids. This legislation applies across the UK.

the maximum penalty for supplying cannabis will remain at 14 years' imprisonment.

Under the proposals expected to apply in England and Wales, for most offences of cannabis possession, a police warning will be sufficient, together with confiscation of the drug. Where there are additional considerations, or where there is repeat offending, the case could proceed to court. The police will retain the power of arrest, to be used in exceptional circumstances. Similar proposals are expected to apply in Scotland.

Terrorism

In the light of the attacks in the United States in September 2001 (see page 76), the Government announced its intention to strengthen the existing counter-terrorism provisions of the *Terrorism Act 2000*. Further measures were contained in the *Anti-Terrorism Crime and Security Act 2001*. Taken together, the two Acts have resulted in new permanent UK-wide anti-terrorist legislation (replacing the system of separate and temporary legislation for Northern Ireland and Great Britain), while a new definition of terrorism has been adopted covering ideological and religious motivation for terrorist acts. Provisions in the Acts include:

- a new offence of inciting terrorist acts abroad from within the UK;

- new powers to seize suspected terrorist cash at borders;

- a new judicial authority to consider applications for extensions of detention of terrorist suspects;

- specific offences relating to training for terrorist activities;

- new offences on weapons of mass destruction;

- better security at airports and nuclear sites; and

- an extension of police powers to detain and question those suspected of terrorist offences.

England and Wales

Policing

The following section deals with police powers only. The structure of the police service in England and Wales is described on page 196.

Police powers and procedures are defined by legislation and accompanying codes of practice. Evidence obtained in breach of the codes may be ruled inadmissible in court. The codes must be available in all police stations.

Stop and search

Police officers can stop and search people and vehicles if they reasonably suspect that they will find stolen goods, offensive weapons or implements that could be used for burglary and other offences. The officer must record the grounds for the search and the person searched is entitled to a copy of the officer's report. Some 714,000 stop and searches were carried out by the police in England and Wales in 2000/01.

Arrest

The police may arrest a suspect on a warrant issued by a court, but can also do so without a warrant for arrestable offences (those for which the sentence is fixed by law or for which the term of imprisonment is five years or more).

Detention and questioning

Suspects must be cautioned before the police can ask any questions about an offence. For arrestable offences, a suspect can be detained in police custody without charge for up to 24 hours. Someone suspected of a serious arrestable offence can be held for up to 96 hours, but not beyond 36 hours unless a warrant is obtained from a magistrates' court.

Charging

Once there is sufficient evidence, the police have to decide whether a detained person should be charged with an offence. If the police institute criminal proceedings against a suspect, the Crown Prosecution Service (see page 189) then takes control of the case.

For minor offences, the police may decide to caution an offender rather than prosecute. A caution is not the same as a conviction, and will only be given if the person admits the offence. Under the *Crime and Disorder Act 1998*, cautioning for young offenders has been replaced with the final warning scheme.

If the police decide to charge someone, that person may be released on bail to attend a magistrates' court. If not granted police bail, the defendant must be brought before a magistrates' court (or, if under 18, a youth court) as soon as possible. There is a general right to bail, but magistrates may withhold it. If bail is refused, an accused person has the right to apply again, subject to some limitations, to the Crown Court or to a High Court judge. In certain circumstances, the prosecution may appeal to a Crown Court judge against the granting of bail by magistrates.

Complaints

Members of the public can make complaints against the police if they feel they have been treated unfairly or improperly. Of the 31,000 complaints in England and Wales completed in 2000/01, roughly a third were resolved locally without investigation, one-third were dispensed with without investigation and one-third were investigated.

The investigation of the more serious cases in England and Wales is supervised by the Police Complaints Authority. A new independent body, intended to be the core component of a new complaints system, will replace the Police Complaints Authority from April 2004.

Community relations

Measures introduced to promote better relations between the police and the communities they serve include:

- an extension of the race relations legislation – through the *Race Relations (Amendment) Act 2000* (see pages 94–5). This outlaws direct and indirect discrimination in all public authorities (including the police), and places a duty on them to promote race equality;

- citizenship classes in schools, to be introduced into the National Curriculum (see pages 105–7) in England and Wales in 2002, to ensure that pupils are taught about the cultural diversity of Britain;

- enforcing specific criminal offences of racially aggravated violence, harassment and criminal damage; and

- a programme to reform the use by the police of their powers to stop and search people (with the aim of ensuring these powers are used fairly).

In 1999 the Government set employment targets for the recruitment, retention and progression of minority ethnic police officers in England and Wales. The targets are intended to ensure that by 2009 forces will reflect their local population. At the end of September 2001 there were 3,386 officers from minority ethnic backgrounds (representing 2.6 per cent of the police service in England and Wales).

Statistics on race and the criminal justice system can be found on the Home Office website (*www.homeoffice.gov.uk/rds/index*).

The prosecution process

The Crown Prosecution Service (CPS) is responsible for prosecuting people in England and Wales who have been charged by the police with a criminal offence. Although it works closely with the police, it is a governmental body independent of them. Its role is to:

- advise the police on possible prosecutions;

- review prosecutions started by the police to ensure that the right defendants are prosecuted on the correct charges before the appropriate court;

- prepare cases for court;

- prosecute cases at magistrates' courts; and

- instruct counsel to prosecute cases in the Crown Court and higher courts.[2]

When deciding on whether to go ahead with a case, Crown Prosecutors must first be satisfied that there is enough evidence to provide a realistic prospect of conviction against each defendant on each charge. If there is enough evidence, prosecutors must then decide whether it is in the public interest to proceed. A prosecution will usually take place unless there are public interest factors against it clearly outweighing those in favour.

Court procedures

There are two types of criminal offence. Summary offences are the least serious and may be tried only in a magistrates' court. Indictable offences are subdivided into 'indictable only' (such as murder, manslaughter or robbery) which must be tried on indictment[3] at the Crown Court by judge and jury,

---

2 A number of CPS lawyers are qualified to appear in some cases in the Crown Court and other higher courts.

3 An indictment is a written accusation against a person, charging him or her with serious crime triable by jury.

Figure 14.4 The prosecution process, England and Wales

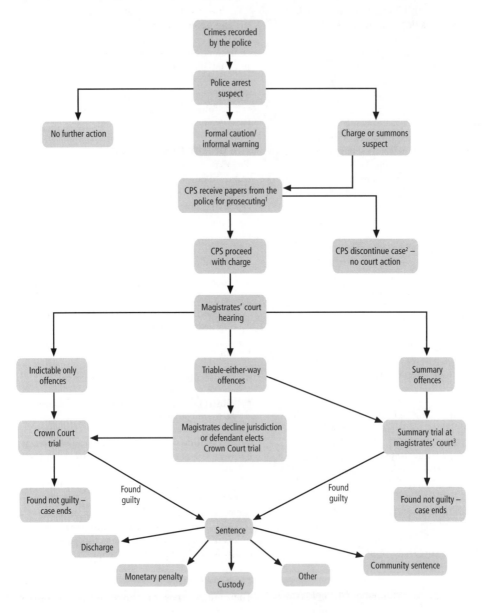

1 Although the majority of prosecutions are handled by the Crown Prosecution Service, other organisations can also bring prosecutions.
2 A case will be under continued review, and may be discontinued at any stage before the hearing at the magistrates' court or the prosecution may offer no evidence. In addition, the charge may be altered up to the final decision of the court.
3 Magistrates may commit to the Crown Court for sentence.
Source: *A Guide to the Criminal Justice System in England and Wales,* Home Office, 2000.

and 'either-way', which may be tried either summarily or on indictment.

Either-way offences, such as theft and burglary, can vary greatly in seriousness and a magistrates' court must decide whether the case is serious enough to be sent to the Crown Court. If the magistrates decide in favour of summary trial, the accused person currently has the right to a trial by jury in the Crown Court if he or she chooses.

Where an either-way case is to be tried on indictment, the magistrates' court commits it to the Crown Court for trial if it is satisfied that there is a case to answer. In most cases this is accepted by the defence and the magistrates do not need to consider the evidence, but if the defence challenges the case, the magistrates consider the documentary evidence, without witnesses being called.

Magistrates may impose a fine of up to £5,000 and/or a maximum sentence of six months' imprisonment, but can send the offender to the Crown Court if they feel their sentencing powers are not sufficient. These arrangements are currently under review.

Youth courts are specialist magistrates' courts, which sit separately from those dealing with adults. They handle all but the most serious charges against people aged at least ten (the age of criminal responsibility) and under 18. Young offenders may also be tried in an adult magistrates' court or in a Crown Court, depending on the type of offence they have committed. Only Justices of the Peace who have been specially trained for the job sit in youth courts. Proceedings are held in private.

Trial
The law presumes an accused person is innocent until proved guilty beyond reasonable doubt by the prosecution. Accused people have a right at all stages to stay silent; however, when questioned, failure to mention facts which they later rely upon in their defence may not be helpful to their case. If the defendant pleads guilty, the judge will simply decide upon the appropriate sentence.

Criminal trials normally take place in open court (that is, members of the public and press are allowed to hear the proceedings) unless there are specific reasons why this would not be appropriate. If a not guilty plea is entered, the

prosecution and defence form opposing sides in an 'adversarial' system. They call and examine witnesses and present opposing versions of the case. Strict rules of evidence govern how this may be done. Written statements by witnesses are allowed with the consent of the other party or in limited circumstances at the discretion of the court. Otherwise evidence is taken from witnesses testifying orally on oath. Child witnesses may testify without taking the oath and their evidence must be received by the court unless the child is incapable of giving intelligible testimony. A child in some circumstances can testify via a live TV link or the court may consider a video-recorded interview, subject to the defence having the right to question the child in cross-examination.

Publicly funded legal services
Advice and assistance are available without reference to an individual's means to anyone who is arrested and held in custody at a police station, or other premises, or who appears before a court.

Where a defendant is charged with a criminal offence, he or she may apply for a representation order which will entitle him or her to the services of a solicitor and/or barrister depending on the type of case. There is no means test to decide eligibility for representation. The court must be

---

Support for victims and witnesses
The Victim's Charter sets out how victims of crime in England and Wales should be treated and what they can expect from the criminal justice system. There is also a charter for court users, which describes how the courts work and spells out the standards of service that should be reached in the higher courts.

A government-funded voluntary sector organisation, Victim Support, provides practical help and emotional support to victims of crime with the aid of around 13,000 volunteers. It also runs the Witness Service, which provides income and support to victims and witnesses attending criminal courts in England and Wales. Similar schemes operate in Scotland and Northern Ireland.

Blameless victims of violent crime in England, Wales and Scotland may be eligible for compensation from public funds under the Criminal Injuries Compensation Scheme. In Northern Ireland there are separate statutory arrangements for compensation for criminal injuries, and for malicious damage to property.

satisfied that it is in the interests of justice that publicly funded representation should be granted. At the end of the case, the trial judge has power to order the defendant to pay back some or all of the costs of his or her defence.

In criminal proceedings the Legal Services Commission (see page 199), through the Criminal Defence Service, makes arrangements for solicitors to assist unrepresented defendants in the magistrates' courts and advocacy assistance is also available in some other specified circumstances.

During 2001 over 1.2 million acts of assistance, including offering advice and payment of legal bills, were granted at a total cost of around £360 million.

The jury

In jury trials in England and Wales the judge decides questions of law, sums up the case to the jury, and discharges or sentences the accused. The jury is responsible for deciding questions of fact. The jury's verdict may be 'guilty' or 'not guilty' and the latter would result in an acquittal. Juries may, subject to certain conditions, reach a verdict by a majority of at least 10–2.

If an accused person is acquitted, there is no right of appeal from the prosecution, and the accused cannot be tried again for that same offence. However, an acquittal may be set aside and a retrial ordered if there is proof that a juror has been interfered with or intimidated.

A jury is independent of the judiciary and any attempt to interfere with its members is a criminal offence. People aged between 18 and 70 whose names appear on the electoral register are liable to be chosen at random for jury service. People in certain occupations, such as police officers, lawyers and doctors, are exempted from serving.

Sentencing and appeals

The court will sentence the offender after considering all the relevant information it has on the case, which may include a pre-sentence or any other specialist report, and a mitigating plea by the defence. A fine is the most common punishment, and most offenders are fined for summary offences. A court may also make compensation orders, which require the offender to pay compensation for personal injury, loss or damage resulting from an offence; or impose a conditional discharge, where the offender, if he or

Criminal Justice White Paper

In July 2002 the Government published the criminal justice White Paper *Justice For All*, outlining a programme for reform of the criminal justice system which the Government intends to introduce in England and Wales over the coming years. The White Paper includes proposals designed to rebalance the system in favour of victims, witnesses and communities and to deliver justice for all, by building trust and credibility in the criminal justice system. Among its proposals, it aims to:

- extend sentencing powers of magistrates from 6 to 12 months and require them to sentence all those they have found guilty, rather than committing some to be sentenced in the Crown Court;

- allow defendants to have the right to ask for trial by judge alone in the Crown Court;

- allow trial by judge alone in serious and complex fraud trials, and the possibility of allowing this for some other complex and lengthy trials, or where the jury is at risk of intimidation;

- allow witnesses to refer to their previous and original statements and change the laws on reported evidence ('hearsay');

- introduce an exception to the double jeopardy rule (which prevents defendants from being tried twice for the same offence) in serious cases, where there is compelling new evidence;

- integrate the management of the courts within a single courts administration; and

- codify criminal statutes so as to avoid inconsistencies and overlapping.

she offends again, may be sentenced for both the original offence and for the new one.

A range of community sentences (see box overleaf) are used in cases where a fine or custodial sentence would not be appropriate. A community rehabilitation order requires offenders to maintain regular contact with their probation officer. The aim is to secure the rehabilitation of the offender, protect the public and prevent re-offending. The order can last from six months to three years; an offender who fails to comply without good reason with any of the requirements can be brought before the court again.

Community sentences

- community rehabilitation orders (involving supervision in the community);

- community punishment orders (unpaid work within the community);

- community punishment and rehabilitation orders (elements of both probation supervision and unpaid work);

- curfew orders (requiring the offender to remain at a specified place for specified periods, usually monitored by electronic tagging);

- drug treatment and testing orders (see page 187);

- drug abstinence orders (currently being piloted) which require an offender to abstain from misusing Class A drugs and to undertake drugs tests when instructed; and

- exclusion orders (likely to be introduced in 2003 and monitored by electronic tagging) requiring offenders to stay away from a certain place for specified periods.

The National Probation Service for England and Wales dealt with around 122,100 new offenders in 2001. Just under half this total were starting community rehabilitation orders; a similar proportion was beginning community punishment orders.

Prohibitive anti-social behaviour orders (ASBOs) may be applied to individuals or groups whose threatening and disruptive conduct harasses the local community. Anyone in breach of such an order is guilty of a criminal offence. ASBOs are applicable throughout the UK.

The type of sentence received by offenders has recently been the subject of much debate, stimulated in part by an official report into sentencing options employed by the courts. Proposals in the report have formed part of a wider review of the criminal justice system (see page 192). Table 14.5 shows that 30 per cent of offenders sentenced for indictable offences were given a community sentence in 2000, 25 per cent were given a fine, and 25 per cent a custodial sentence.

Young offenders

The main custodial sentence for 12 to 17 year olds is the detention and training order. It is a two-part sentence which combines a period of custody with a period under supervision in the community. It may last for a minimum of four months to a maximum of two years and there is provision for the custodial element to be shortened or lengthened depending on the young offender's progress.

Table 14.5 Offenders in England and Wales sentenced for indictable offences, 2000

Per cent

	Discharge	Fine	Community sentence	Suspended sentence	Custody	Other	All ('000s)
Theft and handling stolen goods	22	23	32	0	20	2	127.6
Drug offences	16	46	18	1	18	1	45.0
Violence against the person	13	11	40	2	32	3	35.5
Burglary	6	3	38	0	51	1	26.7
Fraud and forgery	18	17	42	2	20	2	19.1
Criminal damage	24	17	40	0	12	7	10.2
Motoring	5	48	23	1	23	1	7.7
Robbery	1	0	23	0	73	1	5.9
Sexual offences	5	3	27	2	62	2	3.9
Other offences	11	41	18	1	19	10	43.2
All indictable offences	16	25	30	1	25	3	324.9

Source: Home Office

There are a range of non-custodial penalties for young offenders (see box). Those aged 16 or 17 may also be subject to most of the adult community sentences.

Non-custodial penalties for young offenders
Penalties include:

- fines and a compensation order, with the offender's parents having to pay;

- a supervision order, where the offender must comply with specific requirements, such as staying in local authority accommodation;

- an attendance centre order, where the offender is required to attend a centre for two to three hours on alternate Saturdays for specific activities;

- a curfew order with electronic tagging;

- a reparation order, requiring young offenders to compensate the victim or victims (if they wish it) of their offence or the community which they have harmed, in some non-financial way; and

- an action plan order, where young offenders are required to comply with an individually tailored programme designed to address their offending behaviour and the factors associated with it.

A new sentence, the referral order, was introduced in 2002 for young offenders convicted in court for the first time and pleading guilty. The court refers the young person to a youth offender panel led by members of the local community who agree a contract with the young person to repair the harm done and prevent further offending.

Complementing the non-custodial penalties for young offenders are parenting orders, which require a parent or guardian to attend counselling and guidance sessions, and may direct them to comply with other requirements; and child safety orders, which place a child under ten who is at risk of becoming involved in crime or is behaving in an anti-social manner under the supervision of a specified, responsible officer.

Appeals

A person convicted by a magistrates' court may appeal to the High Court, on points of law, and to the Crown Court, for his or her trial to be re-heard. Appeals from the Crown Court go to the Court of Appeal (Criminal Division). A further appeal can be made to the House of Lords on points of law of public importance, if permission is given. A prosecutor cannot appeal against an acquittal, but there is a system for reviewing rulings of law and sentences which are too lenient.

The Criminal Cases Review Commission, which is independent of both government and the courts, reviews alleged miscarriages of justice. Referral of a case to this body depends on some new argument or evidence coming to light, not previously raised at the trial or on appeal.

During 2001, a total of 7,440 applications for leave to appeal were received, of which 1,943 were against conviction in the Crown Court and 5,497 against the sentence imposed.

Prison

The Prison Service in England and Wales is an executive agency of the Home Office. There are currently 138 prison establishments (nine of which are run by private contractors).

One in four of those convicted of an indictable offence in 2001 in England and Wales received a custodial sentence (see Table 14.5). Life imprisonment is the mandatory sentence for murder, and is also available for certain other serious offences. The death penalty is no longer available for any offence; it has not been used anywhere in the United Kingdom since 1965.

Prison accommodation ranges from open prisons to high-security establishments. Sentenced prisoners are classified into different risk-level groups for security purposes. Women prisoners are held in separate prisons or in separate accommodation in mixed prisons.

In England and Wales, there have been recent increases in the prison population, which now numbers over 66,000. Measures taken to alleviate potential overcrowding in prisons include greater use of community (non-custodial) sentences for minor offenders; expanding the capacity of prisons and further opportunities for the granting of early release to prisoners (see below).

Prisoners throughout the UK may write and receive letters, be visited by relatives and friends, and make telephone calls. Privileges include a

Figure 14.6 Structure of the criminal justice system, England and Wales

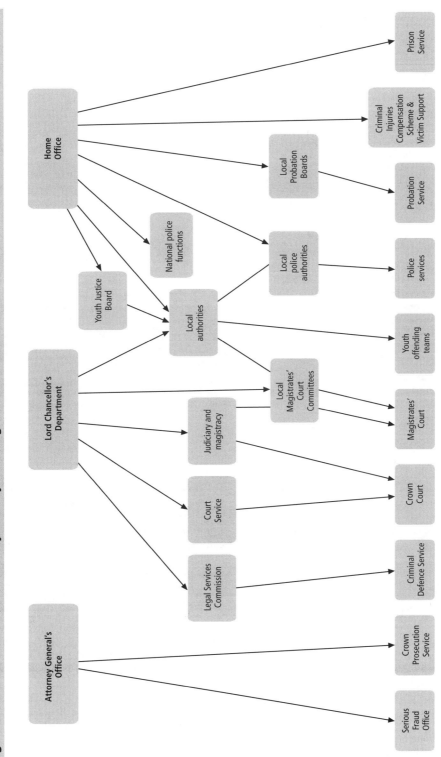

Source: Home Office

personal radio; books, magazines and newspapers; and watching television. Earnable privileges, dependent on good behaviour, include extra and improved visits, higher rates of pay, community visits, and longer periods out of the cell. People awaiting trial in custody have certain rights and privileges not granted to convicted prisoners. Measures to counter drug misuse in prisons include mandatory drug testing.

There are statutory arrangements governing the early release of prisoners. Offenders serving shorter terms (less than four years) may be automatically released at specific points in their sentences, while those detained for longer require Parole Board approval or the consent of a government minister.

Criminal justice agencies

The criminal justice system in England and Wales is made up of personnel working in a number of different agencies, reporting to the Home Office, the Lord Chancellor's Department and the Attorney General's Office, as illustrated in Figure 14.6.

The police service

There are 43 police forces organised on a local basis in England and Wales. The Metropolitan Police Service and the City of London force are responsible for policing London.

Police forces are maintained in England and Wales by local police authorities. In the 41 police areas outside London they normally have 17 members – nine locally elected councillors, three magistrates and five independent members. The authorities set local policing objectives in consultation with the chief constables and local community, while the Government sets ministerial priorities for the police as a whole.

Each force is headed by a chief constable (in London the Commissioner of the City of London Police, and the Commissioner of the Metropolitan Police) appointed by their police authorities with government approval. Independent inspectors of constabulary report on the efficiency and effectiveness of police forces. In 2002 there were in England and Wales 127,231 police officers, 12,068 special constables (part-time volunteers who work in support), and 58,957 civilian staff (including traffic wardens).

National crime bodies

The *National Criminal Intelligence Service* (NCIS) is responsible for collecting and analysing criminal intelligence for use by police forces and other law enforcement agencies in the UK. NCIS co-ordinates the activities of the Security Services in support of the law enforcement agencies against organised crime, and liaises with the International Criminal Police Organisation (INTERPOL), which promotes international co-operation between police forces. It also provides the channel for communication between the UK and EUROPOL (see page 76).

The role of the *National Crime Squad* is to prevent and detect organised and serious crime across police force and national boundaries in England and Wales and to support provincial forces in their investigation of serious crime. It is headed by a Director General, who is accountable to a body known as the Service Authorities.

The *Forensic Science Service* (FSS) is an executive agency of the Home Office that provides scientific support to police forces through its six regional laboratories. It also operates the national DNA database in England and Wales, which is used to match DNA profiles taken from suspects to profiles from samples left at scenes of crime.

The *Serious Fraud Office* prosecutes cases of serious or complex fraud, with teams of lawyers, accountants, police officers and other specialists conducting investigations. The Office has wide powers that go beyond those normally available to the police and prosecuting authorities.

The courts

About 98 per cent of criminal cases are dealt with by magistrates. A *magistrates' court* usually comprises three representatives of the local community who do not have professional legal qualifications, known as lay magistrates or justices of the peace (JPs). They sit with a court clerk who advises them on law and procedure. In some areas a paid professional District Judge (Magistrates' Courts) sits alone instead of the JPs. District Judges (Magistrates' Courts) – who were formerly known as stipendiary magistrates – are becoming more common, although most cases are still dealt with by lay magistrates.

Magistrates' courts committees (MCCs), made up of magistrates selected by their colleagues, are responsible for running the magistrates' courts service locally. During 2000/01 the MCCs were reorganised and their number reduced, improving efficiency and bringing their boundaries into closer alignment with those of other criminal justice agencies, such as the police and the CPS.

The *Crown Court* sits at about 90 venues in England and Wales, in six regional areas called circuits, and is presided over by High Court judges, circuit judges and part-time recorders. The type of judge dealing with a case and instructing the jury of 12 members of the general public will depend on which Crown Court the case is being heard in. Not all Crown Courts handle cases of the same level of seriousness. Judges sat for 87,688 days in the Crown Court in 2001: the bulk of this time was spent by circuit judges (71 per cent) and recorders (23 per cent).

A coroner (usually a senior lawyer or doctor) must hold an inquest if a person died a violent or unnatural death, or died suddenly while in prison or in other specified circumstances. He or she may also need to hold an inquest if the cause of death remains unknown following a post-mortem examination. The *coroner's court* establishes how, when and where the death occurred. A coroner may sit alone or, in certain circumstances, with a jury.

The judiciary

Judges are appointed from the ranks of practising barristers and solicitors. They have independence of office and can be removed only in rare and limited circumstances involving misconduct or incapacity. They are not subject to ministerial control or direction. Full-time judges are generally expected to have previously sat in a part-time capacity (for about 15 days a year) in the same or a similar jurisdiction. Lay magistrates (JPs) are trained in order to give them sufficient knowledge of the law, including the rules of evidence, and of the nature and purpose of sentencing. They are currently advised by legally qualified clerks of court.

The *Lord Chancellor* heads the judiciary and sits as a member of the judicial committee of the House of Lords. He also presides over the upper House in its law-making role and, as a senior Cabinet minister, is in charge of the Lord Chancellor's Department (see page 45).

The *Lord Chief Justice* of England and Wales is second in rank to the Lord Chancellor in the judicial hierarchy. He has some responsibilities for the organisation and work of the criminal courts,

Table 14.7 Numbers[1] in the judiciary in England and Wales (as at 1 January 2002)

Lay magistrates (JPs)	24,526
District Judges (Magistrates' Courts)	95
Recorders	1,326
Circuit judges	614

1 Those spending the bulk of their time on criminal cases. This excludes High Court judges and district judges, who deal primarily with civil cases, and Lord Justices, who sit in the Court of Appeal.
Source: Court Service

including issuing practice directions to the courts and members of the legal professions on criminal law and court procedures.

The *Home Secretary* has overall responsibility for criminal law, the police service, the prison system, the probation service, and for advising the Crown on the exercise of the royal prerogative of mercy.

The *Attorney General* and the *Solicitor General* are the Government's main legal advisers, providing advice on a range of legal matters, including proposed legislation. They may also represent the Crown in difficult or publicly important domestic and international cases.

A wide range of statutory and non-statutory bodies advise the Government. These include the police inspectorates, the Magistrates' Courts Service, the Audit Commission, the Criminal Justice Consultative Committee, law reform bodies such as the Law Commission and ad hoc Royal Commissions and departmental committees. The Youth Justice Board for England and Wales monitors the youth justice system, promotes good practice and advises the Home Secretary on its operation and the setting of national standards.

Prosecution authorities

The Crown Prosecution Service (CPS – see also page 189) is headed by the *Director of Public Prosecutions (DPP)*, who reports to the Attorney General.

Other prosecuting authorities include the Serious Fraud Office (see page 196), which also answers to the Attorney General, and bodies such as the Inland Revenue, Customs and Excise Commissioners, local authorities and trading standards departments, all of which prosecute cases in their own discrete areas of work. Individual citizens may bring private prosecutions for most crimes, but some need the consent of the Attorney General and these cases may be taken over by the DPP.

An Independent Inspectorate (HM Crown Prosecution Service Inspectorate) reports on the performance of the Crown Prosecution Service and the prosecution Group of HM Customs and Excise.

The legal profession
Although people are free to conduct their own cases if they so wish, barristers and solicitors, or other authorised litigators, generally represent the interests of parties to a dispute. Barristers practise as individuals, but join a group of other barristers in Chambers. Solicitors usually operate in partnership with other solicitors, but some are self-employed. Large firms of solicitors employ not only qualified staff, but also legal executives and support staff.

The Bar Council is the professional body representing barristers and the Law Society of England and Wales represents solicitors. The professions are self-regulating, with the professional bodies exercising disciplinary control over their members.

The Legal Services Ombudsman for England and Wales oversees the way in which the relevant professional bodies handle complaints about barristers, solicitors and other legal practitioners.

The Probation Service
In 2001 a unified National Probation Service for England and Wales was formed, led by a National Director who reports directly to the Home Secretary. The service is based in 42 areas, each of which, outside London, has the same boundaries as a police force and Crown Prosecution Service area. The service supervises offenders in the community under direct court orders and on release on licence from custody. It also prepares reports for the courts to assist them in deciding on the most appropriate sentence. Certain young

The Probation Service is developing an alcohol strategy which will build on the existing provision of accredited alcohol and substance misuse programmes and provide a co-ordinated approach to tackling the alcohol misuse and related offending of those offenders under probation supervision.

offenders are supervised by local authority social services departments or youth offending teams.

HM Inspectorate of Probation has both an inspection and an advisory role, and also monitors any work that the Probation Service carries out in conjunction with the voluntary and private sectors.

The Prison Service
Every prison establishment in England and Wales has a board of visitors, comprising volunteers drawn from the local community appointed by the Home Secretary. Boards, which are independent, monitor complaints by prisoners and the concerns of staff, and report as necessary to ministers.

Independent Prisons Inspectorates report on the treatment of prisoners and prison conditions, and submit annual reports to Parliament. Each prison establishment is visited about once every three years.

Prisoners who fail to get satisfaction from the Prison Service's internal request and complaints system may complain to the independent Prisons Ombudsman.

Civil justice
Jurisdiction in civil matters in England and Wales is administered mainly by the county courts and the High Court, the latter handling the more substantial and complex cases. County courts also handle family proceedings, such as divorce, domestic violence and matters affecting children. Most civil disputes do not go to court at all, and most of those which do, do not reach a trial. Many are dealt with through statutory or voluntary complaints mechanisms, or through mediation and negotiation. Arbitration is common in commercial and building disputes. Ombudsmen have the power to determine complaints in the public sector and, on a voluntary basis, in some private sector activities (for example, banking, insurance and pensions).

A large number of tribunals exist to determine disputes. Most deal with cases that involve the rights of private citizens against decisions of the State in areas such as social security, income tax and mental health. Some tribunals deal with other disputes, such as employment. In all, there are some 80 tribunals in England and Wales which together deal with over 1 million cases a year.

Successful actions taken in the civil courts can result in damages being awarded to the individual pursuing the claim. The amount awarded in each case varies according to the circumstances.

Courts

The High Court is divided into three Divisions:

- The *Queen's Bench Division* deals with disputes relating to contracts, general commercial matters (in a specialist Commercial Court), and breaches of duty – known as 'liability in tort' – covering claims of negligence, nuisance or defamation. The Administrative Court has special responsibility for dealing with applications for judicial review of the actions of public bodies, and has the power to declare the action of an individual, department or public body unlawful.

- The *Chancery Division* deals with disputes relating to land, wills, companies and insolvency.

- The *Family Division* deals with matrimonial matters, including divorce, and the welfare of children.

There are 228 county courts handling claims in contract and in tort (and 179 of these also deal with family issues). The majority of claims dealt with concern the recovery and collection of debt. The next most common types of claims relate to recovery of land and personal injury. Magistrates' courts have limited civil jurisdiction: in family matters (when they sit as a Family Proceedings Court) and in miscellaneous civil orders.

Appeals in most civil cases were reformed by the *Access to Justice Act 1999*. The general principle is that appeal 'lies' to the next level of judge in the court hierarchy. A county court appeal lies from a district judge to a circuit judge and from a circuit judge to a High Court judge.

In the High Court appeal lies from a master or district judge of the High Court to a High Court judge and from a High Court judge to the Court of Appeal.

As in criminal cases, appeals from magistrates' courts in civil matters go to the High Court, on

matters of law, or to the Crown Court, if the case is to be re-heard. A further appeal on points of law of public importance would go to the House of Lords.

Proceeding with a claim

There is currently a system of three tracks to which disputed claims are assigned by a judge according to the value and complexity of the case. These are:

- the small claims track, for cases worth less than £5,000, at an informal hearing by a district judge;

- the fast track, for cases from £5,000 to £15,000, with a fixed timetable from allocation to trial; and

- the multi-track, for cases worth over £15,000 or of unusual complexity, which are supervised by a judge and given timetables tailored to each case.

The Civil Justice Council oversees the working of the civil justice system, and makes proposals for its improvement.

Publicly funded legal help

The Legal Services Commission administers the Community Legal Service (CLS), which brings together organisations offering legal and advice services into local networks throughout England and Wales. These include solicitors' firms, Citizens Advice Bureaux (see page 476), law centres, local authority services and other independent advice centres. The CLS Fund provides legal help and representation to qualifying applicants, depending on their personal financial circumstances and the nature of their case. It supports eligible people in cases of divorce, mediation and other family issues, welfare benefits, credit and debt problems, housing and property disputes, immigration and nationality issues, clinical negligence cases, challenges to decisions by government departments and other public bodies, and actions against the police and others.

Recipients may be asked to make a contribution, depending on their personal financial circumstances and the outcome of the case. During 2000/01 there were 1.1 million acts of assistance under the CLS and the total net expenditure was £792 million.

Scotland

The Scottish Executive Justice Department, under the Minister for Justice, is responsible for civil and criminal law and justice, social work services, police, prisons, courts administration, legal aid, and liaison with the legal profession in Scotland. The Department also has responsibility for all matters of the law of Scotland and its operation as it relates to international law and relations with other legal systems, including those of other parts of the United Kingdom. The Scottish Court Service, an executive agency of the Scottish Executive Justice Department, deals with the work of the Supreme Courts and the sheriff courts.

The Lord Advocate and the Solicitor General for Scotland provide the Scottish Executive with advice on legal matters and represent its interests in the courts. Since devolution, the Advocate General for Scotland has provided advice on Scots law to the UK Government.

The role of the Scottish Parliament is to make laws on matters devolved to it (see chapter 4). In these areas, it is able to amend or repeal existing Acts of the UK Parliament and to pass new legislation for Scotland of its own. It can also consider and pass private legislation, promoted by individuals or bodies (for example, local authorities).

Policing

The police in Scotland can arrest someone without a warrant, under wide common law powers, if suspects are seen or reported as committing a crime or are a danger to themselves or others. They also have specific statutory powers of arrest for some offences. In other cases they may apply to a justice of the peace for a warrant. The police may search anyone suspected of carrying an offensive weapon. Someone suspected of an imprisonable offence may be held for police questioning without being arrested, but for no more than six hours without being charged. If arrested, suspects must be charged and cautioned. The case is then referred to the procurator fiscal.

HM Inspectorate of Constabulary for Scotland considers representations from complainants dissatisfied with the way the police have handled their complaints. A consultation paper with proposals for strengthening the independence of the police complaints system in Scotland was published in July 2001.

Distinguishing features of the Scottish legal system

- The Scottish Parliament has legislative competence over most aspects of the law and the legal system in civil and criminal matters, including the prosecution system, the courts administration and certain judicial appointments.

- The Lord Advocate is responsible for the investigation of crime through the Crown Office, and for prosecutions in the High Court, sheriff court and district court.

- Unlike in England, there is no general right of prosecution in Scotland. The prosecution is undertaken by the Lord Advocate in the interests of the public as a whole, and not on behalf of the police or individual citizens.

- The police report details of alleged crimes to the procurator fiscal, who has discretion whether or not to prosecute. Procurators fiscal are also responsible for the investigation of all sudden and suspicious deaths, as there are no coroners in Scotland.

- Scottish juries contain 15 people and reach a verdict by simple majority.

The Scottish Crime Squad performs the same role as the National Crime Squad in England and Wales (see page 196). Forensic services are provided by four regional laboratories, the largest of which is based in Dundee. Police authorities in Scotland are composed of elected councillors.

Criminal justice

Prisons

The Scottish Prison Service is an executive agency. There are currently 17 prison establishments, and an average prison population of around 6,100. Prison accommodation, and the rights and privileges afforded to prisoners in Scotland, are broadly comparable with England and Wales (see page 194).

Prisoners who exhaust the internal grievance procedure may apply to the independent Scottish Prisons Complaints Commissioner.

There are statutory arrangements governing the early release of prisoners. As in England and

Wales, offenders serving terms of less than four years may be automatically released at specific points in their sentences. Those detained for longer require Parole Board approval. In Scotland, ministers are statutorily obliged to give effect to the Parole Board's directions.

Legal aid

The Scottish Legal Aid Board manages legal aid in Scotland. Its main tasks are to grant or refuse applications for legal aid; to pay solicitors or advocates for the legal work that they do; and to advise Scottish ministers on legal aid matters. Where legal aid is granted to the accused in criminal proceedings, he or she is not required to pay any contribution towards expenses.

Scottish law

The legal principles, rules and concepts of Scots law can be traced from diverse sources, including Roman law, canon law and the influences of other European systems. The main sources are judge-made law, certain legal treatises having 'institutional' authority, legislation and EC law. The first two sources are sometimes referred to as the common law of Scotland. Legislation, as in the rest of the UK, consists of statutes (Acts of the UK or Scottish Parliament) or subordinate legislation authorised by the Scottish or UK Parliament.

Advocates (broadly speaking the Scottish equivalent of barristers) have audience in the Supreme Courts. Solicitor-Advocates who are accredited specifically for civil or criminal business also have audience in the Supreme Courts. Solicitors in Scotland (numbering 8,700 in October 2001) have audience in the sheriff and district courts and in the other courts and tribunals. They practise largely in partnerships throughout the country.

The professional body for advocates is the Faculty of Advocates. For solicitors the regulator is the Law Society of Scotland. The Scottish Legal Services Ombudsman oversees the way in which these bodies handle complaints.

Prosecution

The Crown Office and Procurator Fiscal Service provides Scotland's independent public prosecution and deaths investigation service. The Department is headed by the Lord Advocate, assisted by the Solicitor General for Scotland (who are the Scottish Law Officers and members of the Scottish Executive). The Crown Agent, a senior civil servant, is responsible for the running of the Department.

Procurators fiscal and Crown Office officials prepare prosecutions in the High Court which are conducted by the Lord Advocate and the Solicitor General for Scotland; they in turn delegate the bulk of their work to advocates depute, collectively known as Crown Counsel, of whom there are 18.

The police report gives details of alleged crimes to the local procurator fiscal who has discretion whether or not to prosecute. He or she may receive instructions from the Crown Counsel on behalf of the Lord Advocate.

The office of coroner does not exist in Scotland. Instead the local procurator fiscal inquires into sudden or suspicious deaths. When appropriate, a fatal accident inquiry may be held before the sheriff; this is mandatory in cases of death resulting from industrial accidents and deaths in custody. The inquiry has two purposes: to establish the causes of death; and to make recommendations as to how in future the causes and circumstances which led to individual deaths could be avoided.

Criminal courts

There are three criminal courts in Scotland: the High Court of Justiciary, the sheriff court and the district court. Cases are heard under one of two types of criminal procedure:

In *solemn procedure* in both the High Court of Justiciary and the sheriff court, an accused person's trial takes place before a judge sitting with a jury of 15 people selected at random from the general public. The judge decides questions of law and the jury decides questions of fact and may reach a decision by a simple majority. They may decide to find the accused 'guilty', 'not guilty' or 'not proven'; the last two are acquittals and have the effect that the accused cannot be tried again for the same offence.

In *summary procedure* in sheriff and district courts, the judge sits without a jury and decides questions of both fact and law.

Pre-trial hearings (called 'diets') in summary and solemn cases are intended to establish the state of readiness of both the defence and the prosecution.

The *High Court of Justiciary* is the supreme criminal court in Scotland, sitting in Edinburgh, Glasgow and on circuit in other towns. It tries the most serious crimes and has exclusive jurisdiction in cases involving murder, treason and rape.

The 49 *sheriff courts* deal mainly with less serious offences committed within their area of jurisdiction. These courts are organised in six sheriffdoms; at the head of each is a sheriff principal. There are over 100 permanent sheriffs, most of whom are appointed to particular courts. The sheriff has jurisdiction in both summary and solemn criminal cases. Under summary procedure, the sheriff may impose prison sentences of up to three months (although more in some cases) or a fine of £5,000. Under solemn procedure, the sheriff may impose imprisonment for up to three years and unlimited financial penalties.

District courts, which deal with minor offences, are the administrative responsibility of the local authority. The longest prison sentence which can be imposed is generally 60 days and the maximum fine is £2,500. The bench of a district court will usually be made up of one or more Justices of the Peace. A local authority may also appoint a stipendiary magistrate, who must be a professional lawyer of at least five years' standing, and who has the same summary criminal jurisdiction and powers as a sheriff. At present, only Glasgow has stipendiary magistrates sitting in the district court. A government review of the operation of the district courts was announced in May 2000.

A total of 136,800 persons were proceeded against in Scottish criminal courts in 2000; 4 per cent were dealt with under solemn procedure, 60 per cent in sheriff summary courts and 37 per cent in district courts.

Sentencing
In Scotland a court must obtain a social enquiry report before imposing a custodial sentence if the accused is aged under 21 or has not previously served a custodial sentence. A report is also required before making a probation or community service order, or in cases involving people already subject to supervision.

Non-custodial sentences available to the courts include fines, probation orders, community service orders, restriction of liberty orders (monitored by electronic tagging) and supervised attendance orders (which provide an alternative to imprisonment for non-payment of fines, and incorporate aspects of work and training). In 2000 approximately 10 per cent of those sentenced by Scottish courts received either a probation or community service order, and 13 per cent received a custodial sentence.

Children
Criminal proceedings may be brought against any child aged eight or over, but the instructions of the Lord Advocate are necessary before anyone under 16 years of age is prosecuted. Most children under 16 who have committed an offence or are considered to be in need of care and protection may be brought before a Children's Hearing. The hearing, consisting of three people who are not lawyers, determines whether compulsory measures of care are required and, if so, the form they should take. In 2000/01, a total of 2,100 children aged under 16 were referred to a Children's Hearing on offence grounds. Young people aged between 16 and 21 generally serve custodial sentences in young offender institutions.

Probation
In Scotland local authority social work departments supervise offenders on probation, community service and other community disposals – equivalent to community sentences – and ex-prisoners subject to statutory supervision on release from custody.

Appeals
The High Court of Justiciary sits as the Scottish Court of Criminal Appeal. In both solemn and summary procedure, a convicted person may appeal against conviction, or sentence, or both. The Court may authorise a retrial if it sets aside a conviction. There is no appeal from this court in criminal cases. The Scottish Criminal Cases Review Commission is responsible for considering alleged miscarriages of justice and referring cases meeting the relevant criteria to the Court of Appeal for review. Just over 3,100 appeals against conviction or sentence were concluded in 2000, equivalent to 3 per cent of the total number of convictions in that year. Of these appeals, 2 per cent resulted in a conviction being quashed and 11 per cent in a reduction of sentence.

Civil justice
The bulk of the civil business in Scotland is conducted in the sheriff court which has general jurisdiction and sits throughout the country.

The *Court of Session* sits in Edinburgh, and may hear cases from the outset or on transfer from sheriff courts and tribunals on appeal. A leading principle of the court is that cases starting there are both prepared for decision, and decided, by judges sitting alone whose decisions are subject to review by several judges.

In addition to its criminal jurisdiction, the *sheriff court* deals with most civil law cases in Scotland. There is, with very few exceptions, no upper limit to the financial level with which the court can deal, and a broad range of remedies can be granted. Cases may include debts, contracts, reparation, rent restrictions, actions affecting the use of property, leases and tenancies, child protection issues and family actions. There is a right of appeal in some cases from the sheriff to the sheriff principal and then, in some cases, to the Court of Session.

The House of Lords hears relatively few appeals in civil matters from Scotland but, since devolution, the Judicial Committee of the Privy Council (JCPC) has had jurisdiction to consider disputes involving devolution issues. When dealing with Scottish cases, the JCPC usually includes at least two Scottish judges and can sit in London or elsewhere as appropriate.

Civil proceedings

The formal proceedings in the Court of Session are started by serving the defender with a summons or, in sheriff court cases in ordinary actions, an initial writ. A defender who intends to contest the action must inform the court; if he or she fails to do so, the court normally grants a decree in absence in favour of the pursuer. Where a case is contested, both parties must prepare written pleadings, after which a hearing will normally be arranged.

In summary cause actions involving sums between £750 and £1,500[4] in the sheriff court, a summons incorporates a statement of claim. The procedure is designed to let most actions be settled without the parties having to appear in court. Normally, they, or their representatives, need appear only when an action is defended.

Where actions are raised for sums up to £750 there is a special procedure for small claims which allows those who do not have legal advice to raise the claims themselves in the sheriff court. These are broadly restricted to payment actions. The procedure is intended to be simple and to allow for negotiated settlement at the earliest possible time – new rules on summary cause and small claims came into effect in June 2002.

The Scottish Land Court deals with agricultural matters and some environmental issues. The Lands Tribunal for Scotland deals with matters relating to land conditions, right to buy and valuation issues. The Children's Hearing deals with children in need of measures of supervision or care. Other tribunals common to the rest of the United Kingdom deal with unemployment, social security, and asylum and immigration matters.

Northern Ireland

Northern Ireland's legal system is similar to that of England and Wales. Jury trials have the same place in the system, except in the case of offences involving acts of terrorism. In addition, cases go through the same stages in the courts and the legal profession has the same two branches.

People accused of offences specified under emergency legislation (see page 16) are tried in the Crown Court without a jury. The prosecution must prove guilt beyond reasonable doubt and the defendant has the right to be represented by a lawyer of his or her choice. The judge has to set out in a written statement the reasons for conviction and there is an automatic right of appeal to the Court of Appeal against conviction and/or sentence on points of fact as well as of law.

The probation service in Northern Ireland is administered by the government-funded Probation Board, whose membership is representative of the community.

The Northern Ireland Prison Service is an executive agency. There are currently three prison establishments, and an average population (based on monthly counts) in 2001 of 910. Prison accommodation, and the rights and privileges afforded to prisoners in Northern Ireland, are broadly comparable with England and Wales (see page 194).

Every prison has a board of visitors comprising volunteers from the local community appointed

---

4 These levels are currently under review.

by the Secretary of State for Northern Ireland. There are no open prisons in Northern Ireland.

In Northern Ireland, voluntary drug testing in prisons has already been implemented and evaluation of a system of laboratory testing of drug samples will provide the basis for the introduction of mandatory drug testing.

Policing

In November 2001 the Royal Ulster Constabulary became the Police Service of Northern Ireland (PSNI), as part of a series of reforms to the police following the report of the Patten Commission set up under the terms of the 1998 Good Friday Agreement peace accord (see chapter 3). The Chief Constable is accountable to a new Policing Board, made up of ten political nominees and nine independent members appointed by the Secretary of State.

Unlike the rest of Great Britain, police officers in Northern Ireland are issued with firearms for their personal protection. Complaints against the police are investigated by an independent Police Ombudsman.

Administration of the law

The Lord Chancellor is responsible for court administration, while the Northern Ireland Office, under the Secretary of State, deals with policy and legislation concerning criminal law, the police and the penal system. The Lord Chancellor has general responsibility for legal aid, advice and assistance.

The Director of Public Prosecutions for Northern Ireland, who is responsible to the Attorney General, prosecutes all offences tried on indictment, and may do so in other (summary) cases. Most summary offences are prosecuted by the police.

Civil legal aid is administered by the Law Society for Northern Ireland. Where legal aid is granted for criminal cases it is free.

Superior courts

The Supreme Court of Judicature comprises the Court of Appeal, the High Court and the Crown Court. All matters relating to these courts are under the jurisdiction of the UK Parliament. Judges are appointed by the Crown.

The *Court of Appeal* consists of the Lord Chief Justice (as President) and two Lords Justices of Appeal. The High Court is made up of the Lord Chief Justice and five other judges. The practice and procedure of the Court of Appeal and the High Court are virtually the same as in the corresponding courts in England and Wales. Both courts sit in the Royal Courts of Justice in Belfast.

The Court of Appeal has power to review the civil law decisions of the High Court and the criminal law decisions of the Crown Court, and may in certain cases review the decisions of county courts and magistrates' courts. Subject to certain restrictions, an appeal from a judgment of the Court of Appeal can go to the House of Lords. The Criminal Cases Review Commission, which is independent of both government and the courts, reviews alleged miscarriages of justice.

The *High Court* is divided into a Queen's Bench Division, dealing with most civil law matters; a Chancery Division, dealing with, for instance, trusts and estates, title to land, mortgages and charges, wills and company matters; and a Family Division, dealing principally with such matters as matrimonial cases, adoption, children in care and undisputed wills.

The *Crown Court* deals with all serious criminal cases.

Inferior courts

The inferior courts are the county courts and the magistrates' courts, both of which differ in a number of ways from their counterparts in England and Wales.

County courts are primarily civil law courts. They are presided over by one of 14 county court judges, two of whom – in Belfast and Londonderry/Derry – have the title of recorder. Appeals go from the county courts to the High Court. The county courts also handle appeals from the magistrates' courts in both criminal and civil matters. In civil matters, the county courts decide most actions in which the amount or the value of specific articles claimed is below a certain level. The courts also deal with actions involving title to, or the recovery of, land; equity matters such as trusts and estates; mortgages; and the sale of land and partnerships.

The day-to-day work of dealing summarily with minor local criminal cases is carried out in *magistrates' courts* presided over by a full-time, legally qualified resident magistrate (RM). The magistrates' courts also exercise jurisdiction in certain family law cases and have a very limited jurisdiction in other civil cases.

Further reading

The Lord Chancellor's Departments: Departmental Report 2001–2002. The Government's Expenditure Plans 2002–03 to 2003–04. Cm 5408. The Stationery Office, 2002.

Home Office Annual Report 2001–2002. The Government's Expenditure Plans 2002–03 to 2003–2004 and Main Estimates 2002–03. Cm 5406. The Stationery Office, 2002.

A Guide to the Criminal Justice System in England and Wales. Home Office, 2000.

Crime and Criminal Justice in Scotland. Peter Young. The Stationery Office, 1997.

HM Prison Service Annual Report and Accounts 2001–02, The Stationery Office

Justice for All. Cm 5563. Home Office. The Stationery Office, 2002.

Websites

Community Legal Service
www.justask.org.uk

Home Office
www.homeoffice.gov.uk

Legal Services Commission
www.legalservices.gov.uk

Lord Chancellor's Department
www.lcd.gov.uk

Northern Ireland Executive
www.northernireland.gov.uk

Scottish Executive
www.scotland.gov.uk

HM Prison Service (England and Wales)
www.hmprisonservice.gov.uk

WWW.

15 Religion

The United Kingdom is a multifaith society in which everyone has the right to religious freedom. Religious organisations and groups may conduct their rites and ceremonies, promote their beliefs within the limits of the law, own property, and run schools and a range of other charitable activities.

Although religious faith in the UK is predominantly Christian, most of the world's religions are practised. There are large Hindu, Jewish, Muslim and Sikh communities, and also smaller communities of Bahá'í, Buddhists, Jains, and Zoroastrians, as well as followers of new religious movements. On the other hand, many people do not practise any religion and some reject all forms of religious belief. Organisations such as the British Humanist Association and the National Secular Society represent some of the latter views.

Religious traditions in the UK

A distinction is often drawn between 'community size' and 'active membership': the former represents identification with a religion, or a religious ethic, in the broadest sense, and the latter a much closer association. There are an estimated 7.9 million active adult members of religious groups in the UK. Many other people take part in formal religious ceremonies at times of crisis or to mark significant life events such as birth, marriage and death. The 2001 Census of Population included, for the first time throughout the UK since 1851, a question on religion.[1] When the answers to this question have been analysed, they will provide extensive official information on

---

1 Questions about religious beliefs have, however, been asked previously for official purposes in Northern Ireland.

Table 15.1 Belonging to a religion,[1] Great Britain, 2001

Religion	Per cent
Church of England/Anglican	29
Catholic	11
Other Christian	14
Other faiths	4
None	41
Refused/did not answer	1

1 Respondents were asked 'Do you regard yourself as belonging to any particular religion?'.
Source: British Social Attitudes Survey, National Centre for Social Research

Church and state

Christianity has been the most influential religion in the UK, and it remains the declared faith of the majority of the population. Two Churches have a special status with regard to the State. In England, since the rejection by Henry VIII of the supremacy of the Pope in 1534, the Anglican *Church of England* has been legally recognised as the official, or 'established', Church. The Monarch is the 'Supreme Governor' of the Church of England and must always be a member of the Church, and promise to uphold it. A similar position was occupied by the Presbyterian *Church of Scotland* until the early 20th century. This continues to be recognised as the national Church in Scotland, but the Monarch holds no constitutional role in its government, although she is represented at the General Assembly (see page 210) in the office of the Lord High Commissioner. Neither of the established Churches are funded by the State. There are no established Churches in Wales or Northern Ireland. In Wales, the Anglican Church is known as the *Church in Wales*.

patterns of religious identity in the United Kingdom. In the meantime, Table 15.1 gives some indication of religious identity in Great Britain. It suggests that just over half of the population (54 per cent) regard themselves as Christian and 41 per cent regard themselves as belonging to no religion.

The Christian community

The Christian community in the UK consists of many denominations. Of these, the Anglican and Catholic Churches have the largest congregations. Other denominations include Presbyterians, Methodists and Baptists.

The Church of England is part of a worldwide Communion of Anglican churches, 38 in all. The four Anglican churches in the UK are the Church of England, the Church in Wales, the Scottish Episcopal Church, and the Church of Ireland (Northern Ireland). The Church of England has an average weekly church attendance of 1.3 million.

The Catholic Church has an average estimated weekly Mass attendance of over 1 million in England and Wales, around 200,000 in Scotland and 400,000 in Northern Ireland.

The Presbyterian Church of Scotland has an adult communicant membership in the UK of over 610,000.

The rise of the Puritan movement in the 16th and 17th centuries led to a proliferation of nonconformist[2] churches. The term 'Free Churches' is often used to describe these Protestant churches in the UK which, unlike the Church of England and the Church of Scotland, are not 'established' Churches. The major Free Churches include Methodist, Baptist, United Reformed, Salvation Army and a variety of Pentecostal churches.

The British Methodist Church, the largest of the Free Churches, originated in the 18th century following the evangelical revival under John Wesley (1703–91). It has 327,000 adult full members. The present Church is based on the 1932 union of most of the separate Methodist Churches.

2 One who does not conform to the doctrine or discipline of an established Church.

The Baptists first achieved an organised form in the UK in the 17th century. Today they are mainly organised in associations of churches, most of which belong to the Baptist Union of Great Britain (re-formed in 1812) with about 139,000 members. There are also separate Baptist Unions for Scotland, Wales and Ireland, and other independent Baptist Churches.

The third largest of the Free Churches is the United Reformed Church, with some 92,000 members. It was formed in 1972 from the union of the Congregational Church in England and Wales with the Presbyterian Church in England. In 1982 and 2000 there were further unions with the Reformed Churches of Christ and the Congregational Union of Scotland.

Among the other Free Churches are the Presbyterian Church in Ireland, which has around 300,000 members in Northern Ireland; the Presbyterian (or Calvinistic Methodist) Church of Wales, with 42,000 members and the largest of the Free Churches in Wales; the Union of Welsh Independents, with 35,000 members; and a number of independent Scottish Presbyterian churches which are particularly active in the Highlands and Islands.

The Salvation Army was founded in the East End of London in 1865 by William Booth (1829–1912) and has a membership of nearly 51,000. It runs over 800 local church and community centres, and has a strong musical tradition.

The Religious Society of Friends (Quakers), with about 16,000 adult members, was founded in the middle of the 17th century under the leadership of George Fox. Other Unitarians and Free Christians, whose origins go back to the Reformation, belong to a similar tradition. There are two branches of the Christian Brethren, founded in the 19th century: the Open Brethren and the Closed or Exclusive Brethren.

The rich tradition of people of different cultures coming to settle in the United Kingdom since the Middle Ages has also contributed to the diversity of Christian denominations. Christian communities founded by migrants include those of the Orthodox, Lutheran and Reformed Churches of various European countries, the Coptic Orthodox Church, Armenian Church and a number of Churches originating in Africa, such as the Cherubim and Seraphim Churches. These tend to be concentrated in the larger cities, particularly London, and use a variety of languages. The largest is the Greek Orthodox Church, many of whose members are of Cypriot origin.

Other developments within the Christian tradition have included the rise of Pentecostalism and the charismatic[3] movement. A number of Pentecostal bodies were formed in the UK at the turn of the 20th century. The two main Pentecostal organisations in the UK today are the Assemblies of God, and the Elim Pentecostal Church. Since the Second World War immigration from the Caribbean has led to a significant number of Black Majority Pentecostal churches, and these are a growing presence in British (and especially English) church life. The Christian 'house church' movement (or 'new churches') began in the 1970s when some of the charismatics began to establish their own congregations.

Inter-Church co-operation

Churches Together in Britain and Ireland is the main co-ordinating body for the Christian Churches in the UK. It co-ordinates the work of its 33 member organisations, in the areas of social responsibility, international affairs, church life, world mission, racial justice, care of international students and inter-faith relations. Its international aid agencies – Christian Aid, CAFOD and SCIAF[4] – are major charities. Member Churches are also grouped in separate ecumenical bodies, according to country: Churches Together in England, Action of Churches Together in Scotland, Churches Together in Wales (Cytûn), and the Irish Council of Churches.

The Free Churches Group, with 18 member denominations, was incorporated into Churches Together in England in 2001. It promotes co-operation among the Free Churches, especially in hospital chaplaincy and in education matters. The Evangelical Alliance, with a membership of individuals, churches or societies drawn from 20 denominations, represents over 1.3 million evangelical Christians.

Inter-Church discussions about the search for Christian unity take place internationally, as well

as within the UK, and the main participants are the Anglican, Baptist, Lutheran, Methodist, Orthodox, Reformed and Catholic Churches. The Church of England and the Methodist Church published a report in December 2001 on moves that could lead to greater unity between the two Churches. In Scotland, several Churches, including the Church of Scotland, have been pursuing unity through the Scottish Churches' Initiative for Union. Among them is the United Reformed Church, itself the outcome of previous unions. In Wales, recent moves towards a United Free Church have made some progress towards establishing – in one small area – an ecumenical bishop.

Other faith communities

The United Kingdom is home to adherents of many world religions. Immigrants and their descendants are among those who continue to add to this diversity.

The Buddhist community has around 52,000 active members in the UK, including people of British, South Asian and South East Asian background. Various strands of Buddhism from the Mahayana and Theravada traditions are represented.

The Hindu community in the UK originates largely from India. Most British Hindus are of Gujarati or Punjabi origin with smaller numbers from Uttar Pradesh, West Bengal and the southern states of India and Sri Lanka. Others have come from countries to which earlier generations of Indians had previously migrated such as Kenya, Malawi, Tanzania, Uganda and Zambia. The size of the Hindu community is thought to be around 500,000, although some representatives suggest a considerably higher figure (of close to 1 million).

Jews first settled in England at the time of the Norman Conquest. They were banished by royal decree in 1290, but readmitted following the English Civil War (1642–51). Sephardic Jews, who originally came from Spain and Portugal, have been present in the UK since the mid-17th century. The majority of the 283,000 Jews in the UK today, while British born, are Ashkenazi Jews, of Central and East European origin, who emigrated or fled persecution in the Russian Empire between 1881 and 1914, or Nazi persecution in Germany and other European countries from 1933 onwards.

A Muslim community has existed in the UK since the 16th century. By the early 19th century

---

3 A type of Christianity that emphasises personal religious experience and divinely inspired powers.

4 Catholic Agency for Overseas Development and Scottish Catholic International Aid Fund.

Muslim seamen, mainly from Yemen and the Indian subcontinent, had established settlements in several parts of the country, including Cardiff, South Shields and the London Docklands. There was further settlement after the First World War, and again in the 1950s and 1960s as people arrived to meet the shortage of labour following the Second World War. The 1970s saw the arrival of significant numbers of Muslims of Asian origin from Kenya and Uganda. There are well-established Turkish Cypriot and Iranian Muslim communities, and more recently Muslims from Somalia, Iraq, Bosnia and Kosovo have sought refuge in the UK. In addition, there are smaller numbers of English, West Indian and Chinese Muslims. In total, there are thought to be around 1.5 million people who identify themselves as Muslims, the majority of whom are now British-born. Sunni and Shi'a are the two principal traditions within Islam and while both are represented among the Muslim community in the UK, most belong to the Sunni tradition. Sufism, the spiritual aspect of Islam, can be found in both traditions, and members of some of the major Sufi traditions have also developed branches in British cities.

Most of the Sikh community in the UK are of Punjabi origin. A minority came from East Africa and other former British colonies to which members of their family had migrated, but the majority came to the UK directly from the Punjab. There are between 400,000 and 500,000 Sikhs in the UK, making it the largest Sikh community outside the Indian subcontinent.

Jainism is an ancient religion brought to the UK mainly by immigrants from the Gujarat and Rajasthan areas of India. The Zoroastrian religion is mainly represented in the UK by the Parsi community from India. The founders of the UK community originally settled here in the 19th century. The Bahá'í movement originated in Persia in the 19th century. Rastafarianism, with its roots in the return-to-Africa movement, emerged in the West Indies early in the 20th century. It arrived in the UK with immigration from Jamaica in the 1950s.

Other religious groups in the UK were originally founded in the United States in the 19th century, including a number deriving from the Christian tradition. Examples are the Church of Jesus Christ of Latter-Day Saints (the Mormon Church), the Jehovah's Witnesses, the Christadelphians, the Christian Scientists, and the Seventh-day Adventists.

A number of newer religious movements, established since the Second World War and often with overseas origins, are now active in the UK. Examples include the Church of Scientology, the Transcendental Meditation movement, the Unification Church and various New Age groups. INFORM (Information Network Focus on Religious Movements) carries out research and seeks to provide information about new religious movements.

Organisation

The Church of England is divided into two geographical provinces, each headed by an archbishop: Canterbury, comprising 30 dioceses, including the Diocese in Europe; and York, with 14 dioceses. The dioceses are divided into archdeaconries and deaneries, which are in turn divided into about 13,000 parishes, although in practice many parishes are grouped together.

Church of England archbishops, bishops and the deans of some cathedrals are appointed by the Queen on the advice of the Prime Minister. The Crown Appointments Commission, which includes lay and clergy representatives, plays a key role in the selection of archbishops and diocesan bishops. The Archbishops' Council is the centre of an administrative system dealing with inter-Church relations, inter-faith relations, social questions, recruitment and training for the ministry, and missionary work.

The Anglican Archbishops of Canterbury and York, the Bishops of Durham, London and

Dr George Carey will retire as Archbishop of Canterbury on 31 October 2002 after holding office for 11½ years. The Most Revd Rowan Williams, Archbishop of Wales and Bishop of Monmouth, has been nominated as his successor. The main roles of the Archbishop of Canterbury include Diocesan Bishop of Canterbury (Dr Williams will be the 104th), Primate of All England and leader of the Anglican Communion. The Archbishop of Canterbury takes the lead in respect of Anglican relationships with other Christian churches in the UK and abroad, and he also leads in respect of Anglican relationships with other faiths.

Winchester, and the 21 senior diocesan bishops from other dioceses of the Church of England have seats in the House of Lords (see page 34).

With assets of approximately £4 billion, the Church Commissioners are responsible for the management of a large part of the Church of England's invested assets. The Crown appoints a Member of Parliament from the governing party to the unpaid post of Second Church Estates Commissioner, to represent the Commissioners in Parliament. The Church Commissioners currently meet some 20 per cent of the Church of England's total running costs, providing support for parish ministry and the pensions of the clergy. Parishes and dioceses meet the remainder of the Church of England's running costs.

The Church of Scotland has a Presbyterian form of government – that is, government by church courts or councils, composed of ministers, elders, and deacons. The 1,550 congregations are governed locally by courts known as Kirk Sessions. The courts above these are the 'Presbyteries', responsible for a geographical area made up of a number of parishes. The General Assembly, or Supreme Court, meets annually under the chairmanship of an elected moderator, who serves for one year.

There are eight provinces of the Catholic Church in the UK – four in England, two in Scotland, one in Wales and one which includes Northern Ireland. There is a Bishops' Conference of England and Wales, and a Bishops' Conference of Scotland. The Irish Episcopal Conference includes the whole of Ireland. The Bishops' Conference is a permanent institution of the Catholic Church whereby the bishops of a country exercise together pastoral, legislative and teaching offices as defined by the law of the Church.

There are 22 territorial Catholic dioceses in England and Wales and eight in Scotland. Northern Ireland is covered by seven dioceses, some of which have territory in the Irish Republic. Each diocesan bishop is appointed by the Pope and governs according to Canon Law and through reference to a Council of Priests, College of Consultors and a Pastoral Council.

The Network of Buddhist Organisations links various Buddhist educational, cultural, charitable and teaching organisations. The Buddhist Society promotes the principles, but does not adhere to any particular school of Buddhism.

The main administrative bodies for Hindus are the National Council of Hindu Temples (UK) and the Hindu Council UK. Other national bodies serving the Hindu community include Vishwa Hindu Parishad (UK).

The Board of Deputies of British Jews is the officially recognised representative body for the Jewish community. Founded in 1760, it is elected mainly by synagogues, but a growing number of community organisations are also represented. The Board serves as the voice of the community to both government and the wider non-Jewish community. Of the total number of synagogue-affiliated households, most Ashkenazi Jews (60 per cent) acknowledge the authority of the Chief Rabbi. The Reform Synagogues of Great Britain, the Union of Liberal and Progressive Synagogues and the Assembly of Masorti Synagogues together account for most of the remaining synagogue-affiliated community membership.

The Muslim Council of Britain, founded in 1997, represents over 350 established national and regional Muslim bodies as well as local mosques, professional associations and other organisations. The Council aims to promote co-operation, consensus and unity on Muslim affairs in the UK. A number of other representative bodies, such as the Union of Muslim Organisations, aim to develop the social, cultural and economic aspects of Muslim life in the UK. The British Muslim community also has a number of associations of religious scholars – ulema – and shariah councils that provide religious legal rulings on matters such as matrimonial disputes.

The Network of Sikh Organisations (NSO) was formed in 1995 to facilitate co-operation between British Sikhs. It provides a forum for organising the celebration of major events in the Sikh calendar, and works with government departments and a number of national organisations to represent Sikh interests at a national level.

Places of worship

There are 16,000 Anglican churches (the earliest dating from the seventh century) and 42 Anglican cathedrals, which serve as focal points of the dioceses. They have a rich history and significance in British architecture. Examples include Salisbury Cathedral, which has the tallest spire in England at 123 metres.

The Church of Scotland and the Church in Wales both have over 1,500 churches. There are also a large number of churches belonging to other Christian denominations.

Since 1969 over 1,500 churches in England have become redundant and from their disposal, around £31.3 million has been raised. Redundant churches are increasingly being used for residential property or as civic, cultural and community centres. The Churches Conservation Trust, funded jointly by the Government and the Church of England, preserves Anglican churches of particular cultural and historical importance that are no longer used as regular places of worship. At present over 325 churches are maintained in this way. Many outstanding buildings from other denominations and faiths are cared for by the Historic Chapels Trust. The Friends of Friendless Churches is a voluntary organisation also caring for a number of redundant Anglican churches and for chapels and churches in Wales.

In the UK there are numerous Buddhist centres at which meditation or worship take place, although it is not considered essential to go to a temple and worship can take place at home.

The first Hindu temple, or mandir, was opened in London in the 1950s and there are now over 160 in the UK; many are affiliated to the National Council of Hindu Temples (UK). The Swaminarayan Hindu Temple in north London is the largest and was the first purpose-built Hindu temple in Europe.

Jewish synagogues in the UK number slightly fewer than 300, but there are additional congregations that do not have their own synagogue.

There are over 1,000 mosques and numerous community Muslim centres throughout the UK. Mosques are not only places of worship; they also offer instruction in the Muslim way of life, and facilities for education and welfare. They range from converted buildings in many towns and suburbs to the Central Mosque in Regent's Park, London, with its associated Islamic Cultural Centre. The main conurbations in the Midlands, North West and North East of England, and Scotland, Wales and Northern Ireland also have their own central mosques with a range of community facilities.

Continuity and change

Walking tours of the East End of London often pause outside a building on the corner of Fournier Street and Brick Lane. It was originally built in 1742 as a chapel for the Protestant Huguenots who had settled in the area after escaping persecution in France. By 1809 many of the Huguenots had moved on and it became a Methodist chapel. In 1897 it was bought by the Machzikei Hadath society and became the Spitalfields Great Synagogue. The Jewish population in this part of the East End was eventually replaced by Bengalis and in 1975 the building became the London Jamme Masjid (Mosque).

There are over 200 gurdwaras or Sikh temples in the UK, the vast majority being in England and Wales. The largest is in Southall, Middlesex. Gurdwaras cater for the religious, educational, welfare and cultural needs of their community. A granthi is usually employed to take care of the building and to conduct prayers.

In April 2001 the Government announced a new grant for repairs to listed buildings used as places of worship. While not a tax rebate, it will have the same effect as if the level of VAT (value added tax) for repairs had been reduced from 17.5 per cent to 5 per cent.

Religion and society

The influence of Christianity and other religions in the UK has always extended far beyond the comparatively narrow spheres of organised and private worship. Churches, cathedrals and other places of worship make a significant contribution to the architectural landscape of the nation. Religious organisations are actively involved in voluntary work and the provision of social services – many schools and hospitals, for example, were founded by men and women who were strongly influenced by Christianity. Easter and Christmas, the two most important events in the Christian calendar, are the year's major public holidays. Festivals and other events observed by other religions – such as Diwali and Holi (Hindu), the High Holy Days and Passover (Jewish), Ramadan and Eid (Muslim) and Vaisakhi (Sikh) – are adding to the visible diversity of life in the UK today.

In 2002, the Golden Jubilee celebrations marking 50 years of the reign of Queen Elizabeth II included a number of faith-linked events and visits. The programme of royal engagements included visits to a centre or place of worship of each of the main faiths in the UK.

Ceremonies marking life events

Although there are secular alternatives, religious traditions play a major role in commemorating births, marriages, deaths and other important life events.

In 2000 just under 40 per cent of marriages in the UK were solemnised with a religious ceremony, compared with 60 per cent in 1971. Between 1971 and 2000 the number of marriages with civil ceremonies has remained fairly steady while the number of marriages with religious ceremonies has declined (see Figure 15.2).

In England and Wales, 36 per cent of all marriages in 2000 involved a religious ceremony, including over 65,000 marriages solemnised in the Church of England or Church in Wales, over 11,000 Catholic weddings, 13,000 nonconformist weddings and around 2,500 non-Christian religious marriage ceremonies. In Scotland 60 per cent, and in Northern Ireland 75 per cent, of all marriages included a religious ceremony in 2000.

Figure 15.2 Marriages¹ by type of ceremony, UK

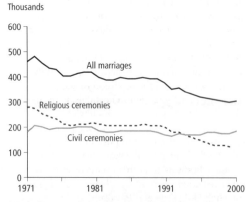

Thousands

1 Includes remarriages for one or both partners.
Source: Office for National Statistics; General Register Office for Scotland; Northern Ireland Statistics and Research Agency

Religious education

In England and Wales all state schools must provide religious education, each local education authority being responsible for producing a locally agreed syllabus. Syllabuses must reflect Christianity, while taking account of the teachings and practices of the other principal religions represented in the UK. State schools must provide a daily act of collective worship. Parents may withdraw their children from religious education and/or collective worship.

In 2000 England had 4,738 state-supported Anglican Church schools and 2,079 Catholic. In addition, there is a well-established tradition of Methodist and Jewish schools, with 28 and 33 state schools provided by each respectively. Recently the Government has helped set up, and given support to, a number of schools reflecting other religious traditions – for example, one Greek Orthodox, one Seventh-day Adventist, four Muslim and two Sikh schools. All the Churches and faith groups involved with the provision of these schools have organisations at national or regional level to provide support and help when opportunities arise to promote new schools.

In Scotland, education authorities must ensure that schools provide religious education and regular opportunities for religious observance. The law does not specify the form of religious education, but it is recommended that pupils should be provided with a broad-based curriculum, through which they can develop a knowledge and understanding of Christianity and other world religions, and develop their own beliefs, attitudes and moral values and practices.

In Northern Ireland a core syllabus for religious education has been approved by the main Churches and this must be taught in all state schools. Integrated education is encouraged and all schools must be open to pupils of all religions, although in practice most Catholic pupils attend Catholic maintained or Catholic voluntary grammar schools, and most Protestant children are enrolled at controlled schools or non-denominational voluntary grammar schools. However, the number of inter-denominational schools is increasing and in 2001/02, 14,980 primary and secondary pupils received their education at 'integrated' schools not attached to any particular religion.

Welfare

Charitable concern is a feature of many religions. Around 3,000 charities have a Christian connection, such as Christian Aid or CAFOD, but there are also many charities involving other religions. Muslim Aid, Islamic Relief, Khalsa Aid (a Sikh charity) and UK Jewish Aid are among the many British-based charities that organise appeals and deliver relief aid globally.

Within the UK the Salvation Army is an important provider of hostel accommodation, and offers other services including work with alcoholics, prison chaplaincy and a family-tracing service. The Quakers have a long tradition of social concern and peacemaking. Trusts with a Quaker history, such as the Cadbury and Rowntree Trusts, support many social initiatives.

The Church Urban Fund, established by the Church of England, is an independent charity which raises money to enable those living in the most disadvantaged urban areas to set up local projects to help alleviate the effects of poverty. Although rooted in the Christian faith, the fund does not restrict its grants on the basis of religious belief.

The General Assembly of the Church of Scotland debates annual reports from its Committee on Church and Nation, on social, economic and political matters, and, through its Board of Social Responsibility, it is the largest voluntary social work agency in Scotland. The Board currently runs projects offering care and support to 4,000 people every day. Churches in Wales and Northern Ireland, and other faith communities, also have a concern for social issues.

In England, the Inner Cities Religious Council, based in the Office of the Deputy Prime Minister, provides a forum in which the Government and faith communities work together on issues relating to urban policy. Chaired by a government minister, the Council includes representatives of the Christian, Hindu, Jewish, Muslim and Sikh faiths. The Churches Regional Network co-ordinates church involvement in Regional Development Agencies and Regional Assemblies.

Churches in Scotland have created a Scottish Churches Parliamentary Office for formal representation of their interests in the Scottish Parliament. In Wales, the Churches have worked together to appoint a Churches National Assembly Liaison Officer to relate to the National Assembly for Wales.

Legal rights and responsibilities

Everyone in the UK has the right to freedom of thought, conscience and religion subject to the law, under Article 9 of the European Convention on Human Rights, which was incorporated into the *Human Rights Act 1998*. In Great Britain religious discrimination will be unlawful in the areas of employment and training under an EC Directive, set to come into effect by December 2003.

The *Anti-Terrorism, Crime and Security Act 2001* has extended existing racially aggravated offences in England and Wales to cover offences motivated by religious hatred.

Discrimination on the grounds of religious belief or political opinion is already unlawful in Northern Ireland. The 1976 and 1989 *Fair Employment Acts* have been updated by the Fair Employment and Treatment (NI) Order 1998 which makes direct and indirect discrimination on grounds of religious belief or political opinion unlawful in employment and training and in the provision of goods, facilities and services.

In addition, under the *Northern Ireland Act 1998*, a public authority, in carrying out its functions relating to Northern Ireland, is obliged to have regard to the need to promote equality of opportunity between persons of different religious beliefs and to have due regard to the desirability of promoting good relations between such persons.

Co-operation between religions

The Inter Faith Network for the UK links a wide range of organisations with an interest in inter-faith relations, including the representative bodies of the Bahá'í, Buddhist, Christian, Hindu, Jain, Jewish, Muslim, Sikh and Zoroastrian communities. The Network promotes good relations between faiths in the UK, and runs a public advice and information service on inter-faith issues. The Council of Christians and Jews works for better understanding among members of these two religions and deals with educational and social issues. The Three Faiths Forum and the Calamus Foundation have as their focus relationships between the Christian, Jewish and Muslim traditions. There are many other organisations in the UK dealing wholly, or in part, with inter-faith issues. These include a growing number of local inter-faith groups and councils.

Churches Together in Britain and Ireland (see page 208) has a Commission on Inter Faith Relations. The Interfaith Unit of the Islamic Foundation was set up with the specific aim of developing better relations between the Muslim and Christian traditions.

> Since November 2000 members of the Buddhist, Orthodox Christian, Hindu, Muslim and Sikh communities have joined other Christian denominations and Jewish leaders at the Cenotaph in London's Whitehall on Remembrance Sunday to represent the many thousands of men and women of different faiths who have lost their lives in conflicts around the world.

Further reading
UK Christian Handbook 2002/2003, ed. Peter Brierley and Heather Wraight. Christian Research.

UK Christian Handbook – Religious Trends 2002/2003, No. 3, ed. Peter Brierley. Christian Research.

Religions in the UK Directory, 2001–03, ed. Paul Weller, Religious Resource and Research Centre at the University of Derby and The Inter Faith Network for the UK, 2001.

Websites

The Inter Faith Network for the UK
www.interfaith.org.uk

ODPM/Inner Cities Religious Council
www.urban.odpm.gov.uk/community/faith/index.htm

16 Culture

The United Kingdom has a diverse cultural heritage, with many artists and performers having contributed to the development of rich traditions in art, music, drama, literature and, more recently, TV, film and radio. Many people come from abroad to visit the UK for cultural reasons. Collections in the UK's museums and galleries are considered among the best in the world. British popular music has enjoyed success at home and overseas.

Culture 50 years ago

Much of the cultural life of Britain was, 50 years ago, still being rebuilt after the Second World War. Years of planning began for a new national theatre, which was eventually built alongside the Royal Festival Hall on London's South Bank. Public funding for the arts was being channelled through the newly founded Arts Council. The image of Britain as presented through films made at the time may have been over reliant on stereotypical images such as the friendly policeman and the London smog, but these familiar and comforting images probably reflected the needs of a nation still recovering after the Second World War. Television was still very much in its infancy, with mainstream broadcasts transmitted for only one hour each afternoon and then later from 8.30–10.00 pm in contrast with the 24-hour coverage of today's major networks.

Participation

Revenue and employment

Recent economic estimates made by the Department for Culture, Media and Sport (DCMS) (see page 226) suggest that the creative industries accounted for nearly 8 per cent of UK gross domestic product in 2000, and were providing nearly 2 million jobs in December 2001.

In 2001, cinemas took £550 million at the box office in Great Britain, compared with £507 million in 2000. An estimated 45,000 people were employed in the film and video industry in 2000 and exports in 1999 were worth around £653 million.

Turnover in the music industry as a whole was estimated at over £4 billion in 2000 (with exports worth £1.3 billion). It employed about 120,000 people. In 2001, nearly 226 million pop albums and 60 million pop singles were sold in the UK domestic market, generating a turnover of £1,231 million.

Audiences

With the exception of the cinema, the percentage of the population who attend various types of cultural event has remained fairly stable since the late 1980s (see Table 16.1). Admissions to cinemas rose from 137 million in 2000 to 141 million in 2001, reaching their highest level since 1972.

Attendance at many major museums and galleries in England also rose between 2000/01 and 2001/02 (see Table 16.2). Attendance may have been boosted by the re-introduction of free admissions.

Churches and cathedrals are also an important part of the nation's cultural heritage, attracting many visitors. Over 1 million people were estimated to have visited York Minster and Canterbury Cathedral in 2000. Strathclyde Country Park in Scotland, Kew Gardens in Richmond, the Botanic Gardens in Belfast and the National Botanic Gardens in Carmarthenshire are also popular destinations for people with an

Table 16.1 Attendance[1] at cultural events, Great Britain

					Percentages
	1987/88	1991/92	1997/98	1998/99	2000/01
Cinema	34	44	54	56	55
Plays	24	23	23	22	23
Art galleries/exhibitions	21	21	22	22	21
Classical music	12	12	12	12	12
Ballet	6	6	6	6	6
Opera	5	6	6	6	6
Contemporary dance	4	3	4	4	4

1 Per cent of resident population aged 15 and over attending 'these days'.
Source: Target Group Index, BMRB International

Table 16.2 Visits to national museums and galleries in England, 2001/02

	Number of visits million	Per cent change over 2000/01
Tate Gallery[1]	5.5	−18
British Museum	4.8	2
National Gallery	4.8	2
National Museum of Science & Industry	3.1	11
Natural History Museum	2.1	24
Victoria and Albert Museum (V&A)	1.9	42
Imperial War Museum	1.6	0
National Portrait Gallery	1.5	23
National Maritime Museum	1.0	25
National Museums & Galleries on Merseyside	0.8	16
Royal Armouries	0.3	42
Wallace Collection	0.2	−8

1 Combined figures for Tate Britain, Tate Modern, Tate Liverpool and Tate St Ives.
Source: Department for Culture, Media and Sport

Government expenditure on the arts is distributed through a number of channels. DCMS has overall responsibility for public expenditure in this area. Table 16.3 shows how DCMS expenditure is allocated. Local government, the arts councils (see page 226), the Scottish Executive, the Welsh Assembly Government and education and library boards in Northern Ireland also fund arts projects. More details on how finance is distributed are given on pages 225–8.

Table 16.3 Department for Culture, Media and Sport expenditure on selected areas of cultural life

			£ million
	1991/92	1996/97	2001/02[1]
Museums, galleries and libraries[2]	333	336	373
Historic buildings (England)	n/a	162	141
The arts (England)	212	195	253
Tourism (UK)	44	46	67

1 Data are estimated outturn.
2 Includes museums and galleries (England), libraries (UK) and museums' library archives (UK).
Source: Department for Culture, Media and Sport

interest in gardening and horticulture. Windsor Castle, the Tower of London and the Roman baths in Bath are among the country's top ten heritage attractions.

Expenditure

Figures from the ONS Family Expenditure Survey show that the culture and leisure industries are strong growth areas for the economy: in 2000/01 the average household spent more on leisure goods and services (including holidays) than food (see chapter 22).

Cultural highlights of the past year

- Free admission to many major national museums and galleries was re-introduced in December 2001. The policy of charging for

Films

Two recent successful films have been *The Lord of the Rings: The Fellowship of the Ring* and *Harry Potter and the Philosopher's Stone*. Both films were adapted from children's books and released in November 2001. They proved to be instant successes with adults and children alike. Although largely filmed in New Zealand, many of the people involved in the production of *The Lord of the Rings* were British. *Harry Potter and the Philosopher's Stone* was produced in Hollywood, but again drew on British filmmaking expertise for its success. Musical soundtracks from both films have also proved popular. By mid-2002 the films had become, respectively, the third and second highest grossing films of all time in the UK. *Gosford Park*, directed by Robert Altman, was also produced during the year to critical acclaim, picking up five Golden Globe nominations. *Star Wars: Attack of the Clones* and *Spiderman* were other major film releases in 2002.

admissions to museums was dropped as a part of the Government's commitment to encourage greater participation in the arts.

- To commemorate the Queen's Golden Jubilee, two free concerts were held in June 2002 in the grounds of Buckingham Palace: The Prom at the Palace on 1 June, featuring the BBC Symphony Orchestra; and The Party at the Palace, featuring, among others, Paul McCartney, Cliff Richard and Atomic Kitten.

- Big Arts Week, held from 15 to 22 June, involved 1,700 artists working in 5,000 schools, volunteering with local pupils on a range of creative projects. It was launched with the support of many artists including the sculptor Anthony Gormley. The aim of the initiative, which will be repeated in 2003, is to inspire more schoolchildren to involve themselves in the arts.

Awards

A selection of major award winners is given on page 218).

British actors and filmmakers have enjoyed success at Hollywood's Oscars in recent years. In 2002 Jim Broadbent was named best supporting actor for his performance in *Iris*, Julian Fellowes won best original screenplay for *Gosford Park* and

Peter Owen was awarded an Oscar for best make-up for *The Lord of the Rings*.

Cultural events

Arts centres

Over 200 arts centres in the UK give people the chance of seeing a range of art forms and taking part in activities, especially educational projects. Nearly all the centres are professionally managed, but use the services of volunteers. The Pier Arts Centre at Stromness (Orkney) and Dundee Contemporary Arts (which has two galleries, two cinemas, a print studio and activity rooms) are two of the centres supported by the Scottish Arts Council. Centres funded by the Arts Council of Wales include the Chapter Arts Centre in Cardiff and the Aberystwyth Arts Centre, which helps to promote international artists and collaborations.

Festivals

Some 500 professional arts festivals take place in the UK each year. Their appeal has broadened – for example, whereas classical music once dominated music festivals, there are now those that offer jazz, folk, pop, rock, world and early music as well. Around 60 festivals concentrate on poetry, and other festivals are devoted to the visual arts, such as the Liverpool Biennial.

The 2002 Edinburgh International Festival featured performances of music, theatre, opera and dance, as well as lectures and discussions. The Edinburgh Festival Fringe, with a wide variety of programmes (including street events), takes place alongside the main events. In recent years it has proved a fertile training ground for comedians and actors who have progressed to successful careers elsewhere. Other annual Edinburgh events include the International Film Festival, the International Book Festival and the International Jazz and Blues Festival.

The Aldeburgh Festival, founded by Benjamin Britten, focuses on classical music. The Hay Festival, held in Hay-on-Wye, originally focusing on literature – the town is renowned for its second-hand bookshops – has broadened its range in recent years and its programme now includes musical events and contributions from guest speakers. Film festivals include the annual London Film Festival, and newer festivals such as the Leeds Children's Film Festival and the Brief Encounters short film festival in Bristol.

Table 16.4 Selected major award winners, United Kingdom, 2002

Award	Category	Title of work	Winner
Turner Prize (2001) *(Art)*		*The Lights Going On and Off*	Martin Creed
Whitbread Prizes *(Literature)*	Children's & Overall	*The Amber Spyglass*	Philip Pullman
	Biography	*Selkirk's Island*	Diana Souhami
	Poetry	*Bunny*	Selima Hill
	First Novel	*Something Like a House*	Sid Smith
	Novel	*Twelve Bar Blues*	Patrick Neate
Booker Prize (2001) *(Literature)*		*True History of the Kelly Gang*	Peter Carey[1]
Brit Awards *(Popular Music)*	Best Male Artist		Robbie Williams
	Best Female Artist		Dido
	Best Group		Travis
	Best Newcomer		Blue
Mercury Music Prize			Ms Dynamite
BAFTA Awards *(Film)*	Best Film	*The Lord of the Rings*	
	Best Director	*The Lord of the Rings*	Peter Jackson[1]
	Best Actor	*A Beautiful Mind*	Russell Crowe[1]
	Best Actress	*Iris*	Judi Dench
BAFTA Awards *(TV and Video)*	Best Drama Series	*Cold Feet*	
	Best Soap	*EastEnders*	
	Best Comedy	*The Office*	
	Best Feature	*Faking It*	
	Innovation	*Double Taker*	
	Best Actor	*Perfect Stranger*	Michael Gambon
	Best Actress	*My Beautiful Son*	Julie Walters
Olivier Awards *(Theatre)*	Best Director	*Henry VI Parts I, II and III* and *Richard III*	Michael Boyd
	Best Actor	*Privates on Parade*	Roger Allam
	Best Actress	*Private Lives*	Lindsay Duncan
	Best New Opera	*Boulevard Solitude*	
	Best New Musical	*My Fair Lady*	
	Outstanding Achievement		Trevor Nunn

1 Winners from outside the UK.

Live performance

Drama

Some of the UK's 300 professional theatres are privately owned, but most belong to local authorities or to not-for-profit organisations.

In England, the Royal National Theatre on the South Bank in London relies in part on public subsidy for support, allowing it to take greater artistic risks and offer cheaper tickets than unsubsidised theatres in London's West End.

Elsewhere in London, revivals of classic musicals have proved a recent success. Other, more literary, lower-budget plays have also proved popular with audiences. The Almeida Theatre and the Donmar Warehouse are two of London's leading independent theatres. The Globe Theatre – a reconstruction of Shakespeare's playhouse – is another notable theatrical venue. The Royal Shakespeare Company, based at Stratford-upon-Avon, presents spring and autumn seasons of Shakespeare's plays in a repertory programme.

Regional theatre
A number of successful productions were staged in regional theatres in England during 2002. After a period of general decline, some significant increases in audience numbers were recorded during the year. Among the highlights of the 2002 season in English regional theatre were productions of *Edward II* in Sheffield, *1984* in Newcastle upon Tyne, *Singing in the Rain* at the West Yorkshire Playhouse, and *Rita, Sue and Bob Too* from the Out of Joint Touring Theatre.

Northern Ireland has six major theatre spaces, including the Opera House and Waterfront Hall in Belfast and the new Millennium Forum in the city of Londonderry/Derry. It also has several independent theatre companies specialising in productions of new work.

In Scotland, the Royal Lyceum Theatre and the King's and Festival Theatres in Edinburgh, and the Citizen's Theatre Glasgow, have full programmes covering a wide range of productions. The Traverse Theatre in Edinburgh is Scotland's leading centre for new writing.

Clwyd Theatr Cymru in Mold is the national English-speaking theatre company for Wales. A new Welsh language theatre company is currently being planned and the Sherman Theatre in Cardiff has a focus on theatre for young audiences.

Music

There are four symphony orchestras with a public subsidy based in London: the largest of these, the London Symphony Orchestra, performs at the Barbican. Other symphony orchestras include two at the British Broadcasting Corporation (BBC), one at English National Opera and one at Covent Garden. Smaller chamber groups, such as the London Mozart Players, the Academy of St Martin-in-the-Fields and the English Chamber Orchestra, also perform regularly.

Outside London, the Bournemouth Symphony, Manchester's Hallé Orchestra and the Royal Liverpool Philharmonic are other well-known and highly rated English orchestras. The Royal Scottish National Orchestra and the Scottish Chamber Orchestra each give many performances a year. The Ulster Orchestra is Northern Ireland's only fully professional orchestra. In Wales the BBC National Orchestra of Wales offers a year-round programme of orchestral and choral music featuring the BBC National Chorus of Wales.

English and Welsh choral societies have done much to foster the oratorio tradition at the leading music festivals. English ecclesiastical choral singing is a speciality of the choirs of cathedrals and Oxford and Cambridge colleges.

Three well-established events in the classical musical calendar are the Leeds International Piano Competition for young pianists, the biennial Cardiff Singer of the World Competition and the biennial BBC Young Musicians contest.

The series of Promenade Concerts (the 'Proms'), in the Royal Albert Hall in London, is the world's largest music festival. In September 2002 the last night of the Proms was staged with a link to Belfast with the Ulster Orchestra playing at the City Hall.

British artists achieving commercial success in 2001 included the female pop star Dido, who had the highest selling album in the UK. Robbie Williams and David Gray also released hit albums in 2001. Other popular British artists include the south London garage band So Solid Crew, Travis, and the 'virtual' band Gorillaz.

Foreign artists, including those from the United States, have always flourished in the British pop charts. In recent years, Madonna, Kylie Minogue and U2 have maintained their long-term appeal. In 2001 Shaggy had the biggest selling single 'It wasn't me', and Irish boy band Westlife accumulated two UK number one singles. Other international artists achieving commercial success in the UK include the nu metal band Limp Bizkit, Strokes and Destiny's Child.

Folk music has always been strong in all parts of the UK. In Northern Ireland, for example, bands perform in pubs and clubs, playing fiddles and other traditional Celtic instruments. Scottish and Welsh festivals uphold Gaelic and Celtic traditions in music and song.

London's Royal Opera House (ROH) at Covent Garden staged over 20 operas in 2001/02 and attracts performers with international reputations. Glyndebourne Opera (East Sussex), which relies on private patrons for its summer season, is another prestigious venue. Other country house opera ventures include Garsington (Oxfordshire), where the stage is a garden terrace, Longborough (Gloucestershire) and Castleward Opera in County Down (Northern Ireland).

Dance

In 2001 English National Ballet was based at the Coliseum; in 2002 it is performing under the same roof as the Royal Ballet in Covent Garden. Other important ballet companies include Birmingham Royal Ballet and Northern Ballet Theatre.

Scottish Ballet has embarked on a new era of classical and contemporary dance, and Dance Base, Scotland's new national centre for dance, opened in Edinburgh in 2001. Contemporary dance companies with established reputations are Diversions, Spring Loaded and the Richard Alston Dance Company. Siobhan Davies and Wayne McGregor are currently two of Britain's leading choreographers.

Broadcast performance

Television

Television is an enormously popular medium for the communication of cultural experiences, now that 99 per cent of households own a television set, and the average person watches around 20 hours of programmes a week.

There is a wide variety in the kinds of television programme broadcast on terrestrial television. 'Soaps', such as *EastEnders* and *Coronation Street* (long-running serials screening several episodes a week and often focusing on family relationships), consistently attract the highest audiences. Quiz shows (*Who Wants to be a Millionaire?* and *The Weakest Link*, among the most notable examples) have maintained their popularity, along with police and detective series such as *Midsomer Murders* and *A Touch of Frost*. Hospital dramas such as *Casualty* and *Holby City* also achieve high ratings. Football has a strong presence on television. Films, documentaries and lifestyle programmes, focusing on cookery and home improvements, are among other types broadcast. More details on the pattern of television watching, and the range of stations available to audiences, can be found in chapter 17.

Radio

Radio 50 years ago
Holders of the 12 million radio receiving licences in the UK tuning in to 'home' radio stations at the start of the 1950s were given three choices: they could listen to the Home Services, the Light Programme, or the Third Programme, all broadcast by the BBC.

Characteristic items on the BBC Home Services radio stations included 'news bulletins, broadcasts to schools, religious services, plays, symphony concerts, brains trusts, music-hall and variety talks'. The object of the Light Programme was to 'entertain its listeners and to interest them in the world at large without failing to be entertaining'. The object of the Third Programme was to 'broadcast without regard to length or difficulty the masterpieces of music, of art and of letters which lend themselves to transmission in sound'.

The BBC broadcasts each week 156 hours of classical and other music (both live and recorded) on Radio 3. BBC Radio 1 broadcasts rock and pop music, and much of the output of BBC Radio 2 is popular and light music. Among the independent stations, Classic FM offers mainly classical and Virgin Radio plays rock and pop. Much of the output of the UK's local radio stations is popular and light music, news and information. More details on the pattern of radio listening, and the range of new digital stations available to listeners, can be found in chapter 17.

BBC Radio 4's output is mainly talk-based and includes a wealth of drama, documentary discussions and full-length plays. Latest estimates indicate that radio programmes reach 91 per cent of the adult population aged 15 and over, with BBC local and national stations taking just over half of the audience share.

Visual arts

A feature of cultural life in Britain recently has been the building or refurbishment of arts centres, many of them outside London. Prominent among these have been:

- the reopening of the Manchester Art Gallery;

- the opening in Gateshead of BALTIC, The centre for Contemporary Arts;

- the reopening of the Walker Art Gallery in Liverpool;

- the opening of a new £5 million exhibition centre at one of the UK's most important archaeological burial sites in Sutton Hoo, near Woodbridge in Suffolk;

- the complete refurbishment of the British Galleries at the Victoria and Albert Museum in London;

- the reopening of the Women's Library and Heritage Centre in east London; and

- major restoration work at the Coliseum, home of the English National Opera, providing a 40 per cent increase in public space, as well as extra room for education activities.

Museums and galleries

Over 77 million visits a year are made to the UK's 1,800 registered museums and galleries which include the major national museums, about 600 independent museums, 500 receiving support from local authorities, and others supported by universities, the armed services, the National Trust

and English Heritage (see Table 16.2). In addition to displaying their permanent collections, museums and galleries also stage temporary exhibitions, the largest attracting hundreds of thousands of visitors. The number of museums has expanded considerably since 1980, when there were 800.

The English national museums and galleries are:

- British Museum, housing one of the most comprehensive collections of European and world culture (*www.thebritishmuseum.ac.uk*).

- Natural History Museum (*www.nhm.ac.uk*).

- Victoria and Albert Museum (concentrating on fine and decorative arts – *www.vam.ac.uk*).

- National Museum of Science & Industry (*www.nmsi.ac.uk*) including the Science Museums in London and Wroughton, the National Railway Museum (York) and the National Museum of Photography, Film and Television (Bradford). Their exhibits commemorate the role played by the UK in the industrial and technological revolutions of the 19th and 20th centuries.

- National Gallery (*www.nationalgallery.org.uk*). Western painting from about 1260 to 1900 – a collection of worldwide importance, including the Leonardo da Vinci cartoons and *The Haywain* by Constable.

- Tate Britain (*www.tate.org.uk/britain*) devoted to British art since the 15th century, with additional collections in Liverpool and St Ives, Cornwall (St Ives School and modern art).

- Tate Modern (*www.tate.org.uk/modern*).

- National Portrait Gallery, containing pictures, sculptures and photographs of people who have shaped Britain's past (*www.npg.org.uk*).

- Imperial War Museum (*www.iwm.org.uk*) which has three sites in London and one at Duxford (which includes the American Air Museum) in Cambridgeshire.

- Royal Armouries (*www.armouries.org.uk*), the UK's oldest museum, which has exhibits in the Tower of London (relating to the Tower's history), Leeds (arms and armour) and Fort Nelson, near Portsmouth (artillery).

- National Army Museum (*www.national-army-museum.ac.uk*).

- Royal Air Force Museum (*www.rafmuseum.org.uk*).

- National Maritime Museum (*www.nmm.ac.uk*).

- Wallace Collection (*www.the-wallace-collection.org.uk*) – paintings, furniture, arms and armour, and *objets d'art*.

- National Museums & Galleries on Merseyside (*www.nmgm.org.uk*).

Particularly important collections outside the national museums are recognised through 'designation'. Designated collections outside London range from the social history collections at Beamish open air museum to the fine art collections of the Barber Institute in Birmingham. Within London, designated collections include the Museum of London; the Courtauld Institute Galleries (containing masterpieces of 14th to 20th-century European painting); and London's Transport Museum.

In Scotland the national collections are held by the National Museums of Scotland (*www.nms.ac.uk*) and the National Galleries of Scotland (*www.nationalgalleries.org*). The former include the Royal Museum, the Museum of Scotland, the Scottish National War Museum and the Scottish Agricultural Museum, in Edinburgh; the Museum of Flight, near North Berwick; and the Museum of Costume at Shambellie House near Dumfries.

The National Galleries of Scotland comprise the National Gallery of Scotland, the Scottish National Portrait Gallery, the Scottish National Gallery of Modern Art, and the Dean Gallery, housing the Paolozzi gift of sculpture and graphic art, as well as renowned Dada and Surrealist collections. The National Galleries also have deposits at Paxton House near Berwick upon Tweed and Duff House in Banff.

The National Museum of Wales in Cardiff (*www.nmgw.ac.uk*) has a number of branches, including the Museum of Welsh Life at St Fagans, the Slate Museum at Llanberis and the National Waterfront Museum, Swansea, which is currently under development and will be housed in Swansea's Maritime Quarter.

The Museums and Galleries of Northern Ireland (*www.magni.org.uk*) comprise the Ulster Museum in Belfast, the Ulster Folk and Transport Museum in County Down, and the Ulster-American Folk Park in County Tyrone.

Architecture and design

The Royal Institute of British Architects, with about 28,000 members, has been promoting and advancing architecture since receiving its Royal Charter in 1837. Among the many notable examples of modern British architecture, the Magna Science Adventure Centre outside Rotherham was awarded the prestigious Stirling Prize for architecture in 2001.

Better design in the fashion, film, computing and manufacturing industries and in other areas, is supported and encouraged in the UK by the Design Council, an independent organisation working with partners in business, education and government to inspire and enable the effective use of design.

Crafts

'Crafts' in the United Kingdom is an umbrella term covering a huge range of activities, from the making of pots and rugs to handmade toys and other personal and household products.

The Crafts Council is the official organisation for crafts in England. Its objectives include raising the profile of crafts in England and abroad, and strengthening and developing the craft economy in support of craftspeople. The Crafts Council also organises the annual Chelsea Crafts Fair and other programmes from its London venue; and co-ordinates British groups at international fairs. Craft Forum Wales supports craft business groups in Wales. Craftworks, an independent company, is the craft development agency for Northern Ireland. The Arts Council of Northern Ireland funds crafts promotion. In Scotland, the Scottish Arts Council has a Crafts Department, which promotes crafts and helps craftworkers.

The written word

Despite the growth of television and the Internet, demand for books remains strong. In 2001 British publishers issued over 119,000 separate titles (including new editions). The UK book industry exported books worth £1,195 million in 2001.

Fictional works of literature are just part of the range of books on offer. Non-fiction, in particular gardening, lifestyle, and travel books, as well as books tied to particular television series, are consistently among the lists of best-selling titles. The top ten best-selling titles of 2001 in Great Britain were as follows:

1. *Harry Potter and the Philosopher's Stone* J K Rowling

2. *Harry Potter and the Goblet of Fire* J K Rowling

3. *Harry Potter and the Chamber of Secrets* J K Rowling

4. *Harry Potter and the Prisoner of Azkaban* J K Rowling

5. *Bridget Jones's Diary* Helen Fielding

6. *A Child Called 'It'* Dave Pelzer

7. *Chocolat* Joanne Harris

8. *Happy Days with the Naked Chef* Jamie Oliver

9. *White Teeth* Zadie Smith

10. *Man and Boy* Tony Parsons

Among the leading trade organisations are the Publishers Association (PA), which has 200 members; and the Booksellers Association, with about 3,300 members. The PA, through its international division, promotes the export of British books. The Welsh Books Council promotes the book trade in Wales in both Welsh and English and the Gaelic Books Council supports the publication of books in Gaelic. The Book Trust encourages reading and the promotion of books through an information service and a children's library.

Literary and philological societies

Societies to promote literature include the English Association, the Royal Society of Literature and the Welsh Academy (Yr Academi Gymreig). The leading society for studies in the humanities is the British Academy for the Promotion of Historical, Philosophical and Philological Studies (the British Academy).

Other specialist societies are the Early English Text Society, the Bibliographical Society and several devoted to particular authors, such as Jane Austen and Charles Dickens. The Poetry Society sponsors poetry readings and recitals, as does the Scottish Poetry Library. London's South Bank Centre and the British Library run programmes of literary events.

Libraries and archives

Local authorities in Great Britain and education and library boards in Northern Ireland have a duty to provide a free lending and reference library service. There are almost 5,000 public libraries in the UK. In Great Britain more than 34 million people (58 per cent of the population) are registered members of their local library, and of these around 20 per cent borrow at least once a week. Those who are not registered members can also use their local library facilities. About 406 million books and 39 million audio-visual items were borrowed from UK public libraries in 2000/01. The Government is advised on library and archives policy by Resource (see page 227).

Many libraries have collections of CDs, records, audio- and video-cassettes, DVDs and musical scores for loan to the public, while a number also lend from collections of works of art, which may be originals or reproductions. Most libraries hold documents on local history, and all provide services for children, while reference and information sections, and art, music, commercial and technical departments are among the other facilities available.

The information role is important for all libraries: nearly all have personal computers for public use and, in May 2002, 70 per cent had Internet connections. A government initiative under the New Opportunities Fund is providing £20 million for information and communications technology training of library staff and £50 million for enabling library material to be stored and accessed in digitised form. The Government intends to link all public libraries and connect them to the National Grid for Learning (see page 116) by the end of 2002.

The British Film Institute (*bfi*) maintains the J Paul Getty Conservation Centre, which contains over 275,000 films and 200,000 television programmes, together with extensive collections of stills, posters and designs. The *bfi* National Library houses a large collection of film-related books, periodicals, scripts and other written materials.

The British Library and national libraries

The British Library (BL), the national library of the UK, is custodian of one of the most important research collections in the world (150 million items spanning 3,000 years). It is housed in the largest wholly publicly funded building constructed in the UK in the 20th century. The total floor space is approximately 100,000 square metres. The basements, the deepest in London, have 340 km of shelving for 15 million books. There are 11 reading areas, three exhibition galleries and a conference centre with a 250-seat auditorium. British publishers are legally obliged to deposit a copy of their publications at the BL. The National Libraries of Scotland and of Wales, the Bodleian at Oxford and the Cambridge University Library (and the Library of Trinity College, Dublin) can also claim copies of all new British publications.

The reading rooms in the British Library are open to those who need to see material (for example, manuscripts, newspapers, journals, stamps, maps and CD-ROMs as well as books) that is not readily available elsewhere and to those whose work or studies require the facilities of the national library.

The British Library's Document Supply Centre at Boston Spa is the national centre for inter-library lending within the UK and between the UK and other countries.

Manuscripts and other records

The Historical Manuscripts Commission (HMC) gives information and advice about historical papers outside the public records. It also advises private owners, grant-awarding bodies, record offices, local authorities and the Government on the acquisition and maintenance of manuscripts. The Commission maintains the National Register of Archives (the central collecting point for information about British historical manuscripts) and the Manorial Documents Register, both of which are available to researchers.

The Public Record Office (PRO) in Kew (Surrey) houses the records of the superior courts of law of England and Wales and of most government departments, as well as manuscripts of historical documents, such as the *Domesday Book* (1086) and autograph letters and documents of the

sovereigns of England. Public records, with a few exceptions, are available for inspection by everyone 30 years after the end of the year in which they were created.

From April 2003 the Historical Manuscripts Commission and the Public Record Office will combine to form a new organisation, the National Archives. The National Archives of Scotland in Edinburgh and the PRO of Northern Ireland in Belfast serve the same purpose.

Education and training

The National Curriculum specifies that all children at school should receive training in the arts, music and literature (see page 107). For many, involvement in art classes, the school play or orchestra is the first time their interest in culture is awakened. The Government is keen to encourage artistic talent at school. In England, Artsmark, an initiative from the Department for Education and Skills (DfES) and the DCMS in conjunction with the Arts Council of England (see page 226), gives formal recognition to schools which achieve a certain standard in the cultural education they offer. Additional initiatives to encourage cultural excellence in schools include:

- the Music Standards Fund, receiving £270 million from the DfES between 1999 and 2004. Some £60 million a year from the DfES Standards Fund has been used to protect and expand a range of music services, such as buying musical instruments for schools, providing instrumental tuition and providing extra training for teachers;

- the National Foundation for Youth Music, funded by Lottery grants and donations from other sources including the British Phonographic Industry; and

- the Space for Sport and Arts programme, allocating up to £130 million to enable pupils and the wider community in deprived areas to participate in art-based and sporting activities by providing new (or modernising existing) facilities in primary schools. The programme will run until 2004.

In Scotland, education is the responsibility of the Scottish Executive Education Department (SEED).

Expressive arts are a key component of the pre-school and 5–14 curricular guidelines, and are available as examination subjects at Standard Grade, Higher and Advanced Higher levels.

For those wishing to pursue a career in the arts, training available at post-16 tends to concentrate on particular specialisms. The DCMS and DfES allocate £19 million a year in grants for drama and dance students for tuition and maintenance. Over 800 students a year cover their tuition fees in this way, on the same basis as other higher and further education pupils. All training must be at accredited institutions and towards recognised qualifications, with annual evaluation by the DCMS and DfES to ensure that standards are maintained. Competition to enter all the Schools of Performing Arts is keen.

The Royal National Theatre's Education Programme encourages access to drama on a national level through youth theatre projects, touring productions, workshops, rehearsed readings, work in schools and a nation-wide membership scheme.

Professional training in music is given at universities and conservatories. Nearly a third of the players in the European Community Youth Orchestra come from the UK. There is also a National Youth Jazz Orchestra, a Scottish Youth Jazz Orchestra and a network of other youth jazz orchestras and wind bands.

Professional training for dancers and choreographers is provided mainly by specialist schools, while all government-funded dance companies provide dance workshops and education activities.

The National Film and Television School is financed jointly by the Government and the film, video and television industries. It offers postgraduate and short course training for directors, editors, camera operators, animators and other specialists.

Most practical education in art and design is provided in the art colleges and fine and applied art departments of universities and in further education colleges and private art schools. Some of these institutions award degrees at postgraduate level. The Royal College of Art in London is the only wholly postgraduate school of art and design

in the world. Art is also taught to degree level at the four Scottish art schools.

University courses concentrate largely on academic disciplines, such as the history of art. The Courtauld and Warburg Institutes of the University of London and the Department of Classical Art and Archaeology at University College London are leading institutions. The Society for Education through Art, among other activities, encourages schools to buy original works by organising an annual 'Pictures for Schools' exhibition.

Innovations

The Government's 24-hour museum website (*www.24hourmuseum.org.uk*) provides a gazetteer of all UK museums and galleries, a magazine, search facilities and educational resources. SCRAN (*www.scran.ac.uk*), the Scottish Cultural Resources Access Network, is a history and culture site providing access to images, films, sounds and virtual reality records from museums, galleries, archives and media.

Culture online (*www.cultureonline.gov.uk*), another government initiative, will increase digital access to and participation in English arts and cultural activities. DCMS will assume initial responsibility for culture online.

A growing number of operas, concerts, ballets and plays can now be viewed via the Online Classics WebPages (*www.onlineclassics.net*). The British Library has put on its Internet catalogue details of more than 10 million documents from the past 500 years, including books, journals and reports. The National Library of Wales has established a substantial digitisation programme in order to make available online copies of large numbers of items from its collections. Art created and shown solely online has also expanded in recent years – encouraged, for example, by the Institute of Contemporary Arts.

Administration

The expression of creativity is primarily a personal or group activity, but there is also an official and commercial side to culture. Many artists and performers engaged in cultural activity rely on subsidies and funding from government and other patrons of the arts. The Government has a role in protecting the rights of authors through copyright legislation; providing a regulatory framework for cultural activities in areas such as film classification; and encouraging greater public participation in the arts.

Public sector involvement in the arts is expressed in a number of different ways: through the work of the four Administrations directly responsible for culture in England, Wales, Scotland and Northern Ireland; through local government support for local initiatives; or through intermediate groups such as the Arts Councils, which act independently from the Government but are nonetheless publicly funded and take on the role of patrons of the arts.

DCMS has policy responsibilities within government for the arts, broadcasting, the built heritage, creative industries, film, museums, galleries and libraries, the National Lottery (see page 263), press freedom and regulation, sport and tourism.

DCMS aims to improve the quality of life for all through cultural activities and to strengthen the creative industries. It works, in partnership with others, towards:

- creating an efficient and competitive market by removing obstacles to growth and unnecessary regulation so as to promote Britain's success in the fields of culture, media, sport and tourism, both in the UK and abroad;

- broadening access to cultural events and to the built environment;

- raising the standards of cultural education and training;

- ensuring that everyone has the opportunity to achieve excellence in areas of culture and to develop talent, innovation and good design; and

- maintaining public support for the National Lottery and ensuring that the objective of the Lottery Fund supports DCMS and other national priorities.

The Welsh Assembly Government has responsibility for the arts in Wales and has published a culture strategy, 'Creative Future'. The Scottish Executive's National Cultural Strategy provides the basis for the administration of the arts in Scotland. In Northern Ireland, responsibility for the arts rests with the Department of Culture, Arts and Leisure.

Local authorities

Although policy is formulated by the four UK administrations, many new initiatives are carried out at a local level. Local authorities maintain about 500 museums and art galleries, and a network of public libraries. They also provide grant aid for professional and amateur orchestras, theatres, and opera and dance companies. Fourteen authorities are piloting Local Cultural Strategies, a DCMS scheme to bring cultural issues into the heart of local government planning.

The Arts Councils

The independent Arts Councils of England, Scotland, Wales and Northern Ireland are the main channels for the distribution of government grants and Lottery funding to the visual, performing and community arts and to literature. They give financial assistance and advice not only to the major performing arts organisations, but also to small touring theatre companies, experimental performance groups and literary organisations. The Arts Councils also commission research into the impact of the arts on society and develop forward strategies.

The Arts Council of England funds the major national arts-producing organisations in England, including the Royal Opera, the Royal Ballet, the Birmingham Royal Ballet, English National Opera (ENO), the Royal Shakespeare Company (RSC), the Royal National Theatre and the South Bank

Reform of the Arts Council of England
In April 2002, the Arts Council of England and the ten Regional Arts Boards joined together to form a single development organisation for the arts in England. The objective is to build a national force for the arts which will deliver more funding and a higher profile for artists and arts organisations. Boundaries for the Arts Council regional offices are being adjusted to match those for government regional offices.

Centre and the main touring companies, such as Opera North and English National Ballet.

New funding announced in early 2001 by the Arts Council of England made an extra £25 million available for theatre companies, spread over two financial years. Nearly 200 individual venues are benefiting from substantial increases in their grants, with 85 touring companies sharing over £4 million.

Resource: The Council for Museums, Archives and Libraries

'Resource' is the strategic agency working with, and on behalf of, museums, archives and libraries across the UK, and advising the Government on policy issues. It is currently in the process of establishing regional agencies in each of the nine English regions. Resource provides funding through these agencies and their predecessors (which include the Area Museum Councils). It has responsibility for a number of other initiatives, including:

- the portable antiquities scheme, set up to record archaeological objects;

- schemes for museum registration and designation of collections (see page 222);

- an initiative to establish a new framework for England's regional museums; and

- the Acceptance in Lieu scheme, whereby pre-eminent works of art may be accepted by the Government in settlement of tax and allocated to public galleries.

Film Council and *bfi*

The Film Council channels the majority of public funding for film production in the UK. It has a wide remit, with both cultural and industry objectives: to develop film culture in the UK, and to create a coherent structure for the UK film industry. The Council also helps to fund the British Film Office in Los Angeles, which acts as an information service to promote both British exports and the advantages of British studios to US film-makers. Recently, the responsibilities of the British Film Office were broadened to include television programmes and commercials.

The moving image as an art form is promoted by the British Film Institute (*bfi*), Scottish Screen, the Northern Ireland Film Commission and Sgrîn, the Media Agency for Wales.

Government help for the film industry allows, until 2005, a 100 per cent tax write-off on the production and acquisition costs, in the year the costs were incurred, for British movies with budgets of up to £15 million. Films which cost more than £15 million can be written off over three years against tax liabilities once the film has been completed.

The Film Council is responsible for distributing £150 million of Lottery and government grant to the UK film industry during 2000–03. Its New Cinema Fund is making £1.5 million available to radical and innovative filmmakers who wish to use the latest digital technology. The £10 million Premiere Production Fund is geared towards the making of popular mainstream films and the £5 million Film Development Fund is targeted at the development stage of film-making.

Cinema licensing and film classification

Public cinemas must be licensed by local authorities, which have a legal duty to prohibit the admission of children to unsuitable films, and may prevent the showing of any picture. In assessing films the authorities normally rely on the judgement of an independent non-statutory body, the British Board of Film Classification (BBFC), to which all items must be submitted. Films passed by the BBFC are put into one of the following categories:

- U (universal), suitable for all;

- PG (parental guidance), in which some scenes may be unsuitable for young children;

- 12, 15 and 18, for people of not less than those ages; and

- Restricted 18, for restricted showing only at premises to which no one under 18 is admitted – for example, licensed cinema clubs.

The BBFC is also legally responsible for classifying videos under a system similar to that for films. It is an offence to supply commercially a video which has not been classified or to supply it in contravention of its designation. Responsibility for the work of the BBFC lies with the DCMS.

Authors' copyright and performers' protection

Original literary, dramatic, musical or artistic works (including computer programs and databases), films, sound recordings, cable programmes, broadcasts and the typographical arrangement of published editions are automatically protected by copyright in the UK if they meet the legal requirements for protection. The copyright owner has rights against unauthorised reproduction, distribution, public performance, rental, broadcasting and adaptation of his or her work (including putting material on the Internet without permission). In most cases the author is the first owner of the copyright, and the term of copyright in literary, dramatic, musical and artistic works is for the life of the author and for 70 years thereafter. There are similar rules governing copyright on films. Sound recordings and broadcasts are protected for a period of 50 years.

National Lottery
The introduction of the National Lottery in 1994 significantly altered the funding of arts events in the United Kingdom. During the early years of the Lottery, the focus of arts funding was chiefly on major capital projects. Some shift in emphasis occurred from 1998 onwards, with the allocation of funds to smaller, local projects. According to an official report on the first seven years of the Lottery's operation, by September 2001:

- the Arts Councils across the United Kingdom had awarded over 21,000 grants worth a total of nearly £1.8 billion;

- the Arts Council of England had awarded over £1.45 billion to over 15,000 projects, including 80 new and almost 600 refurbished arts venues, and over 600 projects worth £300 million, which are intended to benefit children and young people;

- the Scottish Arts Council had made nearly 2,500 grants worth over £154 million;

- the Arts Council of Wales had awarded over £97 million to 2,700 projects; and

- the Arts Council of Northern Ireland had made nearly 700 awards worth over £40 million.

In addition, the DCMS has established the National Endowment for Science, Technology and the Arts (NESTA), which uses the income generated by £200 million of Lottery funds to support projects and inventions in the arts and sciences. Since its inception, it has allocated more than £20 million to over 200 people and projects.

Sponsorship

Total UK business investment in the arts in 2000/01 was £114 million. With many Lottery-backed arts buildings now in operation, business help for new developments fell from £45.7 million in 1999/2000 to £9 million in 2000/01. Sponsorship in kind rose from £11.3 million in 1999/2000 to £18.1 million in 2000/01.

Arts & Business promotes and encourages partnerships between business and the arts. It has over 350 business members and manages the Arts & Business New Partners Programme on behalf of the Arts Council of England and the DCMS.

Many arts organisations also benefit from the fund-raising activities of friends and groups and from private individuals' financial support. For example, theatre companies have traditionally relied on the support of 'angels', individual sponsors investing often quite small amounts of money to meet the costs of putting on a show, in the prospect of subsequently recouping their investment from box office proceeds.

Further reading
Department for Culture, Media and Sport: Annual report 2002. Cm 5423. The Stationery Office, 2002.

Websites

Department for Culture, Media and Sport
www.culture.gov.uk

Artsonline
www.artsonline.com

Arts Council of England
www.artscouncil.org.uk

Arts Council of Wales
www.artswales.org.uk

Scottish Arts Council
www.scottisharts.org.uk

Arts Council of Northern Ireland
www.artscouncil-ni.org

Public Record Office
www.pro.gov.uk

WWW.

17 The media and communications

Long-established media for communication, such as the press and postal services, have altered relatively little over the last 50 years. Many others, particularly those concerned with the broadcast media and telecommunications industries, have experienced widespread and fundamental change. Much of this has occurred over the past decade. With the advent of digital television and radio, alongside continuing expansion of cable and satellite television, there has been a proliferation of new public service and independent channels. The Internet, unimaginable 50 years ago, is another medium still undergoing rapid expansion, with more households gaining access and an increasing range of services.

Television

Figure 17.1 gives a broad indication of the type of programmes on the five main UK terrestrial channels. Drama, factual and education, entertainment, and news and weather programmes dominate the coverage. Around a third of primetime broadcasting output in 2001 was devoted to drama programmes; arts and religion programmes in the same year accounted together for less than 2 per cent of broadcasting time. Between 1997 and 2001 the percentage of primetime television given to drama and factual programmes fell slightly, whereas time allocated to entertainment programmes rose over the same period, to account for over a fifth of broadcast output in 2001.

There are five public service broadcasters in the UK: the BBC (British Broadcasting Corporation), the ITV network, Channel 4, Channel 5, and S4C (Sianel Pedwar Cymru), which broadcasts in Wales. They each have a statutory public service remit, which governs the minimum level of different types of programming they should provide.

Figure 17.1 Types of programmes shown on United Kingdom terrestrial television,[1] 1997 and 2001

Per cent of broadcasting time

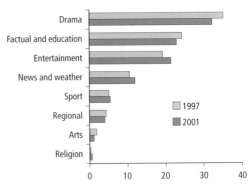

1 At primetime viewing (6 pm – 10.30 pm) for all five UK terrestrial broadcasters.
Source: Independent Television Commission

Local television services operate under licence making use of spare frequencies as and when they are available. There are ten local delivery operators with 15-year licences and five local delivery operators with five-year licences in the UK. These services began in 1998.

BBC
The BBC broadcasts 17,000 hours of television each year on its two analogue domestic channels to national and regional audiences. BBC ONE is the channel of broad appeal (documentaries and current affairs, features, drama and light entertainment, sport, religion and children's programmes), while BBC TWO aims for more innovation and originality in its programming.

Network programmes are made at, or acquired through, Television Centre in London and six bases throughout the UK (Glasgow in Scotland, Cardiff in Wales, Belfast in Northern Ireland, and Birmingham, Bristol and Manchester in England). Programmes are also commissioned from independent producers – the BBC must ensure that at least 25 per cent of its original programming comes from the independent sector.

Education is a central component of the Corporation's public service commitment. A range of programmes is broadcast for primary and secondary schools, further education colleges and the Open University (see page 112), while other educational programmes cover numeracy, literacy, language learning, health, work and vocational training. Books, pamphlets, computer software, and audio and video materials supplement the programmes. Details of the digital television channels available from the BBC can be found on page 232.

ITV network

The ITV network's analogue services are broadcast on Channel 3 as ITV1. There are 15 regionally based independent television companies, which are licensed to supply programmes in the 14 independent television geographical regions.

There are two licences for London, one for weekdays and the other for the weekend. A separate company licensed by the Independent Television Commission (ITC) (see page 235) provides a national breakfast-time service, transmitted on the ITV network. All Channel 3 licences have been renewed for a further ten-year period from 1999, 2000 and 2001.

Programmes are broadcast 24 hours a day throughout the country. A shared national and international news service is provided by Independent Television News (ITN).

ITV1 companies are obliged to operate a national programme network. The ITV network centre, which is owned by the companies, independently commissions and schedules programmes.

Operating on a commercial basis, licensees derive most of their income from selling advertising time. Their financial resources and programme production vary considerably, depending largely on the population of the areas in which they operate. Newspaper groups can acquire a controlling interest in ITV companies, although measures are in force to deter any undue

Participative shows

Pop Idol, a musical talent competition staged over a number of weeks with one contestant from a shortlist of solo performers 'voted off' each week by the television audience, proved to be one of the biggest media events in the UK in 2001/02. The two finalists, Will Young and Gareth Gates, attracted record numbers of telephone votes for any televised event (over 4 million each), and achieved immediate success as solo performing artists. *Big Brother*, *Soapstars* and *Survivor* are other examples of shows with an 'interactive' element that achieved high ratings during the course of the year.

concentrations of media ownership (see page 240).

Channel 4 and S4C

Channel 4 provides a national 24-hour television service. It is a statutory corporation, licensed and regulated by the ITC, and funded by selling its own advertising time. Its remit is to provide programmes with a distinctive character and to appeal to tastes and interests not generally catered for by ITV1. It must present a proportion of educational programmes, and encourage innovation and experiment. Channel 4 commissions programmes from the ITV companies and independent producers, and also buys programmes from overseas. In February 2001 it announced a restructure and launched a new incorporated company, 4Ventures, to manage all its film and other new business activities.

In Wales the fourth analogue channel is allocated to S4C, which is regulated by the Welsh Fourth Channel Authority. Members of the Welsh Authority are appointed by the Government. S4C must ensure that a significant proportion of programming – the majority aired between 6.30 pm and 10 pm – is in the Welsh language. At other times it transmits Channel 4 programmes. In 1998 S4C launched a digital service incorporating analogue Welsh programmes and additional material.

Channel 5

The UK's newest analogue terrestrial channel went on air in 1997, its ten-year licence having been awarded by competitive tender to Channel 5 Broadcasting Ltd. Channel 5 serves about 80 per cent of the population and is supported by advertising revenue.

Text services

Teletext is a text-based data service, broadcast on Channels 1 to 5 using the spare signal capacity in analogue terrestrial television services. Most main television sets in the home are capable of decoding teletext signals, which are displayed as text and simple graphics. Teletext services include regularly updated information on a variety of subjects, including news, sport, travel, weather and entertainment.

The BBC broadcasts its 'Ceefax' teletext service within the BBC ONE and TWO signals. For ITV1, Channel 4, and Channel 5, the teletext service is provided under ten-year broadcasting licences, granted by the ITC. All terrestrial channels provide subtitles for people with hearing difficulties on most of their programmes.

Digital terrestrial television (DTT)

A single frequency carrying the signals of several digital services is called a multiplex. The signal can be received by a standard aerial, but has to be converted into sound and vision by using a decoder, either incorporated into the television set or in a separate digital adaptor attached to a television.

There are six terrestrial multiplexes capable of supporting services nationwide. One is operated by the BBC and the other five are licensed by the ITC.

Since November 1998, the following services have been available: one multiplex operated by the BBC; one multiplex operated by Digital 3&4, supporting services from ITV, Channel 4 and Teletext; and one multiplex operated by S4C Digital Network, supporting services from S4C, Channel 5 and other broadcasters.

The remaining three multiplexes were operated from November 1998 to April 2002 by ITV Digital to support pay-TV services. ITV Digital ceased broadcasting in 2002 and as a result the licences for its multiplexes were handed back to the ITC. In August 2002 the ITC granted the licence for these three multiplexes to new operators. All DTT services are now free-to-view.

Services from the public service broadcasters which are available on analogue terrestrial are also broadcast on DTT. Additional services available on DTT include:

- BBC News 24 (a 24-hour news channel);

- BBC Choice, a supplementary service for a younger audience to complement and enhance the network schedules;

- BBC Parliament (coverage of proceedings in the House of Commons, House of Lords, the Parliament in Scotland and the assemblies in Wales and Northern Ireland);

- BBC FOUR (in-depth coverage of culture, the arts, science, history, business and current affairs);

- two daytime children's channels, CBBC and, for the under fives, CBeebies;

- ITV2 (an additional service from the ITV network); and

- S4C2 (an additional service from S4C).

Future plans for DTT include an extended range of digital services on the three multiplexes previously held by ITV Digital.

Digital switchover

The Government intends eventually to cease analogue terrestrial television transmission, and to reallocate the broadcasting spectrum currently used for analogue television. It believes that switchover could start as early as 2006 and be completed by 2010.

The UK leads the world in uptake of digital television. Services are available to over 96 per cent of households. By the end of June 2002, over 37 per cent of households (9.3 million) were accessing digital television via either DTT, satellite or cable.

Non-terrestrial television

There are two main non-terrestrial television delivery systems (platforms) in the UK – digital satellite and cable-access television (CATV). These are funded mainly by subscription income. Both platforms offer packages of subscription-only television services, including some premium services such as movie and sports channels and pay-per-view events. Both cable and satellite are required to carry the public service channels at no additional cost to the viewer.

On both platforms, the selection of channels available via subscription is broadly similar, but there are some services which are unique to each platform. Available services include Eurosport, Cartoon Network, UK Gold (repeat programmes from TV archives), E4 (additional services from Channel 4) and the Discovery Channel (science and nature documentaries).

Foreign language services are also provided, some of them designed for ethnic minorities within the UK, and others aimed primarily at audiences in other countries. Viewers in the UK can similarly receive a variety of television services from other European countries.

Cable-access television

Cable-access television services are delivered to consumers via underground networks of cables. The signals are decoded using a converter box, which is rented from the cable provider. Cable customers can also access telephone services and, in the case of digital cable, broadband Internet services.

Around 13 million homes in the UK are passed by cable, mostly in urban and suburban areas. The two main cable providers are ntl and Telewest. Both networks are in the process of converting from analogue to digital – currently, there are 2 million homes subscribing to digital CATV, and 1.4 million homes subscribing to analogue CATV.

Analogue CATV systems can carry around 65 television services, as well as a range of telecommunications services. Digital CATV currently carries up to around 100 services (TV and radio), and additionally offers the viewer interactive services.

Digital satellite

Also referred to as 'direct to home', satellite television signals are received via a specially designed antenna (or 'dish') mounted on the outside of a building, and are decoded using either a set-top box or an integrated digital television.

Most satellite television in the UK is provided by British Sky Broadcasting (BSkyB), which had 6.1 million subscribers by the end of June 2002. Sky Television was launched in 1989 as an analogue-only service, and began simultaneous digital broadcasting in 1998. In October 2001 the analogue signal was switched off, and the renamed Sky Digital became the first digital-only TV platform in the UK. The platform has been fully interactive since 1999.

Around 200 services (TV and radio) are currently available on the platform. Most of the more popular channels are accessible only by subscription to BSkyB, but there is also a wide variety of free-to-view channels. Customers can choose to buy a BSkyB installation without a subscription to access free-to-view only. If viewers wish to access the existing UK public service television channels without paying a subscription, they can request free of charge a smart card which gives access to these services.

Interactive digital services

Satellite, digital cable and DTT all offer interactive services. The level and complexity of these services depend on the platform and the equipment that the customer has installed.

Interactive services range from electronic programme guides and digital text (an enhanced version of teletext), to home shopping, video-on-demand,[1] home banking, e-mail and Internet access. Interactive television can also involve participating in TV quiz shows, voting in polls, or viewing sports coverage from different camera angles using the remote control.

Radio

Radio's popularity has shown no signs of diminishing, with 91 per cent of the adult population listening regularly each week. News and music form the bulk of the output of radio stations.

The BBC has five national radio networks, which together transmit all types of music, news, current affairs, drama, education, sport and a range of features programmes. There are also 39 BBC local radio services covering England and the Channel Islands, and national radio services in Scotland, Wales and Northern Ireland, including Welsh and Gaelic language stations. In spring 2002, BBC radio took a 53 per cent share of the total UK radio audience.

There are three national commercial radio stations (see page 234). Around 260 independent local radio (ILR) services also supply music, local news

---

1 Video-on-demand enables viewers to dial into a video library, via a cable or telephone network, and call up a programme or film of their choice, which is then transmitted to that household alone.

and information, sport, education and consumer advice. The first (and only) national commercial digital radio multiplex started in 1999. This has since been joined by 36 local digital multiplexes providing a wide range of services.

BBC network radio
BBC network radio, broadcasting to the whole of the UK, transmits nearly 44,000 hours of programmes each year on its five networks.

- Radio 1 is a contemporary music station, serving a young target audience. It had just over 8 per cent of the overall radio audience share during spring 2002;

- Radio 2 offers a broad range of music, light entertainment, documentaries, public service broadcasting and popular culture (15 per cent of audience share);

- Radio 3 covers classical and jazz music, drama, documentaries and discussion (1 per cent share);

- Radio 4 offers news and current affairs coverage, complemented by drama, science, the arts, religion, natural history, medicine, finance and gardening features; it also carries parliamentary coverage and cricket in season on Long Wave, and BBC World Service programmes overnight (11 per cent share);

- Radio 5 Live broadcasts news, current affairs and extensive sports coverage (nearly 5 per cent share).

New BBC digital radio stations launched during 2002 are:

- 1Xtra, broadcasting contemporary black music for a young audience;

- Network Z comedy, drama, readings and children's programmes;

- BBC World Service;

- 6 Music, broadcasting contemporary and classic pop and rock music;

- Five Live Sports Extra; and

- BBC Asian Network, a station for the Asian communities in the UK.

BBC World Service
The BBC World Service broadcasts in 43 languages (including English) worldwide. It has an estimated global weekly audience of 150 million listeners. The core programming of news, current affairs, business and sports reports is complemented by cultural programmes, including drama, literature and music.

While maintaining shortwave broadcasts for mass audiences, BBC World Service is making programmes more widely available on FM frequencies and delivering services in major languages through digital broadcasting and on the Internet.

Programmes in English and many other languages are made available by satellite for rebroadcasting by agreement with local or national radio stations, networks and cable operators.

BBC Monitoring, the international media monitoring arm of BBC World Service, provides transcripts of radio and television broadcasts from 150 countries. As well as providing a vital source of information to the BBC, this service is used by other media organisations, government departments, the commercial sector and academic institutions.

Independent national radio
There are currently three independent national radio services, whose licences were awarded by the Radio Authority (see page 235) through competitive tender, and which broadcast 24 hours a day:

- Classic FM, which broadcasts mainly classical music, together with news and information;

- Virgin 1215, which plays rock and pop music (and is supplemented by a separate Virgin station which operates under a local London licence); and

- Talk Sport, a speech-based service.

Independent local radio
Independent local radio (ILR) stations broadcast a wide range of programmes and news of local interest, as well as music and entertainment, traffic reports and advertising. There are also stations serving minority ethnic communities. The Radio Authority awards independent local radio licences in an open competition. The success of local

Sutton Hoo in Suffolk was the burial site of Anglo-Saxon kings of East Anglia. In 1939 Basil Brown, a local archaeologist, opened the largest burial mound on the site. He discovered a ship burial containing, among many items, weapons and ornaments. Most of the objects date from the 7th century AD.

March 2002: a new visitors' centre is opened by the poet Seamus Heaney. He holds a reconstruction of a helmet found on the site.

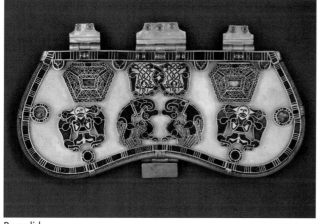

Purse lid.

Pattern-welded sword.

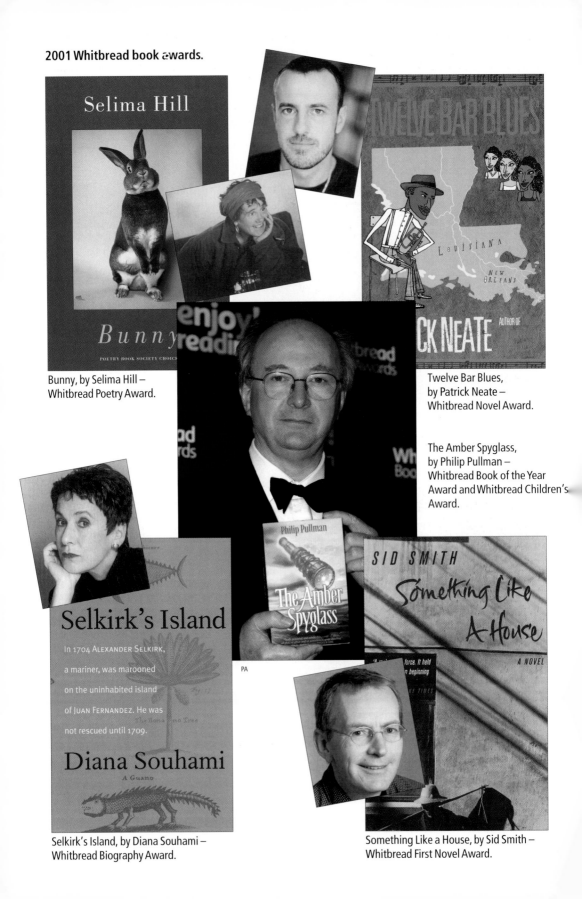

2001 Whitbread book awards.

Bunny, by Selima Hill –
Whitbread Poetry Award.

Twelve Bar Blues,
by Patrick Neate –
Whitbread Novel Award.

The Amber Spyglass,
by Philip Pullman –
Whitbread Book of the Year
Award and Whitbread Children's
Award.

Selkirk's Island, by Diana Souhami –
Whitbread Biography Award.

Something Like a House, by Sid Smith –
Whitbread First Novel Award.

February 2002: the Women's Library opens at its new site in the East End of London. The library was founded 75 years ago as the Fawcett Library and has a collection of over 60,000 books and pamphlets on women's history, together with numerous photographs, posters and other memorabilia.

The new home of the library is on the site of the former Whitechapel Public Baths and Wash Houses, built in 1846.

PHOTOGRAPHY BY PETER COOK / VIEW.
WRIGHT AND WRIGHT ARCHITECTS

PHOTOGRAPHY BY RICHARD DAWSON

DOUG HALL / IMAGE COURTESY OF GATESHEAD COUNCIL / BALTIC

July 2002: BALTIC, The Centre for Contemporary Art, opens at Gateshead Quays on the South Bank of the River Tyne. The centre, a former grain warehouse, has been redesigned to accommodate 3,000 sq m of arts space.

DOUG HALL / IMAGE COURTESY OF GATESHEAD COUNCIL /BALTIC

November 2001: the British Galleries open at the Victoria and Albert Museum, London. The new galleries provide a chronological survey of British design, art and culture from 1500 to 1900.

Top: Breathless, 2001, by Cornelia Parker (b. 1956). Silver-plated brass musical instruments suspended on stainless steel wire. This is the only contemporary exhibit.

Centre: the Great Bed of Ware, c.1590. 'The nation's oldest and most famous bed' measures 3.4 m long by 3.1 m wide. It started life in an inn, and is mentioned in Shakespeare's Twelfth Night.

Top right: Henry VIII's writing desk. English, painted and gilded wood.

Right: High backed chair, c.1900, designed by Rennie Mackintosh (1868–1928).

February 2002: the Great Britain curling team arrive back in Glasgow after their victory at the Winter Olympics in Salt Lake City.

June 2002: England captain David Beckham and Trevor Sinclair celebrate after scoring a penalty in a World Cup match at the Sapporo Dome, Japan. England reached the quarter finals.

June 2002: Lennox Lewis retains the World Heavyweight Championship, beating Mike Tyson in an 8th round knockout in Memphis, Tennessee.

April 2002: Record-breaking National Hunt jockey Tony McCoy.

July–August 2002: the XVII Commonwealth Games, Manchester.

Kanukai Jackson (England) – winner of two gold medals and two silver medals in gymnastics. PA

Sue Gilroy (England) – winner of the women's wheelchair table tennis. PA

Graeme Randall (Scotland) – winner of the 81 kg judo title. PA

Nicole Cook (Wales) – winner of the women's road race. PA

PA

Top left: Martin Millar and David Calvert (Northern Ireland) – winners of the open full bore rifle pairs.

Centre left: Simon Archer and Jo Goode (England) – winners of the badminton mixed doubles.

Bottom left: Ashia Hansen (England) – winner of the triple jump.

Below: John Robertson (Scotland) – one of the winners of the lawn bowls men's triples.

PA

PA

PA

Running for fun

March 2002: nearly 3,000 children from schools in County Durham take part in a cross-country run.

April 2002: participants in the London Mini Marathon, which is run over 4.3 km on the same day as the adult race.

licence applications is in part determined by the extent to which applicants widen choice and meet the needs and interests of the people living in the area, and in part by whether they have the necessary financial resources for the eight-year licence period. Local radio stations do not have guaranteed slots on digital local radio multiplexes.

Digital radio

Commercial national digital radio services now cover nearly 85 per cent of households in the UK. The Radio Authority has awarded one national multiplex licence in the UK carrying ten programme services. It has also awarded licences for 36 local digital multiplexes, which will carry about 250 commercial radio stations between them.

Regulation of broadcast media

The Department for Culture, Media and Sport is responsible for government policy on broadcasting. Two authorities, the BBC and ITC (Independent Television Commission), accountable to Parliament but otherwise independent in their day-to-day operations, oversee television services.

BBC

The BBC's constitution, finances and obligations are governed by Royal Charter and Agreement. Its Board of Governors appoints the Director-General, who heads the bodies in charge of the daily running of the Corporation. The Board of Governors is also responsible for regulating programme content.

In 2000 the Government announced new funding plans for the BBC over the period to 2006/07, aimed at ensuring that the Corporation can continue to meet its public service obligations and operate effectively in a competitive market.

Independent Television Commission

The ITC is an independent statutory body responsible for licensing and regulating all commercial television services (including BBC commercial services) operating in, or from, the UK, including those delivered by non-terrestrial platforms. It does not make, broadcast or transmit programmes.

The ITC must ensure that a wide range of commercial television services is available throughout the UK and that they are of a high quality and appeal to a variety of tastes and interests. It must also ensure fair competition in the provision of these services, and compliance with the rules on media ownership.

The ITC regulates the various television services through licence conditions, codes and guidelines. The codes cover programme content, advertising, sponsorship and technical standards. If a licensee does not comply with the conditions of its licence or the codes, the ITC can impose penalties. These range from a formal warning or a requirement to broadcast an apology or correction, to a fine. In extreme circumstances, a company's licence may be shortened or revoked.

Non-public service broadcasters must comply with the ITC's programmes, advertising and sponsorship codes, but they are not subject to any positive programming obligations.

The Gaelic Broadcasting Committee is an independent statutory body committed to ensuring that a good selection of quality television and radio programmes is broadcast in Gaelic for reception in Scotland. Its members are appointed by the ITC, in consultation with the Radio Authority. The Committee is responsible for the distribution of government money to programme makers through the Gaelic Broadcasting Fund.

Radio Authority

The Radio Authority's licensing and regulatory remit covers all independent radio services, including national, local, cable, satellite and restricted services. Its three main tasks are to plan frequencies, appoint licensees with a view to broadening listener choice, and regulate programming and advertising. It has published codes covering engineering, programmes, news and current affairs, and advertising and sponsorship, to which its licensees must adhere. Satellite radio services must be licensed by the Radio Authority if they are transmitted from the UK for general reception within the country, or if they are transmitted from outside, but are managed editorially from within, the UK.

The Radio Authority also issues restricted service licences (RSLs). Short-term RSLs, generally for periods of up to 28 days, are for special events or

Draft Communications Bill

Following a review of the future regulation of broadcasting and telecommunications, which took account of the implications of the increasing convergence of the two sectors, the Government published in May 2002 a draft Communications Bill. The main proposals are:

- the establishment of a new unified, independent regulator – the Office of Communications (Ofcom) – combining the functions of the Broadcasting Standards Commission, Independent Television Commission, Office of Telecommunications (Oftel, see page 242), Radio Authority and the Radiocommunications Agency;

- a requirement for Ofcom to establish and maintain a 'content board' to ensure that the public's interest in the nature and quality of TV and radio programmes is properly represented within OFCOM's structure;

- making the BBC subject to Ofcom's regulation with regard to standards, while retaining the Board of Governors in the role of overseeing the Corporation's public service remit and upholding its political and editorial independence;

- granting Ofcom powers concurrent with those of the Office of Fair Trading to promote effective competition in the communications services sector for the benefit of consumers;

- removing the requirement for licensing telecommunications systems (see page 241);

- allowing spectrum trading to secure more efficient use of the available radio spectrum; and

- overhauling rules governing media ownership (see page 240).

Consultation on the draft Bill closed in August 2002 and it is expected that full legislation will take place in the next parliamentary session.

trial services, and long-term RSLs, primarily for student and hospital stations, broadcast to specific establishments.

Licences

The ITV licences for Channel 3 are awarded for a ten-year period by competitive tender to the highest bidder (who has to have passed a quality threshold). Licensees must provide a diverse programme service designed to appeal to a wide range of tastes and interests. Each company plans the content of the programmes to be broadcast in its area. These are produced by the company itself, by other programme companies, or are bought from elsewhere. As with the BBC, at least 25 per cent of original programming must come from the independent sector.

Broadcasting standards

The independence of the broadcasting authorities carries certain obligations concerning programme content. Broadcasters must try to achieve a wide and balanced range of subject matter, impartiality in controversial issues and accuracy in news coverage, and must not offend against good taste. Broadcasters must also obey the law relating to obscenity and incitement to racial hatred.

The BBC, the ITC and the Radio Authority apply rules on impartiality, the portrayal of violence, and standards of taste and decency in programmes, particularly during hours when children are likely to be viewing or listening. Television programmes broadcast before 9 pm (or 8 pm on certain cable and satellite services) must be suitable for a general audience, including children.

Broadcasting Standards Commission (BSC)

The BSC, a statutory body, monitors standards and fairness on television and radio (both terrestrial – independent and BBC channels – and satellite). It considers complaints received from the public, and adjudicates on claims of unfair treatment in broadcasts and of unwarranted infringement of privacy in programmes or in their preparation. In 2000/01 the Commission received 358 fairness complaints, of which 114 were within its remit; 80 complaints were considered further, of which 40 per cent were upheld in part or in full. The BSC also received 7,183 complaints about standards, of which 6,124 were within its remit; 5,119 complaints were pursued, of which 9 per cent were upheld in part or in full.

European agreements

The UK has implemented two European agreements on cross-border broadcasting – the European Community Broadcasting Directive and the Council of Europe Convention on Transfrontier Television. These oversee the free flow of television programmes and services throughout participating countries, setting minimum standards on advertising, sponsorship, taste and decency, and the portrayal of sex and violence. If a broadcast meets these standards, no participating country may prevent reception in its territory.

Commercial activities

The domestic services of the BBC are financed almost wholly by a licence fee. All households or premises with a television set must buy an annual licence. This costs £112 for colour and £37.50 for black and white in 2002/03, although households with a member aged 75 and over have been entitled to free licences since 1 November 2000. Licence income is supplemented by profits from the commercial activities of BBC Worldwide (see below). BBC World Service's radio broadcasting operations (see page 234) are financed by a grant from the Foreign & Commonwealth Office.

BBC Worldwide
BBC Worldwide Ltd. is the main commercial arm, and a wholly owned subsidiary, of the BBC. It was formed in 1994 to co-ordinate the Corporation's commercial activities (television, publishing, product licensing, the Internet and interactive services), which are not funded by the licence fee. Its role is to generate money that can be reinvested in public service programming for the benefit of UK licence payers.

BBC Worldwide is Europe's largest exporter of television programmes, the world's biggest television channel operator based outside the United States, and the UK's third largest publisher of consumer magazines. These activities accounted for turnover of £660 million in 2001/02, which in turn delivered £106 million back to the BBC for reinvestment in programming and other services.

It operates 15 commercial channels in the UK and overseas. These include the wholly owned BBC World (news and information), BBC Prime (entertainment) and BBC America channels, and 12 other channels in joint ventures with other companies (Discovery Communications, Flextech, FOXTEL and Pearson). Together, they reach about 460 million households across the world.

BBC Worldwide is the market leader in audio publishing. It also operates online services (beeb.net).

Advertising and sponsorship
The BBC may not raise revenue from broadcasting advertisements or from commercial sponsorship of programmes on its public service channels. It must not give publicity to any firm or organised interest except when this is necessary in providing effective and informative programmes. It does, however, cover sponsored sporting and artistic events. Advertising and sponsorship are allowed on all commercial television and radio services, subject to controls. The ITC and the Radio Authority operate codes governing advertising standards and programme sponsorship, and can impose penalties on broadcasters that do not comply.

Advertisements on independent television and radio are broadcast in breaks during programmes as well as between programmes, and must be distinct and separate from them. Advertisers are not allowed to influence programme content.

Political advertising and advertisements for betting (other than the National Lottery, the football pools, bingo and amusement arcades) are prohibited. All tobacco advertising is banned on television and radio. Religious advertisements may be broadcast on commercial radio and television, provided they comply with the guidelines issued by the ITC and the Radio Authority.

Television advertising
Television advertising in Britain began in 1955. The first commercial was for Gibbs SR toothpaste. The presenter commercial, with a celebrity endorsing the virtues of a particular product, became a standard format. In the 1970s there was a change of emphasis in advertising techniques, with viewers being invited to share in the lifestyles and values of the characters using the product on screen. In the 1990s advertising became increasingly sophisticated as budgets grew. Companies spent £4.1 billion in 2001 on the purchase of TV advertising. Making TV advertisements has also become an established training ground for a number of successful film producers.

Sponsorship in independent broadcasting
In return for their financial contribution, sponsors receive a credit associating them with a particular

programme. The ITC's Code of Programme Sponsorship and the Radio Authority's Advertising and Sponsorship Code aim to ensure that sponsors do not exert influence on the editorial content of programmes and that sponsorships are made clear to viewers and listeners. News and current affairs programmes on television may not be sponsored. References to sponsors or their products must be confined to the beginning and end of a programme and around commercial breaks; on television the references must not appear in the programme itself. All commercial radio programmes, other than news bulletins and any news desk presentation, may be sponsored.

The ITC permits masthead programming (programmes with the same title as a magazine and made or funded by its publishers) on all UK commercial television services.

Audience research

The BBC and the commercial sector are required to monitor the state of public opinion about the programmes and advertising that they broadcast. This is done through the continuous measurement of the size and composition of audiences and their opinions of programmes. For television, this work is undertaken through BARB (the Broadcasters' Audience Research Board). Joint research is undertaken for BBC radio and for commercial radio by RAJAR (Radio Joint Audience Research).

The press

The UK has a long tradition of a free and often outspoken press. Before the emergence of broadcast media, newspapers were for many the principal means of keeping up to date with the news.

On an average weekday it is estimated that around 55 per cent of people aged 15 and over in the UK read a national morning newspaper (59 per cent of men and 50 per cent of women in 2001/02). Over 80 per cent of adults read a regional or local newspaper every week. National papers have an average (but declining) total circulation of some 12 million on weekdays and about 13 million on Sundays. There are more than 1,300 regional and local newspaper titles.

While newspapers are almost always financially independent of any political party, they can express obvious political leanings in their editorial coverage, which may derive from proprietorial and other non-party political influences. There are around 100 regional press publishers – ranging from those owning just one title (about half of them) to a few controlling more than 100 each.

In addition to sales revenue, newspapers and periodicals earn considerable amounts from advertising. Indeed, the press is the largest advertising medium in the UK. The British press receives no subsidies from the State.

The national press

The national press consists of ten morning daily papers and ten Sunday papers. At one time London's Fleet Street area was the centre of the industry, but now all the national papers have moved their editorial and printing facilities to other parts of London or away from the capital altogether. Editions of many papers, such as the *Financial Times*, *Sun*, *Guardian* and *Daily Mirror*, are also printed in other countries.

National newspapers are often described as broadsheet or tabloid papers on the basis of differences in style and content. Many newspapers have colour pages and most produce extensive supplements as part of the Saturday or Sunday edition, with articles on personal finance, travel, gardening, home improvement, food and wine, fashion and other leisure topics. Increasing competition from other media in the delivery of news, information and entertainment has had an effect on the national press, with a gradual decline in circulation discernible for many titles.

Most national newspaper groups have set up Internet websites, building on editorial, directory and advertising services, to develop networks of additional special interest sites to cater for a growing readership.

Regional newspapers

Most towns and cities throughout the UK have their own regional or local newspaper. These range from morning and evening dailies to Sunday papers and others which are published just once a week. They mainly include stories of regional or local interest, but the dailies also cover national and international news, often looked at from a local viewpoint. In addition, they provide a valuable medium for local advertising. Circulation figures for the period July–December 2001 indicate that the regional press sells nearly

41 million paid-for newspapers and distributes over 29 million issues of free titles each week. Over 90 per cent of local and regional titles are now available online.

London has one paid-for evening paper, the *Evening Standard*. Its publisher (Associated Newspapers) also produces a free daily newspaper, *London Metro*, launched in 1999. There are also local weekly papers for every district in Greater London; these are often different local editions of one centrally published paper.

Around 650 free distribution newspapers, mostly weekly and financed by advertising, are published in the UK. Top free weekly titles include the *Manchester Metro News, Nottingham & Long Eaton Topper and Edinburgh Herald & Post*.

There is a broadly based daily and weekly newspaper industry in Scotland covering local, Scottish and UK as well as international issues. The *Daily Record* has the highest circulation and there are also broadsheet newspapers including the *Scotsman* (based in Edinburgh) and the *Herald* (in Glasgow). The press in Wales includes Welsh-language and bilingual papers; Welsh community newspapers receive an annual grant as part of the Government's wider financial support for the Welsh language. Newspapers from the Irish Republic, as well as the British national press, are widely read in Northern Ireland.

Many newspapers and magazines in the UK are produced by minority ethnic communities. Most are published weekly, fortnightly or monthly. A Chinese newspaper, *Sing Tao*, the Urdu *Daily Jang* and the Arabic *Al-Arab*, however, are dailies. Afro-Caribbean newspapers include *The Gleaner, The Voice, New Nation* and *Caribbean Times*, each published weekly. The *Asian Times* is an English language weekly for people of Asian descent. Publications also appear in other languages, particularly Bengali, Gujarati, Hindi and Punjabi. The fortnightly *Asian Trader* is a successful business publication, while *Cineblitz International* targets those interested in the South Asian film industry.

The periodical press

There are around 9,000 separate periodical publications that carry advertising. They are generally classified as either 'consumer' titles, offering readers leisure-time information and entertainment, or 'business and professional' titles,

which provide people with material of relevance to their working lives. Within the former category, there are general consumer titles, which have a wide appeal, and specialist titles, aimed specifically at groups of people with particular interests, such as motoring, sport or music. A range of literary and political journals, appearing monthly or quarterly, caters for a more academic readership. There are also many in-house and customer magazines produced by businesses or public services for their employees and/or clients.

Press institutions

Trade associations include:

- the UK Publishing Media, representing those involved in local, regional and national newspapers and publishers of business, professional and consumer magazines;

- the Scottish Daily Newspaper Society;

- the Scottish Newspaper Publishers Association; and

- the Associated Northern Ireland Newspapers.

Other organisations representing the views of those working in the media include:

- the Society of Editors;

- British Society of Magazine Editors;

- National Union of Journalists;

- Graphical Paper and Media Union;

- Foreign Press Association; and

- the Press Association, the national news agency of the UK and Irish Republic.

A number of other British and foreign agencies and news services have offices in London, and there are smaller agencies based in other British cities. Most regional agencies are members of the National Association of Press Agencies.

Press Complaints Commission

A policy of press self-regulation, rather than statutory control or a law of privacy, operates in the UK. The Press Complaints Commission, a non-statutory body whose 16 members are drawn from both the public and the industry, deals with complaints about the content and conduct of newspapers and magazines, and operates a Code of Practice agreed by editors covering inaccuracy, invasion of privacy, harassment and misrepresentation by the press. The Commission's jurisdiction also extends to online versions of newspaper and magazine titles by publishers that already subscribe to the Code.

In 2001 the Commission received 3,033 complaints, a 36 per cent increase on the previous year. Over half (56 per cent) of the complaints related to national newspapers, 26 per cent to regional newspapers, 7 per cent to newspapers specific to Scotland, 4 per cent to magazines and the remaining 7 per cent to publications in Northern Ireland and to agencies. Most complaints breaching the Code are resolved by editors following the intervention of the Commission. It had to adjudicate on just 41 complaints – upholding 19 and rejecting 22.

The press and the law

There is no state control or censorship of the newspaper and periodical press, and newspaper proprietors, editors and journalists are subject to the law in the same way as any other citizen. However, certain statutes include sections which apply to the press. There are laws governing the extent of newspaper ownership in television and radio companies (see below), the transfer of newspaper assets, and the right of press representatives to be supplied with agendas and reports of meetings of local authorities.

There is a legal requirement to reproduce the printer's imprint (the printer's name and address) on all publications, including newspapers. Publishers are legally obliged to deposit copies of newspapers and other publications at the British Library (see page 224).

Publication of advertisements is governed by wide-ranging legislation, including public health, copyright, financial services and fraud legislation. Legal restrictions are imposed on certain types of prize competition.

Laws on contempt of court, official secrets and defamation are also relevant to the press. A newspaper may not publish anything which might influence the result of judicial proceedings. The unauthorised acquisition and publication of official information in such areas as defence and international relations, where such unauthorised disclosure would be harmful, are offences under the Official Secrets Acts. These are restrictions on publication generally, not just through the printed press. Most legal proceedings against the press are libel actions brought by private individuals.

Advertising practice

Advertising in all non-broadcast media, such as newspapers, magazines, posters, sales promotions, cinema, direct mail, and electronic media (such as CD-ROM and the Internet) is regulated by the Advertising Standards Authority (ASA). The ASA is an independent body whose role is to ensure that advertisers conform to the British Codes of Advertising and Sales Promotion. These require that advertisements and promotions are legal, decent, honest and truthful; are prepared with a sense of responsibility to the consumer and society; and respect the principles of fair competition generally accepted in business.

The ASA monitors compliance with the Codes and investigates complaints received. Pre-publication advice is available to publishers, agencies and advertisers from the Committee of Advertising Practice. If an advertisement is found to be misleading or offensive, the ASA can ask the advertiser to change or remove it. Failure to do so can result in damaging adverse publicity in the ASA's monthly report of its judgements, the refusal of advertising space by publishers, and the loss of trading privileges. Advertisers found guilty of placing irresponsible or offensive posters can face a two-year period of mandatory pre-vetting. The ASA can also refer misleading advertisements to the Director General of Fair Trading (see page 341), who has the power to seek an injunction to prevent their publication.

Media ownership

Legislation in 1990 laid down rules enabling the ITC and Radio Authority to keep ownership of the broadcasting media widely spread and to prevent undue concentrations of single and cross-media ownership, in the broader public interest. The *Broadcasting Act 1996* relaxed those rules, both within and across different media sectors, to reflect the needs and aspirations of the industry against the background of accelerating technological change, by:

■   allowing for greater cross-ownership between newspaper groups, television companies and radio stations, at both national and regional levels; and

- establishing 'public interest' criteria by which the regulatory authorities can assess and approve (or disallow) mergers or acquisitions between newspapers and television and radio companies.

The 1996 Act overturned the rule that no one company could own more than two of the ITV (Channel 3) licences; instead, a new limit was set whereby no company could control franchises covering more than 15 per cent of the total television audience. Local newspapers with more than a 50 per cent share of their market may now own a local radio station, providing at least one other independent local radio station is operating in that area. An additional regulation is the Office of Fair Trading's limit of 25 per cent on any company's share of television advertising revenue. Newspaper transfers and mergers are subject to the consent of the Secretary of State for Trade and Industry, usually after reference (where the total paid-for daily circulation of newspapers owned by the proprietors involved is 500,000 or more) to the Competition Commission.

Relaxing the media ownership rules

Proposals for changes in media ownership rules included in the draft Communications Bill are:

- scrapping those rules preventing single ownership of ITV and more than one national commercial radio licence;

- not allowing any newspaper group with over 20 per cent of the national market a significant stake in ITV;

- the introduction of a parallel regional rule preventing anyone owning all the newspapers and the regional ITV licence in any region or major city; and

- the introduction of a scheme to ensure that at least three commercial local or regional media voices exist in addition to the BBC in almost every local community.

Telecommunications

Turnover of the UK telecommunications services sector grew by 8 per cent in 2001 to £45.4 billion.

In 2002, 163 service providers held a public telecommunications operator licence, and 62 providers held a cable licence.

Telephone services

Telephone calls from fixed links were 22 per cent higher in 2001, at 300 billion call minutes, than in 2000 (see Table 17.2). This mainly reflects a big increase in Internet call volumes during the year, whereas voice call volumes were down. Oftel (see page 242) estimates that Internet calls now account for 44 per cent of fixed call volumes. A telephone is one of the most popular consumer durable goods in the home. According to Oftel, around 95 per cent of households have a fixed telephone, while a further 4 per cent of households are thought to use a mobile phone instead. However, more existing customers are installing second lines in their home, often for Internet use, and 5 per cent of households have more than one fixed line. There are 35.3 million fixed lines, but since October 2000 there have been more mobile subscribers than fixed lines.

BT, which became a private sector company in 1984, remains the biggest fixed-line UK operator, although competitors have increased their share of the market, especially the business market. BT runs one of the world's largest public telecommunications networks, including about 29 million exchange lines. Turnover from continuing businesses in 2001/02 totalled £18.4 billion. In 2001 it demerged its BT Wireless operations, including its mobile phone operations, to form a separate company, MMO_2.

The two main cable operators are ntl and Telewest. By the end of April 2002 cable operators had installed around 5.2 million telephone lines in the UK.

A variety of new telecommunications services has emerged. For example, many companies offer their customers information services using 0845 and 0800 telephone numbers – over 100 operators supply such services to companies. In September 2001 Oftel gave the go-ahead for the expansion of directory enquiry (DQ) services, currently provided mainly by BT through numbers such as 192. In May 2002 a lottery was held to assign new six-digit DQ numbers among operators, and around 300 numbers were allocated. Services using the new numbers are due to be launched in October 2002, with the existing numbers being withdrawn by August 2003.

Table 17.2 Telecommunications statistics, UK

	Call minutes 2001 (million)	Percentage change in call minutes between 2000 and 2001
Fixed link		
Local calls	75,945	–6
National calls	54,947	7
International calls	8,073	9
Calls to mobile phones	13,440	19
Other calls[1]	147,599	54
All calls[2]	300,004	22
Cellular services		
UK calls	43,089	26
Outgoing international calls	574	37
Calls while abroad	970	15
All calls	44,633	26

1 Other calls include number translation services, premium rate calls, directory enquiries, operator calls, the speaking clock, public payphones and calls to Internet Service Providers (ISPs).
2 Figures may include a small amount of double counting, as in some instances calls supplied by an operator to a reseller may be counted by both operator and reseller.
Source: *Oftel Market Information*

Mobile communications

At the end of 2001 there were some 44.9 million mobile phone users in the UK, 12 per cent more than a year earlier. Call volumes are continuing to rise, but at a slower rate as the market reaches maturity. Text messaging is growing in popularity, and the volume of text messages handled by cellular network operators grew by 56 per cent in 2001. About 69 per cent of subscribers at the end of 2001 were using pre-paid packages.

The four network suppliers in the UK are Orange (part of France Telecom), MMO$_2$, Vodafone and T-Mobile (a subsidiary of Deutsche Telekom and formerly known as One 2 One), with 12.4 million, 11.1 million, 11.0 million and 10.4 million subscribers respectively at the end of 2001. There are also around 50 independent service providers. Vodafone is one of the world's largest mobile phone operators. It had over 101 million customers worldwide through its operations in 28 countries in March 2002.

The next development in mobile phone services will be the 'third generation' services, which will provide users with high-speed access to the Internet, e-mail facilities, video conferencing and access to a large number of information services. Five operators have licences in the UK: the four network operators, together with Hutchison 3G. Services are expected to begin later in 2002 and to become widely available in 2003.

Regulation

Oftel (the Office of Telecommunications), a non-ministerial government department headed by the Director General of Telecommunications, is the independent regulatory body for the telecommunications industry. It promotes competition in telecommunications networks and services, and carries out regular reviews of markets. It is encouraging greater broadband and narrowband Internet access. During 2002/03 Oftel will be undertaking work in preparation for the proposed new Office of Communications (see page 236), which would take over its functions.

In April 2002 the European Commission set out a new European regulatory framework for European electronic communications. The framework is contained in four EC directives, covering all telecommunications and broadcasting networks in the EU, and will take effect in each Member State in July 2003. Before implementation, country regulators will be reviewing the telecommunications markets to assess the need for regulation, and in the UK Oftel will be conducting an intensive examination of market competition.

The Internet

The Internet plays an increasingly important role in the provision and distribution of information and entertainment. Broadly speaking, it is a loose collection of computer networks around the world and links thousands of academic, government and public computer systems, giving access to a wealth of stored information and other resources. No one owns the Internet and there is no centralised controlling or regulating body.

The use of the Internet in the UK is growing rapidly (see Figure 17.3). According to the ONS Expenditure and Food Survey, in the first quarter of 2002 an estimated 10.7 million households (42 per cent) in the UK could access the Internet from home, over three times the number in the first quarter of 1999. Nearly all access the Internet through a home computer, although a small proportion access the Internet in another way, such as through digital television or a mobile phone. Many people use the Internet at work, in education establishments and in libraries; 99 per cent of secondary schools and 96 per cent of primary schools in England are connected to the Internet.

A growing number of homes and businesses are using high-speed broadband connections to the Internet. According to Oftel, there were over 700,000 such connections in the UK by the beginning of July 2002. Over 20,000 broadband connections are being added a week.

According to the National Statistics Omnibus Survey, 55 per cent of adults in Great Britain had accessed the Internet at least once by April 2002, equivalent to 25 million adults. Over

Figure 17.3 Households with home access[1] to the Internet, UK

Per cent

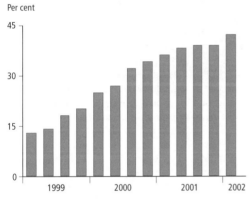

1 Data before the second quarter of 2000 are for home access via computers only.
Source: Omnibus Survey, Office for National Statistics

Index of Internet Connectivity

The ONS has developed a new Index of Internet Connectivity. In the 12 months to June 2002 the number of subscriptions to the Internet in the UK rose by 17 per cent. Dial-up connections accounted for 94 per cent in June 2002 and permanent connections 6 per cent, although the latter are growing very rapidly. The proportion of subscriptions using free access has been falling and in June 2002 represented 30 per cent of subscriptions, while those paying a fixed rate for unmetered access has been growing and accounted for 34 per cent; a further 19 per cent used billed access for call minutes.

Table 17.4 Internet activities: adults who have accessed the Internet, by purpose, Great Britain[1]

Per cent
April 2002

Selected activities	
Communication	
Using e-mail	76
Using chat rooms or sites	17
Information search and online services	
Finding information about goods or services	76
Finding information related to education	38
Playing or downloading games	11
Playing or downloading music	19
Downloading other software	19
Purchasing goods, services and banking	
Buying or ordering tickets, goods or services	38
Personal banking, financial or investment activities	28
Others	
General browsing or surfing	61
Using or accessing government or official services	17
Looking for work	20

1 Personal use only.
Source: Omnibus Survey, Office for National Statistics

three-quarters of adults who have accessed it for private use have used it to find information about goods or services or for e-mail (see Table 17.4). Among those purchasing tickets, goods or services (38 per cent), the most popular purchases in the three months prior to interview were flights and holiday accommodation (35 per cent), books or magazines (24 per cent), tickets for events (23 per cent), and music or CDs (20 per cent).

There are over 700 Internet Service Providers (ISPs), of which BT has the biggest market share (23 per cent in May 2002), followed by Freeserve and AOL (20 per cent each).

The BBC's Internet, interactive and new media offerings were renamed BBCi in November 2001 to provide a single gateway to the BBC's web, interactive TV and hand-held computer services. It is estimated that over 6 million people are regular users of the BBCi website (*www.bbc.co.uk*), which was launched in 1997 and now offers more than 1 million pages of content, including news, sport, weather and a wide range of other topics.

With the rapid growth in the Internet, many UK public and private sector bodies have established websites containing information about their operations and services provided. Two of the main government websites are the UK online Citizen Portal providing a single point of entry to government information and services, *www.ukonline.gov.uk*, and the National Statistics website (*www.statistics.gov.uk*).

Postal services

The Post Office, founded in 1635, pioneered postal services and was the first to issue adhesive postage stamps as proof of advance payment for mail. Under the *Postal Services Act 2000*, the Post Office ceased to be a statutory authority and its business was transferred to a successor company, Consignia plc, wholly owned by the Government.

Consignia (*www.consignia.com*) serves its UK customers through three main operations – Royal Mail, Parcelforce Worldwide and Post Office Ltd – and employs some 220,000 people. The Act gave Consignia greater commercial freedom, while introducing through licensing the requirement to provide a universal postal service throughout the UK, involving the daily delivery and collection of mail at a uniform, affordable price.

In June 2002 Consignia announced a pre-tax loss of £1.1 billion, together with a three-year renewal plan which involves a reduction of around 30,000 in its workforce. It also announced its intention to change the corporate name to Royal Mail Group plc by the end of 2002.

Competition and regulation
Under the 2000 Act, a new independent regulator, the Postal Services Commission (known as 'Postcomm'), was established. Following consultation, Postcomm announced in May 2002 a timetable for introducing competition in respect of items weighing less than 350 grams and costing less than £1 to post. The Royal Mail used to have a monopoly of such items, but is now licensed by Postcomm to provide these services. Competition will be introduced in three stages:

- from 1 January 2003 bulk mail above 4,000 items per mailing (from a single user at a single site in a similar format) will be opened to competition – this market is estimated to

be worth around £1.4 billion a year and represents about 30 per cent of the UK letter market by value;

- from 1 April 2005 the bulk mail threshold will be adjusted to open up a total of 60 per cent of the market by value; and

- from 1 April 2007 all restrictions on market entry will be abolished.

Postcomm is also seeking to adopt a 'light touch' regulatory regime for other licensed operators. By July 2002 it had issued ten interim short-term licences. Interim licences will be replaced by long-term standard licences from January 2003.

Consignia's operations
Royal Mail delivers to 27 million addresses in the UK, handling around 82 million items each working day. In 2001/02 it processed more than 20.6 billion inland letters and 628 million outgoing international letters. The volume of mail has continued to grow despite competition from other forms of communication. Mail is collected from over 110,000 posting boxes, and from Post Office branches and large postal users. The UK postcode system allows mechanised sorting down to part of a street on a delivery round and, in some cases, to an individual address.

Parcelforce Worldwide provides a door-to-door overnight delivery service throughout the UK and an international service to 239 countries and territories. Express services are available to over 220 countries and territories. It handles 150 million packages a year and is modernising its handling facilities.

The UK network of some 17,500 Post Office branches (of which around 600 are directly run by Post Office Ltd) handles a wide range of transactions, with a total value of over £150 billion in 2001/02. It acts as an agent for Royal Mail and Parcelforce Worldwide, government departments and local authorities. Post Office branches also provide banking services for six UK banks as well as National Savings and Investments, and Post Office Ltd is developing its provision of personal banking services.

About 28 million customers visit a Post Office branch each week, with 16 million using them to collect benefit payments. However, this business is expected to decline from April 2003 when new arrangements start to take effect which will mean that benefits will be paid directly into bank accounts. Under new universal banking services (see page 454), benefit recipients and pensioners can continue to have their money paid in cash at their local Post Office branch, and a number of banks will be making their basic bank accounts accessible through Post Office branches. A restructuring programme is expected to reduce the urban network of 9,000 offices by around 3,000.

Further reading

Department for Culture, Media and Sport: Annual report 2002. Cm 5423. The Stationery Office, 2002.

A New Future for Communications. Department of Trade and Industry and Department for Culture, Media and Sport. Cm 5010. The Stationery Office, 2000.

Websites

Department for Culture, Media and Sport
www.culture.gov.uk

Department of Trade and Industry
www.dti.gov.uk

British Broadcasting Corporation (BBC)
www.bbc.co.uk

Broadcasting Standards Commission
www.bsc.org.uk

Channel 4
www.channel4.com

Consignia
www.consignia.com

Independent Television Commission (ITC)
www.itc.org.uk

ITV (Channel 3)
www.itv.co.uk

Office of Telecommunications (Oftel)
www.oftel.gov.uk

Periodical Publishers Association
www.ppa.co.uk

Postal Services Commission
www.psc.gov.uk

Radio Authority
www.radioauthority.org.uk

www.

18 Sport and recreation

Sport is a popular leisure activity. According to the results from the ONS UK 2000 Time Use Survey, about 80 per cent of the population reported doing some type of physical activity in the four weeks prior to the survey. The top three activities reported were walking for at least 2 miles (3.2 km) or 1 hour, by 12 per cent of respondents, swimming (9 per cent) and keep fit (7 per cent). The time use diaries of participants in the survey showed that more time was spent in sports and physical activities (an average of 16 minutes a day) than in watching sport on television (4 minutes a day).

Commonwealth Games

The Commonwealth Games were held in Manchester in July and August 2002 and attracted about 5,250 athletes from 72 Commonwealth nations and dependencies who participated in 14 individual sports and three team sports. This was the largest multi-sport event ever held in the UK. The centrepiece of the new facilities for the Games was the £110 million City of Manchester Stadium, funded by Manchester City Council and Sport England. Its seating capacity for the Games was 38,000. After the Games extra seating will be added to raise capacity to 48,000 and from 2003 the stadium will be the new home for Manchester City Football Club. The Manchester Aquatic Centre, costing £32 million, was also built for the Games and hosted the swimming and diving events.

Athletes from the home country teams won a total of 231 medals at the Commonwealth Games:

	Gold	Silver	Bronze	Total
England	54	51	60	165
Scotland	6	8	16	30
Wales	4	15	12	31
Northern Ireland	2	2	1	5

UK sportsmen and sportswomen hold over 50 world titles in a variety of sports, including athletics, professional boxing, rallying, rowing, sailing, snooker and squash. In 2001 able-bodied UK athletes won 76 medals at world and European championships, while athletes with disabilities won 167 medals at this level.

Major events

Many important sporting events are held every year in the UK, including the Wimbledon Lawn Tennis Championships, the FA Cup Final, the Open Golf Championship and the Grand National steeplechase. Major events in the UK in 2002 included the Commonwealth Games in Manchester and the European Champions League Final at Hampden, Scotland's national football stadium. Among the international events to be staged in the UK in 2003 are the World Indoor Athletics Championships and the World Badminton Championships, both of which will take place in Birmingham. Results in 2001/02 of some key sporting events held regularly in the UK are given in Table 18.1.

Popular sports

Statistics for participation in particular sports in this section are usually provided by the relevant governing body.

Angling
Angling is one of the most popular sports in the UK, with an estimated 3.3 million people participating in the sport on a regular basis. There are three governing bodies controlling the three disciplines of the sport: coarse fishing (for freshwater fish other than salmon or trout), game

Table 18.1 Winners of major sporting events in the UK,[1] 2001/02

Athletics
London Marathon (April 2002): *Men* – Khalid Khannouchi (United States); *Women* – Paula Radcliffe

Badminton
All-England Championships (March 2002): *Men* – Cheng Hong (China); *Women* – Camilla Martin (Denmark)

Cricket
Test matches (summer 2002) – England v Sri Lanka 2–0
England v India 1–1
Frizzell County Championship – Surrey
Cheltenham & Gloucester Trophy – Yorkshire
Benson & Hedges Cup – Warwickshire
Norwich Union League – Glamorgan

Equestrianism
Badminton three-day event (May 2002) – Pippa Funnell riding Supreme Rock
Hickstead Derby (August 2002) – Peter Charles riding Corrada (Ireland)

Football
FA Barclaycard Premiership – Arsenal
AXA-sponsored FA Cup Final – Arsenal beat Chelsea 2–0 (May 2002)
Worthington Cup Final – Blackburn Rovers beat Tottenham Hotspur 2–1 (February 2002)
Bank of Scotland Premier League – Celtic
Tennents Scottish Cup Final – Rangers beat Celtic 3–2 (May 2002)
CIS Insurance Cup Final – Rangers beat Ayr United 4–0 (March 2002)

Golf
Open Golf Championship (July 2002) – Ernie Els (South Africa)
Cisco World Matchplay Championship (October 2001) – Ian Woosnam

Horse racing
Vodafone Derby (June 2002) – High Chaparral, ridden by Johnny Murtagh (Ireland), trained by Aidan O'Brien (Ireland)
Martell Grand National (April 2002) – Bindaree, ridden by Jim Culloty, trained by Nigel Twiston-Davies

Motor racing
British Grand Prix (Formula 1) (July 2002) – Michael Schumacher (Germany)
Network Q Rally of Great Britain (November 2001) – Marcus Gronholm (Finland)

Motorcycling
World Superbike Championship, British Round 1 (May 2002) – Race 1: Colin Edwards (US); Race 2: Troy Bayliss (Australia), British Round 2 (July 2002) – Race 1: Colin Edwards (US); Race 2: Colin Edwards (US)

British Motorcycle Grand Prix (July 2002) – 500 cc: Valentino Rossi (Italy); 250 cc Marco Melandri (Italy); 125 cc Arnaud Vincent (France)

Speedway – British Grand Prix (June 2002) – Ryan Sullivan (Australia)

Rowing
University Boat Race (March 2002) – Oxford

Rugby league
Tetley's Super League Final (October 2001) – Bradford Bulls beat Wigan 37–6
Kellogg's Nutri-Grain Challenge Cup Final (April 2002) – Wigan beat St Helens 21–12

Rugby union
Lloyds TSB Six Nations Championship – France
Zurich Premiership – Leicester
Powergen Cup Final (April 2002) – London Irish beat Northampton 38–7
Welsh/Scottish League – Llanelli
WRU Principality Cup Final (May 2002) – Pontypridd beat Llanelli 20–17

Snooker
Embassy World Championship Final (May 2002) – Peter Ebdon beat Stephen Hendry 18–17
UK Championship Final (December 2001) – Ronnie O'Sullivan beat Ken Doherty (Ireland) 10–1

Squash
British Open Championships Finals (April 2002) – *Men:* Peter Nicol beat John White 15–9, 15–8, 15–8; *Women:* Sarah Fitz-Gerald (Australia) beat Tania Bailey 9–3, 9–0, 9–0

Tennis
Wimbledon Finals (July 2002): *Men's singles* – Lleyton Hewitt (Australia) beat David Nalbandian (Argentina) 6–1 6–3 6–2; *Women's singles* – Serena Williams (US) beat Venus Williams (US) 7–6 6–3

1 UK sportsmen and sportswomen unless otherwise indicated.

fishing and sea fishing. Coarse fishing is the biggest of the three governing bodies, with around 200,000 members. Each discipline organises competitions. The rivers and lochs in Scotland, and the lakes and clear rivers in Wales and Northern Ireland are the main areas for salmon and trout fishing.

Athletics

In the UK athletics incorporates many activities, including track and field events, cross-country and road running, race walking, and fell and hill running. Mass participation events, notably marathons and half marathons, are very popular. Many runners are sponsored, raising considerable amounts for charities and other good causes.

The largest UK marathon is the London Marathon each April, with over 32,000 runners competing in the 2002 event. The Great North Run, a half marathon, takes place between Newcastle upon Tyne and South Shields each autumn.

The governing body for the sport is UK Athletics (*www.ukathletics.net*). It has made successful bids to host major championships, including the World Indoor Championships, which will be held at Birmingham in 2003, and the European Cross Country Championships, to be held in Edinburgh in 2003.

The 2002 London Marathon featured record-breaking performances in both the men's and the women's events. In the men's event, Khalid Khannouchi of the United States broke the world marathon record, winning in 2 hours 5 minutes 38 seconds. Paula Radcliffe of the UK, in her first marathon, recorded the second fastest time by a woman. Her winning time (2–18–56) was the fastest ever time set in a race without the assistance of male pacemakers and the quickest time for a first marathon.

In October 2001 Paula Radcliffe retained her world half-marathon championship in Bristol, and in March 2002 her 8 km world cross-country title in Dublin. In August 2002 she won the 10,000 metres at the European Championships in Munich, one of seven gold medals won by UK athletes. British track and field athletes held world records in two events in mid-2002: Jonathan Edwards in the triple jump and Colin Jackson in the 110 metre hurdles.

Badminton

Badminton takes its name from the Duke of Beaufort's country home, Badminton House, where the sport was first played in the 19th century. The game is organised by the Badminton Association of England and the Scottish, Welsh and Irish (Ulster Branch) Badminton Unions. The Badminton Association of England (*www.baofe.co.uk*) has a coach education system to develop coaches for players of all levels and a development department with a network of part-time county development officers.

The All England Badminton Championships, staged at the National Indoor Arena in Birmingham, is one of the world's leading tournaments. Birmingham is also staging the 2003 World Badminton Championships in May, with around 700 competitors from 50 countries.

Basketball

Over 3 million people participate in basketball in the UK. The English Basketball Association (England Basketball) is the governing body in England, with similar associations in Wales, Scotland and Ireland (Ulster Branch). All the associations are represented in the British and Irish Basketball Federation, which acts as the co-ordinating body for the UK and the Irish Republic.

The leading clubs play in the British Basketball League and the National Basketball League, which cover four divisions for men and two for women, while there are also leagues for younger players in the RAF Junior/Cadet League and the Passerelle competition. Mini-basketball has been developed for players under the age of 12. Wheelchair basketball for people with disabilities is played under the same rules, with a few basic adaptations, and on the same court as the running game.

England Basketball (*www.englandbasketball.co.uk*) runs various development schemes for young people which aim to increase participation and improve the quality of basketball. With support from National Lottery funds, some 10,000 outdoor basketball goals have been installed in parks and play areas in England. An outdoor basketball initiative has also been established in Northern Ireland.

Bowls

The two main forms of bowls are lawn flat green (outdoor and indoor) and crown green. About

6,000 flat green outdoor lawn bowling clubs are affiliated to the English, Scottish, Welsh and Irish Bowling Associations, which, together with the Women's Bowling Associations for the four countries, play to the laws of World Bowls. Crown green, indoor, English bowls federation and short mat bowls have their own separate associations. The World Bowls Tour now organises bowls at the professional level. A new single world governing body, World Bowls Ltd, has been set up, with headquarters in Edinburgh. The 2004 World Bowls Championship will be held at Northfield in Ayr.

At the 2002 world indoor championships, held in Hopton-on-Sea (Norfolk), Tony Allcock won the singles title for the third time, while Hugh Duff and Paul Foster won the pairs title.

Boxing

Boxing in its modern form is based on the rules established by the Marquess of Queensberry in 1865. In the UK boxing is both amateur and professional, and strict medical regulations are applied in both.

There are separate amateur boxing associations in England, Scotland and Wales, and boxing in Northern Ireland is controlled by the Irish Amateur Boxing Association (Ulster Provincial Council). The associations organise amateur boxing championships as well as training courses for referees and coaches.

Professional boxing in the United Kingdom is controlled by the British Boxing Board of Control (*www.bbbofc.com*). The Board appoints referees, timekeepers, inspectors, medical officers and representatives to ensure that regulations are observed, and that contests take place under carefully regulated conditions.

In mid-2002 the UK had three world champions (as recognised by organisations of which the British Boxing Board of Control is a member). Lennox Lewis retained his world heavyweight titles in June 2002 when he knocked out Mike Tyson of the United States in the eighth round of their contest in Memphis, Tennessee. Joe Calzaghe successfully defended his World Boxing Organisation (WBO) super-middleweight title at the Cardiff International Arena in April 2002. Johnny Nelson is the WBO world cruiserweight champion.

Chess

There are local chess clubs and leagues throughout the UK, and chess is also played widely in schools and other educational establishments. Domestic competitions include the British Championships, the National Club Championships and the County Championships. The Hastings Chess Congress, which started in 1895, is the world's longest running annual international chess tournament. A number of UK chess players, including Michael Adams and Nigel Short, feature among the world's grand masters.

The governing bodies are the British Chess Federation (*www.bcf.org.uk*), which is responsible for chess in England and for co-ordinating activity among the home nations, the Scottish Chess Association and the Welsh and Ulster Chess Unions.

Cricket

The rules of cricket became the responsibility, in the 18th century, of the Marylebone Cricket Club (MCC), based at Lord's cricket ground in north London. The MCC still frames the laws today. The England and Wales Cricket Board (ECB) (*www.ecb.co.uk*) administers men's and women's cricket in England and Wales. The Scottish Cricket Union (*www.scu.org.uk*) administers cricket in Scotland. The Irish Cricket Union governs the sport in Ireland, with both the Northern Cricket Union and the North West Cricket Union as constituent bodies.

There is a network of First Class cricket, minor county cricket and club games with a variety of leagues. Eighteen county teams play in the four-day Frizzell County Championship and the one-day Norwich Union League, both in two divisions. Two other main one-day competitions are held: the Cheltenham & Gloucester Trophy and the Benson & Hedges Cup. The latter event will be succeeded in 2003 by a new competition to be

In June 2002 the Cheltenham & Gloucester Trophy fourth round match between Surrey and Glamorgan became the highest scoring game in the history of one-day cricket. Surrey's total of 438 for 5 in 50 overs was the biggest in one-day cricket, while the Glamorgan response of 429 was the second highest score. The Surrey batsman Alistair Brown hit 268 runs off 160 balls, the highest individual score in a one-day match.

played in the evenings with counties divided into three regional groups of six, and the winners and best runner-up will contest the final at Lord's.

Each summer two visiting teams play Test cricket against England in a number of five-day Test Matches; a ten-match one-day triangular competition, the NatWest Series, is also contested. In 2002 the visiting teams were Sri Lanka and India. The other Test-playing countries are Australia, Bangladesh, New Zealand, Pakistan, South Africa, the West Indies and Zimbabwe. A team representing England usually tours one or more of these countries outside the UK cricket season. In mid-2002 England was ranked fifth in the International Cricket Council (ICC) rankings of Test-playing nations.

Cycling
British Cycling (*www.britishcycling.org.uk*) has 17,000 members and 1,200 affiliated clubs, and is the internationally recognised governing body for British cycle sport. Wales and Northern Ireland have separate federations affiliated to British Cycling. Cycling Time Trials (*www.rttc.org.uk*) has around 970 member clubs. In 2001 over 180,000 rides were completed in time trials in England and Wales. CTC (*www.ctc.org.uk*), with 70,000 members, campaigns to improve cyclists' rights and representation, and offers advice on all aspects of cycling except racing. Local CTC groups run regional and national cycling events for riders of all abilities. CTC Scotland, CTC Cymru and CTC Northern Ireland region perform similar roles.

The British team finished second in the medals table at the World Championships in Copenhagen in September 2002. Individual gold medals were won by Chris Hoy and Chris Newton, while Chris Hoy, Craig McLean and Jamie Staff won the team sprint event.

Equestrianism
Leading equestrian events are held at a number of locations throughout the year. The Badminton Horse Trials is one of the UK's largest sporting events, attracting around 250,000 spectators. The major show jumping events include the Horse of the Year Show, which in October 2002 will be held for the first time at the National Exhibition Centre in Birmingham, and the Hickstead Derby in West Sussex.

The British Equestrian Federation (BEF) (*www.bef.co.uk*) is the governing body of horse

sports in the UK. It co-ordinates the major policy interests of common concern of its 12 member organisations, which together represent a total of over 165,000 competitive and recreational riders. These associations act as the governing bodies of the different sporting disciplines in the UK and oversee the organisation of national events. The British Horse Society, which includes Riding Clubs, is responsible for promoting training, road safety, rights of way and the welfare of horses, while the Pony Club provides training for children.

At the European three-day event championships in Pau (France) in October 2001, the British team of Jeanette Brakewell, William Fox-Pitt, Pippa Funnell and Leslie Law retained the team title. Pippa Funnell rode Supreme Rock to take the individual title, repeating their 1999 victory. She became the first rider to win the title twice on the same horse. The same British team then won the bronze medal in the three-day event at the World Equestrian Games at Jerez in Spain in September 2002, and Jeanette Brakewell, riding Over to You, won the silver medal in the individual event.

Exercise and fitness
Exercise and fitness covers a wide variety of activities, including exercise to music, aqua exercise, weight training and circuit training. The Keep Fit Association (KFA) (*www.keepfit.org.uk*), which has 900 teachers and a membership of 8,500, promotes fitness through movement, exercise and dance for people of all ages and abilities. Its certificated training scheme for KFA teachers is recognised by local education authorities. The KFA also offers professional development in a number of specialist areas. Autonomous associations serve Scotland, Wales and Northern Ireland.

Field sports
Field sports in the UK include hunting, shooting, stalking, ferreting, falconry and hare coursing. There are over 300 recognised packs of quarry hounds in the UK, of which more than 180 are foxhound packs recognised by the Masters of Fox Hounds Association. Most hunts organise 'point-to-point' race meetings (see page 253). The Countryside Alliance promotes, among several other issues, the interests of field sports.

Following the report in 2000 of the Committee of Inquiry into Hunting with Dogs in England and

Wales, there have been a number of parliamentary votes, most recently in March 2002 when the House of Commons supported a ban on hunting with dogs but the House of Lords rejected a ban. The Government has initiated a six-month consultation period, with hearings in public in September 2002. Two key principles are being addressed: the prevention of cruelty and the concept of 'utility', so that a specific form of hunting would have to be useful for achieving a specific purpose or purposes. The consultations are to contribute to the preparation of a new Bill that the Government proposes to bring forward for Parliament to consider on further free votes.

In Scotland the Scottish Parliament has passed legislation to ban hunting with dogs. This came into force in August 2002.

Football

Association football is controlled by separate football associations in England, Wales, Scotland and Northern Ireland. In England 314 clubs are affiliated to the Football Association (FA) (*www.thefa.com*) and about 42,000 clubs to regional or district associations. The FA, founded in 1863, and the Football League (*www.football-league.co.uk*), founded in 1888, were both the first of their kind in the world. In Scotland there are 79 full and associate clubs and nearly 6,000 registered clubs under the jurisdiction of the Scottish Football Association (*www.scottishfa.co.uk*). Founded in 1880, the Irish Football Association (*www.irishfa.com*) is the fourth oldest in the world and has 600 affiliated clubs.

In England the FA Premier League comprises 20 clubs. A further 72 professional clubs play in three main divisions run by the Football League. Over 2,000 English League matches are played during the season, from August to May. Three Welsh clubs play in the Football League, while the National League of Wales contains 18 mostly semi-professional clubs. In Scotland 12 clubs play in the Scottish Premier League, while a further 30 clubs play in the Scottish Football League, which has three divisions. In Northern Ireland, 20 semi-professional clubs play in the Irish Football League. Attendance at English League matches in 2001/02 was about 27.7 million. The major knock-out competitions are the FA Cup (sponsored by AXA) and the Worthington Cup in England, the Tennents Scottish Cup and the CIS Insurance Cup in Scotland, the Irish Cup and the Welsh FA Cup.

In England and Wales, licences issued by the Football Licensing Authority (FLA) require all clubs in the Premier League and those in the First Division of the Football League to have all-seater grounds. Clubs in the second and third divisions of the Football League have to ensure that any terracing for standing complies with the highest safety standards, as outlined in guidance from the FLA.

The FA will open a new National Football Centre in Burton-on-Trent in 2003. The Football Foundation, a partnership funding body including the Government, the FA and the FA Premier League, was established in 2001 and is seeking to improve access to the sport for children and amateurs. It has distributed over £11 million to grass-roots football.

The Government works closely with the police, football authorities and the governments of other European countries to implement crowd control measures. Under the *Football (Disorder) Act 2000*, orders banning individuals from attending football matches can be imposed for between two and ten years. Anyone subject to a domestic or international ban has to surrender his or her passport when major international 'away' games involving England are imminent. The 2002 FIFA World Cup Finals were notable for the good behaviour of fans, and there were no public order problems involving England supporters.

Michael Owen, who plays for Liverpool, was voted European Footballer of the Year in 2001. David Beckham, who plays for Manchester United and is the current England captain, was runner-up in the FIFA World Player of the Year.

In the FIFA World Cup in 2002 England reached the quarter-finals of the competition, with wins over Argentina and Denmark before being beaten by Brazil, the eventual winners, by 2 goals to 1.

Scotland and Ireland are jointly bidding to host the 2008 European Football Championship.

Gaelic Games

Gaelic Games, popular in Northern Ireland, cover the sports of Gaelic football, ladies' Gaelic football, handball, hurling, camogie (women's hurling) and rounders. There are over 800 clubs (incorporating more than 3,500 teams) in Northern Ireland affiliated to the Gaelic Athletic

Association, the Ladies Gaelic Football Association and the Camogie Association, the official governing bodies responsible for Gaelic Games.

Golf

Since 1897 the rules of golf have been administered worldwide (excluding the United States and Mexico) by The Royal and Ancient Golf Club (R & A) (*www.randa.org*), which is situated at St Andrews. Club professional golf is governed by the Professional Golfers' Association (PGA) (*www.pga.org.uk*) and tournament golf by the European PGA Tour and the European Ladies Professional Golfers' Association. The home country governing bodies for men's amateur golf are affiliated to the R & A and are represented on the Council of National Golf Unions, which is the UK co-ordinating body responsible for handicapping and for organising home international matches. Women's amateur golf in Great Britain is governed by the Ladies' Golf Union.

The main tournament of the British golfing year is the Open Championship, one of the world's four 'majors'. The Ryder Cup is played between male professional golfers of Europe and the United States every two years, although the 2001 event was postponed in the aftermath of the terrorist attacks of 11 September in the United States. The Europe team regained the Ryder Cup in September 2002 at The Belfry, securing victory by 15½–12½ points.

Other important competitions include the World Matchplay Championship at Wentworth; the Walker Cup and Curtis Cup matches for men and women amateurs respectively, played every two years between Great Britain and Ireland and the United States; and the Solheim Cup for women professionals, played between Europe and the United States.

There are over 2,000 golf courses in the UK. The most famous is the Old Course at St Andrews, while others include Royal Lytham and St Anne's, Royal Birkdale and Muirfield (which staged the 2002 Open Championship).

Greyhound racing

Greyhound racing is one of the UK's most popular spectator sports, with about 4 million spectators a year. The rules for the sport are drawn up by the National Greyhound Racing Club (NGRC), the sport's judicial and administrative body. The representative body is the British Greyhound Racing Board.

Meetings are usually held three times a week at each track, with at least ten races a meeting. The main event of the year is the Greyhound Derby, run in June at Wimbledon Stadium, London. Tracks are issued with a betting licence by local authorities. There are 31 major tracks that operate under the rules of the NGRC and around 25 independent tracks.

Gymnastics

Gymnastics is divided into eight main disciplines: men's artistic and women's artistic gymnastics, rhythmic gymnastics, sports acrobatics, general gymnastics, sports aerobics, trampolining, and gymnastics and movement for people with disabilities. The governing body for the sport is British Gymnastics, to which 984 clubs are affiliated. It is estimated that between 7 million and 8 million schoolchildren take part in some form of gymnastics every day as part of the National Curriculum.

Highland Games

Scottish Highland Games, which take place between May and September, cover a wide range of athletic competitions, including running, cycling and dancing. The heavyweight events are the most popular and include throwing the hammer, tossing the caber and putting the shot. Over 70 events of various kinds take place throughout Scotland, the most famous being the annual Braemar Gathering.

The Scottish Games Association is the official governing body responsible for athletic sports and games at Highland and Border events in Scotland.

Hockey

Club hockey has been played in some form in England since the 1830s. By the 1880s there were several clubs playing regular matches in the London area, and these came together to found the Hockey Association in 1886. English Hockey (*www.hockeyonline.co.uk*) governs men's and women's hockey in England, and there are similar single associations in Scotland (*www.scottish-hockey.org.uk*), Wales and Northern Ireland. However, English Hockey has experienced financial problems, and in May 2002 its member clubs voted to hand over the running of the sport to a new limited company, Hockey England Ltd. Cup competitions and leagues exist at national, divisional or district, club and school levels, both indoors (six-a-side) and outdoors, and there are regular international matches and tournaments.

The National Hockey Stadium in Milton Keynes is the main venue for all major hockey matches played in England.

Horse racing

Horse racing takes two main forms – flat racing and National Hunt (steeplechasing and hurdle) racing – and there are meetings throughout the year. There are 59 racecourses in Great Britain and about 13,000 horses in training. Point-to-point racing, restricted to amateur riders on horses which are qualified by having gone hunting, takes place between January and June.

The Derby, run at Epsom, is the principal event in the flat racing calendar. Other classic races are the 2,000 Guineas and the 1,000 Guineas, both held at Newmarket; the Oaks (Epsom); and the St Leger (Doncaster). The meeting at Royal Ascot in June is another significant flat racing event. The most important National Hunt meeting is the National Hunt Festival held at Cheltenham in March, which features the Gold Cup and the Champion Hurdle. The Grand National, run at Aintree, near Liverpool, since the 1830s, is the world's most famous steeplechase. The race is televised around the world, with an estimated total audience of approximately 500 million in 150 countries in 2002.

The British Horseracing Board (BHB) (*www.bhb.co.uk*) is the governing body for racing and is responsible for strategic and financial planning, the fixture list, race programmes, relations with the Government and the betting industry, and central marketing. The Jockey Club is the regulatory authority and is responsible for licensing, disciplinary matters and security.

In April 2002 Tony McCoy broke the record for the number of winners in a season when he rode his 270th winner in a hurdle race at Warwick – his eventual total for the 2001/02 National Hunt season was 289. This broke the previous record, achieved in 1947 by Sir Gordon Richards, still the most successful UK jockey ever with 4,870 career wins. In August 2002 Tony McCoy became the most successful National Hunt jockey ever when he rode his 1,700th winner, breaking the record previously held by Richard Dunwoody.

Ice hockey

Ice hockey is a popular indoor sport, with over 2 million spectators each season. There are two professional leagues, with seven teams in the Ice Hockey Superleague and a further 12 teams in the Findus British National Ice Hockey League. The English Premier League is a development league, with ten teams in its Premier Division while there are also two lower divisions (North and South). There are around 11,500 players in the UK. The sport is particularly popular in Northern Ireland.

Ice-skating

Ice-skating has four main disciplines: ice figure (single and pairs), ice dance, speed skating and synchronised skating. Competitive participation in ice-skating is concentrated among the under-25s, and it is one of the few sports that attracts more female than male participants. Recreational skating is enjoyed by people in a wide range of ages, and by a growing number of skaters with various levels of disability. The governing body is the National Ice Skating Association of UK Ltd. The Association has 75 affiliated clubs and over 4,500 individual members. There are over 70 rinks in the United Kingdom, including a new National Ice Centre in Nottingham. The Centre has two rinks and caters for many ice sports, including free skating, ice dance, synchronised skating, ice hockey and short track speed skating.

Martial arts

Various martial arts, mainly derived from the Far East, are practised in the UK, such as judo, karate, kendo, taekwondo and tang soo do. Judo is popular not only as a competitive sport and self-defence technique, but also as a means of general fitness training. There is an internationally recognised grading system, which is in operation through the sport's governing body, the British Judo Association (*www.britishjudo.org.uk*).

Motor-car sports

Four-wheeled motor sport includes motor racing, autocross, rallycross, rallying and karting. In motor racing the Formula 1 Grand Prix World Championship is the pinnacle of the sport. The British Grand Prix takes place at Silverstone (Northamptonshire) in July.

The governing body for four-wheeled motor sport in the UK is The Royal Automobile Club Motor Sports Association, which issues licences for competitors and events. It also organises the British Grand Prix and the Rally of Great Britain, an event in the World Rally Championship.

The UK has had more Formula 1 world champions than any other country, the most recent being the 1996 champion Damon Hill. David Coulthard was runner-up in the 2001 World Championship and in September 2002 was in fifth place in the 2002 championship. In May 2002 he won the Monaco Grand Prix to record his 12th career victory. Richard Burns won the 2001 World Rally Championship and former winner Colin McRae was runner-up. During 2002 Colin McRae became the most successful rally driver when winning his 25th World Championship rally.

UK race car constructors have enjoyed outstanding success in Grand Prix, World Rally and many other forms of racing. The UK produces around 75 per cent of the world's single-seat racing cars, including a large proportion of the cars used in the US Indy and Champ Car series. A survey, partly funded by the Department of Trade and Industry and the Regional Development Agencies and carried out in 2000 by the Motorsport Industry Association, estimated that the British motorsport engineering and services industry generates an annual turnover of £5 billion (of which exports account for over 50 per cent) and employs over 40,000 people in more than 2,500 businesses.

Motorcycle sports

Motorcycle sports include road racing, moto-cross, grass track, speedway, trials, drag racing, enduro (endurance off-road racing), hill climb and sprint. There are between 40,000 and 50,000 competitive motorcyclists in the UK.

The governing bodies of the sport are the Auto-Cycle Union (ACU) (*www.acu.org.uk*), for Great Britain, and the Motor Cycle Union of Ireland (in Northern Ireland). The major events of the year include the Isle of Man TT Races, the British Road Race Grand Prix, two rounds of the World Superbike series, and the British Superbike series. The ACU also provides race training through the ACU Race Academy, providing approved instructors for riders of all ages.

In 2002 Dougie Lampkin won his sixth successive outdoor title in the world motorcycle trials championship.

Mountaineering

The representative body for climbers, hill walkers and mountaineers in the United Kingdom is the British Mountaineering Council (BMC) (*www.thebmc.co.uk*), which works closely with the Mountaineering Councils of Scotland and Ireland. Their main areas of work include access and conservation, training and the provision of advice and information. The BMC estimates that the number of active climbers is around 400,000. There are over 300 mountaineering and climbing clubs in the UK, and three National Centres for mountaineering activities run by the Sports Councils (see page 261).

Netball

Netball is the largest female team sport in England, with 56,000 registered participants over 16 years old in over 3,500 clubs that are members of the All England Netball Association (AENA). Over 2,500 schools are members of AENA, providing a playing base in schools of over 1 million. The sport is played almost exclusively by women and girls, although male participation has increased in recent years.

The AENA (*www.england-netball.co.uk*) is the governing body in England, with Scotland, Wales and Northern Ireland having their own organisations. National competitions are staged annually for all age groups, and England plays a series of international matches against other countries, both in England and overseas.

Rowing

Rowing is organised by many schools, universities and rowing clubs throughout the UK and takes place on inland waterways and on the coast. The boats used range from singles and pairs to fours and eights. The governing bodies are the Amateur Rowing Association (ARA) (*www.ara-rowing.org*) in England, with similar bodies in Scotland, Wales and Northern Ireland. The ARA is also the governing body for representative international teams for Great Britain, in World and Olympic competition.

The Head of the River Race is the largest event of its kind, with more than 420 eights racing in procession on the Thames. Similar events are run throughout the winter months for fours, pairs and singles. The University Boat Race, between two eights from Oxford and Cambridge, has been rowed along the same course almost every year since 1836. The National Championships are held at the National Water Sports Centre at Holme Pierrepont in Nottinghamshire, with a series of races over 2,000 metres. At the Henley Regatta in Oxfordshire crews from all over the world compete each July in various kinds of race over a straight course of about 2.1 km.

At the World Championships in Seville in September 2002 the British team won six medals, including three gold medals. Matthew Pinsent and James Cracknell successfully defended their men's coxless pairs title. The men's coxed four – Tom Stallard, Luka Grubor, Steve Trapmore and Kieran West, coxed by Christian Cormack – and the women's lightweight coxless pair of Naomi Ashcroft and Leonie Barron were the other gold medallists.

Rugby league

Rugby league (a 13-a-side game) originated in 1895 following the breakaway from rugby union (see below) of 22 clubs in the north of England, where the sport is still concentrated. There are 30 professional clubs in the UK, with about 2,000 professional players, and some 400 amateur clubs with a total of around 40,000 players.

The governing body of the professional game is the Rugby Football League (*www.rfl.uk.com*), while the amateur game is governed by the British Amateur Rugby League Association. The major domestic club match of the season is the Challenge Cup Final. Matches in the two main leagues are played in the summer. The Tetley's Super League consists of 12 clubs – 11 from the north of England and one from London – while 18 clubs play in the Northern Ford Premiership, which is due to split into two divisions from 2003.

Rugby union

Rugby union football (a 15-a-side game) originated at Rugby School in the first half of the 19th century. The sport is played under the auspices of the Rugby Football Union (RFU) (*www.rfu.com*) in England (the International Rugby Board internationally) and parallel bodies in Wales, Scotland and Ireland. In 2001 the RFU and the Premiership Clubs in England formed a joint venture, England Rugby Ltd, to manage their international and professional game together. Each of the four home unions has separate national league and knock-out competitions for its domestic clubs, while in 2001/02 the two professional sides in Scotland played in a league with Welsh clubs. From 2002/03 they have been joined by a newly formed third Scottish professional team and by teams from the four Irish provinces to form the Celtic League. Leicester were European club champions for a second

successive year when winning the Heineken Cup in May 2002, defeating Munster in the final in the Millennium Stadium, Cardiff.

The Six Nations Championship is contested by England, Scotland, Wales, Ireland (a team from the Irish Republic and Northern Ireland), France and Italy. Overseas tours are undertaken by the national sides and by the British and Irish Lions, a team representing Great Britain and Ireland.

Sailing

Sailing in the UK includes yacht and dinghy racing and cruising, powerboat racing, motor cruising, jet skiing and windsurfing on inland and offshore waters. The RYA (Royal Yachting Association) (*www.rya.org.uk*) is the national governing body for boating in the UK and aims to make boating in all its forms as accessible as possible. The Association also includes RYA Sailability, the charity for disabled sailors, and administers the RYA Yachtmaster training scheme. According to RYA, about 2.2 million people participate in the sport. Among well-known yachting events in the UK are Cowes Week and the Fastnet Race.

Snooker

Snooker was invented by the British in India in 1875 and is played by approximately 7 million people in the UK. British players have dominated the major professional championships. The main tournament is the annual Embassy World Championship, held at the Crucible Theatre in Sheffield. In May 2002 Peter Ebdon won his first world title, defeating the seven-times world champion Stephen Hendry in the final by 18 frames to 17 in the closest finish for eight years. The 2001 world champion Ronnie O'Sullivan also won the UK Championship in York in December 2001 to become the fifth person to win the world and UK titles in the same year.

World Snooker (*www.worldsnooker.com*) organises professional events and holds the copyright for the rules. The representative body for women is the World Ladies' Billiards and Snooker Association.

Squash

Squash derives from the game of rackets, which was invented at Harrow School in the 1850s. The governing body for squash in England is England Squash (*www.englandsquash.com*), while there are separate governing bodies in Wales, Scotland and Ireland (Ulster Branch). The British Open

Championships is one of the major world events in the sport, and in April 2002 it was held in Manchester.

The number of players in the UK is estimated at over 1.5 million, of whom more than 500,000 compete regularly in inter-club league competitions. There are nearly 9,000 squash courts in England, provided mainly by squash clubs, commercial organisations and local authorities.

Peter Nicol is the current men's world squash champion. In January 2002 he regained the world number one position when winning the Memorial US Open in Boston, his third victory in this event.

Swimming

Swimming is a popular sport and form of exercise for people from all age groups. Competitive swimming is governed by the Amateur Swimming Association (ASA) (*www.britishswimming.org*) in England and by similar associations in Scotland and Wales. Together these three associations form the Amateur Swimming Federation of Great Britain Ltd, which co-ordinates the selection of Great Britain teams and organises international competitions. Instruction and coaching are provided by qualified teachers and coaches who hold certificates awarded mainly by the ASA. Swimming in Northern Ireland falls under the auspices of Swim Ireland.

Zoe Baker set a new world record for the 50 metre breaststroke during the Commonwealth Games in July 2002. She was one of 11 gold medallists from the home countries in the swimming events at the Commonwealth Games.

Table tennis

Table tennis originated in England in the 1880s. Today it is played by all age groups, and in a variety of venues, ranging from small halls to specialist, multi-table centres. It is also a major recreational and competitive activity for people with disabilities. The governing body in England is the English Table Tennis Association (*www.etta.co.uk*) and there is also an English Schools Association. Separate associations exist in Scotland, Wales and Ireland (where the association covers both Northern Ireland and the Irish Republic).

Tennis

The modern game of tennis originated in England in 1873 and the first championships were played at Wimbledon in 1877. The governing body for tennis in Great Britain is the Lawn Tennis Association (LTA) (*www.lta.org.uk*), to which Tennis Wales and Tennis Scotland are affiliated. Tennis in Northern Ireland is governed by Tennis Ireland (Ulster Branch).

The Wimbledon Championships, held within the grounds of the All England Club, are one of the four tennis 'Grand Slam' tournaments. Prize money totalled £8.8 million in 2002. The club is in the process of a major redevelopment programme. The UK's leading player is Tim Henman (a Wimbledon semi-finalist in 1998, 1999, 2001 and 2002), who secured his ninth title on the main tennis tour when winning in Adelaide (Australia) in January 2002.

About 2.8 million people play tennis in the UK, according to the latest LTA survey. There are national and county championships, and national competitions are also organised for schools. The profits from the Wimbledon Championships – £32 million in 2001 – are allocated to the LTA for investing in British tennis. The LTA has a five-year plan for developing the game and improving tennis facilities in Great Britain, with the aim of expanding participation and club membership, improving coach education and producing more world-class tennis players.

Winter sports

Skiing takes place in Scotland from December to May and also at several English locations when there is sufficient snow. The five established winter sports areas in Scotland are Cairngorm, Glencoe, Glenshee, the Lecht and Nevis Range. All have a full range of ski-lifts, prepared ski-runs and professional instructors. The governing body in Scotland is Snowsport Scotland (*www.snsc.demon.co.uk*).

There are over 115 artificial or dry ski-slopes throughout the UK. The British Ski and

At the 2002 Winter Olympics in Salt Lake City in the United States the women's curling team defeated Switzerland in the final to take the gold medal, the UK's first at the Winter Olympics since 1984. The Great Britain team in the event was Rhona Martin, Fiona MacDonald, Janice Rankin, Debbie Knox and reserve Margaret Morton. Alex Coomber won the bronze medal in the women's bob skeleton.

Snowboard Federation is the representative body for international competitive skiing and snowboarding. The four home country ski councils are responsible for the development of the sport.

Sports policy

A 'Sports Cabinet', headed by the Secretary of State for Culture, Media and Sport and including the ministers responsible for sport in England, Wales, Scotland and Northern Ireland, is involved in identifying strategic priorities for sport, which is a devolved function.[1]

In February 2002 the Government announced that the Cabinet Office Performance and Innovation Unit and the Department for Culture, Media and Sport (DCMS) would carry out a joint study examining long-term sports policy. The project team will develop an overall strategy for guiding government decisions on sports policy, including major events, and review the institutional structure and financial arrangements in the context of the Government's wider objectives, which include health, crime reduction and social cohesion.

Features of the Government's existing sports policy are:

- an increase in the budget for sport, with extra funds to extend the network of School Sports Co-ordinators (of whom there are over 700), to help governing bodies with modernisation and to support the UK Sports Institute (see page 260);

- the allocation of £750 million, through the National Lottery's New Opportunities Fund, for improving sports facilities in schools in the UK, with all these facilities being available for use by the wider community;

- investment of £130 million, under the Space for Sport and Arts scheme, in building new indoor sports and arts facilities in primary schools in the most deprived areas of England;

- the creation by 2005 of 250 Specialist Sports Colleges, of which 101 are in operation and a further 40 had been designated by June 2002; and

- maintaining funding for elite sportsmen and sportswomen.

Sporting excellence

As well as the Specialist Sports Colleges, two main schemes are designed to promote sporting excellence:

- *The World Class Performance Programme* provides support to the UK's most talented athletes to enable them to improve their performance and win medals in major international competitions.

- *The World Class Events Programme* aims to ensure that major international events can be attracted to, and staged successfully in, the UK. About £1.6 million a year is available to help support the cost of bidding for, and staging, events.

Sport on television and radio

Major sporting events (such as the Olympic Games) receive extensive television and radio coverage in the UK and are watched or listened to by millions of people. Football matches attract very high ratings, especially when the UK's national teams are involved in the final stages of international tournaments. For example, around 15.8 million people (excluding those in pubs and clubs) were estimated to have watched the quarter-final between England and Brazil in the 2002 FIFA World Cup Finals. A number of other sports, including rugby, horse racing, cricket and athletics, also achieve high ratings figures. Several of the UK's leading sports events, such as the Grand National and FA Premier League football matches (see pages 253 and 251 respectively), are watched on television by viewers in many other countries.

Organisation and administration

Sports Councils

Government responsibilities and funding for sport and recreation are largely channelled through five sports councils:

- the United Kingdom Sports Council, operating as UK Sport;

---

1 Most of the strategies and funding programmes in this section relate to England, but there are usually similar programmes in Wales, Scotland and Northern Ireland.

Protected coverage

In the Government's view, there are some leading sporting occasions to which everyone should have access. These are on a protected list (Group A) and cannot be shown on subscription channels unless they have first been offered to the UK's universally available free-to-air broadcasters (the BBC, the ITV network and Channel 4). Live coverage of events on the Group B list may be shown by satellite and cable channels on the condition that an acceptable level of secondary coverage – a combination of delayed coverage and edited highlights – is made available to the universally available free-to-air channels. The current list is:

Group A events (with full live coverage protected)
Olympic Games
FIFA World Cup football finals
European Football Championship finals
FA Cup Final
Scottish FA Cup Final
The Grand National
The Derby
Wimbledon Tennis Championships finals
Rugby League Challenge Cup Final
Rugby World Cup Final

Group B events (with secondary coverage protected)
Cricket Test matches played in England
Wimbledon Tennis Championships (other than the finals)
Rugby World Cup Finals tournament (other than the Final)
Six Nations Rugby Union matches involving home countries
Commonwealth Games
World Athletics Championships
Cricket World Cup – final, semi-finals and matches involving home nations' teams
Ryder Cup
Open Golf Championship

- the English Sports Council, operating as Sport England;

- the Sports Council for Wales;

- the Scottish Sports Council, operating as **sport**scotland; and

- the Sports Council for Northern Ireland.

UK Sport takes the lead on those aspects of sport and physical recreation that require strategic planning, administration, co-ordination or representation for the UK as a whole. Its main functions include:

- co-ordinating support to sports in which the UK competes internationally (as opposed to the four home countries separately);

- tackling drug misuse in sport;

- co-ordinating policy for bringing major international sports events to the UK; and

- representing UK sporting interests overseas at international level.

All the Sports Councils distribute Exchequer and Lottery funds. UK Sport focuses on elite sportsmen and sportswomen, while the home country Sports Councils are more concerned with the development of sport at the community level by promoting participation, giving support and guidance to providers of sports facilities, and supporting the development of talented sportsmen and women, including people with disabilities. They also manage the National Sports Centres (see page 261).

Sports governing bodies

Individual sports are run by over 400 independent governing bodies. Some have a UK or Great Britain structure, while others are constituted on an individual home country basis. In Northern Ireland almost half of the sports are part of an all-Ireland structure, which covers both Northern Ireland and the Irish Republic. The functions of governing bodies include drawing up rules, holding events, regulating membership, selecting and training national teams, and producing plans for their sports. There are also organisations representing people who take part in more informal physical recreation, such as walking. Most sports clubs in the UK belong to, or are affiliated to, an appropriate governing body.

Governing bodies that receive funding from the Sports Councils are required to produce development plans, from the grass roots to the highest competitive levels. In order to have access to Lottery funds for their top athletes, they need to prepare 'world-class performance' plans with specific performance targets.

A number of international federations have their headquarters in the UK: the Commonwealth Games Federation and federations for badminton, billiards and snooker, bowls, cricket, curling, golf, netball, sailing, squash, tennis and wheelchair sports.

Other sports organisations

Central Council of Physical Recreation (CCPR)
The CCPR (*www.ccpr.org.uk*) is the largest sport and recreation federation in the world, comprising 202 UK bodies and 64 English associations, most of which are governing bodies of sport. The British Sports Trust is the charity arm of the CCPR that runs a volunteer sports leadership programme, in which some 55,000 people participated in 2001. The Scottish Sports Association, the Welsh Sports Association and the Northern Ireland Sports Forum are equivalent associations to the CCPR. Their primary aim is to represent the interests of their members to the appropriate national and local authorities, including the Sports Councils, from which they may receive some funding.

British Olympic Association (BOA)
The BOA, comprising representatives of the 35 national governing bodies of Olympic sports, organises the participation of British teams in the Olympic Games, sets standards for selection and raises funds. The BOA is supported by sponsorship and by donations from the private sector and the general public, and works closely with UK Sport. It contributes to the preparation of competitors in the period leading up to the Games, such as arranging training camps, and has programmes to support national governing bodies and their athletes in areas such as acclimatisation, psychology and physiology. Its British Olympic Medical Centre at Northwick Park Hospital in Harrow provides medical services for competitors before and during the Olympics. The BOA's educational arm aims to educate youngsters about the Olympic Games and the Olympic movement.

Women in sport
UK Sport has set up the UK Co-ordinating Group on Women in Sport, which held its first meeting in November 2001. Its overall aim is to raise participation by women in sport at all levels, from grass-roots to high-performance, and increase the number of women involved in coaching, managing and administering sport.

The Women's Sports Foundation (*www.wsf.org.uk*) promotes opportunities for women and girls in sport and active recreation. Its activities include advising on key issues and campaigning for changes in policy. Together with Sport England, it has developed a national action plan on women's sport development.

Sport for people with disabilities
Sport for people with disabilities is organised by a wide range of agencies in the UK. Some organisations promote the needs of people with a particular type of disability across a range of sports. These include the British Amputee and Les Autres Sports Association, British Blind Sport, British Wheelchair Sports Foundation, Cerebral Palsy Sport and the United Kingdom Sports Association for People with Learning Disability. The British Deaf Sports Council organises sporting opportunities for people with hearing impairment and co-ordinates British interests at the World Deaf Games.

In addition, the English Federation of Disability Sport, Disability Sport Cymru, Scottish Disability Sport and Disability Sport Northern Ireland are responsible for the general co-ordination and development of sport for people with disabilities. A number of sports already have a degree of integration: archery, athletics, cricket, cycling, equestrianism, football, judo, powerlifting/ weightlifting, rugby union, sailing, swimming and wheelchair tennis/table tennis. The Commonwealth Games in Manchester in 2002 (see page 246) was the first major sports event in the world to include an integrated programme of events for people with disabilities.

The British Paralympic Association (BPA) ratifies selection, and funds and manages the Great Britain Paralympic Team in the winter and summer Paralympic Games. In May 2002 UK Sport announced a £1.7 million investment programme to support the British team for the 2004 Paralympic Games in Athens, including multi-sport preparation camps, to be held twice a year, to help the athletes experience similar conditions and climate to those expected in Athens.

Funding

National Lottery
Between 1994, when the National Lottery (see page 263) started, and September 2001, 62 sports

in the UK received funding and the Sports Councils awarded nearly 17,000 grants worth nearly £1.6 billion. Money has gone to improve sporting opportunities, provide new sporting facilities in schools (see page 257) and elsewhere, support current and potentially future elite performers, and to stage major events. For example, in projects to improve sporting opportunity, over £1 billion of Lottery funds have been invested in over 3,300 community facilities in England, while in Wales over 6,400 awards totalling more than £89 million have been made by the Sports Council for Wales.

Programmes to help sporting talent include:

- sportscotland's Talented Athlete Programme, which provides financial support to top performers and those with high potential – by 31 March 2002 over 2,600 awards had been made with a total value of about £10.2 million;

- Sport England's Active Sports Partnerships, under which over £2 million has been awarded for facilities and equipment, targeting nine sports, including athletics, basketball and rugby union, in a five-year development programme aiming to help young people to get more from their involvement in sport; and

- the Dragon Sport initiative, introduced by the Sports Council for Wales to increase after-school clubs and sporting opportunities for primary schoolchildren and to recruit parents to help organise after-school sport.

Sponsorship
Sport benefits from sponsorship, which may take the form of financing specific events or championships, such as horse races or cricket leagues, or support for sports organisations or individual performers. Motor sport and football receive the largest amounts of private sponsorship. Sponsorship is encouraged by a number of bodies, including the Institute of Sports Sponsorship, which comprises some 100 UK companies involved in sponsoring sport.

SportsAid
SportsAid raises funds to help encourage and support young people and disabled people with sporting talent. Financial grants are provided on an individual basis, with each application being assessed on the criteria of talent and need. Those receiving funds must usually be aged between 12 and 18, but there is no age limit for disabled people. The Scottish Sports Aid Foundation, SportsAid Cymru/Wales and the Ulster Sports and Recreation Trust have similar functions.

Foundation for Sport and the Arts
The Foundation for Sport and the Arts, set up by the football pools promoters in 1991, funds mainly small-scale projects in sport and the arts, and has made awards to schemes benefiting over 100 sports. This initiative followed a reduction in pools betting duty, made on the proviso that the money forgone by the Government was paid into the Foundation. In April 2002 the Government abolished pools betting duty and replaced it with a 15 per cent tax on pools companies' gross profits. The Foundation will continue in its current form at least until April 2004.

Sports facilities

The UK has a range of world-class sporting facilities including 13 National Sports Centres, operated by the home country Sports Councils. A number of major facilities have been improved in recent years, including the Millennium Stadium in Cardiff, the Wimbledon tennis complex and several football grounds. New facilities were built in Manchester for the Commonwealth Games (see page 246). In September 2002 the Football Association announced the start of work on a £757 million project to rebuild the football stadium at Wembley (London), which will seat 90,000 and is due to open in 2006.

United Kingdom Sports Institute
The United Kingdom Sports Institute (UKSI) has been set up under the strategic direction of UK Sport and in partnership with the home country Sports Councils, with funding mainly from the National Lottery. It provides facilities and integrated support services to elite athletes and teams, and those with exceptional potential. Its Athlete Career and Education (ACE UK) programme is designed to enhance athletes' personal development and sporting performance. All sports have access to the UKSI's services, although it concentrates on Olympic sports and those minority sports that lack a commercial element. The UKSI central services team is part

of UK Sport and based in London. It co-ordinates a network of regional centres in England and national institutes in Scotland, Wales and Northern Ireland.

UKSI regional and national network

England

In England the UKSI network is managed by the English Institute of Sport (EIS), part of Sport England. The EIS, officially launched in May 2002, consists of nine regional multi-sport sites, together with 35 satellite centres. Four of the key centres are based around National Sports Centres: Crystal Palace (London), Bisham Abbey (Berkshire), Lilleshall (Shropshire) and the National Water Sports Centre at Holme Pierrepont in Nottinghamshire. The other network centres are based around the Don Valley Stadium in Sheffield, Gateshead International Stadium, Manchester Sports City, the University of Bath, and Norwich Sports Park.

The EIS is investing £120 million in developing sporting facilities. Its biggest single capital investment is a £28 million project to improve facilities at the Sheffield site, due for completion in 2003. These facilities will include the National Indoor Athletics Centre; the national netball centre; special facilities for badminton, judo and table tennis; and provision for sports science and sports medicine.

Wales

The centre of the UKSI network in Wales is the Welsh Institute of Sport in Cardiff, which is the premier venue in Wales for top-level training and for competition in many sports. The Institute, which is run by the Sports Council for Wales, has close links with other specialist facilities, including the National Watersports Centre at Plas Menai in north Wales, a centre of excellence for sailing and canoeing; the national indoor athletics centre at the University of Wales Institute, Cardiff; and the cricketing school of excellence at Sophia Gardens, Cardiff. A National Swimming Centre will open in Swansea in spring 2003 and shortly afterwards a National Velodrome will open in Newport.

Plas y Brenin National Mountain Centre, in Snowdonia National Park in north Wales, is run by Sport England. It offers courses in canoeing, rock climbing, mountaineering, orienteering, skiing and most other mountain-based activities,

and is the UK's leading training institution for mountain instructors.

Scotland

The network supported by **sport**scotland comprises the Scottish Institute of Sport, which opened its new base at Stirling in May 2002, and six area institutes. The institutes have provided support for over 180 athletes in nine 'core' sports: athletics, badminton, curling (including support for the Winter Olympics gold medallists – see page 256), football, golf, hockey, judo, rugby and swimming.

The network also includes three National Sports Centres, run by **sport**scotland, which provide training and coaching facilities for a range of sports: Glenmore Lodge near Aviemore, which caters for outdoor sports, such as canoeing, mountaineering, mountain biking, orienteering and skiing; Inverclyde in Largs, which caters for 23 sports; and the Scottish National Water Sports Centre on the island of Great Cumbrae in the Firth of Clyde.

Northern Ireland

The Sports Council for Northern Ireland has announced a partnership with the University of Ulster for the development of a Northern Ireland network centre of the UKSI. This will involve creating high-quality training facilities and support services, primarily at the University's Jordanstown campus, with the establishment of links with nearby facilities.

The Tollymore Mountain Centre in County Down, run by the Sports Council for Northern Ireland, offers courses in mountaineering, rock climbing, canoeing and outdoor adventure. Leadership and instructor courses leading to nationally recognised qualifications are also available.

Local facilities

Local authorities are the main providers of basic sport and recreation facilities for the local community, including indoor sports centres, parks, lakes, playing fields, playgrounds, tennis courts, natural and artificial pitches, golf courses and swimming/leisure pools. Commercial facilities include health and fitness centres, tenpin bowling centres, ice-skating and roller-skating rinks, squash courts, golf courses and driving ranges, riding stables and marinas.

There are an estimated 110,000 amateur sports clubs in the UK. Some cater for indoor recreation, but more common are those providing sports facilities, particularly for bowls, cricket, football, rugby, hockey, tennis and golf. The Government is encouraging clubs to apply for charitable status (see chapter 9), which offers tax reliefs and tax exemption for fundraising income. For those clubs that cannot, or do not wish to, become charities, the 2002 Budget included a package of tax measures giving clubs access to tax reliefs similar to those available to charities.

The Government has also announced its intention to allocate £20 million from the Capital Modernisation Fund (see page 349) to provide new or refurbished community sports facilities.

Support services

Coaching

The organisation sports coach UK works closely with sports governing bodies, local authorities, and higher and further education institutions. Supported by the Sports Councils, it provides a comprehensive range of services for coaches in all sports. In 2001, some 30,000 coaches and schoolteachers participated in its programmes. A task force has reviewed coaching in England and in July 2002 produced a report with proposals designed to increase the pool of talented coaches and to introduce a national coaching certificate. The Government is to invest £25 million over the three years from 2003/04 in the development of coaching.

Volunteering

Sport England has developed its Volunteer Investment Plan, which aims to create a pool of accredited volunteers working in sports clubs. In April 2002 the DCMS Leadership and Volunteering in School and Community Sport programme, known as Step into Sport, began. The programme will train up to 60,000 people aged 14 to 19 to act as sports leaders in their schools and local sports clubs. It is run by a consortium of the Youth Sport Trust, the British Sports Trust (see page 259) and Sport England. Up to 8,000 older volunteers will train alongside the young volunteers. Some 10,000 volunteers assisted in the organisation of the Commonwealth Games in July–August 2002.

Sports medicine

The National Sports Medicine Institute of the United Kingdom (NSMI) serves as the national focus for all those concerned with sport and exercise medicine. It aims to provide optimum levels of safety and care in order to enhance the ability of those engaged in exercise and sport from grass-roots to international levels. The NSMI is funded through contracts with the Sports Councils and it also generates income from its services, many of which are developed or delivered through collaboration with other organisations.

Modern sports medicine facilities are being set up as part of the UKSI's regional and national network of world-class facilities and services to elite athletes.

Sports science

The development of sports science support services for the national governing bodies of sport is being promoted by the Sports Councils, in collaboration with the BOA and sports coach UK, in an effort to raise the standards of performance of national squads. The type of support provided may be biomechanical (human movement), physiological or psychological.

Drug misuse

UK Sport aims to prevent doping and achieve a commitment to drug-free sport and ethical sporting practices. In January 2002 it launched a national anti-doping strategy, in line with the International Standard for Doping Control endorsed by the World Anti-Doping Agency. The strategy calls on sports to publish a commitment in their constitution to drug-free sport; inform and, where relevant, test their athletes; publicise targets and achievements; and establish an independent disciplinary process. Many leading sports in the UK, such as football, cricket and rugby union, already comply with the strategy.

UK Sport's Anti-Doping Directorate co-ordinates an independent drugs-testing programme and is responsible for reporting the results to the appropriate governing body. In 2001/02 over 6,000 drug tests were conducted in over 40 sports, of which 1.7 per cent of tests were reported to the appropriate sports governing body for further investigation. Nearly half of the 101 reports concerned stimulants, of which a large proportion were for prescribed substances for those suffering from illnesses or allergies. In January 2002 UK Sport launched a new online drug information service to complement the existing information provided for competitors and officials. The online database draws on information from 102 sports and lists some 2,100 substances and 4,300 products on the UK Sport website (*www.uksport.gov.uk/did*).

Betting and gaming

A survey carried out by the National Centre for Social Research for a consortium representing the gambling industry, the Home Office and other regulatory authorities, and GamCare (the national centre addressing the social impact of gambling), was published in 2000. It found that 72 per cent of adults in Great Britain gamble at least once a year. The National Lottery was by far the most popular gambling activity in the UK and some 65 per cent of the adult population had bought Lottery tickets in the year leading up to the survey.

National Lottery

Of every pound spent on the National Lottery, 28 pence goes to good causes. Since its launch in the UK in 1994, the Lottery has raised over £11.7 billion for good causes, and more than 115,000 awards have been made. Lottery money is divided among the following areas – health, education, environment, arts, sport and heritage.

The National Lottery is run by Camelot Group plc, a private sector consortium, operating under a seven-year licence from 27 January 2002. Online tickets and scratchcards are available from around 25,000 retail outlets across the UK.

In May 2002 Camelot relaunched the Lottery, with new game formats and the relaunch of existing games. The Lottery now involves a series of games, including the Saturday and Wednesday main Lotto game and a variety of scratchcard games.

The National Lottery Commission regulates the Lottery, selects the operator, sets the terms of its licence and ensures that it complies with those terms. It is headed by five commissioners and its duties are to protect players' interests, ensure the Lottery is run properly, and maximise the amount raised for good causes.

In June 2002 the DCMS issued a consultation paper, which included a range of options for

Following an independent review of the controls on gambling, published in 2001, the Government issued its response, *A Safe Bet for Success – Modernising Britain's Gambling Laws*, in March 2002. The main reforms proposed, which would cover Great Britain,[2] would involve:

- the establishment of a single regulator, the Gambling Commission, for all gambling operators;

- all gambling premises to be licensed by local authorities;

- licensing for the first time of online gambling, such as on the Internet or through interactive TV;

- relaxation of the controls on the operation of the UK's casinos, bingo clubs and betting offices; and

- a new licensing framework for gaming machines – amusement machines would be for use by anybody, while gaming machines would be for adults only and confined to places where access could be controlled effectively.

Measures are also planned to keep crime out of gambling, ensure a fair deal for the punter, tackle problem gambling and ensure that children and the vulnerable are protected. An industry-funded gambling trust would support the prevention of problem gambling and finance treatment programmes.

Legislation is planned to implement the key elements of the Government's proposals, but meanwhile some changes will be introduced within the existing gambling legislation (for example, relaxing some of the controls on bingo).

changes to the current system of licensing and regulation of the Lottery – for example, consideration of whether there might be scope for more competition in running the Lottery, and examination of the scope for streamlining day-to-day regulation.

In July 2002 the DCMS published a consultation paper on Lottery funding, setting out a number of issues for consideration on how the Lottery could

2 Northern Ireland has its own gambling law.

be enhanced and developed, and how to ensure that funding is fairly distributed to all areas and communities in the UK. These issues include increasing public awareness on how Lottery money is spent, making the Lottery more responsive to the needs and priorities of communities, and ensuring the long-term sustainability of Lottery projects.

Further reading

The Government's Plan for Sport. Department for Culture, Media and Sport, 2001.

Review of Lottery Funding – A Consultation Paper on Lottery Distribution Policy. Department for Culture, Media and Sport, 2002.

Review of Lottery Licensing and Regulation. Department for Culture, Media and Sport, 2002.

A Safe Bet for Success – Modernising Britain's Gambling Laws. The Government's Response to the Gambling Review Report. Cm 5397. Department for Culture, Media and Sport. The Stationery Office, 2002.

Websites

Department for Culture, Media and Sport
www.culture.gov.uk

Department of Culture, Arts and Leisure (Northern Ireland)
www.dcalni.gov.uk

UK Sport
www.uksport.gov.uk

Sport England
www.sportengland.org

sportscotland
www.sportscotland.org.uk

Sports Council for Northern Ireland
www.sportni.org

Sports Council for Wales
www.sports-council-wales.co.uk

19 The environment

The environment can be defined as anything outside an organism in which that organism lives. Our environment includes not only our natural and geological surroundings, but also buildings, the atmosphere and even noise.

The UK environment

The UK has over 100,000 separate species of plants and animals, out of a global total estimated at between 5 million and 15 million. The natural vegetation of much of the country is deciduous forest dominated by oak. However, after many thousands of years of human activity, only scattered woodlands and areas of wild or semi-wild vegetation lie outside enclosed cultivated fields (see Table 19.1). The moorlands and heathlands which occupy around a quarter of the land area of the UK, while appearing natural, are as much the product of human activity as is farmland.

The UK's native fauna has also been dramatically affected by human activity, and all native large carnivores, such as wolves, are now extinct.

Table 19.1 Land by agricultural and other uses, UK, 2000

Per cent

	Agricultural land				Urban land and land not otherwise specified[3]
	Crops and bare fallow	Grasses and rough grazing[1]	Other[2]	Forest and woodland	
England	30	34	5	8	22
Wales	3	70	1	13	13
Scotland	7	60	2	16	14
Northern Ireland	4	76	1	6	13
United Kingdom	19	48	3	11	18

1 Includes grasses over and under five years old, and sole right and common rough grazing.
2 Set-aside and other land on agricultural holdings, such as farm roads, yards, buildings, gardens and ponds. Excludes woodland on agricultural holdings which is included in 'Forest and woodland'.
3 Figures are derived by subtracting land used for agricultural and forestry purposes from the land area. Figures include land used for transport and recreation, and non-agricultural, semi-natural environments, such as sand dunes, grouse moors and non-agricultural grasslands, and inland waters.
Source: Department for Environment, Food & Rural Affairs; Forestry Commission; Forest Service

However, small carnivores, such as badgers, foxes and stoats, are common in most rural areas, and rodents and insectivores are also widespread. Native herbivores include red and roe deer. There are only eight species of amphibians and six species of reptiles native to the UK. In contrast some 200 species of bird are found, more than half of which are migratory. Both fresh and salt waters contain a wide variety of fish species.

Responsibility for environmental affairs

The government departments with overall responsibility for countryside policy and environmental protection are shown in the box below. In England, Wales and Scotland (but not in Northern Ireland) non-departmental environment agencies are responsible for regulation and enforcement matters.

Many local authorities, voluntary organisations and charities are also involved in environmental conservation and protection.

Pollution control

Executive responsibility for pollution control is divided between local authorities, central government and the devolved administrations. Central government and devolved administrations make policy, promote legislation and advise pollution control authorities on policy implementation. Local authorities are responsible for:

- collection and disposal of domestic waste;

- keeping the streets clear of litter;

- controlling air pollution from domestic premises and, in England and Wales, from many industrial premises;

- reviewing, assessing and managing local air quality; and

- noise and general nuisance abatement.

Environmental legislation

Conservation and the countryside (see pages 269–76)

The primary conservation legislation in Great Britain is the *Wildlife and Countryside Act 1981*, which provides for a range of measures to protect plants and animals from damage and destruction. It was strengthened by the *Countryside and Rights of Way Act 2000*, which gave ministers and departments in England and Wales a statutory duty to have regard to the conservation of biological diversity in carrying out their functions, and contained new measures for the conservation and protection of habitats and wildlife. It also created a new statutory right of access, giving people greater freedom to explore the open countryside, while also providing safeguards for landowners.

Government departments and main non-departmental public bodies with responsibility for the environment

England
Department for Environment, Food & Rural Affairs (DEFRA)
Environment Agency
Countryside Agency (CA)
English Nature
English Heritage

Northern Ireland
Department of the Environment (DOE)
Department of Agriculture and Rural Development (DARD)
Environment and Heritage Service (EHS)
Council for Nature Conservation and the Countryside (CNCC)

Scotland
Scottish Executive Environment and Rural Affairs Department (SEERAD)
Scottish Environment Protection Agency (SEPA)
Scottish Natural Heritage (SNH)
Historic Scotland (an agency of the Scottish Executive Education Department)

Wales
Welsh Assembly Government
Environment Agency Wales
Countryside Council for Wales (CCW)
Cadw: Welsh Historic Monuments Executive Agency

Major conservation and recreation areas

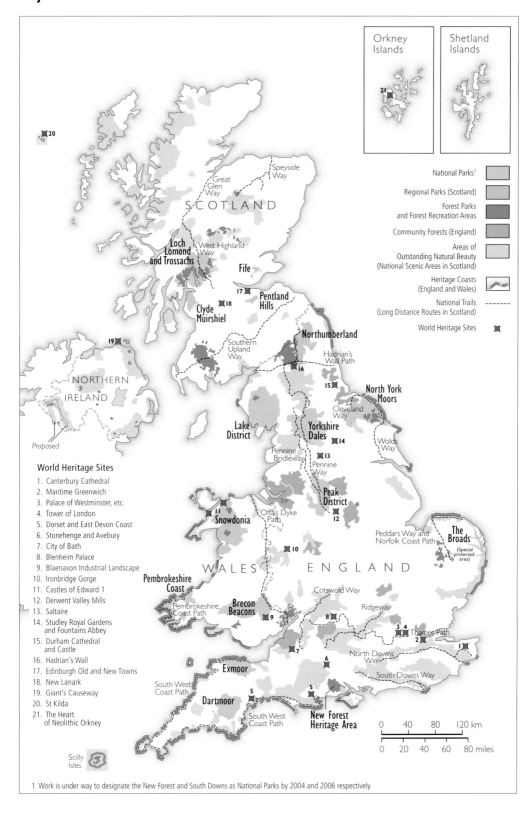

Orkney Islands

Shetland Islands

National Parks[1]

Regional Parks (Scotland)

Forest Parks and Forest Recreation Areas

Community Forests (England)

Areas of Outstanding Natural Beauty (National Scenic Areas in Scotland)

Heritage Coasts (England and Wales)

National Trails (Long Distance Routes in Scotland)

World Heritage Sites

Speyside Way

Great Glen Way

S C O T L A N D

Loch Lomond and Trossachs

West Highland Way

Fife

Pentland Hills

Clyde Muirshiel

Southern Upland Way

Northumberland

Hadrian's Wall Path

NORTHERN IRELAND

Proposed

North York Moors

Cleveland Way

Lake District

Yorkshire Dales

Wolds Way

Pennine Bridleway

Pennine Way

Peak District

World Heritage Sites

1. Canterbury Cathedral
2. Maritime Greenwich
3. Palace of Westminster, etc.
4. Tower of London
5. Dorset and East Devon Coast
6. Stonehenge and Avebury
7. City of Bath
8. Blenheim Palace
9. Blaenavon Industrial Landscape
10. Ironbridge Gorge
11. Castles of Edward 1
12. Derwent Valley Mills
13. Saltaire
14. Studley Royal Gardens and Fountains Abbey
15. Durham Cathedral and Castle
16. Hadrian's Wall
17. Edinburgh Old and New Towns
18. New Lanark
19. Giant's Causeway
20. St Kilda
21. The Heart of Neolithic Orkney

Snowdonia

Offa's Dyke Path

W A L E S   E N G L A N D

Peddars Way and Norfolk Coast Path

The Broads (Special protected area)

Pembrokeshire Coast

Pembrokeshire Coast Path

Brecon Beacons

Cotswold Way

Ridgeway

Thames Path

Exmoor

South West Coast Path

North Downs Way

South Downs Way

Dartmoor

South West Coast Path

New Forest Heritage Area

Scilly Isles

| 0 | 40 | 80 | 120 km |

| 0 | 20 | 40 | 60 | 80 miles |

1 Work is under way to designate the New Forest and South Downs as National Parks by 2004 and 2006 respectively.

December 2001: New Lanark, Lanarkshire (top) and the Dorset and East Devon Coast are declared World Heritage Sites.

New Lanark, on the banks of the River Clyde in Scotland, was founded in 1785 as a purpose-built village for textile workers and subsequently managed by Robert Owen, who provided housing, healthcare and educational opportunities in the hope of creating a model community.

The 'Jurassic Coast' of Dorset and East Devon is rich in fossils and has long been an area of great scientific interest.

April 2002: peat extraction ceases at Thorne Moor, South Yorkshire. Two months previously the Government announced an agreement, reached between English Nature and the private company involved, to stop peat extraction at the Moor and two other sites.

March 2002: opening of the 20 km Durham Coastal Footpath. Fourteen organisations worked together to regenerate the coast following the closure of the local coal mining industry.

M JONES

At the height of coal production, which ceased in 1993, 2.4 million tonnes of spoil from local mines were being tipped into the North Sea every year.

ENGLISH PARTNERSHIPS

July 2002: Loch Lomond and the Trossachs become Scotland's first national park. FORESTRY COMMISSION

Industrial pollution control

There are two pollution control regimes for the UK: Local Air Pollution Control (LAPC), which regulates emissions to air; and Integrated Pollution Control (IPC), which regulates emissions to land and water, as well as air.

A new Pollution Prevention and Control (PPC) regime, which implements an EC Directive on Integrated Pollution Prevention and Control (IPPC), has been introduced. It succeeds IPC and part of LAPC and will be fully established by 2007.

Under both old and new regimes, regulators are required to ensure that pollution from industry is prevented or reduced through the use of best available techniques, subject to assessment of costs and benefits. The characteristics of each installation and its local environment must be considered.

Under PPC, the issuing of integrated permits will apply to more industrial activities than was previously the case. These include animal rendering, the food and drink industry, and intensive livestock installations. Regulators are also required to take into account a wider range of environmental impacts (including noise, energy efficiency and site restoration) when issuing integrated permits.

A Pollution Inventory for England and Wales, administered by the Environment Agency, provides details of emissions to air, water and land from processes regulated under IPC, and their contributions to national emission levels. The data are updated annually and can be found on the Agency's website (*www.environment-agency.gov.uk*). The implementation of the IPPC Directive will increase the number of sites reporting from 2,000 to around 7,000 in 2003. A similar inventory will be developed to include information on emissions from PPC installations.

Waste management (see pages 277–9)

Waste management in Great Britain is governed by the *Environmental Protection Act 1990* (as amended) and the Waste Management Licensing Regulations 1994. A licence is required by anyone wanting to deposit, recover, or dispose of waste. Licences are issued by the Environment Agency and SEPA. In Northern Ireland responsibility for waste regulation lies with the DOE. A duty of care requires waste producers, and anyone else with responsibility for waste, to take all reasonable steps to keep their waste safe. If they give their waste to someone else they must be sure that those people are authorised to take it and can transport, recycle or dispose of it safely. Failure to comply with either the licensing requirements or a duty of care is an offence.

Local authorities are responsible for the collection and disposal of all household waste and some commercial waste. In 'two-tier' areas (see page 7), district councils are responsible for collection, and county councils for disposal, while in unitary areas the council has both roles.

The disposal of radioactive waste in the UK is regulated by the *Radioactive Substances Act 1993*. This Act makes the Environment Agency in England and Wales and SEPA in Scotland responsible for regulating the safe use and storage of radioactive materials and the management of waste. The DOE is responsible for regulating radioactive waste in Northern Ireland.

Noise (see pages 285–6)

In Great Britain, the primary legislation used to take action against the producers of noise that causes nuisance is the *Environmental Protection Act 1990*. Under the *Housing Act 1996*, local authorities in England and Wales have powers to deal with anti-social behaviour by tenants, including noise. In Scotland, action against noisy neighbours is taken under earlier legislation. The *Crime and Disorder Act 1998* introduced Anti-Social Behaviour Orders in England, Scotland and Wales, which can be used against any person who is causing harassment, alarm or distress to others, including noise nuisance.

An EC directive specifies the maximum noise level of certain new equipment for use outside.

Air pollution (see pages 281–5)

Ambient air pollution is controlled and regulated by a number of different pieces of legislation, depending on the source of emissions.

Sustainable development

The widely used definition of sustainable development is 'development which meets the needs of the present without compromising the ability of future generations to meet their own needs'. It springs from an awareness that economic development in the past tended to mean more pollution and the wasteful uses of resources.

The year 2002 marked the tenth anniversary of the UN Conference on Environment and Development, held in Rio de Janeiro. The 'Earth Summit' focused global attention for the first time on the links between environmental problems, economic conditions and social justice, and from it emerged a commitment to sustainable development. It set in motion integrated approaches to social, economic and environmental management in many countries. In September 2002 most UN members, including the UK, attended the World Summit on Sustainable Development (Rio+10) in Johannesburg, South Africa (*www.johannesburgsummit.org*). The summit sought to identify areas for further action and examined the obstacles to the implementation of Agenda 21 (the plan of action adopted at Rio).

The Government's sustainable development strategy for the UK, *A better quality of life*, was launched in 1999, with its own interpretation of sustainable development: 'ensuring a better quality of life for everyone, now and for generations to come'. It identified a core set of around 150 indicators of sustainable development and a subset of 15 headline indicators to provide an overview of progress. The headline indicators cover economic and social, as well as environmental, concerns (see box). The Government reports annually on progress towards sustainable development, and the 2001 report, *Achieving a Better Quality of Life*, was published in March 2002. It showed how progress was being made across the range of indicators. Since 1999, all or part of six headline indicators had remained on the right track, including economic output, greenhouse gas emissions, air quality, river water quality, and vehicle theft and domestic burglary. The trend for another four – investment, employment, poverty and social exclusion, and woodland bird populations – had improved. Violent crime, waste and road traffic, however, remained high. Farmland bird populations were still at an unacceptably low level.

The principal body responsible for encouraging and promoting sustainable development within the UK is the Government's Sustainable Development Unit within DEFRA (*www.sustainable-development.gov.uk*). The independent Sustainable Development Commission acts as an advocate for action, and reviews progress.

Headline indicators of sustainable development

Economic: economic output (gross domestic product at constant prices); investment (as a percentage of gross domestic product); and employment.

Social: poverty and social exclusion; education (qualifications at age 19); health (expected years of healthy life); housing (the proportion of homes not meeting standard decency criteria, which include minimum levels of repair, facilities and thermal comfort); and crime.

Environmental: climate change (greenhouse gases); air quality (days of air pollution); road traffic; river water quality; wildlife (farmland and woodland bird populations); land use (percentage of new homes on previously developed land); and waste (arisings and management).

In its Programme for Government (see page 15), the Northern Ireland Executive stated that 'Sustainable Development will be a key theme running throughout work and priorities'. Some specific strategies include: the Regional Development Strategy, which will influence the future distribution of activities through the region; the *Growing for a Green Economy* strategy, which seeks to achieve sustainable economic development through more efficient business practices; and the Northern Ireland Biodiversity Strategy.

In Wales, the Assembly has adopted a Sustainable Development Scheme, *Learning to Live Differently*, which provides a framework for all its work. This is reflected in the Assembly Government's corporate strategy document *Plan for Wales 2001* and other key strategies, including *Farming for the Future – A new direction for farming in Wales* (see page 397) and the *Transport Framework for Wales* (see page 326). The Assembly has also introduced its own list of sustainable development indicators.

The Scottish Executive Programme for Government commits the executive to make sustainable development the basis of all its activity. The Executive has identified resource use, energy, travel and social justice as priority areas for action.

The Sustainable Development Research Network (SDR) (*www.sd-research.org.uk*) is funded by DEFRA. Its goal is to contribute to sustainable development in the UK by facilitating better use of evidence and research in policy making. Its first conference was held in December 2001.

The Royal Commission on Environmental Pollution (*www.rcep.org.uk*) is an independent standing body that advises the Government on dangers to the environment, suggesting ways of integrating environmental objectives with other economic and social objectives in order to achieve sustainable development. It has produced 23 reports so far, on a variety of topics, such as climate change and environmental standards.

Land

Protecting countryside and wildlife

DEFRA is responsible for policy on wildlife and countryside in England. It sponsors three non-departmental public bodies: the Countryside Agency, English Nature and the National Forest Company. The devolved administrations sponsor similar bodies in Wales, Scotland and Northern Ireland. DEFRA also sponsors the Joint Nature Conservation Committee (JNCC), a committee of three statutory nature conservation agencies (English Nature, Scottish Natural Heritage and the Countryside Council for Wales).

Government funded countryside and wildlife agencies and budgets for 2002/03	
The Countryside Agency *www.countryside.gov.uk*	£93 million
English Nature *www.english-nature.org.uk*	£63 million[1]
Scottish Natural Heritage *www.snh.org.uk*	£49 million[1]
The Countryside Council for Wales *www.ccw.gov.uk*	£50 million
Environment and Heritage Service *www.ehsni.gov.uk*	£40 million
Joint Nature Conservation Committee *www.jncc.gov.uk*	£5 million

1 In 2001/02

The *Countryside Agency* is the statutory body in England whose aims are to conserve and enhance the countryside; promote social equality and economic opportunity for the people who live there; and help everyone, wherever they live, to enjoy this natural asset. The Agency is currently in the process of compiling the Countryside Character database, which will develop a landscape typography that provides a deeper insight into the components of the English countryside. Once finalised, it will be used to assess the impact on the landscape of changes in agricultural practices, new housing, industrial development, transport infrastructure, and mineral extraction.

English Nature promotes the conservation of England's wildlife and natural features, and provides advice to the Government on nature conservation. The Scottish Executive sponsors *Scottish Natural Heritage* (SNH), a body with both the nature conservation duties and powers of English Nature, and the countryside and landscape powers of the Countryside Agency. The *Countryside Council for Wales* (CCW) has responsibilities in Wales for landscape and nature conservation, and for countryside recreation. In Northern Ireland, the *Environment and Heritage Service*, an agency within the Department of the Environment, protects and manages the natural and built environment. It also has an environmental protection role. English Nature, CCW and SNH are also responsible for providing advice and information to the Government and the public on nature conservation, for notifying land as being of special interest due to its wildlife and geological features, and for establishing National Nature Reserves (NNRs).

The JNCC is the statutory committee through which English Nature, CCW and SNH exercise their joint functions. These include providing advice on amendments to the *Wildlife and Countryside Act 1981* and on the development and implementation of policies that affect nature conservation in Great Britain and internationally; establishing common standards for the monitoring of, and research into, nature conservation; and analysis of the information produced. At the international level, the JNCC provides technical advice to government and others to aid implementation of global and European conservation obligations, for example the Convention on Biological Diversity (see page 275) and the EC Birds and Habitats Directives.

Voluntary organisations are well represented in conservation work. Although they are funded largely by subscription, private donations and entrance fees, many receive government support and grants, sometimes in recognition of statutory responsibilities that they perform.

The *National Trust* (*www.nationaltrust.org.uk*), a charity established in 1895 with nearly 2.9 million members, owns and protects places of historic interest and natural beauty for the benefit of the nation. It cares for around 250,000 hectares of land in England, Wales and Northern Ireland, including forests, fens, moorland, downs, farmland, nature reserves and stretches of coastline. It is responsible for 200 historic houses, 160 gardens, 40,000 ancient monuments and archaeological remains, and 46 villages. Some 2.6 million people visit National Trust 'pay for entry' properties each year and an estimated 50 million visits are made annually to its coasts and countryside properties.

The separate *National Trust for Scotland* (*www.nts.org.uk*) owns 127 properties and 74,000 hectares of countryside. Established in 1931, it is supported by a membership of 250,000 and over 2 million people visit its properties each year.

National Parks, Areas of Outstanding Natural Beauty and National Scenic Areas

National Park status recognises the national importance of the area concerned in terms of landscape, biodiversity and as a recreational resource. However, the name National Park does not signify national ownership: most of the land in National Parks is owned by farmers and other private landowners. Each Park is administered by an independent National Park Authority.

The primary objective of Areas of Outstanding Natural Beauty (AONBs) is the conservation and enhancement of the natural beauty of the landscape, although many of them also fulfil a wider recreational purpose. Designation started in 1956 with the Gower peninsula in Wales, and the most recent addition was the Tamar Valley in Cornwall in 1995. The *Countryside and Rights of Way Act 2000* gave authorities and communities greater powers to improve the conservation of AONBs.

National Parks and AONBs are designated by the Countryside Agency and the CCW, subject to

The history of Britain's National Parks

In the early 20th century a growing appreciation of the outdoors, nature and the open air, and the benefits of physical exercise, led to demands for more access to the countryside. As towns and cities expanded and more land was enclosed, conflict between landowners and public interest groups grew. A conference of recreation, conservation and amenity groups was held in 1935 to discuss how to deal with these issues, and from it emerged the Standing Committees on National Parks (SCNP). Pressure from this forum eventually led to the *National Parks and Access to the Countryside Act 1949*, which allowed for the setting up of National Parks to preserve and enhance natural beauty and to provide recreational opportunities for the public.

The first two National Parks – the Lake District and the Peak District – were designated in 1951, and a further eight followed during the course of the decade. The Norfolk and Suffolk Broads were designated in 1988, and two further parks are in the process of designation in England: the New Forest and the South Downs. The parks are now nationally important recreational resources, attracting approximately 100 million visitors a year.

The Scottish Parliament passed the *National Parks (Scotland) Act* in July 2000, paving the way to establish Scotland's first National Park – Loch Lomond and the Trossachs – which was formally inaugurated in July 2002.

confirmation by the Secretary of State for Environment, Food and Rural Affairs or National Assembly for Wales.

In Northern Ireland the Council for Nature Conservation and the Countryside advises the Government on natural landscapes and the designation of AONBs. In addition to the nine already designated, two more areas – Erne Lakeland and Fermanagh Caveland – have been proposed.

Scotland has four regional parks and 40 National Scenic Areas (NSAs), which together cover around 11,000 square kilometres. The main purpose of NSAs is to give special attention to the best scenery in Scotland when new development is being considered. Certain developments in the areas are subject to consultation with SNH and, in the event of a disagreement, with the Scottish Executive.

Table 19.2 National Parks and other designated areas, 2001

	National Parks			AONBs and NSAs		
	Number	Area (sq km)	% of total area	Number	Area (sq km)	% of total area
England	8	9,936[1]	8[1]	36	20,439	15
England/Wales[2]	.	.	.	1	326	.
Wales	3	4,129	20	4	715	4
Scotland	1	1,865	2	40	10,018	13
Northern Ireland	.	.	.	9	2,849	20

1 Includes area covered by water in the Broads.
2 Cross-border AONB.
Source: CA, CCW, SNH, EHS

Forest and country parks

There are 17 forest parks in Great Britain, covering nearly 3,000 square kilometres, which are administered by the Forestry Commission (see page 406). The Countryside Agency recognises over 200 country parks and more than 250 picnic sites in England. A further 35 country parks in Wales are recognised by the CCW, and there are 36 country parks in Scotland. Northern Ireland has eight forest parks, three forest drives and over 40 minor forest recreation sites. All are administered by the Forest Service, an agency of DARD.

Tree preservation and planting

Tree Preservation Orders enable local authorities to protect trees and woodlands. Once a tree is protected, it is, in general, an offence to cut down or carry out most types of work to it without permission. Courts can impose substantial fines for breaches of such Orders. Replacement trees must be planted where protected trees are felled in contravention of an Order or are removed because they are dying, dead or dangerous.

Tree planting is encouraged through various grant schemes, including the Forestry Commission's Woodland Grant Scheme (see page 406), and the planting of broadleaved trees has greatly increased since the 1980s. Just under 14,000 hectares of new woodland were planted in the UK in 2001/02.

Major afforestation projects involving the Forestry Commission, the Countryside Agency and 58 local authorities include the creation of 12 Community Forests in and around major cities, with a total designated area of 450,000 hectares. These forests help to restore areas scarred by industrial dereliction, create sites for recreation, sport and environmental education, and provide new habitats for wildlife. In 2000/01, about 640 hectares of new woodlands were created in Community Forest areas, bringing the total since 1991 to over 8,000 hectares.

The Welsh Assembly Government has a woodland strategy, which is managed by the Forestry Commission. The strategy focuses on community woodlands, the environmental management of existing woodland, and the contribution that woodlands make to rural, social and economic development.

Other organisations involved in protecting existing woods and planting new areas of woodland include voluntary bodies such as the Woodland Trust, which owns over 1,100 woods across the UK covering 18,300 hectares and, since 1976, has planted over 4 million trees.

Public rights of way and open country

England has about 188,700 km of rights of way,[1] including 146,600 km of footpaths. There are 15 long-distance walking routes in England and Wales, designated as National Trails. Twelve have been fully developed and three are in the process of being completed. There are three Long Distance Routes in Scotland, which fulfil the same function (see map).

About 17 per cent of the rights of way in England may be lawfully used by horseriders and cyclists. The Pennine Bridleway – the first section of which

---

1 Where the general public has legal title to go across someone else's property.

opened in May 2002 – will be the first long-distance trail designed specifically for them.

County, metropolitan and unitary councils in England and Wales (see page 7) are responsible for keeping public rights of way signposted and free from obstruction. Public paths are usually maintained by these 'highway authorities', which also supervise landowners' duties to repair stiles and gates on footpaths. In Scotland planning authorities are responsible for asserting and protecting rights of way. Subject to public consultation (and, if necessary, a public inquiry) local authorities in Great Britain can create paths, close paths no longer needed for public use, and divert paths to meet the needs of either the public or landowners. Farmers in England and Wales are required by law to restore any cross-field public paths damaged or erased by agricultural operations.

Common land in England and Wales totals more than 550,000 hectares. The open character of commons has made them popular for informal recreation although significant areas are still important for agriculture. Four-fifths of common land is privately owned and although only 20 per cent has a legal right of public access, there is also *de facto* access. The CA and the CCW have important roles to play in preparing for the new access rights set out in the *Countryside and Rights of Way Act 2000* (see page 266). For example, the CA is preparing maps of all open country and registered common land in England, and hopes to have conclusive maps completed by 2005.

Commons are largely unimproved and therefore have high amenity and wildlife value; many are protected by law and by nature conservation designations. For example, around half of the common land in England is found within National Parks (see page 270) and a similar amount is designated as Sites of Special Scientific Interest (SSSIs) (see page 274). Ministerial consent is usually required to undertake work on commons or to enclose areas by fencing.

The coast

The UK has 12,429 km of coastline, representing about 30 per cent of the North Sea and Atlantic seaboard of Western Europe. The coastline is very indented and includes 163 estuaries. No location is more than 125 km from tidal waters. About 75 per cent of the European chalk coast is located in the UK.

Local planning authorities are responsible for planning land use at the coast; they also aim to safeguard and enhance the coast's natural attractions and preserve areas of scientific interest. The policy for the protection of the coastline against erosion and flooding is administered by DEFRA and the devolved administrations. Operational responsibility lies with local authorities and, in England and Wales, the Environment Agency.

DEFRA and the Welsh Assembly Government are jointly funding a project which aims to predict how the coastline in England and Wales will be changed by processes such as erosion and landslip. This will help local operating authorities update their shoreline management plans and coastal defence systems and provide information for longer-term decisions on coastal management.

Certain stretches of undeveloped coast of particular beauty in England and Wales are defined as Heritage Coast. There are 45 Heritage Coasts, protecting 1,553 kilometres, about 35 per cent of the total length of coastline (see map).

The National Trust (see page 270), through its Neptune Coastline Campaign, raises funds to acquire and protect stretches of coastline of great natural beauty and recreational value. Around £36 million has been raised since 1965 and the

Regeneration of the Durham coast

After 100 years of waste tipping by the coal industry, the coastline of County Durham was heavily polluted. Mining started in the area in the 1840s, and continued until the last pit closure in 1993. In total, over 40 million tonnes of waste from the mining was tipped on the coast. Of just over 17 kilometres of coast, more than 12 kilometres were affected by spoil.

Through the Turning the Tide programme, the derelict land has been transformed. With £10.5 million funding (including £4.5 million from the Millennium Commission), 1.3 million tonnes of spoil have been removed, and 80 hectares of land regenerated. A footpath and cycle track have been established along the coastline, and over 100 environmental and community programmes have been completed. Thirteen kilometres of the coastline were awarded Heritage Coast status in March 2001.

Trust now protects around 960 kilometres of coastline in England, Wales and Northern Ireland. The National Trust for Scotland cares for more than 400 kilometres of the Scottish coastline and protects other stretches through conservation agreements.

In 1993 English Nature launched its 'Estuaries Initiative' with the objective of securing Estuary Management Plans for 50 per cent by number, and 80 per cent by area, of England's estuaries. That objective has been reached and English Nature will continue to support those partnerships which have been successful.

There are also 29 informal marine consultation areas in Scotland. In addition, SNH has established the Focus on Firths initiative to co-ordinate management of the main Scottish estuaries. In Wales the CCW provides grants to the Arfordir (or Coastal) Group, which is concerned with the sustainable management of the whole coast of Wales.

Wildlife protection

The protection of wildlife is an essential element of the UK Government's sustainable development agenda. DEFRA intends to bring 95 per cent of all nationally important wildlife sites in England into a favourable condition by 2010, compared with the 60 per cent of sites currently estimated to be in that state.

All wild bird species in Great Britain, except for a few pest and quarry species, are protected under the *Wildlife and Countryside Act 1981*. Certain birds may be killed or taken at specific times of year, which are detailed in the Act, or under a licence issued under the Act.

Other species are protected under the 1991 Act by Order of the Secretary of State when in his or her opinion the animal or plant is in danger of extinction or likely to become so endangered unless conservation measures are taken; or when protection is needed to comply with international legislation. Similar provisions apply under the Nature Conservation and Amenity Lands Order in Northern Ireland.

The JNCC is required to review Schedules 5 and 8 (protected animals and plants respectively) of the Act every five years and consult on the level of protection given to plant and animal species. From the review stems advice on which the Secretary of State bases his or her decisions. Following the

third review, carried out in 1997/98, 11 species of animal were given full protection. These included the basking shark – the largest fish in UK waters – the water vole, the marsh fritillary butterfly and the southern damselfly. A total of 17 plant species were given protection, including the flamingo moss, hedgehog fungus and wild bluebell. The fourth review took place in 2001/02, and decisions are expected in early 2003.

Bird populations are good indicators of the state of wildlife in the countryside, since they are widely distributed and are near the top of the food chain. There are concerns about the decline in certain bird species, as modern farming and forestry methods have removed the food supply they need for breeding and surviving the winter. A British Trust for Ornithology (BTO) survey found that populations of 20 of Britain's most common birds have dropped by more than 50 per cent in the last 25 years. However, the annual BTO/JNCC/RSPB Breeding Bird Survey conducted in 2000 found that more species (45) had increased since 1994 than had decreased (18).

DEFRA will provide funding up to 2007 for agri-environment schemes to restore farmland habitats (see page 398). It is also funding a study led by the BTO to investigate the long-term declines of the house sparrow and starling, both of which have declined by more than 50 per cent since the 1970s. The UK Biodiversity Action Plan (see page 275) includes targets to reverse bird population decline.

Figure 19.3 Populations of wild birds, UK

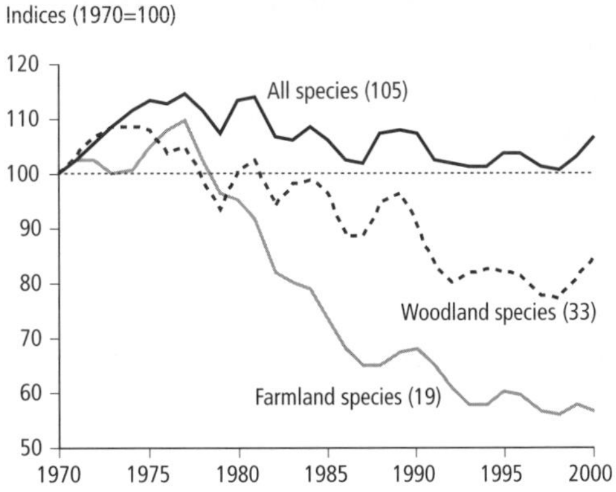

Indices (1970=100)

Source: Royal Society for the Protection of Birds, British Trust for Ornithology and Department for Environment, Food & Rural Affairs

Twenty-five species have been identified for targeting, including the skylark, grey partridge, corn bunting, song thrush and bullfinch.

Wildlife crime

Wildlife crime takes many forms and has been increasing in recent years. Examples include theft of eggs from birds of prey, illegal shooting, trapping, poisoning, digging up of wild plants, and the illicit trade in endangered species. The most significant organised criminal activities involve the trafficking in endangered species and their by-products, and the taking and keeping of species within the UK. The extent of such criminality is unknown, but in 2000 HM Customs and Excise seized 1,783 live animals and made 443 separate seizures of endangered species or their by-products.

DEFRA and the Scottish Executive manage a team of around 100 wildlife inspectors. Their main roles are to verify information submitted in support of applications to keep or trade in wildlife species; and to check that people are complying with the administrative controls contained in certain wildlife legislation. There are also specialist wildlife officers in almost every police force in the UK.

The Partnership for Action Against Wildlife Crime, chaired by the police and DEFRA (*www.defra.gov.uk/paw*), provides a forum for communication and co-operation between the statutory enforcement authorities and non-governmental organisations which have an active interest in wildlife law enforcement.

The UK's first National Wildlife Crime Intelligence Unit was established in April 2002, within the Specialist Intelligence Branch of the National Criminal Intelligence Service. Jointly funded by DEFRA, the Association of Chief Police Officers, the Home Office and the Scottish Executive, it is intended that the Unit will provide law enforcement agencies with the information they need to target and disrupt wildlife crimes and the criminals involved. It will also act as a focal point for the gathering and analysing of intelligence on serious wildlife crime at regional, national and international levels.

Much of UK law in relation to wildlife crime is shaped by international regulations. The Convention on International Trade in Endangered Species (CITES – see page 276) regulates trade in endangered species. It prohibits trade of around 800 species and controls that of a further 23,000, and is implemented in the EU by the European Union Wildlife Trade Regulations. In England and Wales, the *Countryside and Rights of Way Act 2000* introduced stronger measures to combat wildlife crime, including greater powers for police officers and DEFRA wildlife inspectors, and new penalties, including jail sentences of up to six months and fines of up to £5,000. In Scotland, the *Protection of Wild Mammals (Scotland) Act* came into force on 1 August 2002. Among other things, the Act bans hunting with dogs in Scotland (see page 251).

Habitat protection

Habitat protection is mainly achieved through the networks of Sites of Special Scientific Interest (SSSIs) in Great Britain, and Areas of Special Scientific Interest (ASSIs) in Northern Ireland. Sites are protected for their plants, animals or

Table 19.4 Areas in the UK protected for their wildlife, 31 March 2002

Type of site[1]	Number of sites	Area (sq km)
National Nature Reserves	395	2,451
Local Nature Reserves	780	454
Sites of Special Scientific Interest (SSSIs) (Great Britain)	6,565	22,861
Areas of Special Scientific Interest (ASSIs) (Northern Ireland)	196	916
Statutory Marine Nature Reserves	3	213
Areas protected by international agreements		
Candidate Special Areas of Conservation (cSACs)[2]	567	23,590
Special Protection Areas (SPAs)	234	13,116
Ramsar sites	144	7,588

1 Some sites may be included in more than one category.
2 As at December 2001.
Source: Joint Nature Conservation Committee

geological or physiographical features. Some SSSIs and ASSIs are of international importance and have been designated for protection under the EC Wild Birds and Habitats Directives or the Ramsar Convention (see page 276). In England, the Government's target is to bring 95 per cent of SSSIs into favourable condition by 2010. Most SSSIs and ASSIs are privately owned, but about 40 per cent are owned or managed by public bodies such as the Forestry Commission, the Ministry of Defence and the Crown Estate.

English Nature, the CCW and SNH have powers to enter into land management agreements with owners and occupiers of SSSI land, where this is necessary to support the management of their natural features. The CNCC advises on the establishment and management of land and marine nature reserves and the declaration of ASSIs in Northern Ireland. The Northern Ireland Programme for Government includes a commitment to have a policy and legislation framework in place for the protection of ASSIs by July 2003.

The *Countryside and Rights of Way Act 2000* improved the protection and management of SSSIs in England and Wales, by giving enhanced powers to the conservation agencies, including powers to refuse consent for damaging activities. The agencies in England and Wales also have powers to develop management schemes, in consultation with owners and occupiers of SSSIs, and to serve a management notice to require works to be done where necessary. The maximum penalty for deliberate damage to an SSSI is £20,000 in a magistrates' court, with unlimited fines in the Crown Court.

Wildlife Trusts (*www.wildlifetrusts.org*) and the Royal Society for the Protection of Birds (RSPB – *www.rspb.org.uk*) play an important part in protecting wildlife throughout the UK. The Wildlife Trusts have 2,400 nature reserves covering 76,270 hectares. The 47 independent trusts have nearly 400,000 members, and are mainly based in counties in England and Wales, with the whole of Scotland covered by the Scottish Wildlife Trust. The RSPB manages 176 reserves covering 121,082 hectares. It is the largest voluntary wildlife conservation body in Europe, with over 1 million members.

Biodiversity, species recovery and reintroduction

The UK is one of 183 Parties to the Convention on Biological Diversity Treaty, agreed at the Rio Earth

Peat bog preservation

In February 2002 the Government announced an agreement, reached between English Nature and the private company involved, to stop peat extraction at three sites: Wedholme Flow, Thorne Moor and Hatfield Moor. These sites represent about one-third of the total surviving area of lowland peatland in England. Peatlands are unique environments, acidic and low in nutrients, where only specialised wildlife can survive and natural decay can barely take place. Many provide homes to important and unusual species, often in large numbers – over 3,000 species of insect have been found on Thorne Moor alone. All three sites are part of the Natura 2000 network proposed to the European Commission in recognition of their ecological importance under the terms of the Habitats Directive (see page 276).

Summit (see page 268). The Parties have agreed to develop national strategies and programmes for the conservation and sustainable use of biological diversity and to ensure the fair and equitable sharing of benefits from the use of genetic resources. While the prime focus for implementation is at national level, much activity is under way internationally to elaborate the Convention's obligations, share experience and help identify good practice. The next meeting of the Parties will be in 2004.

As part of the UK Biodiversity Action Plan (*www.ukbap.org.uk*), 391 species and 45 habitat action plans have been established and are at various stages of implementation. In addition, over 160 local biodiversity action plans are in preparation or being implemented.

The National Biodiversity Network Trust (*www.searchnbn.net*) is a charity representing 11 voluntary and public organisations. The trust aims to bring together biodiversity information to meet a wide range of conservation, research, educational and public participation needs.

English Nature held its Species Recovery Programme (SRP) tenth anniversary conference in December 2001. The SRP started with attempts to save 13 threatened species of plants and animals – it is now involved with more than 400 species.

The Royal Botanic Gardens at Kew (see page 384) has been successful for many years in the reintroduction of species. Its Millennium Seed Bank in the Wellcome Trust Millennium Building, at Wakehurst Place, West Sussex, holds seeds of 1,312 native UK wild plants and trees – 90 per cent of British plant species. It aims to hold 10 per cent of the world's flowering flora, principally from dryland regions, by 2010 and 20 per cent by 2020. The Royal Botanic Garden Edinburgh (RBGE) (see page 384) promotes conservation programmes for rare plants in Scotland and for coniferous trees worldwide, maintaining genetically diverse populations in cultivation at many sites, as pools for eventual reintroduction to the wild. RBGE's Living Collections consists of 6 per cent of the world's flowering plant species in cultivation and also includes 1,400 threatened plants.

International action

The EC Habitats Directive, adopted in 1992, aims to promote biodiversity through the conservation of natural habitats and wild flora and fauna. It includes a range of measures relating to the conservation and protection of species and habitats; the most stringent obligations relate to the selection, designation and protection of a series of sites, Special Areas of Conservation (SACs). It is envisaged that these sites will make a significant contribution to conserving the 169 habitat types and 623 species identified by the Directive as being most in need of conservation in a European context. In the UK 76 such habitat types have been identified, as have 51 species (four of which are now extinct and a further six occur as vagrants or introductions).

SACs, along with the similar Special Protection Areas (SPAs), set up under the earlier Birds Directive primarily to protect avian species, will form the UK component of the Europe-wide Natura 2000 network.

Advice to the Government on which sites should be SACs or SPAs has been provided by the statutory conservation agencies (see page 269) and co-ordinated by the JNCC. By the end of March 2002, 567 candidate SACs (cSACs), covering 23,590 square kilometres, had been submitted, and 234 SPAs, at 13,116 square kilometres, had been classified.

The UK funds the Darwin Initiative, a small grants programme which uses UK biodiversity expertise to help countries rich in biodiversity, but poor in resources, with the conservation and sustainable

use of their biodiversity. This includes helping them meet their obligations under the Biodiversity Convention.

The UK is also a member of the World Conservation Union and of several international Conventions and Directives, some of which are described below:

■ The IUCN – *the World Conservation Union* – is the largest nature conservation body in the world, having a membership of nearly 1,000 governmental and non-governmental organisations. Its purpose is to influence, encourage and help societies throughout the world to conserve the integrity and diversity of nature and to ensure that any use of natural resources is equitable and ecologically sustainable.

■ The *Convention on Wetlands of International Importance* (the *Ramsar Convention*) (*www.ramsar.org*) is an intergovernmental treaty covering all aspects of wetland conservation and use.

■ *CITES* (*www.cites.org*) regulates trade in endangered species by means of a permit system.

■ The *Convention on the Conservation of Migratory Species of Wild Animals* (the *Bonn Convention*). This convention co-ordinates international action on a range of endangered migratory species.

Land quality, waste, recycling and litter

Land quality

Land quality in the UK is relatively good, but faces pressure from a range of factors, including urbanisation, localised erosion, declining organic content and contamination.

Contaminated land is the legacy of an industrial age that generated wealth but also caused much pollution. The Environment Agency estimates that some 300,000 hectares of land in Great Britain are contaminated to some degree. Government policy emphasises the importance of voluntary action to clean up contaminated land, and most attempts to clean up sites occur when they are redeveloped.

Many of the 391 species identified in the UK Biodiversity Action Plan depend on the right type and quality of soil for their survival, and a good balance of soil types is required to support the existing range of ecosystems, landscapes and agriculture. In 2001 the former Department for the Environment, Transport and the Regions, and Ministry of Agriculture, Fisheries and Food jointly published a draft soil strategy for England promoting the sustainable use of soil and raising public awareness of the importance of soil as part of the environment. The strategy set out five actions:

- to ensure that all policies and programmes which affect soil take into account the strategy's aims and objectives;

- to develop a national set of key soil indicators to help provide assessments of, for example, the extent of soil lost to development;

- to review current soil monitoring and develop a national framework for this activity;

- to examine existing soil research, and recommend ways to improve its co-ordination; and

- to set a five-year goal for evaluating the success of the soil strategy.

Waste management and disposal

The UK produces over 400 million tonnes of waste each year, the majority of which comes from agricultural, industrial and construction sources. However, a considerable amount of waste is produced by households – 89 per cent of an estimated 28.2 million tonnes of municipal waste in England in 2000/01. Commercial activities produce 25 million tonnes of waste a year. Nearly two-thirds of waste from households, commerce and industry is disposed of to landfill, a method which makes little practical use of waste.[2] In the case of municipal waste, 12 per cent was recycled or composted in 2000/01; but the majority, 78 per cent, was disposed of in landfill (see Table 19.5).

The Government's *Waste Strategy 2000 for England and Wales* set out its views on waste and resource management, and the changes needed to make waste management more sustainable during the next 20 years. It requires action by many different organisations – including local authorities, the waste industry and the business sector – and by individuals.

2 Some landfill sites produce gas that is used for energy.

Table 19.5 Management of municipal waste, England, 2000/01

	Thousand tonnes	%
Landfill	22,055	78
Incineration with energy from waste	2,479	9
Refuse-derived fuel manufacture	67	–
Recycled/composted	3,454	12
Other	95	–
Total	**28,150**	**100**

Source: Department for Environment, Food & Rural Affairs

The Recycling Fund is an important part of the Strategy. Councils in England can bid for a share of the £140 million available through the fund from 2002/03 to 2003/04 to help them meet their recycling and composting targets.

The Cabinet Office Performance and Innovation Unit launched a review into waste strategy in January 2002.

By 2005 the Government aims to reduce the amount of UK industrial and commercial waste disposed of in landfill sites to 85 per cent of 1998 levels and, in England, to recycle or compost at least 25 per cent of household waste, increasing to 33 per cent by 2015. Between 1999/2000 and 2000/01 the amount of household waste recycled increased from 10.3 per cent to 11.2 per cent. Meeting these targets would go some way towards meeting the Government's obligation under the EC Landfill Directive, which requires the UK to reduce landfill of biodegradable municipal waste to two-thirds of its 1995 level by 2020.

The landfill tax (see page 357) credit scheme enables landfill site operators in the UK to channel up to 20 per cent of their landfill tax liability into environmental bodies, to be used for approved projects. Examples include reclamation of polluted land, research and education activities to promote re-use and recycling, provision of public parks and amenities, and restoration of historic buildings.

Scotland has its own waste strategy – *the National Waste Strategy: Scotland* – the objectives of which include: ensuring that waste is disposed of without endangering human health and without harming the environment; establishing an integrated and adequate network of waste disposal installations;

encouraging the prevention or reduction of waste production; and encouraging the recovery of waste. Eleven local area plans are to be integrated into a National Waste Plan by autumn 2002.

Northern Ireland has a similar waste management strategy, designed to help achieve sustainable waste management and to meet the targets for diversion away from landfill. The main goal is a reduction of 25 per cent for biodegradable municipal waste going to landfill by 2010, increasing to 50 per cent by 2013 and 75 per cent by 2020 (all set against 1995 levels). A Planning Policy Statement on planning and waste management will be published in 2002.

In June 2002 the Welsh Assembly Government launched *Wise about waste: the national waste strategy for Wales*, which establishes a programme designed to change waste management practice in Wales over the next ten years. It seeks to minimise the production of waste and its impact on the environment, and, where practicable, the use of energy from waste and landfill, while maximising the use of unavoidable waste as a resource. The strategy includes specific targets for public bodies to reduce their waste arisings by 10 per cent from the 1998 level by 2010, and targets for local authorities to have 40 per cent of waste recycled/composted by the same date. Additional funding will be provided by the Assembly Government to local authorities to help meet the recycling and composting targets – a total of £79 million from 2001 to 2004/05.

The EC Directive on Packaging and Packaging Waste stipulates that at least 50 per cent of the UK's packaging waste must be recovered and at least 25 per cent recycled. All packaging must be recoverable through recycling, incineration with energy recovery, composting or biodegradation. By the end of 2000, 42 per cent of packaging waste was recovered and 36 per cent recycled. For 2002, the Government has set a 59 per cent recovery target.

The Waste and Resources Action Programme (WRAP) aims to overcome market barriers to the recovery and recycling of waste – government funding of around £40 million is available to the programme between 2001 and 2004. In Scotland a Strategic Waste Fund has been established to assist local authorities in their implementation of Area Waste Plans. The fund has been allocated £50.4 million over three years (2001–04). Scotland has also allocated £2.1 million to WRAP over this period.

Table 19.6 Recycling levels in the UK: by type of material

	Percentages	
	1990	1998
Paper and board	32	38
Newsprint[1]	26	52
Aluminium cans	5	36
Container glass	15	22
Plastic	–	3

1 Waste paper used in newsprint.
Source: Aluminium Can Recycling Association; British Glass Manufacturers Confederation; British Paper and Board Industry Federation; Paper Federation of Great Britain; British Plastics Federation

Across the UK, banks are available for the public to deposit various waste material for recycling, including bottles, cans, clothes, paper and plastics. In addition, some local authorities provide kerbside collection of recyclable material.

Fridges and freezers
Up to 3 million domestic refrigeration units – fridges, fridge-freezers and freezers – are disposed of in the UK every year. Almost all appliances purchased before 1994 contain Ozone Depleting Substances (ODS – see page 284), used as refrigerants, and these substances are still widely used in blowing agents for the insulation material.

A European Council Regulation came into force in October 2001 which required the removal of ODS from refrigeration equipment before such equipment can be scrapped. At the time, there were no specialised facilities in the UK to carry out this task, leading to concerns about the stockpiling of old fridges before suitable plant could be brought on line. In March 2002 the Environment Agency announced that it would license and regulate suitable ODS processing plant in England and Wales, and by July 2002 five fixed plants were in operation.

Hazardous waste
There is an extensive framework of national and EC legislation on the manufacture, distribution, use and disposal of hazardous chemicals. New and existing chemicals are subject to notification and assessment procedures under EC legislation. Pesticides, biocides and veterinary medicines are subject to mandatory approval procedures.

International movements of hazardous waste are controlled by the Basel Convention on the Control of Transboundary Movements of Hazardous Wastes and their Disposal. The UK is a signatory of the Basel Convention Protocol on Liability and Compensation. Once fully ratified the Protocol requires exporters of hazardous waste to be insured against any damage caused on the journey to the recycler or disposer of that waste.

In Great Britain, the Special Waste Regulations 1996 are the centrepiece of hazardous waste controls. However, since 1996, the Hazardous Waste List that defines the scope of the EC Hazardous Waste Directive has been refined and increased in length. Furthermore, a number of new Directives have been or will be made, which will have an impact on the sector, notably the Hazardous Waste Incineration Directive, the Landfill Directive and the IPC Directive (see page 267).

The Special Waste Regulations were amended in November 2001 to ensure that special wastes are managed from the moment they are produced until they reach their final destination for disposal or recovery.

Litter and dog fouling
It is a criminal offence to leave litter in any public place in the open air or to dump rubbish except in designated places. The maximum fine upon successful prosecution in a magistrates court is up to £20,000 for fly-tipping (illegal dumping of waste) offences. Local authorities can issue £50 Fixed Penalty Notices (FPNs), for litter and dog fouling offences; the maximum fine if FPNs are not paid upon successful prosecution, is £2,500 for littering and £1,000 for dog fouling.

Local authorities have a duty to keep their public land free of litter and refuse, including dog faeces, as far as is practicable. Members of the public have powers to take action against authorities which fail to comply with their responsibilities. In England and Wales local authorities may also make it an offence not to clear up after one's dog in a public place, and issue a fixed penalty fine of £25 under the *Dogs (Fouling of Land) Act 1996*. In Scotland it is an offence to allow a dog to foul in specified places under the *Civic Government (Scotland) Act 1982*.

ENCAMS (*www.encams.org*), formerly the Tidy Britain Group, is the national agency for litter

abatement, working in collaboration with local authorities and the private sector. In 2001 it launched a continuous survey of local environmental quality in England. Conditions being monitored include cleanliness, graffiti, and physical obstructions.

The environment agencies, local authorities, police and ENCAMS have been monitoring the incidence of fly-tipping since the introduction of the landfill tax, and such activity has increased since 1994/95. If indicted to the Crown Court, the maximum penalty for fly-tipping (and other offences relating to waste) is up to five years' imprisonment and/or an unlimited fine.

Buildings and monuments
In England, lists of buildings of special architectural or historic interest are compiled by the Department for Culture, Media and Sport (DCMS) with advice from English Heritage. In Scotland and Wales, buildings are listed by Historic Scotland and Cadw respectively. In Northern Ireland, the EHS has responsibility for listed buildings, following consultation with the advisory Historic Buildings Council (HBC) and the relevant local district council.

It is against the law to demolish, extend or alter the character of any listed building without prior consent from the local planning authority, or the DOE in Northern Ireland, or – on appeal or following call-in – the appropriate government minister. A local planning authority can issue a 'building preservation notice' to protect for six months an unlisted building which it considers to be of special architectural or historic interest and which is at risk, while a decision is taken on whether it should be listed.

There are around 1 million archaeological sites or 'find spots' of all types currently recorded in England. English Heritage assesses known archaeological sites in England in order to identify those that should be afforded statutory protection. It makes its recommendations to the DCMS, which maintains the schedule of ancient monuments. The schedule now has about 19,300 entries (about 35,400 sites). Similar arrangements exist to identify buildings and ancient and historic monuments eligible for statutory protection in Scotland and Wales. In Northern Ireland the EHS assesses all known archaeological sites in order to identify those sites which should be afforded statutory protection. It then makes

Table 19.7 Listed buildings and scheduled monuments, May 2002

	Listed buildings	Scheduled monuments
England	443,000	19,281
Wales	26,762	3,422
Scotland[1]	46,025	7,506
Northern Ireland	8,000	1,525

1 As at 16 August 2002.
Source: Department for Culture, Media and Sport, Cadw: Welsh Historic Monuments, Scottish Executive and EHS

recommendations to the Historic Monuments Council (HMC) and maintains the schedule.

English Heritage is directly responsible for the maintenance, repair and presentation of 409 historic properties in public ownership or guardianship, and gives grants for the repair of other important ancient monuments and historic buildings. In 2001/02 it gave out £27 million in grant aid. Most of English Heritage's properties are open to the public, and there were nearly 5.5 million visits to staffed properties in 2001/02. Its *Images of England* project will provide access via the Internet to one of the largest digital libraries in the world, containing pictures of England's 370,000 listed historic buildings. Government funding for English Heritage in 2002/03 is £115.4 million.

In Scotland and Wales, Historic Scotland, which cares for over 330 monuments, and Cadw, with 127 monuments, perform similar functions. There were nearly 3 million visitors to Historic Scotland's properties where admission is charged in 2000/01 and 1.1 million to Cadw properties in 2000. The DOE in Northern Ireland has 189 historic monuments in its care, managed by the EHS.

Local planning authorities have designated more than 9,000 conservation areas of special architectural or historic interest in England and there are 504 in Wales, 602 in Scotland and 58 in Northern Ireland. These areas receive additional protection through the planning system, particularly over the proposed demolition of unlisted buildings.

The National Heritage Memorial Fund (NHMF) helps towards the cost of acquiring, maintaining or preserving land, buildings, objects and collections that are of outstanding interest and of importance to the national heritage. In addition, its trustees are responsible for distributing the heritage share of the proceeds from the National Lottery (see page 263). The first requests for lottery money were received in 1995 and, by July 2002, more than £2.0 billion had been awarded from the Heritage Lottery Fund in more than 9,350 capital and revenue grants.

Many of the royal palaces and all the royal parks are open to the public; their maintenance is the responsibility of the DCMS and Historic Scotland. Historic Royal Palaces, the Royal Household and the Royal Parks Agency carry out this function on behalf of the Secretary of State in England.

Industrial, transport and maritime heritage

As the first country in the world to industrialise on a large scale, the UK has a rich industrial heritage, including such sites as the Ironbridge Gorge (now a World Heritage site – see below), where Abraham Darby (1677–1717) first smelted iron using coke instead of charcoal.

Several industrial monuments in Scotland are in the care of the First Minister, including Bonawe Iron Furnace, the most complete charcoal-fuelled ironworks surviving in Britain; the working New Abbey Corn Mill; and Dallas Dhu Malt Whisky Distillery.

The UK pioneered railways, and has a fine heritage of railway buildings and structures. A large number of disused railway lines have been bought by railway preservation societies, and there are several railway museums.

A voluntary body, the Maritime Trust, preserves vessels and other maritime items of historic or technical interest. In all, about 400 historic ships are preserved in the UK, mostly in private hands. The *National Heritage Act 2002* extended English Heritage's remit to include securing the preservation and increasing the understanding of archaeological sites of all types in the marine zone.

World Heritage sites

The World Heritage List was established under the United Nations Educational, Scientific and Cultural Organisation's 1972 World Heritage Convention in order to identify and secure lasting protection for sites of outstanding universal value (*www.unesco.org/whc*). The UK currently has 24

World Heritage sites (see map), including three in Overseas Territories – St George in Bermuda, Henderson Island and Gough Island wildlife reserve. Four sites were inscribed by the World Heritage committee in 2001. The Dorset and East Devon Coast is an area of both natural beauty and scientific interest, while Derwent Valley Mills, New Lanark and Saltaire date from the Industrial Revolution, when they were developed as textile communities.

Air and the atmosphere

Air quality

Air quality has improved considerably since the smogs of the 1950s. The first step towards these improvements was the introduction of the *Clean Air Act* in 1956, which controlled smoke from industrial and domestic coal burning, a major source of pollution at the time. Since then, the replacement of coal by natural gas and electricity for domestic heating, tighter regulation and structural changes in industry, and the introduction of progressively more stringent standards for vehicle exhaust emissions, have all led to considerable improvements in air quality. For example, in 1970, 8.9 million tonnes of carbon monoxide (CO) and 6.5 million tonnes of sulphur dioxide (SO_2) were emitted into the air in the UK. By 2000 these emissions had fallen to 4.2 million and 1.2 million tonnes respectively.

Industrial processes with the potential for producing pollutants are subject to regulation under IPC and IPPC (see page 267). Processes with a significant but lesser potential for air pollution require approval, in England and Wales from local authorities, in Scotland from SEPA and in Northern Ireland from the Chief Pollution Inspector or relevant district council, depending on the process. Local authorities also control emissions of dark smoke from commercial and industrial premises, and implement smoke control areas to deal with emissions from domestic properties.

Under the provisions of the *Environment Act 1995*, the Government is required to publish an Air Quality Strategy setting out its policies for managing ambient air quality in the UK, particularly in relation to reducing air pollution and any remaining risks to people's health and the natural and built environment. The current strategy contains air quality standards and

objectives for eight pollutants of particular concern to human health: nitrogen dioxide, PM_{10} (particulate matter that is less than 10 microns in diameter), SO_2, CO, ozone, lead, benzene and 1,3-butadiene. Dates for achieving the various objectives across the UK have been set between 2003 and 2008.

In September 2001 DEFRA and the devolved administrations published a consultation paper which included proposals for tighter objectives for benzene, CO and PM_{10}, and a new objective for polycyclic aromatic hydrocarbons. These were the same throughout the UK except for PM_{10}, where a tougher objective was proposed for Scotland than elsewhere, because air quality there is generally better. Conversely, a less stringent objective was proposed for London. The new objectives came into force in Scotland in June 2002 through the Air Quality (Scotland) Amendment Regulations 2002, and separate arrangements for the rest of the UK will come into effect in due course.

The UK has an automatic air quality monitoring network with 122 sites covering much of the country, in both urban and rural areas. A number of new sites have been established in recent years, mainly in urban areas to provide more comprehensive coverage of air quality in UK towns and cities.

In the UK in 2001 there was an average of 21 days per site in urban areas when air pollution was recorded as moderate or higher, compared with 16 days in 2000 and 28 days in 1999. The main causes of moderate or higher air pollution at urban sites are ground level ozone, PM_{10} and SO_2. Ground level ozone is formed from chemical reactions of other pollutants such as nitrogen oxides (NO_x) and volatile organic compounds (VOCs). Pollution caused by PM_{10} and SO_2 has fallen significantly since 1993, so that ozone is now the principal cause of these criteria being exceeded in urban areas. In rural areas, air pollution was recorded as moderate or higher on 30 days on average per site in 2001 compared with 25 days in 2000. This series can be volatile from year to year, and there is no clear trend. This reflects variability in levels of ozone, which is overwhelmingly the main pollutant in rural areas.

Air Quality Bulletins provide the public with hourly updates of air pollution data from the national monitoring network. These give the concentrations of the main pollutants, together with an air pollution forecast. The information features on television and radio weather reports, and appears in many national and local newspapers. Information can also be accessed through the UK's Air Quality Archive website (*www.airquality.co.uk*).

Vehicle emissions

Measures to reduce pollution from road transport are seen as vital to achieving the objectives set out in the UK Air Quality Strategy. Progressively tighter standards for fuels and vehicle emissions mean that urban road transport emissions of CO, NO_x and particulates are projected to fall by around 70 per cent between 1995 and 2015.

Vehicle emissions standards are governed by a series of EC Directives enforced in the UK under the Motor Vehicles Construction and Use and Type Approval Regulations. All new petrol-engined passenger cars in the UK are fitted with catalytic converters, which typically reduce emissions by over 75 per cent. These measures to reduce vehicle emissions from new vehicles have been accompanied by improvements in fuel quality with, for instance, reductions in components such as benzene and sulphur, which have an environmental impact, and the phasing out of leaded petrol. People in the UK who own vehicles registered after February 2001 pay vehicle excise duty according to the amount of carbon dioxide (CO_2) their car produces and the type of fuel it uses (see page 356).

Compulsory testing of emissions from vehicles is a key element in the UK's strategy for improving air quality. Metered emission tests and smoke checks feature in the annual 'MoT' roadworthiness test. Enforcement checks carried out at the roadside or at operators' premises also include a check for excessive smoke. The Vehicle Inspectorate (see page 314) carried out 90,345 roadside emissions checks in 2001/02 (on cars, coaches, goods vehicles, buses and taxis), and 4,063 vehicles failed. The equivalent figures for 2000/01 were 85,300 and 3,482 respectively. Local councils in England and Wales which have designated air quality management areas have the power to enforce vehicle exhaust emissions standards, by roadside testing, in those areas. The Scottish Executive will introduce similar powers, available to all Scottish local authorities, by the end of 2002, and the Welsh Assembly Government is consulting on extending them to local authorities in Wales.

Climate change

Several gases naturally present in the atmosphere keep the Earth at a temperature suitable for life by trapping energy from the Sun – the 'greenhouse' effect. However, emissions from human activities are increasing the atmospheric concentrations of several greenhouse gases, causing global warming and climate change. Globally the temperature rose by about 0.6°C during the 20th century. In England, four of the five warmest years since records began in 1659 occurred in the 1990s, with 1990 and 1999 being the joint warmest years ever. Research at the Hadley Centre, part of the Met Office, is focused on improving climate predictions and investigating the causes of recent climate change. Results from its latest climate model suggest that, with the current levels of increase in greenhouse gases, the global mean sea level will rise by between 9 and 88 cm by 2100 and there will be a rise in average global temperature of up to 6°C over the next 100 years.

Possible impacts of climate change in the UK could include a rise in average temperatures of about 3°C by 2100 and an increase in rainfall of up to 10 per cent over England and Wales and 20 per cent over Scotland by the 2080s. Models suggest that autumns and winters will get wetter, and spring and summer rainfall patterns will change making the north-west of England wetter and the south-east drier.

The most significant greenhouse gas emitted by the UK is CO_2, followed by methane (CH_4) and nitrous oxide (N_2O). Although still comparatively low, there has been an increase in emissions of hydrofluorocarbons (HFCs), which have a high global warming potential, as consumption grew in response to the phasing out of ozone-depleting substances under the Montreal Protocol (see page 284). HFCs were virtually unused before 1990, but their emissions accounted for nearly 3 per cent of total UK greenhouse gas emissions in 1998 and then fell to about 1.4 per cent in 2000 in response to pollution control regulations.

Control of global and regional air pollution requires international co-operation and action. The first international action dealing with climate change dates from the Rio Earth Summit (see page 268), at which the UN Framework Convention on Climate Change (UNFCCC) was adopted, calling for the stabilisation of greenhouse gas concentrations in the atmosphere at a level that would prevent dangerous man-made interference with the climate system. At the third Conference of the Parties to the Framework Convention, held in Kyoto in 1997, richer countries established a Protocol agreeing legally binding targets to reduce emissions of the basket of six main greenhouse gases: CO_2, methane, N_2O, HFCs, perfluorocarbons (PFCs) and sulphur hexafluoride. The Protocol committed developed nations to a 5.2 per cent reduction in greenhouse gas emissions below 1990 levels by 2008–12. The European Union agreed to a collective reduction target of 8 per cent. At a subsequent meeting in June 1998, the Member States agreed to share out the EU's target to reflect national circumstances. Individual countries' targets range from a reduction of 28 per cent for Luxembourg to a permitted increase of 27 per cent for Portugal. The UK, along with its EU partners, ratified the Kyoto Protocol on 31 May 2002.

Beddington Zero Energy Development, south London

The BedZED housing development in Sutton, Surrey (*www.bedzed.org.uk*), (see also page 303), is one of the first developments in the UK to incorporate thinking on sustainable development into every aspect of construction. The development is designed to use energy from renewable sources generated on site, and aims to be the first large-scale 'carbon neutral' community – in other words it will not add additional carbon to the atmosphere.

Constructed on a former sewage works, features of BedZED include:

- selection of building materials from natural, renewable or recycled sources wherever possible;

- a combined heat and power unit to produce all the development's heat and electricity from tree waste (which would otherwise have gone to landfill);

- energy efficient designs for all buildings; and

- a water strategy, making the most of rain and recycled water, which enables mains consumption to be cut by a third.

---

3 Emissions of non-carbon based gases are weighted for global warming potential.

Figure 19.8 Emissions of greenhouse gases, UK

Million tonnes carbon equivalent

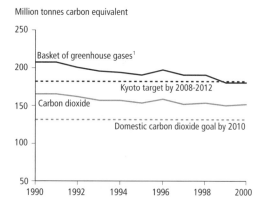

1 Emissions of the basket of greenhouse gases (CO_2, CH_4, N_2O, HFCs, PFCs, SF_6) are presented based on their global warming potential.
Source: NETCEN

The UK is on course to meet its legally binding target, a reduction of 12.5 per cent by 2008–12. Emissions of the basket of greenhouse gases, weighted by global warming potential, fell by 13.2 per cent between the 1990 base year (when the UK emitted 159 million tonnes of carbon as CO_2, 21 million tonnes of carbon equivalent[3] of methane and 19 million tonnes of carbon equivalent of N_2O) and 2000. However, provisional figures suggest that emissions of CO_2, the main greenhouse gas, increased by about 1.5 per cent between 2000 and 2001. This was mainly due to increased use of coal in power stations because of higher gas prices during late 2000 and 2001.

In July 2001 the UK attended the second part of the sixth Conference of the Parties to the UNFCCC in Bonn to discuss the details of the Kyoto Protocol. Among the issues agreed were extra funding for poorer countries for climate-change-related activities, rules on how to make the Protocol workable, and tighter targets for countries that fail to meet their emission reduction targets. Further talks in Marrakesh in November 2001 produced agreement on a text which, following the political agreement in Bonn, provides a legal framework for the Protocol.

The Government and the devolved administrations published *Climate Change: The UK Programme* in 2000. It sets out how they intend to meet the UK's legally binding Kyoto target and move towards a domestic goal of a 20 per cent cut in CO_2 emissions by 2010. The programme also seeks to move the UK towards a more sustainable, lower carbon economy, ensuring that all sectors of the economy and all parts of the UK play their part.

The integrated package of policies and measures contained in the programme includes the climate change levy, which applies to sales of electricity, coal, natural gas and liquefied petroleum gas to the non-domestic sector (see page 434). It aims to encourage business energy efficiency and is expected to prevent at least 5 million tonnes of carbon emissions by 2010. The package includes:

- extra money for improving business use of energy;

- emissions trading (see box);

- reform of the building regulations;

- EU-level voluntary agreements with manufacturers to increase fuel efficiency in vehicles;

- a target to deliver 10 per cent of the UK's electricity from renewable sources of energy by 2010; and

- the promotion of energy efficiency in the domestic sector.

The programme also looks at what the UK may need to do to adapt to the effects of climate change.

As part of its contribution to ocean climate monitoring, the UK has commissioned research to assess the rapid collapse of the western Antarctic ice sheet. The Government has also funded an instrument to provide highly accurate temperature readings for the sea surface, one of ten in the ENVISAT environmental monitoring satellite, which was launched in March 2002.

The ozone layer

Stratospheric ozone is a layer of gas, about 10 to 50 kilometres above the Earth's surface, that protects it from the more harmful effects of solar radiation. British scientists first discovered ozone losses over much of the globe, including a 'hole' in the ozone layer over Antarctica, in 1985. This 'hole' has been growing steadily and its edges now reach

Emissions trading

Emissions trading schemes are designed to allow businesses to reduce their emissions of greenhouse gases in the most economically efficient way.

The UK scheme is the world's first economy-wide greenhouse gas trading scheme. It works by giving individual companies and installations a cap, which when added together form an overall emissions cap for the trading scheme. As long as the aggregate target is achieved, the individual emission contributions do not matter. Participating companies can either meet their individual target by reducing their own emissions; reduce their emissions below their target and sell or bank the excess 'emissions allowances'; or let their emissions remain above target, and buy emissions allowances from other participants. Across the whole scheme those with low-cost emission reduction opportunities will tend to sell allowances to those with higher cost options, thereby minimising the overall cost of delivering a set of environmental benefits.

Thirty-four organisations, including some of the largest businesses, have joined the UK scheme, which started in April 2002. Over the five years of the scheme, the companies have agreed to cut their greenhouse gas emissions by more than 12 million tonnes of CO_2. This represents over 5 per cent of the planned reduction in the UK's annual emissions by 2010.

beyond the Antarctic continent to the tip of South America. Similar, but less dramatic, thinning of the ozone layer occurs over the North Pole each year as well. Ozone depletion is caused by man-made chemicals containing chlorine or bromine, such as chlorofluorocarbons (CFCs), hydrochlorofluorocarbons (HCFCs) and halons. These chemicals have been used in aerosol sprays, refrigerators and fire extinguishers.

In an effort to repair this damage, over 170 countries have ratified the Montreal Protocol, an international treaty for the protection of the stratospheric ozone layer. This is enforced in the UK by an EC Regulation.

Acid rain

The pollutant gases SO_2 (mainly from power stations), NO_x (from road transport and power stations) and ammonia (NH_3 – mainly from livestock) can be carried over long distances before

Table 19.9 Emissions of SO_2, NO_x and VOCs, UK

Thousand tonnes

	Emissions in 1990	Emissions in 2000
Sulphur dioxide	3,721	1,165
of which: from Large Combustion Plants (LCPs)	2,930	899
Nitrogen oxides	2,763	1,512
of which: from LCPs	846	341
Volatile Organic Compounds	2,508	1,498[1]
PM_{10}	313	172[2]

1 Excludes emissions from 'natural' sources i.e. forests.
2 Excludes resuspension.
Source: Department for Environment, Food & Rural Affairs

being deposited directly on to vegetation and soil or being washed out as acid rain. Acidification results when sensitive ecosystems are not capable of neutralising the deposited acidity. In the UK, the ecosystems that are most sensitive to acidification are located in the northern and western uplands. The damaging effects of high levels of acid deposition on soils, freshwater, trees, and buildings, have been demonstrated by scientific research.

The National Expert Group on Transboundary Air Pollution advises the Government and devolved administrations on biological and chemical trends in the UK environment and the prospects for ecosystem recovery as a result of current and projected transboundary air pollution. In 2001 it published its draft report for comment, *Transboundary Air Pollution: Acidification, Eutrophication and Ground Level Ozone in the UK.*

The UK is a party to the UNECE (United Nations Economic Commission for Europe) Convention on Long Range Transboundary Air Pollution, which was set up in 1979 in response to evidence that acidification of lakes in Scandinavia was linked to emissions of SO_2 from other countries in Europe, including the UK. Under the Convention, there have been a number of protocols to reduce emissions of acidifying pollutants. The latest Gothenburg Protocol, signed in December 1999, tackles the three environmental problems of acidification, eutrophication[4] and ground-level

ozone (summer smog). Under the Protocol, the UK agreed annual emission ceilings of 625 kilotonnes for SO_2, 1,181 kilotonnes for NO_x and 297 kilotonnes for NH_3, to be achieved by 2010. By comparison, UK emissions in 2000 were 1,165 kilotonnes for SO_2, 1,512 kilotonnes for NO_x, and 297[5] kilotonnes for NH_3 (see Table 19.9). The Protocol also sets a ceiling of 1,200 kilotonnes for VOCs (for example, solvents used in industry, domestic products, dry cleaning, paints and fumes at petrol pumps). VOCs contribute to the formation of ground-level ozone, and in 2000 the UK emitted 1,498 kilotonnes of these compounds.

Running in parallel with the UNECE Gothenburg Protocol is the EC National Emission Ceilings Directive (NECD), provisionally agreed in June 2001, which is intended to tackle the harmful effects to human health and the environment from transboundary air pollution. The NECD sets ceilings for 2010 for the same four pollutants. The figures negotiated commit the UK to further cuts in SO_2 and NO_x emissions, reducing the ceilings to 585 kilotonnes and 1,167 kilotonnes respectively.

Noise

Noise, whether from the house next door or from aircraft flying overhead, can seriously affect people's quality of life. DEFRA is responsible for the co-ordination and development of policies and the promotion of initiatives to address the problem of noise in England. The Welsh Assembly Government, Scottish Executive and the DOE in Northern Ireland have equivalent responsibilities.

Local authorities have a duty to inspect their areas for 'statutory nuisances', including noise nuisance from premises and vehicles, machinery or equipment in the street. They must take reasonable steps to investigate complaints, and serve a noise abatement notice where it is judged to be a statutory nuisance. There are specific provisions in law to control noise from construction and demolition sites, to control the use of loudspeakers in the streets and to enable individuals to take independent action through the courts against noise nuisance.

The Chartered Institute of Environmental Health found that there were just over 118,000 neighbour noise incidents reported in 2000/01 in England and Wales, by far the largest category of

4 The process by which pollution from sewage or fertilisers stimulates excessive growth of algae. Death and decomposition of the algae depletes the oxygen content of the water, resulting in the death of fish and other animals.

5 Excluding emissions classified under 'Nature'.

noise complaints received by councils. Almost half of the complaints substantiated were dealt with informally. The Government completed a consultation on a proposed national ambient noise strategy in spring 2002. The strategy will include mapping the main sources and areas of noise to enable policy to take better account of the implications of noise sources for rural areas. The first stage is expected to be completed by 2004, and £13 million has been allocated for this.

The Noise Incidence Survey (NIS) and the Noise Attitude Survey (NAS) are undertaken by DEFRA to establish a baseline for, and monitor changes in, the noise climate in Britain. They were conducted nationally in 2000/01 and 1999/2000 respectively, following up similar surveys in 1990 and 1991.

The NIS generates objective assessments of the pattern of the noise exposure of the population. It found that over the last decade changes in outdoor noise level and exposure to noise have been small. Typical outdoor sound levels during the day decreased between 1990 and 2000, while there has been a slight worsening of levels during the night.

The NAS found that 21 per cent of respondents reported that noise spoilt their home life to some extent. Road traffic noise could be heard by 84 per cent, and 40 per cent were bothered, annoyed or disturbed by it to some extent. The proportion of respondents who reported being adversely affected by noise from neighbours has increased over the last ten years. The survey found that 81 per cent of respondents heard noise from neighbours and/or other people nearby and 37 per cent were bothered, annoyed or disturbed to some extent. However, 69 per cent reported general satisfaction with their noise environment.

Compensation may be payable for loss in property values caused by physical factors, including noise from new or improved public works such as roads, railways and airports. Highway authorities (in Scotland, local road authorities and the Scottish Executive, in Wales the Assembly Government and local authorities, and in Northern Ireland, DARD's road service) are required to make grants available for the insulation of homes when they are subject to specified levels of increased noise caused by new or improved roads. Equivalent regulations exist for railways.

The Department for Transport is to carry out a major study to reassess attitudes to aircraft noise, and will ensure that both environmental and aviation interests can contribute to the oversight of the project.

Radioactivity

Man-made radiation represents about 15 per cent of the total exposure to ionising radiation of the UK population – most radiation occurs naturally (for example from the radon gas given off by some rock formations, particularly granite). A large proportion of the exposure to man-made radiation comes from medical sources, such as X-rays. This and other man-made radiation is subject to stringent control. Users of radioactive materials must be registered by the Environment Agency, SEPA or the Chief Radiochemical Inspector in Northern Ireland as appropriate. The Health and Safety Executive (HSE – see page 137) is responsible for regulating safety at civil nuclear installations. The National Radiological Protection Board (NRPB) advises on health risks posed by radiation and how to guard against them.

Radioactive waste management

All solid radioactive waste in the UK is either disposed of in suitable facilities on land or safely stored pending the adoption of a final management strategy. The Government and devolved administrations started a major programme of consultation and research, *Managing radioactive waste safely*, in 2001, which aims to arrive at such a strategy. Radioactive wastes vary widely in nature and level of activity, and the methods of management reflect this. Most solid waste – of low radioactivity – is disposed of at the shallow disposal facility at Drigg in Cumbria. Some small quantities of very low-level waste are disposed of at authorised landfill sites. Some intermediate-level waste is stored at nuclear licensed sites, usually those sites where it is generated, but most of the UK's inventory is at Sellafield in Cumbria. High-level or heat-generating waste is stored in either raw (liquid) or vitrified (glass-like) form. Once vitrified it will be stored for at least 50 years to allow it to cool to a safe temperature for final management.

International commitments

An EC Directive lays down basic standards for the protection of the health of workers and the general public against the dangers arising from ionising radiation. The provisions of the Directive are implemented in the UK through a number of Acts including the *Radioactive Substances Act 1993*. The UK is also a Contracting Party to the International Joint Convention on the Safety of Spent Fuel Management and on the Safety of Radioactive Waste Management.

The contracting parties to the Oslo and Paris Convention on the Protection of the Marine Environment of the North East Atlantic (OSPAR), including the UK, have agreed to reduce radioactive discharges to the North East Atlantic so that by 2020 concentrations of radioactive substances in the marine environment would be almost reduced to historic levels.

In July 2002 the Government and the devolved administrations published the *UK Radioactive Discharge Strategy 2001–2002*, which set out how the UK will implement OSPAR. The Government is also consulting on new statutory guidance to the Environment Agency on the regulation of radioactive discharges from licensed nuclear sites in England. Similar arrangements will apply in other parts of the UK.

Water

Freshwater environment

Freshwater habitats in the UK include rivers, lakes and ponds, and wetlands such as fens, bogs and reedbeds. Many invertebrates and all amphibians native to the UK are dependent on fresh waters, and there are 38 native species of freshwater fish. In addition, a large number of bird species, and two 'rare or threatened' mammals, the otter and water vole, depend on aquatic habitats.

Despite the high rainfall in the UK, there are limited natural and man-made capacities for storage, and the country's high population density means there is relatively little water per person. Available resources of water include rivers, reservoirs and underground aquifers, but these must be carefully managed. The Environment Agency's strategy for water resource management considers both environmental and socio-economic factors (see chapter 28).

Marine environment

The seas around the UK support a wide variety of plants and animals, and are a source of both food and fuel. However, marine life and the food chain can be put at risk by pollution and overfishing.

DEFRA and the devolved administrations have responsibility for protecting the UK's seas and coastal waters. In May 2002 DEFRA published *Safeguarding Our Seas* – the first marine stewardship report, which set out the Government's strategy for the conservation and sustainable development of the marine environment.

Government policy is not to permit any deposit of waste in the sea when there is a safe land-based alternative, unless it can be demonstrated that disposal at sea is the best practicable option. Disposal of sewage sludge at sea ceased at the end of 1998. The only types of waste that are now routinely considered for deposit in the sea are dredged material from ports and harbours, and small quantities of fish waste.

Through the OSPAR Convention the UK and other contracting parties have put in place strategies which aim to promote diversity and tackle the threats posed to the marine environment by hazardous substances, eutrophication and offshore industries.

Decisions about which areas of the UK Continental Shelf should be made available for petroleum licensing take account of advice from the JNCC. Where areas are made available for exploration and development, special conditions may be imposed on the licence holders to minimise or avoid any impact on the marine environment. These conditions are agreed with the JNCC.

The Maritime and Coastguard Agency (see page 324) is responsible for dealing with spillages of oil or other hazardous substances from ships at sea. The various counter-pollution facilities for which it is responsible include remote-sensing surveillance aircraft; aerial and seaborne spraying equipment; stocks of oil dispersants; mechanical recovery and cargo transfer equipment; and specialised beach cleaning equipment. The Agency has an Enforcement Unit at its headquarters in Southampton for apprehending ships making illegal discharges of oil and other pollutants off the British coast. The maximum fine for pollution from ships is £250,000 in cases heard in magistrates' courts.

Water quality

In the UK, about 96 per cent of the population live in properties connected to a sewer, and the waste water from the majority of these properties is given secondary treatment[6] or better. Continued investment in the sewerage system and improving sewage treatment standards will be made up to 2005, and is expected to deliver:

- greater compliance with the EC Bathing Waters Directive;

- at least secondary treatment for all significant discharges from sewage treatment works;

- improved compliance with river quality objectives; and

- improvements to almost 4,700 Combined Sewer Overflows (CSOs) that are currently regarded as unsatisfactory due to their environmental impact.

Water quality in England and Wales has continued to show steady improvement in recent years.

Scottish ministers published a consultation paper in June 2001, entitled *Rivers, Lochs, Coasts: the Future for Scotland's Waters*, which contains proposals for a new approach to the sustainable management of the natural water environment in Scotland and for implementing the EC Water Framework Directive. A second consultation paper, *The future for Scotland's waters, proposals for legislation*, followed in February 2002. Primary legislation to implement the Directive was introduced in the Scottish Parliament in June 2002.

In November 2000 the Government published a draft Water Bill which includes measures to improve customer protection, by setting up an independent consumer council; improvements to water conservation and drought planning; and improvements to the water abstraction licensing system in England and Wales. For details on the water supply industry and the Drinking Water Inspectorate, see page 447.

---

6 The preliminary treatment of sewage involves screening to remove rags, grit and other solids. Primary treatment involves a physical and/or chemically enhanced settlement of suspended solids not removed by preliminary treatment. Secondary treatment involves 'biological' treatment – using bacteria to break down the biodegradable matter in waste water.

Table 19.10 Rivers[1] of good or fair chemical water quality[2]

Percentage of total river lengths

	1990[3]	2000
England	83	94
Wales	98	99
Northern Ireland	95	96
Scotland[4]	96	96

1 Excludes tidal rivers in England and Wales.
2 Figures are three-year averages ending in the year shown.
3 1991 in Northern Ireland.
4 Owing to different methodologies, figures from Scotland are not directly comparable with the rest of the UK.
Source: Department for Environment, Food & Rural Affairs

Discharges to inland waters, coastal waters and groundwaters

All discharges to water in the UK are regulated. In England and Wales the Environment Agency controls water pollution by issuing legally binding documents, known as consents, for all effluent discharges into controlled waters (groundwaters, inland and coastal waters). The effluent quality is monitored against the conditions set within the consents. The Agency maintains public registers containing information about water quality, performance and compliance, consents, authorisations and monitoring. Trade effluent discharges to the public sewers are controlled by the water companies.

In Scotland, controlling water pollution is the responsibility of SEPA; appeals are dealt with by the Scottish Executive and trade effluent discharges to the public sewer are controlled by Scottish Water.

In Northern Ireland, the EHS is responsible for controlling water pollution. In 2001 a cost recovery scheme of application fees in respect of all discharges to waterways and underground strata was introduced. In addition, from 2002/03, annual charges are payable by those industries that discharge effluent to waterways and underground strata that are subject to compliance sampling by the EHS.

In 2000, the Environment Agency responded to 47,840 reports of environmental pollution in England and Wales; 36,406 were substantiated. The number of category 1 (the most significant) incidents fell to 77 in 2000, the lowest number since records began in 1997. In 2000/01, SEPA substantiated 2,345 routine water pollution incidents in Scotland; the DOE responded to 2,582 reports in Northern Ireland, of which 1,701 were substantiated.

Under the 1999 Groundwater Regulations, certain listed dangerous substances may only be disposed of to land following prior investigation and authorisation. An authorisation will not be granted if the investigation reveals that List I substances could enter, or List II substances could pollute, groundwater. The regulations also give the Environment Agency (in England and Wales) and SEPA (in Scotland) powers to stop activities which might cause groundwater pollution.

One of the major causes of water pollution is oil leaking from storage tanks. The Control of Pollution (Oil Storage) (England) Regulations 2001 require commercial and industrial oil stores to have secondary containment, such as a 'bund' (surrounding wall) or a drip tray.

Diffuse pollution from agriculture
Agricultural nutrients, pesticides, microbes from livestock manure, and soil erosion from agricultural land all cause water pollution. In England, the Government is conducting a review to identify cost effective measures to tackle such problems.

One aspect of this wider problem is nitrate pollution arising from the application of inorganic fertiliser and manure on farmland. The designation of Nitrate Vulnerable Zones (NVZs), under the EC Nitrates Directive, is intended to reduce or prevent this pollution. An area is designated as an NVZ when the nitrate concentrations in its ground or surface water exceed or are likely to exceed 50 mg/litre. Sixty-eight NVZs were designated in England and Wales in 1996, and a further two in Scotland and three in Northern Ireland. The Government and the devolved administrations are now in the process of designating additional NVZs. In England, together with existing zones, these will cover 55 per cent of the country, while in Scotland, the Executive announced the designation of some 14 per cent of the total area of Scotland as NVZs in June 2002.

Farmers in NVZs are required to follow rules (known as 'Action Programme Measures'), controlling the timing and rate of application of fertilisers and organic manure. This will have the effect primarily of safeguarding drinking water supplies, and, secondarily, of curtailing wider ecological damage in the form of eutrophication of freshwater and saline waters.

Bathing waters and coastal sewage discharges
Bathing water quality is influenced by natural factors (such as temperature, salinity and sunlight), discharges from coastal sewerage treatment works, storm water overflows and river borne pathogens (that is, pollutants that could affect human health), and run-off from urban and agricultural land. Over the past 11 years the overall quality of UK bathing waters has improved considerably. In 2001, 95 per cent of UK waters complied with the mandatory coliform (bacteria, found in the intestine and faeces of most animals) standards of the EC Bathing Waters Directive, compared with 94 per cent in 2000 and 77 per cent in 1990. The North East and Thames regions in England achieved 100 per cent compliance. Wales, Scotland and Northern Ireland achieved 93, 85 and 81 per cent respectively.

The Scottish Executive launched a bathing water strategy in 2002, to help in its aim of meeting European bathing water standards on all 60 Scottish bathing waters. The SE has identified nine bathing waters as sensitive under the EC Urban Waste Water Treatment Directive; the Welsh Assembly has identified 24 Welsh bathing waters; and DEFRA has declared 180 coastal areas in England. The identification confirms that advanced treatment has been or will be provided to discharges into the bathing waters from local waste water treatment works.

In 2002 ENCAMS (see page 279) gave Seaside Awards (*www.seasideawards.org.uk*) to 317 beaches in the UK for meeting appropriate standards of water quality and beach management. The Awards provide information about a wide range of beaches in the UK and are given to beaches that comply with the EC Bathing Waters Directive mandatory standards, are clean, safe and well managed; and provide appropriate information about water quality.

The European Blue Flag Campaign (*www.blueflag.org*) is an initiative of the Foundation of Environmental Education in Europe and is administered in the UK by ENCAMS. To be considered, a beach must have attained the guideline standard of the EC Bathing

Waters Directive before being assessed for 24 other criteria, including beach cleanliness, dog control, wheelchair access, the provision of life-saving equipment and other facilities. In 2002, 83 beaches in the UK were awarded a 'Blue Flag', compared with 55 in 2001, and 27 marinas won recognition in the 'Blue Flag' for marinas category.

Business and the consumer

Business has an important role to play in environmental matters. A DEFRA survey found that in 1999 UK industry spent an estimated £4.1 billion on environmental protection expenditure. This is spending by companies where the primary aim is to reduce environmental pollution, for example reducing emissions to air or water, to protect soil and groundwater or to prevent noise and vibration.

The *Envirowise* (*www.envirowise.gov.uk*) programme promotes the use of better environmental practices that reduce business costs for industry and commerce. It provides information and advice on environmental technologies and techniques by means of publications, events and a freephone UK helpline. In 2001 it helped businesses generate savings of £178 million and reduce solid waste by 1.6 million tonnes. It works in partnership with the Energy Efficiency Best Practice Programme (EEBPP) (see page 446), which supports energy efficiency measures.

Other government initiatives to encourage environmentally sound practices include:

- the Climate Change Projects Office, launched in May 2001, which exists to help UK firms tackle climate change and take advantage of new opportunities and markets in low carbon technology;

- the Sustainable Technologies Initiative (STI), which provides financial support for developing new technologies that will help businesses to be more efficient in their use of resources, and produce less waste and pollution; and

- the Advisory Committee on Business and the Environment (ACBE) (*www.defra.gov.uk/environment/acbe*), which provides a forum

for government and business to discuss environmental issues. The ACBE was instrumental in the establishment of the *Carbon Trust* in April 2001 (see page 446).

Environmental management systems

An environmental management system provides organisations with a tool to help them control and minimise the impact of their products, services and activities on the environment. Two recognised models exist. One is the international management system, ISO 14001, the other the EU Eco-Management and Audit Scheme (EMAS), which is based on the international standard but additionally requires the reporting of environmental performance. Both require auditing by an accredited independent third party. In the UK accreditation is provided by the UK Accreditation Service (UKAS).

Many leading companies now address environmental issues in their annual reports and over 90 such companies publish separate environmental performance reports. To encourage the top 350 UK businesses to report publicly on their major environmental impacts, the Government has produced guidance to help companies measure and report on greenhouse gas emissions, water consumption and waste.

Environmental labelling

Consumers often rely on the information given on product labels when trying to choose environment-friendly goods. To help them, the Government encourages accurate and relevant environmental labelling, as part of an integrated approach to reduce the environmental impact of consumer products. Through DEFRA, it also administers the voluntary EU ecolabelling award scheme in the UK. The voluntary Green Claims Code sets out guidance for businesses that make environmental claims about their products, and provides an introduction to ISO 14021 – the international standard on environmental labelling.

The Government's Market Transformation Programme aims to encourage the take-up of more energy-efficient domestic appliances. The mandatory EU energy labelling scheme provides graded information on product performance, and EU measures have also resulted in the removal of inefficient appliances from the market.

Further reading

Achieving a Better Quality of life 2001. DEFRA, 2002.

Climate Change: The UK Programme. Department of the Environment, Transport and the Regions, 2000.

Digest of Environmental Statistics. DEFRA. Available only on the Internet: *www.defra.gov.uk/environment/statistics/des/index.htm*

Environment in your Pocket 2001. DEFRA, 2001.

Municipal Waste Management Survey 2000–2001. DEFRA, 2002.

Regional Quality of Life Counts, 2001. DEFRA, 2002.

The State of the Countryside 2002. Countryside Agency, 2002.

Websites

Department for Environment, Food & Rural Affairs
www.defra.gov.uk

Scottish Executive Environment Group
www.scotland.gov.uk/environment

Welsh Assembly Government: Environment
www.wales.gov.uk/subienvironment

Countryside Information System
www.cis-web.org.uk

Environment Agency
www.environment-agency.gov.uk

Scottish Environment Protection Agency
www.sepa.org.uk

Department of the Environment (Northern Ireland)
www.doeni.gov.uk

Environment and Heritage Service (Northern Ireland)
www.ehsni.gov.uk

WWW.

20 Housing, planning and regeneration

The United Kingdom is a relatively densely populated country, with 242 people per square kilometre in 2001. The number of households is projected to increase (in England, for example, from 20.2 million in 1996 to 24.0 million in 2021). These changes, together with an increase in the population and the demands of a growing economy, mean there are pressures on land use. In 2001 a buoyant housing market led to average UK house prices being almost twice that of 1993. Various measures were introduced which attempted to help certain groups, such as nurses, to buy homes in areas where accommodation was particularly expensive. Throughout the UK a number of programmes continue to work to regenerate areas which have been in decline and in need of investment.

Housing

Following a government reorganisation in 2002, the Office of the Deputy Prime Minister (ODPM) has taken over responsibility for determining housing policy in England and supervising the housing programme. Responsibility for housing policy in Wales, Scotland and Northern Ireland rests with the devolved administrations. They all work with local authorities (which are responsible for preparing local housing strategies) and with the private and voluntary sectors. Social housing (housing at below market rent) is provided by local authorities, registered social landlords (RSLs) – most of which are housing associations – and the Northern Ireland Housing Executive (NIHE). RSLs are registered by the Housing Corporation (in England), the National Assembly for Wales (NAW) and Communities Scotland, through

which bodies they also receive government funding. In Northern Ireland, the Housing Division of the Department for Social Development funds the NIHE and the housing association movement, and has regulatory powers over both.

The Government issued a housing policy statement in December 2000, *The Way Forward for Housing*, which set out its strategy for ensuring that everyone in England has the opportunity to

---

The decent home standard

In order to set and monitor progress against its decent social housing target for England, the former Department for Transport, Local Government and the Regions (DTLR) established the decent home standard. A decent home is one which:

- meets the current statutory minimum for housing, which at present is the 'fitness standard';

- is in a reasonable state of repair;

- has reasonably modern facilities; and

- provides a reasonable degree of thermal comfort through effective insulation and efficient heating.

It is estimated by ODPM that in England in April 2001, 1.7 million social rented homes (40 per cent of the social housing stock) were below a decent standard. Further information on the decent home standard can be found on the ODPM website.

live in a 'decent home' (see box). The aim is to deliver greater quality and choice across the housing market, through improving the quality of stock in all tenures; improving the quality of housing services; delivering affordable housing where it is needed; and giving people greater choice over where they live. As part of its 2000 Spending Review, the Government set a target to bring all housing provided by local authorities and RSLs in England up to decent home standard by 2010, with a third of improvements taking place by 2004. By 2003/04 annual capital investment in housing will be more than £4 billion, compared with just over £1.5 billion planned spending in 1997/98.

The Government's 2002 Spending Review (see page 350) announced an additional £1.4 billion over three years to help provide well-designed, affordable homes where they are needed, improve stock conditions in both the social and the private sectors, and tackle the problem of low demand that is causing homes to be abandoned in certain areas.

In addition, the *Supporting People* programme, a policy and funding framework for the delivery of housing support services in England, will begin in 2003. The programme aims to help vulnerable people improve their quality of life by delivering housing support services to complement existing care services. It is hoped that a wider range of people will be able to live independently in their own homes than at present. Supporting People will be delivered on a partnership basis involving local government, other local statutory agencies, users, providers and voluntary agencies.

Better Homes for People in Wales, which sets out the National Assembly's plans for a national housing strategy for Wales, was published in September 2001. The strategy placed emphasis on improving the quality of rented housing, both social and private, continuing support for sustainable home ownership, tackling homelessness, providing help and advice for elderly and disabled people, meeting the needs of disadvantaged households and eradicating fuel poverty by 2010.

The *Housing (Scotland) Act 2001* contained a series of reforms on tenancy rights in the social rented sector, including a modernised right to buy (see page 300) and improved arrangements for tenant involvement. It established a single tenancy (the

Scottish secure tenancy) for tenants of both local authorities and RSLs; provided an enhanced strategic housing role for local authorities; and established Communities Scotland, an executive agency of the Scottish Executive, as a single regulator of providers of social housing. It also strengthened and extended the rights of homeless people, and introduced changes to the system of improvement and repairs grants.

In Northern Ireland a new housing Bill was sent out for consultation in March 2002 and was introduced into the Assembly in June 2002. Key proposals include: a more flexible system of grants to deal with unfit housing, particularly in rural areas; measures to deal more effectively with anti-social behaviour; and stricter controls on houses in multiple-occupancy.

Housing stock and housebuilding

In 1951 there were 14 million dwellings in the United Kingdom. By 2001 the number had increased to 25 million. The peak for housebuilding in the UK was in 1968 when total

Housing in 1952

The damage caused to the nation's housing stock during the Second World War exacerbated existing shortages:

'Out of about 13 million houses in the United Kingdom at the outbreak of war in 1939, nearly 4.5 million were damaged or destroyed by enemy action: 210,000 houses were totally destroyed, 250,000 were so badly damaged as to be rendered uninhabitable, and 4 million received slight damage. The number of houses completed between September 1939 and May 1945 (most of which were under construction on the day war broke out) did not exceed 200,000' (Britain Yearbook 1949–50).

By 1952 the Government was still dealing with the consequences and the provision of new housing became a major post-war priority:

'In January 1952 the Government decided that there should be no fixed limit to the housing programme. House production would be expanded over the next three years as rapidly as the resources of materials and labour that could be made available would allow' (Britain Yearbook 1954).

Figure 20.1 Housebuilding completions, UK, 2000/01

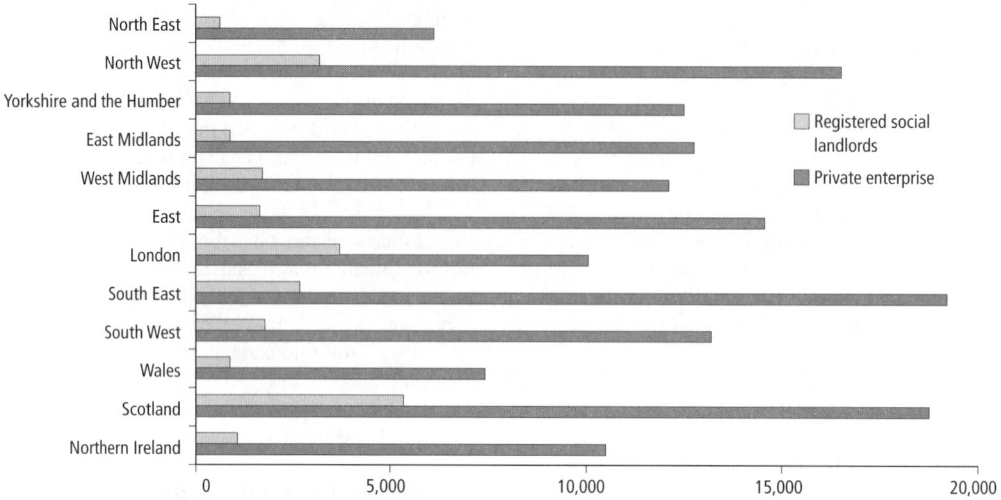

North East
North West
Yorkshire and the Humber
East Midlands
West Midlands
East
London
South East
South West
Wales
Scotland
Northern Ireland

■ Registered social landlords
■ Private enterprise

0   5,000   10,000   15,000   20,000

Source: Office of the Deputy Prime Minister, National Assembly for Wales, Scottish Executive and Department for Social Development, Northern Ireland

completions amounted to 426,000 dwellings: 226,000 completed by private enterprise and 200,000 by the public sector (primarily local authorities). In 2000/01 there were 178,000 completions in the UK. While local authorities are no longer major developers of new housing, they still play an important role as landlords. RSLs (predominantly housing associations) dominate building in what is now called the social sector, although in 2000/01 private sector enterprise was responsible for 86 per cent of all dwellings completed. Figure 20.1 shows the number of homes built in Wales, Scotland, Northern Ireland and the English regions in 2000/01. Scotland had the most completions (when private and social housing are added together). However, the number of homes completed per 1,000 resident households ranged from five in London to 18 in Northern Ireland.

The type of dwellings built has changed over the last century. Terraced housing was the norm before the First World War and over a third of the current stock of terraced housing dates from before 1919. Between 1919 and 1944 there was an expansion in the number of semi-detached dwellings. After 1965 the private sector began to build more detached houses, while a large number of purpose-built flats were provided in the public sector. Figure 20.2 illustrates the type of accommodation households were living in, by 2000/01.

To minimise greenfield development (that is, building on land that has not previously been developed) and to encourage urban regeneration, the Government wishes to see unoccupied homes brought back into use. The number of empty homes in England fell from 868,600 in 1993 to 755,100 in 2001. Four-fifths of vacant dwellings are private housing, with about half of these having been vacant for six months or more. Some dwellings are vacant for short periods between purchase and sale or re-let (known as

Figure 20.2 Households, by type of dwelling occupied, UK, 2000/01

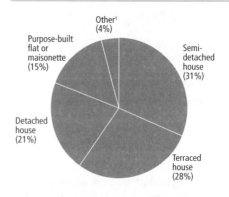

Other[1] (4%)
Purpose-built flat or maisonette (15%)
Semi-detached house (31%)
Detached house (21%)
Terraced house (28%)

1 Includes converted flats.
Source: General Household Survey, Office for National Statistics, and Continuous Household Survey, Northern Ireland Statistics and Research Agency

Table 20.3 Tenure of dwellings in the UK, 2001[1]

	Owner-occupied[2]	Rented from local authority[3]	Rented privately or with job or business	Per cent Rented from registered social landlord
England	70	13	10	7
Wales	72	15	9	4
Scotland	63	24	7	6
Northern Ireland	73	19	5	3
United Kingdom	**69**	**15**	**10**	**6**

1 As at 31 March for England and Wales. Figures for Scotland and Northern Ireland are for 31 December 2000.
2 Including dwellings being purchased with a mortgage or loan as well as those owned outright.
3 Including Scottish Homes and the Northern Ireland Housing Executive.
Source: Office of the Deputy Prime Minister, National Assembly for Wales, Scottish Executive and Department for Social Development, Northern Ireland

'transactional vacancies'), but others may be vacant for longer pending demolition or renovation.

Home ownership

Between 1981 and 2001 the number of owner-occupied dwellings in the United Kingdom increased by more than 40 per cent, while the number of rented dwellings fell by around 15 per cent. By 2001 over 17 million dwellings were owner-occupied, more than double the number of rented dwellings, which numbered 8 million (see also Table 20.3).

The increase in the proportion of dwellings that are owner-occupied is in part due to a number of schemes that aim to increase low-cost home ownership. In England these include the Right to Buy, Right to Acquire and Voluntary Purchase Grants, which offer tenants in social housing a discount against the market value of the homes they rent if they are eligible and choose to buy them. In addition, funding to support low-cost ownership is provided through the Housing Corporation and local authorities, including:

- *Conventional Shared Ownership*, which allows people to part buy and part rent homes developed by RSLs. The scheme allows people to increase their share of ownership in their home over time;

- *Do-It-Yourself Shared Ownership*, which is funded by local authorities in partnership with RSLs and enables people to select a house in the private market and then part

own and part rent it, with the RSL taking on ownership of the rented share of the property;

- *Homebuy*, which allows people to buy a home in the private market with an equity loan from an RSL for 25 per cent of the value of the property. The loan is repayable, at 25 per cent of the current market value, when the home is sold; and

- the *Cash Incentive Scheme*, in which local authorities offer cash grants to its existing tenants for the purchase of a home in the private market.

Properties defined as being owner-occupied fall into two legal categories, either freehold (predominantly houses) or leasehold (mainly flats). Under a freehold, the purchaser has legal ownership of the dwelling and the land it is sited on for an indefinite period. A leasehold provides the purchaser with ownership of the dwelling for a fixed period, during which time ownership of the land remains with the freeholder. On expiry of the lease, ownership of the dwelling reverts to the freeholder. During the period of the lease, leaseholders must pay the freeholder ground rent and property maintenance costs. The freeholder is legally responsible for maintaining the structural condition of the building and ensuring that it is adequately insured.

The *Commonhold and Leasehold Reform Act 2002* introduced 'commonhold', a new form of tenure for multi-occupied properties where people own their individual unit outright. The Act also provides new rights for residential leaseholders in England and Wales, including a right for leaseholders to manage their properties and the extension of the existing right to buy their freehold. Leaseholders in blocks of flats are entitled to buy the freehold of their property jointly, with other leaseholders in their property.

In addition, the new Act provides a range of safeguards to leaseholders including the right to challenge unreasonable service at a Leasehold Valuation Tribunal (LVT). The LVTs currently deal with a wide range of disputes involving residential leasehold property, such as disputes over valuation for the purposes of buying the freehold or renewing the lease, and the appointment of managing agents.

In Wales, local authorities and housing associations operate a low-cost home ownership scheme allowing purchasers to buy a home for 70 per cent of its value, the balance being secured as a charge on the property. The Northern Ireland Co-ownership Housing Association administers a 'buy half, rent half ' (shared ownership) scheme. By September 2002 it had helped 17,000 people become homeowners. Over 98,700 NIHE tenants have bought their homes.

In Scotland, Communities Scotland administers a Housing Association Grant for low-cost home ownership. The grant is used to bridge the shortfall between the cost of provision and locally assessed market value.

Key workers
The Starter Home Initiative (SHI), set up in 2000, aims to help key workers in England, particularly teachers, police officers, nurses and other essential health workers, to buy homes within a reasonable distance of their workplace in areas where high house prices are undermining recruitment and retention. The Government is making £250 million available over the years 2001/02 to 2003/04 in support of the scheme, mainly through RSLs. Types of assistance vary and include equity loans, interest-free loans and shared ownership. The first key workers assisted under the scheme moved into their homes in 2001.

Mortgage loans
A feature of home-ownership in the United Kingdom is the relatively high proportion of homes purchased with a mortgage. Approximately

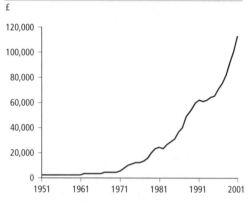

Figure 20.4 Average house prices,[1] UK

1 Current prices, not adjusted for inflation.
Source: Office of the Deputy Prime Minister

three-quarters of house purchases are financed with a mortgage loan facility. In 2001, 77 per cent of loans for home purchase were obtained through banks and 18 per cent through building societies, with 5 per cent through other lenders.

Lenders differ in the amount that they are willing to lend relative to annual income. In 2001 the ratio of the average advance to income for all borrowers was 2.25 – 2.35 for first-time buyers and 2.23 for existing owner-occupiers moving to another home.

Those who are buying a house can choose from a variety of different types of mortgage, the most common being repayment and interest-only. With repayment mortgages, the debt and the interest are both repaid during the life of the mortgage (usually 25 years). Around 72 per cent of all new mortgages were standard repayment mortgages in 2001. Interest-only mortgages, which include endowment policies, ISAs (individual savings accounts) and personal pensions, account for the bulk of other mortgages. Since the late 1980s there has been a decrease in the popularity of endowment mortgages because of the possibility that investments may not grow fast enough to repay the capital borrowed. In 1988, 83 per cent of new mortgages for house purchase were of this type but by 2001 this had fallen to 10 per cent.

In 2000/01 average weekly mortgage payments for owner-occupiers ranged from £40 in Northern Ireland to £95 in London. The number of properties taken into possession by mortgage lenders in the United Kingdom in 2001 was 18,280, 20 per cent fewer than in 2000. The

Table 20.5 Average dwelling prices by region, 2001

£

Region	Bungalow	Detached house	Semi-detached house	Terraced house	Flat/maison-ette	All dwellings	% increase on 2000
North East	79,281	116,619	60,170	45,945	55,129	69,813	9.2
North West	95,386	139,939	75,486	54,486	71,033	82,402	5.7
Yorkshire and the Humber	87,588	127,888	65,334	52,775	61,523	76,368	5.8
East Midlands	91,274	134,679	68,850	58,028	56,582	87,280	10.0
West Midlands	111,508	162,802	78,857	65,879	70,675	97,650	10.4
East	118,186	202,021	118,771	96,546	78,346	127,858	14.3
London	196,184	331,324	213,228	187,493	150,571	182,325	11.5
South East	169,281	254,138	146,033	117,133	93,906	156,964	9.9
South West	130,157	185,670	107,483	87,641	83,917	118,639	13.8
England	121,577	182,487	104,220	92,193	109,380	119,563	11.7
Wales	87,675	126,644	66,922	53,079	60,369	79,628	10.2
Scotland	89,983	121,705	66,255	58,190	56,229	73,570	5.2
Northern Ireland	82,441	124,012	76,529	57,302	40,493	79,885	10.2
United Kingdom	**113,419**	**173,295**	**99,412**	**87,470**	**97,871**	**112,835**	**11.1**

Source: Survey of Mortgage Lenders; Office of the Deputy Prime Minister

number of mortgage accounts in arrears also fell, by 6.5 per cent for mortgages with long-term arrears (over 12 months).

The average dwelling price of properties bought and sold in the United Kingdom in 2001 was £112,835 (see Figure 20.4), although there were marked regional variations with buyers in London and the South East paying the most for their property (see Table 20.5). Dwelling prices also vary according to type, with detached houses being the most expensive.

In December 2001 the Treasury announced that it intended to give the Financial Services Authority (FSA) responsibility for regulating the selling of residential mortgages, including the provision of advice associated with the sales process. The FSA will authorise mortgage lenders and administrators, and intermediaries who advise on and arrange mortgages, regulate mortgage advertising and require firms to disclose the main features of loans clearly and openly. Statutory regulation of mortgages will begin in mid-2004.

In September 2001 the Scottish Executive announced the introduction of a Mortgage to Rent Scheme, designed to allow families in mortgage difficulties to avoid repossession and to become tenants in their own homes. Funding of £8.4 million is available for the scheme in the period to 2003/04. Another measure to help people experiencing difficulties with mortgage payments is contained in the *Mortgage Rights (Scotland) Act 2001*. This provides for people in mortgage debt to seek suspension of the creditor's right of enforcement if, in the view of the court, it is reasonable to do so.

Rented housing

As owner-occupation has increased, the number of dwellings that are rented has decreased. In 2001, 21 per cent of UK households were renting from the social sector (local authorities and RSLs), while 10 per cent were renting privately.

Private rented sector

In its policy statement *The Way Forward for Housing*, the Government set out its strategy to encourage good practice in England through voluntary accreditation schemes for landlords, via the development of the national Approved Lettings Scheme. The Government has also proposed the mandatory national licensing of housing in multiple occupation in order to improve the standard of this type of housing. The Government also plans to allow local authorities to license private landlords if they chose.

'Assured' and 'shorthold' (in Scotland, 'short assured') tenancies are the commonest forms of arrangement for the letting of houses and flats by private landlords. If the tenancy is shorthold, the landlord can regain possession of the property six months after the beginning of the tenancy, provided that he or she gives the tenant two months' notice requiring possession. If the tenancy is assured, the tenant has the right to remain in the property unless the landlord can prove to the court that he or she has grounds for possession. In an assured tenancy, the landlord does not have an automatic right to repossess the property when the tenancy comes to an end. In both types of tenancy the landlord can charge a full market rent.

2002 transfers

In 2002 two of the largest local authority landlords, Glasgow City Council and Birmingham City Council, carried out ballots of their tenants. The tenants voted on whether they were in favour of their homes continuing to be owned and managed by the local authority or whether they preferred the option of transferring them to a single local housing association (in Glasgow) or a network of local community landlords (in Birmingham). The elections were conducted by postal vote and were decided by a simple majority.

Glasgow voted 'Yes' to transfer

Number of tenants voting – 50,802 (64.4 per cent).

Proportion voting for transfer to a housing association – 58.3 per cent.

Proportion voting against transfer – 41.7 per cent.

Birmingham voted 'No' to transfer

Number of tenants voting – 61,593 (65.5 per cent).

Proportion voting for transfer to community landlords – 33.2 per cent.

Proportion voting against transfer – 66.8 per cent.

Social housing

Much of the Government's expenditure on social housing is provided as subsidies to local authorities to help pay for the costs of nearly 3.7 million rented council homes in the UK. More than 2,000 housing associations, most of them RSLs, provide other social housing (see also Table 20.3). RSLs manage and build new homes with the aid of government grants administered through the Housing Corporation, the Welsh Assembly Government, Communities Scotland and NIHE.

Government policy aims to promote a wider range of social landlords through stock transfers. In England and Wales a Large Scale Voluntary Transfer (LSVT) Programme has been running since 1988. By July 2002, almost 650,000 dwellings had been transferred from local authorities to RSLs with the support of tenants and the approval of the appropriate Secretary of State. The transfers generated £4.5 billion in capital receipts, and raised over £10 billion in private finance. Plans for 2002/03 involve 26 local authorities and 182,831 dwellings. An Order allowing local authorities on an LSVT programme up to two financial years in which to transfer came into effect in February 2002. In Scotland, three local authorities are expected to transfer their entire stock of around 101,000 dwellings to RSLs in 2002/03.

Local authorities in Wales own around 200,000, or approximately 15 per cent, of all Welsh homes. By law they have to manage their own stock efficiently and, in consultation with their tenants, address current housing needs and demands.

The Scottish Executive has provided local authorities with £148.5 million in capital allocations for 2002/03. Communities Scotland plans to invest £215 million in Scotland's housing to help build 4,700 new and improved homes. The majority of the homes will be for rent from RSLs, and the remainder will be offered to first-time buyers. In Northern Ireland the Government's contribution to housing of £170 million in 2001/02, supplemented by rental income and capital receipts, meant that gross resources available were £620 million. Under the *Housing (Scotland) Act 2001*, the Executive has powers to place government investment in housing under council control, thus enhancing the role of local authorities. The first local authority to receive funding will be Glasgow City Council in April 2003. This means that local authorities are able to

Housing then and now

Prefabricated housing helped to meet post-war shortages – some remained in use for several decades. This photo was taken in south London in the early 1950s.

January 2002: demolition of two tower blocks in East London. In the 1960s and early 1970s, high-rise housing was seen as a solution to continuing shortages and slum conditions in inner-city areas.

April 2002: the Beddington Zero Energy Development Development in Sutton, Surrey, provides a mixture of homes at affordable rents and full or shared ownership. Designed with environmental sustainability in mind, the development includes workspaces, sports and childcare facilities.

The wind cowls contain heat exchanges. Fresh air coming into the property is warmed slightly by stale air going out.

Motorways and major roads

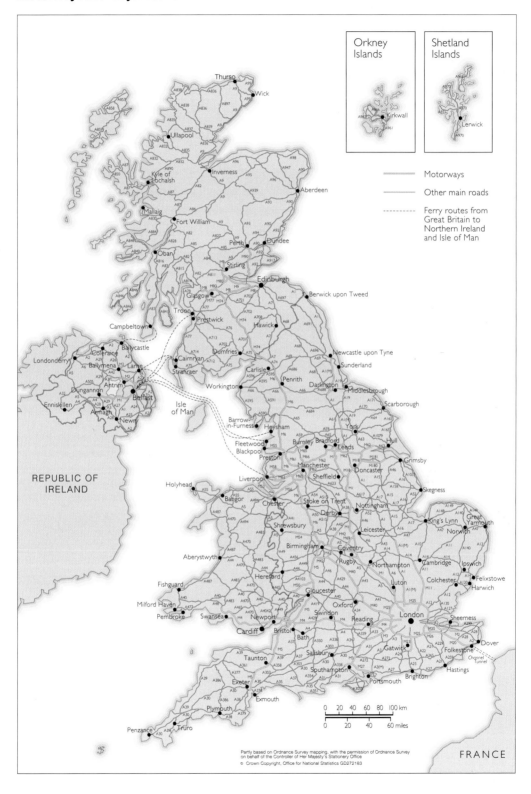

Passenger railway network

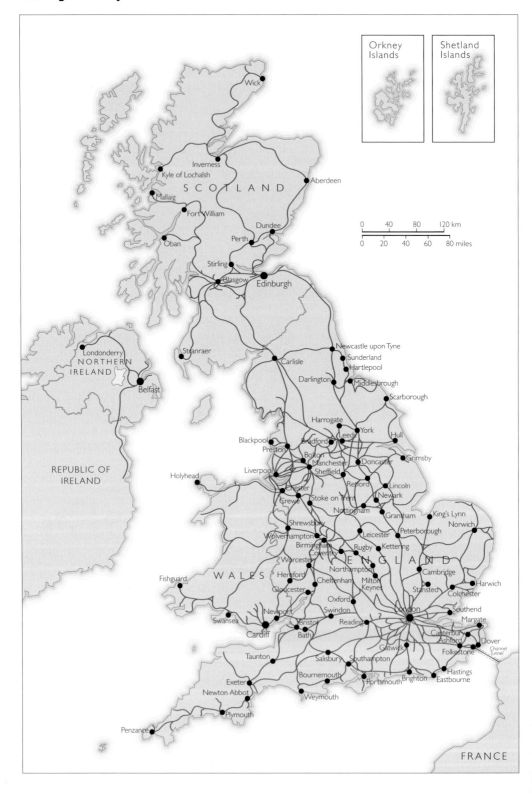

Orkney Islands

Shetland Islands

Wick

Inverness
Kyle of Lochalsh
Mallaig
Fort William
Oban
Dundee
Perth
Stirling
Glasgow Edinburgh

SCOTLAND

Aberdeen

0   40   80   120 km
0 20 40 60 80 miles

Londonderry
NORTHERN IRELAND
Belfast

Stranraer

Carlisle

Newcastle upon Tyne
Sunderland
Hartlepool
Darlington Middlesbrough
Scarborough

REPUBLIC OF IRELAND

Harrogate
Blackpool
Preston
Bolton
Liverpool
Holyhead
Chester
Crewe
Stoke on Trent
Bradford Leeds York Hull
Manchester Doncaster Grimsby
Sheffield
Retford Lincoln
Newark
Nottingham Grantham

Shrewsbury
Wolverhampton
Birmingham
Coventry
Worcester
Hereford
Gloucester
Newport
Swansea
Cardiff Bath
Bristol

Leicester Kettering Peterborough
Rugby Northampton
Milton Keynes
Cheltenham
Oxford
Swindon Reading
Cambridge

King's Lynn
Norwich
Stansted Colchester Harwich

WALES

ENGLAND

Fishguard

Taunton
Exeter
Newton Abbot
Plymouth
Penzance
Weymouth
Salisbury Southampton
Bournemouth
Portsmouth Brighton Eastbourne
Gatwick
London
Canterbury
Ashford Dover
Folkestone
Channel Tunnel
Southend
Margate
Hastings

FRANCE

distribute funds currently allocated to housing associations via Communities Scotland.

The Northern Ireland Housing Executive, the regional strategic housing authority for Northern Ireland, is the landlord of 116,000 properties, nearly one-third of rented properties in Northern Ireland. It is responsible for assessing the need for, and arranging the supply of, social housing.

Registered social landlords

Registered social landlords (RSLs) are the major providers of new subsidised homes for those in housing need. They range from almshouses to large housing associations, managing thousands of homes. They also include large-scale voluntary transfer and local housing companies, set up to own and manage council houses transferred from local authorities. The Housing Corporation, which regulates RSLs in England, gives capital grants to provide homes for rent and for sale under shared ownership terms, primarily from the Approved Development Programme (ADP). Local authorities also provide some capital funding in the form of Social Housing Grant. In March 2002 the Housing Corporation announced an expanded ADP for 2002/03, which aims to provide around 22,000 homes at a cost of £1.2 billion. This includes funding for around 800 homes for rent and 740 for sale in London, plus 550 under the Homebuy scheme (see page 295) in the south of England and the Midlands. Planned ADP funding for 2003/04 is £1.2 billion.

In 2002/03 Communities Scotland will invest almost £344 million in the regeneration of Scotland's communities. Of that total, £215 million will be spent on housing projects, helping to complete more than 5,200 new and improved homes already under way and allowing work to start on another 4,700, mainly for rent through housing associations. In addition, Communities Scotland will assist the Scottish Executive in delivering a range of policy initiatives.

The Northern Ireland Housing Executive has continued to transfer its new build programme to registered housing associations. The 2003/04 programme will involve 110 new schemes producing some 1,400 homes.

Improving existing housing

Poor quality housing can have an adverse impact on health and well being. Although primary responsibility for maintaining a property rests

with the owner, the Government can provide help to improve housing quality across all tenures and accepts that some people, especially the elderly and most vulnerable, do not have the resources to keep their homes in good repair. The Regulatory Reform (Housing Assistance) Order, which came into force in July 2002, prescribes how local authorities can offer assistance to homeowners, and private landlords, for the renovation of their properties.

The Government intends to reform the legislation on housing fitness. The current statutory housing fitness standard (set out in the *Housing Act 1985*) is based in part on criteria first introduced approximately 80 years ago. To reflect a more modern approach to health and safety hazards in the home, the Government has developed the Housing Health and Safety Rating System (HHSRS). The HHSRS was made available to local authorities in July 2000 and consultation on enforcement arrangements took place in 2001. Primary legislation will be required to implement these proposals.

In Scotland, the Housing Improvement Task Force was established in March 2001 to undertake a comprehensive examination of the issues affecting the condition and quality of private sector housing and the process of buying and selling houses in Scotland. Its work includes an examination of the statutory and strategic framework for improving private sector housing. It will report its recommendations in early 2003.

Social housing

Most capital expenditure on social housing goes towards renovating and improving existing local authority housing. By 2003/04 resources provided to local authorities in England for housing capital investment will have risen to £2.6 billion a year, from £0.9 billion in 1997/98. This is excluding local authorities' own contributions and the Private Finance Initiative (PFI) which aims to help councils work with the private sector in providing social housing. The Government hopes this, together with the Major Repairs Allowance (MRA), will reduce the amount of poor quality social housing by a third by 2004 and ensure that all council housing is of a decent standard by 2010. The MRA in England ensures authorities have the resources necessary to maintain their stock. Funding for MRA was £1.6 billion in 2001/02 and will be £1.5 billion in 2002/03 and

£1.4 billion in 2003/04 (reflecting an estimated fall in the number of council homes from 2.86 million in 2001/02 to 2.52 million by 2003/04). In November 2001 the Government published its Neighbourhood Renewal Implementation Strategy to outline how it intends to achieve these targets. In Scotland gross resources available to local authorities for investment in their own stock in 2001/02 were an estimated £356 million.

Private housing

Local authorities in England have discretionary grant-giving powers to help homeowners and tenants to repair their properties and assist in the regeneration of communities. Local authorities use these powers to fund around £250 million of repairs for some 70,000 homeowners and tenants a year. The Regulatory Reform (Housing Assistance) Order gives local authorities a general power to deliver private sector housing renewal through grants, loans, loan guarantees and equity release schemes.

Local authorities have similar powers in Scotland. In July 2001 the Scottish Executive announced modifications to this legislation. New types of work will be eligible for grant, and a national test of resources will be introduced, enabling those on the lowest incomes to receive full grant funding for necessary repairs and improvements. In Northern Ireland, funding is allocated through the house renovation grants scheme, administered by the NIHE, on a similar basis to that in England and Wales. In rural areas of Northern Ireland, financial assistance to replace isolated dwellings that cannot be restored is also available.

Rural housing

The Housing Corporation finances a special rural programme to build houses in villages with a population of 3,000 or less. Following the publication of the Rural White Paper *A Fair Deal for England* in November 2000, the Government announced targets for the Corporation to approve 1,600 new homes in small villages by 2003/04. The Corporation will also contribute to the Government's target of approving 9,000 homes a year across all rural districts by 2003/04.

The National Assembly for Wales supports the development of housing in rural areas if it is regarded as a strategic priority by the local authority. The consultation paper – *Better Homes for People in Wales* – commented on the effect of

second homes and the Right to Buy (which has removed many homes from the social housing stock). Concerns have been raised about the ability of local people to access affordable housing. The National Assembly is considering further restrictions on the Right to Buy and Right to Acquire in rural areas in order to safeguard the accessibility of low cost housing for local people.

Communities Scotland's Rural Development Programme provided 1,178 new and improved homes across Scotland in 2001/02 and aims to improve a further 1,266 in 2002/03. To address a shortage of affordable housing in rural areas, the Scottish Executive established the Rural Partnership for Change. Its report in May 2001 made recommendations on identifying the areas affected and strategies to respond to such pressures. The *Housing (Scotland) Act 2001* provides for the limiting of Right to Buy in certain areas by giving Scottish ministers authority to designate an area as being a pressured area when it considers the demand for social housing exceeds that which is available. The Act also contains initiatives to encourage private landlords to bring empty properties back into a suitable condition for renting.

In Northern Ireland, a revised rural housing policy was introduced in April 2000. It included a programme of rural housing needs assessment, the planned development of around 120 new rural dwellings a year, and the improvement or replacement of some 600 rural cottages over the next three to five years.

Homelessness

Local housing authorities in England and Wales have a statutory obligation to ensure that suitable accommodation is available for applicants who are eligible for assistance, have become homeless through no fault of their own and who fall within a priority need group (this is the 'main homeless duty'). Among the priority need groups are families with children, and households that include someone who is vulnerable, for example because of pregnancy, old age, or physical or mental disability.

Where applicants are homeless but not owed the 'main duty' (for example, because they do not fall within a priority need group) the housing authority must ensure that they are provided with advice and assistance in their own attempts to find

Table 20.6 Homeless households in priority need accepted by local authorities, UK, 2000/01

North East	5,220
North West	13,350
Yorkshire and the Humber	9,150
East Midlands	7,370
West Midlands	13,860
East	9,800
London	29,630
South East	14,760
South West	11,210
England	114,350
Wales	4,390
Scotland[1]	18,000
Northern Ireland	6,457

1 As defined in section 24 of the *Housing (Scotland) Act 1987*.
  Figure relates to 1999/2000.
Source: Office of the Deputy Prime Minister; National Assembly for Wales; Scottish Executive; Department for Social Development, Northern Ireland

accommodation. Authorities also have a general duty to ensure that advice about homelessness and the prevention of homelessness is available free of charge to everyone in their district. In most areas, advice about homelessness is available from housing aid centres, Shelter (a charity that offers housing aid to homeless and badly housed people), citizens advice bureaux and other local agencies.

The *Homelessness Act 2002* introduced measures aimed at helping homeless people. Housing authorities must secure accommodation for these groups until a settled home becomes available for them. Local authorities must also have a strategy for preventing homelessness in their district and ensure that accommodation and any necessary support will be available for homeless people. In March 2002, the former DTLR released *More than a roof*, a report outlining the Government's approach to tackling homelessness in England.

Table 20.6, which shows the number of households accepted as being owed the main homeless duty in 2000/01, does not take account of variations in the size of populations or differences in legislation across the UK. In England and Wales, acceptances per 1,000 resident households ranged from 3.5 in Wales to 9.9 in London.

The number of homeless people housed by local authorities in Bed and Breakfast (B&B)

accommodation in England rose from 4,630 in 1997 to 12,290 in 2001. Other types of accommodation used for households accepted under the legislation include hostels, women's refuges, properties owned by private landlords, and dwellings owned by the local authority and let on a non-secure tenancy.

In October 2001 the Government set up a Bed and Breakfast Unit (BBU) with the aim of reducing the use of accommodation where households are placed in one or more rooms on a daily/nightly charged basis and where they have to share bathing, washing, toilet or cooking facilities. In spring 2002 approximately 6,500 families with children were living in B&B hotel-type accommodation. The BBU aims to ensure that no families with children will live in B&B hotels by March 2004, except in an emergency and then for no more than six weeks.

In Wales the Homelessness Commission was set up in November 2000 with representatives from the National Assembly, voluntary organisations, local government groups and other practitioners. The Commission submitted its final report to the Assembly in August 2001 with 91 recommendations. The Assembly published its response to these recommendations in May 2002, along with a draft national homelessness strategy for consultation.

In Scotland there were around 45,000 applications under the homeless persons legislation during 2000/01. At the end of December 2001, 3,931 households were in various forms of temporary accommodation. The *Housing (Scotland) Act 2001* includes a duty on local authorities to assess homelessness in their area and to produce strategies, setting out how they aim to prevent and alleviate homelessness. The Act provides that unintentionally homeless people in priority need are entitled to permanent accommodation and that there is a minimum package of rights for non-priority applicants, including enhanced advice, assistance and access to temporary accommodation. The Act also introduces a statutory right for the applicant to request a review of the local authority's decision and provides that accommodation offered must meet any special needs that he or she may have.

In 2002 the Homelessness Task Force released its final report – *Homelessness: An Action Plan for Prevention and Effective Response* – which sets out an action plan for preventing and tackling homelessness in Scotland. A Homelessness Bill is planned for introduction to the Scottish Parliament in late 2002 which will amend existing Scottish homelessness legislation in the light of the Task Force's recommendations. Funding totalling £38 million has been allocated to fund the homelessness provisions of the 2001 Act and to support the implementation of the Task Force's recommendations.

In Northern Ireland there were 14,164 applications under the homeless persons legislation during 2001/02. A review of homelessness in Northern Ireland was carried out in 2001 and found that it had a higher rate of homelessness than in the rest of the UK. The review made recommendations to prevent homelessness; to help those in temporary accommodation and to assess the specific needs of those who are long-term homeless with a view to supporting them into resettlement.

The Rough Sleepers Unit (RSU), established in April 1999, has responsibility for delivering the target of reducing rough sleeping in England to as near to zero as possible and by at least two-thirds by 2002. In December 2001 it announced that the latter target had been met and estimated that the number of people sleeping rough in England on any single night was around 530. This represents a reduction of 71 per cent since 1998.

Over the three years to 2004, £3.5 million is being made available to support projects whose aim is to reduce the number of people sleeping rough in Wales. In Scotland, the Executive has set a target to remove the need for anyone to have to sleep rough by 2003.

In December 2001 the Government published *Addressing the housing needs of Black and Minority Ethnic People*, an action plan bringing together current and planned ODPM housing policies and initiatives aimed at meeting the housing needs of black and minority ethnic people in England. The Welsh Assembly Government published its own action plan – *Black, Minority Ethnic Housing Action Plan for Wales* – in September 2002.

Land use planning

Planning systems regulate development and land use, and contribute to the Government's strategy for promoting a sustainable pattern of physical development in cities, towns and the countryside.

In Great Britain land use planning is the direct responsibility of local authorities. They prepare development plans and determine most planning applications. The ODPM and the devolved administrations have overall responsibility for the operation of the system. They issue national planning policy guidance, approve structure plans (except in Wales where unitary authorities have this role), decide planning appeals and determine planning applications that raise issues of national importance. In England the ODPM operates through the Government Offices for the Regions and the Planning Inspectorate.

In Northern Ireland, the Department of the Environment (DOE) functions as the single planning authority. The Planning Service, an executive agency within the DOE, is responsible for issuing operational planning, policy and guidance, determining planning applications and preparing development plans.

England

There are just over 400 planning authorities in England – including county councils, district councils, unitary authorities and National Park authorities. The first planning laws were enacted in 1909 and the modern system dates from the *Town and Country Planning Act 1947* and subsequent legislation in 1990 and 1991. The Government's national policy is set out in 25 Planning Policy Guidance notes (PPGs) – covering issues such as housing, transport, sport and recreation – and in 15 Minerals Policy Guidance notes (MPGs) as well as circulars and other guidance.

There are several tiers to the planning system. Central government issues national planning guidance to local authorities and also Regional Planning Guidance (RPG) (based on advice from regional planning conferences). Upper-tier local authorities (such as county councils) produce 'structure plans', which indicate where development should be focused, while lower-tier local authorities (such as district councils) produce 'local plans' with more detailed and site-specific information. Local authorities decide individual planning applications with reference to these plans. They also prepare 'economic development strategies', which can influence the ability of a local plan to achieve its objectives. In

In December 2001 the Government issued a Green Paper – *Planning: Delivering a Fundamental Change* – which proposed changes to the planning system in England. The proposals include the introduction of new local planning frameworks, including action area plans, faster processing of planning applications, and cutting the decision time on appeals to the Secretary of State. The paper aims to simplify the system by replacing the multi-layered structure of planning which currently exists at a national, regional, county and local level, with a two-tier system of local plans and regional plans. It also proposes the creation of Business Zones, where developers would be allowed to build in designated areas without requiring specific planning approval. This would be for low impact developments, which would not put any strain on existing local services or create massive demand for new housing.

London the Mayor has responsibility for production of a 'spatial development strategy' covering development, regeneration and transport issues in the capital.

Planning Policy Guidance Note 3 on Housing provides national planning guidance on the future of housebuilding and development in England. It sets out proposals for planning authorities to recycle brownfield (previously developed) sites and empty properties in preference to greenfield sites. It also encourages planning authorities to use land more efficiently; assist with the provision of affordable housing in both rural and urban areas; and promote mixed-use developments that integrate housing with shops, local services and transport.

The Government's national target is that, by 2008, 60 per cent of additional housing in England should be provided on brownfield land or by re-using existing buildings. In 2002 it released provisional figures showing that in 2001, 61 per cent of new housing had been built on brownfield land. Proportions varied regionally with London having the highest proportion of new houses built on brownfield land, 90 per cent, while in the North East, South West and East Midlands less than 50 per cent were built on brownfield sites.

Wales

National planning policy for Wales has existed since 1996, and in March 2002 the Assembly published Planning Policy Wales (PPW), its first planning policy document. This includes:

Beddington Zero

Developed by the Peabody Trust, the Beddington Zero Energy Development (BedZED) in the London Borough of Sutton is the first large-scale carbon neutral housing development. See also page 283. Built on brownfield land reclaimed from disused industry, BedZED is providing 82 homes for outright sale, shared ownership, affordable rent for key workers and social housing. The first residents moved into their accommodation in April 2002. Key features of the housing include:

- wind cowls with heat exchangers on roofs to provide ventilation;

- super insulation on all external walls, roofs and ground floors, and triple glazed windows, to reduce heat loss; and

- energy-saving appliances in kitchens.

- keeping development away from flood risk areas;

- the possible establishment of Wales' first Green Belt areas;

- development of land and buildings in a way that creates a more accessible environment, including for people with limited mobility;

- guidance on the sustainable use of previously developed land beyond housing needs alone;

- encouraging both rural and farm diversification; and

- proposals to relax the control of developments in the open countryside so that development on farm complexes can be permitted (subject to controls to prevent adverse environmental and transport effects).

Scotland

Legislation for planning policy in Scotland is contained in the *Town and Country Planning Act (Scotland) 1997*. Nineteen National Planning Policy Guidelines (NPPGs) provide statements of Scottish Executive policy on nationally important land use and other planning matters. Circulars provide guidance on policy implementation and Planning Advice Notes provide advice on good practice. In March 2002 the Executive published revisions to *NPPG3: Planning for Housing*, for consultation. The policy aims to provide good quality, well-located new housing consistent with national and local planning policies.

Northern Ireland

The first piece of town and country planning legislation specifically relating to Northern Ireland was the *Planning and Housing Act (NI) 1931*. Policy is currently contained in 11 Planning Policy Statements. In February 2002 a consultation paper was released with proposals for changes to the planning system in Northern Ireland. Its aims include speeding up decision-making (particularly major planning applications) and effective public participation in the planning process. The new legislation is due to be placed before the Assembly later in 2002.

Green Belts

Green Belts are areas of land that are intended to be left open and protected from development. The aim is to control the unrestricted sprawl of large built-up areas, prevent towns from merging with one another, preserve the heritage of historic towns and encourage the recycling of derelict and other urban land, thereby encouraging urban regeneration. Not all Green Belt land is countryside. It can cover small villages comprising a mixture of residential, retail, industrial and recreational land as well as fields and forests. Development on Green Belts is only permitted under exceptional circumstances.

The first major Green Belt was established around the fringes of Greater London following legislation in 1938. Green Belts have also been established around Glasgow, Edinburgh, Aberdeen, Greater Manchester, Merseyside and the West Midlands, as well as several smaller towns. In 1997, there were 14 separate designated Green Belt areas in England, amounting to 1.65 million hectares (about 13 per cent of the land area). Between 1997 and 2000 some 3 per cent of new dwellings were built within Green Belts, but three-fifths of these were on previously developed land.

In Scotland there are six Green Belt areas totalling 156,000 hectares. Two further Green Belts included in the Fife Structure Plan are now approved in principle around St Andrews and part of Dunfermline. There are 245,000 hectares of Green Belt in Northern Ireland; this represents about 18 per cent of the total land area. There are

no Green Belts at present in Wales, but their creation is under consideration.

Development plans

Development plans play an integral role in shaping land use and provide a framework for consistent decision-making. Planning applications are determined in accordance with relevant development plan policies unless 'material considerations' indicate otherwise. In England, local planning authorities are required to prepare development plans in line with the *Town and Country Planning Act 1990*. Regulations, which took effect in 2000, provide a statutory framework for new procedures designed to improve the delivery of development plans. Unless justified by specific local considerations, plans should not conflict with either national or regional policies.

In England, outside metropolitan areas and certain non-metropolitan unitary authority areas, the development plan comprises:

- *structure plans*, which are produced by county councils, some unitary authorities and National Park authorities (in many cases on a joint basis). They set out the key strategic policies and provide a framework for local plans;

- *local plans*, which are produced by district councils, some unitary authorities and National Park authorities, and contain more detailed policies to guide development in a particular local authority area. The plans may include proposals for specific sites; and

- *minerals and waste local plans*, which are produced by county councils, some unitary authorities and National Park authorities (which are usually the development control authorities for these issues).

Within metropolitan areas and in some non-metropolitan unitary authorities, the development plan comprises a single *unitary development plan (UDP)*. There are two parts to the UDP. Part I consists of the local authority's strategic policies for the development and use of land in its area, and forms the framework for the detailed proposals for the use and development of land set out in Part II.

All unitary authorities and National Park authorities in Wales are required to prepare a

UDP for their area. The UDP is the development plan for each county or borough council and each National Park, replacing the structure plan, local plan and any other existing plan. Three-quarters of the land area and almost 80 per cent of the population of Wales are currently covered by area-wide plans. The Assembly is currently considering the replacement of the requirement to produce UDPs with Local Development Plans.

In Scotland, development plans are prepared by local authorities and consist of structure and local plans. In November 2000 the Scottish Executive announced that current arrangements for strategic planning would be reviewed. A consultation paper was issued in June 2001 inviting views on a range of issues, and details of the confirmed proposal for change were published in June 2002. An objective of these changes would be to guide investment in new development and infrastructure by identifying priority areas for physical renewal and regeneration.

The Scottish Executive's Planning Audit Unit works with planning authorities to establish the underlying reasons for contrasting development control performance and to identify best practice in handling planning applications. The work covers development planning as well as development control.

In Northern Ireland, the Planning Service put in place its Development Plan Programme in 1998. This is reviewed annually, and is designed to meet the development planning needs of all districts. In December 2001 the Planning Service launched the Belfast Metropolitan Area Plan 2015 and released a consultation paper concerning land use proposals in the period to 2015 for six council areas: Belfast, Carrickfergus, Castlereagh, Lisburn, Newtownabbey and North Down.

Development control

Development control is the process for regulating the development of land. Most forms of development, such as the construction of new buildings, alterations of existing buildings or changes of land use, require permission from the relevant planning authority. Applications are dealt with on the basis of the development plans and other material considerations, including national and regional guidance.

In 2001/02 district planning authorities in England received 582,000 applications for permission, and made 534,000 decisions, granting permission to 87 per cent of applications. Householder developments accounted for 49 per cent of all decisions in 2001/02, compared with 11 per cent for new dwellings and 18 per cent for commercial and industrial developments. Other decisions involved listed buildings or conservation areas, advertisements, or change of use.

In 2001/02, 65 per cent of all planning decisions in England were made within the statutory eight-week period. The Government's target is for 80 per cent of applications to be dealt with within this timeframe. Similar targets apply in Wales, Scotland and Northern Ireland. New targets in England, for major and minor applications, came into effect in April 2002.

In England, Wales and Scotland, a small number of planning applications are referred for decision to the Secretary of State, the Assembly, or the Scottish ministers, rather than being decided by the local planning authority. In general, this only occurs where the planning issue is of more than local importance. A small number are referred for consideration at a public inquiry, such as the Terminal 5 inquiry at London Heathrow Airport. The public inquiry to establish the need for a fifth terminal at the airport concluded with government approval for the project. Work is expected to begin on the site in 2004.

If a local authority refuses to grant planning permission, grants it with conditions attached or fails to decide an application within eight weeks (or two months in Scotland), the applicant has a right of appeal to the Secretary of State, the Assembly or the Scottish ministers. In August 2000 a package of revised rules and guidance was introduced aimed at speeding up decisions on planning appeals in England. New arrangements came into effect in Wales in 2002.

The Planning Inspectorate serves both the Deputy Prime Minister in England and the National Assembly for Wales on appeals and other casework on planning, housing, the environment, highways and related legislation. It also provides information and guidance to appellants and other interested parties about the appeal process. In 2001/02, over 14,000 planning appeal cases were determined in England and Wales.

In Scotland, the Scottish Executive Inquiry Reporters Unit is responsible for the

Planning Portal Programme
In the *Modernising Government* White Paper, the
Government made a commitment to ensure local
authorities are able to provide electronic delivery of
all their services by 2005. ODPM, the Welsh
Assembly Government and a number of local
authorities are developing the Planning Portal
Programme, which will deliver many planning
services over the Internet
(*www.planningportalprogramme.gov.uk*). The
Planning Portal will provide online planning
guidance and advice and the Planning Casework
Service will allow online submission and tracking of
cases handled by the Planning Inspectorate.

determination of the majority of planning appeals
and organises public local inquiries into planning
proposals and related matters. In Northern
Ireland, the applicant has the right of appeal to
the Planning Appeals Commission. Major
planning applications can be referred to a public
inquiry in certain circumstances.

Regeneration

Regeneration policies aim to enhance both the
economic and social development of communities
through a partnership between the public and
private sectors, with a substantial contribution
from the latter. They support and complement
other programmes tackling social and economic
decline, and initiatives such as Sure Start (see page
103), Health Action Zones (see page 162), the
Crime Reduction Programme (see page 185) and
the work of the Social Exclusion Unit (see page
98). Rundown areas in the UK benefit from
European Union Structural Funds, which assist a
variety of projects in the least prosperous
industrial, urban and rural areas of the European
Union. Over £10 billion of Structural Funds,
including £3 billion covering Objective 1 areas
(see page 340), have been allocated to the UK for
the period 2000–06.

England
In England, the Government and the nine
Regional Development Agencies (RDAs) set out
the priorities for regeneration and ensure that new
programmes aim to enhance and complement
those already in place. RDA strategies, alongside
Regional Planning Guidance overseen by

Government Offices, provide a regional
framework for economic development and
regeneration.

The Department of Trade and Industry is the lead
sponsor of the RDAs, with the Government
Offices (for the Regions) responsible for day-to-
day RDA sponsorship issues. The ODPM and a
number of other departments are responsible for
financing RDAs and for advising them on the
implementation of regional strategies.

RDAs are now supporting regeneration schemes
from a single budget worth £1.55 billion in
2002/03, £1.7 billion in 2003/04 and £2 billion in
2005/06, giving them greater budgetary flexibility
and freedom. Under this new framework, they will
be required to deliver targets set collectively by
government departments.

English Partnerships (EP) together with the RDAs
are the Government's main regeneration agencies.
EP (sponsored by the ODPM) is a key contributor
to delivering the Government's 'Living
Communities' strategy, which was set out in July
2002 and seeks to create new jobs and investment
through sustainable economic regeneration and
development in the English regions. EP had an
operating budget in 2001/02 of £295 million. As
well as delivering the 'Living Communities'
strategy, EP has responsibility for: the Greenwich
Peninsula; the National Coalfields Programme;
Millennium Communities; support for urban
regeneration companies (URC); the English Cities
Fund, the National Land Use Database, and the
production and maintenance of a national
brownfield strategy.

Englishsites.com
English Partnerships manages Englishsites.com, an
Internet service which delivers information on
strategic development sites in England
(*www.englishsites.com*). It provides data on sites
currently available to companies that are
considering expanding, investing or relocating in the
English regions. The database enables landowners
to promote their sites worldwide and currently holds
data on approximately 200 sites. It also allows users
to search for a site using a number of criteria,
including its size, location, distance to motorways
and airports, and the level of grants available.

Urban living

Following recommendations from the Urban Task Force for improving towns and cities, the Government published a White Paper on urban policy, *Our Towns and Cities: The Future – Delivering an Urban Renaissance*, in November 2000. It set out the Government's plans for towns, cities and suburbs, with the aim of encouraging people to return to live in town and city centres, thereby easing the pressure on the countryside and helping to protect it from development. Action has been taken on a number of initiatives set out in the White Paper including:

- the abolition of stamp duty on properties worth up to £150,000 in over 1,200 of the most disadvantaged wards in England;

- a reduction in VAT (value added tax) to 5 per cent on the costs of converting property to residential use and of renovating properties empty for three years or more;

- relief from VAT on the sale of renovated houses that have been empty for ten years or more;

Urban regeneration companies

URCs are independent companies established by local authorities, RDAs, EP and the private sector working in partnership. By spring 2002 three pilot companies – Liverpool Vision, New East Manchester and Sheffield One – had embarked on a programme of urban regeneration and further URCs have been announced in Bradford, Corby, Hull, Leicester, Newport (South Wales), Sunderland, Swindon and the Tees Valley.

The New East Manchester scheme occupies a location that is mainly residential, but includes former industrial land. A draft regeneration framework has been set up with the aims of:

- doubling the existing population to a total of 60,000;

- building 12,500 new homes;

- improving 7,000 existing homes; and

- encouraging investment and employment prospects by establishing business parks.

- the introduction of 100 per cent capital allowances for the costs of creating flats above shops;

- the provision of tax relief for covering the costs of cleaning up contaminated sites;

- proposals to review the planning system, set out in the Green Paper – *Planning: Delivering a Fundamental Change* (see page 303);

- the establishment of the Green Spaces Task Force with the aim of improving the quality of parks, play areas and open spaces; and

- more urban regeneration companies and the establishment of a Neighbourhood Renewal Fund.

The Neighbourhood Renewal Unit (NRU), established in April 2001, is a unit which spans all the key spending government departments. It aims to tackle the core problems of deprived areas by harnessing the support of all sectors to work in partnership; focusing existing services and resources on deprived areas; and giving local residents a central role in its strategy. Based in the ODPM, it provides funding for a number of renewal programmes including £900 million (over three years from 2001) for the Neighbourhood Renewal Fund. Neighbourhood renewal teams based in each of the Government Offices for the Regions support its work (see also page 98).

Rural regeneration

Although most problems arising from dereliction and unemployment occur in urban areas, some rural areas have also been affected by declining employment in traditional sectors, such as mining, agriculture and rurally based defence establishments. Even in areas that appear relatively prosperous, some individuals within these areas may be disadvantaged by poor local services, poor public transport and low wages or seasonal unemployment.

The RDAs outside London are responsible for rural regeneration. The Countryside Agency promotes and advises on conserving and enhancing the countryside, on access to the countryside for recreation, and on the economic and social development of England's rural areas. It also administers a number of grants designed to help meet village needs for transport, shops or other services.

Wales

Following the reduction in steel making capacity, and consequent redundancies, announced in 2001, the Welsh Assembly Government announced funding of £76 million to help stimulate the regeneration of the affected steel communities. Projects include the reopening of the Ebbw Vale rail line for passenger transport, a Community Learning Network and an Urban Regeneration Company for Newport.

Wales will also receive up to £1.2 billion from the European Union to fund a variety of programmes until 2006. These include Objective 1 Funds (see page 340) for West Wales & the Valleys. By March 2002 over £300 million of Objective 1 Funds had been allocated to 470 projects in Wales. The programmes are aimed at developing a stronger, more sustainable economy (especially with an expanded small and medium-sized company sector), better infrastructure, a more highly skilled workforce, and the regeneration of urban and rural communities.

The Assembly Government has allocated £36.7 million to the Local Regeneration Fund (LRF) in 2002/03. The purpose of the Fund is to support sustainable regeneration or development within, or benefiting, the most deprived areas, including the Objective 1 area in West Wales & the Valleys. Some of the money is used to match funding provided by European structural funds.

Communities First is an area-based regeneration programme that will benefit the 100 most deprived electoral wards, and other communities including 32 pockets of deprivation. The programme emphasises the involvement of local people in decision-making through a community-based partnership.

The Welsh Development Agency contributes to economic regeneration across Wales. Its programmes include physical and environmental regeneration activities, such as land reclamation and environmental improvements; activities to provide site development work to assist with business infrastructure; and financial support for community initiatives such as the Market Towns Initiative and the Small Towns and Villages programmes.

Scotland

In Scotland the Social Inclusion Partnership (SIP) programme, established in 1999, involves 48 local partnerships tackling the problems that disadvantaged groups and communities face across rural and urban Scotland. The SIPs are multi-agency partnerships, consisting of all relevant local public agencies, the voluntary and private sectors, and representatives from the community. The SIPs are supported over three years from 2001/02 by £169 million from the Social Inclusion Partnership Fund. In June 2002 the Scottish Executive launched its community regeneration statement, 'Better Communities in Scotland: closing the gap', which sets out how it intends to help deprived communities.

The Better Neighbourhood Services Fund (BNSF) is a programme designed to improve services in Scotland's most disadvantaged neighbourhoods and among its most disadvantaged groups. By 2002 the Scottish Executive had approved funding for all 12 BNSF authorities. A total of £90 million has been allocated to the fund over three years: £20 million in 2001/02, £30 million in 2002/03 and £40 million in 2003/04.

Scottish Enterprise is the main economic development agency for Scotland, covering 93 per cent of the population from Grampian to the Borders. It contributes to economic regeneration

Crown Street Regeneration Project
The Crown Street Regeneration Project set out to regenerate a major derelict site within a mile of Glasgow city centre. It aims to achieve sustainable improvements by working in partnership with the public sector and actively involving the local communities. Seventeen hectares of derelict land have been reclaimed and 810 mixed-tenure houses and 2,600 square metres of business space provided. Crown Street is scheduled for completion by autumn 2003.

In December 2001 the Welsh Development Agency embarked on a £2.5 million regeneration scheme of the derelict Six Bells Colliery in Blaenau Gwent. During the 1950s the colliery employed around 1,650 men and output peaked at 500,000 tonnes of coal a year. It was closed in 1988. The 15 hectare site will be used for the construction of housing and a school, and the creation of a recreation area for the village of Six Bells.

in Scotland through a number of schemes such as the Crown Street Regeneration Project.

Communities Scotland also has a responsibility for regeneration. It works closely with a number of partners, in particular local authorities. The planned budget for Communities Scotland for 2002/03 is over £300 million, of which £80 million is specifically for regeneration schemes.

Communities Scotland plans to invest £65 million in housing regeneration projects in Glasgow in 2002/03. The funding will be targeted at Glasgow's nine priority areas for regeneration – the SIP areas – and will provide new terraced homes with gardens for people living in poor quality tenement flats. Funding of £5 million will also be targeted at improving poor housing in areas where there are large minority ethnic communities.

Northern Ireland

The Department for Social Development (DSD) administers the Urban Development Grant (UDG) scheme, which promotes job creation, inward investment and environmental improvement in priority areas of Belfast and Londonderry/Derry by stimulating the development of vacant, derelict or underused land or buildings. In Belfast, priority is currently given to schemes within those deprived areas covered by the Belfast Regeneration Office, while UDG in Londonderry/Derry is targeted at the City Centre and Waterside Business District. Outside the two major cities the Department runs the Urban Development Programme on behalf of the International Fund for Ireland. It has similar aims to UDG and is available within existing commercial areas of towns and villages.

Underused or derelict land and buildings in selected areas of towns and cities are identified for planning and regeneration by the DSD via *Comprehensive Development Schemes*. It also has responsibility for the Laganside Corporation, a non-departmental public body managing the regeneration of Belfast's riverside and waterfront areas.

The Making Belfast Work Initiative had an annual budget of around £13.7 million and provided £262 million for a variety of projects between 1988 and the end of 2001/02. The Londonderry Regeneration Initiative had an annual budget of £2.7 million and from its launch in 1988 to the end of 2001/02 provided £36 million for a variety of projects in the most deprived and disadvantaged areas.

The Community Regeneration and Improvement Special Programme (CRISP), which is jointly funded by DSD and the International Fund for Ireland, is aimed at assisting community-led regeneration in the most disadvantaged smaller towns and villages in Northern Ireland. CRISP provides a financial package of measures to deliver economic, physical and social benefits to these deprived communities. Since 1990 over 72 projects have been approved with funding of over £56 million.

The Community Property Development Scheme and Second Community Projects form part of the International Fund for Ireland's Urban Development Programme in Northern Ireland. The primary objective of these schemes is to stimulate economic activity by encouraging cross-community groups to regenerate key properties in the most rundown areas outside Belfast and Londonderry/Derry. Twenty projects have been approved under this scheme with grants totalling £5.5 million.

The Rural Development Programme in Northern Ireland began in 1991. In 2001 the NIHE announced the 2001–06 phase of the programme, which seeks to develop social, economic and cultural initiatives for people living in Northern Ireland's rural communities. The programme targets all parts of Northern Ireland outside the Metropolitan Area of Belfast, the city of Londonderry/Derry and the 20 towns with populations greater than 5,000.
.

Further reading

Delivering a Fundamental Change. Green Paper. DTLR, 2001.

DTLR Annual Report 2002: The Government's expenditure plans 2002–03 to 2003–04. The Stationery Office, 2002

English Partnerships: Annual Report and Financial Statements. English Partnerships.

The Housing Corporation: Annual Review. The Housing Corporation.

Housing Statistics (annual). Office of the Deputy Prime Minister. The Stationery Office.

More than a roof: A report into tackling homelessness. DTLR, 2002.

Our Towns and Cities: The Future – Delivering the Urban Renaissance. Department of the Environment, Transport and the Regions, 2000.

Social Trends (annual). Office for National Statistics. The Stationery Office.

Websites

Office of the Deputy Prime Minister
www.odpm.gov.uk

Scottish Executive
www.scotland.gov.uk

National Assembly for Wales/ Welsh Assembly Government
www.wales.gov.uk

Northern Ireland Executive
www.nics.gov.uk

English Partnerships
www.englishpartnerships.co.uk

Council of Mortgage Lenders
www.cml.org.uk

Housing Corporation
www.housingcorp.gov.uk

Communities Scotland
www.communitiesscotland.gov.uk

Northern Ireland Housing Executive
www.nihe.gov.uk

21 Transport

Introduction

The terrorist attacks in the United States on 11 September 2001 had an immediate impact on international travel to the UK. For example, there were nearly 1 million, or 16 per cent, fewer overseas visitors to the UK in the fourth quarter of 2001 than in the corresponding quarter of 2000. Although the first quarter of 2002 saw a recovery, the number of overseas visitors was still 8 per cent below the same period in 2001.

The end of 2001 and beginning of 2002 saw some important events in the rail industry. Railtrack (see page 317) was placed into administration in October 2001. Since then the administrator has been responsible for ensuring the normal operation of the industry. In January 2002 the Strategic Rail Authority (SRA – see page 318) published its ten-year strategic plan for the railways, which is expected to involve expenditure of £67.5 billion.

The new Department for Transport (DfT) was created in May 2002 to focus solely on transport issues. It took on all the transport responsibilities of the former Department for Transport, Local Government and the Regions (DTLR).

Travel trends

British residents travelled on average around 11,000 kilometres a year within Great Britain in 1999–2001. They made an average of 1,019 trips a year, spending 360 hours, the equivalent of 15 days travelling.

Travel by car accounted for 85 per cent of passenger mileage in Great Britain in 2001. Since the early 1970s, the proportion of households with regular access to one car has remained relatively

Table 21.1 Passenger transport in Great Britain: by mode[1]

			Billion passenger-kilometres	
	1991	1996	2000	2001
Buses and coaches	44	44	45	46
Cars, vans and taxis	582	606	618	624
Motorcycles, mopeds and scooters	6	4	5	5
Pedal cycles	5	4	4	4
All road	**638**	**658**	**672**	**679**
Rail[2]	39	39	47	n/a
Air[3]	5	6	8	8
All modes[4]	**681**	**703**	**726**	**734**

1 Figures for 2000 and 2001 have been produced on a different basis to that used previously and are not directly comparable with those for earlier years.
2 Financial years. Includes former British Rail companies, urban rail systems and underground railways.
3 Scheduled and non-scheduled services. Excludes air taxi services, private flying and passengers paying less than 25 per cent of the full fare. Includes Northern Ireland and the Channel Islands.
4 Excluding travel by water within the UK (including the Channel Islands), estimated at 0.7 billion passenger-kilometres in 2000.
Source: *Transport Statistics Great Britain 2002*

stable, while the proportion with more than one has grown, from 7 per cent in 1970 to 26 per cent in 1999–2001.

Roads

The total road network in Great Britain in 2000 was 391,701 kilometres. Trunk motorways (those motorways that are the direct responsibility of the central administration rather than the local authority) accounted for 3,465 kilometres of this, less than 1 per cent, and other trunk roads for 11,742 kilometres, or 3 per cent. However, motorways carry 20 per cent of all traffic, and trunk roads another 16 per cent. Combined, they carry over half of all goods vehicle traffic in Great Britain. In Northern Ireland the road network is over 24,788 kilometres, of which 114 kilometres are motorways.

The number of licensed vehicles on Britain's roads has increased over sixfold since 1952 (see Table 21.3). By far the biggest factor in this growth has been the increase in private cars.

Motor traffic in Great Britain increased significantly in the mid-1990s, although growth has slowed somewhat in recent years. However, total traffic levels still grew by 1.3 per cent between 2000 and 2001 (see Table 21.2).

Congestion

About 7 per cent of the network of the Highways Agency (see page 313) in England experiences regular heavy peak and occasional non-peak congestion, and a further 13 per cent sees heavy congestion on at least half the days in the year.

Traffic congestion also occurs in many towns and cities throughout the UK in the main morning

Table 21.3 Motor vehicles licensed in Great Britain

	1952	Thousands 2001
Private cars	2,221	23,899
Goods vehicles[1]	450	422
Motorcycles	812	882
Public transport vehicles	119	89
Total[2]	**4,464**	**29,747**

1 Included agricultural and showmans' vehicles in 1952.
2 Total includes Crown and exempt vehicles, and other vehicles.
Source: Department for Transport

and evening peak periods and for much of the day in central London. Traffic management schemes aim to reduce congestion through measures such as traffic-free shopping precincts, bus lanes and other bus priority measures, red routes with special stopping controls, and parking controls. The DfT has a target to reduce congestion on the inter-urban road network and in large urban areas in England to below 2000 levels by 2010, as part of its commitment to the Government's Sustainable Development Programme (see page 267).

Local authorities in London and the rest of England and Wales can introduce congestion charging schemes for road users or a levy on workplace parking. The net revenue generated from charges can be retained for at least ten years, provided that it is used to fund local transport improvements. Provision for urban congestion charging schemes also exists in Scotland. Authorities must consult local people and businesses, make improvements to public transport and obtain ministerial approval before starting schemes. The first such scheme – in the historic centre of Durham – began in 2002. Revenue from this scheme is being used to fund improvements to the city's bus services. A similar

Table 21.2 Motor vehicle traffic in Great Britain: by road class[1]

	1991	1996	2000	Billion vehicle-kilometres 2001
Motorways	61	74	94	95
Built-up[2] major roads	79	81	77	77
Non built-up major roads	117	126	128	130
Minor roads	154	162	169	171
All roads	**412**	**443**	**468**	**474**

1 Figures for 2000 and 2001 are not directly comparable with those for previous years.
2 Built-up roads are those with a speed limit of 40 mph or less (irrespective of whether there are buildings or not).
Source: Department for Transport

scheme is also planned for Edinburgh, but will not commence before 2006.

A congestion charging scheme is planned to start in central London in February 2003. Owners of vehicles entering or moving around a 21 square kilometre area will be charged £5, payable in advance or on the day by telephone, Internet, post or at retail outlets. Weekend and evening travel will remain uncharged. The aim is to reduce traffic in central London by 10 to 15 per cent, and delays by 20 to 30 per cent. The scheme is expected to raise £130 million a year.

Traffic information

Traffic information is provided throughout Great Britain by a variety of means, such as the media, roadside signs and in-vehicle systems. Information sources include roadside sensors, the traffic police and highway authorities, and data are collated by organisations such as the Automobile Association (AA) and the Royal Automobile Club (RAC), and by information service providers like Integrated Traffic Information Services (ITIS), Metro Networks and Trafficmaster.

Local traffic control centres across Great Britain help to manage traffic and provide information about conditions. Centres covering wider areas exist in Scotland and Wales.

The Highways Agency has entered into a public-private partnership (PPP – see page 350) with Traffic Information Services to set up and run the Traffic Control Centre (TCC). The TCC is intended to provide a co-ordinated national information service to travellers in England by early 2003. Up-to-the-minute details will be available via variable message signs, the Highways Agency information line, the Internet, the media and commercial driver information services.

Road safety

There were 4 per cent fewer road deaths and 16 per cent fewer serious casualties in Great Britain in 2001 compared with the average for the years 1994–98. Road traffic increased by 7 per cent over the same period. In 2001 there were 228,825 road accidents involving personal injury in Great Britain, 2 per cent fewer than in 2000, of which 34,749 involved death or serious injury. There were 3,443 deaths in road accidents, 37,094 serious injuries and 272,509 slight injuries.

Overall, Great Britain has one of the best road safety records in the world. Even so, the

Average car speeds[1] on Great Britain's roads in 2000	
Motorways	70 mph
Dual carriageways	70 mph
Single carriageways	45 mph
Urban 30 mph limit zones	32 mph
Urban 40 mph limit zones	37 mph

Traffic speeds in central and inner London showed a marked variation from the national picture. For example, the average speed in central London during the daytime off-peak period in 1997–2000 was 10 mph.

Government has set a target of reducing the number of people killed or seriously injured on the roads by 40 per cent by 2010, compared with the average level for 1994–98. A higher target reduction, of 50 per cent, has been set for deaths and serious injuries to children. Measures that have been, or are being, taken include:

- creating more 20 mph (32 km/h) zones around schools and in residential areas – a further 28 such schemes, at a cost of £3.5 million, were approved in December 2001;

- enforcing road traffic law more effectively, with greater use of speed cameras, which will be made more visible to drivers;

- the mandatory fitting of seat belts in new coaches and minibuses from October 2001; and

- improving road safety education, for example through a network of road safety schemes for children, funded from some £10 million set aside over three years for increases and improvements in child pedestrian training.

Local authorities in England and Wales are now required to include specific road safety measures as part of their Local Transport Plans (see page 325), while local authorities in Scotland are expected to set out in their Local Transport Strategies plans for reducing road casualties.

---

1 These are 'spot' speeds. Measurements tend to be taken where traffic is relatively free-flowing.

A major study of the safety of Europe's roads was published in February 2002. EuroRAP (the European Road Assessment Programme) (*www.eurorap.org*), led by the AA, gave safety 'star' ratings to 833 major UK roads, and a further 2,000 in the Netherlands, Sweden and Spain. EuroRAP shows the safety performance of these routes in relation to the amount of traffic. The system is intended to allow planners to make changes to lessen the risk of the four major causes of fatal accidents – head-on crashes, accidents at junctions, collisions with vulnerable road users and hitting objects at the side of the road. Of the roads assessed in the UK, 23 received no stars; 90 received one; 213 two stars; 415 three stars; and 92 gained the top four-star rating. Roads with no stars have accident rates ten times higher than the best performing roads in the four-star category.

Standards

Minimum ages for driving in the UK are:

- 16 for riders of mopeds, drivers of small tractors, and disabled people receiving a mobility allowance;

- 17 for drivers of cars and other passenger vehicles with nine or fewer seats (including that of the driver), small motorcycles, and goods vehicles not over 3.5 tonnes maximum authorised mass (MAM);

- 18 for goods vehicles weighing over 3.5, but not over 7.5, tonnes MAM; and

- 21 for passenger-carrying vehicles with more than nine seats, goods vehicles over 7.5 tonnes MAM and large motorcycles.

About 32 million people hold a full driving licence for a car. New drivers of motor vehicles must pass both a computer-based touch screen theory test and a practical driving test in order to acquire a full driving licence. In 2000/01, just over 1.3 million driving tests were conducted in Great Britain by the Driving Standards Agency (DSA), the national driver testing authority. The average pass rate was nearly 53 per cent. The DSA also supervises professional driving instructors, the compulsory basic training scheme for learner motorcyclists and a voluntary register for instructors of drivers of large goods vehicles.

Before most new cars and goods vehicles are allowed on the roads, they must meet safety and environmental requirements, based primarily on standards drawn up by the European Union (EU). The Vehicle Certification Agency is responsible for ensuring these requirements are met through a process known as 'type approval'.

The Vehicle Inspectorate is responsible for ensuring the roadworthiness of vehicles, through their annual testing. It also uses roadside and other enforcement checks to ensure that drivers and vehicle operators comply with legislation. In Northern Ireland the Driver and Vehicle Testing Agency is responsible for testing drivers and vehicles.

Road haulage

Most freight in Great Britain is carried by road, which accounts for 81 per cent of goods by tonnage and 64 per cent in terms of tonne-kilometres.

An operator's licence is required for operating goods vehicles over 3.5 tonnes gross weight in the UK. About 88 per cent of the 106,700 licences in issue are for fleets of five or fewer vehicles, and there are around 440,000 heavy goods vehicles (HGVs) in the UK. Road haulage traffic by HGVs amounted to 149 billion tonne-kilometres in Great Britain in 2001, 20 per cent more than in 1991. Road hauliers are tending to use larger vehicles carrying heavier loads – 87 per cent of the traffic, in terms of tonne-kilometres, is now carried by vehicles of over 25 tonnes gross weight.

International road haulage has grown rapidly. In 2001 about 2.4 million road goods vehicles travelled by ferry or the Channel Tunnel to mainland Europe, a 3 per cent increase over 2000. Of these, over 510,000 were powered vehicles registered in the UK. UK vehicles carried 13.8 million tonnes internationally and 97 per cent of this traffic was with the EU.

The Government has a long-term strategy for freight in the UK. This seeks to reduce the extent to which economic growth generates additional lorry movements, by improving efficiency, making the most of rail, shipping and inland waterways, and improving interchange links between the different types of transport. Measures introduced include an increase in the maximum weight of lorries on domestic journeys to 44 tonnes. The Freight Facilities Grant scheme, which provides assistance towards capital costs associated with moving freight by inland waterway rather than road, has been extended to coastal and short sea movements.

Bus services

In 2000/01 some 4,309 million passenger journeys were made on local bus services in Great Britain, nearly 11 per cent fewer than in 1990/91. However, journey numbers have been increasing in recent years, from a low of 4,248 million in 1998/99. In contrast, passenger journeys in London (which accounts for nearly a third of bus journeys in Great Britain) in 2000/01 were some 15 per cent higher than ten years earlier. There have also been increases in bus use in Scotland in recent years. The ten-year plan (see page 325) target for bus use in England is growth of 10 per cent in passenger numbers by 2010 from 2000 levels.

There are around 85,000 buses and coaches in Great Britain, of which 25 per cent are minibuses, while 20 per cent are double-deckers. Most local bus services are provided commercially, with 84 per cent of bus mileage outside London operating on this basis. Local authorities may subsidise services which are not commercially viable but which are considered socially necessary.

Operators

Almost all bus services in Great Britain are provided by private sector concerns, apart from 17 bus companies owned by local authorities. Transport for London is responsible for providing or procuring public transport in the capital. It oversees more than 700 bus routes run by about 25 companies under contract.

Five main groups operate bus services: Arriva, FirstGroup, Go-Ahead Group, National Express and Stagecoach. All also run rail services and some have expanded into transport services in other countries, notably the United States.

In Northern Ireland almost all road passenger services are operated by subsidiaries of the publicly owned Northern Ireland Transport Holding Company (NITHC), collectively known as 'Translink'. Citybus Ltd operates services in Belfast, and Ulsterbus Ltd runs most of the services in the rest of Northern Ireland, carrying 20 million and 47 million passengers a year respectively.

Services

Local authorities in England and Wales are required to develop bus strategies as part of their Local Transport Plans (LTPs – see page 325). Although there is no statutory requirement in Scotland, local authorities are expected to set out their views on bus services in their Local Transport Strategies. Outside London statutory backing also exists for 'bus quality partnerships' and 'quality contracts' between local authorities and bus operators. Similar partnerships have already been developed voluntarily in around 130 towns and cities, and have led to better services with higher-quality buses, and typically 10 to 20 per cent greater passenger use. Authorities have powers to promote joint ticketing and to work with Train Operating Companies on bus/rail ticketing.

Bus priority measures, such as bus lanes, are becoming more extensive, while in some areas innovative measures, such as guided busways (with buses travelling on segregated track) are being adopted. Around 70 park and ride schemes – in which car users park on the outskirts of towns and travel by public transport to the centre – are in operation in England and Scotland, and are being increasingly used to relieve traffic congestion. Over 100 new schemes are envisaged over the next ten years. Similar schemes operate in Wales and Northern Ireland.

The Rural Bus Subsidy Grant (RBSG) has funding of £136 million between 2001/02 and 2003/04. The grant is for the provision of new or enhanced local bus services in England. In addition, a total of £60 million over the same period has been allocated for the Rural Bus Challenge, an annual competition in which local authorities bid for project funding. The Scottish Executive's £6 million Rural Transport Fund is funding over 350 new and improved rural bus services. The Urban Bus Challenge plays a similar role in towns and cities in England to the RBSG, and has been allocated £46 million from 2001/02 to 2003/04.

The Welsh Assembly Government is allocating more than £7.5 million to local authorities in 2002/03 under its Local Transport Services grant to increase the number and range of subsidised bus services and to support community transport projects.

Ninety-four per cent of local authorities offered a half-fare concessionary scheme for the elderly in England in 2001, while 90 per cent offered a similar concession to disabled people and 60 per cent to blind people. The remainder either had flat-fare schemes or schemes offering free travel, such as in London. Since April 2002, travel on local bus services in Wales has been free for pensioners and disabled people, while in Scotland, free off-peak local bus fares will be available for elderly and disabled people from October 2002.

Coaches account for much of the non-local mileage operated by public service vehicles, which totalled 1,503 million vehicle-kilometres in 2000/01. Organised coach tours and holiday journeys account for about 60 per cent of coach travel in Great Britain. High-frequency scheduled services, run by private sector operators, link many towns and cities, and commuter services run into London and some other major centres each weekday. The biggest coach operator, National Express, has a national network of scheduled coach services and carries more than 15 million passengers each year.

Taxis

There are about 98,000 licensed taxis in England and Wales (mainly in urban areas), around 20,000 in Scotland, and about 3,100 in Northern Ireland. In London (which has over 24,000 taxis) and several other major cities, taxis must be purpose-built to conform to strict requirements. In many districts, taxi drivers have to pass a test of their knowledge of the area.

Private hire vehicles (PHVs or 'minicabs') may only be booked through the operator and not hired on the street. There are about 76,000 in England and Wales, outside London, 8,000 in Scotland and over 2,100 in Northern Ireland. Licences have been required for PHV operators in London since October 2001 (bringing the capital in line with the rest of England and Wales). Over 1,800 operators have so far been licensed, and it is estimated that there are around 40,000 drivers and a similar number of vehicles. Transport for London is working on the details for the second and third phases of licensing – covering drivers and vehicles respectively.

Cycling and motorcycling

The use of two-wheeled transport in Great Britain is much less common than 50 years ago. In 1952, 11 per cent of distance travelled was on pedal cycles, and a further 3 per cent on motorcycles. By 2001, these figures had both fallen to only 1 per cent.

The National Cycling Strategy aims to increase the number of pedal cycle journeys fourfold by 2012 (based on 1996 figures). The Cycling Forum for

England is co-ordinating the implementation of the strategy, which has been endorsed by the Government. The Scottish Cycle Forum co-ordinates implementation in Scotland, while Wales and Northern Ireland have their own strategies. The DfT announced its own target of trebling the number of cycling journeys by 2010, as part of the Government's ten-year plan. Cycling strategies form part of Local Transport Plans and Strategies, and include measures to make cycling safer and more convenient.

The National Cycle Network currently provides 9,600 kilometres of cycling and walking routes throughout the UK. Developed by the transport charity Sustrans (*www.sustrans.org.uk*), the network will cover 16,000 kilometres when it is completed in 2005. Over a third of the network will be entirely free from motor traffic by utilising old railway lines, canal towpaths, river paths and derelict land. The remainder will follow existing roads, with traffic calming and cycle lanes being implemented where necessary. Fifty per cent of users are cyclists and 48 per cent pedestrians. Sustrans estimates that more than half of all network users making functional journeys could have chosen a car instead of cycling or walking.

After a long period of decline since the early 1960s, there has been a resurgence in motorcycling in the UK over the last few years. The number of licensed motorcycles has risen from a low of 594,000 in 1995 to around 882,000 in 2001, the highest figure since 1988.

Walking

People in the UK are walking less than in the past, with fewer journeys on foot and many more by car. The Government wishes to reverse this trend, and expects local authorities to give more priority to walking. Almost all local authorities included walking strategies in their LTPs and Strategies (see page 325), many identifying targets to encourage walking through a variety of initiatives. LTP funding is likely to be used to make walking safer and more accessible, for example by improving pavement and footway maintenance, removing obstructions and improving pedestrian crossings.

Home Zones are residential streets in which the road space is shared between the drivers of motor vehicles and other road users, with the wider needs of residents (including people who walk or cycle, and children) in mind. The aim is to change the way that streets are used, for example by encouraging people to walk rather than use their cars, and improve the quality of life of local residents. Thirteen pilot schemes are in operation across Great Britain; one, in Northmoor, Manchester, has already seen a significant drop in car speeds, by up to 10 mph. The Government announced the winners of its Home Zones Challenge in January 2002, when it awarded £30 million to 61 projects.

Safe routes to school projects (*www.saferoutestoschool.org*) aim to encourage and enable children to walk and cycle to school. They combine practical measures, such as redesigns of roadspace to provide for cyclists and pedestrians and 20 mph speed limits near schools, with educational measures, for example cycle training for children and an emphasis on the health benefits of walking and cycling.

The Scottish Executive has provided local authorities with an additional £20 million for cycling, walking and safer streets projects through its Public Transport Fund.

Road programme

The maintenance, operation and improvement of most of the national road network in England is the responsibility of the Highways Agency (*www.highways.gov.uk*), an executive agency of DfT. In London, responsibility lies with the Greater London Authority. In Wales, Scotland and Northern Ireland responsibility for the motorway and trunk road network rests with the devolved administrations.

The Highways Agency is responsible for 9,404 kilometres of motorway and trunk roads in England. However, some 500 kilometres of this network are in the process of being transferred to relevant local authorities. The Agency's budget is £1.77 billion in 2002/03. In addition, local authorities had a budget of nearly £1.9 billion in 2000/01 for maintaining roads. In Scotland, the motorway and trunk road programme for 2001–04 will cost £680 million.

The Highways Agency's 2002/03 programme includes plans to:

- spend £740 million on maintenance. To ease congestion, 90 per cent of routine maintenance will be carried out at night;

- spend £698 million on major road projects, including eight schemes intended to ease congestion and improve safety;

- award a PPP (see page 350) contract to build and run a 53-km section of the A1(M) in Yorkshire; and

- carry out a programme of small-scale congestion and safety improvements across the network, including junction improvements, cycleways and noise mitigation.

Fifty years of travel trends

Passenger travel was 734 billion passenger-kilometres in Great Britain in 2001 (see Table 21.1), compared with 218 billion passenger-kilometres in 1952.

The major trend of the last 50 years has been the increase in journeys by cars, vans and taxis, which accounted for 85 per cent of passenger mileage in 2001 compared with 27 per cent in 1952. Only 15 per cent of households had regular use of a car in 1952; by 2001 this figure had risen to 73 per cent. In contrast, people in Britain are cycling much less than 50 years ago. In 1952, pedal cycles accounted for 11 per cent of all passenger miles, compared with under 1 per cent in 2001.

Another major trend over the last 50 years has been the growth in air travel. In 1952 there were 2.8 million terminal passengers at UK airports. This figure had grown to 181 million passengers by 2001.

Railways

Railtrack is responsible for operating all track and infrastructure in Great Britain. Its assets include 32,000 kilometres of track; 40,000 bridges, tunnels and viaducts; 2,500 stations; and connections to over 1,000 freight terminals. Railtrack was placed into administration in October 2001 when the High Court found it was unable (or likely to be unable) to pay debts of £3.3 billion which it had accrued. Since then the administrator has been responsible for ensuring normal operation of the railway.

A successor company, Network Rail (a company limited by guarantee), has made an offer to the administrator to bring administration to an end. Network Rail would have the interests of the travelling public as its priority and would invest any operating profit back into the railway network.

Most railway services in the UK are now operated by the private sector. Apart from 15 major stations operated directly by Railtrack, nearly all stations and passenger depots are leased to the passenger Train Operating Companies (TOCs) that run passenger services under franchise. There are currently 25 TOCs. Many franchises are for seven years, but some are for 10, 12 or 15 years.

The TOCs, such as First Great Western, South West Trains and GNER, lease their rolling stock from the three main rolling stock companies: Angel Trains, HSBC Rail and Porterbrook Leasing. Freight services are run by four companies, and there are a number of infrastructure maintenance companies.

There are also over 100 other passenger-carrying railways, often connected with the preservation of steam locomotives. Services are operated mostly on a voluntary basis and cater mainly for tourists and railway enthusiasts.

Rail regulation and strategy

The regulation of Britain's railways is the responsibility of two organisations: the Strategic Rail Authority (SRA) and the Office of the Rail Regulator (ORR). The two organisations have common statutory purposes but different powers to achieve them. The SRA is subject to directions and guidance from the Government, while the ORR is independent.

The SRA is responsible for providing strategic leadership to the rail industry; allocating government funding to the railways; negotiating, awarding and monitoring the franchises for operating rail services; and a number of other statutory functions, in particular relating to customer protection. Government support to the rail industry amounted to approximately £1.2 billion in 2000/01.

The Rail Regulator provides independent economic regulation of the monopoly and dominant elements of the rail industry, particularly Railtrack's stewardship of the national rail network. In addition, the Regulator licenses the railway operators, approves or directs agreements governing access to track, stations and depots, and enforces competition law in connection with the provision of rail services.

A new refranchising programme was published by the SRA in December 2001. It is designed to help

The SRA strategic plan

The SRA's ten-year plan for the railways sets out the changes required by 2010 to meet the Government's targets for rail – a 50 per cent increase in passenger-kilometres, reductions in overcrowding, and an 80 per cent increase in freight tonne-kilometres. Utilising government funding of £33.5 billion, the plan mixes short, medium and long-term goals in an attempt to bring major improvements for passengers. Key points include £400 million for a Rail Performance Fund to co-invest with rail companies in short-term schemes to improve reliability, £430 million for local passenger improvements, and a National Rail Academy to develop staff training in core skills. Changes to be delivered within four years include:

- replacement of slam-door Mark 1 coaches with new stock, providing extra capacity;

- track and signalling improvements at 100 locations;

- improved station facilities; and

- revenue support schemes for rail freight to encourage competition.

deliver the Government's ten-year plan targets. Wherever franchises are replaced or extended, new contracts will target provision of better facilities, higher performance incentives for operators and better compensation arrangements for passengers when things go wrong. The SRA is also examining the longer term benefits of fewer franchises where two or more existing franchisees share the use of one London terminus. One such combined franchise, 'Greater Anglia', will be awarded from 2004.

Rail safety

There have been a number of fatal rail accidents in recent years, including incidents at Southall (London) in 1997, Ladbroke Grove, near Paddington (London), in 1999, Hatfield (Hertfordshire) in 2000 and Potters Bar (Hertfordshire) in 2002. Nevertheless, there is evidence that some trends in railway safety are improving. Health and Safety Executive (HSE) figures show that in 2000/01 significant train accidents (that is, most collisions and derailments involving passenger trains) were the second lowest on record – 0.27 per million train miles run. Five people were killed in train accidents in 2001/02, compared with 17 in 2000/01.

Measures being taken to improve the safety of the railway network include:

■ the fitting of the train protection and warning system (TPWS) to the national network by the end of 2003;

■ the development of plans to fit the new European automatic train protection (ATP) system as lines that are included in the European high-speed network are upgraded;

■ investment in new rolling stock; and

■ the development of a new national safety plan to improve safety management and ensure best practice.

Passenger services

The passenger network (see map) comprises a fast inter-city network, linking the main centres of Great Britain; local and regional services; and commuter services in and around the large conurbations, especially London and the South East. Passenger traffic is growing (see Table 21.4) and on the national railways rose by 2 per cent in 2001/02 to 39.1 billion passenger-kilometres, representing some 956 million passenger journeys.

According to the SRA's Public Performance Measure, an average of 78 per cent of scheduled services ran to timetable in 2001/02.

Table 21.4 Passenger traffic on rail,[1] underground and selected light rail services in Great Britain

| | Million passenger-kilometres | | |
	1991/92	1996/97	2001/02
National railways	32,500	32,100	39,100
London Underground	5,895	6,153	7,451
Glasgow Underground	39	40	44
Docklands Light Railway	32	86	207
Greater Manchester Metro	–	86	n/a
Tyne and Wear Metro	277	254	238
Croydon Tramlink	–	–	99
Centro West Midlands Metro	–	–	50
Stagecoach Supertram	–	29	n/a

1 Excludes Heathrow Express.
Source: *Transport Statistics Great Britain 2002*

Freight

Rail freight traffic in Great Britain totalled an estimated 19.7 billion tonne-kilometres, representing the carriage of 94.4 million tonnes in 2001/02. Over 80 per cent of traffic by volume is in bulk commodities, mainly coal, coke, iron and steel, building materials and petroleum. The two largest operators are English, Welsh & Scottish Railway (EWS), which also runs trains through the Channel Tunnel; and Freightliner, which operates container services between major ports and inland terminals.

The Government and the devolved administrations are keen to encourage more freight to be moved by rail, to relieve pressure on the road network and to bring environmental benefits. Grants are available to encourage companies to move goods by rail or water rather than by road.

Northern Ireland

Northern Ireland Railways, a wholly owned subsidiary of the NITHC (see page 315), operates the railway service on about 338 kilometres of track and handled 6.2 million passenger journeys in 2001/02. The NITHC is currently undertaking a programme to improve the railway network, with increased expenditure provided by the Department for Regional Development. The award of a £73 million contract to build new rolling stock was announced in February 2002, the largest single such investment in Northern Ireland.

Channel Tunnel

The Channel Tunnel was opened to traffic in 1994. It is operated by Eurotunnel, a UK-French group, under a concession from the British and French Governments. As well as managing the infrastructure of the Channel Tunnel – tunnels, terminals and track – Eurotunnel operates a drive-on, drive-off shuttle train service, with separate shuttles for passenger and freight vehicles, between terminals near Folkestone and Calais. In 2001 the service carried just over 2.5 million cars (down 11 per cent on 2000), nearly 1.2 million goods vehicles (up by 9 per cent) and 75,400 coaches (down by 5 per cent).

Eurostar high-speed train services are operated jointly by Eurostar (UK) Ltd, French Railways and Belgian Railways under the commercial direction of Eurostar Group Ltd. Frequent services connect London (Waterloo) and Paris or Brussels, taking approximately 3 hours and 2 hours 40 minutes respectively. Trains also serve Ashford International (Kent), Calais, Lille, Disneyland Paris, Bourg St Maurice in the French Alps (in the winter) and Avignon (in the summer). Eurostar carried 7 million passengers in 2001.

Channel Tunnel Rail Link
The first section of the Channel Tunnel Rail Link (CTRL) is under construction between the Channel Tunnel terminal and Fawkham Junction (Kent), and is planned to be completed in 2003. Construction work on the second section to St Pancras (London) is in progress, and is due to open in 2006. The whole project is forecast to cost an estimated £5.2 billion. Eurostar trains will be able to travel in the UK at speeds of 300 km/h (185 mph), reducing journey times by 35 minutes. High-speed domestic services will also operate from Kent to London. New international stations for the CTRL will be built at Stratford in east London and Ebbsfleet in Kent.

Underground railways
London's 'tube' network is run by London Underground Ltd (LUL – *www.thetube.com*), serving 275 stations on 408 kilometres of railway. In 2001/02, 953 million passenger journeys were made on the network. The Glasgow Underground, a heavy rapid transit system, operates on an 11 km circle in central Glasgow.

Under an expected public-private partnership (PPP), responsibility for maintaining and upgrading LUL's infrastructure will transfer to the private sector, while LUL will continue to have responsibility for safety and for all aspects of operating passenger services across the network. Three private sector infrastructure companies (Infracos) will work under contract to LUL for a

30-year period. Ownership of LUL's assets – for example, trains, stations, track and tunnels – will remain with the public sector LUL; the Infracos will lease the assets for the period of the contracts. The PPP is expected to provide about £16 billion of investment over 15 years. LUL will become part of Transport for London once the PPP is in place.

Light railways and tramways
There has been a revival in interest in tram/light rail services in recent years, and a number are now in operation (see Table 21.5). Government plans indicate a growing role for tramways, with the provision of up to 25 new lines in major cities and conurbations.

The £180 million Nottingham Express Transit system, which will run for 13 kilometres, will open in 2003. Construction will commence in 2003 on a £190 million light rail system in South Hampshire and the £500 million Leeds Supertram, while work on the Bristol Light Rail Transit will start in 2004. Approval has also been given for three extensions, costing over £500 million, of the Manchester Metrolink.

Air travel

The number of passengers carried into and out of UK airports has trebled in the last 20 years. Air transport movements and freight have more than doubled. According to the DfT, these trends look set to continue, as the number of air passengers is growing by between 4 and 5 per cent a year and the freight market by 7 per cent.

Traffic on UK-owned airlines, 2001	
Aircraft-kilometres flown	1,512 million
Passengers uplifted[2]	104 million
Passenger-kilometres flown	249 billion
Cargo and mail uplifted	925,000 tonnes
Cargo- and mail-kilometres flown	5,196 million

UK airlines are entirely in the private sector, as are most of the major airports. In recent years

Table 21.5 Light rail systems in operation in the UK, 2002

	Number of stations	Length of route (km)
Centro (West Midlands)	23	20
Croydon Tramlink (London)	38	28
Docklands Light Railway (London)	34	27
Manchester Metrolink	36	39
Sheffield Supertram	47	29
Tyne and Wear Metro	58	77

Source: Department for Transport

2 Passenger and cargo movements are counted every time an aircraft takes off, that is, on every stage of a journey rather than once for the whole journey.

low-cost or 'no-frills' airlines have become increasingly popular. Day-to-day responsibility for the regulation of civil aviation rests with the Civil Aviation Authority (CAA – *www.caa.co.uk*).

The terrorist attacks in the United States on 11 September 2001 had an impact on air travel in the UK. However, figures suggest that this was less severe than was originally feared; for example, passenger numbers in the fourth quarter of 2001 were down only 7 per cent on the same period in 2000. Long-haul, especially transatlantic, services were worst hit, but short-haul European and domestic services, especially among low-cost carriers, have proved more resilient. The attacks prompted a working group, comprising DfT, the Home Office, Metropolitan Police, HM Customs and HM Immigration, to examine security at airports. The recommendations in the group's report were subsequently accepted by the Government. Measures implemented by May 2002 included stiffer regulations concerning security passes and the extension of counter-terrorism checks on staff. In the longer term, enhanced CCTV coverage will also be introduced at airports and the co-operation and co-ordination of those involved in airport security will be improved. The working group will continue to meet to review progress.

Airlines

British Airways

British Airways is the world's largest international airline. During 2001/02 its turnover from airline

Table 21.6 Passenger traffic at the UK's main airports[1]

| | Million passengers | | |
	1991	1996	2001
London Heathrow	40.2	55.7	60.4
London Gatwick	18.7	24.1	31.1
Manchester	10.1	14.5	19.1
London Stansted	1.7	4.8	13.6
Birmingham	3.2	5.4	7.7
Glasgow	4.2	5.5	7.2
London Luton	2.0	2.4	6.5
Edinburgh	2.3	3.8	6.0
Belfast International	2.2	2.4	3.6
Newcastle	1.5	2.4	3.4
Aberdeen	2.0	2.3	2.5
East Midlands	1.1	1.8	2.4

1 Terminal passengers, excluding those in transit.
Source: Civil Aviation Authority

operations was £8.3 billion, and the British Airways group carried over 40 million passengers on its fleet of 360 planes, achieving an occupancy of 70 per cent on its main scheduled services. The airline's worldwide network covers 244 destinations in 97 countries, and its main operating bases are London's Heathrow and Gatwick airports.

British Airways was one of the founders, together with American Airlines, Canadian International Airlines, Cathay Pacific and Qantas, of the 'Oneworld' alliance. The alliance now has eight member airlines and serves 571 scheduled destinations in 135 countries or territories.

Other UK Airlines

BMI, formerly British Midland, is the second largest scheduled carrier and operates an extensive network of scheduled services with 57 aircraft, carrying 6.7 million passengers in 2001. Britannia Airways is the world's biggest charter airline and carried 7.9 million passengers in 2001 on its 31 aircraft. Virgin Atlantic operates scheduled services to 21 overseas destinations with 34 aircraft. Low-fare 'no-frills' airlines operating in the UK include easyJet and Go; easyJet acquired Go in August 2002.

Airports

Of the 150 or so licensed civil aerodromes in the UK, nearly a quarter handle more than 100,000 passengers a year each. In 2001 the UK's civil airports handled a total of 182.3 million passengers (181.2 million terminal passengers and 1.1 million in transit), and 2.1 million tonnes of freight.

Heathrow is the world's busiest airport for international travellers and is the UK's most important for passengers and air freight, handling 60.4 million passengers (excluding those in transit) and 1.2 million tonnes of freight in 2001. Gatwick is the world's sixth busiest international airport and has the world's busiest single runway. Stansted is the fastest growing airport in Europe, with terminal passengers increasing by 15 per cent in 2001.

Ownership and control

BAA plc is the world's largest commercial operator of airports. It handles almost 200 million passengers a year worldwide, 122 million in its seven UK airports alone. Overseas, BAA manages all or part of 11 airports, including six in

Australia. The UK's second largest operator is TBI, which has an interest in 37 airports worldwide.

Highland and Islands Airports Ltd (HIAL) owns ten airports in Scotland. These airports receive considerable investment from the Scottish Executive to ensure the continued provision of 'lifeline' services to remote areas.

All UK airports used for public transport must be licensed by the CAA for reasons of safety. Stringent requirements, such as adequate firefighting, medical and rescue services, have to be satisfied before a licence is granted.

Airport development
Investment to expand passenger facilities is in progress at many UK airports. Planning permission for Heathrow Terminal 5 was given in November 2001, where BAA plans to invest £4.1 billion. Planning conditions include a limit on flight numbers of 480,000 at Heathrow, compared with 457,000 in 2001. Even with this limit, a capacity of 90 to 100 million passengers a year is envisaged. Also at Heathrow, a £100 million redevelopment of departure facilities at Terminal 3 is scheduled for completion in 2002. Expansion at Gatwick's two terminals over the next ten years is designed to raise annual capacity to around 40 million passengers.

Among other large-scale projects at UK airports are a £360 million expansion plan at Birmingham Airport, which will increase capacity to around 10 million passengers a year, and a £200 million investment programme at Stansted to increase capacity to around 15 million passengers a year.

In July 2002 the Government published a consultation document on the future development of air transport in the south-east and the east of England. This examined a number of options for dealing with forecast demand, ranging from no development other than that already in the planning system; extension of Heathrow with another short runway for regional transport; one, two or three new runways at Stansted; and the development of a new airport at Cliffe in Kent.

Air traffic control
Civil and military air traffic control over the UK and the surrounding seas, including much of the North Atlantic, is undertaken by National Air Traffic Services Ltd (NATS – www.nats.co.uk), working in collaboration with military controllers.

NATS is a PPP, in which the Government's partner is the Airline Group, a consortium of seven UK airlines. The Airline Group has a 46 per cent share of the company (with rights giving it voting control), the Government 49 per cent, and NATS employees 5 per cent. The CAA retains responsibility for air safety regulation, and also regulates the PPP.

To cope with the rapid growth in air traffic, NATS is in the process of replacing the three previous UK centres for civil and military *en route* air traffic control operations with two major new centres. Swanwick (Hampshire) opened in January 2002, while a new Scottish centre at Prestwick will replace the existing one in 2009. Controlling around 322,000 square kilometres of airspace above England and Wales, Swanwick will handle up to 6,000 flights a day during busy periods.

NATS announced a £1 billion investment plan in April 2002. Among other things, it is intended that the plan will enable the company to handle a 50 per cent increase in flights, from 2 million to 3 million, by 2010/11, and reduce NATS' attributable delays to less than one minute per flight.

Air safety
The CAA is responsible for safety standards on UK airlines. It certifies aircraft and crews, licenses air operators and air travel organisers, and approves certain air fares and airport charges. To qualify for a first professional licence, a pilot must pass a full-time course of instruction approved by the CAA or have acceptable military or civilian flying experience. Every company operating aircraft used for commercial air transport purposes must possess an Air Operator's Certificate, which the CAA grants when it is satisfied that the company is competent to operate its aircraft safely. All aircraft registered in the UK must be granted a certificate of airworthiness by the CAA before being flown. The CAA works closely with the Joint Aviation Authorities, a European grouping of aviation safety regulation authorities.

The DfT's Air Accidents Investigation Branch (AAIB) investigates accidents and serious incidents in UK airspace and those that occur overseas to aircraft registered or manufactured in the UK. In 2001 the AAIB was involved in the investigation of 322 civil aviation accidents/ incidents worldwide and provided technical assistance to military aircraft accident investigations on five occasions.

Inland waterways

Inland waterways are now used mainly for leisure and general recreation, but they have a number of other important roles: as a heritage and environmental resource, as a catalyst for regeneration, and in land drainage and water supply.

Some inland waterways still carry freight: in 2000, 49.0 million tonnes of goods were lifted and 1.7 billion tonne-kilometres of goods were moved. The Thames was the busiest inland waterway route.

The UK's waterways are managed by about 30 different navigation authorities. British Waterways (*www.britishwaterways.co.uk*), a public corporation sponsored by the Department for Environment, Food & Rural Affairs and the Scottish Executive, is the largest, responsible for some 2,600 kilometres of fully navigable waterways, about half the UK total.

British Waterways has embarked on the biggest ever programme of waterway restorations – over 480 kilometres of canals and waterway structures will be restored or built in two phases. The first, to open over 350 kilometres of canals and structures in eight projects, will be fully completed in 2002. Projects included the restoration of the Anderton Boat Lift, built in 1875, which opened to the public in March 2002, and the Millennium Link project to connect Glasgow and Edinburgh, which opened in May 2002. The second phase, covering ten further projects, includes the first new canal to be designed in a century – the Bedford and Milton Keynes Waterway. Funding for the programme comes from a wide range of partnerships and public support.

The cross-border body Waterways Ireland is responsible for the management, maintenance, development and restoration of the inland navigable waterways system throughout Ireland, principally for recreational purposes.

Shipping and ports

It is estimated that about 95 per cent by weight (75 per cent by value) of the UK's foreign trade is carried by sea. The UK fleet has declined considerably in tonnage terms in the last 25 years, reflecting changing trade patterns, removal of grants, and greater competition. International revenue (including freight revenue) earned by the UK shipping industry in 2000 was £3.8 billion and represented over 5 per cent of the total export of services from the UK.

At the end of 2001 there were 594 UK-owned merchant trading ships of 100 gross tonnes or more, with a total tonnage of 12.0 million deadweight tonnes. There were 140 vessels totalling 4.7 million deadweight tonnes used as oil, chemical or gas carriers, and 454 vessels totalling 7.4 million deadweight tonnes employed as dry-bulk carriers, container ships or other types of cargo ship, together with 37 passenger ships. In all, 75 per cent of UK-owned vessels are registered in the UK, the Channel Islands, the Isle of Man or British Overseas Territories such as Bermuda.

The Government is implementing a series of measures aimed at reviving the shipping industry and reversing the downward trend in the UK fleet. For example, shipping can now be taxed on the basis of tonnage, as occurs in a number of other countries. Other measures include more training and career opportunities for seafarers.

Cargo services

International revenue earned by the UK shipping industry in 2001 was £3.7 billion: £2.8 billion from freight (£2.1 billion on dry cargo and passenger vessels and £0.7 billion on tankers and liquefied gas carriers); £0.3 billion from charter receipts; and £0.6 billion from passenger revenue. Nearly all scheduled cargo-liner services from the UK are containerised. British tonnage serving these trades is dominated by a relatively small number of companies. Besides the carriage of freight by liner and bulk services between the UK and the rest of Europe, many roll-on, roll-off services carry cars, passengers and commercial vehicles.

Passenger services

Over 30 million passenger journeys a year take place on international and domestic ferry services linking Great Britain with Ireland and mainland Europe. A further 18 million passengers are carried on ferry services to many of Britain's offshore islands, such as the Isle of Wight, Isle of Man, Orkney and Shetland, and the islands off the west coast of Scotland.

323

P&O Ferries is the UK's largest ferry operator, with a fleet of about 50 ships operating on 18 routes around the UK coast. Cross-Channel services are operated by roll-on, roll-off ferries, high-speed catamarans and high-speed monohulls.

Maritime safety

The DfT's policies for improving marine safety and pollution control are implemented by the Maritime and Coastguard Agency (MCA), which inspects UK ships and foreign ships using UK ports to ensure that they comply with international safety, pollution prevention and operational standards. In 2001, 117 foreign-flagged ships were detained in UK ports.

In 2001 the MCA was alerted to 12,514 incidents and 16,487 people were assisted, including 4,852 who required rescuing. In an emergency, HM Coastguard co-ordinates facilities, such as its own helicopters; cliff rescue teams; lifeboats of the Royal National Lifeboat Institution (RNLI, a voluntary body); aircraft, helicopters and ships from the armed forces; and merchant shipping and commercial aircraft.

The MCA has set up a Search and Rescue service for the River Thames at Tower Pier in London and there are now four lifeboat stations operated by the RNLI along the river. Three – at Tower Pier, Chiswick Pier and Gravesend – are manned continuously, while the fourth at Teddington is operated using volunteers.

Some locations around the UK are potentially hazardous for shipping. There are over 1,000 marine aids to navigation around the UK coast and responsibility for these rests with three regional lighthouse authorities. Measures to reduce the risk of collision include the separation of ships into internationally agreed shipping lanes. This applies, for example, in the Dover Strait, one of the world's busiest seaways, which is monitored by radar from the Channel Navigation Information Service near Dover.

By the end of 2001 the majority of ports had complied with the Government's Port Marine Safety Code, which is designed to ensure the highest standards of marine safety in UK ports. The DfT has also issued a Guide to Good Practice on port marine operations. It gives guidance on a national standard by which harbour authorities can measure how they discharge their legal duties for the safety of navigation.

Ports

There are about 70 ports of commercial significance in Great Britain, while several hundred small harbours cater for local cargo, fishing vessels, island ferries or recreation. There are three broad types of port: those owned and run by boards constituted as trusts; those owned by local authorities; and company-owned facilities.

Associated British Ports (ABP) is the UK's largest port owner and operates 21 ports, including Cardiff, Grimsby and Immingham, Hull, Ipswich, Newport, Port Talbot, Southampton and Swansea. Other major facilities owned by private sector companies include Felixstowe, Harwich and Thamesport (all owned by the Hong Kong group Hutchison Whampoa).

The Government intends to assist ports in maintaining competitiveness, and to develop nationally agreed safety standards; to promote environmental best practice; and to build on the approach detailed in its ten-year plan for transport, which recognised the importance of port hubs within integrated transport systems.

Port traffic

A total of 566 million tonnes (Mt) of freight traffic was handled in UK ports in 2001, a 1 per cent reduction on 2000. Traffic through the 52 major UK ports (generally those handling over 1 million tonnes a year) accounted for 97 per cent (548 Mt) of the total. Inwards traffic rose by 13 Mt to 329 Mt while outward traffic fell by 20 Mt to 236 Mt.

The main ports, in terms of total tonnage handled, are shown in Table 21.7. Forth, Milford Haven and Sullom Voe mostly handle oil, while the principal destinations for non-fuel traffic are London, Felixstowe, Grimsby and Immingham, Tees and Hartlepool, and Liverpool. Crude oil now accounts for one-third of all port traffic.

By far the most important port for container traffic is Felixstowe (which handles about two-fifths of this type of traffic), while Dover is the leading port for roll-on, roll-off traffic. Dover is also the major arrival and departure point for sea passengers, handling well over half of all international movements to and from the UK. The top four UK ports are among the ten largest ports in northern Europe.

Table 21.7 Traffic through the principal ports of Great Britain

	1991	1996	Million tonnes 2001
Grimsby and Immingham	40.2	46.8	54.8
Tees and Hartlepool	42.9	44.6	50.8
London	52.8	52.9	50.7
Forth	22.9	45.6	41.6
Southampton	31.5	34.2	35.4
Milford Haven	35.7	36.6	33.8
Sullom Voe	35.9	38.2	31.5
Liverpool	24.8	34.1	30.3
Felixstowe	16.1	25.8	28.4
Dover	12.0	13.2	19.1

Source: Department for Transport

Northern Ireland has four main ports, at Belfast, Larne, Londonderry and Warrenpoint. Belfast handles around three-fifths of Northern Ireland's seaborne trade.

Transport policy

Underpinning the Government's transport policy is its ten-year transport spending plan, launched in 2000, which currently envisages public spending and private investment in transport of some £181.9 billion, including: £64.8 billion for railways in Great Britain, £58.7 billion for local transport in England, £25.6 billion for transport in London, £21.2 billion for strategic roads in England and £11.6 billion on future projects and other transport areas. The Government intends to issue a first-year report of the plan in autumn 2002. The devolved administrations are developing their own transport strategies.

Under the *Transport Act 2000* (see box), Local Transport Plans (LTPs) have been drawn up by local transport authorities in England (outside London), and by Welsh authorities. In Scotland all local authorities have produced Local Transport Strategies and Strathclyde Passenger Transport a public transport strategy.

The London Mayor is responsible for delivering integrated transport in the capital. The Mayor's Transport Strategy was published in July 2001, and recognises that an increase in the capacity of London's transport system cannot be based on the private car. It aims to increase the capacity of the

Transport Act 2000
Closely linked to the targets of the ten-year plan, this Act provided for the establishment of the Strategic Rail Authority (see page 318) and the NATS PPP (see page 322). It requires local authorities to prepare five-year plans to improve their local transport facilities; enables local authorities outside London to introduce road charges and workplace parking levies to help tackle congestion; gives local authorities new powers to improve local bus services; and requires them to offer concessionary fares for all pensioners and certain groups of disabled people.

The *Transport (Scotland) Act 2001* provides local authorities with additional powers to enable them to develop an integrated transport system at the local level. The Act contains many provisions similar to those in the Transport Act for England and Wales.

Underground and rail systems by up to 50 per cent over 15 years, two-thirds of which is to come from major new projects such as extensions and improvements to the East London Line and Thameslink. The Strategy also aims to increase the capacity of the bus system by 40 per cent over ten years, and supports the principle of congestion charging in central London, due to be introduced in February 2003 (see page 313).

Authorities in London produce Local Implementation/Borough Spending Plans in line with the Strategy, for which funding of at least £130 million a year from 2003/04 is envisaged. Transport for London will be responsible for delivering the Strategy.

Each year, capital allocations to English authorities are made in the LTP capital settlement. Funding of £8.4 billion is envisaged from 2001/02 to 2005/06. The 2002/03 settlement distributed £1.5 billion to local authorities, including:

- £1.2 billion for new small-scale transport schemes, covering road safety, bus priority measures, park and ride, encouraging cycling and walking, as well as road maintenance and bridge strengthening schemes; and

- funding for 23 major new projects, such as improved public transport interchanges, six new bypasses, and four relief roads.

The Government has announced its intention to introduce a Safety Bill covering travel by rail, air, sea and on the roads.

Wales

The Welsh Assembly Government's Transport Framework for Wales, published in November 2001, sets the context within which the Assembly Government's decisions relating to transport will be taken. It aims to provide a better co-ordinated and sustainable transport system, including improved public transport.

Programmes have been set out under the Framework for rail, roads and local transport:

- The SRA's ten-year Strategic Plan for railways in Wales identifies the important role to be played by the Assembly Government in the planning of railways. Some £60 million is being invested in the rail infrastructure over the next five years.

- The Trunk Road Forward Programme aims, among other things, to support economic growth, secure environmental protection and reinforce links between North and South Wales. It includes a number of major schemes, the start dates of which will be phased in over the next six years.

- Building on a £300 million investment announced in January 2001, a further £130 million has been provided for major new local transport projects in 2002/03. These include distributor roads, bus services to rural areas and the ULTRA driverless taxi scheme in the Cardiff Bay area.

Scotland

Expenditure on transport of £1,029 million is planned in 2002/03, up from £986 million in 2001/02. Priorities include: creating an integrated transport system; encouraging the use of public transport; tackling congestion; moving freight off the roads on to both the railways and waterways; and maintaining affordable lifeline services to islands and other remote areas.

The Executive's Transport Delivery Report was issued in March 2002. It recognises the major challenges facing transport in Scotland for the future – congestion, greater integration and completing missing transport links. Ten priority projects are identified, including:

- a new 15-year Scottish passenger rail franchise, from April 2004;

- developing rail links for Glasgow and Edinburgh airports;

- addressing congestion problems in Aberdeen; and

- completing motorway links on the A8 and A80.

Northern Ireland

An important element of the Regional Development Strategy is the development of five key transport corridors: strategic long-distance routes connecting a number of towns to the major regional 'gateways', including links to transport corridors within the Belfast metropolitan area.

Within this context, the Minister for Regional Development has published the Regional Transportation Strategy for Northern Ireland 2002–2012, which takes into account the ten-year plan and the wider priorities of the Northern Ireland Programme for Government. Aiming to contribute to a long-term goal of a modern, sustainable, safe transport system, the £3.5 billion Strategy seeks to balance investment across the region. Among the areas to be targeted are:

- the regional strategic transport network, where, for example, Northern Ireland has a low proportion of motorway compared with the rest of the UK;

- the Belfast metropolitan area; and

- rural areas, for example modernising the rural bus fleet.

Further reading

The Future Development of Air Transport in the United Kingdom: A National Consultation: South East and East of England. Department for Transport, 2002. *www.airconsult.gov.uk*

National Travel Survey: 1999/2001 Update. Department for Transport, 2002.

Transport 2010: The Ten-Year Plan. Department of the Environment, Transport and the Regions, 2000.

Transport Statistics Great Britain, annual report. The Stationery Office.

Websites

Department for Transport
www.dft.gov.uk

Northern Ireland Department for Regional Development
www.drdni.gov.uk

Scottish Executive
www.scotland.gov.uk

Transport for London
www.transportforlondon.gov.uk

Welsh Assembly Government
www.wales.gov.uk

WWW.

22 Economic and business framework

Structure and performance

The value of all goods and services produced in the UK economy for final consumption is measured by gross domestic product (GDP). In 2001 GDP at current market prices – 'money GDP' – totalled £988 billion. Average annual growth in GDP at 1995 market prices over the past five years has been 2.8 per cent (see also Table 22.1).

UK – then and now

	1951	£ million 2001	% change
At current market prices			
Final consumption expenditure	12,677	845,928	+6,573
Gross capital formation	2,586	164,048	+6,244
GDP	14,661	988,014	+6,639
At 1995 market prices			
Final consumption expenditure	214,985	744,175	+246
Gross capital formation	32,276	152,043	+371
GDP	246,623	845,552	+243

Output

In 2001 growth in the UK economy continued for the tenth consecutive year. GDP at constant market prices rose by 1.9 per cent, slightly below its post-war average of around $2^1/_2$ per cent a year. Quarterly growth weakened during the year and there was only slight growth in the fourth quarter. Strong growth in domestic demand more than accounted for the overall expansion, driven by a 4.1 per cent rise in household consumption. Gross fixed capital formation fell marginally in 2001, although general government investment increased by 10.9 per cent; business investment

declined marginally following rapid expansion over previous years. In the 2002 Budget, HM Treasury expected trend GDP growth of $2^3/_4$ per cent a year in the period 2002 to 2004.

Recent decades have generally seen growth dominated by the service sector (see chapter 29). In 2001, at constant basic prices – that is, adjusted for inflation, and excluding taxes and subsidies on products – output of the service industries increased by 3.4 per cent, with particularly strong growth in post and telecommunications (9.6 per cent) and in business services (7.0 per cent). There was also a strong performance by the construction industry, with growth of 3.6 per cent. However, production industries' output fell by 2.1 per cent, with manufacturing declining by 2.3 per cent, the first such decline since 1991. Manufacturing (see chapter 27) contributed 17.5 per cent of GDP in 2001, compared with over a third in 1950.

The UK experienced lower economic growth than all its major competitors in the 1970s and, apart from Germany and France, in the 1980s, according to the Organisation for Economic Co-operation and Development (OECD). By the 1990s, although the UK's growth slowed, this gap had narrowed significantly.

Annual average GDP growth

	1970s	1980s	Per cent 1990s
UK	2.4	2.3	2.1
EU	3.4	2.2	2.0
G7	3.6	2.9	2.4

Source: National Accounts of OECD countries

Household income and expenditure

Total resources (income) of the household sector – including non-profit institutions serving households – rose by 6.1 per cent in 2001 to £996 billion. Gross disposable income – after

Table 22.1 Gross domestic product and gross national income, UK

	1991	1996	1999	2000	£ million 2001
Final consumption expenditure					
Households	359,616	473,800	569,481	603,557	631,010
Non-profit institutions	11,096	18,385	22,150	23,027	24,255
General government	121,403	146,779	166,614	177,801	190,663
Gross capital formation					
Gross fixed capital formation	105,179	125,762	153,501	158,918	162,244
Changes in inventories	−4,927	1,771	6,060	5,595	1,441
Acquisitions less disposals					
of valuables	−97	−158	231	5	363
Total exports	135,940	223,091	236,609	265,135	268,451
Gross final expenditure	728,210	989,430	1,154,646	1,234,038	1,278,427
less Total imports	−142,061	−227,216	−252,187	−283,623	−290,912
Statistical discrepancy	0	0	0	0	499
GDP at current market prices	**586,149**	**762,214**	**902,459**	**950,415**	**988,014**
Net income from abroad[1]	−6,819	−2,684	282	5,532	5,756
Gross national income at					
current market prices	**579,330**	**759,530**	**902,741**	**955,947**	**993,770**
GDP at 1995 market prices	650,085	738,046	804,713	829,517	845,552
GDP index at 1995					
market prices (1995 = 100)	90.4	102.6	111.9	115.3	117.6

1 Includes employment, entrepreneurial and property income.
Source: ONS Quarterly National Accounts

Figure 22.2 Percentage change in GDP at 1995 market prices, UK

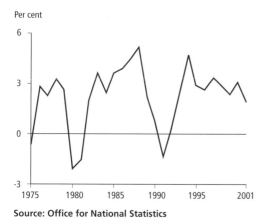

Per cent

Source: Office for National Statistics

deductions, including taxes and social contributions – totalled £686 billion. In 1995 prices, real household disposable income – the amount of money the household sector has available for spending after taxes and other

deductions – rose by 6.6 per cent over the year, the strongest increase since 1988. Wages and salaries increased by 5.9 per cent during 2001 to £478 billion, and accounted for over 59 per cent of household primary income. Over the year, rises in compensation of employees, social benefits and property income outstripped interest payments, social contributions and final consumption expenditure. Household net financial wealth fell by 16 per cent in 2001 to £2,011 billion. The household saving ratio – saving as a percentage of total available households' resources – rose substantially between 2000 and 2001, from 4.2 per cent to 6.2 per cent, although it remains low relative to the rates seen during most of the 1990s.

In 2001 household final expenditure – spending by the household sector on products or services to satisfy immediate needs or wants – rose by 4.1 per cent at constant prices to £568 billion, representing 76.3 per cent of the total £744 billion final consumption expenditure. This was the sixth consecutive year of strong growth. Expenditure on durable and semi-durable goods rose particularly strongly, by 12.5 per cent and 8.9 per cent

Table 22.3 Output by industry – gross value added,[1] UK

	1995 (£ million)[2]	At current basic prices 2001 (£ million)[2]	% contribution 2001[2]	% change at 1995 basic prices 1995–2001
Agriculture, hunting, forestry and fishing	11,766	8,241	0.9	−11.8
Mining and quarrying	16,369	25,665	2.9	1.6
Manufacturing[3]	139,789	153,132	17.5	2.8
Electricity, gas and water supply	15,586	15,713	1.8	14.1
Construction	33,005	47,327	5.4	13.7
Wholesale and retail trade	74,612	106,766	12.2	27.1
Hotels and restaurants	18,252	29,359	3.4	−3.4
Transport, storage and communication	51,340	70,252	8.0	46.3
Financial intermediation[4]	40,089	46,034	5.3	26.0
Adjustment for financial services	−23,215	−39,367	−4.5	44.4
Real estate, renting and business activities	119,052	209,837	24.0	37.2
Public administration and defence	39,756	42,096	4.8	0.0
Education	34,208	52,659	6.0	8.3
Health and social work	42,051	61,410	7.0	18.3
Other services	27,247	45,101	5.2	25.9
Total gross value added	**639,908**	**874,227**	**100.0**	**17.2**

1 Represents the difference between the value of the output of goods and services produced by a company and its intermediate consumption – the value of the goods and services or raw materials used up in the production of such output.
2 At current basic prices.
3 See Table 27.3 for an industry breakdown.
4 The activity by which an institutional unit acquires financial assets and incurs liabilities on its own account by engaging in financial transactions on the market.
Source: ONS Quarterly National Accounts and *United Kingdom National Accounts 2002 – the Blue Book*

respectively, although growth in services was only 1.1 per cent.

Table 22.4 shows the pattern of household final consumption expenditure. Since 1995, in real terms, growth has been strongest in the durable and semi-durable goods categories, much less so in non-durable goods and services. By purpose, communication, recreation and culture, clothing and footwear, and household goods and services have shown the most significant growth. On the other hand, spending on health has shown the smallest increase.

Investment

Gross fixed capital formation represents investment in assets, primarily by businesses, which are used repeatedly or continuously over a number of years to produce goods, such as machinery used to create a product. Total investment at constant 1995 prices fell marginally by 0.4 per cent in 2001 (see Table 22.5), compared with the 1.9 per cent increase in 2000. Business investment fell by 0.7 per cent in 2001 and, at

13.4 per cent of GDP, was slightly down on its share in 2000.

General government investment rose by 10.9 per cent in 2001 following a smaller 3.9 per cent increase in 2000, and is forecast by HM Treasury to accelerate further in 2002, with growth remaining in double digits in both 2003 and 2004.

UK whole economy investment has accounted for a smaller share of GDP than for other industrialised countries – 16.4 per cent of GDP (at current prices) in 2001, compared with a G7 average of 19.0 per cent – but strong growth of business investment until recently has helped to reduce this gap.

International trade

International trade plays a key role in the UK economy. The UK is the world's fourth largest trading nation, with exports accounting for 27 per cent of GDP in 2001. EU countries took 58.1 per cent of UK exports of goods in 2001 and supplied 51.7 per cent of imported goods. See

Table 22.4 Household final consumption expenditure, UK

	1995 (£ million)[1]	2001 (£ million)[1]	% contribution 2001[1]	% change at 1995 market prices 1995–2001
UK domestic				
Food and drink	49,790	60,262	9.6	12.7
Alcohol and tobacco	18,776	25,361	4.0	7.4
Clothing and footwear	28,030	37,355	5.9	49.8
Housing	81,412	112,717	17.9	7.7
Household goods and services	26,287	37,194	5.9	34.1
Health	6,835	9,456	1.5	0.8
Transport	62,733	91,804	14.5	29.1
Communication	9,067	13,827	2.2	88.8
Recreation and culture	51,075	76,754	12.2	62.8
Education	6,197	10,012	1.6	17.8
Restaurants and hotels	50,383	70,686	11.2	10.2
Miscellaneous	52,329	75,539	12.0	17.9
Total	**442,914**	**620,967**	**98.4**	**25.1**
of which:				
Durable goods	51,092	76,534	12.1	68.4
Semi-durable goods	50,848	75,742	12.0	59.8
Non-durable goods	124,466	152,785	24.2	9.4
Services	216,508	315,906	50.1	15.6
Net tourism	453	10,043	1.6	
Total UK national	**443,367**	**631,010**	**100.0**	**28.1**

1 At current market prices.
Source: ONS Quarterly National Accounts

Table 22.5 Gross fixed capital formation at constant 1995 prices, UK

	1996	1999	2000	£ million 2001
Transport equipment	11,833	14,154	12,640	14,684
Other machinery and equipment	49,691	68,367	72,753	70,970
Dwellings	21,868	21,826	22,070	21,154
Other buildings and structures[1]	35,422	40,699	40,145	40,071
Intangible fixed assets	4,162	4,097	4,378	4,447
Gross fixed capital formation	**122,976**	**149,143**	**151,986**	**151,326**
of which:				
Business investment[2]	84,510	111,951	113,973	113,149
General government	11,147	10,153	10,548	11,695
Public corporations	1,618	1,295	1,506	1,624
Private sector	25,701	25,744	25,959	24,858

1 Including costs associated with the transfer of ownership of non-produced assets.
2 Excluding dwellings and costs associated with the transfer of non-produced assets; these are included under the private sector.
Source: ONS Quarterly National Accounts

Table 22.6 Mergers and acquisitions involving UK companies

	1991	1996	1999	2000	2001
Acquisitions abroad by UK companies					
Number	550	442	590	557	371
Value (£ million)	9,688	13,377	111,193	181,285	41,473
Acquisitions in the UK by foreign companies[1]					
Number	146	133	252	227	162
Value (£ million)	6,667	9,513	60,860	64,618	24,382
Acquisitions in the UK by UK companies					
Number	506	584	493	587	492
Value (£ million)	10,434	30,742	26,163	106,916	28,994

1 Includes acquisitions by foreign companies routed through their existing UK subsidiaries.
Source: Office for National Statistics

chapter 24 for full details of the UK's balance of payments position.

Mergers and acquisitions

In 2001 expenditure on acquisitions abroad by UK companies fell sharply by 77 per cent from the record level seen in 2000 (see Table 22.6). Two significant reported transactions were in the telecommunications sector – the acquisition of Viag Interkom GmbH by British Telecommunications for a reported £4.4 billion and of Eircell 2000 by Vodafone Group for £2.6 billion. Expenditure on acquisitions in the UK by foreign companies also fell sharply – by 62 per cent – from the record level in 2000. Significant reported acquisitions in 2001 included that of the software group Sema by Schlumberger Investments for £3.6 billion and of the oil company Lasmo by Eni SpA for £2.7 billion.

Inflation

Three main measures of retail price inflation are used in the UK:

- the all items Retail Prices Index (RPI), the main domestic measure of prices in the UK. RPI inflation measures the average change from month to month in the prices of goods and services purchased by most households in the UK and is commonly called 'headline' inflation;

- the RPI excluding mortgage interest payments (RPIX), which is used to calculate 'underlying' inflation, the target measure set by the Government (see page 334); and

- the harmonised index of consumer prices (HICP), calculated for each Member State of

the European Union for the purposes of European comparisons; it is also used to derive inflation rates for the eurozone and the EU as a whole.

Retail Prices Index

The RPI is compiled using a large and representative 'basket' of more than 650 goods and services sampled each month to see how prices are changing. Each year a review of the composition of this 'basket' is undertaken. New items are added to represent new or increasing areas of spending, while other items are deleted as spending on them falls. For the 2002 review some of the changes included:

In	Out
Frozen prawns	Loose tea
Aluminium stepladders	Pipe tobacco
Pet flea drops	Shower curtains
Sunglasses	Blank audio cassettes
Dumb-bells	Darts

Annual underlying inflation (RPIX) has fluctuated considerably in the last 25 years or so, peaking at 20.8 per cent in the year to May 1980. However, it was much lower in the 1990s, and since 1993 has been in a relatively narrow range, from around 2 per cent to 3.5 per cent. In 2001 it averaged 2.1 per cent, and has been below the Government's current target of 2½ per cent – set in May 1997 – since April 1999, in all but two months.

In 2001 the all items RPI averaged 1.8 per cent: goods inflation averaged 0.3 per cent and services inflation 3.8 per cent. UK inflation on the HICP

Figure 22.7 RPI inflation, UK (all items)[1]

Per cent

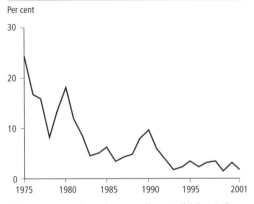

1 Annual percentage change in the Retail Prices Index, all items.
Source: Office for National Statistics

measure was 1.2 per cent, the lowest in the EU. This was significantly below the EU average of 2.3 per cent and it has remained below the average during the first half of 2002.

Having risen by 11.5 per cent in 2000, producer input prices for materials and fuels purchased by manufacturing industry declined by 0.3 per cent in 2001 as a whole, as prices fell in the second half of the year and into early 2002. Producer output

price inflation was 2.6 per cent in 2000 as a whole, reducing to just 0.2 per cent in 2001, as output prices fell towards the end of the year, driven by a decline in the price of oil. They continued at this lower level into the early part of 2002.

Labour market

Figures released in July 2002 show that employment reached a record level of 28.51 million in the three months to May 2002, 179,000 higher than in the same period a year earlier, and representing an employment rate of 74.7 per cent. According to the International Labour Organisation measure, unemployment, at 1,572,000 in the three months to May 2002, was 100,000 higher than a year earlier. This represented 5.2 per cent of the workforce, well below the figure (7.6 per cent) for all EU countries. For full details see chapter 11.

Economic strategy

The main elements of the Government's economic strategy, designed to deliver high and stable levels of economic growth and employment, are as set out in the 2002 Budget:

■ delivering macroeconomic stability;

■ meeting the productivity challenge;

Table 22.8 Consumer price indices and producer prices, UK

	1991	1996	1999	2000	2001
Consumer prices					
RPIX (January 1987 = 100)	130.3	152.3	164.3	167.7	171.3
RPI (January 1987 = 100)	133.5	152.7	165.4	170.3	173.3
of which:					
Goods	125.7	144.3	151.2	151.6	152.1
Services	139.3	170.4	187.8	194.4	201.7
HICP (1996 = 100)	87.2	100.0	104.8	105.6	106.9
Producer prices (1995 = 100)					
Output prices					
Manufactured products	87.5	102.6	105.3	108.0	108.2
of which:					
Food, beverages and tobacco	85.0	103.3	106.4	107.8	110.1
Petroleum products	85.2	107.2	127.4	149.7	142.0
Input prices[1]					
Materials purchased	86.1	99.7	83.0	94.2	92.8
Fuels purchased	100.0	91.7	89.1	86.7	94.6

1 Includes the climate change levy from April 2001.
Source: ONS Consumer Price Indices, Producer Prices

- increasing employment opportunity for all (see chapter 11);

- building a fairer society;

- delivering high quality public services; and

- protecting the environment.

HM Treasury is the department with prime responsibility for the Government's monetary and fiscal frameworks. It is also responsible for wider economic policy, which it carries out in conjunction with other government departments, such as Trade and Industry, Education and Skills, Work and Pensions, and Transport.

The Government's policy on UK membership of the European single currency (see page 60) remains as set out by the Chancellor of the Exchequer in his statement to Parliament in October 1997. The determining factor underpinning any decision is the national economic interest and whether the economic case for joining is clear and unambiguous. The Government has set out five economic tests which must be met before any decision to join can be made. The five tests are:

- sustainable convergence between Britain and the economies of the single currency;

- whether there is sufficient flexibility to cope with economic change;

- the effect on investment;

- the impact on the UK financial services industry; and

- whether it is good for employment.

A comprehensive and rigorous assessment of the five tests will be made within two years of the start of this Parliament (June 2001). On the basis of the assessment, the Government will decide whether the five tests have been met. If a decision to recommend joining is taken by the Government, it will be put to a vote in Parliament and then to a referendum of the British people.

Economic stability

The Government's central economic objective is to raise the economy's sustainable rate of growth, and achieve rising prosperity, through creating economic and employment opportunities for all. It has established frameworks for the operation of both monetary and fiscal policy in order to achieve low and stable inflation and sound public finances, and seeks to ensure the co-ordination of monetary and fiscal policy by setting mutually consistent objectives for both.

The Bank of England's Monetary Policy Committee (see page 452) is responsible for setting interest rates to meet the Government's inflation target of $2^1/_2$ per cent, as defined by the 12-month change in RPIX. Official interest rates peaked at $7^1/_2$ per cent in 1998, compared with a peak of 15 per cent in 1989 in the previous economic cycle. More recently, they have been held at 4 per cent since November 2001, as weak external demand and investment have been balanced by buoyant household consumption.

Fiscal policy

The *Code for Fiscal Stability* sets out the five key principles of fiscal management at the heart of the Government's fiscal policy framework:

- *transparency* in setting fiscal policy objectives, the implementation of fiscal policy and the publication of the public accounts;

- *stability* in the fiscal policy-making process and in the way that fiscal policy impacts on the economy;

- *responsibility* in the management of the public finances;

- *fairness,* including between present and future generations; and

- *efficiency* in the design and implementation of fiscal policy, and in managing both sides of the public sector balance sheet.

The Code also requires the Government to state its objectives and fiscal rules through which it operates fiscal policy based on these principles. The objectives are:

- over the medium term, to ensure sound public finances and that spending and taxation impact fairly both within and between generations; and

- over the short term, to support monetary policy and, in particular, to allow the 'automatic stabilisers' to play their role in smoothing the path of the economy.

These objectives are implemented through the Government's two fiscal rules, against which the performance of fiscal policy can be judged, and which are set out in its Economic and Fiscal Strategy Report (see below):

- *the golden rule* – over the economic cycle, the Government will borrow only to invest and not to fund current spending; and

- *the sustainable investment rule* – public sector net debt as a proportion of GDP will be held over the economic cycle at a stable and prudent level. Other things being equal, net debt will be maintained below 40 per cent of GDP over the economic cycle.

These fiscal rules promote economic stability by ensuring sound public sector finances, while allowing flexibility in two key respects:

- the rules are set over the cycle, allowing fiscal balances to vary between years in line with the cyclical position of the economy; and

- the interaction of the two rules promotes capital investment while ensuring sustainable public finances in the longer term.

The fiscal framework also recognises that projections of the current budget and net debt involve a considerable element of uncertainty. Projections of the public finances are therefore deliberately based on prudent assumptions for key economic variables. These assumptions, which include the trend rate of growth, the level of unemployment, and oil and equity prices, are audited by the National Audit Office (NAO – see page 350) under a three-year rolling review to ensure they remain both reasonable and cautious. This minimises the need for unexpected changes in direction in taxation or spending.

Sound public finances are a prerequisite for sustainable investment in public services. The fiscal rules are the foundation of the *public spending framework* (see chapter 23) and have

important consequences for the structure of the budgeting regime.

The Budget

The role of the Budget is to:

- provide an update on the state of the economy and the public finances and to present new forecasts for each;

- set out the Government's economic and fiscal objectives; and

- report on the progress the Government has made towards achieving its objectives, and set out the further steps it is taking to meet them.

It is usually published in March, although in 2002 it was published in April. In a major speech to Parliament, the Chancellor of the Exchequer reviews the nation's economic performance and describes the Government's economic objectives and the economic policies it intends to follow in order to achieve them. In accordance with the *Code for Fiscal Stability*, the 2002 Budget report comprised two documents:

- the Economic and Fiscal Strategy Report (EFSR), setting out the Government's long-term goals and the comprehensive strategy it is pursuing to achieve them, the progress that has been made so far, and the further steps the Government is taking in the 2002 Budget to advance its long-term goals; and

- the Financial Statement and Budget Report (FSBR), providing a summary of each of the main Budget measures and how they affect the Budget arithmetic, and updated forecasts of the economy and the public finances.

Under the *Code for Fiscal Stability*, the Government is committed to publishing a Pre-Budget Report (PBR) at least three months prior to the Budget (usually in the previous November). The PBR provides an opportunity for the Government to consult the public on specific policy initiatives under consideration for the forthcoming Budget, as well as presenting an interim update on the outlook for the economy and the public finances, taking account of economic and other developments since the previous Budget.

Industrial and commercial policy

The Department of Trade and Industry (DTI) aims to increase UK competitiveness and scientific excellence in order to generate higher levels of sustainable growth and productivity. It has four specific objectives:

- to promote enterprise, innovation and higher productivity;

- to make the most of the UK's scientific, engineering and technological capabilities;

- to create strong and competitive markets within a fair and effective regulatory framework; and

- to assist the competitiveness of UK companies through export promotion and inward investment.

Competitiveness

In February 2001 the DTI published the second in its series of UK competitiveness indicators, including international comparisons with other members of the G7 and the OECD. In March 2002 a web-based version was launched (*www.dtistats.net/competitiveness*), and this is updated on a regular basis. According to the indicators, the UK is a relatively open economy, with a high level of both inward and outward investment. Among other UK strengths noted at the time the web-based version was launched:

- the growth in GDP per head was the second highest of the G7 countries over the most recent economic cycle;

- knowledge-based industries, such as aerospace, pharmaceuticals and telecommunications, were responsible for 54 per cent of output in 2000, with the UK having a higher share of knowledge-based exports than any other G7 country;

- the science base was highly productive and of high quality;

- venture capital investment as a proportion of GDP was higher than in any other EU country;

- the percentage of business connected to digital networks was the highest in the G7; and

Enterprise Bill

The Enterprise Bill was introduced into Parliament in March 2002. It contains a number of provisions designed to foster enterprise, promote competition and increase productivity in the UK. These include:

- the removal of ministerial involvement from most decisions on mergers and market investigations, with the intention of making the competition regime more transparent and predictable for business;

- criminal penalties for those who operate cartels;

- legislative weight to a new right for consumer groups to make 'super-complaints' to the Office of Fair Trading (OFT), to which the OFT would have to respond within 90 days;

- the power to enable the OFT to refer markets to the Competition Commission where it appears they may not be working well;

- reforms to strengthen the legal rights of parties harmed by anti-competitive behaviour;

- a formal role for the competition authorities to alert government to existing and proposed regulations that may have anti-competitive effects; and

- modernisation of insolvency law, to provide those bankrupts who have failed through no fault of their own with a second chance while introducing a tougher regime for those who have been reckless or dishonest (see page 345).

- progress had been made in improving skills.

The indicators also found that there were areas for improvement. For example, the UK invested less than other G7 countries and UK business was less innovative, entrepreneurial and risk-taking, while UK workers were relatively less skilled than in other EU countries. Productivity continued at a level below that of the UK's main competitors. In 2001 the UK registered a weaker productivity performance than in 2000, with the annual rise in productivity falling from 1.9 to 1.0 per cent (see Table 22.9), as firms tended to retain labour despite weaker external demand. The DTI plans to publish in October 2002 a document summarising the UK's performance against the main drivers of productivity.

Table 22.9 Productivity and unit wage costs, UK

					1995 = 100
	1991	1996	1999	2000	2001
Output per job					
Whole economy	88.4	101.7	105.8	107.8	108.9
Production	82.8	100.2	106.5	112.0	114.0
Manufacturing	86.2	99.4	105.0	110.8	112.9
Unit wage costs					
Whole economy	96.9	101.4	110.9	113.4	117.9
Manufacturing	94.8	105.0	112.6	111.7	114.3

Source: Office for National Statistics

Enterprise, innovation and business support

The DTI promotes enterprise and innovation by encouraging successful business start-ups and offering businesses a number of support services. Most support is designed to assist business, especially small and medium-sized enterprises (SMEs), to expand and invest, and to adopt best practice.

The DTI has reviewed business support arrangements and confirmed the role of the Small Business Service (SBS), an agency of the DTI, in organising the delivery of help for SMEs. In addition, the Secretary of State is advised by the Small Business Council, a non-departmental public body with 20 members, most of whom are entrepreneurs with experience of running an SME.

The Business Link network, which reports to the SBS, covers 45 areas throughout England formed by partnerships between local enterprise agencies, local authorities, chambers of commerce and some commercial organisations with wider interests. In addition, the network can be accessed nationally via a contact number and associated website (*www.businesslink.org*). Business Link, which offers information and advice on a wide range of subjects, is the 'gateway' to a network of business support organisations, as well as to information from the public, private and voluntary sectors. The main advice services are delivered by personal business advisers, who either give advice or arrange appointments with the relevant experts. The SBS plans to spend some £140 million on the network services in 2002/03.

Elsewhere in the UK similar business support arrangements apply:

- in Scotland, the Small Business Gateway offers a package of measures designed to improve the quality and consistency of public sector support for new and small businesses in the Scottish Enterprise area, which covers the lowland areas of the country, while the Business Information Source of Highlands and Islands Enterprise operates equivalent services;

- in Wales, following a review of business support services, the Welsh Development Agency is working with its partners to develop a new single gateway for business support; and

- in Northern Ireland, firms are helped by Invest Northern Ireland (see page 340).

Business finance

Small businesses can face particular difficulties accessing finance. The Government is working in partnership with the private sector to help to address weaknesses in the finance market for SMEs. The Enterprise Fund is a partnership with the private sector to deliver and develop risk capital programmes to support SMEs. Funding for SMEs includes:

- the Small Firms Loan Guarantee Scheme, which offers guarantees on loans to small firms with viable business proposals that are unable to obtain conventional finance as they lack security to offer against a loan. For established businesses that have been trading for two years or more, the SBS provides a guarantee of 85 per cent on loans of up to £250,000 and for other businesses, including start-ups, the guarantee is 70 per cent on loans of up to £100,000. Since the scheme started in 1981 around 80,000 loans, valued at £3 billion, have been guaranteed;

- new Regional Venture Capital Funds, which are being established in each region of England to encourage small businesses with high growth potential – the first five are already in operation. They operate as public-private partnerships (see page 350), with investment from the Government of up to £80 million and from the European Investment Fund of £53 million. Private sector funding of at least £187 million is being sought;

- the UK High Technology Fund, which is a 'fund of funds', managed by a private equity firm. It has £20 million of government investment and has secured £106 million of private sector funding. The Fund has committed over £114 million to eight venture capital funds that specialise in investing in early-growth, high-technology companies, and investments have been made in 69 firms;

- the £75 million SBS Business Incubation Fund, which opened for applications in October 2001 and is available until 2004/05. It is providing loans to those in the English regions setting up or running business incubation projects (helping SMEs to survive and grow when they are at their most vulnerable in their start-up and early-growth stages) whose development plans are hindered by a shortfall in funding from other sources; and

- a new programme of Early Growth Funding, which is being developed by the SBS to encourage the provision of relatively small amounts of risk capital for start-up and growth businesses. The SBS will invest up to £50 million over three years to help up to 1,000 businesses.

In addition, the £100 million Phoenix Fund helps to tackle social exclusion by encouraging entrepreneurship in disadvantaged areas and in groups under-represented in business ownership.

The Queen's Awards for Enterprise

The Queen's Awards for Enterprise scheme (*www.queensawards.org.uk*) has three categories: the Award for International Trade, which recognises export achievement and outstanding performance in other forms of international trading; the Award for Innovation; and the Award for Sustainable Development, which recognises commercially successful products, services and approaches to management that have major benefits for the environment, society and the wider economy. All UK organisations that operate regularly as a 'business unit' and can meet the criteria are eligible to apply. Awards are made annually and are valid for five years. The Queen makes the awards on the advice of the Prime Minister, who is assisted by an advisory committee that includes representatives of government, industry and commerce, and trade unions. Successful organisations may fly the Queen's Award flag at their principal premises and are entitled to use the Queen's Award Emblem on their stationery, packaging, goods and advertising. In 2002, 131 Awards were granted: 85 for International Trade, 37 for Innovation and nine for Sustainable Development.

Information and communications technology

The Government is keen to ensure that the UK benefits fully from the growth of the Internet (see page 242) and of 'e-commerce'. Its e-commerce strategy is being taken forward by the Office of the 'e-Envoy', within the Cabinet Office. This aims to make the UK a leading e-commerce nation, and to provide all government services electronically and in a customer-focused way by the end of 2005. By mid-2002 over 50 per cent of government services were online. The Government's website (*www.ukonline.gov.uk*) is a portal for over 1,000 government department and agency websites and 17 per cent of Internet users in the UK have accessed government websites or e-government services online.

The ONS e-commerce survey of UK businesses indicates that in 2001, excluding the financial sector, there were £18.4 billion of sales made online, that is, over the Internet. This represented 1.0 per cent of total sales by the non-financial sectors of the UK economy. Sales by firms in the non-financial sectors over electronic networks other than the Internet were provisionally estimated at £182 billion in 2001. The survey found that 50 per cent of businesses reported use of the Internet in 2001:

- 12 per cent had permanent Internet connections;

- 17 per cent of those not already online in 2001 planned to be during 2002;

- 39 per cent of businesses had their own website;

- 49 per cent used e-mail in 2001;

- 64 per cent used personal computers, work stations or terminals in 2001; and

- of those online, 7 per cent were selling online and 25 per cent were purchasing online, while 9 per cent and 10 per cent of businesses were selling and purchasing via other electronic networks respectively.

Regional development

The Government's view is that all regions and communities should have the opportunity to share in the UK's prosperity. Its regional policy aims to facilitate economic growth in the regions, and to create the conditions to enable regional and local initiatives to work. Financial help is focused on the Assisted Areas, covering some 16.5 million people in Great Britain and all 1.7 million people in Northern Ireland. Regional Selective Assistance (RSA) is the main instrument of government support to industry in the Assisted Areas in Great Britain, and is now focusing more on high-quality, knowledge-based projects that provide skilled jobs. In 2001/02, 477 offers of RSA grants totalling £246 million were accepted in Great Britain in support of projects with total investment of £1.46 billion, which is expected to create or safeguard 38,000 jobs.

England

Nine Regional Development Agencies (RDAs) in England (see also chapter 2) aim to stimulate economic development and regeneration; promote business efficiency, investment, competitiveness and employment; raise the level of skills; and contribute to the achievement of sustainable development. The RDAs have developed regional economic strategies, which are designed to secure better and more sustainable economic performance for their regions. They work closely with the Government Offices for the Regions on economic development and regeneration programmes. The work of the

RDAs is currently scrutinised by voluntary regional chambers.

Funding for the RDAs is £1.55 billion in 2002/03, rising to £2.0 billion in 2005/06. From April 2002 RDA funding is being provided under a single cross-departmental framework to give the agencies greater flexibility to concentrate their resources according to regional priorities. The DTI is the lead sponsoring department, with a number of other departments contributing to the RDAs' single programme. RDAs have to meet a number of targets set by these departments, including targets on economic development, regeneration and skills development.

The Government's plans for decentralising power and strengthening regional policy in England were set out in a White Paper, *Your Region, Your Choice: Revitalising the English Regions* (see page 10), published in May 2002. The White Paper:

- confirms greater freedom and flexibility for the RDAs;

- sets out an enhanced role for the regional chambers;

- gives extra responsibilities to the Government Offices; and

- in the longer term, offers regions the chance to vote in a referendum to have an elected assembly which would be responsible for setting priorities, delivering regional strategies and allocating funding.

Scotland

In Scotland the Scottish Executive Enterprise and Lifelong Learning Department, which has overall responsibility for development of the Scottish economy, operates a range of schemes to support business. Scottish Enterprise and Highlands and Islands Enterprise are the lead economic development agencies in lowland and highland Scotland respectively, operating mainly through the network of Local Enterprise Companies (LECs), which are wholly owned subsidiaries of the national agencies. The enterprise networks are focusing on three main aspects of raising productivity: encouraging entrepreneurship, raising skill levels and improving international links. Joint working with other economic development partners is developing through a network of Local Economic Forums, which consider local needs within the national framework and aim to deliver a co-ordinated approach to local economic development.

Wales

In December 2001 the National Assembly for Wales issued its new national economic development strategy, 'A Winning Wales', including:

- a greater focus in the Welsh economy on innovation, enterprise, skills and ICT;

- a commitment to an improved planning system;

- greater emphasis on sustainable development; and

- developing the theme of working in partnership with others.

The Welsh Development Agency (WDA) is the lead body for economic development. Its business plan is drawn up within the policy framework of the national economic development strategy. The WDA is focusing its activities on encouraging businesses to increase the level of value added, on supporting innovation and encouraging entrepreneurship and e-commerce.

In 2001/02 over £109 million in RSA grants were offered to 235 investment projects in Wales. Business support schemes have been simplified, and a new Assembly Investment Grant, providing grants of between £5,001 and £50,000 to small and medium-sized enterprises, was introduced in April 2002.

Northern Ireland

A new agency, Invest Northern Ireland, was set up in April 2002 to promote and support innovation and entrepreneurship in the Northern Ireland economy. The agency has become responsible for the business support aspects of the Northern Ireland Tourist Board, the company development programme element of the Department of Enterprise, Trade and Investment, and the functions of three bodies: the Industrial Development Board, the Local Enterprise Development Unit and the Industrial Research and Technology Unit.

European Union regional funding

The EU seeks to promote economic and social cohesion, reducing disparities between the regions and countries of the Union. The principal responsibility for helping poorer areas remains with national authorities, but the EU provides additional funding and targets the worst affected areas through its Structural Funds. The major fund is the European Regional Development Fund (ERDF), which supports regional competitiveness, training, economic development and innovation.

The UK is due to receive about £10.7 billion from the Funds in 2000–06. This is supporting a range of projects, designed to encourage businesses to grow, create suitable conditions for inward investment and new jobs, assist the most disadvantaged areas and the socially excluded, and help people to learn new skills.

The highest level of assistance is available to areas with 'Objective 1' status, where GDP is less than 75 per cent of the EU average. In the UK about £3 billion is allocated to four Objective 1 areas: Cornwall & the Isles of Scilly, Merseyside, South Yorkshire, and West Wales & the Valleys. There is a special programme in Northern Ireland and a transitional funding programme in the Highlands and Islands of Scotland; both areas used to have Objective 1 status.

Aid is also available to areas qualifying for 'Objective 2' status, which covers industrial and urban areas in need of regeneration, declining rural areas, and depressed areas dependent on fisheries. About 13.8 million people in the UK are in Objective 2 areas and a further 6 million benefit from transitional programmes.

Competitive markets

The Enterprise Bill (see page 336) includes measures to implement the Government's plans to strengthen the UK's overall competition regime, as set out in the White Paper *Productivity and Enterprise – A World Class Competition Regime*, published in July 2001. These include:

- new regimes for investigating mergers and markets, with decisions taken in a large majority of cases by independent competition authorities (see page 341) against a new competition-based test within a more transparent and accountable framework, and with the end of ministerial involvement in these decisions;

- new criminal penalties to deter those who dishonestly engage in cartels covering the most serious forms of anti-competitive activity, such as agreements to fix prices, share markets, limit production and rig bids; and

- enabling those harmed by anti-competitive behaviour to bring claims for damages before a specialist competition body, the Competition Appeal Tribunal.

Office of Fair Trading

The Office of Fair Trading (OFT) (*www.oft.gov.uk*) is a non-ministerial government department headed by the Director General of Fair Trading. It administers a wide range of legislation on competition and on consumer protection (see chapter 29). The *Competition Act 1998*, whose main provisions came into force in March 2000, is enforced by the Director General of Fair Trading and the utility regulators (see page 342) who have concurrent powers in their sectors. The Act introduced two prohibitions:

- of agreements which prevent, restrict or distort competition and which may affect trade within the UK (the Chapter I prohibition); and

- of conduct by undertakings that amounts to an abuse of a dominant position in a market and may affect trade in the UK (the Chapter II prohibition).

The Chapter I and II prohibitions are based on articles 81 and 82 of the Treaty of Rome. An agreement will infringe the Chapter I prohibition only if it has as its object or effect an appreciable prevention, restriction or distortion of competition in the UK. The Director General takes the view that an agreement will generally have no appreciable effect on competition if the parties' combined share of the market does not exceed 25 per cent, although there will be circumstances when this is not the case. Under the Act, the Director General has the power to impose financial penalties of up to 10 per cent of turnover in the UK for up to three years on an undertaking that has infringed either prohibition.

The OFT has already imposed the first penalties under the Act on a pharmaceuticals firm found to have abused its dominant position in the supply of

drugs for cancer patients. At the end of 2001 over 40 cases under the Act were under consideration. The OFT has also begun to take action to promote competition in specific markets. It has launched studies into competition in the markets for consumer IT goods and services, pharmacies, extended warranties for electrical goods, and the estate agency market in England and Wales. The market for extended warranties for electrical goods has now been referred to the Competition Commission for further investigation, as has the market for private dentistry, following the first 'super-complaint' (see page 336) by the Consumers' Association.

Competition Commission

The Competition Commission (*www.competition-org.uk*) has two main arms:

- a reporting arm, which investigates various aspects of monopolies and mergers referred by the Director General of Fair Trading or a utility regulator; and

- an Appeal Tribunals arm, which hears appeals against decisions of the Director General of Fair Trading and the regulators made under the prohibition provisions of the *Competition Act 1998*.

Its report on small business banking (see page 454) found that a complex monopoly existed and proposed a series of remedies.

Mergers and monopolies

A merger qualifies for investigation if it involves the acquisition of assets of more than £70 million or the creation or enhancement of a 25 per cent share of the supply of a particular good or service in the UK or a substantial part of it. There is a voluntary procedure for pre-notification of proposed mergers. Qualifying mergers are considered by the Director General of Fair Trading, who currently advises the Secretary of State for Trade and Industry on whether the merger should be referred to the Competition Commission. The Secretary of State's policy is to follow the advice of the Director General on reference, unless there are exceptional circumstances. In general, a reference to the Competition Commission will be made where the merger raises competition concerns. However, most mergers are cleared without being referred to the Competition Commission. Under the Enterprise Bill, the final decision in merger cases (apart from those raising exceptional public interest issues) would be made by the Competition Commission.

If the Competition Commission finds that a merger could be expected to operate against the public interest, the Secretary of State can prohibit it, allow it, or allow it subject to certain conditions being met. Where the merger has already taken place, action can be taken to reverse it. There are special provisions for newspaper and water company mergers.

The European Commission has exclusive jurisdiction in mergers which meet certain domestic, EC and global turnover thresholds. The Commission can ban mergers if it concludes that they would create or strengthen a dominant market position which would significantly impede effective competition within the EU or a substantial part of it; alternatively, it may negotiate undertakings to correct the adverse effect.

The Director General of Fair Trading and those utility regulators with parallel powers may examine scale and complex monopolies,[1] and make a reference to the Competition Commission to establish whether a monopoly operates, or may be expected to operate, against the public interest.

Sectoral regulators

There are a number of bodies which regulate particular industries or sectors formerly in public ownership, including the Office of Gas and Electricity Markets (see page 443), the Office of Water Services (see page 447), the Office of Telecommunications (Oftel – see page 242) and two regulatory bodies for the railways: the Strategic Rail Authority and the Office of the Rail Regulator (see page 318). Each regulator operates within a framework of statutory objectives, an important feature of which is to protect and promote the interests of consumers, for example through ensuring effective competition.

---

1 A scale monopoly exists where a single company (or a group of interconnected companies) supplies or acquires at least 25 per cent of the goods or services of a particular type in all or part of the UK. A complex monopoly exists where a group of companies which are not connected and together account for at least 25 per cent of the supply of, or acquisition of, any particular description of goods or services in all or part of the UK engage in conduct which has, or is likely to have, the effect of restricting, distorting or preventing competition.

EU Single Market

The Government is working with the European Commission and other Member States to ensure effective competition within the Single Market (see page 366). It is looking to improve the way the market operates through wide-ranging economic reforms which target 'weak areas' (those areas where the Single Market does not work as well as it could) identified by the Commission. By the end of May 2002, 98.5 per cent of Single Market measures had been incorporated into UK law.

Corporate affairs

The UK has around 3.7 million businesses including many large companies. In 2001 there were 3,540 UK businesses employing 500 or more people (see Table 22.10), representing 39.6 per cent of total employment by UK businesses and 41.2 per cent of turnover. A small number of large companies and their subsidiaries are responsible for a substantial proportion of total production in some sectors. This is particularly true for chemicals, pharmaceuticals, motor vehicle assembly and aerospace.

Table 22.10 UK private sector and public corporations, 2001

	Number of enterprises	% of enterprises	% of employment
Enterprises with employees	1,149,955	30.7	87.2
Number of employees:			
1–4	747,655	20.0	9.9
5–9	200,315	5.3	6.3
10–19	112,690	3.0	6.9
20–49	54,845	1.5	7.5
50–99	18,145	0.5	5.5
100–199	7,895	0.2	4.9
200–249	1,625	0.0	1.6
250–499	3,245	0.1	5.0
500+	3,540	0.1	39.6
Enterprises with no employees[1]	2,596,420	69.3	12.8
All enterprises	**3,746,370**	*100.0*	*100.0*

1 Sole proprietorships and partnerships comprising only the self-employed owner-manager(s) and companies comprising only an employee director.
Source: Small Business Service

Table 22.11 Top UK companies by market capitalisation, 2002[1]

Company/business sector	Market capitalisation (£ million)[2]
BP/oil & gas	141,008
GlaxoSmithKline/pharmaceuticals & biotechnology	102,092
Vodafone/telecommunication services	88,860
HSBC Holdings/banks	76,347
AstraZeneca/pharmaceuticals & biotechnology	61,086
Royal Bank of Scotland/banks	54,357
Shell Transport & Trading/oil & gas	51,612
Lloyds TSB/banks	40,322
Barclays/banks	36,305
Diageo/beverages	30,862
HBOS/banks	29,119
BT/telecommunication services	24,401
Anglo American/mining	17,256
CGNU[3]/life assurance	17,031
Tesco/food & drug retailers	16,944
Unilever/food producers & processors	16,445
British Sky Broadcasting/media & photography	15,829
British American Tobacco/tobacco	14,785
Rio Tinto/mining	14,778
Abbey National/banks	14,770

1 As at 28 March.
2 Market capitalisation represents the number of shares issued multiplied by their market value.
3 Now Aviva.
Source: FT 500 Survey

According to a *Financial Times* survey of the world's 500 largest companies in March 2002, 41 were UK-based, with a market capitalisation of US$1,498 billion (£1,052 billion). Of the top 20 UK companies by market capitalisation, six were banks and there were two each in oil and gas, telecommunication services, pharmaceuticals and biotechnology, and mining (see Table 22.11). BP, the biggest UK company, was the eighth largest in the world and the second largest oil and gas company. In the other most valuable sectors, by market capitalisation:

- the UK had four representatives in the world's top ten banks – HSBC Holdings, Royal Bank of Scotland, Lloyds TSB and Barclays;

- GlaxoSmithKline was the world's third largest pharmaceuticals and biotechnology company, and AstraZeneca ranked sixth; and

- Vodafone was the world's second biggest telecommunication services company.

Value added scoreboard

To complement 'scoreboards' on research and development and on capital expenditure, the DTI published in May 2002 the UK's first company wealth creation league table, which includes the 500 largest UK firms and the 300 largest European companies by added value. Five UK companies featured in the top 15 wealth creators in Europe: Shell, BP, HSBC, GlaxoSmithKline and BT. The total annual value added for the UK 500 was £427 billion.

Small firms play an important part in the UK economy: around 43 per cent of the private sector workforce work for companies employing fewer than 50 people. About 2.6 million businesses are sole traders or partners without employees, while a further 747,655 businesses employ one to four people (see Table 22.10). Together these 3.3 million enterprises account for 89.3 per cent of the number of businesses, 22.7 per cent of business employment and 15.4 per cent of turnover. In 2001 there were 345,000 business start-ups in the UK.

Private sector firms predominate in the economy. The public sector has become much less significant following the privatisation since 1979 of many public sector businesses, including gas, electricity supply, coal and telecommunications. The remaining major nationalised industries are Consignia (see page 244), BNFL (British Nuclear Fuels) and the Civil Aviation Authority.

Company profitability

Company profitability, in terms of the net rate of return on capital employed, was 11.6 per cent in 2001, compared with 12.5 per cent in 2000 (see Figure 22.12). Among the individual sectors:

- the net rate of return for UK Continental Shelf companies fell slightly, from 35.7 per cent in 2000 to 34.2 per cent in 2001, although it remained at a historically high level, reflecting a combination of high oil and gas prices and high levels of output;

- service companies' net rate of return, at 12.9 per cent, was the lowest since 1993

Figure 22.12 Profitability of UK companies

Annual net rate of return (%)

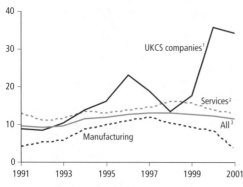

1 Those involved in the exploration for, and production of, oil and natural gas from the UK Continental Shelf (UKCS).
2 Excludes financial service sector companies.
3 Also includes other sectors (such as construction, electricity and gas supply, agriculture, mining and quarrying).
Source: Office for National Statistics

and compared with the recent peak of 16.2 per cent in 1998; and

- the net rate of return for manufacturing firms fell from 8.6 per cent in 2000 to 3.6 per cent in 2001, representing the lowest annual rate of return since 1984.

Corporate structure

At the end of March 2002 there were about 1,491,500 'live' companies registered in Great Britain with the Registrar of Companies. Companies incorporated overseas with a place of business or branch in Great Britain must also register. Most corporate businesses are 'limited liability' companies, in which the liability of members is restricted to contributing an amount related to their shareholding (or to their guarantee where companies are limited by guarantee). Since April 2001 a firm has been able to be incorporated as a limited liability partnership, with the organisational flexibility and tax status of a partnership but with limited liability for its members.

Companies may be either public or private; about 12,400 are public limited companies (plcs). A company must satisfy certain conditions before it can become a plc. It must be limited by shares and meet specified minimum capital requirements.

Private companies are generally prohibited from offering their shares to the public.

Company law and corporate governance

Company law is designed to meet the need for proper regulation of business, to maintain open markets and to create safeguards for those wishing to invest in companies or do business with them. It takes account of EC Directives on company law, and on company and group accounts and their auditing.

A three-year fundamental review of company law led by an independent steering group of experts was completed in July 2001. The review recommended the development of a modern framework of company law that would encourage both competitiveness and accountability. In July 2002 the Government published in a White Paper *Modernising Company Law* its response to the review's major recommendations and its core proposals to reform company law. It will consult on further proposals for the reform of company law as soon as practicable.

In August 2002 new regulations came into force which give shareholders a right to an annual vote on company directors' pay, with the intention of strengthening accountability, transparency and the links between pay and company performance. A quoted company is required, as part of the annual reporting cycle, to publish a report on directors' remuneration. This must include full details of directors' remuneration, including details of the performance criteria for share options and long-term incentive schemes, a justification of any compensation payments when a contract is terminated, and a graph showing company performance. A company must put a resolution to shareholders on this remuneration report at each annual general meeting. In April 2002 the Government commissioned an independent review of the role and effectiveness of company non-executive directors, which is expected to report around the end of 2002.

Insolvency

The Government wants a modern insolvency regime that supports enterprise and encourages responsible risk-taking. The *Insolvency Act 2000* provided small firms in financial difficulty with the option of a moratorium to agree a rescue plan with their creditors, and introduced disqualification undertakings whereby unfit company directors may agree a period of disqualification without the need to go to court, so speeding up the process. Major changes to insolvency law are contained in the Enterprise Bill, now before Parliament. The Bill would:

- reduce the duration of bankruptcy from three years to a maximum of 12 months for those who do not represent a risk to the public or commercial interests, while at the same time providing more effective protection against those who do – it would also remove many restrictions currently applying to bankrupts that the Government considers are irrelevant and outdated;

- reform corporate insolvency law by restricting the use of administrative receivership and streamlining administration;

- abolish the Crown's preferential rights to recover unpaid taxes ahead of other creditors; and

- modernise the financial regime of the Insolvency Service.

Regulation of business

The Government is working towards ensuring high standards of regulation across the UK by changing the culture of regulation through institutional and procedural reforms, lifting barriers to enterprise by removing or relaxing specific regulations, and improving communications with business. In February 2002 it announced a Regulatory Reform Action Plan (*www.cabinet-office.gov.uk/regulation/actionplan/index.htm*), with over 250 measures. Among these are changes to simplify and consolidate fire safety legislation; a Green Paper to reform the planning system, including speeding up the planning process for business (see page 303); and reforms to reduce restrictions on the operation of credit unions and to develop their role as financial institutions (see page 457).

The Cabinet Office's Regulatory Impact Unit (*www.cabinet-office.gov.uk/regulation*) works to ensure that new and existing regulation is necessary, meets the principles of better regulation, and imposes the minimum burden. The Regulatory Impact Unit helps to ensure that regulatory impact assessments are prepared for proposals that have an effect on business, charities and the voluntary sector. These assess the cost, benefit and risk, as well as considering all the available options to achieve the policy goals, including non-regulatory alternatives. Each government department has a minister responsible for its regulatory reform programme. The Ministerial Panel for Regulatory Accountability takes a strategic overview of the regulatory system to tackle instances where progress on regulatory reform is blocked.

The Better Regulation Task Force advises the Government to ensure that regulation and its enforcement conform to the principles of good regulation. In 2001/02 the Task Force conducted reviews of employment regulations, local delivery of central government policy, higher education, and scientific research and regulation. In its 2002/03 work programme the Task Force will study the problems small firms face when doing business with the public sector, independent regulators, alternatives to state regulation, and producer responsibility and waste.

Industrial associations

The CBI (Confederation of British Industry) (*www.cbi.org.uk*) is the largest business organisation in the UK. With a membership comprising companies and trade associations, it represents some 200,000 firms which employ about 7.5 million people. The CBI's objective is to help create and sustain the conditions in which British business can compete and prosper, both in the UK and overseas. Examples of its work include lobbying to minimise the burden of regulation, and campaigning to spread best practice. The CBI also offers a wide range of advisory services, including a series of regular economic surveys. It is the British member of the Union of Industrial and Employers' Confederations (UNICE). The CBI has 13 regional offices in the UK and offices in Brussels and Washington.

The British Chambers of Commerce (BCC) (*www.chamberonline.co.uk*) is a national network of chambers of commerce, which are local, independent, non-profit-making organisations funded by membership subscriptions. With over 2,500 staff covering more than 100 locations, the network provides a wide range of services for its membership of over 135,000 businesses. Services provided include business training, commercial services, export-related services, financial services and access to information resources. The BCC represents business views to the Government at national and local levels and is also part of the global network of chambers of commerce.

The Institute of Directors (IoD) (*www.iod.com*) has around 55,000 members in the UK. It provides business advisory services on matters affecting company directors, such as corporate management, insolvency and career counselling, and represents the interests of members to authorities in the UK and EU.

Enterprise Insight (*www.enterpriseinsight.co.uk*), a government-supported initiative launched in 2000 and led by a company owned jointly by the BCC, CBI and IoD, is aiming to encourage more positive attitudes to enterprise among young people aged 5 to 30 and to develop their entrepreneurial skills. Up to 1,000 'ambassadors' from business are helping to develop closer links between schools and the business community.

The Federation of Small Businesses is the largest pressure group promoting the interests of the self-employed and small firms. The Federation has over 168,000 members, and provides them with expert information and guidance on subjects such as taxation, employment, health and safety, and insurance.

Trade associations represent companies that produce or sell a particular product or group of products. They exist to supply common services, regulate trading practices and represent their members in dealings with government departments. For information on trade associations and trade unions see chapter 11.

Further reading

Budget 2002. The Strength to Make Long-term Decisions: Investing in an Enterprising, Fairer Britain. Economic and Fiscal Strategy Report and

Financial Statement and Budget Report April 2002. HM Treasury. The Stationery Office, 2002.

Modernising Company Law. Cm 5553. 2 vols. Department of Trade and Industry. The Stationery Office, 2002.

Modern Company Law for a Competitive Economy. Final Report of the Company Law Review Steering Group. 2 vols. Department of Trade and Industry, 2001.

Productivity and Enterprise: Insolvency – A Second Chance. Cm 5234. Department of Trade and Industry. The Stationery Office, 2001.

Productivity and Enterprise: A World Class Competition Regime. Cm 5233. Department of Trade and Industry. The Stationery Office, 2001.

Trade and Industry: The Government's Expenditure Plans 2002–03 to 2004–05 and Main Estimates 2002–03. Cm 5416. The Stationery Office, 2002.

United Kingdom National Accounts – the Blue Book (annual). Office for National Statistics. The Stationery Office.

Websites

Department of Trade and Industry
www.dti.gov.uk

HM Treasury
www.hm-treasury.gov.uk

National Statistics
www.statistics.gov.uk

WWW.

23 Public finance

The UK Government's spending and revenue are now over £400 billion a year. The main categories of expenditure and of receipts are shown in Table 23.5 and Figure 23.6 respectively on pages 351 and 352.

Since 1998/99 there has been a surplus on the public sector current budget, which reached £21.3 billion in 2000/01 (see Table 23.1). However, it fell back to £7.7 billion in 2001/02, primarily reflecting a fall in receipts from financial corporations and lower growth in other receipts, especially of corporation tax. Receipts from the latter were little changed, reflecting weaker global economic growth in 2001 and the resulting weak profitability of non-financial corporations.

Fiscal policy framework

The fiscal policy framework is designed to ensure sound public finances, which are a prerequisite for sustainable investment in public services. The *Code for Fiscal Stability* sets out the five key principles of fiscal management – transparency, stability, responsibility, fairness and efficiency – and government objectives are implemented through two fiscal rules which are the foundation of the spending framework and are designed to promote economic stability:

- *the golden rule* – over the economic cycle, the Government will borrow only to invest and not to fund current spending; and

- *the sustainable investment rule* – public sector net debt as a proportion of gross domestic product (GDP) will be held over the economic cycle at a stable and prudent level – generally below 40 per cent of GDP.

The fiscal framework also recognises that projections of the current budget and net debt involve a considerable element of uncertainty. Projections of the public finances are therefore deliberately based on prudent assumptions for key economic variables. These assumptions, which include the trend rate of growth, the level of unemployment, and oil and equity prices, are audited by the National Audit Office (NAO – see page 350) under a three-year rolling review to ensure they remain both reasonable and cautious. This minimises the need for unexpected changes in direction in taxation or spending.

Public spending framework

The key elements of the public spending framework are:

- three-year Departmental Expenditure Limits (DELs), designed to ensure that government departments plan and manage resources more effectively over the medium term;

- Annually Managed Expenditure (AME), which covers those elements of spending that cannot reasonably be subject to firm

Table 23.1 Key fiscal indicators, UK

	1996/97	1999/2000	2000/01	2001/02
Public sector				
Surplus on current budget (£ billion)	−23.1	20.0	21.3	7.7
Net investment (£ billion)	5.3	4.4	5.4	8.8
Net borrowing (£ billion)	28.4	−15.7	−15.9	1.2
Net debt (£ billion)	348.5	340.1	305.9	310.9
Net debt as a percentage of GDP	*43.7*	*36.2*	*31.3*	*30.4*

Source: *Financial Statistics*

Table 23.2 Trends in Total Managed Expenditure, UK

	1971/72	1981/82	1991/92	1996/97	2001/02	2002/03
In nominal terms (£ billion)	25.1	124.9	251.9	317.2	390.1	418.4
In real terms (£ billion)[1]	220.5	291.5	332.7	368.2	399.5	418.4
Per cent of GDP	42.5	48.1	42.3	41.0	39.0	39.9

1 At 2002/03 prices.
Source: *2002 Spending Review*

multi-year pre-set limits and are instead subject to annual scrutiny as part of the Budget process (see chapter 22);

- separate resource (current) and capital budgets for each department, consistent with the distinction in the fiscal rules – departments are required to manage their resource and capital budgets separately, removing the bias against investment which was present in the previous spending regime; and

- Public Service Agreements, through which each department is committed to deliver challenging targets that focus on outcomes.

DELs and AME sum to Total Managed Expenditure, the main concept in the management of public expenditure.

Other features of the framework include:

- ten-year plans for the National Health Service (see page 162) and for transport (see page 325);

- a National Asset Register to improve the utilisation of the public sector asset base;

- flexibility to allow departments to retain resources not fully spent by the end of the financial year, so assisting departments in managing their budgets and avoiding wasteful end-of-year spending surges;

- Resource Accounting and Budgeting (RAB) procedures, which became fully operational in April 2001 and apply the financial reporting practices of the private sector and much of the rest of the public sector to government departments' accounts, estimates and budgets. They are designed to improve efficiency and focus more on departmental objectives and outputs in terms of resources used rather than the money available for spending; and

- central funds, including the Invest to Save Budget and the Capital Modernisation Fund, which reward innovative ideas on a competitive basis.

Table 23.3 Components of Total Managed Expenditure, UK

					£ billion
	Provisional outturn				Plans
	2001/02	2002/03	2003/04	2004/05	2005/06
Resource Budget	213.2	228.5	249.3	263.7	283.1
Capital Budget	18.3	21.3	25.2	27.6	30.1
less depreciation	−9.7	−10.1	−11.1	−11.5	−12.2
Departmental Expenditure Limits	221.8	239.7	263.5	279.8	301.0
Annually Managed Expenditure	168.4	178.7	191.2	201.7	210.4
of which:					
Social security benefits	101.8	105.3	110.6	116.3	121.1
Locally financed expenditure	20.5	20.7	22.0	23.2	24.5
Central government gross debt interest	22.2	20.9	23.0	22.9	22.8
Total Managed Expenditure	390.1	418.4	454.6	481.5	511.4

Source: *2002 Spending Review*

Public expenditure

In terms of 2002/03 prices, Total Managed Expenditure rose from £220.5 billion in 1971/72 to £399.5 billion in 2001/02 (see Table 23.2). During this period it peaked as a proportion of GDP at 49.9 per cent in 1975/76, but by 1999/2000 had fallen to 37.4 per cent, before rising to 39.0 per cent in 2001/02. Total Managed Expenditure is projected to rise to £418.4 billion in 2002/03 and to reach £474.6 billion by 2005/06 when in nominal terms it would be £511.4 billion (see Table 23.3).

Spending priorities

Social security is the biggest single element of public spending, involving expenditure of £105 billion (nearly 25 per cent of spending) in 2002/03, followed by spending on the National Health Service (NHS) of £68 billion and on education of £54 billion (see Table 23.5).

In the April 2002 Budget the Government set overall spending limits for the three years to 2005/06 (see box on page 350). In addition, it announced a substantial increase in investment to place the NHS on a sustainable long-term financial footing and ensure that resources are available for reform (see chapter 13). The Budget provided for spending on the NHS in the UK to grow by 7.4 per cent a year on average in real terms over the five years to 2007/08.

Local authorities in the UK are estimated to have spent nearly £99 billion in 2001/02, around a quarter of public expenditure. The main categories of expenditure are education, law and order, personal social services, housing and other environmental services, and transport.

Public expenditure is planned and controlled on a departmental basis, except where devolved responsibility lies with the Scottish Parliament, the National Assembly for Wales and the Northern Ireland Assembly. The Scottish Parliament has limited financial authority to vary tax revenue in Scotland (see chapter 4). In 2000/01 the estimated outturn for the current and capital budgets of the devolved administrations totalled £14.7 billion in Scotland, £7.6 billion in Wales and £5.4 billion in Northern Ireland. See Table 23.4 for expenditure by country when other expenditure has been allocated.

Net public investment in the UK rose substantially in 2001/02 to £8.8 billion (see Table 23.1). There

Table 23.4 Identifiable expenditure on services[1] by country, 2000/01

	Expenditure (£ billion)	£ per head
England	226.4	4,529
Scotland	28.4	5,558
Wales	15.6	5,302
Northern Ireland	10.9	6,424
Total identifiable expenditure, UK	281.4	4,709
Non-identifiable expenditure,[2] UK	40.4	677
Total expenditure on services, UK	**321.8**	**5,386**

1 Expenditure on services differs from Total Managed Expenditure in that it excludes debt interest payments, net public service pensions and a number of accounting adjustments.
2 Expenditure, such as on defence and overseas aid, that is incurred on behalf of the UK as a whole.
Source: *Public Expenditure Statistical Analyses 2002–03*

are two central funds supporting innovative public investment projects:

- the Capital Modernisation Fund, which is aimed at improving delivery of public services, with funds allocated to departments on a competitive basis. Some £3.9 billion has been allocated to 116 projects, such as the new NHS walk-in centres and IT Learning Centres in major city areas; and

- the Invest to Save Budget, which provides venture capital for the public sector – over £300 million has been allocated to 335 partnership projects across central government and the wider public and voluntary sectors.

The Office of Government Commerce (OGC) was set up as an independent office of HM Treasury in April 2000 to modernise procurement in central civil government and to deliver substantial improvements in value for money. Its primary target is to work with central civil government to deliver £1 billion of value-for-money gains from commercial activities by the end of 2002/03. More than a third of this target was achieved in 2001/02 (the first year of operation), with £433 million of gains reported. OGC is engaged in a number of activities to modernise and promote best procurement practice, based on a collaborative approach with departments. These include helping departments to develop their skills for successful delivery; setting standards for

Spending Review 2002
In July 2002 the Government published its 2002 Spending Review, setting spending plans and targets for the period 2003/04 to 2005/06. Total DEL spending is set to rise by an average of 5¼ per cent a year in real terms in this period, so that by 2005/06 DELs will be £61 billion higher than in 2002/03 (see Tables 23.3 and 23.5). Public sector net investment is planned to rise to £24 billion by 2005/06, representing 2 per cent of GDP.

The 2002 Spending Review focused on the priority areas of raising productivity, extending opportunity, establishing stronger and more secure communities, and Britain's position in the world. Three-quarters of the additional spending in 2005/06 will go to the Government's key priorities of education, health, transport, housing and tackling crime. Additional resources allocated include:

- in *education* an increase in spending in the UK of £14.7 billion a year by 2005/06 compared with 2002/03, raising education's share of GDP to 5.6 per cent by 2002/03, compared with 5.1 per cent in 2002/03;

- a substantial increase in spending on *health*, to £109 billion by 2007/08, or 9.4 per cent of GDP (compared with 7.7 per cent in 2002/03);

- expected growth in UK *transport* spending of 8.4 per cent a year in real terms over the period

to 2005/06, in line with the ten-year plan for transport (see chapter 21), to improve rail travel and tackle road congestion;

- an extra £1.3 billion a year for *housing* investment by 2005/06 compared with 2002/03;

- *crime*, where, for example, spending on police in England will be around £1.5 billion a year higher by 2005/06 than in 2002/03;

- *defence*, which will grow by 1.2 per cent a year in real terms over the three years to 2005/06; and

- *international aid*, which will account for 0.40 per cent of gross national income by 2005/06, compared with the level of 0.32 per cent in 2002/03.

New Public Service Agreements, for 2003 to 2006, were published as part of the Government's spending plans. They contain about 130 'headline' performance targets. Targets have been set for each department, with independent audit and inspection arrangements to monitor progress. Public service providers will have flexibility and discretion to innovate, respond to local conditions and meet differing consumer demands within this framework of targets and accountability arrangements. The Prime Minister's Delivery Unit and HM Treasury are working with departments to support them in producing delivery plans for all their targets by October 2002.

departments' own good practice; ensuring the success of large, novel and/or complex projects; and working with suppliers to achieve value for money.

Examination of public expenditure

Examination of public expenditure is carried out by select committees of the House of Commons. The committees study in detail the activities of particular government departments and question ministers and officials. The Public Accounts Committee considers the accounts of government departments, executive agencies and other public sector bodies, and examines reports by the Comptroller and Auditor General on departments and their use of resources.

Audit of the Government's spending is exercised through the functions of the Comptroller and Auditor General, the head of the National Audit Office. The NAO's responsibilities include

certifying the accounts of all government departments and executive agencies, and those of many other bodies receiving public funds. It reports to Parliament on the results of its investigations of the financial operations of these organisations and of the economy, efficiency and effectiveness with which public resources have been used.

Public-private partnerships

The Government sees public-private partnerships (PPPs) as a key factor in the delivery of high-quality public services, by bringing in private sector management, finance and ownership with the intention of improving the value for money, efficiency and quality of these services. The PPPs cover a variety of arrangements, including joint ventures; outsourcing; the sale of equity stakes in government-owned businesses; and the Private Finance Initiative (PFI), in which the public sector specifies the service needed, in terms of the

Table 23.5 Main departmental allocations[1] under the Spending Review 2002

	2002/03	2003/04	2004/05	£ billion 2005/06	Annual average growth rate (per cent)
Total Departmental Expenditure Limits	**239.7**	**263.5**	**279.8**	**301.0**	**5.2**
of which:					
Education and Skills	23.2	25.6	27.8	31.1	7.6
Health	58.0	63.9	70.3	77.3	7.3
of which: National Health Service	55.8	61.3	67.4	74.4	7.4
Transport	7.7	10.7	11.2	11.6	12.1
Office of the Deputy Prime Minister	6.0	6.7	7.2	7.6	5.2
Local government	37.7	40.7	42.8	45.9	4.2
Home Office	10.7	12.3	12.7	13.5	5.6
Defence	29.3	30.9	31.8	32.8	1.2
Trade and Industry	4.7	5.1	5.1	5.5	2.8
Work and Pensions	7.0	7.5	7.8	7.8	1.1
Scotland	18.2	19.7	20.9	22.3	4.4
Wales	9.4	10.3	10.9	11.8	5.1
Northern Ireland Executive[2]	6.4	6.8	7.2	7.6	3.3
Selected allocations by function					
Education (UK)	53.7	58.6	62.9	68.4	5.7
National Health Service (UK)	68.1	74.9	82.2	90.5	7.3
Transport (UK)	12.0	15.4	15.8	16.4	8.4
Housing (England)	4.9	5.5	5.7	5.9	4.2
Criminal justice (England and Wales)	14.7	16.4	17.2	18.3	5.0

1 Departmental Expenditure Limits are given for selected departments – those with DELs over £5 billion in 2005/06.
2 There is a separate DEL for the Northern Ireland Office.
Source: *2002 Spending Review*

outputs required, and private sector companies compete to meet the requirements. Over 500 PFI projects, with a combined capital value of over £22 billion, were signed between mid-1997 and mid-2002 in a variety of areas, including schools, colleges, hospitals, local authorities, defence IT and property management. Major PPP projects include the Channel Tunnel Rail Link (see page 320) and a scheme for investment in the London Underground (see page 320). Partnerships UK, owned jointly by the public and private sectors, supports public authorities in the development and implementation of PPP and PFI projects.

Debt management

The Government meets its borrowing needs by selling debt to the private sector. In 2001/02 UK public sector net debt was £310.9 billion, 12 per cent below the peak of £352.9 billion in 1997/98. As a proportion of GDP, it declined from 41.6 per cent in 1997/98 to 30.4 per cent in 2001/02, and is the lowest level of any G7 country. 'Core debt', a new measure of net debt excluding fluctuations in the economic cycle, is now being published and in 2000/01 was estimated at 31 per cent of GDP.

The objective of the Government's debt management policy is to minimise, over the long term, the cost of meeting the Government's financing needs, taking into account risk while ensuring that debt management policy is consistent with the aims of monetary policy. Operational responsibility for managing government debt rests with a Treasury agency, the United Kingdom Debt Management Office (DMO).

Gilt-edged stock

The major debt instrument, government bonds, is known as gilt-edged stock ('gilts'), as government securities are judged by the market as having the lowest risk of default. Gilts include 'conventionals', which generally pay fixed rates of interest and redemption sums; and index-linked stocks, on which both principal and interest payments are linked to movements in the Retail Prices Index. Gilt issues are primarily by auction. The annual Debt and Reserves Management Report sets out the framework for issuing gilts for the forthcoming fiscal year. The DMO, on behalf of the Government, is aiming for gilts sales of £22.4 billion in 2002/03, compared with gilts sales of £13.7 billion in 2001/02.

At the end of December 2001 holdings of central government marketable securities were estimated at £286.1 billion. This comprised £204.4 billion of conventional gilts, £70.5 billion of index-linked gilts and £11.2 billion of Treasury Bills (short-term securities issued as part of the DMO's cash management operations). Insurance companies and pension funds hold 61 per cent of gilts, other UK financial institutions 12 per cent, UK households 7 per cent and holders in the rest of the world 18 per cent.

Main sources of revenue

Government revenue is forecast to be £407 billion in 2002/03. The main sources (see Figure 23.6) are:

- taxes on income (together with profits), which include personal income tax, corporation tax and petroleum revenue tax (see page 435);

- taxes on expenditure, which include VAT (value added tax) and customs and excise duties;

- National Insurance contributions (see chapter 12); and

- taxes on capital, which include inheritance tax, capital gains tax, council tax and non-domestic rates (also known as business rates).

Taxation policy

The primary aim of tax policy is to raise sufficient revenue for the Government to pay for the services that its policies require and to service its

Figure 23.6 Projections of UK government receipts 2002/03

Total receipts: £407 billion

£ billion

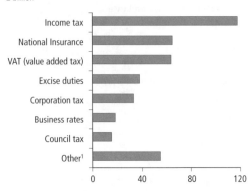

1 Includes capital taxes, stamp duties, vehicle excise duties and some other tax and non-tax receipts (such as interest and dividends).
Source: HM Treasury, Budget 2002

April 2002 Budget
Among the main measures announced in the April 2002 Budget were:

- a cut in the starting rate of corporation tax from 10 per cent to zero, a reduction in the small companies' rate, and a new 25 per cent tax credit to boost research and development by large companies (see page 355);

- changes to the North Sea oil and gas tax regime (see page 435), so that companies will pay a 10 per cent supplementary charge on North Sea profits and will receive a 100 per cent first-year allowance for capital expenditure. The Government has also announced its intention to abolish the system of North Sea royalties; and

- confirmation of arrangements for a new Child Tax Credit and a new Working Tax Credit (see page 354).

debt, while keeping the overall burden of tax as low as possible. The Government has based its tax policy on the principles of encouraging work, raising investment, and promoting fairness and opportunity. It has taken measures designed to improve productivity, increase employment opportunities, tackle child and pensioner poverty, and protect the environment.

Collection of taxes and duties

The Inland Revenue assesses and collects taxes on income, profits and capital, and stamp duty (see Table 23.7). Its National Insurance Contributions Office is responsible for collecting National Insurance contributions. HM Customs and Excise collects around £100 billion a year in taxes and duties (see Table 23.8), including VAT, environmental taxes and alcohol, oils, tobacco and gambling duties. Local authorities collect the main local taxes, such as council tax.

Most wage and salary earners pay their income tax under a Pay-As-You-Earn (PAYE) system whereby tax is deducted and accounted for to the Inland Revenue by the employer, in a way which enables most employees to pay the correct amount of tax during the year.

Under the self-assessment system for collecting personal taxation, around 8.5 million people – primarily higher-rate taxpayers, the self-employed and those receiving investment income – are

Table 23.7 Inland Revenue taxes and duties

			£ million
	1996/97	2000/01	2001/02
Net receipts by Board of Inland Revenue			
Income tax and capital gains tax combined	70,202	104,537	106,231
Corporation tax	27,787	32,421	32,357
Inheritance tax	1,558	2,223	2,348
Stamp duties	2,467	8,165	7,101
Petroleum revenue tax	1,729	1,518	1,307
Total	**103,743**	**148,862**	**149,345**

Source: Inland Revenue and Office for National Statistics

Table 23.8 Main Customs and Excise taxes and duties

			£ million
	1996/97	2000/01	2001/02
Payments by HM Customs and Excise into the Consolidated Fund[1]			
VAT	46,644	58,501	61,032
Duties on:			
hydrocarbon oils	17,174	22,630	21,916
tobacco	8,039	7,648	7,754
beer	2,629	2,850	2,899
wine and made wine	1,274	1,814	1,982
spirits	1,593	1,842	1,918
betting, gaming and lottery	1,441	1,510	1,434
Customs duties and agricultural levies	2,300	2,097	2,042
Insurance premium tax	671	1,707	1,861
All payments[2]	**82,351**	**102,169**	**104,855**

1 Those bringing in over £1 billion in 2001/02 are listed in the table.
2 Among the other taxes and duties included are air passenger duty, climate change levy and landfill tax.
Source: HM Customs and Excise

required to complete an annual tax return for the Inland Revenue. Such taxpayers may calculate their own tax liability, although they can choose to have the calculations done by the Inland Revenue if they return the form by the end of September.

The UK has agreements governing double taxation with over 100 countries. They are intended to avoid double taxation arising, to deal with cross-border economic activity, and to prevent fiscal discrimination against UK business interests overseas. They also include provisions to counter tax avoidance and evasion.

Tax Law Rewrite Project
The Tax Law Rewrite Project, established in 1996, involves rewriting the UK's primary direct tax legislation so that it is clearer and easier to use, but without changing its general effect. It also involves a revision of the PAYE regulations. The first rewritten item was the *Capital Allowances Act 2001*, and the second will be the Income Tax (Earnings and Pensions) Bill, due to be introduced into Parliament later in 2002, governing taxation of employment and of charging provisions for pension and social security income.

Taxes on income

Income tax
Income tax is the biggest single contributor to government receipts, bringing in net receipts of £103 billion in 2001/02. In general, it is charged on all income originating in the UK – although some forms of income, such as child benefit, are exempt – and on all income arising abroad of people resident in the UK. Income tax is imposed for the year of assessment beginning on 6 April. The tax rates and bands for 2001/02 and 2002/03 are shown in Table 23.9. Of around 28.3 million income taxpayers, 3.0 million are expected to pay tax only at the starting rate of 10 per cent in 2002/03, 21.7 million at 22 per cent and 2.8 million at 40 per cent, while 0.8 million taxpayers will pay a marginal rate of 20 per cent on their savings.

Allowances and reliefs reduce an individual's income tax liability. All taxpayers are entitled to a personal allowance against income from all sources, with a higher allowance for the elderly (see Table 23.9). One of the most significant reliefs, which is designed to encourage people to save towards their retirement, covers contributions

Tax credits
Currently there are a number of tax credits, including the Children's Tax Credit (CTC), introduced in April 2001, which is currently worth up to £529 a year for families with one or more children under 16 living with them; the credit is reduced where the main earner in the family is a higher rate taxpayer. In April 2002 a higher rate of CTC, worth up to £1,049 a year, was introduced for families in the year of a child's birth, to recognise the extra costs associated with having a baby. The Working Families' Tax Credit (WFTC – see chapter 12) is designed to provide a guaranteed minimum income for working families.

From April 2003 the Government plans to introduce a new system with the aim of supporting families, tackling child poverty and making work pay. Two new tax credits are planned:

- the *Child Tax Credit*, which will integrate all the existing income-related elements of support for children currently included in the WFTC, the Disabled Person's Tax Credit (DPTC) and Income Support or Jobseeker's Allowance, as well as the existing CTC; and

- the *Working Tax Credit*, which will include the adult elements of WFTC and DPTC, and extend in-work support to workers without children or disabilities.

to pension schemes. Personal tax-free saving is also encouraged through the Individual Savings Account (ISA) (see page 460).

Corporation tax
Corporation tax is payable by companies on their income and capital gains. The UK's main rate of corporation tax, 30 per cent, is lower than any other major industrialised country. Two changes to the lower rates took effect in April 2002, reducing the starting rate of 10 per cent to zero for the smallest companies (so that companies with annual profits of up to £10,000 will no longer pay corporation tax) and cutting from 20 per cent to 19 per cent the small companies' rate levied on firms with annual profits between £50,000 and £300,000. A sliding scale of relief is allowed for companies with annual profits between £10,000 and £50,000 and between £300,000 and £1.5 million, so that the overall average rate paid by these firms is up to

Table 23.9 Tax allowances and bands, UK

		£
	2001/02	2002/03
Income tax allowances		
Personal allowance:		
age under 65	4,535	4,615
age 65–74	5,990	6,100
age 75 and over	6,260	6,370
Income limit for age-related		
allowances	17,600	17,900
Married couple's allowance[1]		
for those born before 6 April 1935	5,365	5,465
age 75 and over	5,435	5,535
minimum amount	2,070	2,110
Children's tax credit[1]	5,200	5,290
baby rate[2]	–	10,490
Blind person's allowance	1,450	1,480
Bands of taxable income[3]		
Starting rate of 10 per cent	0–1,880	0–1,920
Basic rate of 22 per cent	1,881–29,400	1,921–29,900
Higher rate of 40 per cent	over 29,400	over 29,900

1 The rate of relief for these allowances is restricted to 10 per cent.
2 For babies born on or after 6 April 2002, in the first year of the child's life. Includes Children's Tax Credit.
3 The rate of tax applicable to savings income in the basic rate band is 20 per cent. For dividends the rates applicable are 10 per cent for income below the basic rate upper limit and 32.5 per cent above that.
Source: Inland Revenue

19 per cent and between 19 per cent and 30 per cent respectively.

A consultation document containing further government proposals to reform and modernise the corporation tax regime was published in August 2002. The views of business and other interested parties are being sought on three areas: the tax treatment of capital assets not covered by earlier changes; rationalisation of the way in which various types of income are taxed; and differences in the tax treatment of trading and investment companies.

Some capital expenditure – on machinery and plant, industrial buildings, agricultural buildings and scientific research, for example – may qualify for relief in the form of capital allowances. There is a 40 per cent first-year allowance for expenditure on machinery or plant by small or medium-sized businesses. Small businesses can also claim 100 per cent first-year allowances on investments in information and communications technology (ICT) between 1 April 2000 and 31 March 2003, so enabling them to write off immediately the entire cost against their taxable income. In April 2002 a new research and development (R&D) tax credit was introduced for large companies, complementing a similar credit for small and medium-sized firms. The credit, payable at a rate of 25 per cent, will provide an additional £400 million a year support for investment in new technology by UK industry. There are also 100 per cent allowances for investments in qualifying environmental technologies (including allowances that are part of the climate change levy package – see page 434) and a 150 per cent tax credit for expenditure on restoring contaminated land.

Taxes on capital

Capital gains tax

Capital gains tax (CGT) is payable by individuals and trusts on gains realised from the disposal of assets. It is payable on the amount by which total chargeable gains for a year exceed the exempt amount (£7,700 for individuals and £3,850 for most trusts in 2002/03). Gains on some types of asset are exempt from CGT, including the principal private residence, government securities, certain corporate bonds, and gains on holdings of Personal Equity Plans and Individual Savings Accounts (see page 460). For individuals, CGT in 2002/03 will be payable at 10 per cent, 20 per cent or 40 per cent, depending on a person's marginal income tax rate.

CGT taper relief, introduced in 1998, reduces the amount of the chargeable gain depending on how long an asset has been held, with a higher rate of relief for business assets than for non-business assets. Subsequent changes to taper relief, particularly on business assets, have been introduced with the intention of encouraging investment and promoting enterprise. The current CGT taper reliefs reduce the percentage of the gain that is chargeable for a business asset from 100 per cent for assets held for less than one year to 25 per cent for assets held for two years or more. For non-business assets the chargeable gain falls from 100 per cent for assets held for less than three years to 60 per cent for assets held for ten years or longer.

Inheritance tax

Inheritance tax is charged on estates at the time of death and on gifts made within seven years of death; most other lifetime transfers are not taxed. There are several important exemptions, including transfers between spouses, and gifts and bequests to UK charities, major political parties and heritage bodies. In general, business assets and farmland are exempt from inheritance tax, so that most family businesses can be passed on without a tax charge.

Tax is charged at a single rate of 40 per cent above a threshold (£250,000 in 2002/03). Only about 4 per cent of estates each year become liable for an inheritance tax bill.

Taxes on expenditure

Value added tax (VAT)

VAT, which contributes about 58 per cent of Customs and Excise receipts, is a tax on consumer expenditure, which is collected at each stage in the production and distribution of goods and services. The final tax is payable by the consumer. The standard rate is 17.5 per cent, with a reduced rate of 5 per cent on a number of goods and services, including domestic fuel and power, children's car seats, women's sanitary products and the installation of energy-saving materials in homes.

Certain goods and services are relieved from VAT, either by being charged at a zero rate or by being exempt:

- Under zero rating, a taxable person does not charge tax to a customer but reclaims any VAT paid to suppliers. Among the main categories where zero rating applies are goods exported to other EU countries; some foods; water and sewerage for non-business use; domestic and international passenger transport; books, newspapers and periodicals; construction of new residential buildings; young children's clothing and footwear; drugs and medicines supplied on prescription; specified aids for handicapped people; and certain supplies by or to charities.

- For exempt goods or services, a taxable person does not charge any VAT but is not entitled to reclaim the VAT on goods and services bought for his or her business. The main categories where exemption applies are many supplies of land and buildings;

financial services; postal services; betting and gaming (where there are some exemptions); lotteries; much education and training; and health and welfare.

Recent Budgets have contained measures designed to help new and small businesses, allowing them to manage their entry into the VAT system, reduce their VAT administrative burden and improve their cash flow. The annual level of turnover above which traders must register for VAT was raised to £55,000 in the April 2002 Budget. Under a new optional scheme, small businesses with an annual turnover of up to £100,000 do not now have to account for VAT on each purchase and sale, but instead are able to calculate their net VAT liability by applying a flat rate percentage to their total annual turnover. This will be extended in April 2003 to businesses with an annual turnover of up to £150,000.

Excise duties

Vehicle excise duty: since March 2001 VED for new cars has been determined according to the carbon dioxide emissions of the vehicle and the type of fuel used. Initially there were four VED bands, but in the 2002 Budget a fifth band was introduced, with a further discount for the most efficient vehicles. The annual VED rate for cars registered after March 2001 now ranges from £70 to £155 for cars using petrol, and £80 to £160 for those using diesel, and for cars using cleaner fuels the overall duty varies from £60 to £150. For cars registered before 1 March 2001 VED is determined according to engine size. The standard rate is £160, with a lower rate of £105 for cars up to 1,549 cc. Under the new system of VED for goods vehicles, which came into operation in December 2001, seven broad rate bands replaced around 100 different rates. This is intended to better reflect the environmental and road damage caused by goods vehicles. The annual standard rate ranges from £165 to £1,850 (£160 to £1,350 for lorries with reduced pollution certificates). Duty on buses varies according to seating capacity.

Insurance premium tax: this is levied at 5 per cent on most general insurance, with a higher rate of 17.5 per cent on travel insurance and on insurance sold by suppliers of cars and domestic appliances.

Air passenger duty: for flights to UK and to European Economic Area (EEA) destinations, the duty is £5 for the lowest class and £10 for any other class; the equivalent rates to non-EEA

The main announcements in the April 2002 Budget on excise duties included:

- an increase on tobacco duty, in line with inflation;

- no change in the duty on the main road fuels and on road fuel gases, although a new lower rate for biodiesel was introduced;

- no change in the main vehicle excise duty (VED) rates (see page 356), but with some changes, including a new low-carbon VED rate for cars with the lowest emissions and reforms to VED for motorcycles and vans to reflect environmental benefits;

- no change on the duty on spirits, for the fifth Budget in succession;

- a cut in beer duty for small brewers from June 2002, with a 50 per cent cut for those producing up to 500,000 litres a year and lower rates of duty worth more than £120,000 for breweries producing up to 3 million litres a year; and

- confirmation of the abolition of the pool betting duty (on football pools) and its replacement by a 15 per cent tax on pools promoters' gross profits (stakes less winnings). The Government announced its intention to consider abolition of the tax on bingo stakes and its replacement by a gross profits tax on bingo companies; a consultation document on bingo duty was published in August 2002.

destinations are £20 and £40 respectively. All flights from airports in the Scottish Highlands and Islands are exempt from duty in recognition of their remoteness and dependence on air travel. From 1 November 2002 the lower rates of duty applying to EEA destinations will be extended to all countries applying to join the EU (see page 61) and to Switzerland.

Betting, gaming and lottery duties: these are charged on off-course betting, pool betting, gaming in casinos, bingo and amusement machines. Rates vary with the particular form of gambling. In October 2001 a 15 per cent tax on bookmakers' gross profits replaced general betting duty of 6.75 per cent on total stakes. On the National Lottery (see page 263) there is a 12 per cent duty on gross stakes, but no tax on winnings.

Landfill tax: this is levied at £13 a tonne, with a lower rate of £2 a tonne for inert waste.

Aggregates levy: introduced in April 2002, this is applied at £1.60 a tonne on the extraction of sand, gravel and rock for use as aggregate.

Climate change levy: since April 2001 this has been levied on the non-domestic use of energy at the rate of 0.43p per kilowatt-hour (kWh) for electricity, 0.15p per kWh for gas, 0.96p per kilogramme (kg) for liquefied petroleum gas and 1.17p per kg for solid fuels. All revenues are recycled back to business through a reduction in employers' National Insurance contributions and additional support for energy efficiency measures (see page 445). An 80 per cent discount is available to energy-intensive business sectors that have agreed targets with the Government for increasing energy efficiency and reducing greenhouse gas emissions.

Stamp duty

Some transfers are subject to stamp duty. Transfers of shares generally attract duty at 0.5 per cent of the cost, while certain types of document, such as declarations of trust, generally attract a small fixed duty of £5. Transfers by gift and transfers to charities are exempt. Duty on land and property is payable at 1 per cent of the total price when above £60,000, 3 per cent above £250,000 and 4 per cent over £500,000. Property transfers of up to £150,000 in the UK's most disadvantaged areas are exempt from stamp duty, and stamp duty is to be abolished for all non-residential transfers in these areas, subject to EU state aid approval. The system of stamp duty on land and buildings is to be reformed, and the Government issued a consultative document in April 2002.

Local authority taxation

Domestic property in Great Britain is generally subject to the council tax, one of the main sources of income for local authorities (see page 53). Each dwelling is allocated to one of eight valuation bands, based on its capital value (the amount it might have sold for on the open market) in April 1991. Discounts are available for dwellings with fewer than two resident adults, and those on low incomes may receive council tax benefit of up to 100 per cent of the tax bill (see page 154). In 2002/03, in England the average council tax for a Band D dwelling (occupied by two adults) is £976 (compared with £901 in 2001/02): £895 in

London, £1,017 in other metropolitan areas and £984 in shire areas. In Scotland the average Band D dwelling council tax is £971 and in Wales £762.

Non-domestic rates (also known as business rates) are a tax on the occupiers of non-domestic property. The rateable value is assessed by reference to annual rents and reviewed every five years. Separate non-domestic rates are set for England, Wales and Scotland, and collected by local authorities. They are paid into separate national pools and redistributed to local authorities in proportion to their population.

In Northern Ireland, rates – local taxes on domestic and non-domestic properties – are based on the value of the property. For 2002/03 the average domestic rates bill in Northern Ireland will be £499.

Further reading
2002 Spending Review. Opportunity and security for all: Investing in an enterprising, fairer Britain. New Public Spending Plans 2003–2006. Cm 5570. HM Treasury. The Stationery Office, 2002.

Budget 2002. The Strength to Make Long-term Decisions: Investing in an Enterprising, Fairer

Britain. Economic and Fiscal Strategy Report and Financial Statement and Budget Report April 2002. HM Treasury. The Stationery Office, 2002.

Inland Revenue Statistics. Contains statistics on taxes administered by the Inland Revenue. Available only on the Internet at *www.inlandrevenue.gov.uk/stats*

Annual Reports
Debt and Reserves Management Report. HM Treasury.

Public Expenditure Statistical Analyses. HM Treasury. The Stationery Office.

Websites

HM Treasury
www.hm-treasury.gov.uk

Inland Revenue
www.inlandrevenue.gov.uk

HM Customs and Excise
www.hmce.gov.uk

WWW.

24 International trade and investment

Trade has been of vital importance to the British economy for hundreds of years. Although it has under 1 per cent of the world's population, the UK was the fourth largest trading nation in 2001, accounting for 5.1 per cent of world trade in goods and services. In 2001, 53 per cent of the UK's export trade in goods and services and 52 per cent of its import trade was with fellow members of the European Union, the world's largest established trading group. The UK exports more per head than either the United States or Japan. Its sales abroad of goods and services were 27 per cent of gross domestic product at market prices in 2001. Investment income and receipts from trade in services (such as financial services, business services, travel, transport and communications) accounted for 51 per cent of total UK current account credits and for 44 per cent of equivalent debits. The UK consistently runs large surpluses on these accounts.

Trade in goods and services – then and now		
		£ million
	1951	2001
Exports of goods	2,779	191,644
Imports of goods	3,471	225,178
Balance of trade in goods	–692	–33,534
Exports of services	860	76,807
Imports of services	828	65,734
Balance of trade in services	32	11,073

Balance of payments

The balance of payments (see Table 24.1) is an account of all the economic transactions between the UK and the rest of the world. It records inward and outward transactions, the overall net flow of transactions between UK residents and the rest of the world, and how that flow is funded. Economic transactions include:

- *exports and imports of goods*, such as oil, agricultural products, machinery and consumer goods;

- *exports and imports of services*, such as international transport, travel, financial and business services;

- *income flows*, such as dividends and interest earned by non-residents on investments in the UK and by UK residents investing abroad;

- *financial flows*, such as investment in shares, debt securities, loans and deposits; and

- *transfers*, such as payments to, and receipts from, EU institutions, foreign aid and funds brought by migrants to the UK.

The balance of payments is made up of the following accounts:

- the *current account*, which comprises trade in goods and services (Table 24.2), income (investment income and compensation of employees – for example, locally engaged staff in UK embassies and military bases abroad) and current transfers (such as food aid) (Table 24.8);

- the *capital account*, which comprises capital transfers and the acquisition and disposal of non-produced, non-financial assets (such as copyrights);

- the *financial account*, which covers the flow of direct, portfolio and other investment and reserve assets (Table 24.9); and

- the *international investment position*, which measures the UK's stock of external financial assets and liabilities (Table 24.10).

Table 24.1 UK balance of payments summary[1]

	1991	1996	1999	2000	£ million 2001
Current account					
Trade in goods and services	−6,121	−4,125	−15,578	−18,488	−22,461
Income	−3,307	1,204	2,536	9,312	9,162
Current transfers	−1,231	−5,788	−6,687	−10,032	−7,154
Current balance	−10,659	−8,709	−19,729	−19,208	−20,453
Capital account	290	736	943	1,823	1,499
Financial account	5,269	5,515	19,735	13,993	19,291
Net errors and omissions[2]	5,100	2,458	−949	3,392	−337

1 Balance of payments basis.
2 Amount necessary to bring the sum of all balance of payments entries to zero.
Source: ONS Balance of Payments

Table 24.2 UK external trade in goods and services[1]

	1991	1996	1999	2000	£ million 2001
Exports of goods	103,939	167,196	166,166	187,936	191,644
Exports of services	32,001	55,895	70,443	77,199	76,807
Exports of goods and services	135,940	223,091	236,609	265,135	268,451
Imports of goods	114,162	180,918	193,538	218,262	225,178
Imports of services	27,899	46,298	58,649	65,361	65,734
Imports of goods and services	142,061	227,216	252,187	283,623	290,912
Balance of trade in goods	−10,223	−13,722	−27,372	−30,326	−33,534
Balance of trade in services	4,102	9,597	11,794	11,838	11,073
Balance of trade in goods and services	−6,121	−4,125	−15,578	−18,488	−22,461

1 Balance of payments basis.
Source: ONS Balance of Payments

Table 24.1 summarises the UK's balance of payments position over recent years. In 2001 the current account was in deficit by £20.5 billion, compared with a £19.2 billion deficit in 2000. A sharp widening in the deficit on goods and services was largely offset by a reduced deficit in current transfers. The capital account surplus fell from a record £1.8 billion in 2000 to £1.5 billion in 2001.

Trade in goods and services

Table 24.2 summarises the UK's trade in goods and services over recent years. More detailed analyses for 2001 can be found in subsequent tables. In 2001, UK exports of goods amounted to £191.6 billion and imports to £225.2 billion, giving a deficit on trade in goods of £33.5 billion, slightly higher than in 2000 and the largest deficit on record. The surplus on trade in services in 2001 (£11.1 billion) compares with a £11.8 billion surplus recorded in the previous year. Figure 24.3 shows the position over the past 30 years.

Commodity composition of goods

UK exports of goods are dominated by manufactures – finished manufactures and semi-manufactured goods – which in 2001 accounted for the same proportion (84 per cent) of exports as they did in 1971. Oil exports, which had risen as a proportion of total exports from 4 per cent in 1971 to 21 per cent in 1984, have subsequently declined to 8 per cent (see Table 24.4).

Figure 24.3 UK balance of payments in goods and services

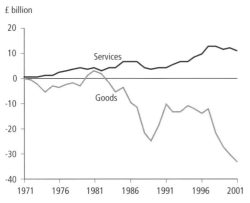

£ billion

Source: Office for National Statistics

Historically the UK was predominantly an importer of foods and basic materials. Over the last 30 years, however, imports of manufactures have grown rapidly. Between 1971 and 2001 the share of finished manufactures in total imports rose from 27 per cent to 60 per cent. The UK has not had a surplus on manufactured goods since 1982. Basic materials fell from 12 per cent of total imports in 1971 to 3 per cent in 2001. Food, beverages and tobacco accounted for 22 per cent of imports in 1971 compared with only 8 per cent in 2001.

Machinery and transport equipment accounted for 46 per cent of exports and 44 per cent of imports in 2001. Aerospace, chemicals and electronics have become increasingly significant export sectors, while textiles have declined in relative importance. Sectors with a significant positive balance of trade in 2001 included fuels, chemicals and mechanical machinery, while those with a relatively large negative balance included food, crude materials, road vehicles and clothing.

Geographical breakdown of goods
Most of the UK's trade in goods is with other developed countries (see Table 24.5). In 2001, 85 per cent of UK exports were to other member countries of the Organisation for Economic Co-operation and Development (OECD), and 81 per cent of imports came from the same countries. The proportion of goods export trade with the European Union was 58 per cent, while goods imports from the EU accounted for 52 per cent of the total.

EU countries accounted for eight of the UK's top ten export markets in 2001 and for seven of the top ten leading suppliers of goods to the UK (see Table 24.6). The United States remained the UK's largest single destination and was also its largest single supplier. Two of the biggest percentage increases in 2001 were in exports to the Irish Republic (which rose by over 12 per cent) and imports from China (over 20 per cent).

Trade in services
Trade in services covers the provision of services between UK residents and non-residents, and transactions in goods which are not freighted out of the country in which they take place – for example, purchases for local use by foreign forces in the UK and by UK forces abroad and purchases by tourists. There has been a surplus recorded for trade in services every year since 1966, although in 2001 this was £0.8 billion lower than the record level achieved in 2000. Exports fell slightly by 0.5 per cent to £76.8 billion in 2001, with imports rising slightly by 0.6 per cent to £65.7 billion (see Table 24.2). There were strong surpluses in business and financial services, while travel and transport contributed the largest deficits (see Table 24.7).

Income and transfers

Earnings on UK investment abroad rose by 3.4 per cent to £138.8 billion in 2001, while debits (earnings of foreign-owned assets in the UK) also increased, by 3.8 per cent, to £129.8 billion, giving a surplus of £9.0 billion, a slight fall from 2000 (see Table 24.8). The surplus on direct investment income of £15.8 billion, down a little from the £17.5 billion surplus in 2000, was partly offset by a £7.0 billion deficit on other investment income (including earnings on reserve assets). The deficit on current transfers fell from £10.0 billion in 2000 to £7.2 billion in 2001 (see Table 24.1).

Inward and outward investment

The UK has an open economy, with no restrictions on the outward flow of capital. Outward investment helps develop markets for UK exports while providing earnings in the form of investment income (see above). Inward investment is promoted by Invest UK (see page 369). This inward investment is seen as a means of

Table 24.4 Commodity composition of trade in goods, UK, 2001[1]

	Exports	Imports	£ million Balance
Food, beverages and tobacco	9,754	18,785	−9,031
Food and live animals	5,546	14,378	−8,832
of which: Meat and meat preparations	430	2,732	−2,302
Dairy products and eggs	625	1,242	−617
Cereals and animal feeding stuffs	1,394	1,967	−573
Vegetables and fruit	418	4,138	−3,720
Beverages	3,272	2,875	397
Tobacco	936	1,532	−596
Basic materials	2,622	6,461	−3,839
Crude materials	2,470	5,935	−3,465
of which: Wood, lumber and cork	73	1,158	−1,085
Pulp and waste paper	82	611	−529
Textile fibres	439	396	43
Metal ores	848	2,006	−1,158
Animal and vegetable oils and fats	152	526	−374
Oil	14,926	9,534	5,392
Other fuels	1,551	1,272	279
Semi-manufactured goods	51,002	53,558	−2,556
Chemicals	28,123	23,043	5,080
of which: Organic chemicals	6,141	5,655	486
Inorganic chemicals	1,654	1,193	461
Colouring materials	1,549	986	563
Medicinal products	9,448	6,225	3,223
Toilet preparations	2,762	2,279	483
Plastics	3,468	4,108	−640
Manufactures classified chiefly by material	22,879	30,515	−7,636
of which: Wood and cork manufactures	267	1,354	−1,087
Paper and paperboard manufactures	2,096	4,919	−2,823
Textile manufactures	3,040	4,352	−1,312
Iron and steel	2,894	3,170	−276
Non-ferrous metals	3,053	3,842	−789
Metal manufactures	3,873	4,348	−475
Finished manufactured goods	110,750	134,283	−23,533
Machinery and transport equipment	88,431	98,804	−10,373
Mechanical machinery	24,729	18,860	5,869
Electrical machinery	42,412	44,180	−1,768
Road vehicles	14,134	26,470	−12,336
Other transport equipment	7,156	9,294	−2,138
Miscellaneous manufactures	22,319	35,479	−13,160
of which: Clothing	2,600	9,213	−6,613
Footwear	491	2,241	−1,750
Scientific and photographic	7,943	7,707	236
Unspecified goods	1,039	1,285	−246
Total	**191,644**	**225,178**	**−33,534**

1 Balance of payments basis.
Source: ONS Balance of Payments

January 2002: Stephen Hawking at a symposium held to celebrate his 60th birthday and his contributions to physics and cosmology.

PA

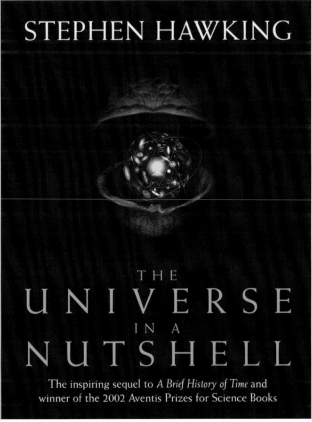

June 2002: Stephen Hawking wins the Aventis General Prize for Science Books with his sequel to A Brief History of Time.

PUBLISHED BY BANTAM PRESS, A DIVISION OF THE RANDOM HOUSE GROUP

March 2002 (National Science Week): a model of DNA (believed to be the world's biggest) goes on display in a Staffordshire shopping mall. 3,000 children helped to build the model, taking over six hours.

James Watson (left) and Francis Crick with the model of DNA they built at Cambridge in 1953.

December 2001: Tim Hunt (left) from the Imperial Cancer Research Fund (now Cancer Research UK) receives the Nobel Prize in medicine, which he won jointly with Sir Paul Nurse and Leland Harwell (from the US) for their work on key regulators of the cell cycle.

PA

Sir Paul Nurse (left) congratulates Sir Vidiadhar (VS) Naipaul, who has just received the Nobel Prize in literature.

PA

March 2002: a colony of 'living' robots goes on show at the Magna Science Adventure Centre, Rotherham. The robots, which are divided into predator and prey, are part of an experiment into artificial evolution.

GUZELIAN

MAGNA

SHARAN DOORBAR

The centre opened in 2001 when it won the Stirling Award for Architecture 'Building of the Year'.

Table 24.5 Distribution of trade in goods, UK, 2001[1]

| | Value (£ million) | | | % | |
	Exports	Imports	Balance	Exports	Imports
European Union	111,315	116,497	−5,182	58.1	51.7
Other Western Europe	7,182	12,513	−5,331	3.7	5.6
North America	33,816	35,048	−1,232	17.6	15.6
Other OECD countries	10,914	17,418	−6,504	5.7	7.7
Oil-exporting countries	6,476	3,983	2,493	3.4	1.8
Rest of the world	21,941	39,719	−17,778	11.4	17.6
Total	**191,644**	**225,178**	**−33,534**	**100.0**	**100.0**

1 Balance of payments basis.
Source: ONS Balance of Payments

Table 24.6 UK trade in goods – main markets and suppliers, 2001[1]

	Value (£ million)	% share of UK trade in goods
Main markets		
United States	29,600	15.4
Germany	23,987	12.5
France	19,529	10.2
Netherlands	14,807	7.7
Irish Republic	14,027	7.3
Belgium and Luxembourg	10,042	5.2
Italy	8,525	4.4
Spain	8,485	4.4
Sweden	4,010	2.1
Japan	3,744	2.0
Main suppliers		
United States	29,713	13.2
Germany	28,657	12.7
France	19,284	8.6
Netherlands	15,123	6.7
Belgium and Luxembourg	12,893	5.7
Italy	9,881	4.4
Irish Republic	9,450	4.2
Japan	9,154	4.1
Spain	6,917	3.1
Hong Kong	5,815	2.6

1 Balance of payments basis.
Source: ONS Balance of Payments

improving UK productivity through the introduction of new technology, knowledge, products and management styles into the UK.

Table 24.9 shows that in 2001 there was a net inflow of UK investment of £19.3 billion. Direct investment abroad was £23.7 billion, compared with a record £168.6 billion in 2000, a year of exceptional merger and acquisition activity (see also Table 22.6). Direct investment in the UK was £43.8 billion in 2001, compared with £79.1 billion in the previous year. This fall was primarily in equity capital transactions, reflecting lower merger and acquisition activity taking place in the year. In 2001 direct investment in the UK exceeded UK direct investment abroad for the first time since 1990.

The UK's stock of external liabilities exceeded its assets by £40 billion at the end of 2001 (see Table 24.10). Direct investment abroad stood at £645 billion, 5.8 per cent higher than a year earlier, while direct investment in the UK was £347 billion, a 13.3 per cent increase – giving a net balance of £298 billion.

International direct investment

According to the United Nations Conference on Trade and Development (UNCTAD) *World Investment Report 2001*, the UK was the world's largest outward direct investor in 2000 and was ranked third at attracting inward investment (see Table 24.11). It accounted for 21 per cent of all inward investment into the EU in 2000 and 32 per cent of its outward investment (inclusive of intra-EU flows). There are over 20,000 foreign investors in the UK, including 5,500 from the United States.

Table 24.7 UK trade in services, 2001

	Value (£ million)			%	
	Exports	Imports	Balance	Exports	Imports
Transport	12,220	15,808	−3,588	15.9	24.0
Travel	12,632	26,382	−13,750	16.4	40.1
Communications	1,276	1,741	−465	1.7	2.6
Construction	114	47	67	0.1	0.1
Insurance	3,832	763	3,069	5.0	1.2
Financial services	12,988	3,032	9,956	16.9	4.6
Computer and information services	2,408	784	1,624	3.1	1.2
Royalties and licence fees	5,666	4,101	1,565	7.4	6.2
Other business services	23,082	10,269	12,813	30.1	15.6
Personal, cultural and recreational services	1,070	703	367	1.4	1.1
Government	1,519	2,104	−585	2.0	3.2
Total	**76,807**	**65,734**	**11,073**	**100.0**	**100.0**

Source: ONS Balance of Payments

Table 24.8 UK income and transfers, 2001

	Credits	Debits	£ million Balance
Income			
Compensation of employees	1,049	869	180
Investment income	138,831	129,849	8,982
of which:			
Earnings on direct investment	43,844	28,075	15,769
Earnings on portfolio investment	34,897	34,686	211
Earnings on other investment[1]	60,090	67,088	−6,998
Total	**139,880**	**130,718**	**9,162**
Current transfers			
Central government	4,912	7,403	−2,491
Other sectors	11,271	15,934	−4,663
Total	**16,183**	**23,337**	**−7,154**

1 Including earnings on reserve assets, that is short-term assets which can be very quickly converted into cash.
Source: ONS Balance of Payments

Table 24.9 UK financial account summary[1]

	1991	1996	1999	2000	£ billion 2001
UK investment abroad[2] (net debits)	24.1	217.6	199.9	504.2	282.1
of which: Direct investment abroad	9.3	22.3	125.0	168.6	23.7
Investment in the UK[2] (net credits)	29.4	223.1	219.7	518.2	301.3
of which: Direct investment in the UK	9.2	17.6	55.2	79.1	43.8
Net transactions[2] (net credits less net debits)	5.3	5.5	19.7	14.0	19.3
of which: Direct investment	−0.1	−4.7	−69.8	−89.5	20.1

1 Balance of payments basis.
2 Also includes portfolio and other investment.
Source: ONS Balance of Payments

Table 24.10 UK international investment position summary[1]

	1991	1996	1999	2000	£ billion 2001
UK assets	943.1	1,628.1	2,413.5	2,981.5	3,175.9
of which: Direct investment abroad	128.1	201.6	428.1	609.9	645.2
UK liabilities	945.7	1,697.5	2,494.0	3,018.6	3,215.7
of which: Direct investment in the UK	128.6	152.6	250.3	306.6	347.5
Net international investment position	−2.6	−69.4	−80.5	−37.0	−39.9
(assets less liabilities)					
of which: Direct investment	−0.6	49.0	177.8	303.3	297.7

1 Balance of payments basis.
Source: ONS Balance of Payments

Table 24.11 Largest foreign direct investment sources and recipients, 2000

	Value (US$ billion)	World share (%)
Outward investment		
United Kingdom	250	21.7
France	173	15.0
United States	139	12.1
Belgium and Luxembourg	83	7.2
Netherlands	73	6.3
Hong Kong	63	5.5
Spain	54	4.7
Germany	49	4.3
Canada	44	3.8
Switzerland	40	3.5
European Union	773	67.2
World	**1,150**	**100.0**
Inward investment		
United States	281	22.1
Germany	176	13.8
United Kingdom	130	10.2
Belgium and Luxembourg	87	6.8
Hong Kong	64	5.0
Canada	63	5.0
Netherlands	55	4.3
France	44	3.5
China	41	3.2
Spain	37	2.9
European Union	617	48.5
World	**1,271**	**100.0**

Source: UNCTAD, *World Investment Report 2001*

Recent inward investment announcements have included:

- Guardian Industries, one of the world's largest glass makers from the US, which is to build a new factory in Goole, Yorkshire, creating more than 300 jobs;

- Arius 3D Inc, the Canadian 3D scanning specialist, which is to set up a 3D digital imaging centre in Dundee, creating 250 jobs; and

- Ryobi Aluminium Costing (UK) of Japan, which is expanding its plant in Carrickfergus, Northern Ireland, creating 76 new jobs.

International trade policy

The Department of Trade and Industry (DTI) pursues the UK's interest in international trade policy, working closely with EU partners and drawing on the UK's bilateral relations and membership of international organisations such as the World Trade Organisation. The Common Commercial Policy co-ordinates the external trade of all EU Member States. In consultation with other departments, together with a wide range of business, consumer and other civil society interests, the DTI seeks to:

- create a framework for free and fair trade;

- minimise barriers to the free movement of goods, services and international investment across the world;

- promote open, dynamic and sustainable markets; and

- ensure coherence between commercial, financial, environmental and social policies.

European Union

The free movement of goods, people, services and capital is a fundamental principle of the EU, and the basis of the Single European Market. In the Government's view, benefits of the Single Market include:

- a wider market for UK goods, comprising nearly 380 million consumers, and making up around 40 per cent of world trade;

- lower prices, brought about by greater competition and liberalisation;

- better consumer protection;

- the sale of goods throughout the EU without expensive re-testing in every country, as a result of the harmonisation and mutual recognition of standards;

- a significant reduction in export bureaucracy – in effect the Single Market is a domestic market for European business; and

- the right of UK citizens to work, study or retire in all other Member States – around 750,000 Britons live in other EU countries.

The European Commission set out its Internal Market Strategy in 1999 and conducts an annual review. The 2002 review, endorsed by the Internal Market, Consumer and Tourism Council, focuses on those target actions which have the most significant contribution to make, and largely reflects UK views on priorities for action to improve the operation of the Single Market. These include completion of work by the end of 2002 on Community Patents and on public procurement. In the longer term, the UK is helping to take forward work on other key elements in the Strategy, such as on services and plans to simplify the regulatory environment.

More than 92 per cent of Single Market Directives have now been implemented in all Member States. At the Stockholm European Council in March 2001, EU Heads of Government agreed that no more than 1.5 per cent of directives should be

overdue in any Member State by the time of the Barcelona European Council in March 2002. Heads of Government decided in Barcelona that this 1.5 per cent target should be retained, and agreed in addition that all directives whose implementation was more than two years overdue should be addressed by the Thessalonika European Council in spring 2003.

The framework for ensuring the even and effective enforcement of Single Market rules involves encouraging co-operation between national administrations, setting up contact points for businesses and citizens, and improving the efficiency of the Commission's complaints procedure. In the UK, the DTI's Action Single Market (*www.dti.gov.uk/europe/asm*) is a contact point for UK business and citizens and a first port of call for similar units in other Member States when Single Market problems arise. Initiatives for simplifying national and Community rules include SLIM (Simpler Legislation for the Internal Market) and the European Business Test Panel, which allows for consultation of business during the drafting stage of new legislation.

World Trade Organisation (WTO)

The WTO (*www.wto.org*) aims to promote an open and liberal trading system, where barriers to free trade – such as high import duties or subsidies – are minimised. It was established in 1995 (when it replaced the General Agreement on Tariffs and Trade) and currently has a membership of 144 countries, with 28 negotiating to join. At the fourth Ministerial Conference in Doha, Qatar, in November 2001, members agreed to accept China and Taiwan into the WTO. The Ministerial Declaration, the *Doha Development Agenda*, adds new negotiations on industrial goods, the environment, subsidies and anti-dumping to existing ones on agriculture and services. More negotiations are envisaged after two years' study on investment, competition, transparency in government procurement and trade facilitation. A fifth Ministerial Conference will be held in Cancun, Mexico, in September 2003.

The DTI monitors actions by other countries which represent obstacles to UK exports and wherever possible seeks to resolve problems bilaterally in conjunction with EU partners. Where efforts to resolve problems by negotiation fail, the initiation of a WTO dispute settlement action, again through the EU, may be necessary.

US restrictions on imported steel
The United States announced on 5 March 2002 that it would impose a range of tariff measures severely restricting imports of steel products from the rest of the world, to take effect on 20 March. EU trade commissioners requested immediate WTO dispute settlement action, the first step of which was a 60-day consultation period with the US. That consultation period did not produce a resolution of the issues and a WTO disputes panel has now been set up. Brazil, China, Japan, Korea, New Zealand, Norway and Switzerland have all joined the panel hearing complaints against the US. The EU has also taken safeguard action to protect the domestic steel market from injury that would be caused by a surge of imports into the EU, diverted from the US market.

Developing countries

The DTI works closely with the Department for International Development (DFID) and other government departments to ensure that developing countries participate in, and benefit from, the world trade system. An inter-departmental Working Group on Trade and Development, chaired by the DTI, meets regularly to ensure consistency of approach.

The EU and the 76 African, Caribbean and Pacific (ACP) countries are party to the Cotonou Partnership Agreement, signed in June 2000 in Cotonou, Benin. This sets out a framework for economic and political co-operation, development aid and trade, and gives the ACP countries tariff-free access, subject to certain safeguards, to the EU for almost all industrial and agricultural products. After a transitional period of eight years, during which the ACP countries will continue to enjoy their current preferential access to the EU, new WTO-compatible arrangements will be put in place. Negotiations on these new trading arrangements were due to start in September 2002.

The EU also operates a Generalised System of Preferences (GSP), available to nearly all developing countries and applying to industrial products, including textiles and certain (mainly processed) agricultural products. The EU Member States negotiated a new, more generous, GSP scheme which took effect on 1 January 2002.

Other recent developments have included:

- a proposal by the European Commission, agreed by the General Affairs Council in

February 2001, to open up immediately duty- and quota-free access for all exports from Least Developed Countries, except arms. Only three products – sugar, rice and bananas – are treated differently, with full duty-free access being phased in gradually in the period up to 2009; and

- working within the Commonwealth to build a stronger system of world trade which works for the benefit of countries at all stages of development.

Special trading arrangements

The multilateral trading system provides the foundation for the EU's common commercial policy. However, the EU has preferential trading arrangements with a number of groups of countries, including:

- those in Central and Eastern Europe preparing for possible EU membership (see page 61);

- virtually all non-EU member countries with Mediterranean coastlines (see page 65); and

- former dependent territories (ACP countries – see above).

New trade relationships with countries and regions of Latin America and the Gulf Cooperation Council are being pursued. A free trade agreement with Mexico came into force in July 2000, an Association Agreement encompassing free trade with Chile was initialled in June 2002 and negotiations for a new agreement with Mercosur (Argentina, Brazil, Paraguay and Uruguay) are continuing.

Partnership and co-operation (non-preferential) agreements have been concluded with ten states of the former Soviet Union. Non-preferential co-operation agreements have also been made with countries in South Asia, the Andean Community, the Central American States, as well as the People's Republic of China and the Association of South East Asian Nations.

Controls on trade

Import controls
Following the completion of the Single European Market, all national quantitative restrictions were abolished. However, the EU does restrict imports

of textiles and clothing, steel, footwear and ceramics from certain countries under EU import regimes using licensing controls; these are also used to monitor imports and deter quota fraud.

Imports into the UK may also be subject to prohibition or restriction, either as a result of UN resolutions (for example, imports of rough diamonds from Angola, Liberia and Sierra Leone) or for reasons of national security. These include firearms and ammunition, nuclear materials, landmines and chemical weapons.

The DTI's Import Licensing Branch (ILB) has responsibility for issuing import licences for goods that DTI controls in accordance with UK and EC law. Its principal customers are UK and other EC importers dealing in goods that are controlled. In 2001/02 ILB issued over 343,000 licences.

Other products may be prohibited or restricted to protect human, animal or plant life or health. Examples include certain drugs, explosives, endangered wildlife and derived products (under the CITES Convention, see page 274), pornographic material, counterfeit and pirated goods and certain agricultural, horticultural and food products. These are controlled and enforced by other government departments such as the Department for Environment, Food & Rural Affairs, and HM Customs and Excise.

Export controls

Strategic export controls apply to a range of goods, components, spare parts and technologies and include the following:

- military equipment, such as arms, ammunition, bombs, tanks, imaging devices, military aircraft and warships;

- nuclear-related items, including nuclear materials, reactors and processing plant;

- dual-use goods – goods designed for civil use but which can be used for military purposes – such as certain materials, machine tools, electronic equipment, computers, telecommunications equipment, cryptographic goods, sensors and radar, navigation and avionics equipment, marine equipment and space and propulsion equipment;

- chemical weapons precursors, and related equipment and technology;

- certain micro-organisms, biological equipment and technology; and

- goods used in programmes involved in weapons of mass destruction and missiles used for their delivery.

Other export controls cover animals and plants (under CITES); cultural goods such as works of art or antiques; and drug precursors.

Licences to export goods subject to strategic export control are issued by the DTI acting through its Export Control Organisation (ECO). The ECO also issues licences for the export or supply of goods and certain services that are controlled following the imposition of trade sanctions by the United Nations or the EU.

The *Export Control Act 2002* represents the outcome of a wide-ranging review of the existing framework governing export controls. The Act provides:

- new powers to introduce controls on trafficking and brokering in arms and on the transfer of sensitive technology by intangible means – such as by e-mail or fax; and

- increased transparency and accountability in the arms export control regime, by setting clear limits for the first time on the Government's power to impose export controls, and by providing for parliamentary scrutiny of new controls introduced under the Act.

Government services

The Government provides a wide range of advice and practical support to meet the needs of overseas inward investors and exporters.

British Trade International

British Trade International (BTI) brings together the work of the Foreign & Commonwealth Office and the DTI on international trade and investment. It aims to enhance the competitiveness of companies in the UK through overseas sales and investments and to maintain a high level of inward direct investment. BTI delivers its services through two operating arms, Trade Partners UK and Invest UK, responsible for trade development and inward investment respectively.

BTI combines:

- all trade development and promotion work undertaken in the English regions by international trade teams, working with the English Regional Development Agencies (RDAs), Small Business Service (SBS) and Business Link network, as well as many private sector partners;

- trade support services provided nationally;

- inward investment development work within the UK in collaboration with the national development agencies and the English RDAs;

- the trade and inward investment work of embassies and other diplomatic posts; and

- national co-ordination of trade development across other government departments, the devolved administrations and the English regions.

The Group Chief Executive reports to the Secretaries of State for Foreign & Commonwealth Affairs and Trade and Industry, and to the BTI Board, which is chaired by the Minister for International Trade and Investment.

Each of the devolved administrations, through Scottish Development International (*www.scottishdevelopmentinternational.com*), WalesTrade International (*www.walestrade.com*) and Invest Northern Ireland (*www.investni.com*), sits on the BTI Board. The devolved administrations provide their own supplementary programmes to suit local businesses, as well as accessing national programmes.

Trade Partners UK

Trade Partners UK (*www.tradepartners.gov.uk*) provides national co-ordination across government departments, the devolved administrations and the English regions on international trade, and a voice within government for exporters and companies investing overseas.

Invest UK

Invest UK (*www.invest.uk.com*) is the only government agency promoting the whole of the

> Trade UK (*www.tradeuk.com*) is a free online service for overseas customers to help find products and services from UK companies. Over 60,000 UK businesses can be searched by name, product or service, with links to 34,000 websites and 50,000 e-mail addresses.

UK as an inward investment location. Operating through a network of offices in British diplomatic posts abroad, and with partners in development agencies throughout the UK, it:

- aims to attract, retain and add value to investment by communicating the benefits of the UK for potential investors; and

- identifies and approaches potential investors and assists them with all aspects of locating and expanding in the UK.

Table 24.12 UK inward investment cases and effect on jobs

	1999/2000	2000/01	2001/02
UK figures			
Inward investment decisions	757	869	764
New jobs created	52,783	71,488	34,087
Invest UK			
Active cases	604	655	1,103
Inward investment decisions in which it was significantly involved	145	219	131
New jobs created	15,519	16,909	3,692

Source: Invest UK

Latest figures on inward investment decisions notified to Invest UK and new jobs expected to be created are shown in Table 24.12. In 2001/02 around a third of these investment projects were from companies with an existing presence in the UK. The largest single investor country was the United States, with 38 per cent of projects, followed by Japan (8 per cent) and Canada (7 per cent). The UK is particularly successful at attracting investment in industries linked to the knowledge-driven economy – computer software, Internet, telecommunications, electronics and e-business sectors. These form the largest category of foreign direct investment, with some 239 projects (31 per cent). Other main sectors for UK inward investment are the automotive sector, pharmaceuticals and financial services.

Export Credits Guarantee Department (ECGD)

ECGD (*www.ecgd.gov.uk*), the UK's official export credit agency, provides facilities, which are broadly complementary to those available from the private sector. Its principal roles are threefold: to provide support for capital goods and project exports sold on medium and long-term credit; to provide reinsurance for UK exports sold on short terms of payment; and to provide insurance for UK companies investing overseas. ECGD's purpose is to benefit the UK economy by helping exporters of UK goods and services win business and UK firms to invest overseas by providing guarantees, insurance and reinsurance against loss, taking into account the Government's international policies. ECGD is a government department and is responsible to the Secretary of State for Trade and Industry.

Including overseas investment insurance and reinsurance, the total amount of business supported by ECGD in 2001/02 was £3,298 million. Table 24.13 shows the top ten markets, representing 72 per cent of business in the year.

Table 24.13 Top ten markets for ECGD guarantees, 2001/02

	Value (£ million)	% share of total market
Saudi Arabia	1,013	30.7
Chile	286	8.7
Philippines	194	5.9
Indonesia	169	5.1
United States	152	4.6
Turkey	144	4.4
Russia Federation	121	3.7
Canada	107	3.2
India	105	3.2
China	93	2.8
Sub-total	**2,384**	**72.3**
World	**3,298**	**100.0**

Source: ECGD

ECGD's main civil business sectors are shown in Table 24.14. Power generation and transmission

continued to absorb 25 per cent of activity, while business in the water sector increased from 17 per sent to 27 per cent, mainly as a result of overseas investment insurance business.

Table 24.14 ECGD guarantees by main civil business sector

	Per cent	
	2000/01	2001/02
Water	17	27
Power generation and transmission	25	25
Energy	14	13
Transport	13	12
Manufacturing, process plant and equipment	9	10
Telecommunications	6	5
Mining	4	2
Education and medical	2	1
Other	10	5

Source: ECGD

Further reading

Trade and Industry. The Government's Expenditure Plans 2002–03 to 2004–05 and Main Estimates 2002–03. Cm 5416. The Stationery Office, 2002.

British Trade International. The Government's Expenditure Plans 2002–03 to 2004–05 and Main Estimates 2002–03. Cm 5415. The Stationery Office, 2002.

United Kingdom Balance of Payments – the Pink Book 2002. Office for National Statistics. The Stationery Office.

Export Credits Guarantee Department Annual Report and Resource Accounts 2001–02. The Stationery Office, 2002.

Websites

Department of Trade and Industry
www.dti.gov.uk

National Statistics
www.statistics.gov.uk

WWW.

25 Science, engineering and technology

The UK has been at the forefront of many world-class advances in science, engineering and technology. Notable areas of UK achievement include biotechnology, biomedicine, materials, chemicals, electronics and aerospace.

Research and development expenditure

Gross domestic expenditure in the UK on research and development (R&D) in 2000 was £17.5 billion, 1.8 per cent of gross domestic product (GDP). Of this, £15 billion was on civil R&D, with the rest going to defence projects. In real terms, gross domestic expenditure on R&D increased by 2 per cent between 1999 and 2000.

Business enterprise is the largest source of funding, providing 49 per cent of expenditure in

2000 (see Figure 25.1). Other contributions were made by private endowments, trusts and charities. As well as financing R&D carried out within business enterprise itself, business enterprise supports university research and finances contract research at government establishments. Some charities have their own laboratories and offer grants for outside research. Contract research organisations carry out R&D for companies and are playing an increasingly important role in the transfer of technology to British industry.

Total spending on R&D within business enterprise amounted to £11.5 billion in 2000. Business enterprise own funds accounted for 63 per cent, with 9 per cent coming from government and most of the remaining 28 per cent from overseas. Expenditure on R&D within the pharmaceuticals product group accounted for 25 per cent of all spending. Aerospace and the radio, television and

Figure 25.1 Gross domestic expenditure on R&D in 2000, UK

Total: £17.5 billion

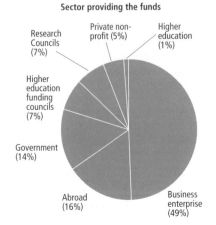

Sector providing the funds

Research Councils (7%)
Private non-profit (5%)
Higher education (1%)
Higher education funding councils (7%)
Government (14%)
Abroad (16%)
Business enterprise (49%)

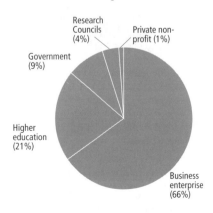

Sector carring out the work

Research Councils (4%)
Private non-profit (1%)
Government (9%)
Higher education (21%)
Business enterprise (66%)

Source: Office for National Statistics

Some notable British achievements during the last 50 years

- In 1953 Francis Crick, together with James Watson of the United States, worked out the structure of DNA using the experimental results of Maurice Wilkins and Rosalind Franklin.

- In 1955 the first atomic clock was built at the National Physical Laboratory in Teddington.

- Sir Bernard Lovell pioneered the science of radio astronomy in the 1950s, and in 1957 Jodrell Bank, the world's first giant radio telescope, opened.

- Interferons – proteins produced in the body to fight infections – were first isolated and named by Alick Isaacs and colleagues in 1957.

- The work of Sir Peter Medawar in the 1950s on acquired immunological tolerance made possible the first successful kidney transplants.

- Artificial hip joints were developed and first fitted by Sir John Charnley at Wrightington Hospital, Lancashire, in 1960.

- In 1962 the first beta-blocker successful in treating angina was introduced, having been synthesised by Sir James Black at ICI.

- Dorothy Hodgkin won the Nobel Prize for Chemistry in 1964 for her work on the structure of penicillin and vitamin B12.

- A new form of telephone message transmission, based on optical fibres, was invented in the UK in 1964.

- In the late 1960s the science of radio-astrophysics was pioneered by Sir Martin Ryle and Antony Hewish. In 1967 their co-worker Jocelyn Bell Burnell discovered pulsars.

- The work of Brian Josephson in the early 1970s was later used to develop high-speed computers.

- The first commercial brain and body scanner relying on computer-assisted tomography, based on a technique developed by Sir Godfrey Hounsfield, was produced in 1972.

- Much of the work on black holes was carried out by Stephen Hawking, who in 1974 showed that they could emit radiation with a thermal spectrum.

- In 1975 César Milstein produced the first monoclonal antibodies – proteins with enormous potential in the diagnosis and treatment of disease. This discovery transformed biological research and created biotechnology.

- The technique of *in vitro* fertilisation, pioneered by Patrick Steptoe and Robert Edwards, led to the birth of the world's first 'test-tube baby' in 1978.

- In the 1980s Professor Michael Green helped to develop the 'superstring' theories, which see the fundamental building blocks of matter and energy as infinitesimal 'strings' rather than points.

- Professor Sir Alec Jeffreys, working at Leicester University, developed the technique of DNA fingerprinting in 1985.

- In 1985 British Antarctic Survey scientists discovered the hole in the ozone layer over the Antarctic. The finding was linked to the growth of chlorofluorocarbons (CFCs) in the atmosphere and led directly to the Montreal Protocol controlling the use of CFCs (see page 284).

- Professor Sir Harold Kroto of Sussex University shared the 1996 Nobel Prize for Chemistry with two US scientists for discovering in 1985 the fullerene molecule – 60 carbon atoms arranged in a symmetrical cage.

- Timothy Berners-Lee did pioneering work in connection with the Internet – he invented the web's address system and layout while working at CERN (see page 387) in 1990.

- Pioneering work on nuclear transfer at the Roslin Institute near Edinburgh resulted in the birth of the world's first cloned mammal, Dolly the sheep, in 1996.

- Scientists at the Sanger Centre in Cambridgeshire played a major role in the international Human Genome Project, being responsible for decoding nearly one-third of the genome in the project's initial stage, completed in 2000.

- Sir Paul Nurse and Tim Hunt, together with a US scientist Lee Hartwell, won the Nobel Prize in Physiology or Medicine in October 2001 for their work on key regulators of the cell cycle.

communication equipment sector each accounted for 9 per cent of spending.

Government role

The Secretary of State for Trade and Industry, assisted by the Minister for Science, has overall responsibility for Science, Engineering and Technology (SET). They are supported by the Office of Science and Technology (OST), part of the Department of Trade and Industry (DTI). The Ministerial Committee on Science Policy provides the framework for the collective consideration of, and decisions on, major science policy issues.

The OST, headed by the Government's Chief Scientific Adviser, is responsible for policy on SET, both nationally and internationally, and co-ordinates science and technology policy across government departments. The Chief Scientific Adviser also reports directly to the Prime Minister.

An independent Council for Science and Technology advises the Prime Minister on the strategic policies and framework for science and technology in the UK. Its members are drawn from academia, business and charitable foundations/institutions.

The policy and management of some aspects of science and technology are reserved to the UK Government, while in other instances this has been devolved to the administrations in Scotland, Wales and Northern Ireland.

The term 'science and engineering base' (SEB) is used to describe the research and postgraduate training capacity based in the universities and colleges of higher education and in establishments operated by the Research Councils (see pages 379–82). Also included are the national and international central facilities (such as CERN – see page 387) supported by the Research Councils and available for use by British scientists and engineers. There are also important contributions from private institutions, chiefly those funded by charities. The SEB is the main provider of basic research and much of the strategic research (research likely to have practical applications) carried out in the UK. It also collaborates with the private sector in the conduct of specific applied research.

The OST, through the Director General of Research Councils, has responsibility for the

Science Budget, and for the government-financed Research Councils. Through the Research Councils, the Science Budget supports research by:

- awarding research grants to universities, other higher education establishments and some other research units;

- funding Research Council establishments to carry out research or provide facilities;

- paying subscriptions to international scientific facilities and organisations; and

- supporting postgraduate research students and postdoctoral Fellows.

The Science Budget also funds programmes of support to the science and engineering base through the Royal Society (see page 388) and the Royal Academy of Engineering (see page 388). The other main sources of funds for universities are the higher education funding councils (see page 386).

Strategy and finance

The Government's policies for science, engineering and technology were set out in the July 2000 White Paper *Excellence and Opportunity – a science and innovation policy for the 21st century*. The White Paper set out the actions being taken by the Government to ensure that UK science remains world class, to open up opportunities for innovation throughout the economy and to increase public confidence in science. High research priorities for 2001/02 to 2003/04 are genomics, e-science and basic technology. Building on the commitments in the White Paper, in July 2002 the Government published *Investing in innovation: A strategy for science, engineering and technology.* This sets out how an additional £1.25 billion investment in science and technology allocated from the 2002 Spending Review (see page 350) will be used. The strategy ties together the increases in science, engineering and technology spending across schools, universities and the research base. It also sets out how the Government plans to improve the way it manages science within Government itself, and contains its response to the Roberts Review of the supply of skilled scientists and engineers (see page 385).

The SEB is chiefly funded through two funding streams, which together are known as the Dual

373

Support Scheme. One stream is provided by the Education Departments through their higher education funding councils. The other stream is provided by the DTI/OST through the Research Councils, which award programme and project grants for specific research programmes, both to universities and to their own institutions.

Figure 25.2 Planned net government expenditure on SET, UK, 2002/03

Total: £7.8 billion

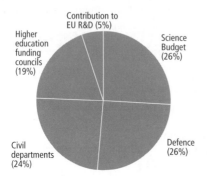

Source: Office of Science and Technology

Planned total government expenditure on SET (both civil and defence) in 2002/03 is £7.8 billion (see Figure 25.2). In the 2002 Spending Review the Government announced that the OST's Science Budget would increase by 10 per cent a year between 2002/03 and 2005/06, from £2.0 billion in 2002/03 to £2.9 billion in 2005/06. This includes an extra £436 million over the three years to fund an expansion in science and engineering research activities. Extra funding is intended to develop the science research infrastructure, and to enable UK scientists and engineers to take forward current world-class research programmes and to move into newly promising areas.

Additional resources would be available for knowledge transfer from the SEB, with funding of £90 million a year by 2005/06 for an enlarged Higher Education Innovation Fund (see page 375).

Foresight programme

The Government's Foresight programme (*www.foresight.gov.uk*) encourages the public and private sectors to work together to identify opportunities in markets and technologies likely to emerge over the next 10 to 20 years. The

programme is co-ordinated by a joint industry/academic steering group headed by the Chief Scientific Adviser. Foresight is guiding government priorities in SET programmes, in overall policy, regulation, and education and training.

A review of the programme in 2001 recommended that resources should be concentrated on fewer areas to allow for deeper analysis and ensure greater impact. The revised programme was launched in April 2002, and is working on three or four projects at a time. The first two pilot projects are:

- the *Flood and Coastal Defence Project*, which draws together experts to advise on factors affecting future impacts and the required response to flooding in the UK. Factors considered will include land use, demographic shifts, socio-economic changes and climate change; and

- the *Cognitive Systems Project*, which will examine recent progress in artificial and cognitive systems and their related disciplines, including computer science, neuroscience, cognitive science and artificial intelligence. It will also look at likely developments in these fields over the next decade, and in particular the rate of progress in the UK's capability to build artificial cognitive systems.

LINK

LINK is the Government's main mechanism for promoting partnership in commercial research between industry and the research base. It focuses on areas of strategic importance for the future of the UK economy. Government departments and Research Councils fund up to 50 per cent of the cost of research projects, with industry providing the balance. Since 1988, 74 LINK programmes have supported 1,500 projects with a total value of some £760 million and involving some 2,400 companies. Recent programmes include manufacturing molecules, health technology devices, and information storage and display.

Science Research Investment Fund

The Science Research Investment Fund, with funding of £1 billion for 2002–04, finances new infrastructure schemes across the spectrum of science and engineering. Money from the Government and the Wellcome Trust (see page

387), is allocated to universities for them to decide priorities; the universities themselves contribute 25 per cent of investment. Projects include: a new biomedical sciences research building at Leicester University; a research institute for medical cell biology at the new Royal Infirmary of Edinburgh; an environmental engineering and bioremediation centre at Queen's University Belfast; and a research institute for molecular medicine at Leeds University.

University Challenge Fund

The fund is a competitive scheme that has offered financing to 57 universities to help them in the early stages of turning research into commercial products. The first round of the competition in 1999 saw 15 seed funds being set up worth £45 million. The awards from the second round of the competition in October 2001 allocated a further £15 million.

Science Enterprise Challenge

Twelve Science Enterprise Centres have been established with £29 million of government funding. The centres support the teaching and practice of entrepreneurship among science faculties and students, and promote links between universities and business. Awards worth £15 million were announced in October 2001. This funding will help establish a new centre and expand the 12 existing centres.

Higher Education Innovation Fund (HEIF)

The HEIF is run in partnership by DTI/OST, the Higher Education Funding Council for England (HEFCE) and the Department for Education and Skills (DfES). The aim is to enable higher education institutions to respond to the needs of business, through developing capacity in universities to liaise with business and the community, and through large collaborative projects to strengthen university-business partnerships. In October 2001 awards totalling £80 million were announced, with 89 bids being funded. Additional resources are being allocated to the HEIF under the Spending Review 2002, and overall resources for knowledge transfer are planned to rise from £64 million in 2002/03 to £114 million in 2005/06.

Faraday Partnerships

The Faraday Partnerships scheme (*www.faradaypartnerships.org.uk*) is intended to improve the exploitation of SET in the UK. The partnerships bring together universities,

independent research organisations, industry associations and manufacturers, with support from DTI, the Department for Environment, Food & Rural Affairs (DEFRA) and some of the Research Councils. There are 24 partnerships, including six announced in September 2002.

Space activities

The UK's civil space programme is brought together through the British National Space Centre (BNSC) (*www.bnsc.gov.uk*), a partnership of government departments and the Research Councils. BNSC's key aims are to develop practical and economic uses of space, to promote the competitiveness of British space companies in world markets, to maintain the UK's position in space science, to foster the development of innovative technology and to improve understanding of the Earth's environment and resources. These are realised primarily by collaboration with other European nations through the European Space Agency (ESA). BNSC's policy and aims are set out in detail in the publication *Space Strategy 1999–2002: New Frontiers*.

Through BNSC, the Government spends around £180 million a year on space activities. About three-quarters of this is channelled through ESA for collaborative programmes on Earth observation, telecommunications and space science, much of which returns to the UK through contracts awarded to British industry. The remaining quarter of the space budget is spent on international meteorological programmes carried out through the European Meteorological Satellite Organisation (EUMETSAT); developing experiments (such as the Beagle 2 Mars Lander) for ESA satellites; and on the national programme, which is aimed at complementing R&D supported through ESA. Around half of the British space programme is concerned with satellite-based Earth observation (remote sensing) for commercial and environmental applications.

The UK is also a major contributor to ESA's latest Earth observation satellite, ENVISAT, launched in March 2002. This carries a new generation of radar and radiometer systems as well as other scientific environmental instruments, some of which have been either designed or constructed in Britain. The first pictures recorded by ENVISAT were beamed down to scientists at the end of March 2002.

A quarter of the UK's space budget is devoted to space science led by the Particle Physics and

Astronomy Research Council, in support of astronomy, planetary science and geophysics. The UK is contributing substantially to the SOHO mission to study the Sun; to the Cluster mission launched in 2000 to study solar-terrestrial relationships; to the Infrared Space Observatory, which is investigating the birth and death of stars; and to the Cassini Huygens mission, a seven-year programme to send a probe to Saturn and its moon Titan, launched in 1997. It is also participating in XMM, ESA's X-ray spectroscopy mission to investigate X-ray emissions from black holes.

The UK is also developing the Geostationary Earth Radiation Budget instrument, which is intended to provide accurate measurements of the energy source for the Earth's climate and, together with the National Aeronautics and Space Administration (NASA), the High Resolution Dynamics Limb Sounder, which will provide measurements of upper atmosphere trace chemicals and temperature.

Living planet programme
ESA's £400 million Living Planet environmental research programme, to help scientists understand and predict the Earth's environment and humankind's effects upon it, was launched in 1999. BNSC is contributing £67 million to this programme. The first project to benefit will be the British CRYOSAT mission, due to be launched in 2004, which will study the effects of global warming on the polar ice caps and floating Arctic sea ice. UK environmental scientists also have a significant interest in a second mission, which will measure soil moisture and ocean salinity.

Two new centres of excellence in Earth observation will use satellites and models to help forecast environmental change and play a role in exploiting data from ENVISAT and the Living Planet programme. The Data Assimilation Research Centre will forecast changes in the Earth's systems, while the Centre for Polar Observation Modelling will measure changes in polar ice which could cause rising sea levels and changes in ocean circulation.

Industrial and intellectual property
The Government supports innovation through the promotion of a national and international system for the establishment of intellectual property

rights. These matters are the responsibility of the Patent Office, an executive agency of the DTI. The Office is responsible for the granting of patents, and registration of designs and trademarks. In 2001 it received over 30,500 applications for patents and almost 61,000 applications for trademarks.

The Patent Office encourages worldwide harmonisation of rules and procedures, and the modernisation and simplification of intellectual property law. International patenting arrangements include the European Patent Convention and the Patent Co-operation Treaty. For trademarks the European Community Trademark System and the Madrid Protocol provide means of extending rights beyond the UK's borders. The Patent Office Central Enquiry Unit and the website (*www.patent.gov.uk*) offer detailed information about intellectual property rights.

Departmental responsibilities

The DTI publication *The Forward Look 2001 Government-funded science, engineering and technology* outlines the policy and expenditure details for government departments and Research Councils, learned societies and other bodies in relation to their SET activities. The activities of the main government departments involved in SET are detailed below.

Department of Trade and Industry
In 2002/03 DTI's planned expenditure on SET is £429 million: £289 million on R&D and £140 million on technology transfer. Expenditure covers innovation and technology for a number of industrial sectors, including aeronautics, biotechnology, chemicals, communications, engineering, environmental technology, IT, space (see page 375), and nuclear and non-nuclear energy.

Funding for innovation embraces the development, design and financing of new products, services and processes, exploitation of new markets, creation of new businesses and associated changes in management of people and organisational practices. Through its Innovation Unit, a mixed team of business secondees and government officials, DTI seeks to promote a culture of innovation in all sectors of the economy.

Technology and knowledge transfer

DTI also aims to increase collaboration and the flow of knowledge between the SEB and businesses; improve access to sources of technology and technological expertise; improve the capacity of business to use technology effectively; and increase the uptake of the latest technology and best practice techniques.

One example of a technology and knowledge transfer mechanism is TCS (previously known as the Teaching Company Scheme), which is funded by DTI, two other government departments, five Research Councils and the devolved administrations, and by the participating companies. As well as facilitating technology and knowledge transfer, TCS also provides business-based training and experience for high-calibre graduates. They work in companies on two-year projects that are central to the needs of the businesses and are jointly supervised by personnel from the knowledge base and the companies. There are around 900 individual TCS Programmes, each involving one or more graduates, with around 90 per cent of the programmes involving small and medium-sized enterprises (SMEs).

To help UK companies remain competitive in an increasingly global market, DTI's International Technology Service (ITS) (see *www.globalwatchonline.com*) enables UK companies to become aware of, and gain access to, new technological developments and management practices not present in the UK. The ITS highlights developments and opportunities overseas; and assists companies to access technology, set up licensing agreements and collaborative ventures, and gain experience of new technology and leading management practices.

Smart

The Smart scheme in England, operated by the Small Business Service (an agency of the DTI), provides grants to help individuals and small businesses research and develop technologically innovative new products or buy external consultancy to improve their use and exploitation of technology.

Over 800 offers of help under Smart were made in England in 2001/02. Separate Smart schemes are operated in Scotland, Wales and Northern Ireland.

Aeronautics

DTI's Civil Aircraft Research and Technology Demonstration Programme (CARAD) supports research and technology demonstration in aeronautics as part of the industrial exploitation of science programme. CARAD is part of the national aeronautics research effort, with most of the supported research work being conducted in industry, and with significant involvement of QinetiQ (see page 378). Universities and other research organisations receive about 7 per cent of funding. CARAD and earlier programmes have supported a range of projects, including aluminium and composite airframe materials, more efficient and environmentally friendly engines, and advanced aircraft systems.

National Measurement System

DTI is responsible for the National Measurement System (NMS), which funds science and technology programmes in measurement science, including materials metrology. In 2002/03 DTI expects to invest £59 million on the NMS. The NMS provides world-class measurement standards and calibration facilities. These enable businesses and public authorities to make accurate measurements which are nationally and internationally accepted. Although most of the work is carried out at the National Physical Laboratory, the Laboratory of the Government Chemist, the National Engineering Laboratory and the National Weights and Measures Laboratory, DTI is taking steps to increase competition in these programmes and to work more closely with business in order to identify its future needs.

British Standards Institution

The DTI works closely with the British Standards Institution (BSI), the national standards body which is independent of the Government, to promote UK trade and technology interests. DTI support for BSI is directed particularly towards European and international standards, which account for over 90 per cent of the Institution's work. It also provides support for the United Kingdom Accreditation Service (UKAS), the sole national body recognised by the Government to accredit organisations that test, calibrate, inspect and certify against standards. DTI's contribution to BSI and UKAS was £7.2 million in 2001/02.

Ministry of Defence (MoD)

The Government invests about £450 million a year in technological research to ensure that the UK's armed forces stay ahead of threats from potential adversaries. The MoD has a research budget and also a much larger equipment procurement budget. Planned net expenditure on SET for 2002/03 is £2.4 billion.

All MoD research used to be carried out by its Defence Evaluation and Research Agency (DERA), but in July 2001 DERA was disbanded and replaced by two new organisations: Defence Science and Technology Laboratory (Dstl) and QinetiQ plc. Dstl carries out research in key areas, provides a high-level overview of defence science and technology, acts as an in-house source of impartial advice and manages international research collaboration.

About 75 per cent of DERA's staff were transferred to QinetiQ plc, currently a wholly government-owned company. The Government is selling the company, while initially retaining a financial stake.

Department for Transport (DfT)

The DfT funds research to inform the evidence base for all its major policy and operational responsibilities: transport integration, roads and local transport; and railways, aviation and shipping. Total planned expenditure for 2002/03 is £52 million, including spending by its executive agencies.

Department for Environment, Food & Rural Affairs (DEFRA)

DEFRA co-ordinates its research programme with the devolved administrations and the Research Councils. The programme supports the Department's wide-ranging responsibilities for protecting the public in relation to farm produce and animal diseases transmissible to humans; protecting and enhancing the rural and marine environment; reducing risks from flooding and coastal erosion; improving animal health and welfare; and encouraging modern, efficient and competitive agriculture, fishing and food industries.

The budget for research expenditure in 2002/03 is £147 million, including support for the Royal Botanic Gardens, Kew (see page 384). Through the Darwin Initiative, British expertise is being made available to assist countries that are rich in biodiversity but have insufficient financial or technical resources to implement the Biodiversity Convention.

Department of Health (DH)

The DH supports R&D to provide the evidence needed to inform policy and practice in public health, healthcare and social care. It delivers this objective through:

- National Health Service (NHS) R&D funding, which supports projects funded by other non-commercial R&D sources (including charities) carried out in the NHS, and also specific health and social care projects meeting the identified research needs of the DH and the NHS;

- a Policy Research Programme (PRP), directly commissioned by the DH; and

- ad hoc project funding from other DH R&D budgets and support for non-departmental public bodies (NDPBs).

The DH expects to spend some £572 million on research in 2002/03: £507 million on NHS R&D, £35 million on the PRP and about £30 million involving the NDPBs and ad hoc budgets.

Department for International Development (DFID)

DFID commissions and sponsors knowledge generation and sharing in natural resources, health and population, engineering, education and social sciences. Financial provision in 2002/03 is around £105 million, covering research projects and programmes that respond to identified development needs and that help build research capacity in developing countries.

DFID also contributes to international centres and programmes generating knowledge on development issues. These contributions include support for the EU Framework Programmes (see page 386), which sponsor research and technological development in renewable natural resources, agriculture, health and information technologies; for the Consultative Group on International Agricultural Research (CGIAR); and for the World Health Organisation which administers programmes that include international research and the strengthening of research capacity.

Scottish Executive

The majority of the Scottish Executive's support for the science base is disbursed by the Scottish

Higher Education Funding Council. In total this amounts to some £180 million for 2002/03 – £132 million for research and £48 million to support the strategic development of the sector. The Scottish Executive spends about £130 million directly on agricultural and fisheries research, health, biological, environmental, economic and social science. A large proportion of this goes to the Scottish Agricultural and Biological Research Institutes, the Fisheries Research Service and the Scottish Agricultural College. In addition, the UK Research Councils contribute around £150 million to Scottish research institutions and around £100 million is contributed by other UK government sources.

In August 2001 the Executive launched *A Science Strategy for Scotland*. In accordance with the strategy, the Executive has established an independent Scottish Science Advisory Committee, to advise it on strategic science matters.

Northern Ireland Executive

In addition to participating in the Dual Support Scheme and other UK-wide initiatives, the Northern Ireland Executive is part funding the Support Programme for University Research (SPUR). This is a joint public/private programme, under which some £44 million is being invested in research over the period 2001/02 to 2004/05. A substantial percentage of the programme expenditure will be on science-related projects, most notably the new £14.5 million Centre for Molecular Biosciences at the University of Ulster. In Northern Ireland, Invest Northern Ireland has a similar role to that of DTI's Innovation Unit, supporting industrial R&D, technology transfer and innovation.

Research Councils

There are seven Research Councils. Each is an autonomous body established under Royal Charter, with members of its governing council drawn from universities, professions, industry and government. The Councils support research, study and training in universities and other higher education institutions. They also carry out or support research, through their own institutes and at international research centres, often jointly with other public sector bodies and international organisations. They provide awards to about 15,000 postgraduate students in science, social sciences, engineering and technology. In addition

Table 25.3 Research Councils budget, 2002/03

	£ million
Engineering and Physical Sciences Research Council	498
Medical Research Council	454
Natural Environment Research Council	274
Biotechnology and Biological Sciences Research Council	268
Particle Physics and Astronomy Research Council	223
Economic and Social Research Council	97
Council for the Central Laboratory of the Research Councils	101

Source: Research Councils

to funding from the OST, the Councils receive income from research commissioned by government departments and the private sector.

Following the Quinquennial Review of the Research Councils in 2001, a new strategy group, Research Councils UK (RCUK), was launched in May 2002 to develop a stronger strategic framework for science.

Research Councils UK

RCUK is a strategic partnership set up to champion science, engineering and technology. It is supported by the seven UK Research Councils and aims to:

- create a common framework for research, training and knowledge transfer;

- provide a single focus for dialogue with stakeholders;

- provide the focus for independent scientific advice from the Research Councils to the Government;

- promote collaboration to deliver scientific and strategic goals; and

- harmonise procedures to give stakeholders a more efficient service.

The RCUK strategy group is chaired by the Director General of Research Councils and includes the chief executives of the seven Councils.

Engineering and Physical Sciences Research Council (EPSRC)

The EPSRC (*www.epsrc.ac.uk*), the largest Research Council in terms of remit, promotes and supports high-quality basic, strategic and applied research and related postgraduate training in engineering and the physical sciences. It also provides advice, disseminates knowledge and promotes public understanding in these areas. Its remit is delivered through ten programme areas: engineering; infrastructure and the environment; innovative manufacturing; chemistry; physics; mathematics; information technology and computer science; materials; the boundary between the EPSRC and the life sciences; and public awareness of SET. The EPSRC also manages programmes in basic technology and e-science on behalf of all the Research Councils.

Photonic crystal fibres

Photonic crystal fibres are being developed at Bath and other universities. In these 'holey fibres' light is guided by a regular array of micro or nanosized air holes which run the length of the fibre; these greatly enhance the capabilities of optical fibre. In telecommunications, these fibres could transmit many times more power than existing systems, reducing costs for oceanic links by removing the need for amplifiers or repeaters. Other applications are expected to include high-power lasers, amplifiers and medical imaging.

Medical Research Council (MRC)

The MRC (*www.mrc.ac.uk*) (see also chapter 13, page 179) is the main source of public funds for biomedical, health services and related research and training aimed at maintaining and improving public health. The Council has three major institutes: the National Institute for Medical Research, the Laboratory of Molecular Biology and the Clinical Sciences Centre. It has 29 smaller MRC Units, an MRC Health Services Research Collaboration (a collaborative arrangement based in the Department of Social Medicine in Bristol University and involving groups in seven other universities) and five grant-funded Centres. Most of these are attached to higher education institutions or hospitals throughout the UK. The MRC also has laboratories overseas, in The Gambia and Uganda.

About half the MRC's research expenditure is allocated to its own institutes and units, with the rest going mainly on grant support and research training awards to teams and individuals in higher education institutions. The Council works closely with the health departments, the major charities, industry and international collaborators.

Genetics

The MRC Human Genetics Unit in Edinburgh has developed a new imaging technique, Optical Projection Tomography (OPT). It allows new insights into the structure of tissues that will help the understanding of what genes do and where and when they function. It will be used initially to aid research on the function of genes in mice. In the past, genome sequencing projects have successfully identified many thousands of genes. This new technique is expected to find out what all these genes do and their contribution to health and disease.

Natural Environment Research Council (NERC)

The NERC (*www.nerc.ac.uk*) funds and carries out scientific research in the sciences of the environment. *Science for a sustainable future 2002–2007* is the strategy document that identifies priority areas for NERC, including:

- *Earth's life-support systems* – water, biogeochemical cycles and biodiversity;

- *climate change* – predicting and mitigating the effects; and

- *sustainable economies* – identifying and providing sustainable solutions to the challenges associated with energy, land use and the effects of natural hazards.

Robot under ice

Autosub, a revolutionary £5 million submarine robot, was designed and built at Southampton Oceanography Centre (a NERC partnership with the University of Southampton). Results of Autosub's first mission under the Antarctic sea ice were published in March 2002. Before its advent, it was impossible to investigate under sea ice for more than a few metres. The 7 m long, torpedo-shaped Autosub travelled 27 km inside the edge of the ice and made the first ever continuous measurement of ice thickness.

NERC trains the next generation of environmental scientists. It also provides a range of facilities for use by the wider environmental science community, including a marine research fleet. NERC's wholly owned research centres are the British Geological Survey, the British Antarctic Survey, the Centre for Ecology and Hydrology, and the Proudman Oceanographic Laboratory. NERC also supports 13 collaborative centres in UK universities.

Biotechnology and Biological Sciences Research Council (BBSRC)

The BBSRC (*www.bbsrc.ac.uk*) supports basic and strategic research and research training in the non-medical life sciences. The scientific themes of its research committees are biomolecular sciences; genes and developmental biology; biochemistry and cell biology; plant and microbial sciences; animal sciences; agri-food; and engineering and biological systems. As well as funding research in universities and other research centres, the BBSRC sponsors eight research institutes.

Centre for Novel Agricultural Products

The Centre for Novel Agricultural Products was opened in summer 2002 at the University of York, where it is an integral part of work on bioscience development. The Centre seeks to identify valuable genes, determine their function and define realistic commercial opportunities for their use – taking basic research through to application. Research projects already in progress include:

- new methods of oil production from plants;

- molecular understanding of spider silk production; and

- biodegradation of explosives.

Particle Physics and Astronomy Research Council (PPARC)

The main task of the PPARC (*www.pparc.ac.uk*) is to encourage and support a balanced and cost-effective research programme into fundamental physical processes. It funds UK research, education and training in its four broad areas of science: particle physics, astronomy, solar system science and particle astrophysics.

The PPARC provides funds to universities to undertake research and facilities to enable that research to take place. Facilities are provided on a national and international basis, the latter including bodies such as the European Organisation for Nuclear Research (CERN) and the European Space Agency.

European Southern Observatory

In July 2002 the UK formally joined the European Southern Observatory (ESO) project, which has nine other member states. UK astronomers now have access to some of the world's most advanced telescopes and a major stake in future developments, including the Atacama Large Millimetre Array (ALMA) and the vast 100 m Overwhelmingly Large Telescope project. UK astronomers will be able to use the four 8.2 m and several 1.8 m telescopes that comprise the Very Large Telescope (VLT) facility, which is the world's largest and most advanced optical telescope, located at the Paranal Observatory in the Atacama desert in Chile. The PPARC negotiated the terms of the agreement under which the UK joined ESO and is also making an additional contribution, including support for a new 4 m Visible and Infrared Survey Telescope (VISTA). VISTA, which will be installed at the Paranal Observatory, is being financed using a grant awarded to 18 UK universities and is designed to be capable of rapidly mapping large areas of the sky to a great depth.

Economic and Social Research Council (ESRC)

The ESRC (*www.esrc.ac.uk*) supports research and training in the social sciences. Research funded by the ESRC is conducted in higher education institutions or independent research establishments. The Council has seven priority themes: economic performance and development; environment and human behaviour; governance and citizenship; knowledge, communication and learning; lifecourse, lifestyles and health; social stability and exclusion; and work and organisations.

Council for the Central Laboratory of the Research Councils (CCLRC)

The CCLRC (*www.cclrc.ac.uk*) promotes scientific and engineering research by providing facilities and technical expertise, primarily to meet the needs of the research communities supported by the other Research Councils. Its budget for 2002/03 is £101 million, of which £73 million comes through agreements with other Research

381

The domestic management of terrorist attacks

Following the terrorist attacks in the United States on 11 September 2001 (see page 75), research began in August 2002 on a new ESRC-funded research initiative into the domestic management of terrorist attacks in the UK. More than £600,000 has been allocated to three individual projects:

- *the UK response* – a comprehensive analysis of the current state of the UK response to the possible threat of a terrorist attack;

- *the public, risks and lessons from the United States* – an examination of the options for responding to the threat of terrorist attacks on the UK; and

- *knowledge resourcing for civil contingencies* – examination of the civil vulnerabilities of UK society, including the UK's position as a globally networked, knowledge-intensive society.

Councils and £28 million from contracts and agreements with the EU, overseas countries, and other industries and organisations.

The CCLRC is responsible for the Rutherford Appleton Laboratory (RAL) in Oxfordshire; the Daresbury Laboratory (DL) in Cheshire; and the Chilbolton Facility in Hampshire. These centres provide facilities too large or complex, and technologies too specialised, to be housed by individual academic institutions. RAL is the home of the DIAMOND project, a new synchrotron light source to be operational in 2007. Among other resources, RAL also hosts ISIS (the world's leading source of pulsed neutrons and muons); the high-power Central Laser Facility with some of the world's brightest lasers; and specialist e-science, instrumentation, accelerator and space technology centres. DL hosts the Synchrotron Radiation Source and advanced computing facilities, and Chilbolton provides infrastructure for experimental work undertaken by the CCLRC's Radiocommunications Research Unit.

Following its quinquennial review, the CCLRC will have a new strategic role from April 2003. Under the strategic direction of RCUK, the CCLRC will act as the focus for large-scale facilities for neutron scattering, synchrotron radiation and high-power lasers. It will also co-ordinate the development of policies and strategies to provide access for UK scientists to large-scale facilities in these scientific areas, both nationally and internationally.

New high-performance computing centre

In July 2002 an agreement to manage access to a new supercomputer was agreed between the EPSRC and a consortium led by the University of Edinburgh, with the CCLRC and IBM. The contract will cost £53 million and will be mostly funded by the EPSRC, with additional funding from the NERC and BBSRC. The service, due to start in December 2002, will be used by UK scientists to solve a wide range of previously inaccessible problems, ranging from the very small – such as the nature of matter – to the global, with simulations of the Earth. In addition, the service is expected to help engineers design new and safer structures, and aircraft. New advances are also envisaged in the human genome project, and in new fields of research, such as biomolecular electronics.

Public engagement in science

The Government seeks to raise the status of SET among the general public, by increasing awareness of the contribution of SET to the UK's economic wealth and quality of life. To this end, the Government supports activities such as the annual science festival of the British Association (BA) and National Science Week, and offers grants to science communicators through a scheme administered by the Royal Society.

Science festivals are a growing feature of local co-operative efforts to further the understanding of the contribution made by science to everyday life.

Cheltenham Festival of Science

The first Cheltenham Festival of Science, a five-day event in May 2002, was attended by an estimated 24,000 people. The festival was promoted by Cheltenham Arts Festivals and will continue as part of their annual calendar. The pleasure of science, the theme of the festival, aimed to engage the interest of families and schoolchildren. The festival had 26 events and talks, including debates on genetic modification, as well as a free hands-on interactive exhibition aimed at younger visitors.

The longest established annual science festival to be held in a single location is the Edinburgh International Science Festival. Activities such as these help to ensure continued interest in SET among young people making their educational and career choices, and to enhance the public's ability to relate to scientific issues in general and to make informed judgements about scientific developments.

Science and the public

Science and the public, published in 2000 and sponsored by the OST and the Wellcome Trust, brought together research on the provision of science communication with research exploring public attitudes to SET.

The survey found that the British public generally supported science. For example:

- three-quarters of people said they were amazed by the achievements of science;

- only a fifth claimed that they were not interested in science;

- 72 per cent agreed that, even if it brought no immediate benefits, scientific research that advances knowledge was necessary and should be supported by the Government; and

- in general, scientists were well respected, with 84 per cent of respondents stating that scientists and engineers made a valuable contribution to society.

Science year

Science year has been extended to run from September 2001 to July 2003. It is a UK-wide education initiative, managed by the National Endowment for Science, Technology and the Arts

Aventis Prize for Science Books
The winner of the international science book prize in 2002 was Stephen Hawking with *The Universe in a Nutshell*. It is the first time in five years that a British writer has won it. Stephen Hawking is a physicist who became famous in 1988 through his book *A Brief History of Time*. He is currently Lucasian Professor of Mathematics at Cambridge University. The prize for the best science book for children under 14 was awarded to Richard Walker for the *Dorling Kindersley Guide to the Human Body*.

and funded by the Department for Education and Skills (DfES). It is focusing particularly on those aged 10 to 19 and the adults around them (especially their teachers), and aims to raise awareness of the wide range of subjects and careers that are underpinned by science and technology.

Science year was launched with The Giant Jump. Over 1 million children jumped up and down at the same time, in the largest simultaneous jump ever, and measured the effects on home-made seismometers.

Science and Engineering Ambassadors (SEAs)
The Science and Engineering Ambassadors project was launched by the DfES and DTI in January 2002. Individuals with backgrounds in science, engineering, technology and mathematics go into schools to help teachers develop the curricula and to act as role models for the young. SEAs are administered across the UK by SETNET, the Science, Technology, Engineering and Mathematics Network (*www.setnet.org.uk*) and delivered through a network of 53 SET points.

National Science Week

National Science Week is an annual event co-ordinated by the British Association (see page 388) and held throughout the UK each March. Organisations participating in 2002 included hospitals, schools, industry and museums. Among the events were a balloon launch from the steps of the Royal Albert Hall in London – scientific principles were used to predict where the balloons would land – and Footprints, an Amoeba Theatre production to promote genetics to students.

DNA day
As part of National Science Week, the world's largest model of DNA, standing at 10.78 m, was built by teams from Daresbury Laboratory (see page 381) and Keele University at the Potteries Shopping Centre in Stoke-on-Trent. Some 3,000 schoolchildren, and celebrities from science, politics and the arts built base pairs for the model.

Zoological gardens

The Zoological Society of London (ZSL) (*www.zsl.org*), an independent conservation, science and education charity founded in 1826, runs London Zoo in Regent's Park (London). It also owns and runs Whipsnade Wild Animal Park in Bedfordshire. ZSL is responsible for the Institute of Zoology, which carries out research in support of conservation. The Institute's work covers topics such as ecology, reproductive biology and conservation genetics. ZSL also operates in overseas conservation projects, and is concerned with practical field conservation, primarily in East and Southern Africa, the Middle East and parts of Asia. Other well-known zoos in the UK include those in Edinburgh, Bristol, Chester, Dudley and Marwell (near Winchester).

Botanic gardens

The Royal Botanic Gardens, Kew (*www.kew.org.uk*), founded in 1759, are based at Kew in south-west London and at Wakehurst Place (Ardingly, in West Sussex). They contain one of the largest collections of living and dried plants in the world. Research is conducted into all aspects of plant life, including physiology, biochemistry, genetics, economic botany and the conservation of habitats and species.

Titanic flowering

One of the most spectacular plants to be found in the wet tropics zone of the Princess of Wales Conservatory, at Kew Gardens, is the titan arum (*Amorphophallus titanum*). In May 2002 this giant plant, over 2 m in height and a possible world record of 75 kg in weight, burst into flower; two more from the same batch of seeds have repeated the majestic flowering. The Titan arum blooms very rarely in cultivation and plants very often grow for many years without producing a flower. The central spike-like spadix gave off a pungent aroma described as a mixture of rotting flesh and excrement.

The Royal Botanic Garden in Edinburgh (*www.rbge.org.uk*) was established in 1670 and is the national botanic garden of Scotland. Together with its three associated specialist gardens, it has become an internationally recognised centre for taxonomy (classification of species); for the conservation and study of living and preserved plants and fungi; and as a provider of horticultural education.

A National Botanic Garden and research centre for Wales (*www.gardenofwales.org.uk*) has been developed on a site on the Middleton Hall estate at Llanarthne, near Carmarthen, and was opened in 2000 – the first botanic garden to be built in Britain for two centuries.

Scientific museums

The Natural History Museum (*www.nhm.ac.uk*) is one of the UK's most popular visitor attractions (with 2.1 million visitors in 2001/02), with exhibitions devoted to the Earth and the life sciences. It is also a world-leading centre in the fields of taxonomy and biodiversity. It is founded on collections of 70 million specimens from the natural world, and has 500,000 historically important original works of art. There are 350 scientists, and research projects are active in 60 countries. In September 2002 the opening of phase one of the Darwin Centre made a further 12 million specimens accessible to the public for the first time. The museum also offers an advisory service to foreign institutions.

The Science Museum (*www.nmsi.ac.uk*), which had 3.1 million visitors in 2001/02, promotes the public understanding of the history of science, technology, industry and medicine. The collections contain many of the icons of the scientific age with objects as diverse as Crick and Watson's DNA model and Stephenson's *Rocket*.

These two museums are in South Kensington, London. Other important collections include those at the Museum of Science & Industry in Manchester, the Museum of the History of Science in Oxford, and the Royal Scottish Museum, Edinburgh.

In Belfast, the W5 Interactive Discovery Centre (*www.w5online.co.uk*) is located within Northern

Magna Science Adventure Centre

Magna (*www.magnatrust.org.uk*) is the UK's first Science Adventure Centre. It is located in Rotherham in South Yorkshire. Visitors can explore displays on Earth, Air, Fire and Water, and have a chance to create their own adventure through hands-on interactive challenges. There are four Adventure Pavilions, two shows and an outdoor adventure park. Magna runs workshops and events aimed at different age groups and tailored to different levels of education. Since March 2002 a colony of 'Living Robots' has been on show, featuring 'predator' and 'prey' robots, special effects and commentary. The robots have the goal of obtaining enough energy to survive and breed.

Ireland's Millennium project, Odyssey. Opened in March 2001, it has over 100 hands-on, high-technology exhibits and attracted 245,000 visitors in its first year.

Workforce

The DTI report *Maximising Returns – to science, engineering and technology careers*, published in January 2002, estimated that the number of SET graduates in the working age population increased between 1992 and 2000 by 19 per cent, from 1.1 million to 1.3 million. However, owing to the increase in the number of graduates overall, the proportion holding an SET degree has declined from 32 per cent to 25 per cent. Although the number of women SET graduates is increasing, in 2000 men outnumbered women by more than four to one.

The study found that less than half of male SET graduates and approximately a quarter of female SET graduates were employed in key SET occupational groups (as defined by the study), such as engineers, scientists and computer programmers. They may, however, be engaged in related occupations such as sales and marketing.

According to the 2000 ONS Business R&D Survey, the number of staff employed on R&D in UK businesses decreased by 5 per cent between 1999 and 2000, to 145,000 (see Table 25.4). Scientists and engineers accounted for 59 per cent of the staff.

In 1999/2000 there were nearly 82,000 full-time staff employed in SET within higher education, 69 per cent of whom were male. Of those teaching and carrying out research, 74 per cent were male. Women were more likely to be involved in research only (38 per cent), rather than teaching and research (26 per cent).

The Promoting SET for Women Unit within OST was established in 1994 in response to a report which found that women were under-represented in the SET sectors, especially at senior levels, a finding confirmed in the 2002 Roberts Review (see box). The Unit has highlighted the benefits to business of providing a working environment sensitive to the needs of women scientists and engineers, many of whom have to combine a career with family responsibilities. It seeks to

Table 25.4 Employment in R&D within UK businesses, 2000

	Thousands
Scientists and engineers	86
Technicians, laboratory assistants and draughtsmen	30
Administrative, clerical, industrial and other staff	30
Total	**145**

Source: Office for National Statistics

Roberts Review

The 'Roberts Review', published in *SET for Success, the supply of people with science, technology, engineering and mathematic skills*, in April 2002, found that compared to other countries, the UK has a relatively large, and growing, number of students studying for scientific and technical qualification. This growth primarily reflected increases in those studying IT and the biological sciences, and there were downward trends in the numbers studying mathematics, engineering and the physical sciences. The review made recommendations to deal with a number of issues including:

- a shortage of women choosing to study subjects such as mathematics, engineering and the physical sciences;

- poor experiences of science and engineering education, coupled with a negative image of careers in the sector;

- insufficiently attractive career opportunities in research; and

- science and engineering graduates and postgraduates did not have the transferable skills required by R&D employers.

The Spending Review 2002 (see page 350) provides for additional investment of £100 million a year by 2005/06 paid via the Science Budget. This is to enable the OST to take forward the key recommendations of the Roberts Review, with the intention of ensuring a strong future supply of skilled scientists and engineers. Measures include attracting students in schools and universities to science through improved pay and training for PhD students and postdoctoral researchers, together with better teaching and research facilities.

ensure that careers information for girls and women is widely available and to promote good employment practices, such as the provision of childcare facilities and job sharing. The Unit's website (*www.set4women.gov.uk*) promotes SET for girls and women, and gives details of the Unit's activities. In the *Maximising Returns* report, the DTI estimated that around 24,000 women SET graduates returned to employment in 2000, and that about a third of them returned to SET occupations.

Research in higher education institutions

Universities carry out most of the UK's long-term strategic and basic research in science and technology. The higher education funding councils provide the main general funds to support research in universities and other higher education institutions in Great Britain. These funds pay for the salaries of permanent academic staff, who usually teach as well as undertake research, and contribute to the infrastructure for research. The quality of research performance is a key element in the allocation of funding. In Northern Ireland institutions are funded by the Department for Employment and Learning.

The Research Councils also finance basic and strategic research in higher education institutions. The other main channels of support are industry, charities, government departments and the EU.

Science Parks
Science Parks encourage and support the start-up, incubation and growth of innovation-led, high-growth, knowledge-based businesses. They have formal or operational links to a higher education institution or other major research centre. The UK Science Park Association (*www.ukspa.org.uk*) numbers 61 such initiatives, which together host over 1,500 firms employing over 30,000 people.

International collaboration

European Union
The EU's Sixth Framework Programme for Research and Technical Development (FP6), published in June 2002, has a budget of €17.5 billion for the four years to 2006. Framework programmes are the EU's main instrument for funding research. There are

seven key areas within FP6, funding research in genomics and biotechnology for health; information society technologies; nanotechnologies and nanosciences; aeronautics and space; food safety; sustainable development; and economic and social sciences. Framework programmes also provide support for mobility, fellowships, infrastructures and the continuation of nuclear research under Euratom.

FP6 is a key mechanism in realising a European Research Area, which aims to regroup all EC support for better co-ordination of research and innovation policies, at national and EU levels. The UK is actively engaged in the development of a common European Space Strategy involving ESA, the EU and others.

The six grant-giving Research Councils, in association with the UK universities, maintain the UK Research Office in Brussels which aims to promote UK participation in European research programmes. The CCLRC receives funds from the EU to make its facilities available to researchers from other Member States.

Other international activities
Over 800 UK organisations have taken part in EUREKA (*www.eureka.be*), an industry-led scheme to encourage European co-operation in developing advanced products and processes with worldwide sales potential. There are 33 members of EUREKA, including the 15 EU countries and the European Commission. Some 650 projects are in progress, involving firms, universities and research organisations. Examples of projects in 2002 involving UK organisations include:

- development of medicinal uses of cannabis extracts;

- generic e-trading software;

- environmentally friendly plant growth regulators and protection agents for use in organic agriculture; and

- automatic digitalisation and classification of sound.

The COST programme (European co-operation in the field of scientific and technical research) is a multilateral agreement involving 33 countries (including all the EU Member States, many

Mediterranean, Central European and Eastern European countries and Israel). Its purpose is to encourage co-operation in national research activities across Europe, with participants from industry, academia and research laboratories. The UK participates in the majority of COST actions and in the management of the programme.

Another example of international collaboration is CERN, home to the European laboratory for particle physics, based in Geneva, where the Large Hadron Collider is due to be completed by 2006. Scientific programmes at CERN aim to test, verify and develop the 'standard model' of the origin and structure of the Universe. There are 20 member states. The PPARC leads UK participation in CERN and the CCLRC co-ordinates several aspects of UK research community involvement. The EPSRC provides the UK contribution to the costs of access by UK researchers to the high-flux neutron source at the Institute Laue-Langevin and to the European Synchrotron Radiation Facility, both in Grenoble. These responsibilities are to transfer to the CCLRC from April 2003.

The PPARC is a partner in the European Incoherent Scatter Radar Facility within the Arctic Circle, which conducts research on the ionosphere. NERC has a major involvement in international programmes of research into global climate change organised through the World Climate Research Programme and the International Geosphere-Biosphere Programme. It also supports the UK's subscription to the Ocean Drilling Program.

The Medical Research Council pays the UK subscription to the European Molecular Biology Laboratory (EMBL), which has its home research base at Heidelberg. The European Bioinformatics Institute, an outstation of the EMBL, at Hinxton, near Cambridge, provides access to important molecular biology, sequencing and structural databases. The MRC is also responsible for the UK's subscriptions to the International Agency for Cancer Research, Lyon.

BBSRC and MRC pay the UK subscription to the Human Frontiers Science Program, which promotes international collaboration in two areas: brain functions and biological functions through molecular level approaches.

The Research Councils have a number of bilateral arrangements to promote international collaboration. For example, the BBSRC has

agreements with its equivalent organisations in France, the Netherlands, the United States, Canada, China, Japan, the Republic of Korea and India, and supports travel, workshops and other activities to encourage international links.

The UK is a member of the science and technology committees of such international organisations as the Organisation for Economic Co-operation and Development (OECD) and North Atlantic Treaty Organisation (NATO), and of various specialised agencies of the United Nations, including the United Nations Educational, Scientific and Cultural Organisation (UNESCO). The Research Councils and the Royal Society are members of the European Science Foundation – an association of 70 major national funding agencies in 27 European countries.

The UK Government also enters into bilateral agreements with other governments to encourage closer collaboration in SET. Staff in British Embassies, High Commissions and British Council offices conduct government business on, and promote contacts in, SET between the UK and overseas countries; and help to inform a large number of organisations in the UK about developments and initiatives overseas. The FCO has a London-based Science and Technology unit, whose tasks include the management of the overseas network of science attachés, and the recruitment and training of new attachés.

The British Council promotes 'cutting edge' UK science through events, partnership programmes, seminars, exhibitions and information provision.

Other organisations

Charitable organisations

Medical research charities are a major source of funds for medical research in the UK. According to the Association of Medical Research Charities, their members spent more than £640 million in support of medical research in the UK in 2000/01. The two largest contributors are the Wellcome Trust and Cancer Research UK.

The Wellcome Trust is an independent charity, established under the will of Sir Henry Wellcome in 1936. Its mission is to foster and promote research with the aim of improving human and animal health'. To this end, it supports 'blue sky' research and applied clinical research, and encourages the exploitation of research findings for medical benefit. The Trust also seeks to raise awareness of the medical, ethical and social implications of research and to promote dialogue between scientists, the public and policy makers.

To complement the programme of resources announced in the 2002 Spending Review, the Wellcome Trust is committing an additional £280 million for complementary funding for new programmes of science research and improved training for science teachers.

New research facility
The Wellcome Trust Clinical Research Facility was opened at Addenbrooke's Hospital, Cambridge, in January 2002. It is the first of five new facilities being established as part of a £20 million initiative to use the results of research to improve patient care. There are 31 studies in progress at the Addenbrooke's facility, with more planned for the future. Current studies include work on:

- the role of genetic factors in the development of severe childhood obesity; and

- a study of bone protection for stroke victims, who are at greater risk of hip fracture and death from falls.

Professional and learned institutions
There are numerous technical institutions, professional associations and learned societies in the UK, many of which promote their own disciplines or the education and professional well being of their members. The Council of Science and Technology Institutes has ten member institutes representing biology, biochemistry, chemistry, the environment, food science and technology, geology, hospital physics and physics.

Engineering Council
The Engineering Council (UK) (ECUK) was created in March 2002 as the successor of the chartered institution first established in 1982 to promote and regulate the engineering profession in the UK. It is responsible for the Register of Chartered Engineers, Incorporated Engineers and Engineering Technicians, and the Engineers Registration Board. ECUK is supported by 36 professional engineering institutions and

14 professional affiliates. In partnership with the institutions, the Council accredits higher and further education courses and advises the Government on academic, industrial and professional issues. Some 258,000 individuals have satisfied the Council's regulations for registration through their institution as either Chartered Engineers, Incorporated Engineers or as Engineering Technicians.

Royal Society
The Royal Society (*www.royalsoc.ac.uk*), founded in 1660, has 1,236 Fellows and 118 Foreign Members. The Society has three roles: as the national academy of science, as a learned society and as a funding agency for the scientific community. It offers independent advice to government on science matters, acts as an international forum for discussion of ground-breaking scientific research, supports many of the best young scientists and engineers in the UK, facilitates dialogue between scientists and the public, and promotes science education. Its government grant for 2002/03 is £28.7 million.

Royal Academy of Engineering
The national academy of engineering in Great Britain is the Royal Academy of Engineering (*www.raeng.org.uk*), which has 1,206 Fellows and 86 Foreign Members. It promotes excellence in engineering for the benefit of society, and advises government, Parliament and other official organisations. The Academy's programmes are aimed at attracting students into engineering, raising awareness of the importance of engineering design among undergraduates, developing links between industry and higher education, and increasing industrial investment in engineering research in higher education institutions. It has a government grant of £4.8 million in 2002/03.

Other societies
In Scotland the Royal Society of Edinburgh, established in 1783, promotes science by offering postdoctoral research fellowships and studentships, awarding prizes and grants, organising meetings and symposia, and publishing journals. It also acts as a source of independent scientific advice to the Government and others.

Three other major institutions publicise scientific developments by means of lectures and publications for specialists and schoolchildren. Of these, the British Association for the Advancement of Science, founded in 1831, is mainly concerned with science, while the Royal Society of Arts (*www.rsa.org.uk*), dating from 1754, deals with the arts and commerce as well as science. The Royal Institution (*www.ri.ac.uk*), founded in 1799, arranges a large and varied public programme of events to bring science to a wider audience, including the *Christmas Lectures* and the *Friday Evening Discourses*. In 2001 the *Christmas Lectures* celebrated their 175th anniversary. As well as being broadcast in the UK, the lectures are transmitted to other parts of Europe, Japan and Korea.

Further reading

Excellence and Opportunity – a science and innovation policy for the 21st century. Cm 4814. The Stationery Office, 2000.

The Forward Look 2001 Government-funded science, engineering and technology. DTI/OST. Cm 5338. The Stationery Office, 2001.

Invest in Innovation – A strategy for science, engineering and technology. DTI/HMT/DfES, 2002.

Maximising Returns – to science, engineering and technology careers. DTI, 2002 .

SET for success, the supply of people with science, technology, engineering and mathematic skills. HM Treasury, 2002.

Websites

Office of Science and Technology
www.ost.gov.uk

Council of Science and Technology
www.cst.gov.uk

The Wellcome Trust
www.wellcome.ac.uk

Research Councils UK
www.rcuk.ac.uk

26 Agriculture, fishing and forestry

Although agriculture, forestry and fishing together accounted for only 0.7 per cent of the total economy in terms of gross value added in 2001, their impact across the United Kingdom was far greater. Their share of the total economy has fallen from 1.6 per cent in 1995 and 2.9 per cent in 1973 because of a long-term fall in agricultural prices. The UK is about 63 per cent self-sufficient for all food and about 75 per cent for indigenous food.

The outbreak of foot-and-mouth disease (see page 401) in 2001 dealt the farming industry another serious blow, after the severe flooding which affected many parts of the UK during autumn 2000 (the wettest for at least 230 years) and the BSE epidemic. However, 2001 was exceptionally mild and drier than 2000 – this allowed farmers to catch up on work which had fallen behind.

The Forestry Commission published its Millennium Inventory of trees in November 2001. The statistics for 2000 obtained by the inventory have been compared with the figures indicated almost 1,000 years ago by the Domesday Book (see page 488). In 1086 forest cover was estimated to be around 15 per cent. By 1870 it had fallen to below 5 per cent, but has since recovered (see page 405). Similar research in Scotland has found that tree cover has trebled in the last 100 years and is now higher than it was 700 years ago.

Agriculture

In 2001 UK agriculture contributed £6.4 billion to the total economy, employed some 568,000 people and used over three-quarters of the country's land area. Income per full-time worker from agriculture in the UK increased by 3.5 per cent in 2001, slightly above the EU average increase of 3.3 per cent.

In 2000 there were some 286,000 farm holdings in the UK (excluding minor holdings in Wales but including all active farms in Northern Ireland, Scotland and England). These holdings had an

Figure 26.1 Agricultural land use in the UK, 2001

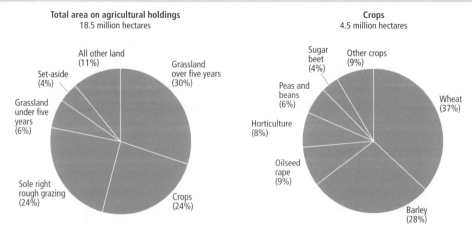

Source: Department for Environment, Food & Rural Affairs

average area of 60.5 hectares. Nearly half of them are smaller than eight European size units (ESUs).[1] About two-thirds of all agricultural land is owner-occupied; the rest is tenanted or rented. Agricultural land represents over 77 per cent of total land area in the UK, compared with 42 per cent for the EU as a whole.

Following a 35 per cent fall in 2000, *total income from farming* in the UK is estimated to have risen by 11 per cent in real terms in 2001, to £1,710 million. The *value of output* (including subsidies directly related to products) was 0.7 per cent (£104 million) higher in current prices than in 2000. Volume was 6 per cent lower, with reduced production of cereals, due to wet weather in the winter of 2000/01, and of livestock, due to the outbreak of foot-and-mouth disease. However, prices received by farmers were 7.1 per cent higher, mainly owing to price rises for milk, potatoes, vegetables, sugar beet, oilseed rape and wheat.

Productivity measures how efficiently inputs are converted into outputs. Since 1973 the productivity of the agriculture industry in the UK has increased by 36 per cent. However, in 2001 the volume of output was 6 per cent lower than in 2000 and inputs hardly changed. Labour productivity decreased by 17 per cent and total factor productivity decreased by 6.1 per cent. This

was mainly due to the measures taken to combat foot-and-mouth disease, poor yields and re-sowing in the arable sector.

Agricultural landlords and tenants

About 35 per cent of agricultural land in England and 23 per cent in Wales is rented. Since 1995 a simplified legal framework for new tenancies, known as farm business tenancies, has allowed landowners to benefit from full income tax relief.

There is a similar proportion of rented land in Scotland, much of it in the Highlands and Islands under crofting tenure (see box), including common grazing. The Scottish Executive is committed to changing the law relating to agricultural tenure by introducing new tenancy options. It is hoped that these will stimulate the rental sector and offer tenants the opportunity to manage their land more flexibly.

Most farms in Northern Ireland are owner-occupied, but the conacre system allows owners not wishing to farm all their land to let it annually to others. Conacre land, about 30 per cent of agricultural land, is used mainly for grazing.

Farmers' markets

The first of around 455 *farmers' markets* now operating in the UK – selling produce directly to consumers – started in Bath in 1997. The National Association of Farmers' Markets (NAFM – *www.farmersmarkets.net*) was established in 1999. NAFM has developed a set of criteria which markets should meet to be recognised as farmers' markets. These include provisions that:

- food must be locally produced (each market will have a definition of local);

- all produce sold must be grown, reared or otherwise produced by the stallholder; and

- information should be available to customers at each market about the rules of the market and the production methods of the producers.

Smallholdings and crofts

In England and Wales, county councils let smallholdings to experienced people who want to farm on their own account, and may also lend working capital to them. In March 2000 there were approximately 4,000 smallholdings in England and 720 in Wales. In Scotland, the Scottish Executive manages a number of estates and holdings, comprising some 103,000 hectares. Almost all this is tenanted croft land.

Crofting is a system of land tenure regulated through the Crofting Acts and found only in the Highlands and Islands of Scotland. A croft is a unit of land subject to these Acts. Crofting agriculture rarely provides a full-time income and most crofters have other employment. An estimated 30,000 family members live on the 17,721 crofts, and croft land covers some 800,000 hectares, accounting for more than 25 per cent of the agricultural land area of the Highlands and Islands. The Crofters Commission develops and regulates the crofting system, and promotes the interests of crofters. The Scottish Executive issued a White Paper in July 2002 containing proposals for legislation on crofting reform.

---

1 ESUs measure the financial potential of the holding in terms of the margins which might be expected from stock and crops: eight ESUs is judged the minimum for full-time holdings.

Table 26.2 Production as a percentage of total new supply¹ for use in the UK

Product	Average 1990–92	1996	1999	2000	2001
Wheat	130	125	113	118	104
Barley	129	126	126	137	109
Oats	106	128	104	119	116
Oilseed rape	97	97	97	83	75
Linseed	137	76	152	303	n/a
Sugar (as refined)	56	63	71	69	63
Potatoes	90	90	90	89	84
Vegetables	77	73	71	71	67
Fruit	19	13	12	10	10
Beef and veal	96	89	80	79	73
Mutton and lamb	98	102	104	100	79
Pork	103	99	100	92	76
Bacon and ham	44	48	51	45	43
Poultrymeat	94	93	90	89	90
Milk	100	100	102	102	103
Butter	65	68	71	64	64
Cheese	66	68	63	63	65
Eggs	95	95	93	91	89

1 Total new supply is home production plus imports less exports.
Source: DEFRA *Agriculture in the United Kingdom 2001*

Production

Home production of the principal foods is shown in Table 26.2 as a percentage by weight of total supplies.

Livestock

About 40 per cent of farms are devoted mainly to dairy farming or to beef cattle and sheep. Most of the beef animals and sheep are reared in the hill and moorland areas of the UK. Among world-famous British livestock are the Hereford, Welsh Black and Aberdeen Angus beef breeds, the Jersey, Guernsey and Ayrshire dairy breeds, the Large White pig breed and a number of sheep breeds. Livestock totals are given in Table 26.3.

Cattle and sheep

Cattle and sheep constitute nearly 35 per cent of the value of the UK's gross agricultural output. Dairy production is the largest part of the sector, followed by cattle and calves, and then sheep and lambs.

In 2001 the average size of dairy herds in England was 82, and 90 in Scotland. The average yield of milk for each dairy cow in the UK was 6,308 litres per year. The total value of milk and milk products for human consumption rose by

18 per cent to £2,818 million, the highest since 1997.

More than half of home-bred beef production originates from the national dairy herd, in which the Holstein Friesian breed predominates. The remainder derives from suckler herds producing high-quality beef calves.

Between June 2000 and June 2001 the total cattle population declined by 4.8 per cent and the value of cattle and calf production fell to its lowest figure for 19 years. This was due primarily to a 10 per cent fall in the value of home-fed production of beef and veal, a decrease in unfinished production work (work in progress on animals to be slaughtered) and a 5.9 per cent fall in subsidy and other payments to beef producers.

The UK has more than 60 native sheep breeds and many cross-bred varieties. The size of the UK breeding flock declined by 12 per cent in 2001 to 17.9 million, due primarily to the effects of foot-and-mouth, but also continuing a decline from 1999. The value of sheepmeat production fell in 2001, again to its lowest for 19 years. This was primarily due to a 32 per cent fall in the value of

Table 26.3 Livestock and livestock products in the UK

	Average 1990–92	1996	1999	2000	2001
Cattle and calves ('000 head)	12,040	12,040	11,423	11,135	10,602
Sheep and lambs ('000 head)	44,392	42,086	44,656	42,264	36,716
Pigs ('000 head)	7,650	7,590	7,284	6,482	5,845
Poultry ('000 head)[1]	135,504	n/a	165,157	169,773	179,880
Milk (million litres)[2]	14,200	13,975	14,303	13,801	14,020
Hen eggs (million dozen)[3]	809	775	743	752	803
Beef and veal ('000 tonnes)	1,001	710	679	706	645
Mutton and lamb ('000 tonnes)	406	383	403	389	265
Pork ('000 tonnes)	792	801	831	725	610
Bacon and ham ('000 tonnes)	191	241	233	209	197
Poultrymeat ('000 tonnes)	1,186	1,476	1,525	1,513	1,564
Butter ('000 tonnes)	137	130	141	132	129
Cheese ('000 tonnes)	320	377	368	340	385
Cream – fresh, frozen, sterilised ('000 tonnes)	241	281	275	270	267
Condensed milk ('000 tonnes)	203	206	177	162	166
Milk powder – full cream ('000 tonnes)	78	83	102	105	89
Skimmed milk powder ('000 tonnes)	138	108	102	83	74

1 Includes ducks, geese and turkeys. In England and Wales a new approach to collecting poultry information has been used. The figures from
   1998 onwards are not therefore directly comparable with previous years.
2 For human consumption. Including the production of dairy products.
3 For human consumption only; does not include eggs for hatching.
Source: DEFRA *Agriculture in the United Kingdom 2001*

home-fed production and a 43 per cent fall in subsidy payments.

Pigs
The value of production of pigs fell by 5.4 per cent in 2001. A fall in the value of home-fed production of pigmeat of 9.9 per cent was partially offset by an increase in the value of unfinished production. Marketing of clean pigs[2] fell by 14 per cent, primarily due to the contraction of the breeding herd in the previous year as a result of poor market returns. The outbreaks of foot-and-mouth disease in 2001 and Classical Swine Fever in autumn 2000 also had an effect.

Poultry
The total UK poultry population in 2001 comprised 112.5 million chickens and other table fowls; 29.9 million birds in the laying flock;

2 Pigs which have not been used for breeding.

Table 26.4 Value of livestock production in the UK, 2001

	£ million	% change on 2000
Cattle and calves	1,809	−9.5
Sheep and lambs	625	−34.9
Pigs	751	−5.4
Poultrymeat	1,317	1.1

Source: DEFRA *Agriculture in the United Kingdom 2001*

12.1 million fowls for breeding; and 12.3 million turkeys, ducks and geese.

Poultrymeat production in 2001 was 1.6 million tonnes, a 3.4 per cent increase on 2000. The increase in value (see Table 26.4) was less than the rise in production because poultrymeat prices fell during 2001.

Crops
Farms devoted primarily to arable crops are found mainly in eastern and central southern England

and eastern Scotland. The main crops are shown in Table 26.5. In the UK in 2001, the area planted to *cereals* – predominantly wheat, barley and oats – totalled 3.0 million hectares, a decrease of 10 per cent on 2000. Wet weather in autumn 2000 hindered planting, and farmers elected to enter extra land into 'set-aside' when alternatives became unviable. The total volume of cereal production fell by 21 per cent and the total value by 14 per cent.

The output value of *oilseed rape* rose by 12 per cent in 2001, due to a slight overall increase in production coupled with an increase in price levels. The value of production of *linseed* fell by 53 per cent, due to lower plantings and a further reduction in subsidy rates. The output value of *sugar beet* rose by 1 per cent.

Large-scale *potato* and *vegetable* cultivation takes place on the fertile soils throughout the UK, often with irrigation. Principal areas include East Anglia and the Midlands. Total area for all potatoes was almost unchanged in 2001, while the overall volume of production was down by 1.9 per cent. However, the value of production increased by 32 per cent, recovering from a low in the previous year, due to higher prices.

Arable Area Payments Scheme
Under this scheme within the Common Agricultural Policy (CAP – see page 399), farmers may claim area payments on cereals, oilseeds, proteins and linseed, and on fibre flax and hemp for fibre. A condition for claiming area payments is that large-scale farmers must 'set aside' a certain percentage of their land, thereby avoiding overproduction, and must comply with the strict rules for managing set-aside. The minimum rate for set-aside for 2001 was 10 per cent of the total area claimed.

In 2001 there were approximately 60,000 claims for area payments in the UK in respect of over 4.3 million hectares of land. Payments of approximately £1 billion were made.

Horticulture
Table 26.6 gives details of the main horticultural products. As at June 2001 the total area devoted to horticulture (excluding mushrooms, potatoes, and peas for harvesting dry) amounted to 172,734 hectares, almost unchanged from the 2000 figure. This area relates to field area and does not take into account the number of crops in the year.

The output value of all horticultural commodities (including seeds and peas harvested dry) in 2001 was £1.9 billion, an increase of 8.1 per cent from 2000, with price rises due to a shortage of supply. The value of production of vegetables increased by 11 per cent, fruit by 7 per cent and ornamentals by 5 per cent.

Genetically modified crops
Now that the location and function of individual crop genes are being discovered, scientists have the chance to alter the genetic make-up of plants by adding or removing specific genes. Some 52.6 million hectares of genetically modified crops were estimated to have been grown in 13 countries across the world in 2001.

The year 2002 is the last in a three-year UK programme of farm-scale evaluations (FSEs), set up to allow independent researchers to study the effect, if any, that the management practices associated with genetically modified (GM) herbicide tolerant crops might have on farmland wildlife, when compared with those used with non-GM crops. Three crops are involved: oilseed rape (both spring and autumn sown); beet (fodder and sugar varieties); and maize. The project has involved between 60 and 75 fields of each crop in total. The sites for the last spring sowing round were announced in January and March 2002. At the end of the programme in 2003/04, the results will be reported, made publicly available and considered by the Government. The FSE programme includes a project to monitor gene-flow, including cross-pollination. There will be no commercial growing of GM crops in the UK at least until the FSEs are completed and the results fully assessed. The results will be one factor which will be taken into account when decisions are taken about the commercial future of GM crop production in the UK.

Food safety
The Food Standards Agency (FSA – see chapter 13) (*www.foodstandards.gov.uk*), launched in 2000, aims to ensure that the food consumers eat is safe, and to offer independent, balanced advice to government throughout the UK. The Meat Hygiene Service, an executive agency of the FSA, is responsible for enforcing legislation on meat hygiene, inspection, animal welfare at slaughter and specified risk materials controls in all licensed abattoirs and cutting premises in Great Britain.

Pesticides
The Pesticides Safety Directorate (PSD), an executive agency of the Department for

May–July 2002: Agricultural Shows.

NIGEL ANDREWS

PHIL SMITH

MIKE WILKINSON

D LOW PHOTOGRAPHERS

Top left: a champion cow at The Royal Bath and West of England Show, Shepton Mallet.

Top right: crowds at The Royal Ulster Agricultural Society Show, Belfast.

Centre left: a black-faced ram at the Royal Highland Show, Edinburgh.

Centre right: judging sheep at the Royal Welsh Show, Llanelwedd, Powys.

Left: Highland cattle at the Royal Highland Show.

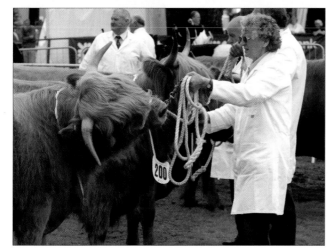

MIKE WILKINSON

November 2001: the National Inventory of Woodland and Trees in England reveals that the oak is the most common broadleaved tree, covering 159,000 hectares and representing 25 per cent of all broadleaved trees.

April 2002: National Inventory of Woodland and Trees for Scotland.

The Sitka Spruce is the main species of conifer, covering 528,000 hectares.

The main broadleaved species, covering 78,000 ha, is the birch.

Farmers Markets

GARETH JONES

GARETH JONES

March 2002: Winchester Farmers' Market, Hampshire. Certification of farmers' markets was introduced to reassure customers that markets are keeping to the principle of local producers selling local products.

GARETH JONES

August 2002: The market at Whetstone, North London. This opened as a new market in 2002.

Table 26.5 Cereals and other crops in the UK

	Average 1990–92	1996	1999	2000	2001
Cereals					
Wheat					
Area ('000 hectares)	2,020	1,976	1,847	2,086	1,635
Production ('000 tonnes)	14,164	16,100	14,870	16,700	11,570
Yield (tonnes per hectare)	7.0	8.1	8.1	8.0	7.1
Value of production (£ million)	1,599	2,315	1,525	1,585	1,222
Barley					
Area	1,404	1,269	1,179	1,128	1,245
Production	7,634	7,790	6,580	6,490	6,700
Yield	5.5	6.1	5.6	5.8	5.5
Value	782	1,183	735	685	726
Oats					
Area	104	96	92	109	112
Production	518	590	540	640	615
Yield	5.0	6.1	5.9	5.9	5.5
Value	54	86	58	65	64
Total¹ for cereals					
Area	3,550	3,359	3,141	3,348	3,014
Production	22,426	24,590	22,120	23,990	18,990
Yield	6.3	6.9	7.0	7.2	6.3
Value	2,439	3,595	2,326	2,338	2,019
Other crops					
Oilseed rape					
Area	417	415	537	402	451
Production	1,234	1,415	1,737	1,157	1,159
Yield	3.0	3.4	3.2	2.8	2.6
Value	292	434	371	246	275
Linseed					
Area	90	54	213	74	31
Production	150	87	302	43	39
Yield	1.7	1.6	1.4	0.6	1.2
Value	46	39	132	34	16
Sugar beet					
Area	196	199	183	173	177
Production	8,917	10,420	10,584	9,079	8,180
Yield	45.6	52.4	58.0	52.5	46.1
Value	324	358	280	252	255
Potatoes					
Area	178	178	178	166	166
Production	6,909	7,228	7,131	6,652	6,528
Yield	38.7	40.7	40.1	40.1	39.4
Value	545	636	750	454	600

1 Also includes rye, mixed corn and triticale.
Source: DEFRA *Agriculture in the United Kingdom 2001*

Table 26.6 Horticulture in the UK

	Average 1990–92	1996	1999	2000	2001
Vegetables¹					
Area ('000 hectares)	185.3	163.0	149.1	137.0	145.1
Value of production (£ million)	979	1,083	962	877	970
Fruit					
Area ('000 hectares)	45.5	38.3	34.2	33.4	33.4
Value (£ million)	275	292	257	228	243
of which:					
Orchard fruit					
Area ('000 hectares)	31.7	26.4	25.3	24.5	24.5
Value (£ million)	149	134	106	83	97
Soft fruit					
Area ('000 hectares)	13.9	11.9	8.9	8.9	8.9
Value (£ million)	125	150	139	133	133
Ornamentals					
Area ('000 hectares)	18.9	19.0	19.7	20.2	20.2
Value (£ million)	519	678	715	672	708

1 Includes peas harvested dry for human consumption.
Source: DEFRA *Agriculture in the United Kingdom 2001*

Environment, Food & Rural Affairs (DEFRA), administers the regulation of agricultural, horticultural, forestry, food storage and home garden pesticides. Its principal functions are to evaluate and process applications for approval of pesticide products for use in Great Britain and provide advice to government on pesticides policy. The PSD aims:

- to protect the health of human beings, creatures and plants;

- to safeguard the environment; and

- to ensure that methods of pest control are safe, efficient and humane by providing effective controls on the sale, supply and use of pesticides.

Exports, marketing and promotion

Exports of food, feed and drink were around £8.6 billion in 2001, compared with £18.4 billion for imports. EU countries accounted for 60 per cent of all UK food and drink exports. The main markets were the Irish Republic (£1.3 billion) and France (£1.0 billion).

Drinks and cereals are key contributors to exports. Drinks were up overall by 2.4 per cent in 2001,

with whisky and other spirits being the main components in the drink category. However, exports of cereals fell by 20 per cent due to short supply.

Food from Britain (FFB – *www. foodfrombritain.com*), an organisation funded by DEFRA on behalf of the four agricultural departments and by industry, provides specialist marketing and international business development services to the food and drink industry. It has a network of 11 international offices, each with local food industry expertise and trade contacts. It also fosters the development of the speciality food and drink industry in the UK through a range of tailored business development and marketing services, delivered nationally by FFB and locally by regional and county food groups.

The British Farm Standard red tractor logo, launched in June 2000, has been designed by the National Farmers' Union as an authoritative mark to identify food that meets high – and independently verified – production standards covering food safety, animal welfare and environmental issues.

Several major agricultural shows are held annually across the UK, including:

- the Royal Show, Stoneleigh, Warwickshire (early July), enabling visitors to see the latest techniques and improvements in British agriculture – some 151,000 visitors attended in 2002;

- the Royal Highland Show, Edinburgh (June), with around 4,000 head of livestock on show and the largest trade exhibition of agricultural machinery in Great Britain – 168,000 visitors in 2002;

- the Royal Welsh Show, Llanelwedd, Builth Wells (late July);

- the Royal Welsh Agricultural Winter Fair, Llanelwedd, Builth Wells, for livestock and carcases (December);

- the Royal Ulster Agricultural Society Show, Belfast (May); and

- the Royal Smithfield Show, London (every other year), for agricultural machinery, livestock and carcases.

Government role

The Department for Environment, Food & Rural Affairs (DEFRA) has a crucial role in promoting sustainable development, rural renewal, and sustainable and competitive food chains, both in England and internationally. It has responsibility for agriculture, fisheries, food, animal welfare issues, environmental protection, and wildlife and the countryside in general. DEFRA administers support policies agreed in Brussels which provide around £3 billion a year to UK agriculture from the European Union (EU) budget.

The Scottish Executive Environment and Rural Affairs Department (SEERAD), the National Assembly for Wales Agriculture Department (NAWAD), and the Department of Agriculture and Rural Development in Northern Ireland (DARD) have varying degrees of responsibility for agriculture and fisheries affairs. Matters not devolved or transferred to the devolved administrations, such as relations with the EU and other international organisations, remain with the Government in London. The work of DEFRA's nine Regional Service Centres in England and SEERAD's eight areas in Scotland relates to payments under domestic and EU schemes, licensing and other services for farmers and growers.

UK agriculture strategy

The Government's aim is to secure a more competitive agriculture industry with a stronger market orientation. In *A New Direction for Agriculture* – published in 1999 – it set out its long-term strategy for the future development of the industry. The strategy is designed to help farming become more competitive, diverse, flexible, responsive to consumer wishes and environmentally responsible. It aims to deliver short-term support to those sectors hit hardest by the continuing farming crisis and longer-term action to encourage industry restructuring and adaptation.

Rural Development Programmes (RDPs) (see page 398) are helping to implement the strategy, investing nearly £3 billion in the UK rural economy from 2001 to 2006.

The RDPs have been supplemented by other measures, in particular the *Action Plan for Farming*, launched in March 2000 in response to the crisis in farm incomes in the UK. The plan provides short-term financial relief and longer-term support for business restructuring and development, improved marketing and food chain co-operation, training and innovation. Although a number of measures in the Action Plan are UK-wide, others are focused on England. The devolved administrations are developing strategies to meet priorities in their own areas. The Scottish Executive published a policy document, *A forward strategy for Scottish agriculture*, in June 2001, and the Welsh Assembly published its strategy for farming in Wales, *Farming for the future*, in November 2001. *A Vision for the future of the Northern Ireland agri-food industry*, produced by the 'Vision' group set up by the Minister of Agriculture and Rural Development, was published in October 2001.

The milk task force

Set up in 2000 by the then Ministry of Agriculture, Fisheries and Food to study and report on the food chain in the milk and dairy sector, the task force was asked to identify those areas where greater efficiencies could be obtained from production and marketing. It published its report in January 2002. The report states the need for greater co-operation and communication between participants in the dairy supply chain, for example in market and scientific research, the promotion of milk and milk products, and the collection and distribution of milk.

The report also identified a number of areas where government action could help the industry become more efficient, for example by simplifying the administration of milk quotas; CAP reform; and accurate labelling of dairy products. The Government published its response to the report in April 2002, agreeing to almost all the recommendations.

Agri-industrial materials (AIMS)

The AIMS section in DEFRA is responsible for the co-ordination and development of plant-based raw materials. Among other things, it aims to encourage the use of crops for energy and industry and stimulate opportunities for renewable raw materials from environmentally acceptable crops. It also provides the secretariat for a new government-industry forum on non-food uses of crops.

Policy Commission report on farming and food

In January 2002 the Policy Commission on the future of farming and food published *Farming and Food*, its response to the Government's request to investigate how a sustainable, competitive and diverse farming and food sector could be created in England. The report makes over 100 recommendations, including:

- radical reform of the CAP (see page 399), for example removing remaining price supports and associated production controls;

- targeting public funds towards environmental and rural development instead of subsidising production;

- setting up a permanent Food Chain Centre to bring together people from each part of the food chain, in order, for example, to develop supply chain analyses and identify how efficiency savings could be made; and

- the setting up of a new national 'champion' body for local food to help the sector expand.

Rural Development Programmes

Although each is different, these programmes have the general aims of conserving and improving the environment, and creating productive and sustainable rural economies. Developing more diverse and competitive rural industries are also central themes. Agri-environment schemes (see below) are key parts of the RDPs, and have seen

substantial expansions in funding. The RDPs will run from 2001 to 2006.

The *England* Rural Development Programme (ERDP) is investing £1.6 billion in rural development and agri-environment measures. The Environmentally Sensitive Areas and Countryside Stewardship Schemes will continue, and four new schemes opened to applications in October 2000: the Rural Enterprise Scheme; Processing and Marketing Grants; the Energy Crops Scheme; and the Vocational Training Scheme.

The *Scottish* Rural Development Programme concentrates on accompanying the CAP and provides measures which support less favoured areas (LFAs), through a new area-based scheme, agri-environment measures, and afforestation. Around £685 million will be spent over the lifetime of the programme. In addition, SEERAD has introduced the Agricultural Business Development Scheme in the Highlands and Islands. It will provide assistance to farmers and crofters for investments in agricultural holdings and diversification projects.

The *Rural Development Plan for Wales* involves investment of around £450 million. The programme will make funds available for schemes such as the Tir Gofal (Land in Care) whole farm agri-environment scheme and the Processing and Marketing Grant Scheme. It includes support for hill farming and a range of forestry and farm woodland initiatives.

The *Rural Development Regulation Plan for Northern Ireland*, which is running from 2000 to 2006, is worth £266 million. It includes the new LFA support scheme and an enhanced agri-environment programme. DARD also manages a Rural Development Programme targeted at the broader rural community. It is expected to be worth about £80 million between 2001 and 2007, and combines several programmes, such as the Northern Ireland Programme for Building Sustainable Prosperity.

Agri-environment schemes

Agri-environment schemes form key parts of the RDPs. They generally make payments for the management of land to maintain, enhance and extend wildlife habitats; conserve historic or geological features; encourage public access; and restore traditional aspects of the countryside. Aiming to make conservation part of management practice, they are funded by the EU and the Government.

The *Environmentally Sensitive Areas* (ESA) scheme offers incentives to farmers to adopt agricultural practices which will safeguard and enhance parts of the country of particularly high landscape, wildlife or historic value. Farmers and land managers enter ten-year agreements to manage land in an environmentally beneficial way in return for annual payments. Grants are also available for capital works, such as hedge laying and the restoration of traditional farm buildings. There are now 22 ESAs in England, covering some 10 per cent of agricultural land; six in Wales (operating under Tir Gofal), ten in Scotland and five in Northern Ireland. In 2001 £71 million was spent in the UK under ESAs.

The *Hill Farm Allowance* (HFA) scheme provides assistance to hill farmers, who face particular difficulties in their activities. Those farming in LFAs are eligible for support under the HFA. Different schemes operate in each of the constituent countries of the UK, and provided a total of £164 million in 2001.

The *Countryside Stewardship* scheme is the main scheme for the wider countryside. Farmers and land managers enter ten-year agreements to manage land in an environmentally beneficial way in return for annual payments. Grants are also available towards capital works, such as hedge laying and planting, or repairing dry stone walls. Around £49 million was spent on the scheme in 2001. In Scotland, the *Rural Stewardship* scheme has replaced both the ESA and Countryside Premium schemes as the main scheme for encouraging environmentally friendly farming practice.

Organic farming schemes offer payments to farmers – in the form of financial help during the conversion process – to aid them in converting to organic farming and to manage their land in some additional environmentally beneficial ways. Total expenditure on these schemes was £35 million in the UK in 2001.

As at June 2002, there were 699,879 hectares of land registered as being farmed organically in the UK. It is estimated that the UK market for organic food is currently worth around £500 million a year.

The Organic Conversion Information Service, funded by DEFRA in England, provides free advice to farmers considering conversion to organic farming. In Scotland SEERAD funds the Scottish Agricultural College to operate a telephone helpline. Standards of organic food production in the UK are set by the UK Register of Organic Food Standards.

The *Farm Woodland Premium Scheme* (partly funded by the EU) aims to encourage farmers to convert productive agricultural land to woodlands by providing payments to help offset agricultural income foregone. The aim is to enhance the environment through the planting of trees, improve the landscape, provide new habitats and increase biodiversity. Between April 1992 and December 2001 a total of 12,223 applications, covering 84,712 hectares, were approved for planting in the UK.

Common Agricultural Policy (CAP)

Total UK expenditure under the CAP and on national grants and subsidies in 2001/02 is forecast to increase by some £2.2 billion compared with in 2000/01, to £5.3 billion. Spending in the UK under the CAP itself is forecast to increase from £2.7 billion in 2000/01 to £2.9 billion in 2001/02. The increase is mainly attributable to the impact of foot-and-mouth disease, and in particular the cost of creating the Livestock Welfare Disposal Scheme (see page 401).

Expenditure in the cereals sector is expected to drop significantly, mainly due to a sharp reduction in intervention buying and reduced expenditure on export refunds. Conversely, expenditure on the milk sector is forecast to grow in 2001/02, mainly due to new expenditure on dairy agrimonetary compensation (see below).

Expenditure under the CAP arable and livestock schemes is protected by the Integrated Administration and Control System (IACS). Controls to prevent and detect fraud and irregularity are major features of the system. These include verification checks of claimed land and animals, including on-the-spot inspections and remote sensing by observation satellites.

In 2000 the Government announced a series of packages of agrimonetary compensation to offset falls in CAP direct payments to the UK resulting from changes in the euro/sterling exchange rate. In 2001 a total of £146 million was paid to farmers in the livestock and dairy sectors, while arable farmers received £29 million.

Figure 26.7 Public expenditure[1] under the Common Agricultural Policy, UK, 2001/02

Total: £2.9 billion

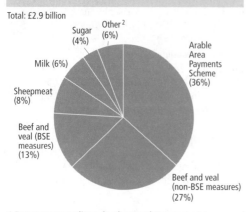

Sugar (4%)
Other[2] (6%)
Milk (6%)
Sheepmeat (8%)
Beef and veal (BSE measures) (13%)
Arable Area Payments Scheme (36%)
Beef and veal (non-BSE measures) (27%)

1 Forecast expenditure by the Rural Payments Agency and agricultural and other departments.
2 Includes cereals and processed goods.
Source: Department for Environment, Food & Rural Affairs

Member States not participating in the European single currency have the opportunity to offer producers, processors and traders the option of CAP payments in euro. Following European Commission approval of its scheme for euro payments, the Government offered CAP market support measures, such as export refunds, to traders and processors from autumn 2001. Further consideration is being given to extending this option to direct aid recipients.

EU legislation permits Member States to recycle, or *modulate*, a proportion of payments made direct to farmers under CAP commodity regimes. Modulation was introduced in 2001 at a flat rate of 2.5 per cent, to help fund the RDP (see page 398). This means that 2.5 per cent of subsidy payments will be reallocated to agri-environment and forestry schemes such as Countryside Stewardship, Tir Gofal, and ESAs (see page 398). The Government is matching the sum reallocated to provide further funding for the RDPs. On an accruals basis, modulation is estimated to have reduced arable and livestock subsidies by £44 million in 2001. In order to secure a significant increase in funds for rural development measures, all direct payments made under CAP commodity regimes between 2001 and 2006 will be modulated.

In December 2000 a comprehensive EU proposal for submission to the World Trade Organisation

(WTO) agriculture negotiations was agreed, meeting a key UK objective in committing the EU to constructive negotiations on continuing trade liberalisation and reform of agricultural policy. The WTO fourth ministerial conference held in November 2001 in Doha (see page 366) contained an important text on agriculture, which commited WTO members to substantial cuts in market protection and domestic subsidies, as well as reductions of export subsidies. It also committed members to take account of environmental, rural development and animal welfare concerns, and negotiate special treatment for developing countries. The timetable for these measures requires rules and commitments to be agreed by March 2003 and for negotiations to be complete by the beginning of 2005.

EU-wide rules on compulsory beef labelling have been implemented. These require fresh, chilled and frozen beef, offered for sale throughout the supply chain, to be labelled with information on place of slaughter and cutting/mincing, and, from 1 January 2002, with full country of origin information (place of birth, raising and slaughter).

Professional, scientific and technical services
A number of organisations are active in service provision:

- in England the Rural Development Service of DEFRA provides scheme implementation services for the ERDP, involving professional and technical work in relation to the enhancement and protection of the environment, including biodiversity and rural development;

- in Scotland the Scottish Agricultural College (SAC) provides professional, business, scientific and technical services in the agriculture, rural business, food and drink, and environmental markets;

- the Department of Agriculture and Rural Development (DARD) has a similar remit in Northern Ireland; and

- Lantra, which is the UK Sector Skills Development Agency (see page 115) for the industry, receives government support under contracts from DEFRA and the Scottish Executive.

Animal health and welfare

Professional advice and action on the statutory control of animal health and the welfare of farm livestock are the responsibility of the State Veterinary Service. It is supported in England and Wales by the Veterinary Laboratories Agency (VLA – *www.defra.gov.uk/corporate/vla*), which also offers its services to the private sector on a commercial basis. Similar support is provided in Scotland by the SAC. In Northern Ireland, DARD's Veterinary Service carries out a similar role to the State Veterinary Service in Great Britain, supported by its Veterinary Sciences Division.

DEFRA works to ensure priority is given to maintaining standards of welfare for animals during

---

Foot-and-mouth disease

A significant outbreak of foot-and-mouth disease occurred in the UK during 2001. By the time that the disease was confirmed in pigs at an abattoir, and in cattle on a neighbouring farm, in Brentwood (Essex) on 20 February 2001, it had already been present in the country, undetected, for two to three weeks – the original outbreak was subsequently found to have been on a farm at Heddon-on-the-Wall, Northumberland. During this time it had already been spread widely throughout the country by large-scale commercial movements of sheep. As a result, cases occurred in many areas, with particular clusters in Cumbria, Dumfries and Galloway, Devon and North Yorkshire, together accounting for over two-thirds of all confirmed cases.

There were 2,030 confirmed cases in 2001, the last being confirmed on 30 September. England had 1,730 cases, Scotland 183, Wales 113 and Northern Ireland four. The disease peaked in March and April and then trailed off from May onwards.

Over the year a total of 4,082,000 animals, on 10,075 premises, were slaughtered for disease control purposes. A further 2,046,000 were slaughtered for welfare reasons (for example because they could not be moved from waterlogged fields), and another 526,000 under the Light Lambs Scheme.

Foot-and-mouth disease is highly virulent in pigs, cattle, sheep and other ungulates, spreading rapidly by contact between animals, transmission via people or transport, or through the air. Strict controls on the movement of animals in affected areas were introduced as was an export ban. Direct compensation payments for foot-and-mouth disease totalled £991 million. In addition, a Livestock Welfare Disposal Scheme was opened as an outlet of last resort for livestock farmers whose animals faced welfare difficulties as a result of the movement restrictions. The scheme provided for the removal and disposal of such animals, and the Government paid a total of £224 million.

A report by the National Audit Office (see page 350), published in June 2002, found that overall the foot-and-mouth outbreak cost the public sector over £3 billion and the private sector more than £5 billion. However, the Treasury has estimated that the net economic effect of the outbreak was less than 0.2 per cent of GDP (less than £2 billion) because expenditure was diverted elsewhere in the economy.

Throughout the crisis the export of livestock and livestock products was banned. Export of pigmeat from provisionally free areas was resumed at the end of October 2001. All remaining trade restrictions on the export of meat, animal products and livestock as a result of foot-and-mouth disease were lifted on 7 February 2002 by the Standing Veterinary Committee of the European Commission (beef exports remain subject to BSE controls).

The UK was declared free of the disease on 14 January 2002.

Three separate, independent, inquiries have reported on the lessons learned from foot-and-mouth; the science of disease control and prevention; and the future of farming and the countryside:

- *Inquiry into the lessons to be learned from the foot-and-mouth disease outbreak of 2001* (*www.fmd-lessonslearned.org.uk*), which reported in July 2002;

- *The Royal Society Inquiry into Infectious Diseases in Livestock*, which also reported in July 2002; and

- *The Policy Commission report on the Future of Farming and Food*, which reported in January 2002 and covered only the situation in England (see page 398).

In Northern Ireland, the Minister of Agriculture and Rural Development commissioned *The independent review of foot-and-mouth in Northern Ireland*, which reported in June 2002.

all stages of production. Work currently being undertaken includes improved welfare conditions for laying hens; broiler chicken welfare standards; a new sheep code and negotiations on pig welfare.

Britain enforces controls on imports of live animals and genetic material, including checks on all individual consignments originating from outside the EU and frequent checks on those from other EU Member States at destination points. Measures can be taken to prevent the import of diseased animals and genetic material from regions or countries affected by disease. Veterinary checks also include unannounced periods of surveillance at ports.

An EC Directive on welfare standards for laying hens will forbid the installation of conventional barren battery cages after 1 January 2003, and ban them from January 2012. Farmers will still be able to use 'enriched' cages which have more space for each bird and include a nest, perch and litter.

Cattle tracing system (CTS)
The British Cattle Movement Service (BCMS) was launched in 1998 in order to record all cattle in the national herd on a CTS database. Cover has been extended to over 98 per cent of the 10 million cattle in the Great Britain herd. Work is in hand to collect the remaining data and apply checks to help ensure that information held on the database is accurate and complete. There is a legal requirement to notify the BCMS of all movements. In Northern Ireland, all cattle and cattle movements are recorded on the Animal and Public Health Information System (APHIS), which has been approved by the EU since 1999 as a fully operational database for cattle traceability.

Tuberculosis (TB) in cattle
The Government's strategy is to find a science-based policy to control TB in cattle. An annual £5 million research programme has been put in place to find out how the disease is spread among cattle and wildlife, including research into improved diagnostic tests and the development of a TB vaccine. An on-farm epidemiological survey, known as TB99, is starting to provide data to help understand the disease and focus future research. DEFRA is also investigating the role that husbandry might play in reducing TB risk. An important element of the Government's strategy is the badger culling trial, designed to establish the contribution that badgers, as opposed to other factors, make in spreading TB to cattle. Field operations were

suspended during the foot-and-mouth outbreak, but restarted in May 2002. It is hoped that the trial will start yielding results by 2004.

BSE inquiry
In October 2000 the Government published the report of the public inquiry into the history of BSE (bovine spongiform encephalopathy) and variant CJD (Creutzfeldt-Jakob disease) and how the diseases were handled by the Government and others in the period up to 20 March 1996. The report found that most of those responsible for responding to the challenge posed by BSE emerged with credit. However, it identified a number of aspects of the response that were inadequate, and set out some fundamental lessons for public policy and administration in the future. The Government published its response to the inquiry report in September 2001. It set out the progress made since March 1996, for example the creation of the Food Standards Agency (see page 179) and the opening up of scientific advisory committees to public scrutiny. The response concluded that, in general, many of the inquiry's findings had already been, or were in the process of being, addressed.

Fur farming
Under the *Fur Farming (Prohibition) Act 2000*, it will be illegal to keep animals solely or primarily for slaughter for their fur from January 2003. The Act covers England and Wales – similar legislation will be introduced in Scotland which will take effect at the same time, and a Bill is being introduced in Northern Ireland. Since January 2002 farmers who incur losses as a result of the ban have been able to submit claims for compensation.

Veterinary medicinal products
The Veterinary Medicines Directorate (*www.vmd.gov.uk*), an executive agency of DEFRA, aims to protect public health, animal health and the environment, and to promote animal welfare, by ensuring the safety, quality and efficacy of all aspects of veterinary medicines in the UK. The Government is advised by the independent scientific *Veterinary Products Committee* on standards to be adopted in the authorisation procedures for veterinary medicines.

The fishing industry

The UK has a major interest in sea fisheries, reflecting its geographical position in the North

East Atlantic, and is one of the EU's largest fishing countries, taking about a fifth of the total catch in major species. It has an interest in more than 100 'total allowable catches' set by the European Commission (see page 404). In 2001 total UK fish supplies amounted to some 718,000 tonnes, with the UK fishing industry supplying around 67 per cent by quantity. Household consumption of fish in the UK in 2000 was estimated at 442,000 tonnes.

Fisheries Departments, in partnership with the European Commission, are responsible for the administration of legislation concerning the fishing industry, including fish and shellfish farming. The *Sea Fish Industry Authority* (*www.seafish.co.uk*), a largely industry-financed body, undertakes some R&D, provides training and promotes the marketing and consumption of sea fish. There are also two government laboratories specialising in fisheries research – one in Aberdeen and one in Lowestoft.

Fish caught and the fishing fleet

UK fishing industry statistics are shown in Table 26.8. Altogether, some 530,000 tonnes of sea fish, with a total value of £488 million, were landed into the UK by both the UK fleet and foreign fishing vessels in 2001. Another major source of supply is the import into the UK in bulk of fish caught by other countries.

In 2001 demersal fish (living on or near the bottom of the sea) accounted for 43 per cent by weight of total landings by British fishing vessels, pelagic fish (living in mid water) for 28 per cent and shellfish for 30 per cent. Landings of all types of fish (excluding salmon and trout) by British fishing vessels into the UK totalled 458,300 tonnes. Haddock and cod represented 14 and 15 per cent of the total value of demersal and pelagic fish landed respectively. The quayside value of landings of all sea fish, including shellfish, by British vessels in 2001 was £424 million.

Catches of crabs, lobsters, scampi and other shellfish have increased to supply a rising demand. In 1985 British fishermen landed 75,000 tonnes of shellfish worth about £65 million. By 2001 landings were 136,200 tonnes worth £167 million.

Some of the species caught by UK fishing vessels find a more favourable market overseas and these species are usually exported or landed directly abroad. In 2001 UK vessels landed directly into non-UK ports 279,500 tonnes of sea fish with a value of £151 million.

Britain aims to achieve the EU target for reducing its fishing fleet by both cutting numbers and limiting the time some vessels spend at sea. At the end of 2001 the UK fleet consisted of 7,721 vessels, including 416 greater than 24.39 m. There are an estimated 14,600 professional fishermen in Britain (see Table 26.8).

A national licensing scheme now limits the shellfish fleet to 3,000, mainly small boats. Minimum landing sizes for shellfish to be introduced across the EU in 2002, and which make it illegal to land a lobster smaller than 87 mm, already apply in the UK.

There is a substantial fish processing industry of around 540 businesses which employ some 22,000 people. At the retail level, there are approximately 1,400 fishmongers. An increasing proportion of all fish (69 per cent by volume and 67 per cent by value, excluding canned produce) is sold through supermarkets. A small proportion of the catch is used to make fish oils and animal feeds.

Aquaculture

Fish farming is a significant industry in remote rural areas on the west coast of Scotland, as well as in Orkney, Shetland and the Western Isles, producing primarily salmon. In addition, species such as cod, halibut and turbot are entering commercial production. Trout is also farmed as a freshwater species, and various shellfish species are produced all round the coast of the UK. In 2000, total value at first sale was estimated at over £350 million, and the industry employed over 3,000 people. Production in 2000 was 130,000 tonnes of salmon, 15,000 tonnes of rainbow trout, and some 14,000 tonnes of mussels, with some farming of oysters, clams and cockles.

Aquaculture is subject to a comprehensive regulatory regime covering such issues as fish and shellfish health and disease control, control of discharges into the marine and riverine environment, site leasing and planning, and the use of medicines and other chemicals.

Common Fisheries Policy

Management of the UK's sea fisheries is subject to the EU's Common Fisheries Policy (CFP). Under the CFP, UK vessels have exclusive rights to fish

Table 26.8 UK fishing industry: summary table

	1991	1996	1999	2000	2001
Fleet size at end of year					
Number of vessels	11,411	8,667	8,039	7,818	7,721
Employment					
Number of fishermen	n/a	19,044	15,961	15,121	14,645
Total landings by UK vessels[1]					
Quantity ('000 tonnes)	787	892	836	748	738
Value (£ million)	496	635	588	550	574
Household consumption					
Quantity ('000 tonnes)	418	471	446	442	n/a

1 Figures relate to landings both in the UK and abroad.
Source: *UK Sea Fisheries Statistics*

within 6 miles of the UK coast. Certain other EU Member States have historic rights in UK waters between 6 and 12 miles. UK vessels have similar rights in other Member States' 6 to 12 mile belts. Between 12 and 200 miles, EU vessels may fish wherever they have access rights. Non-EU countries' vessels may fish in these waters if they negotiate reciprocal fisheries agreements with the EU. UK fishery limits extend to 200 miles or the median line (broadly halfway between the UK coast and the opposing coastline of another coastal state), measured from baselines on or near the coast of the UK.

The primary aim of the CFP is to ensure rational and sustainable exploitation of fish stocks through conservation and management policies designed to protect resources and reflect the needs of the fishing industry. The CFP aims to improve the balance between catching capacity and available resources by regulating the amount of fishing and the quantities of fish caught, through a system of Total Allowable Catches (TACs) based on scientific advice. These TACs are then distributed to Member States according to the system of relative stability. This means that national quota allocations are based each year on a fixed proportion reflecting, among other things, historical fishing patterns. Catch limits are complemented by a series of technical conservation measures intended to achieve more selective fishing, for example by setting rules on minimum landing sizes, minimum mesh sizes and gear design, as well as defining areas of seasonal closures, methods of fishing and target species. Opportunities to fish in third country waters are also secured through the CFP.

Stock conservation plans are in place to help conserve stocks of cod and hake which are currently below safe biological limits. All EU Member States with relevant fishing interests share the burden of reduced fishing effort and increased protection for the stocks.

A thorough review of the CFP is occurring during 2002. It is focusing on the decommissioning of some fishing boats and other measures to help conserve fish stocks.

Fish quotas

EU fisheries ministers set TACs for a wide range of stocks in December each year. The TACs are then divided into Member States' quotas. The UK's separate quotas are then allocated between various groups within the UK fishing fleet. The size and structure of the fishing fleet is governed by a licensing system (see below), and vessels work to an agreed quota of allowable catches, based on scientific assessment of fish stocks. Some allocations are managed by fishermen's organisations, known as Producer Organisations. However, overall responsibility for managing the UK's quotas rests with DEFRA and the other Fisheries Departments in the UK. Quotas, technical conservation and other management measures aim to allow balanced fish populations to renew themselves.

The 2002 quotas were decided at the EU Fisheries Council in December 2001. After pressure from the UK, an agreement was reached which attempted to balance fish stock conservation with fishing jobs, taking into account scientific advice. Key elements of the revised deal included increases in the Irish Sea cod quota (of almost 50 per cent), in the proposed quota for prawn catches in the North Sea, and in monkfish quotas.

Restrictive licensing system for fishing vessels
This system, also operated by the fisheries departments, controls the activities of the UK fishing fleet in accordance with the EU and UK aims on fleet and catch management. All engine-powered UK-registered or owned vessels which fish for profit for sea fish (other than salmon, migratory trout and eels) are required to hold a licence issued by one of the UK fisheries departments. In order to constrain the size of the fleet, additional licences are not granted. Licences must therefore be transferred or aggregated in accordance with detailed rules.

Sea Fisheries Committees
There are 12 Sea Fisheries Committees (SFCs) which regulate local sea fisheries around virtually the entire coast of England and Wales out to 6 miles. SFCs were established in the 19th century and are empowered to make bye-laws for the management and conservation of their districts' fisheries. In Scotland, inshore fisheries are regulated by measures under Scottish legislation, and local management bodies may also be established in statute to regulate specific shellfish fisheries.

Salmon and freshwater fisheries
The Environment Agency produces an annual assessment of salmon stocks and fisheries in England and Wales. The 2001 report found that the declared catch of wild salmon was down slightly from 2000 levels at 153 tonnes. The angling catch was affected by foot-and-mouth disease, when access to many rural areas was limited, and was 17 per cent below the 2000 figure.

Following the Salmon and Freshwater Fisheries Review Group report, the Government increased fisheries grant-in-aid to the Environment Agency by £3 million a year from April 2002. The Agency will be able to increase its work on conserving and restoring salmon stocks, and improving controls over unauthorised transfers of coarse and non-native fish.

Forestry

Land area covered by woodland in 2002 amounted to 16.9 per cent in Scotland, 13.9 per cent in

Table 26.9 Area of woodland by ownership and forest type, UK, as at 31 March 2002

Thousand hectares

	Conifers	Broadleaves[1]	Total productive woodland
Forestry Commission/ Forest Service			
England	156	50	206
Wales	102	11	113
Scotland	450	25	475
Northern Ireland	57	4	61
United Kingdom	765	90	855
Private woodland[2]			
England	215	682	898
Wales	64	111	175
Scotland	603	246	849
Northern Ireland	10	13	22
United Kingdom	892	1,052	1,944
Total			
England	371	733	1,104
Wales	166	122	288
Scotland	1,053	271	1,324
Northern Ireland	67	17	83
United Kingdom	**1,657**	**1,143**	**2,799**

1 Broadleaves include coppice and coppice with standards.
2 Private woodland figures for England, Scotland and Wales are based on the 1995–99 National Inventory of Woodland and Trees (NIWT) and adjusted to reflect subsequent changes. The NIWT did not include Northern Ireland.
Source: Forestry Commission

Wales, 8.5 per cent in England and 6.1 per cent in Northern Ireland. This gives a total of 11.5 per cent for the UK, or 2.79 million hectares, almost double the cover in 1947, compared with 37 per cent for the EU as a whole.

In 2001/02, 27,700 hectares of trees were planted, including both new planting and restocking (see Table 26.10).

Forestry and primary wood processing in Great Britain employed 29,500 people in 1998/99, about 43 per cent of whom were engaged in forest activity.

The UK uses a large amount of timber, paper, board and other wood products each year, equivalent to about 50 million cubic metres under

Table 26.10 New planting and restocking, UK

					Thousand hectares
	1991/92	1996/97	1999/2000	2000/01	2001/02
New planting					
Broadleaf	6.6	9.9	11.4	13.5	10.1
Conifer	11.6	7.7	6.5	5.2	3.8
Total	18.2	17.6	17.9	18.7	13.9
of which:					
Forestry Commission/Forest Service	3.4	0.6	0.3	0.3	0.3
Restocking					
Broadleaf	4.9	3.5	3.3	3.0	2.4
Conifer	11.8	11.6	11.9	12.2	11.4
Total	16.7	15.1	15.2	15.3	13.8
of which:					
Forestry Commission/Forest Service	8.7	8.4	8.8	8.9	9.1

Source: Forestry Commission and Northern Ireland Forest Service

bark. Around 85 per cent of this has to be imported at a cost of about £8 billion – the fourth largest single import commodity. The British timber industry, using wood from sustainable forests, has seen considerable investment in recent years. The volume of wood supplied from Britain's forests each year has more than doubled from 4 million cubic metres over bark standing in the 1970s to around 10 million in 2001. This is forecast to increase to over 15 million cubic metres by 2020, offering scope for further substantial investment in the processing industry.

Very few woodlands in Britain are planted without some form of grant. The Forestry Commission offers grants through the *Woodland Grant Scheme* (WGS), and operates the *Farm Woodland Premium Scheme* (FWPS) on behalf of DEFRA and SEERAD (see page 399). In Wales, there is a joint application form for farmers who enter land into the WGS and FWPS, which is administered by the Welsh Assembly Government. Both schemes aim to encourage the creation of new woodlands and the management of existing woodlands by providing money towards the cost of the work involved, although the FWPS can only be given where the WGS is also payable. Expenditure of £139 million between 2001 and 2006 on the WGS is provided for under the England Rural Development Programme.

The Forestry Commission and forestry policy

The *Forestry Commission* (www.forestry.gov.uk) is the government department responsible for

forestry throughout Great Britain. It is the UK's largest land manager and biggest single provider of countryside recreation. It has a Board of Commissioners with duties and powers prescribed by statute which, following devolution, they exercise separately in England, Scotland and Wales, under the directions of the relevant commission. DEFRA ministers direct the Commissioners' activities in England and, after consultation with Scottish ministers, the Welsh Assembly Government and the Northern Ireland Assembly, represent the UK's forestry interests within the EU and in the wider world. The Commission is responsible for advising ministers and for implementing each country's separate and distinct forestry policy.

The Commission's objectives are to:

- protect Britain's forests and woodlands;

- expand Britain's forest area;

- enhance the economic value of forest resources;

- conserve and improve the biodiversity, landscape and cultural heritage of forests and woodlands;

- develop opportunities for woodland recreation; and

- increase public understanding and community participation in forestry.

The Forestry Commission has two executive agencies. *Forest Enterprise* is responsible for managing the forests and woodlands owned by the nation. It has a total forest estate of 794,000 hectares of woodland with complementary land for grazing, conservation and recreation, and employs around 2,300 staff. A further 3,000 people work in the forests as contractors or are employed by the timber purchasers.

In 2001/02, 1,503 hectares of land were acquired by the Commission. It disposed of 3,090 hectares.

Forest Research aims to deliver high-quality scientific research and surveys, to inform the development of forestry policies and practices, and to promote high standards of sustainable forest management. It is the principal organisation in the UK engaged in forestry and tree-related research.

The Commission is undertaking a review of forestry administration in England, Scotland and Wales, examining options for further decentralisation of forestry policy and management.

Forestry initiatives

The new National Forest (*www.nationalforest.org*) covers 520 sq km of the English Midlands, spanning parts of Derbyshire, Leicestershire and Staffordshire and incorporating the towns of Ashby-de-la-Zouch, Burton upon Trent, Coalville and Swadlincote. The original 6 per cent wooded cover in the area has been doubled, resulting in some 470 new forest sites covering 3,100 hectares. A total of 4 million trees have been planted so far, and 30 million will eventually be planted (60 per cent broadleaf and 40 per cent conifer). The aim is to increase woodland cover to about one-third of the area, with a third remaining in agriculture and the remainder comprising the towns and villages. For Community Forests, see page 271.

Forestry in Northern Ireland

The *Forest Service* (*www.forestserviceni.gov.uk*) is an executive agency within DARD and promotes the interests of forestry through sustainable management and expansion of state-owned forests. It encourages private forestry through grant aid for planting.

The Service offered over 400,000 cubic metres of timber for sale in 2001/02, with receipts of

£4.6 million. Forestry and timber processing employ about 1,050 people. It is estimated that some 2 million people visited Northern Irish forests during the year.

Further reading

Agriculture in the United Kingdom 2001. DEFRA, SEERAD, DARD and NAWAD. The Stationery Office, 2002.

Farming and Food: a sustainable future. Policy Commission, 2002.

Forestry Statistics. Forestry Commission, 2002.

Milk Task Force Report. DEFRA, 2002.

The Report of the BSE Inquiry. The Stationery Office, 2000.

Scottish Agriculture Facts and Figures 2001. Scottish Executive, 2002.

United Kingdom Sea Fisheries Statistics. DEFRA. The Stationery Office.

Statistical Review of Northern Ireland Agriculture 2001. Department of Agriculture and Rural Development, 2002.

Departmental report of the Department for Environment, Food and Rural Affairs, Forestry Commission and the Office of Water Services 2002. Cm 5422. The Stationery Office, 2002.

Websites

DEFRA
www.defra.gov.uk

Department of Agriculture and Rural Development (Northern Ireland)
www.dardni.gov.uk

National Assembly for Wales
www.wales.gov.uk/subiagriculture

Scottish Executive Environment and Rural Affairs Department
www.scotland.gov.uk/who/dept_rural.asp

27 Manufacturing and construction

Introduction

Manufacturing continues to play an important but declining role in the UK economy, accounting for 17.5 per cent of gross value added (GVA)[1] (at current basic prices) in 2001 and for 14.5 per cent of employment (over 3.7 million people) in December 2001. Service industries now generate over four times as much gross domestic product (GDP) and almost five-and-a-half times as much employment.

The regions with the highest proportion of employees in manufacturing are the East Midlands and West Midlands (both 21 per cent). London has the lowest at just 7 per cent. Overseas companies have a strong presence.

The recession in the early 1990s led to a decline in manufacturing output, but it began to rise again in 1993. By 2000, the volume of output was over 13 per cent above the level in 1992, but then fell by 2.3 per cent in 2001. Some industries, notably electrical and optical equipment – where output was up by 68 per cent between 1992 and 2001 – and chemicals and man-made fibres (up 31 per cent), have achieved substantial growth following the recession. However, output of some other sectors was below the 1992 level – textiles and

Manufacturing and construction output – then and now

	1995 = 100		% change
	1951	2001	
Manufacturing	47.4	102.8	+117
Construction	45.1	113.7	+152

textile products, for example, was 34 per cent down.

Relative sizes of enterprises are shown in Tables 27.2 and 27.3, with output and investment, industrial production and employment in Tables 27.4 to 27.6.

The construction industry contributed 5.4 per cent of GVA in 2001. Following a period of marked decline as recession affected the industry in the early 1990s, output picked up and was 18 per cent higher in 2001 than in 1993, and above pre-recession levels for the first time. Output grew strongly, by 3.6 per cent, in 2001.

Manufacturing

An outline of the main manufacturing sectors follows, in order of their significance to the economy in terms of gross value added. For each

---

1 Gross value added represents the difference between the value of the output of goods and services produced by a company and the value of the goods and services or raw materials used up in the production of the output.

Table 27.1 Manufacturing, UK[1]

	Number of enterprises	Total turnover	GVA at basic prices	Total employment	Total net capital expenditure
		£ million	£ million	Thousand	£ million
1998	169,376	460,563	149,906	4,354	20,399
1999	170,196	461,829	150,313	4,230	18,295
2000	167,476	474,459	151,096	4,091	17,313

1 Includes coke, refined petroleum products and nuclear fuel (see chapter 28).
Source: ONS Annual Business Inquiry

Table 27.2 Manufacturing – size of UK businesses by turnover, 2002

Annual turnover (£ thousand)	Number of businesses	Percentage
1–49	22,665	15.5
50–99	24,875	17.0
100–249	31,625	21.7
250–499	20,610	14.1
500–999	16,465	11.3
1,000–1,999	11,565	7.9
2,000–4,999	9,180	6.3
5,000–9,999	3,950	2.7
10,000–49,999	3,900	2.7
50,000+	1,195	0.8
Total	**146,035**	**100.0**

Source: Office for National Statistics, *Size Analysis of United Kingdom Businesses*

Table 27.3 Manufacturing – size of UK businesses by employment, 2002[1]

Employment size	Number of businesses	Percentage
1–9	103,370	71.1
10–19	17,840	12.3
20–49	13,335	9.2
50–99	5,295	3.6
100–199	2,750	1.9
200–499	1,815	1.2
500–999	635	0.4
1,000+	425	0.3
Total	**145,460**	**100.0**

1 Not all businesses have been allocated by employment size – hence the difference in totals between this table and Table 27.2.
Source: Office for National Statistics, *Size Analysis of United Kingdom Businesses*

sector a table summarises key indicators in that sector for the latest available three years. This data is collected by the ONS Annual Business Inquiry (ABI) and allows for the approximate estimation of concepts such as total output and GVA. The 2000 inquiry sampled 69,600 businesses. The figures shown will not be the same as those published in the UK National Accounts, which are subject to a balancing process. ABI figures for employment are collected on a set day in December and will not necessarily match those from the separate ONS Labour Force Survey,

Table 27.4 Output and investment in UK manufacturing, 2001

			£ million
1992 Standard Industrial Classification (SIC) category	GVA at current basic prices	% contribution	Business investment at current prices
Food, drink and tobacco	21,102	13.8	2,212
Textiles, leather and clothing			
Textiles and textile products	5,076	3.3	276
Leather and leather products	702	0.5	33
Wood and wood products	2,368	1.5	227
Pulp, paper and paper products, publishing and printing	21,242	13.9	2,115
Coke, refined petroleum products and nuclear fuel[1]	3,258	2.1	454
Chemicals, chemical products and man-made fibres	16,419	10.7	2,749
Rubber and plastic products	7,512	4.9	754
Other non-metallic mineral products	5,228	3.4	608
Basic metals and fabricated metal products	15,906	10.4	1,213
Engineering and allied industries			
Machinery and equipment not elsewhere classified	12,708	8.3	752
Electrical and optical equipment	19,732	12.9	1,821
Transport equipment	15,242	10.0	2,778
Other manufacturing	6,635	4.3	430
Total	**153,132**	**100.0**	**16,422**

1 Covered in chapter 28.
Source: ONS *United Kingdom National Accounts 2002 – the Blue Book* and ONS Quarterly Business Investment Inquiry

Table 27.5 Index of production, UK

				1995 = 100
1992 SIC category	1996	1999	2000	2001
Food, drink and tobacco	100.9	100.8	99.6	101.2
Textiles, leather and clothing	98.2	82.5	78.3	68.7
Textiles and textile products	98.2	81.9	78.3	67.3
Leather and leather products	98.6	86.6	79.3	79.0
Wood and wood products	98.1	89.7	91.7	90.2
Pulp, paper and paper products, publishing and printing	98.0	99.1	98.9	97.2
Coke, refined petroleum products and nuclear fuel[1]	91.8	79.4	83.3	79.6
Chemicals, chemical products and man-made fibres	100.6	107.4	111.8	116.2
Rubber and plastic products	98.8	100.9	99.9	95.7
Other non-metallic mineral products	96.6	95.7	95.9	96.5
Basic metals and fabricated metal products	99.9	95.2	95.6	92.7
Engineering and allied industries	103.8	114.0	120.3	114.7
Machinery and equipment not elsewhere classified	98.0	90.1	90.2	91.1
Electrical and optical equipment	104.9	126.1	144.5	132.6
Transport equipment	107.7	120.2	115.5	112.4
Other manufacturing	102.0	106.6	104.7	103.8
Total manufacturing	100.7	103.1	105.2	102.8

1 Covered in chapter 28.
Source: Office for National Statistics

Table 27.6 Employee jobs in manufacturing industries, UK

		Thousands, seasonally adjusted, June	
1992 SIC category	1991	1996	2001
Food, drink and tobacco	531	474	493
Textiles, leather and clothing	463	396	251
Wood and wood products	87	85	80
Pulp, paper, printing and publishing	460	465	450
Chemicals and man-made fibres	276	252	235
Rubber and plastic products	202	241	227
Non-metallic mineral, metal and metal products	778	719	631
Machinery and equipment	448	390	353
Electrical and optical equipment	485	499	477
Transport equipment	438	393	389
Coke and nuclear fuel,[1] other manufacturing	210	221	249
Total manufacturing	**4,379**	**4,138**	**3,838**

1 Covered in chapter 28.
Source: ONS *Labour Market Trends*

Table 27.7 Pulp, paper and paper products, publishing and printing, UK

	Number of enterprises	Total turnover	GVA at basic prices	Total employment	Total net capital expenditure
		£ million	£ million	Thousand	£ million
1998	32,505	42,721	18,296	505	1,957
1999	32,884	43,387	19,280	489	1,719
2000	32,621	45,077	19,575	473	1,826

Source: ONS Annual Business Inquiry

which samples approximately 120,000 people in around 61,000 households and which is produced on a continuous basis throughout the year. ABI turnover data will also differ from that collected as part of the ONS Monthly Production Inquiry.

On occasion, statistics in the text and in some of the later tables come from sources other than National Statistics, such as trade associations. Any variations usually reflect differences in coverage of the industry concerned.

Paper, printing and publishing

In 2000 the UK pulp, paper and paper products industry had turnover of £11.8 billion and employed 98,000 people; the publishing and printing industry had turnover of £33.3 billion and employed 376,000 people. Total industry output fell by 1.7 per cent in 2001 and was less than 5 per cent higher than in 1992.

Paper

The paper and board sector is dominated by a small number of medium and large firms – 87 pulp, paper and board mills, employing 17,400 people in 2001, concentrated in north Kent, Lancashire, the West Country and central Scotland. UK production in 2001 was 6.2 million tonnes, 25 per cent higher than in 1991, with 1.2 million tonnes exported, 73 per cent to the EU. Imports amounted to 7.6 million tonnes, 84 per cent of which came from the EU and Norway. Hundreds of different grades of paper and board are converted into a wide range of products for use in industry, commerce, education, communications and distribution, and in the home. A host of speciality papers are produced for industrial use, for example filters and papers, which are subsequently coated, sensitised or laminated. There has been a significant trend towards waste-based packaging grades. Recycled paper made up 63.5 per cent of

Table 27.8 Top ten UK export destinations for books

			£ million
	1999	2000	2001
United States	201.9	212.6	213.1
Irish Republic	65.9	72.9	82.3
Germany	68.4	70.3	78.1
Netherlands	64.7	72.7	69.3
Australia	75.9	69.5	66.9
Spain	45.0	49.1	57.7
France	42.1	40.9	42.0
Japan	38.0	42.2	39.2
Italy	38.3	44.7	35.8
South Africa	33.1	33.3	34.3

Source: Department of Trade and Industry

Table 27.9 UK printing industry: top ten export categories

		£ million
	2000	2001
Books, booklets and brochures	1,019.1	1,028.3
Newspapers and periodicals	402.4	394.2
Single sheets	84.9	103.1
Trade advertising	119.0	101.6
Postcards and greetings cards	69.7	62.6
Printed labels	57.5	56.5
Cartons, boxes, etc	60.8	55.6
Security printing	48.6	35.8
Maps and charts	17.0	26.9
Children's books	15.6	19.9

Source: HM Customs and Excise

the raw material for UK newspapers in 2001, compared with 60.3 per cent in 2000 (including imports).

Printing and publishing

Unlike the paper and board sector, the printing industry in particular has many small businesses – only about 650 firms employ more than 50 people and approximately 90 per cent of firms employ fewer than 20 employees. Much publishing and printing employment and output is carried out in firms based in south-east England. Mergers have led to the formation of large groups in newspaper, magazine and book publishing. The British book-publishing industry is a major exporter, with exports of £1.2 billion in 2001, 2.1 per cent higher than in 2000 (see also Table 27.8). The United States maintained its place as the largest export market, followed by the Irish Republic. There were 119,000 new titles (including new editions) issued in 2001, a 2.2 per cent increase on 2000.

The UK printing industry had an annual turnover of £13 billion, employing 170,000 people in 2001. It has undergone significant technological change recently, with digital technology enabling much greater automation and standardisation. With exports of £2.0 billion and imports of £1.6 billion, the printing industry had a £0.4 billion trade surplus in 2001. Exports are dominated by books and periodicals (see Table 27.9).

Food, drink and tobacco

In 2000 there were nearly 7,900 enterprises employing 527,000 people in the UK food and drink manufacturing and processing industry, with a combined turnover of £65.7 billion. The industry has accounted for a growing proportion of total domestic food supply since the 1940s. The largest concentration of enterprises is in the production of bread, cakes and fresh pastry goods, followed by those engaged in processing and preserving meat and meat products. The greatest number of food and drink manufacturing jobs and facilities are in the South East and London (20.2 per cent of the total for Great Britain),

Scotland (13.6 per cent) and the North West (11.1 per cent). Spirits production gives Scotland the highest concentration of employment in the alcoholic and soft drinks manufacturing industry, with a significant proportion of jobs in its economically deprived rural areas. The biggest food and drinks export category in 2001 was alcoholic drinks, with exports of £3.1 billion, accounting for 36 per cent of the total value of food and drink sales overseas. The largest food-exporting sector was biscuits and confectionery, worth £681 million. As well as the leading companies involved in food and drink manufacturing and processing, there are many specialist small and medium-sized firms, supplying high-quality 'niche' products, often to small retail outlets, such as delicatessens.

Frozen foods and chilled convenience foods, such as frozen potato products and ready-prepared meals, fish and shellfish dishes, salads and pasta, together with yogurts, desserts and instant snacks, have formed some of the fastest-growing sectors of the food market in recent years. The trend towards snacking – eating less, more often – and higher consumption outside the home means that snacks are filling the gap left by the decline of the traditional family meal. Many new low-fat and fat-free items have been introduced, ranging from dairy products to complete prepared meals. Organic foods have also become more widely available. There has been a substantial rise in sales of vegetarian foods (both natural vegetable dishes and vegetable-based substitutes of meat products, where soya plays a big role). For genetically modified foods, see chapter 26.

Bread and morning goods

The UK market is worth over £3 billion each year and is one of the largest sectors in the food industry – total volume is about 2.9 million tonnes, equivalent to over 9 million large loaves

Table 27.10 Food products, beverages and tobacco, UK

	Number of enterprises	Total turnover	GVA at basic prices	Total employment	Total net capital expenditure
		£ million	£ million	Thousand	£ million
1998	8,268	73,482	19,351	541	2,763
1999	8,124	73,655	19,977	542	2,725
2000	7,909	74,105	20,628	534	2,296

Source: ONS Annual Business Inquiry

British bakers have developed a bread containing a range of nutrients more usually found in sprouts and broccoli. This uses a form of vitamin C which survives the cooking process in a form the body can absorb – in traditional baking vitamin C is used as a raising agent, but its benefits are lost. Each slice of bread contains nearly one-fifth of the recommended daily allowance of vitamin C for children. The range of sliced white bread and white rolls also contains vitamins D and B complex. The product was launched in May 2002.

every day. The larger baking companies produce 81 per cent of bread sold in the UK by volume, with in-store bakeries (ISBs) within supermarkets accounting for about 15 per cent and high street retail bakers the remaining 4 per cent. Some ISBs use the bake-off method, where dough is part-baked and frozen, to be baked off later at the retail outlet – this is particularly popular at smaller supermarkets. The two largest bread producers are Allied Bakeries and British Bakeries, with 25 manufacturing sites in mainland Britain and three in Northern Ireland between them. By volume, 76 per cent of bread sold in the UK is white, 16 per cent wholemeal and 8 per cent brown. Morning goods, or bakery snacks (including rolls and baps, scones, teacakes and croissants), account for 25 per cent by volume of the bread market. Sandwiches are the UK's most frequently consumed snack food and have a wider range of distribution outlets than other bread sales. The sandwich market was valued at £3.5 billion in 2001.

Dairy products

Around 24 per cent of household liquid milk supplies in Great Britain are distributed through a doorstep delivery system employing about 11,100 people, although the proportion is declining as supermarkets take a greater share of milk sales. Household consumption of liquid milk per head – 2.1 litres (3.8 pints) a week – is among the highest in the world. Consumption of semi-skimmed (containing between 1.5 and 1.8 per cent fat) and skimmed milk (not more than 0.5 per cent fat) continues to grow, accounting for 68 per cent of total milk sales in 2001. The British dairy industry accounted for 64 per cent of butter and 65 per cent of cheese supplies to the domestic market in 2001, and achieves significant sales overseas. Over 400 different types of cheese are produced in the UK. Cheddar accounts for over 55 per cent of all household cheese purchases; other well-known

varieties include Caerphilly, Cheshire, Double Gloucester, Red Leicester, Stilton and Wensleydale.

Beer

Beer (including lager) production in 2001, at 56.8 million hectolitres, was 2.8 per cent higher than in 2000; beer released for home consumption amounted to 58.2 million hectolitres. Exports were valued at £225 million in 2001, amounting to 3.2 million hectolitres. The brewing industry currently has six major national brewery groups, 44 regional/family brewers and about 400 micro-breweries. Throughout the world brewers use British malt, made almost entirely from home-grown barley. Beer consumption per head in the UK in 2001 was 171 pints, equivalent to 28 million pints sold every day or 10 billion pints a year. Lager accounted for 66 per cent of all sales, up from 64 per cent in 2000, but there is still a strong demand for the vast range of traditional cask-conditioned and brewery-conditioned ales and stouts.

Spirits

Home-produced whisky production in 2001 was 3.69 million hectolitres, a 2 per cent increase on 2000. The Scotch whisky industry is one of the UK's top export earners, with overseas sales worth

Table 27.11 Alcoholic drink production, UK

			Thousand hectolitres
	1991	1996	2001
Beer	59,552	58,072	56,802
Potable spirits			
Home-produced whisky	4,256	4,462	3,692
Other	219	406	676
Released for home consumption			
Beer	63,038	59,894	58,234
Wine of fresh grapes			
Still	6,266	7,326	9,821
Sparkling	316	358	515
Made wine	699	2,293	4,076
Cider and perry	3,713	5,656	5,911
Spirits			
Home-produced whisky	382	321	321
Other[1]	547	495	647

1 Includes imported spirits.
Source: HM Customs and Excise

Table 27.12 Top ten overseas markets for Scotch whisky

Country	2000	2001	% share in 2001
			Thousand bottles
France	136,449	153,941	15.2
Spain	158,905	137,428	13.6
United States	119,172	110,018	10.9
Japan	52,782	70,139	6.9
South Korea	35,876	45,381	4.5
Venezuela	39,556	43,779	4.3
Greece	34,036	38,015	3.8
Thailand	34,054	34,015	3.4
Germany	30,541	34,000	3.4
Australia	31,435	25,674	2.5
Total exports	**989,536**	**1,012,970**	**100.0**
of which:			
European Union	447,573	448,732	44.3

Source: Scotch Whisky Association

£2.3 billion in 2001, 6.4 per cent higher than in 2000. By volume, about 90 per cent of sales was exported to over 200 countries worldwide – the top ten overseas markets are shown in Table 27.12. Some 10,700 people work in the Scotch whisky industry and a further 30,000 are employed in associated sectors, for instance supplying ingredients and materials. There are around 85 malt whisky distilleries in Scotland, the majority in Speyside and in the Highlands, with a further seven on Islay and three in the Lowlands. In addition, seven distilleries produce grain whisky – most Scotch consumed is a blend of malt and grain. Some of the best-known single malt Scotch whiskies include Glenfiddich, Glen Grant, Glenmorangie and Macallan. Gin and vodka production is another important part of the spirits industry, with 64 per cent of UK-produced gin and 28 per cent of vodka exported, worth £204 million in 2001.

Wine, cider and perry

In a highly competitive market, English and Welsh wines have a distinctive local identity. There are nearly 400 commercial vineyards, covering approximately 800 hectares of land, nearly all in the southern half of the two countries. Most of the production is white wine, mainly from Germanic vines. Quality continues to improve with a combination of more experienced winemakers, modern technologies and better winemaking equipment. Cider and perry are made predominantly in the west and south-west of England, notably in Herefordshire, Somerset and Devon. Bulmers, one of the big two UK producers, is the world's largest cider maker.

Soft drinks

The soft drinks industry produces still and carbonated drinks, dilutable drinks, fruit juices and juice drinks, and bottled waters. The UK market was worth £8.6 billion by retail value in 2001, with Coca-Cola Enterprises the largest supplier. Soft drinks are one of the fastest-growing sectors of the grocery trade, responsible for introducing many innovative products each year. In 2001 UK consumption of soft drinks was 12.4 billion litres, compared with 8.3 billion litres in 1989, an increase of almost one-half. Sales of energy and sports drinks reached £750 million in 2001, a fourfold increase since 1996. Bottled waters – natural mineral waters, spring and table waters – experienced the second fastest growth within the sector between 1996 and 2001, averaging increases in volume of 12 per cent a year, and with sales of £900 million in the UK in 2001. Sales of carbonates registered the smallest increase in sales in 2001, with 2 per cent growth.

Tobacco

In 2001 around 7,100 people in the UK were directly employed in tobacco manufacturing, with a further 125,000 jobs indirectly supported in supplier industries and through forward linkages into distribution and retailing. Three major manufacturers supply the market, including British American Tobacco, the second largest tobacco company in the world. UK consumers

Table 27.13 Tobacco – UK sales to trade

	1991	1996	2001
Sales to trade[1]			
Cigarettes (billion)	95.9	81.4	55.7
Handrolling tobacco (tonnes)	4,095	2,220	2,775
Pipe tobacco (thousand kg)	1,805	1,030	590
Cigars (million)	1,445	1,095	892

1 Based on UK manufacturers' sales to the wholesale and retail trade and estimates of imported goods.
Source: Tobacco Manufacturers' Association

Table 27.14 Electrical and optical equipment, UK

	Number of enterprises	Total turnover £ million	GVA at basic prices £ million	Total employment Thousand	Total net capital expenditure £ million
1998	16,026	61,037	19,203	533	2,688
1999	16,618	64,949	19,613	531	1,962
2000	16,443	69,217	21,137	523	2,386

Source: ONS Annual Business Inquiry

spent £14.7 billion on tobacco products in 2001, of which £7.7 billion was accounted for by excise duty. The figures in Table 27.13 show a substantial decline in sales, although in recent years there has been a rapid growth in smuggling and legitimate cross-border shopping. Official estimates of revenue lost through tobacco smuggling in 2000/01 were £3.5 billion, compared with £2.9 billion in 1999/2000. The industry achieved significant export sales – £931 million in 2001 – with Europe, the Middle East and Africa important overseas markets. The UK tobacco industry remains one of the top ten balance-of-payments earners in the UK economy.

Electrical and optical equipment

In 2000, 37 per cent of turnover in this industry was in the radio, TV and communications equipment sector, 23 per cent in office machinery and computers, 23 per cent in electrical machinery

Table 27.15 Electrical and optical equipment – turnover and orders, UK

			£ billion
	1999	2000	2001
Home			
Orders on hand	9.5	11.3	11.6
New orders[1]	35.2	37.6	33.1
Turnover	33.2	35.9	32.8
Export			
Orders on hand	6.6	7.3	4.8
New orders[1]	28.8	31.3	24.0
Turnover	28.4	30.6	26.5
Total			
Orders on hand	16.2	18.5	16.4
New orders[1]	64.0	68.9	57.1
Turnover	61.6	66.6	59.3

1 Net of cancellations.
Source: ONS Monthly Production Inquiry

and 17 per cent in medical, precision and optical equipment and watches. Total output had been rising sharply up to 2000, although it fell by over 8 per cent in 2001; nevertheless it was 68 per cent higher than in 1992. Production of office machinery and computers rose by 281 per cent between 1992 and 2001, while radio, TV and communications equipment output was up by 91 per cent. However, output of medical and optical instruments was only 10 per cent higher, while that of electrical machinery and apparatus rose by just 2 per cent.

Southern England provides a substantial proportion of employment (especially sales and administrative jobs) in these sectors, with Scotland and Wales having been important areas for inward investors. Scotland's electronics industry ('Silicon Glen' – in effect all of central Scotland) directly employed about 41,600 people in 1999. In 2001 electrical and instrument engineering accounted for exports worth £10.8 billion, 58.4 per cent of Scotland's manufactured exports, up from 56.4 per cent in 2000.

Many of the world's leading overseas-based multinational electronics firms have substantial manufacturing investment in the UK. The main electronic consumer goods produced are television sets, with UK production concentrated in the high-value market and with an increasing proportion of widescreen and digital sets. High-fidelity audio and video equipment is also produced.

The computer industry in the UK produces an extensive range of systems for all uses (for information on software, see page 472). There are several multinational computer manufacturers in the UK; others have concentrated on developing new lines for specialised markets.

A broad range of other electrical machinery and apparatus is produced in the UK by both British and foreign companies, covering power plant, electric motors, generators, transformers, switchgear, insulated wire and cable (including optical fibre cables for telecommunications), and lighting equipment.

Recent years have seen the development of electronic service providers – contract electronic manufacturers – manufacturing and assembling products to the specification of other companies. This global trend has encouraged some multinational producers to move away from manufacture to become designers, developers, marketers or sellers of their products; the UK is one of the leading locations in Europe for this type of business.

Communications equipment

Domestic telecommunications equipment manufacturers have invested heavily in facilities to meet rapidly increasing demand for telecommunications services (see chapter 17). The main products are switching and transmission equipment, telephones and terminals. Transmission equipment and cables for telecommunications and information networks include submarine and high-specification data-carrying cables.

The UK is among Europe's leading markets and manufacturing bases for mobile communications (see page 242) and many producers have UK production or design centres. Fibre optics are a UK invention. There has been a general downturn in the telecommunications sector due mainly to the downturn in the world economy. This has led to rationalisation and job losses across the sector.

Another sector of the industry manufactures radio communications equipment, radar, radio and sonar navigational aids for ships and aircraft, thermal imaging systems, alarms and signalling apparatus, public broadcasting equipment and other capital goods. Radar was invented in the UK and British firms are still in the forefront of technological advances. Solid-state secondary surveillance radar is being supplied to numerous overseas civil aviation operators.

Medical electronics

The high demand for advanced medical equipment in the UK stems from its comprehensive healthcare system and extensive clinical research and testing facilities in the chemical, biological, physical and molecular sciences. British scientists and engineers have made important contributions to basic R&D in endoscopy, computerised tomography scanning, magnetic resonance imaging (pioneered in the UK), ultrasonic imaging, CADiagnosis and renal analysis. Firms in the UK medical electronics sector continue their tradition of developing and manufacturing a range of medical equipment for domestic and overseas health sectors.

Instrumentation and control

The instrumentation and control sector covers the design, development and manufacture of scientific and industrial equipment and systems for analysis, measurement, testing and control. The instrumentation sector is generally broken down into six specific categories: navigation and surveying; electronic and electrical testing; laboratory/analytical; process monitoring and control; automotive; and drafting and dimensional measurement. The UK instrumentation and control sector has an estimated annual output of £5 billion, with a trade surplus of £0.8 billion in 2001. The sector is diverse, with over 3,300 enterprises, employing 91,000 people in 2000.

Chemicals and chemical products

The chemicals industry is one of the primary manufacturing sectors in the UK. Over 37 per cent of turnover in 2000 was in the manufacture of basic chemicals, with a further 26 per cent in pharmaceutical products. Sales for a range of chemical products are shown in Table 27.17. The sector underpins much of the rest of UK manufacturing industry, with chemicals being essential supplies for most other industrial processes. Growth in output was strong in 2001 – up 3.9 per cent – and was over 31 per cent higher than in 1992.

It is a diverse industry, with important representation in all principal chemical sectors – ranging from bulk petrochemicals to low-volume, high-value specialised organics. It includes key industrial materials, such as plastics and synthetic rubber, and other products such as man-made fibres, soap and detergents, cosmetics, adhesives, dyes and inks, and intermediate products for the pharmaceutical and a range of other downstream industries.

Table 27.16 Chemicals, chemical products and man-made fibres, UK

	Number of enterprises	Total turnover	GVA at basic prices	Total employment	Total net capital expenditure
		£ million	£ million	Thousand	£ million
1998	4,065	44,800	14,388	273	3,174
1999	4,029	46,264	14,763	261	2,899
2000	3,961	47,404	14,918	247	2,712

Source: ONS Annual Business Inquiry

Table 27.17 Chemicals – UK manufacturers' sales by industry[1]

			£ million
	1999	2000	2001
Basic chemicals and pesticides			
Industrial gases	530	n/a	539
Dyes and pigments	1,049	1,095	1,067
Other inorganic basic chemicals	1,251	1,155	1,159
Other organic basic chemicals	4,152	5,412	5,740
Fertilisers and nitrogen compounds	737	714	596
Plastics in primary forms	3,500	3,775	3,642
Synthetic rubber in primary forms	n/a	351	323
Pesticides and other agrochemical products	725	1,049	1,129
Pharmaceutical products			
Basic products	521	666	705
Preparations	7,298	7,264	7,986
Soaps, detergents; cleaning and polishing preparations	1,922	1,917	1,941
Perfumes and essential oils			
Perfumes and toilet preparations	2,529	2,656	2,584
Essential oils	526	n/a	612
Other chemical products			
Paints, varnishes and similar coatings; printing ink and mastic	2,627	2,600	2,512
Explosives	107	109	n/a
Glues and gelatines	353	318	342
Photographic chemical material	n/a	605	361
Prepared unrecorded media	141	131	n/a
Other chemical products not elsewhere classified	2,315	2,382	2,097
Man-made fibres	673	739	659

1 Where indicated as not available, data have been suppressed to avoid identifying individual enterprises.
Source: ONS PRODCOM (PRODucts of the European COMmunity)

Bulk chemicals

The UK's North Sea oil and gas provide accessible feedstocks for its large organics sector, including such products as ethylene, propylene, benzene and paraxylene. These provide the basic building blocks for the manufacture of many chemical products, including plastics whose strength, durability and light weight have led to their increasing use in transport and packaging applications; and synthetic fibres such as nylon and polyester used in textiles, clothing and home furnishings.

There is substantial inorganics production, including sulphuric acid (947,000 tonnes in 2001), chlorine and caustic soda, based on minerals such as salt, sulphur, and phosphate ores, or reaction between gases. These also serve many other chemical processes.

Formulated products

The UK is strong in formulated consumer products, such as decorative paint, home laundry and cleaning products and personal care items like toothpaste, shampoos and skincare products, as well as a wide range of industrial speciality products such as adhesives, inks and lubricants.

Fine chemicals

Fine chemicals meet specific needs through highly sophisticated product and process development. Active ingredients for the pharmaceutical and agrochemical sectors are at the forefront of this kind of innovation. In recent years, the application of chirality[2] in synthesis has allowed firms to make drugs and agrochemicals more closely tailored to specific targets. Leading-edge research by international pharmaceutical and agrochemical companies in the UK is supported both by a strong academic research capability and a network of specialist manufacturers of 'fine' chemicals. The latter specialise in the highly skilled processes needed to produce commercial quantities of the complex molecules identified by the pharmaceutical and agrochemical companies' research.

Pharmaceuticals

The UK pharmaceuticals industry, largely based in the South East, North West and North East of England, is the world's third largest exporter of medicines, accounting for 12 per cent of the developed world's export market. Research-driven, it is one of the UK's most dynamic industries, of key importance to the economy. Exports in 2001 were worth £10 billion, contributing to a trade surplus of around £2.4 billion. The principal overseas markets are Western Europe, North America and Japan. Recently, the largest growth has been in medicines that act on the cardiovascular system, followed by central nervous system and alimentary tract remedies. The total UK market for pharmaceuticals was estimated to be worth about £9.3 billion in 2001 (of which

prescription medicines accounted for approximately 80 per cent).

Around 355 pharmaceutical companies operate in the UK, with indigenous and US-owned multinationals dominating production. GlaxoSmithKline and AstraZeneca (UK-Swedish) are the two largest UK-based companies (see page 343).

Some 65,000 people are directly employed in the UK pharmaceutical industry, with another 250,000 in related sectors. About a third are engaged in R&D, expenditure on which grew by 162 per cent between 1990 and 2000. The industry invested £3.0 billion in UK-based R&D in 2001, around 25 per cent of all UK manufacturing industry R&D. AstraZeneca and GlaxoSmithKline are the UK's top two companies in terms of R&D expenditure, with the US companies Pfizer, Merck and Eli Lilly, and the Swiss company Novartis also significant investors.

Major developments pioneered in the UK include semi-synthetic penicillins and cephalosporins, both powerful antibiotics, and new treatments for ulcers, asthma, arthritis, meningitis C, cancer, migraine, HIV/AIDS, coronary heart disease, hypertension, fungal infections, erectile dysfunction and schizophrenia. The UK pharmaceuticals industry is second only to the US in the discovery and development of leading medicines, including ten of the world's current top 50 best-selling drugs. There are about 20 new pharmaceutical products launched on the market each year. Among the best-selling drugs produced by the two largest UK-owned companies are:

- GlaxoSmithKline – Seroxat/Paxil (depression), Augmentin (bacterial), Avandia (diabetes), Flixotide/Flovent and Seretide/Advair (asthma); and

- AstraZeneca – Losec/Prilosec (gastric/anti-ulcer), Nexium (successor to Losec), Zestril (hypertension), Seroquel (schizophrenia/Parkinson's disease/Alzheimer's disease) and Zoladex (cancer).

The most significant UK manufacturing investment in 2001 was AstraZeneca's announcement of a planned US$109 million (over £70 million) expansion at Alderley Park/Macclesfield (Cheshire).

---

2 Chiral compounds are mirror images of each other, analogous to left- and right-handed forms. One form may be more effective, or safer, than the other.

Biotechnology

The UK has the leading biotechnology sector in Europe, with over 550 companies (approximately 29 per cent of the number in Europe), employing over 40,000 people. UK companies have a particular strength in healthcare which includes some of the largest biotechnology companies in Europe, such as Celltech, Cambridge Antibody Technology and Oxford GlycoSciences. Of the potential new drugs under development in Europe, around 50 per cent are from publicly quoted UK companies. Companies are clustered particularly around Cambridge, Oxford, London, the South East and Scotland. The industry benefits strongly from the UK's science base. Bioscience research in UK universities is of world renown, and the major research laboratories of leading pharmaceutical multinationals are based here. The UK has a number of world-class research institutes, such as the Sanger Centre in Cambridge, which played an important part in the Human Genome project (see page 372), the Laboratory of Molecular Biology (also in Cambridge) and the Roslin Institute in Edinburgh.

Metals and fabricated metal products

The Industrial Revolution in the UK was based to a considerable extent on the manufacture of iron and steel and heavy machinery – these sectors remain important parts of the industrial economy. However, output fell by 3.0 per cent in 2001 to its lowest level since 1983.

The major areas of steel production are concentrated in south Wales and northern England, with substantial processing in the Midlands and Yorkshire. Major restructuring in the steel industry took place during the 1980s and 1990s. Steel is the most recycled material in the world – more than 80 per cent of scrap steel generated in the UK is recycled.

Total UK crude steel production was 13.5 million tonnes in 2001, 11 per cent down on 2000 and the fourth year of decline after five successive years of growth. British producers delivered 13.0 million tonnes of finished steel in 2001. The main UK markets for steel are in the engineering (24 per cent), construction (22 per cent), automotive (17 per cent) and metal goods industries (14 per cent). The UK steel industry exported 48 per cent of its output in 2001, 71 per cent of which went to other EU countries, with Germany the biggest market. Annual steel industry exports peaked in 1997 at 9.1 million tonnes before falling in successive years to 6.5 million tonnes in 2001, valued at £2.4 billion.

Corus, Europe's second largest steelmaker and the sixth biggest in the world, employed 26,700 people in the UK at the end of December 2001 and produced 83 per cent of the UK's total crude steel. Its output is based on strip mill products, plate, sections, specialist engineering steels, bars, wire rods and tubes.

Products manufactured by other UK steel companies include reinforcing bars for the construction industry, wire rods, hot rolled bars, bright bars, tubes, and wire and wire products. Production of special steels is centred on the Sheffield area and includes stainless and alloy special steels for the aerospace and offshore oil and gas industries.

Steel has had a notable success in the UK construction industry, with its market share in buildings of two or more storeys more than doubling from 30 per cent in the early 1980s to more than 70 per cent today. It has 90 per cent of the single storey market. Total iron and steel sales to the construction sector are £2.3 billion a year and consumption of constructional steelwork 1.1 million tonnes.

Table 27.18 Basic metals and fabricated metal products, UK

	Number of enterprises	Total turnover	GVA at basic prices	Total employment	Total net capital expenditure
		£ million	£ million	Thousand	£ million
1998	32,312	44,399	17,030	545	2,024
1999	32,451	40,879	15,941	535	1,464
2000	32,100	41,623	16,275	510	1,321

Source: ONS Annual Business Inquiry

Several multinational companies have plants in Britain producing non-ferrous metals from both primary and recycled raw materials. The aluminium industry supplies customers in the aerospace, transport, automotive and construction industries. Other important non-ferrous metal sectors are copper and copper alloys, used for electrical wire and cables, power generation and electrical and electronic connectors, automotive components, plumbing and building products, and components for industrial plant and machinery; lead for lead acid batteries and roofing; zinc for galvanising to protect steel; nickel, used principally as an alloying element to make stainless steel and high temperature turbine alloys; and titanium for high-strength, low-weight aerospace applications.

Fabricated metal products include those made by forging, casting, pressing, stamping and roll forming of a wide variety of metals. They are used in many different applications from automotive, aerospace and railway components to construction, domestic appliances, packaging and general hardware. Many of these products are subjected to surface engineering processes, which improve their working performance. These include electroplating, galvanising, anodising and heat treatment.

Transport equipment

Motor vehicles

New UK car registrations rose by 10.7 per cent in 2001 to 2.46 million, beating the previous record set in 1989 by 6.9 per cent. The home-produced share of the UK market in 2001 was 24.2 per cent, compared with 28.3 per cent in 2000. By customer type, the private sector took 49 per cent of the total, the fleet car sector 42 per cent and the business sector 9 per cent. Commercial vehicle registrations, at 313,000, were 5.2 per cent higher than in 2000 and the third highest figure on record.

Two long-standing UK motor vehicle plants ceased production during 2002. The last car manufactured at Vauxhall's Luton plant rolled off the production line in March, 95 years and 10 million cars after the first vehicle built there. Production of cars and vans ended at Ford's Dagenham plant in February after more than 70 years. Almost 11 million cars, trucks and tractors had been built there. However, Ford is investing heavily in its diesel engine plant at Dagenham to enhance its status as Europe's centre for excellence.

Although car production, at 1.5 million, was 9.1 per cent lower than in 2000, it has risen by almost 21 per cent since 1991. Traditional home markets no longer dominate production by vehicle manufacturers – exports accounted for 60 per cent of production in 2001 compared with only 31 per cent in 1990. Despite being 15.9 per cent lower than in 2000, 894,000 passenger cars were produced for export in 2001, more than twice as many as in 1990. Commercial vehicle production in 2001 rose by 11.8 per cent to 193,000, reversing a downward trend since 1997; almost 50 per cent, or 96,000 units, was for export. The sector is dominated by light commercial vehicles (van derivatives of passenger cars).

In 2001 there were two particularly significant all-new model launches, with the BMW Mini produced at its Oxford plant, and the Jaguar 'X' type, produced at Ford's Halewood plant. Both models have made an immediate impact in the UK and also in export markets around the world.

The UK is an increasing force in engine production as a result of major recent investments. BMW's new Hams Hall (West Midlands) plant produces 50 per cent of the company's engines, all for export, while Ford

Table 27.19 Transport equipment, UK

	Number of enterprises	Total turnover £ million	GVA at basic prices £ million	Total employment Thousand	Total net capital expenditure £ million
1998	5,536	62,933	17,157	427	2,948
1999	5,921	63,239	17,955	417	2,749
2000	5,772	61,366	15,968	404	2,608

Source: ONS Annual Business Inquiry

Table 27.20 UK car and commercial vehicle production

Thousands and percentages

	1999	2000	2001
Passenger cars			
Total production	1,786.6	1,641.5	1,492.4
of which:			
1,000cc and under	6.3	5.9	6.3
1,001cc to 1,600cc	43.4	41.2	42.4
1,601cc to 2,500cc	42.5	44.1	42.5
2,501cc and over	7.8	8.9	8.8
Production for export	1,138.5	1,063.0	894.3
of which:			
1,000cc and under	6.7	5.3	6.3
1,001cc to 1,600cc	38.6	35.3	36.9
1,601cc to 2,500cc	44.7	47.9	44.8
2,501cc and over	10.0	11.4	12.0
Commercial vehicles			
Total production	185.9	172.4	192.9
of which:			
Light commercial vehicles	87.2	84.5	88.0
Gross vehicle weight trucks	5.7	7.0	6.4
Motive units	1.5	1.6	1.3
Buses, coaches and minibuses	5.6	7.0	4.3
Production for export	74.9	76.2	96.2
of which:			
Light commercial vehicles	92.5	86.2	90.6
Gross vehicle weight trucks	4.2	5.4	4.8
Motive units	0.3	0.2	0.2
Buses, coaches and minibuses	2.9	8.3	4.4

Source: ONS Motor Vehicle Production Inquiry

produces 20 per cent of its global engines from Bridgend and Dagenham. UK engine manufacturing output is forecast to rise to over 4 million units by 2003, double the 1990 figure, and representing substantial net exports.

Around 330,000 people are employed in vehicle and component production and manufacturing activities in the UK.

The UK has around 40 producers of motor vehicles. This includes volume car producers BMW, Ford (including Jaguar, Land Rover and Aston Martin), Honda, MG Rover, Nissan, Peugeot, Toyota and Vauxhall/IBC and a range of smaller producers targeting specialist markets such as sports and luxury cars. London Taxis

International, owned by Manganese Bronze Holdings, the engineering and automotive components group, produces some 2,500 taxis a year at its Coventry factory.

The main truck manufacturer is Leyland Trucks, owned by PACCAR. Medium-sized vans are manufactured by LDV at Birmingham, Ford at Southampton and by the GM/Renault joint venture at the IBC plant in Luton. The main UK bus manufacturer is TransBus, formed from a merger of the bus manufacturing interests of Mayflower and Henlys, and Optare.

The *automotive components manufacturing* sector is a major contributor to the UK motor industry, with an annual turnover of around £12 billion and employing an estimated 150,000 people. A large proportion of its enterprises are small- and medium-sized, in terms of employment, and many also supply other sectors.

Shipbuilding and marine engineering

The UK *merchant shipbuilding* industry, located mainly in Scotland and northern England, comprises some 17 yards employing around 4,000 people, producing ships ranging from tugs and fishing vessels to fast ferries and large specialist craft for offshore exploration and exploitation work. The industry's current order book is for ten ships. The merchant ship repair and conversion industry, which has a strong presence in the UK, comprises over 60 companies employing 4,000 to 7,000 people depending on workload. Naval construction accounts for a further 7,900 people. Vosper Thornycroft and BAe Systems dominate warship production, and in 2002 received an order to build a further six Royal Navy warships at yards in Glasgow, Barrow-in-Furness and Portsmouth. Overall, shipyards employ about 27,000 people and tend to concentrate around Southampton, Liverpool, Newcastle upon Tyne, Glasgow and Belfast. In addition, the UK has a range of world-class companies in the boat-building sector. A few internationally known builders dominate the market for the supply of luxury motor yachts and cruisers.

The UK marine equipment industry has an annual turnover of £1.7 billion and employs an estimated 16,600 people in about 690 companies. About 62 per cent of its output is exported. Production ranges from traditional marine equipment to sophisticated navigational and propulsion systems, as well as equipment and supplies for the cruise industry.

Oil and gas exploitation in the North Sea has generated a major offshore industry (see page 438). Shipbuilders and fabricators design and build semi-submersible units for drilling, production and emergency/maintenance support; drill ships; jack-up rigs; modules; and offshore loading systems as well as undertaking 'floating production storage and offload' vessel (FPSO) conversions. Harland and Wolff of Belfast is a principal leader in the offshore sector, specialising in drill ships. Many other firms supply equipment and services to the industry, notably diving expertise, consultancy, design, project management and R&D. A number have used their experience of North Sea projects to establish themselves in oil and gas markets throughout the world.

Railway equipment

Over 120 UK enterprises were engaged in manufacturing railway equipment for both domestic and overseas markets in 2000, mainly producing specialist components and systems for use in rolling stock, signalling, track and infrastructure applications. About 5,000 firms are involved in the supply chains, and UK expertise extends to consultancy and project management. Two large multinational train builders, the UK/French-owned Alstom and the Canadian-owned Bombardier, have UK factories and assemble passenger rolling stock here. British-owned companies are involved in producing and exporting signalling and track accessories. Most new trains now being introduced in Britain have a number of foreign-made components, so UK input varies from 5 to 75 per cent of total value. Privatised train operating companies have placed orders for around 4,000 passenger carriages since 1996. One notable order has been for 53 electric tilting trains, due to begin operating on Virgin West Coast routes from London Euston in 2003.

Aerospace and defence

The UK's aerospace industry is one of the few in the world with a complete capability across the whole spectrum of aerospace products and technology. Some 120,000 people were employed in 2000 and turnover was £17.1 billion. The industry contributed £2.1 billion to the UK's balance of payments in 2001.

Farnborough International, held in July every other year and organised by the Society of British Aerospace Companies, is one of the world's premier aerospace business events. At the 2002 show there were 1,260 exhibitors from 32 countries, with trade and public attendance of 290,000. Orders worth £9 billion were announced during the event.

Industry activities cover designing and constructing airframes, aero-engines, guided weapons, simulators and space satellites, materials, flight controls including 'fly-by-wire' and 'fly-by-light' equipment (see page 423), and avionics and complex components, with their associated services. The UK also has one of the largest defence manufacturing industries in the Western world.

Among the leading companies are BAe Systems and Rolls-Royce. BAe Systems is a global systems, defence and aerospace systems company. It employs some 70,000 people (excluding joint ventures) around the world and has annual sales of some £13 billion; its order book in 2001 was £43 billion. It designs and manufactures a range of defence equipment, including military aircraft, surface ships, submarines, communications and electronic systems, and through joint ventures is heavily involved in guided weapons and in civil aerospace.

Engines

Rolls-Royce is one of the world's three leading manufacturers of aero-engines, with a turnover in 2001 of £6.3 billion, including £3.4 billion for its aerospace business and £1.4 billion for defence. More than 55,000 Rolls-Royce civil engines are in service, in over 150 countries. Customers include over 500 airlines, 2,400 corporate and utility operators, and 100 armed forces. In civil aerospace, the Trent family of engines has about half of the available market in the new generation of wide-bodied airliners from Airbus and Boeing. Rolls-Royce is a partner in the low-emission V2500 aero-engine, now in service on the Airbus A320 family. In the defence sector, it produces military engines for both fixed-wing aircraft and helicopters, and is a partner in the EJ200 engine project for the Eurofighter Typhoon; it is also participating in the US/UK Joint Strike Fighter (JSF) programme and in the team developing an alternative main propulsion engine for JSF designs.

Equipment

A number of UK companies produce aerostructures (doors, windows and aircraft body parts), equipment and systems for engines, aircraft propellers, navigation and landing systems, engine and flight controls, environmental controls and oxygen breathing and regulation systems, electrical generation, mechanical and hydraulic power systems, cabin furnishings, flight-deck controls and information displays. BAe Systems is the world's largest manufacturer of head-up displays (HUDs). British firms have made important technological advances, for example, in developing fly-by-wire and fly-by-light technology, in which control surfaces on the wings and elsewhere are moved by means of automatic electronic signalling and fibre optics respectively. UK companies provide radar and air traffic control equipment and ground power supplies to airports and airlines worldwide.

Civil aircraft

BAe Systems has a 20 per cent share of Airbus, with EADS (European Aeronautic Defence and Space Company) controlling the other 80 per cent. Airbus UK is responsible for the design and manufacture of the wings for the whole family of Airbus airliners, from the short- to medium-haul A320 series (the first civil airliner to use fly-by-wire controls) to the large long-range four-engined A340. The company will also design and manufacture the wings for the new A380 'super jumbo' – a twin-deck, twin-aisle jetliner with 555 or more seats – expected to create up to 22,000 new jobs, 8,000 at Airbus UK and in UK suppliers to the programme and a further 14,000 in associated employment. In 2001 Airbus received firm orders for 375 new aircraft worth US$44.7 billion from 32 customers around the world, and in the first half of 2002 had 42 per cent of the world market for large civil aircraft.

Bombardier Aerospace of Canada, the third largest civil aircraft manufacturer in the world, produces a wide range of turboprop and regional jet aircraft and business jets. Bombardier Aerospace Northern Ireland (formerly Short Brothers) employs around 7,000 people. Its Belfast site is engaged in the design and manufacture of major civil aircraft sub-assemblies, advanced engine nacelles, flight controls, and for processes such as composites, metal bonding and computer-aided design/ manufacture, as well as the provision of aviation support services.

Military aircraft and missiles

BAe Systems, EADS and Alenia of Italy are building the Eurofighter Typhoon. BAe Systems also has the Harrier, a vertical/short take-off and landing (V/STOL) military combat aircraft, the Tornado combat aircraft manufactured by Panavia GmbH, a joint venture with EADS and Alenia, and the Hawk fast-jet trainer, all of which have been sold overseas. The company is also part of the Lockheed Martin Joint Strike Fighter team which is manufacturing three variants of the F-35.

BAe Systems co-owns (with EADS and Italy's Finmeccanica) Europe's main guided weapons business, MBDA, which is second only to Raytheon of the US. Another major company operating in the guided weapons sector is Thales, including Thales Air Defence in Belfast.

Helicopters

Agusta Westland manufactures the multi-role EH101 medium-lift helicopter for civilian and military markets – two British variants are the Royal Navy's Merlin HM.1 advanced anti-submarine warfare helicopter and the RAF's Merlin HC.3 combat transport helicopter. It also manufactures the Super Lynx light battlefield and naval helicopter, and is building and supporting the Apache attack helicopter for the UK Army, under licence from Boeing. The company is involved in the successful NH Industries NH-90 support helicopter and a range of civil helicopters through its Italian facilities. It has a joint venture with Bell in the US, which has recently developed the Agusta-Bell AB139 helicopter, selected for the US Coastguard.

Land systems

The UK's main armoured fighting vehicle capability is concentrated in three companies: Vickers Defence Systems, RO Defence (part of BAe Systems) and Alvis. RO Defence is also the UK's main artillery and ordnance company.

Space equipment and services

Around 400 organisations employing about 5,500 people are engaged in industrial space activities, with turnover of £460 million in 2001. UK participation in the European Space Agency, and the British National Space Centre's role in co-ordinating UK space policy (see page 375), has enabled UK-based companies to participate in many leading space projects covering telecommunications, satellite navigation, Earth observation, space science and astronomy. The industry is strong in the development and manufacture of civil and military communications satellites and associated Earth stations and ground infrastructure equipment. In the field of Earth

Table 27.21 Machinery and equipment not elsewhere classified, UK

	Number of enterprises	Total turnover	GVA at basic prices	Total employment	Total net capital expenditure
		£ million	£ million	Thousand	£ million
1998	14,330	35,580	13,414	400	982
1999	14,303	33,306	12,254	367	954
2000	13,931	33,990	12,319	368	858

Source: ONS Annual Business Inquiry

observation, it plays a major role in manufacturing platforms, space radar and meteorological satellite hardware, and in the exploitation of space data imaging products.

The largest British space company is Astrium Limited. Currently jointly owned by BAe Systems and EADS, it is one of the world's major space companies. A leading provider of direct broadcast television satellites, it is involved in all of Europe's space science and Earth observation projects and Europe's launcher and navigation programmes.

Machinery and equipment

Industry output rose by 1 per cent in 2001 but was still almost 4 per cent lower than in 1992 and 1993. Total turnover was £31.8 billion, of which exports accounted for £10.8 billion, or 34 per cent (see Table 27.22). Mechanical machine-building is an area in which British firms excel, especially internal combustion engines, power transmission equipment, pumps and compressors, wheeled tractors, lawnmowers, and construction and earth-moving equipment. The UK is a major producer of industrial engines, pumps, valves and compressors, and of pneumatic and hydraulic equipment. Companies manufacture steam generators and other heavy equipment for power plants.

Alstom, a global specialist in transport and energy infrastructure, is one of the world's leading suppliers of major components for complete power station projects along with the transformers and switchgear needed in transmission and distribution of electricity. In the UK the company's strengths are steam turbine manufacture, switchgear manufacture, industrial gas turbines, and project design and management.

The mechanical lifting and handling equipment industry makes cranes and transporters, lifting devices, escalators, conveyors, powered industrial trucks and air bridges, as well as electronically

Table 27.22 Machinery and equipment – turnover and orders, UK

£ billion

	1999	2000	2001
Home			
Orders on hand	7.4	7.7	7.5
New orders[1]	20.9	20.2	20.8
Turnover	20.5	19.9	20.9
Export			
Orders on hand	3.3	3.6	3.4
New orders[1]	10.6	11.5	10.7
Turnover	10.9	11.1	10.8
Total			
Orders on hand	10.6	11.3	10.9
New orders[1]	31.6	31.7	31.4
Turnover	31.3	31.0	31.8

1 Net of cancellations.
Source: ONS Monthly Production Inquiry

controlled and automatic handling systems. The commercial heating, ventilation, air-conditioning and refrigeration sector is served largely by small and medium-sized firms, although several large multinational companies have sites in Britain.

Tractors and equipment used in agriculture, horticulture, forestry, sports turf and gardens achieved export sales of £1.0 billion in 2001. Most tractor exports were supplied by three major multinationals with plants in the UK; together with JCB Landpower they export to nearly every country in the world. A wide range of specialist golf, parks and sports field machinery, lawn and garden products, and agricultural equipment complement the tractor business.

Machine tools, most of which are computer-controlled, are used in all sectors of manufacturing, including the engineering, aerospace and

Table 27.23 Metalworking machine tools – turnover and orders, UK

			£ million
	1999	2000	2001
Home			
Orders on hand	94	93	105
New orders[1]	440	504	467
Turnover	485	505	455
Export			
Orders on hand	114	197	97
New orders[1]	388	515	354
Turnover	382	432	454
Total			
Orders on hand	208	290	202
New orders[1]	828	1,019	821
Turnover	867	937	909

1 Net of cancellations.
Source: ONS Monthly Production Inquiry

automotive industries. In 2001 total turnover of companies classified to the metalworking machine tools industry was £909 million, of which exports accounted for £454 million, almost 50 per cent (see Table 27.23).

The UK mining and tunnelling equipment industry has a world reputation in the production of coal-cutting and road-heading (shearing) equipment, hydraulic roof supports, conveying equipment, flameproof transformers, switchgear, and subsurface transport equipment and control systems. In construction equipment, the UK has the largest production volume in Europe, around one-third of the total of the principal categories of construction equipment. JCB and a number of major multinational companies contribute to construction equipment exports of over £1.5 billion a year.

The UK has one of the largest engineering construction sectors in the world, serving the whole spectrum of process industries, with particular strengths in oil, gas and related industries. British innovations include computerised colour matching and weave simulation, friction spinning, high-speed computer-controlled knitting machines and electronic jacquard attachments for weaving looms. British companies also make advanced printing machinery and ceramic processing equipment, and other types of production machinery.

The domestic appliances sector includes the manufacture of refrigerators and freezers, dishwashers, washing machines, tumble dryers, vacuum cleaners, floor polishers, microwave ovens and cookers, as well as water heaters and showers, ventilation products and small appliances for the kitchen and bathroom. Energy efficiency and water conservation have progressively improved in home laundry products, and new technology has been applied to many products. Visual design of what were traditionally 'white goods' has changed, giving a new look to kitchens, and modern design has also been applied to vacuum cleaners and small appliances such as kettles and toasters. The UK is Europe's largest manufacturer of tumble dryers, with an annual trade surplus of £20 million in 2000.

Rubber and plastics products

In 2000 the rubber industry had turnover of £3.4 billion and employed around 41,000 people; the plastics industry had turnover of £16.4 billion and employed 205,000 people. Output fell by 4.2 per cent in 2001, although it was over 12 per cent higher than in 1992.

Rubber products include tyres and tubes, pipes, hoses, belting and floor coverings, many of which

Table 27.24 Rubber and plastic products, UK

	Number of enterprises	Total turnover	GVA at basic prices	Total employment	Total net capital expenditure
		£ million	£ million	Thousand	£ million
1998	7,256	20,420	8,062	269	1,102
1999	7,112	19,520	7,554	257	1,088
2000	7,050	19,795	7,636	246	975

Source: ONS Annual Business Inquiry

have applications in the automotive industry. The largest firms in this sector are major tyre manufacturers such as Goodyear, making tyres at its Wolverhampton factory, and Michelin, with factories in Stoke-on-Trent, Dundee and Ballymena. Both companies have been making tyres in the UK since 1927.

Plastics have a multitude of applications. The packaging industry is the largest user, accounting for 36 per cent of the market, followed by the construction (22 per cent), electrical and electronic goods (8 per cent) and transport industries (7 per cent). The UK's plastics industry continues to be a world leader in material specification and design, with new processes allowing stronger plastics to replace traditional materials and develop new applications. Among the larger firms in a sector characterised by many small and medium-sized businesses is British Polythene Industries, Europe's largest producer of polyethylene films, sacks and bags. In the moulded plastics sector, Linpac's output includes trays, fast food packaging, egg cartons and disposable tableware.

Glass, ceramics and building materials

In 2001 industry output rose by 0.6 per cent in 2001 and was 2 per cent higher than in 1992.

Glass

In 2000 the glass and glass products industry had turnover of £2.9 billion and employed 35,000 people. The UK is a world leader in the manufacture of glass. Flat glass is made through the float process, invented by Pilkington in 1952, which manufactures clear, tinted and coated glass for buildings, and clear and tinted glass for vehicles. It is a process that continues to be licensed throughout the world. Pilkington has its own manufacturing operations in 25 countries on five continents and sales to 130 countries. Today,

one in three of the world's new light vehicles has glazing from Pilkington and its associates. The manufacture and supply of building components containing glass, windows, doors, partitioning and cladding is carried out by many other companies operating from within the timber, metal (aluminium and steel) and plastic (UPVC) sectors. The UK also has several leading lead crystal suppliers, such as Waterford-Wedgwood, Dartington and Edinburgh Crystal.

> Pilkington has developed a self-cleaning glass. It is float glass with a special ultra-thin coating on the outside that has a unique dual action. Once exposed to daylight, the coating reacts chemically in two ways: first, it breaks down any organic dirt deposits and second, when rain or water hit the glass, the loosened dirt is washed away without leaving any marks.

Ceramics

'Ceramics' covers tableware, giftware, ornamental ware and catering ware; floor and wall tiles and sanitary ware; clay roofing tiles, clay pipes and land drains; industrial ceramics and refractories; and ceramic materials and machinery. In 2000 the industry – heavily concentrated in the West Midlands – had turnover of £1.9 billion and employed 36,000 people. Domestic tableware production includes fine china, bone china, earthenware and stoneware, and is produced predominantly in the Potteries (Stoke-on-Trent) area of Staffordshire. Wedgwood, Spode and Royal Doulton are among the most famous names in fine bone china, and the UK is one of the world's leading manufacturers and exporters. Important industrial ceramics invented in the UK include some forms of silicon carbide and sialons, which can withstand ultra-high temperatures.

Table 27.25 Other non-metallic mineral products, UK

	Number of enterprises	Total turnover	GVA at basic prices	Total employment	Total net capital expenditure
		£ million	£ million	Thousand	£ million
1998	5,272	11,346	4,904	146	656
1999	5,406	11,710	4,865	145	747
2000	5,386	11,994	5,136	144	621

Source: ONS Annual Business Inquiry

March 2002: workers leave the Vauxhall car factory in Luton on the last day of production of the Vectra car. The factory is closing after nearly 100 years. Around 1,000 workers have transferred to the nearby IBC vehicles van plant, owned by Vauxhall's parent company, General Motors.

The 'Prince Henry' model being manufactured at Luton in 1912.

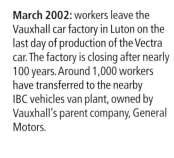

One of the 'Velox' models, c.1950.

May 2002: the Falkirk wheel – a 25 m diameter boat lift – has been designed to reconnect the Forth & Clyde and the Union canals between Glasgow and Edinburgh. It was opened by the Queen during her Golden Jubilee tour of Scotland.

DOUG HALL / BONNEY'S NEWS AGENCY

PA

September 2001: the Gateshead Millennium Bridge is the world's first rotating bridge and the first opening bridge to be built across the Tyne for more than 100 years.

Above: The bridge was assembled at a Tyneside shipyard and transported on a giant barge. It was lifted into position by one of the world's largest floating cranes.

February 2002: the 320 m long Millennium Bridge, London, re-opens to the public after being fitted with 90 dampers to prevent the swaying which was noticeable when it originally opened in June 2000.

REUTERS / STEPHEN HIRD

NIGEL YOUNG / FOSTER AND PARTNERS ARCHITECTS

NIGEL YOUNG / FOSTER AND PARTNERS ARCHITECTS

July 2002: City Hall, the new Greater London Authority headquarters, designed by Foster and Partners. It houses the offices of the Mayor, London Assembly Members and GLA staff.

July 2001:City Hall under construction. Many features of the building, including its shape and alignment, have been designed to save energy.

Table 27.26 Production of building materials and components, Great Britain

	1999	2000	2001
Bricks (millions)	2,939	2,864	2,754
Concrete building blocks (thousand sq m)	87,767	90,219	87,922
Cement (thousand tonnes)[1]	12,697	12,452	11,854
Sand and gravel (thousand tonnes)[2]	88,209	89,234	97,141
Ready mixed concrete (thousand cu m)[1,3]	23,550	23,043	23,008
Slate (tonnes)[4]	98,870	85,858	93,125
Concrete roofing tiles (thousand sq m)	25,972	26,765	24,825

1 UK figures.
2 Sales.
3 Deliveries.
4 Excluding slate residue used for fill.
Source: Department of Trade and Industry – *Construction Statistics Annual 2002*

Building materials

In 2000 the building materials industry had turnover of £7.3 billion and employed 76,000 people. Most crushed rock, sand and gravel quarried by the aggregates industry (some 220 million tonnes in Great Britain in 2000) is used in construction. In 2001, 2.75 billion bricks were produced by, and 2.83 billion bricks were delivered from, sites in Great Britain. Portland cement, a 19th-century British innovation, is a widely used chemical compound throughout the world.

Textiles and clothing

This sector has been adversely affected by imports from low labour-cost suppliers and changing sourcing patterns in the UK high street – in 2001 output of textiles and textile products was 33 per cent below the level in 1995. UK manufacturers have modernised their domestic operations to meet these challenges. In addition, to compete in areas other than price, firms have shifted into higher-value products to benefit from the UK's strengths in fashion, design, product and process innovation, and information technology.

Technical textiles in particular are currently growing at about 7 per cent a year and cover sectors such as medical textiles, geo textiles and electronic textiles. New technologies, largely designed to improve response times and give greater flexibility in production, are used throughout the industry.

The textiles industry has a high degree of regional concentration, reflecting the traditional centres for this sector: cotton textiles in the North West, fine knitwear in Scotland, linen in Northern Ireland, woollens and worsteds in Yorkshire and Scotland, and knitted fabrics in the East Midlands. The clothing industry is more dispersed throughout the UK, but also has significant concentrations in the Midlands, north and east London and the North East.

The UK textile and clothing industry comprises a few multi-process companies, but in the main companies operate vertically. However, small and medium-sized enterprises (SMEs) dominate, some of which subcontract work to other companies or to homeworkers. Two long established companies

Table 27.27 Textile and textile products, UK

	Number of enterprises	Total turnover	GVA at basic prices	Total employment	Total net capital expenditure
		£ million	£ million	Thousand	£ million
1998	13,835	17,364	6,699	326	552
1999	12,971	16,137	5,930	301	460
2000	12,109	14,309	5,412	262	275

Source: ONS Annual Business Inquiry

in the industry are Coats Viyella and Sara Lee Courtaulds (created when the US Sara Lee Corporation bought Courtaulds Textiles in 2000). A number of clothing brands are managing a resurgence, both in the UK and in the international market, particularly micro and SMEs, including those in the cut, make and trim (CMT) sub-sector.

The principal textile and clothing products are yarns, woven and knitted fabrics, interior (including printed) textiles, technical textiles, carpets and a full range of clothing (including knitwear). Tables 27.28 and 27.29 show manufacturers' sales for a range of products. Worsted yarns are finely spun for use mainly in suit fabric and fine knitwear. As well as spinners, weavers and knitters, the sector supports a number of other processes, such as scouring of raw wool and dyeing and finishing of wool, yarn or fabric. British mills also process rare fibres such as cashmere and angora. In addition, the UK produces synthetic fibres, cotton/synthetic mixed yarns and fabrics, and has a large dyeing and finishing sector (which includes fabric printing).

Axminster and Wilton are the main types of woven carpets in the UK, which is recognised for its high-quality products, variety of design and use of new technology. UK companies are also continually improving their capability in the manufacture of higher-volume, lower-value tufted carpets.

Technical textiles are usually defined as such for their performance characteristics. They include non-wovens for filtration and absorbency, textiles used in construction, automotive textiles, sewing thread, rope and medical/healthcare textiles and a very wide range of fabrics used in the automotive, aviation, aerospace and defence sectors.

The clothing industry is more labour-intensive than textiles. British firms have had some success in the growing market for branded street and club-wear. However, total exports fell by 23 per cent between 1996 and 2001 to £2.6 billion.

Table 27.28 Textiles – UK manufacturers' sales by industry[1]

			£ million
	1999	2000	2001
Soft furnishings	444	458	525
Canvas goods and sacks	161	137	137
Household textiles	942	987	893
Carpets and rugs	1,029	973	898
Cordage, rope, twine and netting	80	79	98
Non-wovens excluding apparel	158	n/a	167
Preparation and spinning of textile fibres	891	798	669
Textile weaving	972	902	831
Finishing of textiles	629	575	509
Lace	39	34	28
Narrow fabrics	223	210	189
Other textiles not elsewhere classified	498	516	488
Knitted and crocheted fabrics	n/a	374	n/a
Knitted and crocheted hosiery	363	n/a	306
Knitted and crocheted pullovers, cardigans and similar articles	664	582	413

1 Where indicated as not available, data have been suppressed to avoid identifying individual enterprises.
Source: ONS PRODCOM

Table 27.29 Clothing – UK manufacturers' sales by industry[1]

			£ million
	1999	2000	2001
Leather clothes	14	16	25
Workwear	279	261	253
Men's outerwear	613	421	340
Women's outerwear	1,001	915	790
Men's underwear	437	294	n/a
Women's underwear	779	737	626
Hats	63	n/a	54
Other wearing apparel and accessories	604	568	481
Dressing and dyeing of fur and fur articles	6	5	3

1 Where indicated as not available, data have been suppressed to avoid identifying individual enterprises.
Source: ONS PRODCOM

Wood and wood products

In 2000, over 47 per cent (£2.9 billion) of turnover in the wood and wood products industry was in the manufacture of builders' carpentry and joinery, with a further 18 per cent (£1.1 billion) in saw milling and planing of wood. Also included in this sector are veneer sheets, plywood, laminboard, particle board and fibre board; wooden containers; and cork, straw and plaiting materials.

Table 27.30 Wood and wood products, UK

	Number of enterprises	Total turnover	GVA at basic prices	Total employment	Total net capital expenditure
		£ million	£ million	Thousand	£ million
1998	8,578	5,797	2,270	89	255
1999	8,549	5,838	2,101	89	238
2000	8,363	6,186	2,304	88	227

Source: ONS Annual Business Inquiry

Table 27.31 Leather and leather products, UK

	Number of enterprises	Total turnover	GVA at basic prices	Total employment	Total net capital expenditure
		£ million	£ million	Thousand	£ million
1998	1,208	2,005	689	33	42
1999	1,112	1,837	687	26	38
2000	1,034	1,747	616	21	9

Source: ONS Annual Business Inquiry

Table 27.32 British footwear market

	1999	2000	2001
Volume (million pairs)			
Manufacturers' sales	63	34	34
less Exports[1]	38	37	32
plus Imports	290	280	346
equals Domestic supplies	315	277	348
Value (£ million)			
Manufacturers' sales	1,015	608	584
less Exports[1]	507	486	432
plus Imports	1,923	1,890	2,127
equals Domestic supplies	2,432	2,012	2,279

1 Including re-exports.
Source: British Footwear Association

Leather and leather products

Total sector output in 2001 was 21 per cent below the level in 1995. Leather and leather products accounted for just 0.4 per cent of total manufacturing gross value added in 2000. Almost 60 per cent (£1.0 billion) of turnover was in the footwear industry, with a further 23 per cent (£0.4 billion) in the tanning and dressing of leather. Also included under this sector are the manufacture of luggage, handbags, saddlery and harness.

Britain is home to some of the world's leading footwear brands and most innovative designers – 75 per cent of its production is exported. UK shoemakers are renowned for high-quality formal footwear, directional fashion (such as trainers), casual comfort brands and safety footwear. Around 10,000 people are employed in footwear manufacturing, with a further 5,000 in supply trades. Manufacturers' sales were 34 million pairs in 2001, worth £584 million (see also Table 27.32). The domestic market is, however, dominated by imports, which amounted to 346 million pairs in 2001, or about £5.5 billion at retail prices.

Other manufacturing

In 2000, 58 per cent (£9.4 billion) of turnover in this sector was in the manufacture of furniture, with a further 10 per cent (£1.7 billion) in the recycling of waste and scrap. Also included here are the manufacture of jewellery and related articles, musical instruments, sports goods and games and toys.

Construction

The total value of work done in the construction industry in Great Britain during 2001 was £74.7 billion at current prices: £40.0 billion new work and £34.7 billion repair and maintenance

Table 27.33 Manufacture not elsewhere classified, UK

	Number of enterprises	Total turnover	GVA at basic prices	Total employment	Total net capital expenditure
		£ million	£ million	Thousand	£ million
1998	19,930	15,356	6,153	240	528
1999	20,465	15,798	6,306	243	485
2000	20,551	16,270	6,165	244	484

Source: ONS Annual Business Inquiry

Table 27.34 Construction, UK

	Number of enterprises	Total turnover	GVA at basic prices	Total employment	Total net capital expenditure
		£ million	£ million	Thousand	£ million
1998	179,868	102,441	34,600	1,302	1,819
1999	188,304	111,365	39,150	1,337	1,869
2000	190,832	118,738	40,954	1,342	2,052

Source: ONS Annual Business Inquiry

(see also Table 27.35). The volume of output at constant 1995 prices grew by 3.5 per cent compared with 2000; new work increased by 2.8 per cent and repair and maintenance by 4.5 per cent. The main areas of construction work within the GB industry covered by these statistics are:

- building and civil engineering – ranging from major private sector companies with diverse international interests to one-person enterprises carrying out domestic repairs; and

- specialist work – companies or individuals undertaking construction work ranging from structural steelwork and precast concrete structures to mechanical and electrical services (including the design and installation of environmentally friendly building control systems).

Other areas of construction work not covered in the above statistics include:

- the supply of building materials (see page 427) and components – ranging from large quarrying companies, and those engaged in mass production of manufactured items, to small, highly specialised manufacturers; and

Table 27.35 Value of construction output by type of work, Great Britain

£ million

	1999	2000	2001
New work			
New housing			
Public	1,012	1,319	1,437
Private	7,406	8,666	8,796
Other new work			
Infrastructure	6,200	6,453	7,146
Other public	4,919	4,854	5,330
Other private industrial	3,973	3,716	3,701
Other private commercial	12,076	12,653	13,560
Total	35,587	37,660	39,970
Repair and maintenance			
Housing			
Public	6,485	6,552	6,630
Private	9,885	10,354	10,990
Other work			
Public	5,371	5,685	6,110
Private	8,376	9,424	10,991
Total	30,117	32,016	34,720
All work	**65,704**	**69,676**	**74,690**

Source: Department of Trade and Industry

- consultancy work – companies or individuals engaged in the planning, design and supervision of construction projects.

In 2001 the total value of new orders in Great Britain at current prices was £29.6 billion, of which £7.6 billion was new housing and £22.0 billion other new work (see Table 27.36). The volume of new orders at constant 1995 prices grew by 2.2 per cent over the year, new housing increasing by 1.6 per cent and other new work by 2.4 per cent.

Table 27.36 Value of new orders by type of work, Great Britain

£ million

	1999	2000	2001
New housing			
Public and housing association	969	910	1,084
Private	5,901	6,085	6,525
Total	6,869	6,995	7,610
Other new work			
Infrastructure	4,195	4,992	5,154
Public	3,273	3,815	4,117
Private industrial	2,558	2,589	2,542
Private commercial	9,184	9,729	10,221
Total	19,210	21,124	22,033
All new work	**26,709**	**28,120**	**29,643**

Source: Department of Trade and Industry

Housing

The value of new housing orders in Great Britain in 2001 was 8.8 per cent higher than in 2000 – the private sector accounted for almost 86 per cent of the total compared with 75 per cent in 1993. In 2001 construction of 178,900 dwellings was started in Great Britain. Starts by private enterprise concerns were 161,700, by registered social landlords 16,900, and by local authorities 300. New dwellings completed by sector are shown in Table 27.37.

Project procurement, management and financing

Private and public sector projects are managed in a variety of ways. Most clients invite construction firms to bid for work by competitive tender, having used the design services of a consultant. The successful contractor will then undertake on-site work with a number of specialist

subcontractors. Alternative methods of project procurement have become more common in recent years – for example, contracts might include subsequent provision of building maintenance, or a comprehensive 'design-and-build' service where a single company oversees every stage of a project from conception to completion.

Financing of major projects has also been changing. Traditionally, clients raised the finance to pay for schemes themselves. Today, they often demand a complete service package that includes finance. As a result, larger construction companies are developing closer links with banks and other financial institutions. In public sector construction the Government's Private Finance Initiative/public-private partnerships (see page 350) have also heralded a move away from traditional financing.

Table 27.37 Permanent dwellings completed by sector, Great Britain

Thousands

	1991	1996	2001
Private enterprise	154.4	147.3	140.5
Registered social landlords	20.1	32.1	21.6
Local authorities	10.3	0.9	0.5
Total	**184.7**	**180.3**	**162.6**

Source: Office of the Deputy Prime Minister

Overseas contracting and consultancy

UK companies operate internationally and in any one year British consultants work in almost every country in the world.

UK contractors have pioneered management contracting and design and build, and also the financing mechanisms that have been developed in the domestic market through innovations such as the Private Finance Initiative. During 2001 they won new international business valued at £4.7 billion, 20 per cent more than in 2000 (see Table 27.38). Contractors were particularly successful in North America, their most valuable market, accounting for 38 per cent of all new contracts. Contracts secured during 2001 included:

- widening and upgrading roads in India;

- construction of the Millennium Bridge in Wroclaw, Poland;

Table 27.38 Overseas construction activity by British companies – new contracts

	£ million		%
	2000	2001	2001
Europe	822	870	18.5
of which:			
European Union	618	773	16.4
Middle East	365	334	7.1
Far East	464	734	15.6
of which:			
Hong Kong	276	325	6.9
Africa	117	535	11.4
Americas	1,846	1,931	41.0
of which:			
North America	1,748	1,778	37.7
Oceania	321	308	6.5
Total	**3,935**	**4,712**	**100.0**

Source: Department of Trade and Industry – *Construction Statistics Annual 2002*

- building a station depot for the Kowloon Canton Railway Corporation, Hong Kong, in Tai Wai;

- completing the Kagara Dam project in Nigeria;

- designing and expanding the Bur Juman shopping centre in Dubai;

- completing a 9,000-seat indoor stadium in Yaroslavi, Russia; and

- expanding and renovating Salem Hospital in Oregon in the United States.

The main categories of work in which British consultants are involved include structural commercial (roads, bridges, tunnels and railways); electrical and mechanical services; chemical, oil and gas plants; and water supply.

Websites

Department of Trade and Industry
www.dti.gov.uk

National Statistics
www.statistics.gov.uk

WWW.

28 Energy and natural resources

Energy

UK energy production fell by 3.9 per cent in 2001, although primary energy consumption for energy uses increased by 1.8 per cent. Oil production fell by 7.6 per cent, mainly due to the decline in production from established fields. Production of gas fell by 2.4 per cent. Emergency arrangements for the energy sector are being updated in the light of the events of 11 September 2001 (see page 76). This is being done against the background of testing of current procedures for dealing with the risks to the supplies of the oil, gas, nuclear, coal and electricity industries and the responsible public bodies.

The Government has allocated £267 million over the three years from 2001/02 to 2003/04 to promote new and renewable energy technologies.

Resources

Production of primary fuels in 2001, at 277.6 million tonnes of oil equivalent, was 3.94 per cent lower than in 2000. UK production of crude oil and natural gas liquids (NGLs) decreased by 7.6 per cent to 116.7 million tonnes. Annual production of gas (including gaseous renewables) reached 106.8 million tonnes of oil equivalent, 2.4 per cent lower than in 2000, while petroleum production was down by 7.6. per cent. In 2001 UK refineries produced 0.5 million tonnes more petrol than UK demand. UK coal production has followed a downward trend since 1980. However, production rose by 2.3 per cent in 2001 to 31.9 million tonnes. Coal still supplied a significant proportion of the country's primary energy needs: 33 per cent of the electricity supplied in 2001 was

from coal, while gas supplied 37 per cent and nuclear 22 per cent. Nuclear electricity production was 5.9 per cent higher than in 2000.

For 2001, in value terms, total imports of fuels were 5.6 per cent higher than in 2000, largely owing to a 72 per cent increase in the value of coal and other solid fuel. Exports were 0.7 per cent higher. The value of exports of natural gas increased by 25 per cent, reflecting high world gas prices during 2001 (see page 436).

Overall the UK remains a net exporter of all fuels, with a surplus on a balance of payments basis of £5.7 billion in 2001, £1.4 billion lower than in 2000. The trade surplus in crude oil and petroleum products was £5.4 billion. In volume terms, imports of fuel in 2001 were 16.2 per cent higher than in 2000, while exports were 8.1 per cent higher. The UK had a trade surplus in fuels of 40.2 million tonnes of oil equivalent.

Energy policy

The Cabinet Office Performance and Innovation Unit (PIU) published its *Energy Review* in February 2002, setting out the strategic issues for Great Britain, within the context of tackling global warming, and ensuring competitive energy supplies. In response to the Review, the Government initiated a national debate about sustainable energy. The Department of Trade and Industry (DTI) and Department for Environment, Food & Rural Affairs (DEFRA) launched an energy consultation paper in May 2002, targeted at a wide range of energy stakeholders. In addition, the Government undertook a programme of events to involve members of the general public.

The following assumptions formed the background to the consultation:

- liberalised and competitive markets will continue to be a cornerstone of future energy policy;

- it is vital to maintain security of supply;

- greenhouse gas emissions will need to be reduced significantly during the 21st century – this will need technological innovation, with the potential for the UK to benefit from moving to clean and low-carbon technologies and improving performance in energy efficiency;

- competitiveness and affordability are also key objectives of energy policy; and

- climate change issues and some aspects of security of supply are international questions: the UK cannot therefore only act through domestic policies but must also address these issues through international policies and agreements, particularly through EU market liberalisation and the Kyoto Protocol (see page 283).

The Government proposes to publish a White Paper early in 2003 setting out its approach to future energy policy in the light of the PIU report and the findings from the consultation.

Climate change levy

In April 2001 the Government introduced the climate change levy, a tax on business use of energy, designed to encourage energy efficiency across business, and thus help to bring about lower emissions of greenhouse gases. It is a key component in the Government's Climate Change Programme, and is contributing towards climate change commitments, including the UK's target under the Kyoto Protocol to reduce greenhouse gas emissions by 12.5 per cent below 1990 levels by 2008–12 (see page 283).

The levy is designed to balance environmental gains and the protection of business competitiveness. It is expected to cut carbon emissions by about 5 million tonnes a year by 2010. All revenues, however, are being recycled, mainly through an offsetting cut in employer National Insurance contributions, but also through support for energy efficiency

programmes and renewables (see page 445). To protect the international competitiveness of energy-intensive industries, the Government has provided an 80 per cent discount from the levy for those sectors that agree targets for improving their energy efficiency or reducing carbon emissions.

International developments

Since 1999 the European Union's (EU) Fifth Framework Programme of Research and Technological Development has been the focus of research, development and demonstration of energy technologies in the EU. The EU Energy Framework Programme (EFP) 1998–2002 had six separate components:

- ETAP (shared studies and analyses);

- SYNERGY (international co-operation on security of supply and Kyoto targets);

- ALTENER (renewable energy);

- SAVE (strategic action for vigorous energy efficiency);

- SURE (safe transport of nuclear materials and safeguards); and

- CARNOT (clean and efficient use of solid fuels).

The EFP is to be replaced by the Intelligent Energy for Europe Programme (2003–06) comprising SAVE, ALTENER, STEER (energy aspects of transport) and COOPENER (international co-operation in renewables and energy efficiency).

The European Commission collaborates with specialist international organisations, notably the International Energy Agency (IEA) in Paris, which monitors world energy markets on behalf of industrialised countries and promotes reform of energy markets, both among its members and internationally. The IEA's membership consists of all members of the Organisation for Economic Co-operation and Development except Iceland and Mexico.

The degree to which electricity and gas markets have been opened to competition varies considerably across the EU, with only the UK and a few others allowing all consumers to choose their suppliers. However, agreement was reached to complete the internal energy market at the 2000 Lisbon summit and the Commission subsequently brought forward proposals to bring this about at the start of 2001. Negotiations continue, although it has now been agreed that the non-domestic sector should be totally opened by 2004. The UK Government supports the Commission's proposals and wishes to see their early adoption.

In November 2001 the European Commission issued a Green Paper, *Towards a European strategy for the security of energy supply*, aimed at stimulating debate on the issue of security of supply against the background of increasing EU energy dependence. Among other things it proposes stronger demand management (using taxes and efficiency measures), promotion of renewable energy sources as ways to address the challenges of climate change and over-dependence on fossil fuels, and dialogue with, and promotion of, economic reform in supplier countries. It also underlines the benefits of a liberalised EU energy market and the importance for the single energy market of adequate infrastructure.

Oil and gas exploration and production

In 2001, either through direct use or as a source of energy for electricity generation, oil and gas accounted for 72 per cent of total UK energy consumption, with UK production supplying 97 per cent of gas consumed. About 11 per cent of UK production was exported to Ireland or through the UK–Belgium interconnector although on some winter days imports were required to meet demand. In 2001 output of crude oil and natural

gas liquids in the UK averaged 2.4 million barrels (about 320,000 tonnes) a day, making it the world's tenth largest producer.

The UK Continental Shelf (UKCS) comprises those areas of the seabed and subsoil up to and beyond the territorial sea over which the UK exercises sovereign rights of exploration and exploitation of natural resources. Exports from the UKCS rose by 36 per cent in 2001 to 12.7 billion cubic metres, with gas going to the Netherlands, from the British share of the Markham transboundary field and the neighbouring Windermere field, to the Irish Republic and to Belgium through the UK–Belgium interconnector. About 2.8 billion cubic metres were imported from Norway and from Belgium via the interconnector, representing 2.9 per cent of total supplies in 2001, compared with 2.5 per cent in 2000.

Taxation

The North Sea fiscal regime is a major mechanism for gaining economic benefit for the UK from its oil and gas resources. The Government grants licences to private sector companies to explore for, and exploit, oil and gas resources (see page 436). Its main sources of revenue from oil and gas activities are petroleum revenue tax, levied on profits from fields approved before 16 March 1993; and corporation tax, charged on the profits of oil and gas companies. The 2002 Budget introduced changes to the North Sea tax regime to ensure that it raises a fair share of revenue while promoting long-term investment. Companies will

Table 28.1 Oil statistics, UK

Million tonnes

	1991	1999	2000	2001
Oil production				
Land	3.7	4.3	3.2	2.9
Offshore	83.1	124.0	114.6	105.5
Refinery output	85.5	82.0	82.7	77.0
Deliveries	74.5	72.0	71.2	70.9
Exports				
Crude, NGL, feedstock	55.1	91.8	92.9	88.7
Refined petroleum	19.4	21.7	20.7	19.0
Imports				
Crude, NGL, feedstock	57.1	44.9	54.4	53.5
Refined petroleum	10.1	13.9	14.2	17.0

Source: Department of Trade and Industry

now pay a 10 per cent supplementary charge on North Sea profits and receive a 100 per cent first-year allowance for capital expenditure in the North Sea. As part of the modernisation of the North Sea fiscal regime, the Government intends, subject to consultation on timing, to abolish the Royalty (Royalty is charged at 12.5 per cent of the gross value of oil and gas won in a particular licence area, less an allowance for the costs associated with the conveying, treating and initial storage of the oil and gas) that applies to fields approved before April 1982. Royalty was abolished in the 1980s for all fields given development consent on or after April 1982.

Licensing
In January 2001 the 20th round of offshore licensing was launched inviting applications for blocks in the North Sea. The licence awards in the tenth round of landward licensing will encourage the exploitation of the potential of coal bed methane, either through direct drilling or by tapping into the gases released from abandoned coal workings. By the end of 2001, over 8,000 wells had been, or were being, drilled in the UKCS: 2,172 exploration wells, 1,396 appraisal wells and 4,570 development wells. Some 24 exploration wells and 36 appraisal wells were started in 2001. The Government must approve all proposed wells and development plans.

Production and reserves
Some 233 offshore fields were in production at the end of 2001: 117 oil, 96 gas and 20 condensate (a lighter form of oil). During 2001, 22 new developments were approved. Offshore, these comprised eight oilfields, 12 gasfields and one condensate field; onshore, one gasfield. In addition, approval for 12 incremental offshore developments (elaborations to existing fields) was granted.

Cumulative production to end 2001 was 2.687 billion tonnes, with Forties (335 million tonnes) and Brent (293 million tonnes) the largest-producing fields. Britain's largest onshore oilfield, at Wytch Farm (Dorset), produces 90 per cent of the total crude oils and NGLs originating onshore. Possible maximum remaining UKCS reserves of oil are estimated at 1.43 billion tonnes.

Offshore gas
Natural gas now accounts for over 40 per cent of total inland primary fuel consumption in the UK. In 2001 indigenous production amounted to a record 111 billion cubic metres, 2.5 per cent up on 2000.

Cumulative gas production to the end of 2001 was 1,716 billion cubic metres. Maximum possible remaining gas reserves in present discoveries now stand at just under 1,710 billion cubic metres.

Pipelines
Some 10,928 km of major submarine pipelines transport oil, gas and condensate from one field to another and to shore. Nine landing places on the North Sea coast bring gas ashore to supply a national and regional high- and low-pressure pipeline system some 273,000 km long, which transports natural gas around Great Britain. A 40 km pipeline takes natural gas from Scotland to Northern Ireland; exports to the Irish Republic are conveyed by the Britain–Ireland interconnector. The pipeline from Bacton to Zeebrugge in Belgium (232 km) has an export capacity of 20 billion cubic metres a year and an import capacity of 8.5 billion cubic metres a year.

Economic and industrial aspects
World oil prices declined somewhat in 2001; the average price received by producers from sales of UKCS oil was £126 a tonne, compared with £154 a tonne in the last quarter of 2000. UKCS oil and gas production fell from 2.6 per cent of the UK's gross value added in 2000 to an estimated 2.4 per cent in 2001. Total revenues from the sale of oil (including NGLs) produced from the UKCS in 2001 fell to £14.7 billion, while those from the sale of gas rose to £8.3 billion. Taxes and royalty receipts attributable to UKCS oil and gas rose to some £5.1 billion in 2001/02.

PILOT, the successor to the Oil and Gas Industry Task Force, is a joint initiative between oil and gas companies, the industrial supply chain and the Government. It is seeking to maintain exploration and development momentum on the UKCS in the face of increasing maturity of its oil reserves, and to prolong UK self-sufficiency.

Since 1965 the oil and gas production industry has generated operating surpluses of some £287 billion, of which about £111 billion (including over £24 billion of exploration and appraisal expenditure) has been reinvested in the industry, £100.5 billion paid in taxation, and about £75.5 billion retained by the companies. Total annual income of the oil and gas sector fell slightly to some £24.5 billion in 2001.

Among PILOT's targets are:

- a production level of 3 million barrels of oil equivalent a day in 2010;

- a sustained investment level of £3 billion a year;

- a 50 per cent increase in the value of industry-related exports by 2005;

- additional revenue of £1 billion from new businesses;

- 100,000 more jobs than there would otherwise have been in 2010; and

- prolonged self-sufficiency in oil and gas for the UK.

Production investment in the oil and gas extraction industry rose to some £3.5 billion in 2001. Including exploration and appraisal investment of a further £0.4 billion, it formed about 15 per cent of total British industrial investment and some 2.5 per cent of gross fixed capital investment. In 2001 some 32,000 people were engaged in extraction offshore and onshore by the industry while some 265,000 jobs were supported by the industry. Various initiatives, such as LOGIC (Leading Oil and Gas Industry Competitiveness), are aimed at making the UKCS more attractive to investors and sustaining activity through 2010 and beyond.

The offshore environment

All new developments are assessed under the Offshore Petroleum Production and Pipe-lines (Assessment of Environmental Effects) Regulations, the 'EIA' (Environmental Impact Assessment) Regulations and the Offshore Petroleum Activities (Conservation of Habitats) Regulations 2001. The EIA Regulations apply to the drilling of wells, the installation of pipelines, extended well tests and the development of new fields. Environmental Statements are required for projects that could have a significant impact on the marine environment. The Habitats Regulations additionally apply to activities that are not covered by the EIA Regulations, such as offshore oil and gas surveys, well abandonment and decommissioning operations.

In addition to these assessment procedures, permits are required for a number of offshore

activities. The Offshore Combustion Installations (Prevention of Control of Pollution) Regulations 2001 aim to reduce pollution from installations. The regulations require permits for offshore combustion installations, that is, gas turbines and diesels burning natural gas or diesel fuel predominantly used to generate electricity. Permits are also required for the use and discharge of chemicals during all offshore operations under the Offshore Chemicals (Pollution Prevention and Control) Regulations 2002. A comprehensive review of the environmental regime will take place in 2003 to examine ways of streamlining the current regulations.

During 2001 a total of 93 tonnes of oil, from 435 incidents, was reported to the DTI as a result of accidental spills. About 96 per cent of reports are for a spill of less than 1 tonne. Since 1986 the UK has carried out surveillance flights in accordance with international obligations under the Bonn Agreement. These flights are unannounced and cover all offshore installations on the UKCS. The DTI uses a computer link to the aircraft which transmits photographic images of possible pollution incidents and enables the Department to investigate these as they happen. In addition, an initial study by the Department into the potential for satellite surveillance complemented by aerial surveillance has given encouraging results. The appointment of additional environmental inspectors enabled the number of inspections of offshore installations on the UKCS to be increased significantly in 2001.

Decommissioning

The Petroleum Act 1998 places a decommissioning obligation on the operators of every offshore installation and the owners of every offshore pipeline on the UKCS. Companies have to submit a decommissioning programme for ministerial approval and ensure that its provisions are carried out. In 1998 the OSPAR Convention (see page 287) agreed rules for the disposal of defunct offshore installations at sea. Under the terms of this decision, there is a prohibition on the dumping and leaving wholly or partly in place of offshore installations. Derogations, however, are possible for concrete platforms and for the footings of steel installations with a jacket weight above 10,000 tonnes. All installations put in place after 9 February 1999 must be completely removed. The Government encourages the re-use of facilities and expects operators to show that they have investigated such a course. It also encourages free trade in mature offshore oil and gas assets, as a means of extending field life and maximising economic recovery. By August 2002, 22 decommissioning programmes, covering 25 redundant installations, had been approved by the DTI.

Offshore safety

Offshore health and safety are the responsibility of the Health and Safety Executive (HSE – see page 137). The Offshore Division (OSD) within HSE ensures that risks to people who work in oil and gas extraction are properly controlled. OSD's regulatory tasks range from providing advice and guidance on operational and technical matters to working with industry on reducing releases of hydrocarbon.

The work includes:

- inspecting and auditing offshore operations and onshore oil and gas well operations;

- investigating accidents and complaints;

- assessing safety cases and other notifications, including well operations and some construction operations; and

- providing technical information and statistics.

The Offshore Petroleum Industry Training Organisation and the Norwegian Oil Industry Association have approved the Warsash Maritime Centre in Southampton as a recognised training centre. It offers a range of basic safety and emergency training courses for those employed in the offshore oil and gas industry. The course is a prerequisite that satisfies the United Kingdom Offshore Operators Association guidelines.

Suppliers of goods and services

As the UK offshore oil and gas sector matures, UK supply and manufacturing companies have increasingly turned to work in other industrial sectors and in overseas hydrocarbon producing areas. The Oil and Gas Industry Development Group in the DTI works with the PILOT initiatives and takes other action to help the industry realign to changing market circumstances. In May 2002 a new website containing contact details of over 3,000 companies in the UK oil and gas supply chain was launched. This website is maintained by the DTI and is available for global buyers to seek information on

the capabilities and contact details of UK-based companies in this sector.

Gas supply industry

Structure of the industry

The holder of a gas transporter's licence in Great Britain may not also hold licences for supply or shipping in a fully competitive market.[1] Of the two entirely separate companies formed from the demerged British Gas plc, the supply business is now part of the holding company Centrica plc (which still trades under the British Gas brand name in Great Britain), while the pipeline and storage businesses, most exploration and production, and research and technology (R&T) became part of the holding company BG Group plc. In October 2000 BG Group plc demerged its transport, telecommunications, R&T and other businesses into a separately listed company, Lattice Group plc, while the rest of the group continues as BG Group plc. In April 2002 National Grid plc and Lattice Group announced their intention to merge to create National Grid Transco plc, and in July 2002 the Secretary of State for Trade and Industry cleared the merger.

The national and regional gas pipeline network is owned by Transco, part of Lattice Group, which is responsible for dealing with leaks and emergencies. It has also had a monopoly in gas metering, which the energy regulator, Ofgem (see page 443), plans to open to competition. Shippers participate in balancing supply and demand in the pipeline network, within a regime partly driven by commercial concerns, and utilising gas trading arrangements, which include a screen-based on-the-day commodity market for trading in wholesale supplies of gas. In addition, there are auctions for the allocation of entry capacity into the high-pressure national transmission system; and commercial incentives for Transco to operate and balance the system efficiently. Because of the increasing use of gas for electricity generation, the energy regulator is considering changes to the gas balancing regime – the way gas supply is matched to demand, at present on a daily basis.

In Northern Ireland supplies of natural gas have been available since 1996, when the Scotland to

---

1 Suppliers sell piped gas to consumers; public gas transporters (PGTs) operate the pipeline system through which gas will normally be delivered and shippers arrange with PGTs for appropriate amounts of gas to go through the pipeline system.

Northern Ireland gas pipeline was put into operation. Phoenix Natural Gas Ltd has a combined licence for the conveyance and supply of gas in Greater Belfast. There are proposals both to extend the gas system to other parts of Northern Ireland and for a South–North pipeline from outside Dublin to the Belfast area.

Competition

Since 1994 suppliers other than British Gas have captured 83 per cent of the industrial and commercial gas market. Some 60 companies are licensed to sell gas to the commercial sector.

By December 2001 about 6.8 million (out of 20 million) domestic customers no longer took their gas supply from British Gas and were supplied by one of 23 other companies now in the domestic market. In 2001, a standard credit customer could save, on average, £47 on his or her annual gas bill by changing supplier. (The average annual bill in the UK was £308 in April 2001, including VAT.) Only companies that have been granted a supplier's licence are allowed to sell gas. Licence conditions include providing gas to anyone who requests it and is connected to the mains gas supply. Special services must be made available for elderly, disabled and chronically sick people. Suppliers must offer customers a range of payment options; they are able to set their own charges, but have to publish their prices and other terms so that customers can make an informed choice.

Ofgem (Office of Gas and Electricity Markets) (see page 443) has removed price controls from British Gas Trading, as it considers the market to be competitive. However, it continually monitors the market to ensure that anti-competitive practices do not take place.

Between 1991 and 2001, the average price of gas fell in real terms for domestic gas customers by 23 per cent. Over the same period industrial customers saw prices fall by 15 per cent in real terms (18 per cent excluding the climate change levy – CCL – which came into effect in April 2001).

Consumption and the market

Demand for natural gas in 2001, at 1,119 terawatt hours (TWh), was 0.5 per cent lower than in 2000. Gas used for electricity generation in 2001, at 311.5 TW, was 4.0 per cent lower. Although two new gas-fired power stations started to generate during 2001 and four others made their first full-year contributions, high gas prices led to some stations

operating below full capacity. Consumption in the domestic sector grew by 2.5 per cent to 379.2 TWh in 2001 as a whole, while consumption in the public administration, commerce and agriculture sector grew by 2.4 per cent. Consumption in the industrial sector fell by 1.3 per cent to 192.0 TWh.

Sharp rises in the wholesale prices of gas have occurred since spring 2000, affecting in particular industrial and commercial customers. Between the first quarters of 2000 and 2002 prices paid by industry (excluding the CCL) have increased by 42 per cent in real terms. The major causes have been arbitrage (trading on the price differences) across the UK–Belgium gas pipeline, at a time when continental gas prices are linked to oil prices, which have themselves been at high levels, and the associated tightening of the UK supply/demand balance.

Downstream oil

Oil consumption

Deliveries of petroleum products for inland consumption (excluding refinery consumption) in 2001 included 20.9 million tonnes of petrol for motor vehicles, 16.4 million tonnes of DERV (diesel-engined road vehicles) fuel, 10.3 million tonnes of aviation turbine fuel, 6.5 million tonnes of gas oil (distilled from petroleum) and 2.2 million tonnes of fuel oils (blends of heavy petroleum).

Oil refineries

In 2001 the UK's 13 refineries processed 85 million tonnes of crude and process oils, a slightly lower level than in 2000. About 80 per cent of UK output by weight is in the form of lighter, higher-value products, such as gasoline, DERV and jet kerosene. The UK is much more geared towards petrol production than its European counterparts; this accounts for about a third of each barrel of crude oil, compared with a European average of just over a fifth.

In 2001 UK exports of refined petroleum products fell by 15 per cent to £4.1 billion. Virtually all exports went to partners in the EU and in the International Energy Agency, especially France, Germany and the United States.

Coal

The UK coal industry is entirely in the private sector. The main deep-mine operators in the UK are UK Coal (formerly known as RJB Mining), in England, Tower Colliery in south Wales, and Hatfield Colliery (now owned by Coalpower), in South Yorkshire. UK Coal, Mining Scotland, H J Banks and Company and Celtic Energy, which operates in Wales, are the main opencast operators. In May 2002 there were 29 underground mines in production, including 16 major deep mines, employing around 8,600 workers (including contractors), and 56 opencast sites, employing some 2,600 workers. Opencast production accounts for most of the relatively low-sulphur coal mined in Scotland and south Wales, and contributes towards improving the average quality of coal supplies. Opencast mining is subject to approval by local authorities and can take place only where it can comply with strict environmental guidelines, which stress the highest standards of operation, restoration and aftercare.

Market for coal
In 2001 overall demand for coal, at 64 million tonnes, was up 9.6 per cent on 2000. About 79 per cent was used by the electricity generators, 12 per cent by coke ovens and blast furnaces, 1 per cent by other fuel producers, 3.8 per cent by industry, 4 per cent by domestic consumers and 0.2 per cent by other final consumers. Exports were 550,000 tonnes, while imports amounted to 35.5 million tonnes – mainly of steam coal for electricity generation and coking coal. Total production from British deep mines rose by 0.9 per cent to 17.3 million tonnes in 2001. Opencast output rose from 13.4 million tonnes to 14.2 million tonnes in the same period. The Government's lifting of the stricter consents policy on the building of gas-fired power stations has helped win European Commission approval for the UK Coal Operating Aid Scheme in November 2000. This has allowed for up to £170 million to help the coal industry through short-term energy market problems while its production costs are higher than world market prices for coal.

Clean coal
Cleaner coal technologies reduce the environmental impact of coal used for power and industrial applications by increasing the efficiency of its conversion to energy and reducing harmful emissions, which are the cause of acid rain. Improvements in the efficiency of coal-fired power stations lead directly to reductions of carbon dioxide (CO_2), a major contributor to climate change. The DTI allocation of £12 million during 1999/2000 to 2001/02 to the cleaner coal

research and development (R&D) programme aimed to encourage collaboration between UK industry and universities in the development of the technologies and expertise. The DTI is also developing a sub-commercial underground coal gasification project to meet government criteria on cleaner coal.

Coal Authority
The Coal Authority is a public body sponsored by the DTI. It has five main responsibilities: licensing coal-mining operations; repairing coal subsidence damage; managing coalfield property; managing minewater pollution and other environmental problems associated with coal-mining; and providing information to house buyers, other purchasers of property and local authorities about mining activity near property.

Nuclear power
Nuclear power generates about one-sixth of the world's energy and over a third of Europe's. It substantially reduces the use of fossil fuels that would otherwise be needed for generation. In the UK, nuclear stations generated 90.1 TWh in 2001 and contributed 23 per cent of total electricity generation. The private sector company British Energy owns and operates seven advanced gas-cooled reactor stations – five in England and Wales – and the pressurised water reactor (PWR) at Sizewell B. British Energy's reactors have a declared net capacity of 7,140 megawatts (MW) in England and 2,440 MW in Scotland. British Nuclear Fuels operates six magnox power stations, and five more that are being decommissioned.

Existing nuclear stations are expected to continue to contribute to the country's energy requirements provided they do so to the high safety and environmental standards currently observed. Government projections suggest that nuclear power generation could represent about 17 to 18 per cent of total generation by 2010 and about 7 per cent of total generation by 2020. These projections assume no new build and recognise that plant lifetimes are dependent on safety and economic factors.

In September 2002, as a result of experiencing financial difficulties, British Energy asked the Government for financial support. The Government has provided a short-term loan to British Energy in respect of the period until 29 November 2002. The Government stated that this was in order to give sufficient time to clarify the company's full financial position and to come to a clear view on the options for restructuring the company. The Government's priorities are nuclear safety and security of electricity supplies while protecting the interests of the taxpayer.

British Nuclear Fuels (BNFL)

BNFL is Britain's primary provider of nuclear products and services – including spent fuel management, recycling, reprocessing oxide fuel, decommissioning and cleaning up redundant nuclear facilities, and treating historic wastes to both UK and international customers. The company's turnover in 2001/02 was £2.26 billion. In November 2001, the Government announced that a Liabilities Management Authority (LMA) would be established to take responsibility for most of the UK's public sector civil nuclear liabilities, including those of BNFL. In June 2002 BNFL announced a restructuring, aligning the existing business into two new business groups designed to reflect the company's main customer groups: Nuclear Business Utilities Group and Government Services Business Group. The company restructuring and the LMA will allow BNFL to operate in a more commercially competitive environment and position the company to aim for a public-private partnership (PPP) for the business in the future.

UK Atomic Energy

The main activity of UK Atomic Energy (UKAEA) (*www.ukaea.org.uk*) is the decommissioning of nuclear liabilities. It is committed to do this in a way that achieves value for money without compromising safety. It has integrated plans for the decommissioning and environmental restoration of its sites at Harwell (Oxfordshire), Winfrith (Dorset), Dounreay (Caithness) and Windscale (Cumbria). UKAEA's objective is to restore the sites for conventional use. It also manages the fusion research centre at Culham (Oxfordshire) which forms an integral part of the European Union's research into fusion energy.

Fusion research

Nuclear fusion research in the UK is funded by the Office of Science and Technology and Euratom. The UK Government spends £14.3 million a year on research, of which the main focus is magnetic confinement, based at Culham science centre. The UKAEA operates both Europe's fusion facility – JET (Joint European Torus) – and the UK's domestic programme at Culham. Through the EU, the Euratom/UKAEA Fusion Association

contributes to the international effort to demonstrate the principle of power production from fusion, currently embodied in the International Thermonuclear Experimental Reactor.

Nuclear safety

The safety of nuclear installations is the responsibility of the nuclear operators within a system of regulatory control enforced by HSE. Regulation of nuclear safety is primarily achieved through a system of licensing that requires the licensees to demonstrate that they meet 36 licence conditions to HSE's satisfaction. HSE assesses and inspects the sites to satisfy itself that the licensees meet their responsibilities for safety.

The International Convention on Nuclear Safety has been ratified by 53 countries, including the UK and members at the European Commission. The UK has to submit a report showing how it meets the articles of the Convention, which is the subject of peer review by the other countries that are party to the Convention. The latest UK report for the Convention was prepared in September 2001.

The UK's main contribution to the international effort to improve safety in Central and Eastern Europe and in the former Soviet republics is channelled through the EU's nuclear safety programmes.

Energy consumption

Total UK energy demand was 249 million tonnes of oil equivalent in 2001, of which 11 million were for non-energy use. Transport was the sector with the greatest level of consumption, accounting for 32 per cent of total final consumption. The domestic sector was responsible for 28 per cent of the total, the industrial sector for 20 per cent and the service industries, including agriculture, for 13 per cent. Non-energy use made up the remaining 6 per cent.

Primary energy demand in 2001 was 1.2 per cent higher than in 2000. Primary demand for coal and other solid fuels was 9.0 per cent higher than in 2000, but primary demand for oil and gas fell by 1.1 per cent and 0.5 per cent respectively. On a temperature-corrected basis, which shows what annual intake might have been if the average temperature during the year had been the same as the average for 1961–90, energy consumption

Table 28.2 Inland consumption for energy use (in terms of primary sources), UK

Million tonnes oil equivalent

	1991	1999	2000	2001
Natural gas	55.4	92.5	95.5	95.1
Oil	77.1	76.0	76.1	76.5
Coal	67.1	36.7	38.1	41.5
Nuclear energy	17.4	22.4	19.6	20.8
Hydro-electric power[1]	0.4	0.5	0.5	0.4
Renewables and waste	0.7	2.2	2.4	2.7
Net imports of electricity	1.4	1.2	1.2	0.9
Total[2]	**219.5**	**231.4**	**233.4**	**237.7**

1 Excludes pumped storage. Includes generation at wind stations.
2 Total includes losses of electricity during transmission and distribution.
Source: Department of Trade and Industry

grew by 0.5 per cent in 2001, compared with an increase of 1.1 per cent between 1999 and 2000.

Electricity

England and Wales
In December 2001, 72 companies held generation licences in England and Wales. The New Electricity Trading Arrangements (NETA) took effect in March 2001 (see below). A new electricity licensing regime, including the separation of supply from the distribution networks, was introduced in October 2001. The largest generators are Innogy, PowerGen, AES, British Energy, TXU Europe, Edison Mission Energy, and BNFL's Magnox Generation Group. The National Grid Company plc owns and operates the transmission system, and is responsible for balancing electricity supply and demand.

Distribution – transfer of electricity from the national grid to consumers via local networks – is carried out by the 12 regional electricity companies (RECs). Supply – the purchase of electricity from generators and its sale to consumers – has been fully open to competition since 1999. All consumers in Great Britain are free to choose their electricity supplier.

Cross-border acquisitions and takeovers have become a feature of the European power market. RECs are now restructuring as separate distribution and supply companies, most of them overseas-owned. All the main UK generators are vertically integrating through ownership of supply businesses. British electricity companies continue to invest overseas.

In March 2001 the new wholesale electricity trading arrangements came into operation in England and Wales. NETA, along with plant divestments, has introduced competition into wholesale electricity trading. Generators, suppliers, traders and customers are encouraged to enter into bilateral contracts in forwards and futures markets and short-term power exchanges. Participants are free to trade electricity until 1 hour ahead of real time for any half-hour period. From that point until real time, the market operates through a balancing mechanism run by the National Grid Company plc – because of the need to balance the system on a second-by-second basis. NETA took effect through conditions inserted into generation, supply and transmission licences.

Scotland
Scottish Power and Scottish and Southern Energy generate, transmit, distribute and supply electricity within their respective franchise areas. They are also contracted to buy all the output from British Energy's two Scottish nuclear power stations (Hunterston B and Torness) until 2005. The over 100 kW market in Scotland comprises about 6,750 customers and accounts for around 45 per cent of all electricity consumed. All major suppliers compete in Scotland. In 2000/01, 29.5 per cent of customers in the over 100 kW market obtained their power from holders of second-tier supply licences. In 1999 Ofgem proposed the establishment of BETTA (British Electricity Transmission and Trading Arrangements), an extension of NETA to Scotland and aimed at bringing greater competition to the Scottish market. Included in the BETTA proposals is the creation of a single system operator, which

would monitor the balancing of supply and demand and trading. BETTA is scheduled to be introduced by April 2004.

Northern Ireland

Three private companies, AES (NI) Ltd, Premier Power Ltd and Coolkeeragh Power Ltd, generate electricity from three power stations. Most of the electricity generated is sold to Northern Ireland Electricity plc (NIE), which has a monopoly of transmission and distribution, and a right to supply. The market has been gradually opened up to competition since 1999. In 2001 the right to choose a supplier was extended to 35 per cent of the total market (mainly large industrial and public sector consumers). In addition, a number of second-tier suppliers are now operating.

In April 2002 the grid operator for Northern Ireland and Electricity Supply Board National Grid, the transmission system operator in the Irish Republic, opened three upgraded electricity interconnectors linking the electricity system of Northern Ireland with the Republic. The main North–South interconnector has a capacity to trade 2 x 600 MW of power, enough electricity to power several major towns. The interconnectors enable trade of electricity between Northern Ireland and the Republic and through the Moyle Interconnector (Northern Ireland–Scotland) with regions throughout Britain.

NIE's parent company, the Viridian Group, made a significant contribution towards a competitive Irish market by investing in the North–South interconnectors, the NIE Moyle Interconnector with Scotland and the Huntstown power station near Dublin. The wider interconnection strategy is laying the foundation for a modern, competitive all-island electricity market offering competition and security of supply.

Regulation and other functions

The gas and electricity markets in Great Britain are regulated by Ofgem, which is governed by an authority whose powers are provided under the *Gas Act 1986*, the *Electricity Act 1989* and the *Utilities Act 2000*. Ofgem's principal objective is to protect the interests of gas and electricity customers, wherever appropriate, by promoting effective competition. Other duties and objectives include ensuring that reasonable demands for electricity are met and that electricity and gas licensees are able to finance their statutory obligations. Ofgem is responsible for setting

performance standards for gas and electricity companies, and for price regulation of companies where competition has not yet fully emerged or where there is a natural monopoly.

In Northern Ireland the energy regulator holds two separate statutory appointments: Director General of Northern Ireland Electricity and Director General of Gas Northern Ireland.

Consumption

In 2001 sales of electricity through the public distribution system in the UK amounted to 321.8 TWh. Domestic users took 36 per cent of the total, industry 32 per cent, and commercial and other users the remainder. The average price for electricity in the UK fell by 27 per cent in real terms between 1991 and 2001 for domestic customers. Over the same period industrial customers saw prices fall by 34 per cent in real terms (37 per cent excluding the climate change levy, which came into effect in April 2001). By December 2001, just over 8.0 million customers had chosen a supplier other than their historical local electricity supplier. In 2001 these customers saved an average of £18 on their annual bill over customers who had not changed supplier. The average annual domestic electricity bill in the UK for a customer paying by standard credit (paying monthly in advance by cheque or cash, at a bank or post office) was estimated at £250 in 2001.

Generation

Non-nuclear power stations owned by the UK's major power producers consumed 55.8 million tonnes of oil equivalent in 2001, of which coal accounted for 54.9 per cent and natural gas for 42.7 per cent. Other power companies (for which gas is the most widely used fuel) and over 2,000 small autogenerators (which produce power for their own use) have equal access with the major generators to the grid transmission and local distribution systems. A ten-year programme to control emissions of nitrogen oxides (NO_x) through the installation of low-NO_x burners at 12 major power stations in England and Wales is in progress.

Combined cycle gas turbines (CCGTs)

In 2001 CCGT stations accounted for 33 per cent of the electricity generated by major power producers, compared with 16 per cent in 1995. This increase has been balanced by a fall in coal- and oil-fired generation. CCGT stations, favoured by the smaller, independent producers

Table 28.3 Generation by and capacity of power stations owned by the major power producers in the UK

| | Electricity generated (GWh) | | | % | Output capacity |
	1990	1995	2001	2001	(MW)[1]
Nuclear plant	61,308	88,964	90,093	25	12,486
Other conventional steam plant	230,376	169,866	136,937	39	34,640
Gas turbines and oil engines	432	190	2,472	1	1,323
Pumped storage plant	1,982	1,552	2,356	1	2,788
Natural flow hydro-electric plant	4,393	4,096	3,216	1	1,348
CCGTs	–	48,720	117,183	33	19,349
Renewables other than hydro	4	570	728	–	117
Total	**298,495**	**313,958**	**352,985**	**100**	**73,219**
Electricity supplied (net)[2]	276,003	295,166	331,781	–	–

1 At end-December 2001.
2 Electricity generated less electricity used at power stations (both electricity used on works and that used for pumping at pumped storage stations).
Source: Department of Trade and Industry

and using natural gas, offer cheap generation, and give out almost no sulphur dioxide and some 55 per cent less CO_2 than coal-fired plant per unit of electricity. At the end of March 2002, 27 such stations in the UK (with a total registered capacity of 20.5 GW) were generating power. With the introduction of NETA (see page 442), the Government has lifted restrictions on the building of new CCGTs.

Combined heat and power (CHP)

CHP plants are designed to produce both electricity and usable heat. They convert about 80 per cent of fuel input into useful energy, compared with conventional generation, which wastes at least half the energy content of the fuel and emits considerably more CO_2. CHP thus benefits the environment and contributes to UK climate change targets by reducing emissions of greenhouse gases. It is also used for cooling and chilling.

CHP can be fuelled by a variety of energy sources. It offers particular benefits where there is a regular need for heat as well as electricity – in hospitals, leisure centres and housing developments for example – and can be provided on a local scale. About 83 per cent of CHP plants are less than 1 MW capacity; however, large-scale plant (above 10 MW) represents just under 80 per cent of total CHP capacity. In 2001 over 1,500 CHP schemes supplied more than 4,800 MW of generating capacity and produced a total of 22.3 TWh. This

represents 6 per cent of the UK's total electricity generated (and 6 per cent of electricity consumption in the commercial and industrial sectors). The Government aims to have at least 10,000 MW by 2010. EU strategy is to double CHP's share of the electricity market from 9 per cent in 2001 to 18 per cent by the same year. The Government promotes CHP by administering a quality assurance programme under the Energy Efficiency Best Practice Programme (EEBPP) (see page 445), to assess CHP schemes for exemption from the climate change levy and for other benefits. The Whitehall District Heating system in London includes a CHP plant serving 23 government buildings, among them 10 Downing Street.

Trade

National Grid and Electricité de France run a 2,000 MW cross-Channel cable link, allowing transmission of electricity between the two countries. The link has generally been used to supply 'baseload' power – which needs to be generated and available round the clock – from France to England. Imports met just under 3 per cent of the UK's electricity needs in 2001.

Scotland has a peak winter demand of under 6 GWh and generating capacity of over 9 GW. The additional available capacity is used to supply England and Wales through transmission lines linking the Scottish and English grid systems. This interconnector's capacity is now

1,600 MW, with plans to increase it to 2,200 MW. The 60-km 500 MW undersea interconnector between Scotland and Northern Ireland (see page 443) will allow further exports of power from Scotland.

New and renewable sources of energy

The Government is committed to meeting targets to reduce UK emissions of greenhouse gases (see page 434). It is putting in place measures designed to ensure that the UK exceeds its commitment to reduce emissions of these gases by 12.5 per cent below 1990 levels by 2010. A growth in the proportion of electricity generated from renewable sources will play a vital role in these efforts. The Government aims to increase the percentage of electricity generated from renewable sources from the current level of just under 3 per cent to 10 per cent by 2010, subject to the cost being acceptable to consumers. The Orders for the Renewables Obligation for England and Wales and the associated Scottish Renewables Obligation were implemented in April 2002. These orders will oblige all licensed electricity suppliers to ensure that a specified proportion of their supplies is derived from renewable sources.

The Government is allocating over £260 million during 2001–04 to promote renewables technologies. This includes:

- capital grants of £89 million for offshore wind power, energy crops and small-scale biomass from the DTI and the New Opportunities Fund;

- an expanded DTI R&D programme worth £55.5 million; and

- the allocation of £100 million following the report by the Cabinet Office's Performance and Innovation Unit (see page 433).

Photovoltaics (solar electricity) will also benefit through a major installation programme, the first phase of which has been allocated £10 million. DEFRA will distribute £12.5 million in grants for the further development of energy crops.

A large number of British companies are involved in an expanding global market for renewables technologies, directly employing several thousand people, and with a multi-million-pound export business. A specific government unit, Renewables UK, has been established to help manufacturers of renewable equipment and technology. It will promote the UK as a renewables manufacturing base and support the renewables industries. Based in Aberdeen, it aims to raise awareness of the industry and to take advantage of transferable skills from the established oil and gas industry.

Elean power station at Sutton (Cambridgeshire) is the UK's first straw-fired power plant. With a potential output of 36 MW, it burns 200,000 tonnes of straw a year and generates enough power for 80,000 homes. The world's first commercial wave power station has been commissioned on the coast of Islay, Scotland, following the award of a contract under the Scottish Renewables Obligation. This is the Land Installed Marine Powered Energy Transformer (LIMPET), which has been developed by Wavegen and Queen's University Belfast with EU support, and harnesses oscillating water column technology to provide 500 kW for the national grid.

Wind power

Wind power has a significant role to play in assisting the UK in reducing its carbon dioxide emissions and combating climate change. National Wind Power, PowerGen, RES and Scottish Power plan, develop and operate wind energy projects and together have a considerable portfolio of wind farm projects, both in the UK and overseas.

Total UK wind generating capacity now stands at 500 MW, and wind power provides 0.37 per cent of the UK's electricity demand. Just over 64 MW of wind power was installed in 2001, according to the British Wind Energy Association (BWEA). Nearly 100 MW of wind power construction is confirmed for 2002, which would increase the UK's total installed capacity by about 20 per cent.

Britain's coastal waters offer the potential of an abundant supply of wind power, if it can be harnessed effectively and efficiently. The UK's first offshore wind farm, off the Northumberland coast at Blyth, consists of two 2 MW turbines and began generating power in 2000. It was developed by the Border Wind consortium, with financial help from the Non Fossil Fuel Obligation (which preceded the Renewables Obligation) and an EU grant. The Government is seeking to streamline the planning consent process for wind power. A major step has been the announcement of 18 potential sites as having pre-qualified for leases from the Crown Estates, which could result in a maximum of 540 turbines if all were to go ahead.

Energy efficiency

The Government funds a number of energy efficiency programmes in the UK. Over £200 million of the revenue from the climate change levy in its first two years is going to support energy efficiency measures and renewables, including 100 per cent first-year capital allowances for energy-saving investments. These initiatives are an essential part of the UK strategy for reducing greenhouse gas emissions (see page 434) and achieving the Government's domestic goal of a 20 per cent reduction in carbon emissions by 2010.

The Carbon Trust was set up in 2001 as an independent, non-profit-making company to accelerate the take-up of low-carbon technologies in the non-domestic sector. The Trust's funding is around £50 million a year from the UK Government – partly from recycled receipts from the climate change levy. It has taken over the former non-domestic Energy Efficiency Best Practice Programme (EEBPP), which was the main source of independent authoritative information and advice on energy efficiency and is estimated to have produced energy savings of more than 4 million tonnes of carbon a year by 2000. The Trust has also taken over the administration of the Government's Enhanced Capital Allowance scheme for energy-saving technologies, worth about £130 million in 2002/03, depending on take-up. In addition, it is developing a Low Carbon Innovation Programme that aims to accelerate the development of new and emerging low-carbon and energy-efficient technologies in the UK.

The Energy Saving Trust (EST) was set up by the Government and the major energy companies to work through partnerships towards the sustainable and efficient use of energy. In 2001/02 it received £24.5 million in direct government funding for work with the domestic and small business sectors and £16.4 million on transport-related programmes; its UK-wide programmes brought in an extra £75 million of investment.

Since 1994 the public electricity suppliers (see page 442) have invested nearly £26 million a year in energy efficiency measures under the regulator's successive Energy Efficiency Standards of Performance (EESOP) schemes. The energy companies are increasing their investment in EESOP schemes to about £55 million a year over 2000–02, including scheme delivery costs. Since 1994 EESOP programmes have resulted in more than 500,000 insulation improvements and the sale of 13.5 million energy-efficient light bulbs.

Under the *Utilities Act 2000*, the Government has the power to set such energy efficiency requirements. The Energy Efficiency Commitment (EEC) for 2002–05 commenced in April 2002. The EEC (which is replacing EESOP) places an obligation on energy suppliers to promote improvements in energy efficiency by domestic consumers. It will make a contribution to carbon savings in the domestic sector as part of the UK Climate Change Programme. It will also help the Government achieve its commitment to alleviate fuel poverty by directing 50 per cent of energy savings to lower income consumers.

Fuel poverty

The UK Fuel Poverty Strategy was jointly published in November 2001 by DEFRA and DTI in accordance with the *Warm Homes and Energy Conservation Act 2000*. The general definition of a fuel poor household is one that needs to spend more than 10 per cent of its income on fuel to keep warm. Approximately 4 million households in the UK were in fuel poverty in 2000. The Strategy commits the Government to end fuel poverty for vulnerable households – the elderly, those with children, and the disabled and long-term sick – by 2010. The Government's approach to tackling fuel poverty in England is based on improving energy inefficient homes, reducing fuel bills, and tackling low incomes and unemployment.

The Fuel Poverty Strategy states that 'the Government believes that a substantial majority of the 2.2 to 2.4 million vulnerable fuel poor households in England will require assistance through energy efficiency improvements'. The main programme for the provision of energy efficiency measures in England is the Home Energy Efficiency Scheme (HEES), now marketed as Warm Front Team (WFT). WFT has a budget of over £600 million for the period 2000–04 and is targeted specifically at vulnerable households in the private sector. It offers grants of up to £1,500 for packages of insulation and heating improvements (except central heating) for low-income families with children and for the disabled, and up to £2,500, including packages of insulation and central heating, for those aged 60 and over on low incomes.

In Wales, the Welsh Assembly Government is making over £11 million available to fund HEES during 2002/03, in order to tackle fuel poverty among the estimated 220,000 affected households in Wales. While broadly similar to HEES that operates in England, there are a number of differences. Grant rates are £1,500 for a basic insulation package and £2,700 for heating and insulation. The heating package is also available to lone-parent and chronically sick and disabled households, in addition to the over 60s.

Water supply

About 75 per cent of the UK's water supplies is obtained from mountain lakes, reservoirs and river intakes and about 25 per cent from underground sources (stored in layers of porous rock). South-east England and East Anglia are more dependent on groundwater than any other parts of the UK. Scotland and Wales have a relative abundance of unpolluted water from upland sources. Northern Ireland also has plentiful supplies for domestic use and for industry.

Water put into the public water supply system (including industrial and other uses) in England and Wales averaged 15,259 megalitres a day (Ml/d) in 2000/01. An average of 2,400 Ml/d was supplied in Scotland, and for Northern Ireland the figure was 720 Ml/d. In 1999/2000 the average daily consumption per head was 151 litres.

Some 54,148 Ml/d were abstracted from all surface and groundwaters (for example, rivers and reservoirs) in England and Wales in 1999, of which public water supplies accounted for 16,255 Ml/d. The electricity supply industry took 26,515 Ml/d and agriculture 142 Ml/d.

England and Wales

Water companies
The 24 water companies across England and Wales have statutory responsibilities for public water supply, including quality and sufficiency. Ten of these companies are also responsible for public sewerage and sewage treatment.

The *Water Industry Act 1999* prohibits water companies from disconnecting households and other premises deemed vital to the community.

The 1999 Act also makes provision for the protection of water customers on metered supplies who are vulnerable to hardship because of high bills. These include large low-income families, the elderly and the disabled. Since 1989 water bills have risen by more than a third in real terms. The UK Government's draft Water Bill, published in November 2000, contains clauses to encourage the efficient use of water, including changes to the licensing system for water abstraction (with increased penalties for abstraction and impounding offences), and provisions to improve the regulation of the water industry and promote the interests of consumers.

Watermark (*www.watermark.gov.uk*), a government-backed initiative, aims to develop a database that will give the public sector, which has a water bill of £600 million a year, reliable benchmarks against which to measure its consumption. Such data, it is estimated, could save £60 million of this amount.

During 2000/05 the water companies are required to pay for a capital investment programme costing an estimated £15.6 billion,[2] including £7.4 billion on improving water quality and on meeting new UK and EU environmental standards. The Director General of Water Services, who heads Ofwat (Office of Water Services) (*www.ofwat.gov.uk*), the industry's regulatory body, has determined that the companies' efficiency improvements will mostly fund the investments specified. Household customers saw an average increase of 2.3 per cent in their bills for water and sewerage services for 2001/02, coming after an average 11.3 per cent reduction in their bills for 1999/2000. About 22 per cent of households and 90 per cent of commercial and industrial customers are currently charged for water on the basis of consumption measured by meter. Most homes are still charged according to the rateable value of their property. Provisions made in the *Water Industry Act 1999* have given customers increased choice over whether or not to have their bills based on a water meter. As a result, all water companies now supply free meters to households on request. Average water and sewerage bills were £236 for households without a

---

2 The programme includes dismantling what remains of Victorian sewerage systems; providing new sewers, and tanks to prevent sewage overflows; removal of lead from supply pipes; and replacement of iron water mains, which cause discoloration.

Some minerals produced in Britain

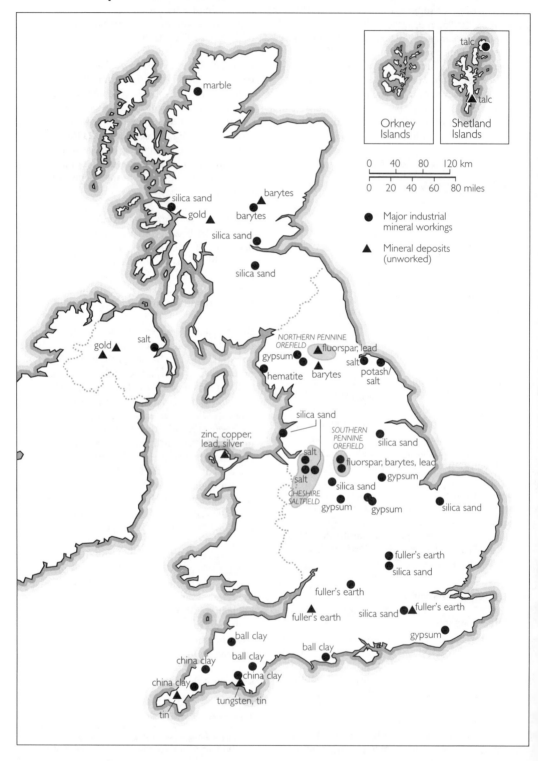

meter (unmeasured) and £198 for households with a meter (measured) in 2002/03.

The main role of the Drinking Water Inspectorate (DWI) is to check that water companies in England and Wales supply wholesome water and comply with the requirements of the Water Quality Regulation. In 2001, 99.86 per cent of the 2.8 million drinking water samples taken met the quality standards. The Water Supply (Water Quality) Regulations 2000 were introduced to implement the European Directive on Drinking Water Quality and require new standards to be met by 2003, with the exception of the final standard for lead, which needs to be met by 2013.

Competition

The UK Government and the National Assembly for Wales intend to extend the opportunities for competition in the water industry in England and Wales and will take steps to safeguard water quality, public health and wider social policies. In July 2002 a joint consultation paper was issued seeking views on the possible extension of opportunities for competition, including the licensing of new entrants into the market for production and retail activities.

In March 2000, the *Competition Act 1998* (see page 341) came into force and strengthened regulators' powers against anti-competitive behaviour. The Act has enabled the shared use of distribution networks (often referred to as common carriage) and Ofwat has actively encouraged water companies to develop access codes. By September 2000 eight 'inset appointments' had been made under which a water company can seek to be appointed to supply a customer in another appointed water company's area. Five of these appointments have involved Anglian Water, and one a new entrant. In August 2000 the UK Government lowered the 'inset' threshold in England from 250 million litres to 100 million litres a year.

Water leakage

Targets are set each year for water companies in England and Wales to reduce leakage. In 2000/01, 3,243 megalitres per day of water put into the supply in England and Wales were lost through leakage, 37 per cent lower than in the peak year of 1994/95.

Scotland

Scottish Water is a new organisation created from the merger of the three former water authorities in Scotland as a result of the *Water Industry (Scotland) Act 2002*. It provides water and waste water services to household and business customers across one-third of the land area in Britain. Scottish Water remains in the public sector and is answerable to the Scottish Parliament.

Scottish Water is the fourth largest water services provider in the UK and the twelfth biggest business in Scotland by turnover. Its assets are valued at £13 billion, and the company serves over 5 million customers with drinking water and also provides sewerage services. It supplies approximately 2.5 billion litres of water a day.

Scottish Water is accountable to a number of regulatory bodies:

- the Water Industry Commissioner for Scotland;

- the Scottish Environment Protection Agency; and

- the Drinking Water Quality Regulator for Scotland.

Northern Ireland

The Water Service is an Executive Agency with the Department for Regional Development. It is responsible for the supply and distribution of drinking water and the provision of sewerage services to over 720,000 domestic, agricultural. commercial and business customers throughout Northern Ireland. It has an annual budget, before capital charges, of £255 million and fixed assets valued at £4.9 billion.

The Water Service envisages expenditure of up to £2.5 billion will be required over 15–20 years to bring water and sewerage services up to standard and to meet increasing demand.

Non-energy minerals

Output of non-energy minerals in 2000 was 306.9 million tonnes, valued at nearly £2.4 billion. The total number of employees in the extractive industry was about 24,900.

The UK is virtually self-sufficient in construction minerals, and produces and exports several

Table 28.4 Production of some of the main non-energy minerals in the UK

	Million tonnes		Production value 2000
	1995	2000	(£ million)
Sand and gravel	101.7	101.6	619
Silica sand	4.3	4.1	51
Igneous rock	57.2	54.1	320
Limestone and dolomite	112.6	97.4	662
Chalk[1]	9.9	9.2	46
Sandstone	19.8	14.9	98
Gypsum	2.0	1.5	13
Salt, comprising rock salt, salt in brine and salt from brine	6.6	5.9	153
Common clay and shale[1]	13.9	10.8	19
China clay[2]	2.6	2.4	234
Ball clay	0.9	1.1	50
Fireclay[1]	0.7	0.6	n/a
Potash	.0.9	1.0	91
Fluorspar	0.1	0.0	4
Fuller's earth	0.1	0.1	7
Slate	0.3	0.5	n/a

1 Great Britain only.
2 Moisture-free basis.
Source: British Geological Survey, *United Kingdom Minerals Yearbook 2001*

industrial minerals, notably china clay, ball clay, potash and salt. The Boulby potash mine in north-east England is the UK's most important non-energy mineral operation. Production in 2001 was 890,000 tonnes, of which 59 per cent was exported. Sales of china clay (or kaolin), the largest export, were 2.4 million tonnes, of which 87 per cent was exported.

The largest non-energy mineral imports are metals (ores, concentrates and scrap – valued at £2.0 billion in 2000), refined non-ferrous metals (£3.9 billion), iron and steel (£2.2 billion), and non-metallic mineral products (£6.6 billion, of which rough diamonds account for £4.4 billion).

Further reading

Annual publications

Digest of Environmental Statistics. Department for Environment, Food & Rural Affairs. Available only on the Internet on the DEFRA website (*www.defra.gov.uk/environment/statistics/des/index.htm*).

Digest of United Kingdom Energy Statistics. Department of Trade and Industry. The Stationery Office.

Energy Report (the Blue Book). Department of Trade and Industry. The Stationery Office.

United Kingdom Minerals Yearbook. British Geological Survey.

Other

Draft Water Resources (EIA) (England and Wales) Regulations 2002 – Consultation document. DEFRA, 2002. Available on the Internet (*www.defra.gov.uk*).

Websites

Department of Trade and Industry
www.dti.gov.uk

Department for Environment, Food & Rural Affairs
www.defra.gov.uk

Northern Ireland Executive
www.northernireland.gov.uk

Scottish Executive
www.scotland.gov.uk

National Assembly for Wales
www.wales.gov.uk

British Geological Survey Minerals UK
www.bgs.ac.uk

Office of Gas and Electricity Markets
www.ofgem.gov.uk

www.

29 Finance and other service industries

The service sector in the United Kingdom continues to grow and accounted for 71.4 per cent of gross value added at current basic prices and for 77.5 per cent of employment in 2001. There were over 22.8 million workforce jobs in the sector at the end of the year.

Financial services and the economy

The UK's financial services sector accounts for around 5 per cent of gross domestic product (GDP) and employs more than 1 million people. UK financial sector net exports reached a record £13.2 billion in 2001.

Service industries – then and now: gross value added at 1995 basic prices

	1995 = 100		% change
	1951	2001	
Service industries	34.9	124.8	+258

Table 29.1 Index numbers of gross value added[1] at basic prices: service industries, UK

				1995=100
	1996	1999	2000	2001
Wholesale and retail trade	106.1	119.3	122.9	127.1
Hotels and restaurants	101.2	102.7	100.4	96.6
Transport, storage and communication	104.3	129.0	140.4	146.3
Financial intermediation[2]	103.8	117.0	121.4	126.0
Adjustment for financial services	106.9	127.6	135.7	144.4
Real estate, renting and business activities	104.8	124.8	130.4	137.2
Public administration and defence	98.8	97.8	98.8	100.0
Education	101.3	105.2	106.7	118.3
Health and social work	103.2	112.9	114.8	118.3
Other social and personal services	105.4	116.4	121.2	125.9
Total	103.6	116.6	120.8	124.8

1 Represents the difference between the value of the output of goods and services produced by a company and its intermediate consumption – the value of the goods and services or raw materials used up in the production of such output.
2 The activity by which an institutional unit acquires financial assets and incurs liabilities on its own account by engaging in financial transactions on the market.
Source: Office for National Statistics

Historically, the heart of the UK financial services industry has been in the 'Square Mile' in the City of London, and this remains broadly the case. Among the major financial institutions and markets in the City are the Bank of England, the London Stock Exchange and Lloyd's insurance market. London is one of the three main financial centres in the world and the premier financial centre in Europe. Scotland (Edinburgh and Glasgow) is the second financial centre in the UK, and one of the main European centres for institutional equities – at the end of 2001 over £326 billion of funds were under management in Scotland. Other sizeable UK financial centres are Leeds, Manchester, Bristol and Birmingham.

International Financial Services London (IFSL) (*www.ifsl.org.uk*) promotes the international activities of UK-based financial institutions and related professional and business services. It also seeks to raise awareness of the UK's leading role in international financial markets and highlight the major contribution of financial services to the UK economy.

Scale of the financial services sector
The UK's trade surplus on financial services is the largest in the world. A report by IFSL in April 2002 confirmed the UK's strong international position in financial services:

- UK banking sector assets reached over £3,400 billion at the end of 2001;

- assets under fund management in the UK were over £2,800 billion in 2000, of which nearly £600 billion was managed on behalf of overseas clients;

- London has the world's second largest derivatives exchange;

- London is the biggest international centre for foreign exchange trading;

- the revenue of UK management consultancies reached £8 billion in 2001, up by £2 billion compared with 1999; and

- five of the ten largest law firms in the world are international law firms based in London.

Bank of England

The Bank of England (*www.bankofengland.co.uk*) was established in 1694 by Act of Parliament and Royal Charter as a corporate body. Its capital stock was acquired by the Government in 1946.

As the UK's central bank, the Bank's overriding objective is to maintain a stable and efficient monetary and financial framework for the effective operation of the economy. In pursuing this goal, it has three main purposes:

- maintaining the integrity and value of the currency;

- maintaining the stability of the financial system; and

- seeking to ensure the effectiveness of the financial services sector.

Under the Bank of England Act 1998, the Court of Directors is responsible for managing the affairs of the Bank, apart from the formulation of monetary policy, and comprises the Governor, two Deputy Governors and 16 non-executive directors. The Court is required to report annually to the Chancellor of the Exchequer.

Monetary policy framework
The Bank's monetary policy objective is to maintain price stability and, subject to that, to support the Government's economic policy, including growth and employment objectives. Price stability is defined in terms of the Government's inflation target (see page 334). The responsibility for meeting this target and for setting interest rates rests with the Bank's Monetary Policy Committee, which comprises the Governor, the two Deputy Governors and six other members. The Committee meets every month and interest rate decisions are announced as soon as is practicable after the meeting; the minutes are published within two weeks and are placed on the Bank's website. The Committee is accountable to the Bank's Court of Directors, to government and to Parliament.

Financial stability
Under the Memorandum of Understanding between the Bank, HM Treasury and the Financial Services Authority, the Bank is responsible for the overall stability of the financial system, and its Financial Stability Committee oversees its work in

this area. In exceptional circumstances, the Bank may provide financial support as a last resort to prevent problems affecting one financial institution from spreading to other parts of the financial system. It also oversees the effectiveness of the financial sector in meeting the needs of customers and in maintaining the sector's international competitiveness.

Other main functions

The Bank, through its daily operations in the money market, supplies the funds which the banking system as a whole needs to achieve balance at the end of each day. By setting the interest rate for these operations, the Bank influences the general level of interest rates as the interest rate at which the Bank deals is quickly passed on through the financial system, which in turn affects the whole pattern of interest rates across the UK economy.

The Bank provides banking services to its customers, principally the Government, the banking system and other central banks. It plays a key role in payment and settlement systems.

Banknotes and coins

In England and Wales the Bank has the sole right to issue banknotes, which are backed by government and other securities. The profit from the note issue is paid directly to the Government. Three Scottish and four Northern Ireland banks may also issue notes, but these have to be fully backed by Bank of England notes.

The circulation of coins is the responsibility of the Royal Mint. At the end of 2000 there were over

22.7 billion coins in circulation in the UK, with a face value of £2.7 billion. Some 2.1 billion circulating coins were issued in the UK in 2000/01.

Banking services

The UK is a major banking centre, and UK banking sector assets were valued at over £3,400 billion at the end of 2001, nearly three times the level in 1991, with over half being owned by overseas banks, mostly from the EU. At the end of March 2002 there were 184 authorised banks incorporated in the UK and a further 113 authorised branches of banks incorporated outside the European Economic Area. In addition, 377 branches of European-authorised institutions were entitled to accept deposits in the UK.

'Retail' banking primarily caters for personal customers and small businesses. Nearly all banks also engage in some 'wholesale' activities, which involve taking larger deposits, deploying funds in money-market instruments, and making corporate loans and investments, while some concentrate on wholesale business. Banks feature strongly among the UK's top companies (see page 343). Six of the top 20 companies by market

Table 29.2 Banknotes in circulation, UK

	Value of notes in circulation end-February 2002 (£ million)	Number of new notes issued in year to end-February 2002 (million)
£5	1,044	233
£10	5,928	292
£20	16,335	419
£50	5,203	11
Other notes[1]	874	–
Total	**29,384**	**955**

1 Includes higher value notes used internally in the Bank, for example, as cover for the note issues of banks of issue in Scotland and Northern Ireland in excess of their permitted issues.
Source: Bank of England

Contribution of banking to the UK economy

A report by IFSL, published in April 2002, found that the banking industry contributed about 3.6 per cent of the UK's GDP and provided around 445,000 jobs, or around 40 per cent of employment in financial services. Banking generated £3.2 billion in overseas earnings in 2001. Other strengths identified by the report included:

- banking sector deposits in the UK were the third largest in the world, being exceeded only by those in Japan and the United States;

- the UK is the world's largest single market for cross-border banking, with nearly 20 per cent of international bank lending in December 2001;

- London is one of the most important centres for onshore private banking and the second most popular destination for offshore wealth after Switzerland; and

- London is the largest investment banking centre in Europe.

capitalisation are banks: HSBC, Royal Bank of Scotland, Lloyds TSB, Barclays, HBOS and Abbey National.

Retail bank services include current accounts, savings accounts, loan arrangements, credit and debit cards, mortgages, insurance, investment products, share-dealing services and 'wealth management' services. Around 92 per cent of households in Great Britain have at least one adult member with a bank or building society or other savings account (see Table 29.3).

'Universal banking services', giving access to the banks' basic bank accounts and a new Post Office card account, are expected to be available through post offices from 2003. The services are intended to tackle financial exclusion and bring those people without bank accounts into the financial mainstream, while ensuring that benefit recipients and pensioners can continue to receive their money in cash at their local post office when such payments are automated in 2003. The major financial institutions have agreed to contribute by making their own basic bank accounts accessible

Table 29.3 Households¹ with different types of account or savings in Great Britain, 2000/01

	Per cent of households
Accounts	
Current account	86
Post Office account	8
Individual Savings Account (ISA)	23
Tax Exempt Special Savings Account (TESSA)	13
Other bank or building society accounts (excluding current accounts, ISAs and TESSAs)	59
Other savings	
Stocks and shares	25
Unit trusts or investment trusts	6
Personal Equity Plans	12
Gilt-edged stock	1
Premium Bonds	26
National Savings Bonds	4
Company share scheme/profit-sharing scheme	5
Save as you earn	1
Any type of account	92

1 Households in which at least one member has an account. Covers accounts held by adults only.
Source: Family Resources Survey, Department for Work and Pensions

at post offices and by making a financial contribution to the cost of running the Post Office card account.

Traditionally, the major retail banks have operated through their local branches, but the number of such branches is falling as banks have taken steps to cut costs. This is partly because more customers are using telephone and Internet banking. According to APACS (see page 455), over 15 million people in the UK accessed their current accounts in 2001 using the telephone, the Internet or interactive digital television. About a third of these used remote banking to initiate 58 million payments in 2001, with the most popular application being the settlement of credit card bills. The UK is the largest European online banking market. Most major banks have introduced Internet banking, either as an additional option for customers or as a separate stand-alone facility.

Supervision

Banks are regulated by the Financial Services Authority (see page 463). They are required to meet minimum standards on the integrity and competence of directors and management, the adequacy of capital and cash flow, and the systems and controls to deal with the risks they experience. If a bank fails to meet the criteria, its activities may be restricted, or it may be closed. These arrangements are intended to strengthen, but not guarantee, the protection of bank depositors, thereby increasing confidence in the banking system as a whole.

Competition

A major review of banking services, *Competition in UK Banking: A Report to the Chancellor of the Exchequer*, published in 2000, recommended a more competitive policy framework for UK banking. In response, the Government announced measures designed to improve competition and deliver benefits to consumers.

In March 2002 the Competition Commission issued a report on small business banking, which found that there was a complex monopoly in the supply of banking services to small and medium-sized enterprises (SMEs) and identified practices carried out by the UK's eight main clearing banks that restricted or distorted competition and operated against the public interest. It recommended a number of changes to the banks' practices with the intention of reducing barriers to entry, improving choice for SMEs and making easier the switching of accounts between banks. The Government has accepted the Commission's report and recommendations, and the Director General of Fair Trading is seeking undertakings from the banks on the proposed changes.

Investment and private banking

London is a major international centre for investment and private banking, and accounts for an estimated 50 per cent of investment banking activity in Europe. Global banks dominate the international market, and most have headquarters or a major office in London.

Investment banks offer a range of professional financial services, including corporate finance and asset management. Advice on mergers and acquisitions accounted for 57 per cent of investment banking revenue originating in the UK in 2001. Equity underwriting accounted for a further 25 per cent, and banks facilitate a wide range of equity finance transactions, such as flotations, the issue or placing of new shares, and management buy-outs.

The UK, along with the United States and Switzerland, is one of the top centres for private banking. Some £360 billion of private client securities are managed by banks, fund managers and stockbrokers in the UK.

Building societies

Building societies are mutual institutions, owned collectively by their savers and borrowers. As well as their retail deposit-taking services, they specialise in housing finance, making long-term mortgage loans against the security of property – usually private dwellings purchased for owner-occupation. Some of the larger societies provide a full range of personal banking services. According to the Building Societies Association (BSA) (*www.bsa.org.uk*), about 15 million adults have building society savings accounts (around 25 million accounts), and over 2.5 million borrowers are buying their homes through mortgage loans from a building society. The chief requirements for societies are that:

- their principal purpose is making loans which are secured on residential property and are funded substantially by their members;

- at least 75 per cent per cent of lending has to be on the security of housing; and

- a minimum of 50 per cent of funds must be in the form of deposits made by individual members.

There are 65 authorised building societies, all of which are members of the BSA, with total assets of over £175 billion and around 2,100 branches. The largest society is the Nationwide, with assets of £75 billion in April 2002.

The number of societies has fallen substantially in recent years as a result of mergers and as several large societies have given up their mutual status and become banks. Many of the remaining societies have taken steps to defend their mutual status, for example, by requiring new members to assign to charity any 'windfall' payments arising from a conversion.

Payment systems

Apart from credit and debit card arrangements, the main payment systems are run by three separate companies operating under an umbrella organisation, the Association for Payment Clearing Services (APACS) (*www.apacs.org.uk*). One system, Cheque and Credit Clearing, covers bulk paper clearings – cheques and paper credits. A second, CHAPS (Clearing House Automated Payment System), is a nationwide electronic transfer service for same-day payments. A third, BACS (formerly Bankers' Automated Clearing Services), covers bulk electronic clearing for direct credits, standing orders and direct debits. A total of 31 banks and building societies are members of one or more clearing companies, while several hundred others obtain access to APACS clearing through agency arrangements with one of the members.

The Government plans legislation to establish a new regulatory framework governing UK payment systems. As a result, the Office of Fair Trading (see page 341) would have new powers to promote competition in payment systems.

Trends in financial transactions

Major changes in the nature of financial transactions have included the rapid growth in the use of plastic cards (which first appeared in 1966) and of automated teller machines (ATMs). According to APACS, there are about 137 million plastic cards in issue in the UK, with 89 per cent of adults holding one or more cards. In 2001 there were over 6.6 billion plastic card transactions in the UK. Most small non-regular payments are still

Table 29.4 Transaction trends in the UK

Million

	1991	1996	2000	2001
Plastic card purchases	1,104	2,413	3,914	4,371
of which:				
Debit card	359	1,270	2,337	2,696
Credit and charge card	699	1,025	1,452	1,558
Store card[1]	46	118	125	117
Plastic card withdrawals at ATMs and counters	1,112	1,656	2,102	2,269
Direct debits, standing orders, direct credits and CHAPS	1,848	2,613	3,470	3,705
Cheques	3,882	3,203	2,700	2,565
of which:				
For payment	3,450	2,901	2,515	2,399
For cash acquisition	432	302	185	166
Total non-cash transactions	7,946	9,885	12,185	12,909
Cash payments[1]	28,022	26,318	27,910	27,860
Post Office Order Book payments and passbook withdrawals	1,061	1,114	880	821
Total transactions	**37,025**	**37,318**	**40,975**	**41,589**

1 Estimated figures.
Source: APACS

made by cash, but the trend is away from cash and cheques towards greater use of plastic cards (see Table 29.4).

Consumers now acquire more than half their cash through withdrawals from ATMs, which in 2001 dispensed £127.7 billion in 2.2 billion transactions. The number of ATMs has more than doubled in the last ten years, to 36,700 at the end of 2001. About two-thirds of adults use ATMs regularly, making on average 70 withdrawals a year.

Direct debit and standing order payments account for nearly 60 per cent of regular bill payments, and 72 per cent of adults have set up at least one direct debit or standing order. Many mortgage and other loan repayments and life insurance contributions are made by direct debit, as are the majority of electricity, gas, water and council tax bills. Direct debit payments rose by 7 per cent to reach 2.2 billion in 2001.

Plastic cards

Debit cards, where payments are deducted directly from the purchaser's bank or building society account, were first issued in 1987 and the number of cards is growing strongly. They are often combined with cheque guarantee and ATM facilities in a single card. About 54 million cards have been issued, and 80 per cent of adults in the UK hold a debit card. Over half of adults are regular users, with each making on average 116 debit card payments in 2001. The total number of debit card payments in the UK was 2.7 billion in 2001, 15 per cent higher than in 2000.

There are about 56 million credit cards (including charge cards) in use in the UK, and 60 per cent of adults have at least one credit card. There are a large number of credit card providers and over 1,300 different brands of card. They have become increasingly popular as a source of consumer credit and are also the most common way for adults to buy goods and services using the Internet.

Fraud losses on UK-issued plastic cards have risen considerably and totalled £411 million in 2001, with counterfeit cards accounting for the biggest proportion of card crime, about 39 per cent. To combat fraud, banks are investing in highly secure chip cards, in which information is contained on a microchip embedded in the card. About 25 million chip cards have been issued. Cash machines and point-of-sale terminals are also being upgraded. By 2005 plastic cards will be authorised in the UK by the customer keying in his or her PIN (personal identification number) rather than by signing a receipt.

National Savings and Investments

National Savings and Investments (NS&I) (*www.nsandi.com*), an executive agency of the Chancellor of the Exchequer, is a source of finance for government borrowing and offers personal savers a range of investments. Formerly known as National Savings, it changed its corporate name in February 2002 to reflect the changes in products provided and enhancements in services to its customers. It is developing new products and services, and in March 2002 launched its first guaranteed equity bond, where the return is linked to the performance of the FTSE 100 index.

Gross sales of NS&I products totalled £10.3 billion in 2001/02 and over £62.4 billion remained invested in NS&I products as at March 2002. Premium Bonds are held by around 23 million people and are entered in a monthly draw, with tax-free prizes (instead of interest) ranging from £50 to a single top prize each month of £1 million. Other savings products include Savings Certificates (both Fixed Interest and Index-linked), Pensioners' Bonds, Children's Bonus Bonds, cash mini ISAs (see page 460), and Ordinary and Investment Accounts (where deposits and withdrawals can be made at post offices).

Friendly societies

Friendly societies have traditionally been unincorporated societies of individuals, offering their members a limited range of financial and insurance services, such as small-scale savings products, life insurance and provision against loss of income through sickness or unemployment. Under the *Financial Services and Markets Act 2000*, the Government removed on 1 December 2001 the remaining restrictions on the activities of friendly society subsidiaries.

At the end of March 2002 there were 237 friendly societies, of which life directive and incorporated societies carrying on long-term business accounted for 95 per cent of the movement's total funds. There were 36 life directive societies, which are subject to the requirement of the EC Life Insurance Directive, and six societies incorporated under the *Friendly Societies Act 1992*.

Credit unions

Credit unions are mutually owned financial co-operatives established under the *Credit Unions Act 1979*. They aim to promote thrift among members, create sources of credit at a reasonable rate of interest, and use and control members' savings for their mutual benefit. There are 700 credit unions registered in Great Britain, with a membership of about 300,000 and assets of around £200 million.

Responsibility for registration and supervision of credit unions passed to the Financial Services Authority (see page 463) in December 2001 and a new regulatory regime for credit unions took effect in July 2002. Among the key features of the regime are that credit unions have to meet a basic test of solvency and maintain a level of initial capital and a minimum liquidity ratio, while for the first time members have protection for their deposits through the Financial Services Compensation Scheme (see pages 463–4).

Private equity/venture capital

Private equity/venture capital companies offer medium- and long-term equity financing for new and developing businesses, management buy-outs and buy-ins, and company rescues. The British Venture Capital Association (BVCA) (*www.bvca.co.uk*) has 169 full members, and represents private equity and venture capital sources in the UK. During 2001, according to a report for the BVCA based on data provided by 97 per cent of its members, UK private equity and venture capital firms invested in a record 1,597 businesses worldwide, although the amount invested, at £6,164 million, was 25 per cent less than in 2000. Of this investment, £4,752 million (77 per cent) was in the UK. The Government is encouraging the further development of venture capital, including new Regional Venture Capital Funds (see chapter 22).

Other credit and financial services

Finance houses and leasing companies provide consumer credit, business finance and leasing, and motor finance. The 109 full members of the Finance and Leasing Association carried out new business worth £74 billion in 2001.

Factoring and invoice discounting comprises a range of financial services, including credit management and finance in exchange for outstanding invoices. The industry provides working capital to nearly 30,000 businesses a year.

Member companies of the Factors & Discounters Association (*www.factors.org.uk*) handled business worth £89 billion in 2001, 16 per cent higher than in 2000.

Insurance

The UK insurance industry is the largest in Europe and the third largest in the world. In 2001 it employed almost 360,000 people in insurance companies, Lloyd's of London, insurance brokers and other related activities, representing in total over a third of all employment in financial services. About 50,000 of these jobs are supported by the London Market, a unique international wholesale insurance market.

Net worldwide premiums generated by the UK insurance industry reached £156 billion in 2001, according to the Association of British Insurers (ABI) (*www.abi.org.uk*). UK risks were £119 billion and overseas risks £37 billion. The industry has almost £1,100 billion invested in company shares and other assets.

Main types of insurance
There are two broad categories of insurance: long-term (such as life insurance), where contracts may be for periods of many years; and general, where contracts are for a year or less. Most insurance companies reinsure their risks; this performs an important function in spreading losses and in helping companies manage their businesses.

UK long-term insurance has been rising more rapidly than general insurance, and in 2001 accounted for £117 billion of net worldwide premiums by the UK industry, compared with £39 billion of general insurance. Life insurance accounted for 40 per cent of long-term premium income, occupational pensions 31 per cent and individual pensions 25 per cent. About 54 per cent of households have life insurance cover.

Motor insurance accounts for over a quarter of general insurance premiums. Other important areas are property insurance, and accident and health insurance. Independent intermediaries distributed 57 per cent of general insurance premiums in 2001, direct selling 21 per cent, company agents 10 per cent and banks and building societies 7 per cent. Direct selling in areas such as motor and household insurance has

increased, reflecting the growth of insurers offering telephone-based and Internet-based services.

Structure of the industry
At the end of 2001, 808 companies were authorised to conduct one or more classes of insurance business in the UK. Nearly 600 companies carry on general business only, 160 are authorised for long-term business only and about 60 are authorised to conduct both types of business. About 400 companies belong to the ABI.

The industry includes both public limited companies and mutual institutions (companies owned by their policyholders), although the mutual sector has gradually contracted. The biggest insurance group in the UK is Aviva (formerly CGNU), while Standard Life is the largest mutual insurer in Europe.

Insurance firms and markets have recently been adversely affected by a number of events, in particular costs arising from the collapse of the World Trade Centre in New York in the terrorist attacks in September 2001 (see page 76) and weak equity markets (see page 462). The Financial Services Authority has relaxed some of its requirements on solvency to ease the position for insurance companies. In addition, the insurance company Equitable Life has experienced particular problems arising from guarantees offered to a number of its policyholders, and closed to new business in December 2000. In 2002 a compromise scheme was agreed to put the company on a more stable footing for the future. The Government has set up an independent inquiry to examine the events at Equitable Life and to consider the lessons that can be drawn for the conduct, administration and regulation of the UK life assurance sector.

The London Market
The London Market is an international wholesale insurance market-place accepting risk from around the world. It is the main centre for world reinsurance business and for marine, aviation, satellite and other forms of transport insurance. It consists of insurance and reinsurance companies, Lloyd's of London, protection and indemnity clubs (originally created to serve the marine industry) and brokers. Gross premiums of the London Market from reported returns were estimated at £20 billion in 2001. Virtually all companies participating in the company sector of

the London Market are members of the International Underwriting Association of London (IUA) (*www.iua.co.uk*), which in mid-2002 had 70 members. Over three-quarters of the companies operating in the London Market are overseas-owned.

Lloyd's of London

Lloyd's (*www.lloydsoflondon.com*) is an incorporated society of private insurers in London. It is not a company but a market for insurance administered by the Council of Lloyd's and Lloyd's Regulatory and Market Boards.

Lloyd's is the world's second largest commercial insurer and third largest reinsurer. For 2002 the Lloyd's market has a capacity to accept premiums of over £12 billion. There are 88 syndicates underwriting insurance at Lloyd's during 2002, covering all classes of business from over 100 countries. Each syndicate is managed by an underwriting agent responsible for appointing a professional underwriter to accept insurance risks and manage claims on behalf of the members. In 2001, although premium income rose sharply, there was an overall loss, reflecting an exceptional series of events, notably the terrorist attack on the United States of 11 September (see page 76) where the estimated net loss for the Lloyd's market was £1.98 billion.

In January 2002 Lloyd's announced a series of proposals to change the market. Following consultation, the reforms were supported in a vote of members in September 2002 and will be implemented in the coming months. A new franchise arrangement is envisaged, under which Lloyd's will be the franchiser and the managing agents will be the franchisees. A single Franchise Board will replace the Regulatory and Market Boards and will help to shape the market's standards and business practices. Other changes include annual accounting, which is intended to improve transparency and efficiency; the development of a range of investment schemes aimed at attracting new capital on a non-membership basis; and from the beginning of 2003 there will be no new 'Names' – members with unlimited liability.

Investment

The UK has considerable expertise in fund management, which involves managing funds on

Table 29.5 Assets and net investment by UK insurance companies, pension funds and trusts

		£ billion
	Holdings at end of 2000 (market values)	Net investment in 2001 (cash values)
Long-term insurance funds	947.1	23.5
General insurance funds	90.2	11.4
Self-administered pension funds	768.4	10.8
Investment trusts	63.7	0.5
Unit trusts and OEICs	235.5	12.2
Adjustment[1]	−185.3	−1.8
Total	**1,919.6**	**56.6**

1 Adjustment to take account of investment of one institutional group in another.
Source: Office for National Statistics

behalf of investors, or advising them how best to invest their funds. The main types of investment fund include pension schemes, life insurance, unit trusts, open-ended investment companies (OEICs) and investment trusts. The assets of these institutions were worth £1,920 billion at the end of 2000 (see Table 29.5), of which UK company securities accounted for £955 billion, UK gilt-edged stock £229 billion and overseas company and government securities £415 billion.

The final report of the Myners review of institutional investment, published in 2001, found that there were a number of distortions affecting institutional investment decision-making and proposed a set of clear principles, which would apply to pension funds and, in due course, other institutional investors. In February 2002 the Government issued three consultation documents covering proposed legislation on pension scheme trustees, including a proposed new duty for trustees and fund managers to intervene in companies where this is in the interests of the beneficiaries, and a requirement for funds to have an independent custodian.

Pension funds

Total assets of UK self-administered pension funds were estimated at about £768 billion at the end of 2000. Pension funds are major investors in securities markets, holding around 20 per cent of securities listed on the London Stock Exchange. Funds are managed mainly by the investment management houses.

Unit trusts and open-ended investment companies

Nearly 2,000 authorised unit trusts and OEICs pool investors' money in funds divided into units or shares of equal size, enabling people with relatively small amounts of money to benefit from diversified and managed portfolios. In April 2002 total funds under management were £240 billion, of which £46 billion represented funds in Personal Equity Plans and £25 billion in Individual Savings Accounts (ISAs). Most unit trusts are general funds, investing in a wide variety of UK or international securities, but there are also many specialist funds.

There are nearly 140 unit trust and OEIC management groups, of which 55 had total fund values exceeding £1 billion in April 2002. Investment fund management groups are represented by the Investment Management Association (IMA) (*www.investmentuk.org*), formed in February 2002 by a merger of the Association of Unit Trusts and Investment Funds and the Fund Managers' Association.

OEICs, set up in 1997, are similar to unit trusts, but investors buy shares in the fund rather than units. By April 2002, 740 OEICs had been set up by 65 management groups, and OEIC funds were worth £97 billion.

Investment trusts

Investment trust companies are listed on the London Stock Exchange and their shares can be bought and sold in the same way as other companies. They invest principally in the shares and securities of other companies. Assets are purchased mainly out of shareholders' funds, although investment trusts are also allowed to borrow money for investment.

There are 395 investment trusts, which form the largest listed sector of the London Stock Exchange. Around 35 per cent of their shares by value are held by private investors. About 305 listed trust companies are members of the Association of Investment Trust Companies (*www.aitc.co.uk*). At the end of May 2002 the industry had £64 billion of assets under management and a stock market capitalisation of £48 billion.

Share ownership

The latest analysis by the Office for National Statistics of share ownership showed that, at 31 December 2000, financial institutions held the bulk of equities. UK financial institutions held shares valued at £881 billion (48 per cent of the total market value of £1,811 billion), with insurance companies holding £381 billion and pension funds £321 billion. Holders from outside the UK had £587 billion (32 per cent). The value of holdings of UK individual shareholders was £290 billion (16 per cent). About 25 per cent of households have at least one adult owning shares (see Table 29.3).

According to ProShare (an independent organisation encouraging share ownership), the number of investment clubs – groups of individuals, usually about 15 to 20 people, who regularly invest in shares – has risen to around 12,000.

Tax-free savings

Tax-free saving is encouraged by the Individual Savings Account (ISA), which in 1999 succeeded Personal Equity Plans (PEPs) and TESSAs (Tax Exempt Special Savings Accounts) as the main method of tax-free saving. ISAs are guaranteed to run until at least April 2009. Until April 2006 each individual can contribute up to £7,000 a year in total. There are three main elements of an ISA:

- cash – up to £3,000 each year – such as in a bank or building society ISA account;

- stocks and shares – up to £7,000 a year in a maxi ISA and £3,000 in a mini ISA (see below); and

- life insurance – up to £1,000 a year.

In addition, savers can roll over capital from a matured TESSA into a cash ISA or a special TESSA-only ISA.

There are two main types of ISA: a maxi ISA, which can include all three elements in a single ISA with one manager; and mini ISAs, which allow savers to have different managers, for the cash, stocks and shares, and life insurance components. Savers can choose to put money into mini ISAs or a maxi ISA, but not both, in each tax year.

In 2001/02 subscriptions were made to about 12.0 million ISAs – 9.5 million mini ISAs and 2.5 million maxi ISAs – attracting £28.5 billion (see Table 29.6).

Table 29.6 Subscriptions to ISAs in the UK

	Subscriptions in 2000/01 (£ million)	Subscriptions in 2001/02 (£ million)	% of subscriptions in 2001/02
Mini ISAs			
Stocks and shares	1,843	1,772	6.2
Cash	13,871	16,831	59.0
Life insurance	99	153	0.5
Total invested in mini ISAs	15,813	18,756	65.7
Maxi ISAs			
Stocks and shares	13,341	9,547	33.4
Cash	606	227	0.8
Life insurance	18	20	0.1
Total invested in maxi ISAs	13,965	9,794	34.3
Total invested in ISAs	**29,778**	**28,549**	**100.0**

Source: Inland Revenue

Sandler review of retail savings

In July 2002 the Sandler review of medium-term and long-term retail savings was published. It found two main problems in the UK savings market: competitive forces in the sector did not work effectively, and savings levels were insufficient, particularly among the less well-off, partly because of the high cost of serving this group. Key recommendations of the review to the Government and the Financial Services Authority (FSA) include:

- a series of simple investment products with regulation of product features, which could be sold outside the current regulatory regime for the sale of, and advice on, investment products;

- reforms to 'with-profits' policies[1] to make their structure and management simpler and more transparent;

- a new model for the provision of independent financial advice, with more stringent investment qualifications for financial advisers;

- tax measures aimed at simplifying the current regime for retail savings products; and

- measures to boost consumer education in financial matters.

The Government will be taking forward the review's suggestions, and intends to consult consumer representatives, the industry and the FSA on these 'stakeholder' products and their design.

Financial markets

London Stock Exchange

The London Stock Exchange (*www.londonstockexchange.com*) is one of the world's leading centres for equity trading, particularly for trade in international equities where in 2001 London accounted for more than half of total cross-border trading. In 2001 turnover in international equities was £3,676 billion and in UK equities £1,905 billion. At the end of 2001, 1,809 UK and 453 international companies were listed on the main market, with a market capitalisation of £1,524 billion and £2,580 billion respectively. A further 629 companies, with a total capitalisation of £11.6 billion, were listed on AIM, the Alternative Investment Market, primarily for small, young and growing companies. The 'techMARK' market brings together 243 of the listed companies engaged in technology or related sectors.

Several other products for raising capital are handled, including Eurobonds (see page 462), warrants, depositary receipts and gilt-edged stock (see page 352). The London Stock Exchange provides a secondary or trading market where investors can buy or sell gilts. Turnover in UK gilts on the Exchange was £2,030 billion in 2001.

The CREST computerised settlement system for shares and other company securities is now

---

1 With-profits products offer equity-related returns, with some protection from market fluctuations.

Share price movements

A range of indices track share price movements on the Exchange. The most widely quoted is the FTSE 100 index (the 'Footsie'), which relates to the 100 largest UK companies, by market capitalisation, listed on the Exchange. Among the other indices often quoted are:

- the FTSE 250 index – the next biggest 250 companies;

- the FTSE 350 index – the largest 350 companies;

- the FTSE All-share – all the companies on the main market;

- the FTSE techMARK 100 – the top 100 companies on the techMARK; and

- the Eurotop 300 – the top 300 companies in Europe.

During 2001 the FTSE 100 fell to a low of 4,434 in September in the aftermath of the terrorist attacks in New York and Washington (see page 76) – stock markets around the world fell substantially in late September but quickly recovered, and the FTSE 100 reached 5,370 in December 2001. However, during summer 2002 it fell back again, reflecting concern about the global economy. By the end of August 2002 the FTSE 100 was 4,227, 39 per cent below the peak of 6,930 in 1999, and during September 2002 it fell below 3,700 to a six-year low.

settling over 300,000 transactions a day with a value of nearly £500 billion.

Other equity exchanges

There are three other, relatively small markets in the City of London for trading equities: Virt-x (formed from a merger of 'Tradepoint' and SWX Swiss exchange), OM London, and OFEX. The OFEX market for small companies became directly regulated for the first time in December 2001.

Bond markets

London is at the centre of the Euromarket (a major market in a variety of currencies lent outside their domestic markets) and houses most of the leading international banks and securities firms. According to IFSL, London-based bookrunners are estimated to account for about 60 per cent of Eurobonds issued and around 70 per cent of trading in the secondary market. CoredealMTS acts as an exchange for transactions involving such bonds.

Foreign exchange market

A survey by the Bank for International Settlements (BIS) in 2001 showed that daily foreign exchange turnover in the UK was US$504 billion and that London was the world's biggest trading centre, with nearly a third of global net daily turnover. Trading in London was down by a fifth since the previous survey in 1998, mainly reflecting the overall fall in global foreign exchange trading. One factor in the decline was the introduction of the euro in 1999, which eliminated cross-trading between the former euro currencies. Dealing is conducted through telephone and electronic links between the banks, other financial institutions and a number of firms of foreign exchange brokers which act as intermediaries.

Bullion markets

London is the world's most liquid 'spot' (immediate) market for gold and the global clearing centre for worldwide gold trading. It is also the global clearing centre for silver. Around 60 banks and other financial trading companies participate in the London gold and silver markets. London fixes the world's gold price twice a day and the world silver price once a day, through the members of the London Bullion Market Association.

Derivatives

Financial derivatives, including 'futures' and 'options', offer a means of protection against changes in prices, exchange rates and interest rates. The UK is the most important 'over the counter' (OTC) market-place, as measured by booking location. According to the BIS, the UK accounted for 36 per cent of the global OTC derivatives market in April 2001, representing average daily turnover of US$275 billion.

In 2001 the London International Financial Futures and Options Exchange (LIFFE) (www.liffe.com) was acquired by the pan-European stock exchange Euronext, which had been formed by the merger of exchanges in Amsterdam, Brussels and Paris. LIFFE has changed its name to Euronext.liffe. It is the second largest derivatives market in the world and also handles trade in commodities such as coffee, cocoa and sugar. LIFFE traded a record 216 million contracts in 2001, 65 per cent more than in 2000. Business worth £375 billion a day was traded through its electronic trading platform, LIFFE CONNECT. The LIFFE market and its broad range of products can now be accessed from 530 locations in 25 countries.

Other exchanges

Other important City exchanges include:

- the *London Metal Exchange* (LME) – the primary base metals market in the world, trading contracts in aluminium, aluminium alloy, copper, lead, nickel, tin and zinc, and handling 59 million lots in 2001;

- the *International Petroleum Exchange* (IPE), the largest energy futures and options market in Europe – in 2001 it became a wholly owned subsidiary of Intercontinental Exchange Inc (ICE) of the United States; and

- the *Baltic Exchange,* the world's leading international shipping market.

The London Clearing House (LCH) clears and settles business at LIFFE, LME, IPE and Virt-x.

Regulation

The *Financial Services and Markets Act 2000,* which came into force on 1 December 2001, created a new framework for the regulation of financial services. It formally established the Financial Services Authority (FSA) (*www.fsa.gov.uk*), which had already been in operation since 1997, as the single regulator for the financial services industry. The FSA became responsible for the regulation of investment business, banks, building societies and insurance companies previously handled by nine regulatory bodies. In May 2001 it acquired responsibility from the London Stock Exchange for acting as the competent authority for listing companies in the UK. A new single Financial Services Compensation Scheme and a single Financial Ombudsman Service have also been set up.

FSA objectives and functions

The FSA's statutory objectives are maintaining confidence in the UK financial system and

promoting public understanding of it, providing an appropriate degree of consumer protection and reducing the potential for financial crime. In delivering these objectives, the FSA has to be efficient and economic, facilitate innovation in financial services, take account of the international nature of financial services business and minimise any adverse effects of regulation on competition.

In November 2001 the Government announced that the FSA would also be given responsibility for regulating the provision of mortgage advice and general insurance broking – it had earlier said that the FSA would become responsible for regulating mortgage lending. Currently the General Insurance Standards Council sets standards for selling general insurance products, while most mortgage lenders and intermediaries are signatories to the voluntary Mortgage Code, which is overseen by the Mortgage Code Compliance Board. The FSA is consulting on these changes, which are expected to take effect in 2004.

During 2001/02 the FSA introduced or announced, among other things:

- proposals intended to enhance consumer choice by reforming the way in which financial advice is provided in the UK, involving the end of the 'polarisation' regime under which financial advisers have to be either 'independent' (offering advice on all products and companies in the market) or 'tied' (representing one company and selling only its products);

- comparative tables for consumers of a range of financial products, including unit trust ISAs, personal pensions (including stakeholder pensions), savings endowments, mortgage endowments and investment bonds;

- plans to strengthen regulation of the insurance industry, including proposals to reform the running of with-profits investments; and

- proposals for a simpler and more practical pricing system for unit trusts and OEICs.

Compensation

The single Financial Services Compensation Scheme (FSCS) (*www.fscs.org.uk*) came into operation in December 2001, replacing eight previous compensation schemes. It provides compensation for:

- *deposits* – when an authorised deposit-taking firm (such as a bank, building society or credit union) goes out of business or the FSA considers that it is unable to repay depositors or likely to be unable to do so. The maximum level of compensation for a customer, covering all of his or her deposits, is £31,700 (100 per cent of the first £2,000 and 90 per cent of the next £33,000);

- *investments* – two kinds of loss are covered: when an authorised investment firm goes out of business and cannot return investments or money, and a loss arising from bad investment advice or poor investment management. The maximum compensation is £48,000 (all of the first £30,000 and 90 per cent of the next £20,000); and

- *insurance* – 100 per cent cover for compulsory insurance (such as third-party motor insurance) and for other insurance (including long-term insurance, such as pensions and life assurance) 100 per cent cover for the first £2,000, with 90 per cent protection for amounts above this threshold.

Financial Ombudsman Service

The Financial Ombudsman Service is a one-stop service for dealing with complaints about financial services firms. The budget for 2002/03 is around £28 million. All firms authorised by the FSA are subject to the Ombudsman's procedures, but consumers have to seek a resolution to a complaint from the firm in the first instance. If the matter is not resolved satisfactorily, they can ask the Ombudsman to intervene.

Introduction to other service industries

The distribution of goods, including food and drink, to their point of sale is a major economic activity. The large wholesalers and retailers of food and drink operate extensive distribution networks, either directly or through contractors.

With rising real incomes, consumer spending on personal and leisure services has increased considerably. Travel, hotel and restaurant services

in the UK are among those to have benefited from long-term growth in tourism. The UK is one of the world's leading tourist destinations, even though the foot-and-mouth outbreak in 2001 and the aftermath of 11 September caused a temporary decline in visitor numbers.

Computer activities and research and development are among the non-financial sectors which experienced strong growth in turnover in 2001 (see Table 29.7).

Table 29.7 Turnover[1] in selected non-financial services

			£ billion
	2000	2001	% change
Motor trades	122.5	125.3	2.2
Wholesale trades	380.1	375.5	−1.2
Hotels and restaurants	52.8	56.6	7.2
Renting	17.3	18.3	5.9
Computer and related activities	40.8	46.2	13.2
Business services	145.9	161.7	10.8

1 Annual data derived from short-term turnover inquiries.
Source: Office for National Statistics

Wholesaling and retailing

In 2002 there were over 107,000 enterprises (see Table 29.8) engaged in *wholesaling* in the UK; 25 per cent were sole proprietors and 15 per cent partnerships. There were 1.18 million employee jobs in the UK in this sector in December 2001 and turnover in 2001 amounted to £375 billion, 1.2 per cent lower than in 2000.

In the food and drink trade almost all large retailers have their own buying and central distribution operations. Many small wholesalers and independent grocery retailers belong to voluntary 'symbol' groups, which provide access to central purchasing facilities and co-ordinated promotions. This has helped smaller retailers to remain relatively competitive; many local and convenience stores and village shops would not otherwise be able to stay in business.

London's wholesale markets play a significant part in the distribution of fresh foodstuffs. New Covent Garden at Nine Elms is the main market for fruit and vegetables, London Central Markets at

Table 29.8 Wholesale and retail VAT-based[1] enterprises in the UK, 2002

Number of enterprises

Turnover[2] (£ thousand)	Wholesale Total	of which: Sole proprietors	Partnerships	Retail Total	of which: Sole proprietors	Partnerships
1–49	16,595	7,925	2,405	18,965	10,865	4,085
50–99	15,320	6,760	2,550	44,550	26,070	12,310
100–249	21,775	6,910	4,175	67,095	29,635	25,420
250–499	14,390	2,715	2,755	33,490	10,070	14,130
500–999	13,085	1,335	1,955	16,915	3,415	5,825
1,000+	26,000	800	1,775	11,380	1,025	2,215
Total	**107,165**	**26,440**	**15,610**	**192,390**	**81,080**	**63,990**

1 Excludes units with zero VAT turnover and all enterprises without a VAT basis.
2 Relates mainly to a 12-month period ending in early 2001.
Source: Office for National Statistics. *Size Analysis of UK Businesses 2002*. Business Monitor PA1003

Smithfield for meat and Billingsgate at Canary Wharf for fish.

The Co-operative Group (CWS) Limited was formed from the merger of the Co-operative Wholesale Society (CWS) and Co-operative Retail Services (CRS) in 2000. As well as food retailing, the Group's operations cover funeral businesses, travel retailing, motor trading and non-food department stores. The merger created the UK's largest mutual retail group, with total sales of £3.2 billion in 2001.

The Co-operative Group has been the principal supplier of goods and services to the Co-operative Movement – comprising 43 independent retail societies and 2,355 stores – and was a founder member of the Co-operative Retail Trading Group (CRTG). Formed in 1993, the CRTG acts as a central marketing, buying and distribution partnership for retail co-operative societies, and now controls all Co-op food trade. Retail co-operative societies are voluntary organisations controlled by their members, membership being open to anyone paying a small deposit on a minimum share.

The *retail sector* accounted for 33 per cent of all consumer expenditure in 2001 and for 11 per cent (2.87 million) of UK employee jobs in December 2001. In 2002 there were over 192,000 retail enterprises in the UK (see Table 29.8); 42 per cent were sole proprietors, 33 per cent partnerships and the remaining 25 per cent companies.

Total retail turnover (including repair of personal and household goods) in 2000 amounted to £218 billion, 4 per cent higher than in 1999. Businesses range from national supermarket and other retail chains to independent corner grocery shops, hardware stores, chemists, newsagents and many other types of retailer. The large multiple retailers have grown considerably, tending to increase outlet size until relatively recently and to diversify product ranges. Some also operate overseas, through either subsidiaries or franchise agreements.

Small independent retail businesses and co-operative societies have been in decline for some time. To help their competitive position, smaller retailers are permitted by the Sunday trading laws to open for longer hours than larger supermarkets and department stores, which are restricted to six hours on Sundays (except in Scotland). Some major supermarket branches now open for 24 hours, six days a week.

The volume of retail sales rose by 28 per cent between 1995 and 2001 (see also Table 29.9). Growth in non-food stores (38 per cent) was higher than in predominantly food stores (18 per cent), with the most significant increase (62 per cent) in household goods stores.

The largest supermarket chains, including Tesco, J Sainsbury, Asda and Safeway, accounted for 62.5 per cent of total grocery sales, worth £103 billion in 2001. Tesco is the largest private sector employer in the UK, employing 195,000 people.

Table 29.9 Volume of retail sales in the UK

					1995 = 100
	1991	1996	1999	2000	2001
Predominantly food stores	90.4	101.9	110.8	113.6	117.7
Predominantly non-food stores					
Non-specialised stores	92.9	106.0	114.7	122.2	129.0
Textile, clothing and footwear stores	88.0	104.3	117.1	124.7	137.3
Household goods stores	87.0	106.8	135.2	148.6	161.6
Other stores	97.1	101.4	113.2	117.0	124.4
Total	91.0	104.4	119.9	127.9	138.1
Non-store retailing and repair	105.7	101.4	115.2	115.6	119.2
All retailing	91.8	103.1	115.6	120.8	128.0

Source: Office for National Statistics

The leading mixed retail chains are found in high streets nationwide. Competition with lower-priced outlets and discount chains has squeezed some of the more traditional suppliers selling a range of items. Several chains of DIY (Do-It-Yourself) stores and superstores cater for people carrying out repairs and improvements to their own homes and gardens; they stock tools, decorating and building materials, kitchen and bathroom fittings, and garden products. Specialist shops, such as those selling mobile telephones, have shown substantial growth.

The large multiple groups have broadened their range of goods and services. Large food retailers have also placed greater emphasis on selling own-label groceries and environmentally friendly products (including organic produce), together with household wares and clothing. In-store pharmacies, post offices, customer cafeterias and dry-cleaners are now a feature of large supermarkets, which also sell newspapers, magazines, books, audio cassettes, pre-recorded videos, compact discs, DVDs and electrical goods. Several large retailers offer personal finance facilities in an attempt to encourage sales, particularly of high-value goods, while others have diversified into financial services. Some supermarkets now offer banking facilities.

Franchising is the granting of a licence by one company (the franchiser) to another (the franchisee), usually by means of an initial payment with continuing royalties. Franchised activities operate in many areas, including cleaning services, film processing, print shops, fitness centres, courier delivery, car rental, engine tuning and servicing, and fast-food retailing. About 200 franchisers are members of the British Franchise Association (BFA) (*www.british-franchise.org*) which conducts an annual survey of franchising. Its findings for 2002 estimated that there were 671 fully fledged business-format franchises, with around 34,500 outlets, accounting for about 325,000 direct jobs in the UK and with annual turnover of £9.2 billion.

Vehicle, vehicle parts and petrol retailing

In December 2001 there were 543,000 employee jobs in the UK in retailing motor vehicles and parts, and in petrol stations. Turnover in the motor trades industry in 2001 amounted to £125.3 billion, 2.2 per cent higher than in 2000 (see Table 29.10).

Most businesses selling new vehicles are franchised by the motor manufacturers. Vehicle components are available for sale at garages which undertake servicing and repair work and also at retail chains and at independent retailers. Drive-in fitting centres sell tyres, exhaust systems, batteries, clutches and other vehicle parts. At the end of 2001 there were 12,201 retail outlets for petrol, a decline of 842 over the year; the top three companies accounted for 36 per cent of the total. The number of petrol stations declined by 11 per cent between 1999 and 2001 alone, reflecting intense competition in the sector, relatively low profit margins and consolidation among operators. This is particularly so in rural areas.

Petrol stations offer other retail services, such as shops, car washes and fast-food outlets (there were

Table 29.10 Turnover[1] in the motor trades industry

£ million

	2000	2001	% change
Sale of motor vehicles	81,550	85,490	4.8
Maintenance and repair of motor vehicles	9,688	9,875	1.9
Sale of motor vehicle parts and accessories	11,665	11,646	−0.2
Sale, maintenance and repair of motorcycles and related parts and accessories	1,959	1,742	−11.1
Retail sale of automotive fuel	17,686	16,543	−6.5
Total	**122,548**	**125,295**	**2.2**

1 Annual data derived from short-term turnover inquiries.
Source: Office for National Statistics

667 quick serve restaurants at the end of 2001), with the aim of increasing business. Approximately 27 per cent of petrol sold in the UK comes from supermarket forecourts, 1,036 of which were operating at the end of 2001.

Shopping facilities

Since 1996, social, economic and environmental considerations have led the Government and local planning authorities to limit new retail developments outside town centres. Out-of-town superstores, retail warehouses and shopping centres were felt to be undermining the vitality and viability of existing town and district centres. Government policy is now to focus new retail development in existing centres and so revitalise them. This is to ensure that everyone has easy access to a range of shops and services, whether or not they have a car; and to enable businesses of all types and sizes to prosper.

All new retail development requires planning permission from the local planning authority, which must consult central government before granting permission for most developments of 2,500 sq m or more. Retailers' attentions have now turned back to town centres, redeveloping existing stores and building smaller outlets. Forecasts show that completion of town centre shopping schemes for 2002/03 are at the highest level reached in the last 50 years.

There are eight regional out-of-town shopping centres (see box), located at sites offering good road access and ample parking facilities. Bluewater is the largest such development in Europe. There are no plans to build any further such out-of-town

Centre	Date opened	Area (sq m)
Merry Hill, Dudley, West Midlands	1985	111,000
MetroCentre, Gateshead, Tyne and Wear	1987	145,000
Meadowhall, near Sheffield	1990	102,000
Lakeside, Thurrock, Essex	1990	107,000
Trafford Centre, Manchester	1998	100,000
Cribbs Causeway, Bristol	1998	65,000
Braehead, near Glasgow	1999	56,000
Bluewater, near Dartford, Kent	1999	160,000

Source: Office of the Deputy Prime Minister

shopping centres, as these are not compatible with government policy.

Home shopping

Traditionally, all kinds of goods and services are purchased through mail-order catalogues. The largest-selling items are clothing, footwear, furniture, household textiles and domestic electrical appliances. Electronic home shopping, using a television and telephone, and 'online' shopping, where personal computers are linked to databases, are growing rapidly. Internet sales in the UK were estimated at £56.6 billion in 2000, and all forms of e-commerce sales at almost £162 billion (5.8 per cent of total sales). The finance and insurance sector had the largest value of e-commerce sales (an estimated £43.7 billion),[2] followed by the wholesale, retail, catering and travel sector (£7.6 billion).

Hotels, restaurants and catering

The hotel and restaurant trades, which include public houses (pubs), wine bars and other licensed bars in addition to all kinds of businesses offering accommodation and prepared food, had 1.65 million employee jobs in the UK in December 2001. Total turnover in 2001 amounted to £56.6 billion, 7.2 per cent higher than in 2000. Hotels and guest houses in the UK range from major hotel groups to small guest houses, individually owned. Holiday centres, including traditional holiday camps with full board, self-catering centres and caravan parks, are run by several companies.

In 2000 there were almost 51,500 enterprises in the UK in the licensed restaurant industry (including fast-food and takeaway outlets), an increase of 3.0 per cent on 1999. Total turnover in 2001 was £18.2 billion, 12.1 per cent higher than in 2000. Restaurants offer cuisine from virtually every country in the world, and several of the highest-quality ones have international reputations. Chinese, Indian, Thai, Italian, French and Greek restaurants are among the most popular. 'Fast-food' restaurants are widespread, many of which are franchised. They specialise in selling hamburgers, chicken, pizza and a variety of other foods, to be eaten on the premises or taken away. Traditional fish and chip shops are another main provider of cooked takeaway food. Sandwich bars are common in towns and cities, typically in areas with high concentrations of office workers.

There were an estimated 49,500 pubs in the UK in 2001, a decline of over 8 per cent since 1990. They accounted for 57 per cent of all fully licensed premises, compared with 65 per cent in 1990.

Turnover was estimated at £14.7 billion in 2000, approaching an annual average of £300,000 per pub. Although brewers still own many of the tightly controlled, and often branded, pub chains, their share has declined to less than 25 per cent of UK pubs. Such breweries either provide managers to run the pubs or offer tenancy agreements and tend to sell only their own brands of beer, although some also offer 'guest' beers. Multiple pub-owning 'pub companies' and venture capital companies account for over 40 per cent of the ownership. The remaining 36 per cent of pubs, called 'free houses', are independently owned and managed – these frequently serve a variety of different branded beers.

Travel agents

Many British holidaymakers travelling overseas buy 'package holidays' from travel agencies, where the cost covers both transport and accommodation. Long-haul holidays to North America, the Caribbean, Australia and New Zealand have gained in popularity in recent years. Some people prefer more independence, and many travel agents will make just the travel arrangements.

In 2001 turnover in the travel agency and tour operator businesses amounted to £18.7 billion, 12.6 per cent higher than in 2000. Around 70 per cent of high street travel agencies are members of the Association of British Travel Agents (ABTA) (*www.abta.com*). Although most are small businesses, a few large firms have hundreds of branches. ABTA's 830 tour operators and 1,700 travel agency companies have over 7,000 offices and are responsible for the sale of more than 90 per cent of UK-sold package holidays.

ABTA operates financial protection schemes to safeguard its members' customers and maintains a code of conduct drawn up with the Office of Fair Trading. It also offers a free consumer affairs service to help resolve complaints against members, and a low-cost independent arbitration scheme for members' customers. The British Incoming Tour Operators Association (*www.bitoa.co.uk*), founded in 1977, represents the commercial and political interests of incoming tour operators and suppliers to the British inbound tourism industry.

---

2 As no sales data are held by ONS for much of the financial sector, turnover from administrative sources was used to supplement the percentages supplied by business and produce the estimates. Accordingly, the estimates for e-commerce in the financial sector have to be treated with caution.

Table 29.11 Spending on tourism in the UK

					£ billion
	1997	1998	1999	2000	2001
Spending by:					
Overseas residents					
Visits to the UK	12.2	12.7	12.5	12.8	11.3
Overseas fares to UK carriers	2.0	1.9	2.1	1.9	2.0
Domestic tourists					
Trips of one night or more	15.1	14.0	16.3	26.1	26.1
Day trips	22.0	31.3	32.0	32.7	33.4
Total	**51.3**	**59.9**	**62.9**	**73.5**	**72.8**

Source: ONS, International Passenger Survey; British Tourist Authority

Tourism and leisure

Tourism is one of the UK's key long-term growth sectors, with total spending in 2001 estimated at £72.8 billion (see Table 29.11). The bulk of tourism services are provided by some 129,000 mainly independent small businesses such as hotels and guest houses, restaurants, holiday homes, caravan and camping parks. In all about 8 per cent of small businesses are engaged in tourism.

A new £40 million tourism initiative entitled 'Only in Britain. Only in 2002' was launched in May 2002 with the aim of attracting 1 million extra visitors and generating an additional £500 million for the British economy in 2002. The campaign focuses on Britain's uniqueness in terms of its diversity, heritage and humour.

Table 29.12 Employment in tourism-related industries, Great Britain, March 2002

	Thousands
Hotels and other tourist accommodation	389
Restaurants, cafés, etc.	534
Bars, public houses and nightclubs	518
Travel agencies/tour operators	129
Libraries/museums and other cultural activities	79
Sport and other recreation activities	408
Total	**2,056**
of which: Self-employment jobs	148

Source: Department for Culture, Media and Sport

There were an estimated 22.8 million overseas visitors to the UK in 2001, 9 per cent fewer than in 2000. They generated earnings of £11.3 billion, 12 per cent lower than in 2000 (see Tables 29.11 and 29.13). A combination of the foot-and-mouth outbreak (see chapter 26) and the aftermath of 11 September are likely to have contributed to this £1.5 billion decline. The number of visitors from North America fell by 13 per cent, those from the European Union by 8 per cent and from all other areas by 9 per cent. The UK's share of world tourism earnings reached 3.4 per cent in 2001 and ranked seventh behind the United States, Spain, France, Italy, China and Germany. Table 29.14 shows that the United States topped the league of overseas visitors to the UK. Business travel, which includes attendance at conferences, exhibitions, trade fairs and other business sites, accounted for 30 per cent of all overseas visits in 2001. London's Heathrow and Gatwick airports, the seaport of Dover and the Channel Tunnel are the main points of entry.

Some 50 per cent of overseas tourists spend at least half of their stay in London, while others venture further afield to see the many attractions in the English regions as well as in Scotland, Wales and Northern Ireland.

Domestic tourism generated £59.5 billion in 2001. For British residents opting to take their main holiday in the UK, 21 per cent choose a traditional seaside destination, such as Blackpool, Bournemouth, Eastbourne, Llandudno and resorts in Devon and Cornwall. Short holiday breaks (up to three nights), valued at £8.1 billion in 2001, make up a significant part of the market.

Table 29.13 Overseas visits to the UK

	1997	1998	1999	2000	Million 2001
By area					
North America	4.10	4.55	4.60	4.87	4.23
European Union	15.30	15.21	14.58	14.02	12.87
Non-EU Europe	2.09	2.17	2.23	2.07	1.99
Other countries	4.03	3.81	3.98	4.25	3.75
By purpose					
Holiday	10.80	10.48	9.83	9.30	7.59
Business	6.35	6.88	7.04	7.32	6.78
Visiting friends or relatives	5.16	5.40	5.64	5.83	5.90
Miscellaneous	3.21	2.99	2.88	2.75	2.57
All visits	**25.52**	**25.75**	**25.39**	**25.21**	**22.84**

Source: ONS, International Passenger Survey

Table 29.14 Top countries of origin for overseas visitors to the UK, 2001

	Visits (thousand)	Spending (£ million)
United States	3,580	2,383
France	2,852	685
Germany	2,309	731
Irish Republic	2,039	548
Netherlands	1,411	387

Source: ONS, International Passenger Survey

The UK's historic towns and cities and its scenic rural and coastal areas continue to have great appeal for domestic and overseas tourists alike. Their popularity reflects a growing interest in British heritage, arts and culture. There are an estimated 6,800 visitor attractions in the UK, which in 2000 attracted 413 million visits, resulting in revenue of £1.4 billion and providing employment for 130,000 people. These attractions include museums, art galleries, historic houses and castles, which together make up 50 per cent of the total, although only one-third of all reported visits. Domestic and foreign tourists play an increasingly important role in supporting the UK's national heritage and creative arts, in addition to the large financial contribution they make to hotels, restaurants, cafés and bars, and public transport.

Activity holidays are often based on walking, canoeing, mountain climbing, or artistic activities. *Youth Hostel Associations* operate a comprehensive network of around 310 hostels in the UK, offering a range of facilities, including self-catering, to families and people of all ages.

Theme parks attract many million visitors a year. Attractions in these parks include spectacular 'white knuckle' rides and overhead cable cars and railways, while some also feature domesticated and wild animals. The British Airways London Eye was the most popular UK attraction charging admission in 2001 (see Table 29.15). Another new attraction, the Eden Project, occupied the third position in its first full year. The largest tourist attraction with free admission (and also the largest overall attraction) was Blackpool Pleasure Beach in Lancashire (see Table 29.16).

Tourism promotion

Tourism in England is the responsibility of the Department for Culture, Media and Sport, and the Scottish Parliament, the Welsh Assembly Government and Northern Ireland Assembly have responsibility for tourism in their respective countries. The government-supported British Tourist Authority (BTA) (*www.britishtouristauthority.org*) promotes Britain through its network of 27 overseas offices, located in markets offering the best potential return and covering 88 per cent of all visitors to Britain. There are separate national tourist boards – in England the English Tourism Council (ETC) (*www.englishtourism.org.uk*), Scotland (*www.visitscotland.com*), Wales (*www.visitwales.com*) and Northern Ireland

Table 29.15 Top UK tourist attractions charging admission[1]

	Visits (million)	
	2000	2001
British Airways London Eye	3.30[2]	3.85
Tower of London	2.30	2.02
Eden Project, St Austell	0.49[3]	1.70
Natural History Museum, London	1.58	1.70
Legoland, Windsor	1.49	1.63
Victoria and Albert Museum, London	1.34	1.45
Science Museum, London	1.34	1.35
Flamingo Land Theme Park and Zoo, North Yorkshire	1.30[4]	1.32[4]
Windermere Lake Cruises, Cumbria	1.17	1.24[4]
Canterbury Cathedral	1.26[4]	1.15[4]
Edinburgh Castle	1.20	1.13
Chester Zoo	1.12	1.06
Kew Gardens	0.86	0.99
Westminster Abbey, London	1.24	0.99
Royal Academy of Arts, London	0.76[4]	0.91

1 Attractions that responded to the survey and gave permission for ETC to publish their figures.
2 Opened to the public in March 2000.
3 Opened partly from spring 2000; official opening in March 2001.
4 Estimated visitor numbers.
Source: English Tourism Council survey of visits to tourist attractions 2001

Table 29.16 Top UK free tourist attractions[1]

	Visits (million)	
	2000	2001
Blackpool Pleasure Beach	6.80[2]	6.50[2]
National Gallery, London	4.90[2]	4.92[2]
British Museum, London[3]	5.47[2]	4.80
Tate Modern, London	3.87	3.55
Pleasureland Theme Park, Southport	2.10[2]	2.10[2]
Clacton Pier	1.00[2]	1.75[2]
York Minster	1.75[2]	1.60[2]
Pleasure Beach, Great Yarmouth	1.50[2]	1.50[2]
National Portrait Gallery, London	1.18	1.27
Poole Pottery	1.13	1.06
Kelvingrove Art Gallery and Museum, Glasgow	1.00[2]	1.03[2]
Tate Britain, London	1.20[2]	1.01
Cannon Hill Park, Birmingham	0.95[2]	0.95[2]
Chester Cathedral	1.00[2]	0.90[2]
Flamingo Family Fun Park, Hastings	0.86[2]	0.90[2]

1 Attractions that responded to the survey and gave permission for ETC to publish their figures.
2 Estimated visitor numbers.
3 Visitor recording method changed in 2001.
Source: English Tourism Council survey of visits to tourist attractions 2001

(*www.discovernorthernireland.com*) – which support domestic tourism and work with the BTA to promote Britain overseas.

The BTA and the national tourist boards inform and advise the Government on issues of concern to the industry. They also help businesses and other organisations to plan by researching and publicising trends affecting the industry. The national tourist boards work closely with regional tourist boards, on which local government and business interests are represented. There are 551 local Tourist Information Centres in England, 80 in Wales, 131 in Scotland and 22 in Northern Ireland. The national tourist boards, in conjunction with motoring organisations, operate accommodation classification and quality grading schemes.

The Government is working with the tourism industry to raise standards of accommodation and service, and to address certain key issues facing the industry. These include: improving visitor attractions; boosting business tourism;

encouraging best practice for the development of workforce skills; and government-industry communication. The Government is also considering how best to support tourism growth which is economically, socially and environmentally sustainable.

Exhibition and conference centres

The UK – along with the United States and France – is one of the world's three leading countries for international conferences. London and Paris are the two most popular conference cities. Many British towns and cities – including several traditional seaside holiday resorts which have diversified to take advantage of the growing business tourism market – have conference and exhibition facilities.

Among the most modern purpose-built centres are the National Exhibition and International Conference Centres in Birmingham; the Queen

Elizabeth II and Olympia Conference Centres, both in London; Cardiff International Arena; and the Belfast Waterfront Hall. In Scotland, Edinburgh, Glasgow and Aberdeen have major exhibition and conference centres. Brighton (East Sussex), Harrogate (North Yorkshire), Bournemouth (Dorset), Manchester, Nottingham and Torquay (Devon) all have exhibition and conference centres. Other important exhibition facilities in London are at the Barbican, Earls Court, Alexandra Palace, Wembley Arena and the ExCel exhibition and conference centre in Docklands.

The Association of Exhibition Organisers (*www.aeo.org.uk*) is the trade body for trade exhibitions and consumer events. It estimates that between 1999 and 2001 exhibitor spending rose from £1.76 billion to £2.04 billion, an increase of 16 per cent.

Table 29.17 UK exhibitions and attendance[1]

	1999	2000	2001
Number of events	817	868	823
Number of visitors (thousand)	10,096	11,082	9,069
Visitors per exhibition	12,357	12,767	11,019

1 Excludes one-day public events; covers only venues of 2,000 sq m and over.
Source: Association of Exhibition Organisers

Of the 823 events recorded in 2001, 56 per cent were trade exhibitions, 42 per cent public (consumer) exhibitions and the remaining 2 per cent a combination of both. Public (consumer) exhibitions attracted 69 per cent of all visitors, trade exhibitions 27 per cent and a combination of both types the remaining 4 per cent. In addition, there were more than 3.1 million visitors to 32 exhibitions held in outdoor venues. A further 1,001 exhibition events (mainly smaller and often regional) took place in 390 venues, attracting an estimated 5 million visitors.

The Department of Trade and Industry (DTI), via its Trade Partners UK operating unit, sponsors the 'Trade fairs and exhibitions UK' website (*www.exhibitions.co.uk*), which offers a comprehensive listing of all consumer, public, industrial and trade exhibitions held in major UK venues.

Rental services

A varied range of rental services, many of which are franchised, are available throughout the UK. These include hire of cars and other vehicles; televisions, video recorders and camcorders; household appliances such as washing machines; tools and heavy decorating equipment (such as ladders and floor sanders); and videos, DVDs and computer games. Retailing of many types of service is dominated by chains, although independent operators are still to be found in most fields. In December 2001 there were 156,000 employee jobs in the UK in the rental sector, with turnover in 2001 amounting to £18.3 billion, 5.9 per cent higher than in 2000.

Computing services

The computing software and services industry comprises businesses engaged in:

- software development;

- systems integration;

- IT consultancy;

- IT 'outsourcing';

- processing services; and

- the provision of complete computer systems.

It also includes companies that provide:

- IT education and training;

- independent maintenance;

- support, contingency planning and recruitment; and

- contract staff.

In December 2001 there were 478,000 employee jobs in the UK in computer and related activities. Turnover of companies in this sector amounted to £46.2 billion in 2001, 13.2 per cent higher than in 2000. British firms and universities have established strong reputations in software R&D. A number of international IT conglomerates, such as Microsoft, have set up R&D operations in the UK. Academic expertise is especially evident in such areas as artificial intelligence, neural networks, formal programming for safety-critical systems, and parallel programming systems.

Software firms have developed strengths in sector-specific applications, including systems for retailing, banking, finance and accounting, the medical and dental industries, and the travel and entertainment industries. Specialist 'niche' markets in which UK software producers are active include artificial intelligence, scientific and engineering software (especially computer-aided design), mathematical software, geographical information systems, and data visualisation packages. Some firms specialise in devising multimedia software. Distance learning, 'virtual reality' and computer animation all benefit from a large pool of creative talent.

One of the biggest users of software is the telecommunications industry (see page 241). The provision of almost all new telecommunications services, including switching and transmission, is dependent on software.

A special one-off survey by ONS in July 2001 estimated the size of the computer services market in Great Britain in 2000 as £32.0 billion (including exports). Table 29.18 shows a breakdown of the activities. There was a further £5.4 billion of sales activity in non-computer (but related) services, the largest of which were wholesaling or retailing of goods (£3.1 billion), and telecommunications services (£1.2 billion).

Table 29.18 Computer services sales by service type, Great Britain, 2000

	£ million	%
IT consultancy	7,687	24.1
Facilities management	5,407	16.9
Systems integration	4,190	13.1
Software maintenance	3,403	10.7
Packaged applications	3,402	10.6
Custom applications	2,875	9.0
Information services	1,789	5.6
Hardware maintenance	1,758	5.5
Non-applications	1,071	3.4
Disaster recovery	317	1.0
Other	53	0.2
Total	**31,951**	**100.0**

Source: Office for National Statistics

Business services

In December 2001 a total of 2.81 million employee jobs in the UK were in the other business activities sector, which includes market research, business and management consultancy activities and advertising, and turnover in 2001 amounted to £161.7 billion, 10.8 per cent higher than in 2000.

Market research

According to the British Market Research Association (BMRA) (*www.bmra.org.uk*), members' turnover grew by 7.1 per cent in 2001 to an estimated £1,147 million, following growth of 9.3 per cent in 2000. UK-owned market research companies include the largest international customised market research specialists. The top ten companies by turnover are shown in Table 29.19 below.

Table 29.19 Top ten UK market research companies[1] by turnover

		£ million
Company	2000	2001
Taylor Nelson Sofres	110.1	119.7
Research International	64.7	73.4
NOP Research Group	68.1	71.9
Millward Brown UK	64.5	67.9
NFO WorldGroup	43.4	45.1
BMRB International	39.5	44.7
Ipsos UK	39.3	40.5
MORI	26.9	33.9
Information Resources	30.9	33.8
The Research Business International	24.8	24.3

1 BMRA members only.
Source: British Market Research Association

Management consultancy

The UK's 60,000 management consultants supply technical assistance and advice to business and government clients. In 2001 revenues for the industry were estimated at £8 billion, with exports in excess of £1 billion. The 40 member firms of the Management Consultancies Association (MCA) (*www.mca.org.uk*), which accounts for over half of UK revenues, earned a record income of £4,345 million in 2001, 17 per cent higher than in 2000 (see Table 29.20). Income from outsourcing activities rose by 49 per cent and

Table 29.20 Management consultancy income[1]

	£ million	
	2000	2001
UK fee income	3,207	3,780
of which:		
Outsourcing	797	1,188
Strategy	490	502
IT systems development	469	487
IT consultancy	465	469
Financial systems	389	391
Production management	218	155
Human resources	151	115
Project management	119	401
Marketing	61	40
Economic/environmental	48	32
Overseas fee income	514	565
Total	**3,721**	**4,345**

1 MCA firms only.
Source: Management Consultancies Association

Table 29.21 UK advertising revenue by medium

Medium	£ million		%
	2000	2001	2001
Press	8,604	8,514	51.5
of which:			
National newspapers	2,252	2,071	12.5
Regional newspapers	2,762	2,834	17.1
Consumer magazines	750	779	4.7
Business and professional magazines	1,270	1,202	7.3
Directories	868	959	5.8
Press production costs	702	670	4.0
Television	4,646	4,147	25.1
Outdoor	810	788	4.8
Radio	595	541	3.3
Cinema	128	164	1.0
Direct mail	2,049	2,228	13.5
Internet	155	166	1.0
Total	**16,988**	**16,548**	**100.0**

Source: *Advertising Statistics Yearbook 2002* – World Advertising Research Center

accounted for over 31 per cent of all UK fee income.

Advertising and public relations

The UK is a major centre for creative advertising, and multinational corporations often use advertising created in the UK for marketing their products globally. British agencies have strong foreign links through overseas ownership and associate networks. British television advertising has received many international awards. According to the Advertising Association (*www.adassoc.org.uk*), total UK advertising expenditure fell by 2.6 per cent in 2001 to £16.5 billion, after nine years' uninterrupted growth (see also Table 29.21).

There are around 1,540 advertising agencies. In addition to their creative, production and media-buying roles, some offer integrated marketing services, including consumer research and public relations. Many agencies have sponsorship departments, which arrange for businesses to sponsor products and events, including artistic, sporting and charitable events.

Government advertising campaigns – on crime prevention, health promotion, armed services recruitment and so on – are often organised by

COI Communications (see page 483), an executive agency of the Government.

The UK's public relations industry has developed rapidly, and there are now many small specialist firms as well as some quite large ones. The Public Relations Consultants Association (*www.martex.co.uk/prca*) membership accounts for 80 per cent of UK fee income. It had 122 members who employed almost 5,400 people in 2001, and generated £401 million of fee income, 6.4 per cent higher than in 2000.

Business support services

One of the major growth areas in the service sector is in support services, reflecting the trend among more and more firms to 'outsource' non-core operations. Initially, operating areas that were outsourced or contracted out were in cleaning, security and catering. However, firms are now outsourcing other activities, such as IT and personnel support services.

Consumer protection

The Government aims to maintain and develop a clear and fair regulatory framework that gives confidence to consumers and contributes to business competitiveness. It works closely with outside bodies that have expert knowledge of consumer issues to develop policies and legislation. A 1999 White Paper, *Modern Markets: Confident Consumers*, set out a range of initiatives aimed at improving consumer protection. Much of the White Paper agenda has now been implemented. The consumer voice has been strengthened with new consumer councils for the energy and postal industries, and a stronger, more modern National Consumer Council. Information and redress have been improved with the launch of Consumer Support Networks and plans to pilot new helplines on consumer advice and debt.

The regulatory regime has been strengthened with the implementation of the Distance Selling Directive and the introduction in June 2001 of Stop Now Orders (see below) to tackle rogue traders for whom existing sanctions are not a sufficient deterrent.

Other measures are being taken forward in the Enterprise Bill (see page 336), introduced into Parliament in 2002. This will create a 'new' Office of Fair Trading (OFT) (*www.oft.gov.uk*) – for the first time with a statutory Board that will reflect the interests, among others, of consumers. The OFT will also be given a range of new duties:

- to promote competition;

- to approve industry codes of practice;

- to educate consumers; and

- to consider 'super-complaints' about markets that are failing consumers (see page 336).

Consumer legislation

- The *Trade Descriptions Act 1968* prohibits misdescriptions of goods and services, and enables regulations to be made requiring information or instructions relating to goods to be marked on, or to accompany, the goods or to be included in advertisements.

- The *Consumer Credit Act 1974* is intended to protect consumers in their dealings with credit businesses. Most businesses connected with the consumer credit or hire industry or which supply ancillary credit services – for example, credit brokers, debt collectors, debt

counsellors and credit reference agencies – require a consumer credit licence. The Director General of Fair Trading is responsible for administering the licensing system, including refusing or revoking licences of those unfit to hold them. He also has powers to prohibit unfit people from carrying out estate agency work; to take court action to prevent the publication of misleading advertisements; to stop traders using unfair terms in standard contracts with consumers; and to take court action against breaches of the Distance Selling Regulations.

- The *Sale of Goods Act 1979* (as amended in 1994) ensures that consumers are entitled to receive goods which fit their description and are of satisfactory quality.

- The *Consumer Protection Act 1987* covers misleading indications about prices of goods. The Act also makes it a criminal offence to supply unsafe products, and provides product liability rights for consumers. The regulatory framework to control product safety is a mixture of European and UK legislation, voluntary safety standards and industry codes of practice.

- The *Stop Now Orders (EC Directive) Regulations 2001* (SNORs) enable the OFT and certain specified bodies – Qualified Entities (QEs) – to take swift action against traders in the UK and in other EU Member States who breach ten existing EC Directives, where those breaches harm the collective interests of UK consumers. The OFT has lead enforcement responsibility for each Directive area, including responsibility for co-ordinating the actions of all QEs and publishing advice and guidelines on how the Regulations work. The Regulations cover consumer credit, unfair contract terms, distance selling, misleading and comparative advertising, doorstep selling, timeshare, package travel and sale of goods.

- The Enterprise Bill will, if enacted, replace parts II and III of the *Fair Trading Act 1973* and will extend the current injunctive powers available to the OFT and other QEs under the SNORs to all UK markets, both goods and services. There will be a similar lead enforcement responsibility for the OFT in ensuring that action is co-ordinated and guidance and information is published. It will also enable the OFT to formally approve business-to-consumer codes of practice.

The marking and accuracy of quantities are regulated by weights and measures legislation. Other law provides for the control of medical products, and certain other substances and articles, through a system of licences and certificates. Changes to existing legislation were introduced at the end of 1998 to strengthen the protection of consumers from unscrupulous doorstep sellers.

The EU's consumer programme covers activities such as health and safety, protection of the consumer's economic interests, promotion of consumer education and strengthening the representation of consumers. The interests of UK consumers on EU matters are represented by a number of organisations, including the Consumers' Association and the National Consumer Council (see below).

Consumer advice and information

Citizens Advice Bureaux deliver advice from over 2,000 outlets across England, Wales and Northern Ireland. They handled 5.7 million enquiries during 2001/02 (see Table 29.22). Their work is co-ordinated by a national association (www.nacab.org.uk) linked to the bureaux by local and regional committees. In 2000/01 an additional 405,000 problems were handled by Citizens Advice Scotland (www.cas.org.uk). Similar assistance is provided by trading standards and consumer protection departments of local authorities in Great Britain and, in some areas, by specialist consumer advice centres.

The National Consumer Council (www.ncc.org.uk), a non-departmental public body receiving much of its funding from the DTI, works to represent consumer interests to policy-makers, regulators and suppliers in the UK and Europe. Associate Councils in Scotland, Wales and Northern Ireland deal with the particular concerns of consumers in those countries.

Consumer bodies for privatised utilities investigate questions of concern to the consumer.

Table 29.22 Citizens Advice Bureaux enquiries, England, Wales and Northern Ireland

Thousand

Category	2000/01	2001/02	% change
Benefits	1,723	1,629	−5.5
Consumer and utilities	1,175	1,194	1.6
Employment	632	601	−4.9
Housing	600	573	−4.5
Legal	479	460	−4.0
Relationships	388	390	0.5
Tax	154	150	−2.6
Other	707	721	2.0
Total	**5,858**	**5,718**	**−2.4**

Source: National Association of Citizens Advice Bureaux

Some trade associations have set up codes of practice. In addition, several organisations work to further consumer interests by representing the consumer's view to government, industry and other bodies. The largest is the *Consumers' Association*, set up in 1957, with 974,000 members in June 2002, funded largely by subscriptions to *Which?* magazine (www.which.net). Over 60,000 subscribers have online access to the complete range of *Which?* publications.

Further reading

Competition in UK Banking: A Report to the Chancellor of the Exchequer. HM Treasury. The Stationery Office, 2000.

Medium and Long-term Retail Savings in the UK: A Review. Sandler review. The Stationery Office, 2002.

Bank of England Annual Report. Bank of England.

Financial Services Authority Annual Report. FSA.

Websites

National Statistics
www.statistics.gov.uk

Appendix A Government departments and agencies

Below is an outline of the principal functions of the main government departments and a list of their executive agencies. An asterisk before a department's name shows that it is headed by a Cabinet minister. Executive agencies are normally listed under the relevant department, although in some cases they are included within the description of the department's responsibilities.

The main contact address, telephone number, fax number and website of each department are also given, together with an e-mail address where available. *The Civil Service Year Book* contains more detailed information.

The UK online Citizen Portal – *www.ukonline.gov.uk* – is a single point of entry to government information and services on the Internet, and gives the public simple access to links to more than 1,000 official websites.

The work of many of the departments and agencies covers the United Kingdom as a whole and is indicated by (UK). Where this is not the case, the abbreviations used are (GB) for functions covering England, Wales and Scotland; (E, W & NI) for those covering England, Wales and Northern Ireland; (E & W) for those covering England and Wales; and (E) for those concerned with England only.

*Cabinet Office
70 Whitehall, London SW1A 2AS
Tel: 020 7276 1234
Website: *www.cabinet-office.gov.uk*

*Prime Minister's Office
10 Downing Street, London SW1A 2AA
Tel: 020 7930 4433
Website: *www.number-10.gov.uk*

*Office of the Deputy Prime Minister
26 Whitehall, London SW1A 2WH
Tel: 020 7944 4400
Website: *www.odpm.gov.uk*
Policies for planning; housing; regeneration; local and regional government; homelessness, urban policy, neighbourhood renewal, social exclusion, regional co-ordination, Government Offices and the fire service.

Executive agencies
Fire Service College
Planning Inspectorate
Queen Elizabeth II Conference Centre
Rent Service

UK territorial departments

*Northern Ireland Office
Castle Buildings, Stormont, Belfast BT4 3SG
Tel: 028 9052 0700 Fax: 028 9052 8473
11 Millbank, London SW1P 4QE
Tel: 020 7210 3000 Fax: 020 7210 0254
Website: *www.nio.gov.uk*
Through the Northern Ireland Office, the Secretary of State for Northern Ireland has direct responsibility for political and constitutional matters, law and order, security, and electoral matters.

Executive agencies
Compensation Agency
Forensic Science Northern Ireland
Northern Ireland Prison Service

*Scotland Office
Dover House, Whitehall, London SW1A 2AU
Tel: 020 7270 6754 Fax: 020 7270 6812
e-mail: scottish.secretary@scotland.gov.uk
Website: *www.scottishsecretary.gov.uk*
Represents Scottish interests within the UK

Government in matters that are reserved to the UK Parliament under the terms of the *Scotland Act 1998*. Promotes the devolution settlement by encouraging co-operation, between both the parliaments and between the UK Government and the Scottish Executive, or otherwise intervenes as required by the Act.

*Wales Office

Gwydyr House, Whitehall, London SW1A 2ER
Tel: 020 7270 0549 Fax: 020 7270 0568
e-mail: wales.office@wales.gov.uk
Website: *www.walesoffice.gov.uk*
The Secretary of State for Wales is the member of the UK Cabinet who takes the lead in matters connected with the *Government of Wales Act 1998*. The Secretary of State is responsible for consulting the Assembly on the Government's legislative programme.

Economic affairs

*Department of Trade and Industry

1 Victoria Street, London SW1H 0ET
Tel: 020 7215 5000
e-mail: enquiries@dti.gov.uk
Website: *www.dti.gov.uk*
Competitiveness; enterprise, innovation and productivity; science, engineering and technology; markets; the legal and regulatory framework for business and consumers. Specific responsibilities include innovation policy; regional industrial policy and the Regional Development Agencies (E); small businesses (E); spread of management best practice; business/education links (E); employment relations; international trade policy; energy policy; company law; insolvency; radio regulation; patents and copyright protection; import and export licensing; relations with specific business sectors.

Executive agencies

Companies House
Employment Tribunals Service
Insolvency Service
National Weights and Measures Laboratory
Patent Office
Radiocommunications Agency
Small Business Service

British Trade International (see page 368) is a body jointly funded by DTI and the Foreign & Commonwealth Office.

Office of Manpower Economics (OME)

Oxford House, 76 Oxford Street,
London W1N 9FD
Tel: 020 7467 7244 Fax: 020 7467 7248
Website: *www.ome.uk.com*
OME is a non-statutory body providing a secretariat for the six public-sector Pay Review Bodies which deal with: school teachers; nurses; doctors and dentists; senior civil servants and the judiciary; the armed forces; and prison officers. It also serves the Police Negotiating Board and the Police Advisory Board, and carries out a range of studies into Civil Service pay levels and other related pay matters.

Office of Science and Technology (OST)

1 Victoria Street, London SW1H 0ET
Tel: 020 7215 3973 Fax: 020 7215 0394
Website: *www.ost.gov.uk*
The Office of Science and Technology (OST) supports the Secretary of State for Trade and Industry and the Minister for Science on issues of science, engineering and technology. Headed by the Government's Chief Scientific Adviser (who reports direct to the Prime Minister), the OST is responsible for policy on science, engineering and technology (SET), both nationally and internationally, and co-ordinates SET policy across government departments. Through the Director General of Research Councils, the OST also has responsibility for the Science Budget, and for the government-financed Research Councils.

*HM Treasury

1 Horse Guards Road, London SW1A 2HQ
Tel: 020 7270 5000
Website: *www.hm-treasury.gov.uk*
Oversight of the framework for monetary policy; tax policy; planning and control of public spending; government accounting; the quality and cost-effectiveness of public services; increasing productivity and expanding economic and employment opportunities; promoting international financial stability and the UK's economic interests; the regime for supervision of financial services, management of central government debt and supply of notes and coins (UK).

HM Customs and Excise

New King's Beam House, 22 Upper Ground,
London SE1 9PJ
Tel: 020 7620 1313
Website: *www.hmce.gov.uk*
A department reporting to the Chancellor of the Exchequer. Responsible for collecting and

accounting for Customs and Excise revenues, including VAT (value added tax); agency functions, including controlling certain imports and exports, policing prohibited goods, and compiling trade statistics (UK).

ECGD (Export Credits Guarantee Department)

PO Box 2200, Exchange Tower, Harbour Exchange Square, London E14 9GS
Tel: 020 7512 7000 Fax: 020 7512 7649
Website: *www.ecgd.gov.uk*
The Export Credits Guarantee Department (ECGD) is a government department responsible to the Secretary of State for Trade and Industry and is the UK's official export credit agency. One of ECGD's main functions – through its export credit guarantees – is to underwrite bank loans to enable overseas buyers to purchase capital and project-related goods and services from the UK, and to insure the return investments made by UK companies in overseas enterprises.

Office of Fair Trading

Fleetbank House, 2–6 Salisbury Square, London EC4Y 8JX
Tel: 020 7211 8000 Fax: 020 7211 8800
e-mail: enquiries@oft.gov.uk
Website: *www.oft.gov.uk*
A non-ministerial department, headed by the Director General of Fair Trading. Administers a wide range of competition and consumer protection legislation, with the overall aim of making markets work well for consumers (UK).

Regional Co-ordination Unit

2nd Floor, Riverwalk House,
157–161 Millbank, London SW1P 4RR
Tel: 020 7217 3495 Fax: 020 7217 3590
Website: *www.rcu.gov.uk*
Strategy development, corporate relations and business development for the nine Government Offices for the Regions (see page 9) (E).

Inland Revenue

Somerset House, Strand, London WC2R 1LB
Tel: 020 7438 6622
Website: *www.inlandrevenue.gov.uk*
A department reporting to the Chancellor of the Exchequer responsible for the administration and collection of direct taxes and valuation of property (GB).

Executive agencies

National Insurance Contributions Office
Valuation Office

National Savings and Investments

Charles House, 375 Kensington High Street, London W14 8SD
Tel: 020 7348 9200 Fax: 020 7348 9432
Website: *www.nsandi.com*
A department in its own right and an executive agency reporting to the Chancellor of the Exchequer. Aims to raise funds for the Government by selling a range of investments to personal savers (UK).

Royal Mint

Llantrisant, Pontyclun CF72 8YT
Tel: 01443 222111 Fax: 01443 623190
Website: *www.royalmint.com*
The Royal Mint is responsible for the production of coins for the United Kingdom and overseas customers. It also produces military and civilian decorations and medals, commemorative medals, and royal and official seals. The Mint manufactures special proof and uncirculated quality coins in gold, silver and other metals, as well as accessories such as paperweights and jewellery.

Legal affairs

*Lord Chancellor's Department

Selborne House, 54–60 Victoria Street, London SW1E 6QW
Tel: 020 7210 8500
e-mail: general.queries@lcdhq.gov.uk
Website: *www.lcd.gov.uk*
Responsibility for procedure and administration of the Crown Court, the Supreme Court and county courts and a number of tribunals under the Court Service; overseeing the locally administered magistrates' courts; work relating to judicial appointments; overall responsibility for the Community Legal Service and Criminal Defence Service and for the promotion of general reforms in the civil law (E & W); policy on and funding for marriage and relationship support; sponsor department for the Children and Family Court Advisory and Support Service and the Legal Services Commission; freedom of information and data protection; data sharing; human rights issues; House of Lords reform; Royal, Church and hereditary issues and Lords Lieutenant and Crown

Dependencies. The Lord Chancellor also has responsibility for the Northern Ireland Court Service, the Law Commission, Office of the Judge Advocate General, Office of the Official Solicitor and Public Trustee, Judicial Studies Board, Office of the Legal Services Ombudsman, the Council on Tribunals, and Magistrates' Court Service Inspectorate.

Executive agencies

Court Service
Public Guardianship Office
Two sister departments – HM Land Registry and the Public Record Office – fall under the Lord Chancellor's responsibility and are run on executive agency lines (see page 483).

Legal Secretariat to the Law Officers

Attorney General's Chambers,
9 Buckingham Gate, London SW1E 6JP
Tel: 020 7271 2400 Fax: 020 7271 2430
e-mail: lslo@gtnet.gov.uk
Website: *www.lslo.gov.uk*
Supporting the Law Officers of the Crown (Attorney General and Solicitor General) in their functions as the Government's principal legal advisers (E, W & NI).

Treasury Solicitor's Department

Queen Anne's Chambers, 28 Broadway,
London SW1H 9JS
Tel: 020 7210 3000 Fax: 020 7210 3004
Website: *www.treasury-solicitor.gov.uk*
A department in its own right and an executive agency reporting to the Attorney General. Provides legal services to most government departments, agencies, and public and quasi-public bodies. Services include litigation; giving general advice on interpreting and applying the law; instructing Parliamentary Counsel (part of the Cabinet Office) on Bills and drafting subordinate legislation; and providing conveyancing services and property-related legal work (E & W).

Crown Prosecution Service

50 Ludgate Hill, London EC4M 7EX
Tel: 020 7796 8000 Fax: 020 7796 8651
Website: *www.cps.gov.uk*
Responsible for deciding independently whether criminal proceedings begun by the police should be continued, and for prosecuting those cases it decides to continue (E & W). The CPS is headed by the Director of Public Prosecutions, who is accountable to Parliament through the Attorney General.

Serious Fraud Office

Elm House, 10–16 Elm Street, London WC1X 0BJ
Tel: 020 7239 7272 Fax: 020 7837 1689
e-mail: public.enquiries@sfo.gov.uk
Website: *www.sfo.gov.uk*
Investigating and prosecuting serious and complex fraud. The Director of the SFO is accountable to Parliament through the Attorney General (E, W & NI).

Defence and external affairs

*Ministry of Defence

Old War Office Building, Whitehall,
London SW1A 2EU
Tel: 020 7218 9000 Fax: 020 7218 6460
Website: *www.mod.uk*
Defence policy and control and administration of the Armed Services (UK).

Defence agencies

Armed Forces Personnel Administration
Army Base Repair Organisation
Army Personnel Centre
Army Training and Recruiting Agency
British Forces Post Office
Defence Analytical Services Agency
Defence Aviation Repair Agency
Defence Bills Agency
Defence Communication Services Agency
Defence Dental Agency
Defence Estates
Defence Geographic and Imagery Intelligence Agency
Defence Housing Executive
Defence Intelligence and Security Centre
Defence Medical Training Organisation
Defence Procurement Agency
Defence Secondary Care Agency
Defence Storage and Distribution Agency
Defence Transport and Movements Agency
Defence Vetting Agency
Disposal Services Agency
Duke of York's Royal Military School
Hydrographic Office
Medical Supply Agency
Met Office
Ministry of Defence Police
Naval Manning Agency
Naval Recruiting and Training Agency
Pay and Personnel Agency
Queen Victoria School
RAF Personnel Management Agency

RAF Training Group
Service Children's Education
War Pensions Agency
Warship Support Agency

*Foreign & Commonwealth Office

King Charles Street, London SW1A 2AH
Tel: 020 7270 3000
Website: *www.fco.gov.uk*
The Foreign & Commonwealth Office provides, through its staff in the UK and through its diplomatic missions abroad, the means of communication between the UK Government and other governments and international governmental organisations on all matters falling within the field of international relations. It is responsible for alerting the UK Government to the implications of developments overseas; for promoting British interests overseas; for protecting British citizens abroad; for explaining British policies to, and cultivating relationships with, governments overseas; for the discharge of British responsibilities to the Overseas Territories; for entry clearance (through UK visas, with the Home Office) and for promoting British business overseas (jointly with the Department of Trade and Industry through British Trade International).

Executive agency
Wiston House Conference Centre (Wilton Park)

*Department for International Development

1 Palace Street, London SW1E 5HE
Tel: 0845 300 4100 Fax: 020 7023 0019
Website: *www.dfid.gov.uk*
Responsibility for promoting sustainable international development and the reduction of global poverty; managing the UK's programme of assistance to developing countries, and for ensuring that government policies affecting developing countries, including environment, trade, investment and agricultural policies, take account of those countries' issues.

Social affairs, the environment and culture

*Department for Culture, Media and Sport

2–4 Cockspur Street, London SW1Y 5DH
Tel: 020 7211 6200 Fax: 020 7211 6032
Website: *www.culture.gov.uk*
The Department has an overall interest in the arts, public libraries and archives, museums and galleries, tourism, sport and the built heritage in England – in Scotland, Wales and Northern Ireland these are the responsibility of the devolved administrations. The Department also has overall responsibility for the film industry and for alcohol and public entertainment licensing in England and Wales. The Department has UK-wide responsibility for broadcasting, press regulation, creative industries, public lending right, gambling and the National Lottery, censorship and video classification. However, the devolved administrations have some operational responsibilities in some of these areas.

Executive agency
Royal Parks

*Department for Education and Skills

Sanctuary Buildings, Great Smith Street,
London SW1P 3BT
Public enquiry office tel: 01928 794248
e-mail: info@dfes.gov.uk
Website: *www.dfes.gov.uk*
Overall responsibility for school, college and university education (E); student support (E & W); youth and adult training policy and programmes (E).

*Department for Environment, Food & Rural Affairs

Nobel House, 17 Smith Square, London SW1P 3JR
Tel: 020 7238 6000
Website: *www.defra.gov.uk*
Responsible for government policies on sustainable development and the environment; agriculture, horticulture, fisheries and food; rural development; the countryside; animal welfare and hunting.

Executive agencies
Central Science Laboratory
Centre for Environment, Fisheries and Aquaculture Science
Pesticides Safety Directorate
Rural Payments Agency
Veterinary Laboratories Agency
Veterinary Medicines Directorate

*Department for Transport

Great Minster House, Marsham Street,
London SW1P 4DR
Tel: 020 7944 8300
Website: *www.dft.gov.uk*
Policies for roads; local transport (E); shipping (E); railways (GB); aviation, including the Civil Aviation Authority (UK).

Executive agencies
Driver and Vehicle Licensing Agency
Driving Standards Agency
Highways Agency
Maritime and Coastguard Agency
Vehicle Certification Agency
Vehicle Inspectorate

*Department of Health
Richmond House, 79 Whitehall,
London SW1A 2NL
Tel: 020 7210 3000 (main switchboard)
Public enquiries: 020 7210 4850
e-mail: dhmail@doh.gov.uk
Website: *www.doh.gov.uk*
National Health Service; personal social services
provided by local authorities; and all other health
issues, including public health matters and the
health consequences of environmental and food
issues (E). Represents UK health policy interests in
the EU and the World Health Organisation.

Executive agencies
Medical Devices Agency
Medicines Control Agency
NHS Estates
NHS Pensions Agency
NHS Purchasing and Supplies Agency

*Home Office
50 Queen Anne's Gate, London SW1H 9AT
Tel 0870 000 1585 Fax: 020 7273 2065
e-mail: public.enquiries@homeoffice.gov.uk
Website: *www.homeoffice.gov.uk*
The Home Office works to reduce crime and the
fear of crime; combat terrorism and other threats
to national security; ensure the effective delivery
of justice; deliver effective custodial and
community sentences; reduce the availability and
abuse of dangerous drugs; regulate entry to and
settlement in the United Kingdom; and support
equal opportunities, including race relations.

Executive agencies
Forensic Science Service
HM Prison Service
Passport and Records Agency (incorporating UK
Passport Service and Criminal Records Bureau)

*Department for Work and Pensions
Richmond House, 79 Whitehall,
London SW1A 2NS
Tel: 020 7238 3000 Fax: 020 7238 0831
Website: *www.dwp.gov.uk*
Responsible for welfare and pensions;
employment and disability issues (GB).

Executive agencies
Child Support Agency
Jobcentre Plus

Regulatory bodies

Financial Services Authority
25 The North Colonnade, Canary Wharf,
London E14 5HS
Tel: 020 7676 1000 Fax: 020 7676 1099
Website: *www.fsa.gov.uk*
Regulatory body for the whole of the financial
services industry (see page 463) (UK).

National Lottery Commission
101 Wigmore Street, London W1U 1QU
Tel: 020 7016 3400 Fax: 020 7016 3464
Website: *www.natlotcomm.gov.uk*
See page 263.

Office of Gas and Electricity Markets (Ofgem)
9 Millbank, London SW1P 3GE
Tel: 020 7901 7000 Fax: 020 7901 7066
Website: *www.ofgem.gov.uk*
Ofgem regulates the gas and electricity industries.
(see page 443) (GB).

Strategic Rail Authority (SRA)
55 Victoria Street, London SW1H 0EU
Tel: 020 7654 6000 Fax: 020 7654 6010
e-mail: secretariat@sra.gov.uk
Website: *www.sra.gov.uk*
See page 318.

Office of the Rail Regulator (ORR)
1 Waterhouse Square, 138–142 Holborn,
London EC1N 2TQ
Tel: 020 7282 2000 Fax: 020 7282 2040
e-mail: rail.library@orr.gov.uk
Website: *www.rail-reg.gov.uk*
See page 318.

Office for Standards in Education (OFSTED)
Alexandra House, 33 Kingsway, London WC2B 6SE
Tel: 020 7421 6800 Fax: 020 7421 6707
Website: *www.ofsted.gov.uk*
See page 120.

Office of Telecommunications (Oftel)
50 Ludgate Hill, London EC4M 7JJ
Tel: 020 7634 8700 Fax: 020 7634 8943
Website: *www.oftel.gov.uk*
See page 242.

Office of Water Services (OFWAT)

Centre City Tower, 7 Hill Street,
Birmingham B5 4UA
Tel: 0121 625 1300 Fax: 0121 625 1400
e-mail: enquiries@ofwat.gov.uk
Website: *www.ofwat.gov.uk*
Economic regulator of the water industry in
England and Wales (see page 447).

Other offices and agencies

COI Communications

Hercules Road, London SE1 7DU
Tel: 020 7928 2345 Fax: 020 7928 5037
Website: *www.coi.gov.uk*
An agency of the Cabinet Office, COI
Communications' main responsibilities include
consultancy, procurement and project
management of marketing communications
activity on behalf of government departments,
agencies and other public sector clients (UK).

Information Commissioner's Office

Wycliffe House, Water Lane, Wilmslow,
Cheshire SK9 5AF
Tel: 01625 545745 Fax: 01625 524510
e-mail: data@wycliffe.demon.co.uk
Website: *www.informationcommissioner.gov.uk*
The *Data Protection Act 1998* sets rules for
processing personal information and applies to
some paper records as well as those held on
computers. It is the Commissioner's duty to
compile and maintain the register of data
controllers and provide facilities for members of
the public to examine the register; promote
observance of the data protection principles; and
disseminate information to the public about the
Act. The Commissioner also has the power to
produce codes of practice and is responsible for
freedom of information.

HM Land Registry

32 Lincoln's Inn Fields, London WC2A 3PH
Tel: 020 7917 8888 Fax: 020 7955 0110
e-mail: enquiries.pic@landreg.gov.uk
Website: *www.landreg.gov.uk*
A government department, executive agency and
trading fund responsible to the Lord Chancellor.
Its main purpose is to register title to land in
England and Wales and to record dealings once
the land is registered. HM Land Registry provides
access to information on over 18 million
registered property titles. It has 24 district land
registries in England and Wales, each providing

land registration services for different counties
and unitary authorities.

Office for National Statistics

1 Drummond Gate, London SW1V 2QQ
Tel: 020 7533 5888 Fax: 01633 652747
National Statistics Public Enquiry Service
Tel: 0845 601 3034
e-mail: info@statistics.gov.uk
Website: *www.statistics.gov.uk*
A government department and an executive
agency accountable to the Chancellor of the
Exchequer. The Director is the National
Statistician and Registrar General for England and
Wales. He is also the Head of the Government
Statistical Service.

Ordnance Survey

Romsey Road, Southampton SO16 4GU
Tel: 023 8079 2000 Fax: 023 8079 2615
Customer helpline tel: 08456 05 05 05
Website: *www.ordnancesurvey.co.uk*
An executive agency and government department
in its own right, which reports through the Office
of the Deputy Prime Minister, providing official
surveying, mapping and associated scientific work
covering Great Britain (GB).

Public Record Office

Ruskin Avenue, Kew, Richmond, Surrey TW9 4DU
Tel: 020 8876 3444 Fax: 020 8878 8905
e-mail: enquiry@pro.gov.uk
Website: *www.pro.gov.uk*
A government department reporting to the Lord
Chancellor. Responsible for the records of the
central government and courts of law dating from
the 11th century. Advises government departments
on the selection of records for preservation and
makes records available to the public (UK).

Northern Ireland Executive

Website: *www.northernireland.gov.uk*

Office of the First Minister and Deputy First Minister

Castle Buildings, Stormont, Belfast BT4 3SR
Tel: 028 9052 8400
Economic policy; equality; human rights;
executive secretariat; liaison with the North/South
Ministerial Council, British-Irish Council, British-
Irish Intergovernmental Conference and Civic
Forum. Liaison with the Northern Ireland Office
on excepted and reserved matters. European
affairs; international matters; liaison with the

International Fund for Ireland; the Executive Information Service; community relations; Programme for Government; public appointments policy; honours; freedom of information; victims; Nolan standards; women's issues; policy innovation; public service improvement.

Department of Agriculture and Rural Development

Dundonald House, Upper Newtownards Road, Belfast BT4 3SB
Tel: 028 9052 0100
Food; farming and environment policy; agri-food development; veterinary matters; Science Service; rural development; forestry; sea fisheries; rivers.

Executive agencies
Forest Service
Rivers Agency

Department of Culture, Arts and Leisure

3rd Floor, Interpoint, 20–24 York Street, Belfast BT15 1AQ
Tel: 028 9025 8825
Responsible for the arts, culture, sport, museums, public libraries, inland waterways, inland fisheries, language diversity, visitor amenities and matters relating to the National Lottery and the Northern Ireland Events Company. DCAL also has responsibility for two agencies and two cross-border implementation bodies which deal with inland waterways and language issues.

Executive agencies
Ordnance Survey
Public Record Office

Department of Education

Rathgael House, Balloo Road, Bangor, County Down BT19 7PR
Tel: 028 9127 9279
Control of the five education and library boards and education from nursery to secondary education; youth services; and the development of community relations within and between schools.

Department for Employment and Learning

39–49 Adelaide House, Adelaide Street, Belfast BT2 8FD
Tel: 028 9025 7777
Higher education; further education; vocational training; employment services; employment law and labour relations; teacher training and teacher education; student support and postgraduate awards; training grants.

Department of Enterprise, Trade and Investment

Netherleigh House, Massey Avenue, Belfast BT4 2JP
Tel: 028 9052 9900
Economic policy development, energy, tourism, mineral development, health and safety at work, Companies Registry, Insolvency Service, consumer affairs, labour market and economic statistics services. DETI also has a role in ensuring the provision of the infrastructure for modern economy.

Executive agencies
General Consumer Council for Northern Ireland
Health and Safety Executive for Northern Ireland
Invest NI
Northern Ireland Tourist Board

Department of the Environment

Clarence Court, 10–18 Adelaide Street, Belfast BT2 8GB
Tel: 028 9054 0540
Most of the Department's functions are carried out by executive agencies. These include: planning; protection and conservation of the natural and built environment; and driver and vehicle testing and licensing. Core departmental functions include: the improvement and promotion of road safety and supporting a system of local government which meets the needs of citizens and taxpayers.

Executive agencies
Driver and Vehicle Licensing (Northern Ireland)
Driver and Vehicle Testing Agency
Environment and Heritage Service
Planning Service

Department of Finance and Personnel

Rathgael House, Balloo Road, Bangor, County Down BT19 7NA
Tel: 028 9127 9657
Control of public expenditure; personnel management of the Northern Ireland Civil Service; provision of central services and advice.

Executive agencies
Business Development Service
Construction Service
Government Purchasing Agency
Land Registers of Northern Ireland

Northern Ireland Statistics and Research Agency
Office of Law Reform
Rates Collection Agency
Valuation and Lands Agency

Department of Health, Social Services and Public Safety

Castle Buildings, Stormont, Belfast BT4 3SJ
Tel: 028 9052 0500
Health and personal social services; public health and public safety.

Executive agency

Health Estates Agency

Department for Regional Development

Clarence Court, 10–18 Adelaide Street,
Belfast BT2 8GB
Tel: 028 9054 0540
Main functions include: strategic planning; transport strategy; transport policy and support, including rail and bus services, ports and airports policy; provision and maintenance of roads; and water and sewerage services.

Executive agencies

Roads Service
Water Service

Department for Social Development

Churchill House, Victoria Square,
Belfast BT1 4SD
Tel: 028 9056 9100 Fax: 028 9056 9240
Departmental functions include: urban regeneration; voluntary and community sector; housing; social policy and legislation; child support; state, occupational and personal pensions; social security policy and legislation.

Executive agencies

Northern Ireland Child Support Agency
Northern Ireland Social Security Agency

Scottish Executive

Scottish Executive

St Andrew's House, Edinburgh EH1 3DG
Tel: 0131 556 8400 Fax: 0131 244 8240 (for all departments)
e-mail: ceu@scotland.gov.uk
Website: *www.scotland.gov.uk*
The Scottish ministers and Scottish Executive are responsible in Scotland for a wide range of

statutory functions. These are administered by six main departments (see below). Along with Corporate Services, Finance and Central Services Department, Legal & Parliamentary Services, and the Crown Office and Procurator Fiscal Service, these departments are collectively known as the Scottish Executive. In addition, there are a number of other Scottish departments for which Scottish ministers have some degree of responsibility: the department of the Registrar General for Scotland (the General Register Office), the National Archives of Scotland and the department of the Registers of Scotland. Other government departments with significant Scottish responsibilities have offices in Scotland and work closely with the Scottish Executive.

Scottish Executive Environment and Rural Affairs Department

Pentland House, 47 Robb's Loan, Edinburgh EH14 1TY
Agriculture and food: plant health, animal health and welfare; land use and forestry; CAP subsidies and commodities. Co-ordination of the Executive's policy on the promotion of rural development and overall responsibility for land reform. Environment, including environmental protection, nature conservation and the countryside; water and sewerage services; waste management, sustainable development, biodiversity, and climate change. Fisheries and aquaculture; control of sea fishing under the CFP; protection of the marine environment. Agricultural and biological research; support of the agricultural and biological science base and funding of related research.

Executive agencies

Fisheries Research Service
Scottish Agricultural Science Agency
Scottish Fisheries Protection Agency

Scottish Executive Education Department

Victoria Quay, Edinburgh EH6 6QQ
Administration of public education; science and technology; youth and community services; the arts; libraries; museums; galleries; Gaelic; broadcasting, sport and tourism. Protection and presentation to the public of historic buildings and ancient monuments.

Executive agencies

Historic Scotland
Scottish Public Pensions Agency
Student Awards Agency for Scotland

Scottish Executive Development Department

Victoria Quay, Edinburgh EH6 6QQ
Housing and area regeneration, social justice
(including equality, voluntary and social inclusion
issues); transport and local roads, National Roads
Directorate; land use planning; building control.

Executive agency
Communities Scotland

Scottish Executive Enterprise and Lifelong Learning Department

Meridian Court, Cadogan Street, Glasgow G2 7AB
and Europa Building, 450 Argyle Street, Glasgow
G2 8LG
Tel: 0141 242 5703 Fax: 0141 242 5477
e-mail: ps/elld@scotland.gov.uk
Industrial and economic development:
responsibility for selective financial and regional
development grant assistance to industry; for the
promotion of industrial development and for
matters relating to energy policy; urban
regeneration and training policy. The Department
is also responsible for policy in relation to Scottish
Enterprise and Highlands and Islands Enterprise.
Lifelong learning: further and higher education;
student support; youth and adult training;
transitions to work; development of the Scottish
University for Industry (learndirect scotland),
Modern Apprenticeships, Careers Scotland; science.

Scottish Executive Health Department

St Andrew's House, Regent Road, Edinburgh
EH1 3DG
Executive leadership of NHSScotland and the
development and implementation of health and
community care policy, in particular: improving,
protecting and monitoring the health of the
people of Scotland, implementing policies which
address health inequalities, prevent disease,
prolong life and promote and protect health;
developing and delivering modern primary care
and community care services; providing hospital
and specialist services; encouraging collaboration
and joint working between health and other
partner organisations; and promoting and
monitoring consistent standards of performance
throughout NHSScotland.

Scottish Executive Justice Department

St Andrew's House, Regent Road, Edinburgh
EH1 3XD
Central administration of law and order
(including police service, criminal justice and
licensing, access to justice and legal aid, the
Scottish Court Service and the Scottish Prison
Service); civil law, fire, home defence and civil
emergency services, judicial appointments and the
European Convention on Human Rights.

Executive agencies
Office of the Accountant in Bankruptcy
Registers of Scotland
Scottish Court Service
Scottish Prison Service

Corporate Services

S1/5 Saughton House, Broomhouse Drive,
Edinburgh EH11 3XD
e-mail: ps/cs/peo@scotland.gov.uk
Human resources, including personnel policy,
propriety, recruitment, staff appraisal and
interchange, pay, employee relations, training and
development, equal opportunities and welfare; estate
management, accommodation services, internal
communications, IT facilities and security matters.

Finance and Central Services Department

St Andrew's House, Edinburgh EH1 3DG
Matters relating to Cabinet business; local
government; Europe and external relations
(including relations with Whitehall); finance;
analytical services; media and communications;
and public service delivery.

Legal & Parliamentary Services

25 Chambers Street, Edinburgh EH1 1LA
Policy on constitutional issues, devolution
settlement and electoral matters. The Scottish
Parliament's powers and procedures, co-
ordination of the Scottish Executive's legislative
programme, liaison with the Scottish
Parliamentary Ombudsman, freedom of
information policy and legislation. Provision of
legal advice and services for the Scottish Executive
through the Office of the Solicitor to the Scottish
Executive. Also responsible for drafting Bills to be
put before Parliament by the Executive and
handling associated work.

Executive agency
National Archives of Scotland

The Crown Office and Procurator Fiscal Service

25 Chambers Street, Edinburgh EH1 1LA
Tel: 0131 226 2626 Fax: 0131 226 6910
Website: *www.crownoffice.gov.uk*

The Crown Office and Procurator Fiscal Service provides Scotland's independent public prosecution and deaths investigation service. Although it is a Department of the Scottish Executive, the independent position of the Lord Advocate as head of the systems of criminal prosecution and investigation of deaths in Scotland is protected by the *Scotland Act 1998*.

National Assembly for Wales/Welsh Assembly Government

National Assembly for Wales
Cynulliad Cenedlaethol Cymru

Cathays Park, Cardiff CF10 3NQ and Cardiff Bay, Cardiff CF99 1NA
Tel: 029 2082 5111
Website: *www.wales.gov.uk*
www.cymru.gov.uk

The Welsh Assembly Government (Llywodraeth Cynulliad Cymru) is responsible for many aspects of Welsh affairs, including agriculture, forestry and fisheries; education; health and personal social services; local government; Welsh language and culture, including the arts, museums and libraries. Also responsible for housing; water and sewerage; environmental protection; the countryside and nature conservation; sport; land use, including town and country planning; transport; tourism; training and enterprise; economic development, business support and regional selective assistance to industry. The Assembly Government is also responsible for over 50 public bodies which discharge functions in these areas in Wales.

Executive Agencies
Cadw: Welsh Historic Monuments
Wales European Funding Office

Appendix B Significant dates in UK history

55 and 54 BC: Julius Caesar's expeditions to Britain

AD 43: Roman conquest begins under Claudius

122–38: Hadrian's Wall built

c.409: Roman army withdraws from Britain

450s onwards: foundation of the Anglo-Saxon kingdoms

597: arrival of St Augustine to preach Christianity to the Anglo-Saxons

664: Synod of Whitby opts for Roman Catholic rather than Celtic church

789–95: first Viking raids

832–60: Scots and Picts merge under Kenneth Macalpin to form what is to become the kingdom of Scotland

860s: Danes overrun East Anglia, Northumbria and eastern Mercia

871–99: reign of Alfred the Great in Wessex

1066: William the Conqueror defeats Harold Godwinson at Hastings and takes the throne

1086: *Domesday Book* completed: a survey of English landholdings undertaken on the orders of William I

1215: King John signs Magna Carta to protect feudal rights against royal abuse

13th century: first Oxford and Cambridge colleges founded

1301: Edward of Caernarvon (later Edward II) created Prince of Wales

1314: Battle of Bannockburn ensures survival of separate Scottish kingdom

1337: Hundred Years War between England and France begins

1348–49: Black Death (bubonic plague) wipes out a third of England's population

1381: Peasants' Revolt in England, the most significant popular rebellion in English history

c.1387–c.1394: Geoffrey Chaucer writes *The Canterbury Tales*

1400–c.1406: Owain Glyndŵr (Owen Glendower) leads the last major Welsh revolt against English rule

1411: St Andrews University founded, the first university in Scotland

1455–87: Wars of the Roses between Yorkists and Lancastrians

1477: first book to be printed in England, by William Caxton

1534–40: English Reformation; Henry VIII breaks with the Papacy

1536–42: Acts of Union integrate England and Wales administratively and legally and give Wales representation in Parliament

1547–53: Protestantism becomes official religion in England under Edward VI

1553–58: Catholic reaction under Mary I

1558: loss of Calais, last English possession in France

1588: defeat of Spanish Armada

1558–1603: reign of Elizabeth I; moderate Protestantism established

c.1590–c.1613: plays of Shakespeare written

1603: union of the crowns of Scotland and England under James VI of Scotland

1642–51: civil wars between King and Parliament

1649: execution of Charles I

1653–58: Oliver Cromwell rules as Lord Protector

1660: monarchy restored under Charles II

1660: founding of the Royal Society for the Promotion of Natural Knowledge

1663: John Milton finishes *Paradise Lost*

1665: the Great Plague, the last major epidemic of plague in England

1666: the Great Fire of London

1686: Isaac Newton sets out his laws of motion and the idea of universal gravitation

1688: Glorious Revolution; accession of William and Mary

1707: Acts of Union unite the English and Scottish Parliaments

1721–42: Robert Walpole, first British Prime Minister

1745–46: Bonnie Prince Charlie's failed attempt to retake the British throne for the Stuarts

c.1760s–c.1830s: Industrial Revolution

1761: opening of the Bridgewater Canal ushers in Canal Age

1775–83: American War of Independence leads to loss of the Thirteen Colonies

1801: Act of Union unites Great Britain and Ireland

1805: Battle of Trafalgar, the decisive naval battle of the Napoleonic Wars

1815: Battle of Waterloo, the final defeat of Napoleon

1825: opening of the Stockton and Darlington Railway, the world's first passenger railway

1829: Catholic emancipation

1832: first Reform Act extends the franchise (increasing the number of those entitled to vote by about 50 per cent)

1833: abolition of slavery in the British Empire (the slave *trade* having been abolished in 1807)

1836–70: Charles Dickens writes his novels

1837–1901: reign of Queen Victoria

1859: Charles Darwin publishes *On the Origin of Species by Means of Natural Selection*

1868: founding of the Trades Union Congress (TUC)

1907: Henry Royce and C S Rolls build and sell their first Rolls-Royce (the Silver Ghost)

1910–36: during the reign of George V, the British Empire reaches its territorial zenith

1914–18: First World War

1918: the vote given to women over 30

1921: Anglo-Irish Treaty establishes the Irish Free State; Northern Ireland remains part of the United Kingdom

1926: John Logie Baird gives the first practical demonstration of television

1928: voting age for women reduced to 21, on equal terms with men

1928: Alexander Fleming discovers penicillin

1936: Jarrow Crusade, the most famous of the hunger marches in the 1930s

1939–45: Second World War

1943: Max Newman, Donald Michie, Tommy Flowers and Alan Turing build the first electronic computer, Colossus I, which was used for breaking enemy communications codes in the Second World War

1947: independence for India and Pakistan: Britain begins to dismantle its imperial structure

1948: the National Health Service comes into operation, offering free medical care to the whole population

1952: accession of Elizabeth II

1953: Francis Crick and his colleague James Watson of the United States discover the structure of DNA

1965: first commercial natural gas discovery in the North Sea

1969: first notable discovery of offshore oil in the North Sea

1973: the UK enters the European Community (now the European Union)

1979–90: Margaret Thatcher is the UK's first woman Prime Minister

1994: Channel Tunnel opened to rail traffic

1999: Scottish Parliament, National Assembly for Wales and Northern Ireland Assembly assume their devolved powers

2001: for the first time, the Labour Party wins a General Election with sufficient MPs to govern for a second full five-year period

2002: the Queen celebrates her Golden Jubilee

Appendix C Obituaries

Her Majesty Queen Elizabeth The Queen Mother, Lady of the Order of the Garter, Lady of the Order of the Thistle, CI, GCVO, GBE

Born 4 August 1900, the Hon. Elizabeth Angela Marguerite Bowes-Lyon, 9th child of Claude George Bowes-Lyon, Lord Glamis and his wife, née Cecilia Nina Cavendish-Bentinck. Married in April 1923 to HRH Prince Albert Frederick Arthur George, Duke of York, 2nd son of King George V and Queen Mary. On the abdication of King Edward VIII 1936 they became King George VI and Queen Elizabeth and Emperor and Empress of India. Their two daughters, Princess Elizabeth Alexandra Mary (now Queen Elizabeth II) and Princess Margaret Rose (see below), were born in 1926 and 1930.

During 1939–45 the King and Queen won admiration for their resolve and inspiration to their people in war. After the King's death in February 1952 and the accession of her elder daughter, Queen Elizabeth became known as Queen Elizabeth The Queen Mother. She was Chancellor of London University (1955–80), Lord Warden of the Cinque Ports and Constable of Dover Castle (1978–2002), Grand Master of the Royal Victorian Order, Colonel-in-Chief of 13 British and Commonwealth regiments and Commandant-in-Chief of Women in the Royal Navy and RAF. She held over 300 patronages, which included support for the arts and also reflected her interest in gardening and country pursuits. From 1950 she established herself as one of the leading owners in National Hunt racing. Her public life, with its wide range of official engagements, and overseas tours, audiences, and investitures, continued almost until her death.

Died 30 March 2002

Her Royal Highness Princess Margaret, Countess of Snowdon, CI, GCVO

Born 21 August 1930, 2nd daughter of the Duke and Duchess of York, later King George VI and Queen Elizabeth (see above). Married 1960 Antony Armstrong-Jones, 1st Earl of Snowdon. Their two children, David, Viscount Linley and Lady Sarah Armstrong-Jones (now Lady Sarah Chatto), were born in 1961 and 1964. Divorced

1978. She was president of the National Society for the Prevention of Cruelty to Children, the Royal National Institute for the Blind and the Royal Ballet. Her other patronages reflected her concern for children's welfare, nursing and the arts.

Died 9 February 2002

Stuart Adamson
Rock singer
Born 1958, died December 2001

Barbara Ansell, CBE
Pioneer of paediatric rheumatology
Born 1923, died September 2001

The Hon. David Astor, CH
Editor of the *Observer*, 1948–75
Born 1912, died December 2001

Field Marshal Sir Nigel Bagnall, GCB, CVO, MC and Bar
Chief of the General Staff, 1985–88
Born 1927, died April 2002

Professor Theo Barker
Authority on history of modern transport
Born 1923, died November 2001

Lord Bauer, FBA (Peter Thomas)
Economist
Born 1915, died May 2002

Roy Boulting
Film producer and director
Born 1913, died November 2001

Michael Bryant, CBE
Actor
Born 1928, died April 2002

Professor Sir Colin Buchanan, CBE
Architect and town planner
Born 1907, died December 2001

Richard Buckle, CBE
Critic and author
Born 1916, died October 2001

Earl of Carnarvon, KCVO, KBE (Henry George Reginald Molyneux Herbert; 7th earl)
Racing manager to The Queen
Born 1924, died September 2001

Field Marshal Lord Carver, GCB, CBE, DSO and Bar, MC (Michael)
Chief of the Defence Staff, 1973–76
Born 1915, died December 2001

Baroness Castle of Blackburn (Barbara Anne)
Labour politician and former Cabinet minister
Born 1910, died May 2002

Wallace John Challens, CBE
Nuclear scientist
Born 1915, died March 2002

Edward Thomas (Ted) Chapman, VC, BEM
Second World War hero
Born 1920, died February 2002

Helen Cherry (Mrs Trevor Howard)
Actress
Born 1915, died September 2001

Anastasios Christodoulou, CBE
Founding Secretary of the Open University
Born 1932, died May 2002

Rt Rev. Alan Clark
Roman Catholic Bishop of East Anglia, 1976–94
Born 1919, died July 2002

Professor Desmond Clark, CBE, FBA
Archaeologist
Born 1916, died February 2002

Charlotte Coleman
Actress
Born 1968, died November 2001

Pat Coombs
Comedy actress
Born 1926, died May 2002

Sir Frank Cooper, GCB, CMG
Civil servant
Born 1922, died January 2002

Joseph Cooper, OBE
Pianist and broadcaster
Born 1912, died August 2001

Group Captain John Cunningham, CBE, DSO and two Bars, DFC and Bar, AE
Nightfighter ace and test pilot
Born 1917, died July 2002

Professor Albinia de la Mare, OBE
Palaeographer
Born 1932, died January 2002

Maurice Denham, OBE
Actor
Born 1909, died July 2002

Kay Dick
Novelist and critic
Born 1915, died October 2001

Professor Arthur Geoffrey Dickens, CMG, FBA
Historian
Born 1910, died July 2001

Jaroslav Drobny
Tennis player; men's Wimbledon champion 1954
Born 1921, died September 2001

Dame Ann Ebsworth, DBE
High Court judge
Born 1937, died April 2002

John Entwistle
Bass guitarist with The Who
Born 1944, died June 2002

Professor John Erickson, FBA
Military historian
Born 1929, died February 2002

Professor Martin Esslin, OBE
Writer and head of BBC Radio Drama, 1963–77
Born 1918, died February 2002

Huw Evans, CB
Economist
Born 1941, died February 2002

Moss Evans
General Secretary, Transport and General Workers' Union, 1978–85
Born 1925, died January 2002

Professor Sir Raymond Firth, FBA
Anthropologist
Born 1901, died February 2002

Bert Foord
Weather forecaster
Born 1930, died July 2001

Barry Foster
Actor
Born 1927, died February 2002

Patrick Fyffe
Comedian ('Dame Hilda Bracket')
Born 1942, died May 2002

Philip Gaskell
Bibliographer and jazz clarinettist
Born 1926, died July 2001

Sir Arthur Gilbert
Fine art collector
Born 1913, died September 2001

Max Glatt
Specialist in addiction medicine
Born 1912, died May 2002

Barbara Goalen
Fashion supermodel
Born 1921, died June 2002

Sir Ernst Gombrich, OM, CBE, FBA
Art historian
Born 1909, died November 2001

Professor George Patrick Goold
Editor of Loeb Classical Library, 1973–99
Born 1922, died December 2001

Alf Gover
Surrey and England cricketer
Born 1908, died October 2001

John Grigg
Writer and historian
Born 1924, died December 2001

Rachel Gurney
Actress
Born 1920, died November 2001

Lord Hailsham of St Marylebone, KG, CH, QC, FRS
(Quintin McGarel Hogg)
Lord Chancellor, 1970–74 and 1979–87
Born 1907, died October 2001

Professor Edward Hall, CBE, FBA
Archaeological scientist and inventor
Born 1924, died August 2001

Ian Hamilton
Poet, critic, biographer
Born 1938, died December 2001

Lord Hamlyn, CBE (Paul Bertrand)
Publisher and philanthropist
Born 1926, died August 2001

George Harrison, MBE
Guitarist, composer, former Beatle
Born 1943, died November 2001

Sir Nigel Hawthorne, CBE
Actor
Born 1929, died December 2001

Major Dick Hern, CVO, CBE
Horseracing trainer
Born 1921, died May 2002

Ben Hollioake
Surrey and England cricketer
Born 1977, died March 2002

Sir Fred Hoyle, FRS
Astronomer
Born 1915, died 20 August 2001

Stratford Johns
Actor
Born 1925, died January 2002

Lord Keith of Kinkel, GBE (Henry Shanks Keith)
Law lord
Born 1922, died June 2002

Lady Khama (née Ruth Williams)
Widow of Sir Seretse Khama, President of
Botswana
Born 1923, died May 2002

Professor Edmund King
Educationalist
Born 1914, died February 2002

Jimmy Knapp
Secretary of Rail, Maritime and Transport Union,
1990–2001
Born 1940, died August 2001

Peter Laslett, CBE
Historian
Born 1915, died November 2001

Erna Low
Tour operator
Born 1909, died February 2002

Leo McKern
Actor
Born 1920, died July 2002

George Mann, CBE, DSO, MC
Middlesex and England cricketer
Born 1917, died August 2001

Tony Miles
Historian and chess player
Born 1955, died November 2001

Spike Milligan (Hon. KBE)
Comedian and writer
Born 1918, died February 2002

César Milstein
Immunologist
Born 1926, died March 2002

Marian Montgomery
Jazz and cabaret singer
Born 1934, died July 2002

Brian Moore
Football commentator
Born 1932, died September 2001

Dudley Moore, CBE
Comic, actor, composer and musician
Born 1935, died March 2002

Katharine Moore
Writer, chronicler of Victorian society
Born 1898, died November 2001

Peggy Mount, OBE
Actress; 'the nation's favourite dragon'
Born 1916, died November 2001

Lord Moyola (James Dawson Chichester-Clark)
Prime Minister of Northern Ireland, 1969–71
Born 1923, died May 2002

Duke of Norfolk, KG, GCVO, CB, CBE, MC (Miles
Francis Stapleton Fitzalan-Howard; 17th duke)
Major-General and premier duke and Earl
Marshal of England
Born 1915, died June 2002

Professor Sir Dimitri Obolensky
Historian
Born 1918, died January 2002

Sir Peter Parker, KBE, LVO
Chairman of British Rail, 1976–83
Born 1924, died April 2002

Max Perutz, OM, CH, FRS
Scientist
Born 1914, died February 2002

Professor Sir John Plumb
Historian
Born 1911, died October 2001

Professor Roy Porter
Historian
Born 1946, died March 2002

Lady Violet Powell
Author
Born 1912, died January 2002

Diane Pretty
Euthanasia campaigner
Born 1958, died May 2002

Bryan Pringle
Actor
Born 1935, died May 2002

Professor (William) Brian Reddaway, CBE, FBA
Professor of Political Economy, Cambridge
Born 1913, died July 2002

Sir Gordon Reece
Public relations consultant
Born 1929, died September 2001

Sir John Saunders, CBE, DSO, MC
Banker
Born 1917, died July 2002

Jack Scott
Test pilot
Born 1908, died April 2002

Richard Seifert
Architect
Born 1910, died October 2001

Anthony Shaffer
Playwright and screenwriter
Born 1926, died November 2001

Sir Peter Shepheard, CBE
Architect and landscape gardener
Born 1913, died April 2002

Dame Sheila Sherlock, DBE
Clinical scientist
Born 1918, died December 2001

Lord Shore of Stepney (Peter David)
Former Labour MP and Cabinet minister
Born 1924, died September 2001

Sir Reo Stakis
Hotelier
Born 1913, died August 2001

John Thaw, CBE
Actor; ('Inspector Morse')
Born 1942, died February 2002

Barry Took
Scriptwriter, comedian and broadcaster
Born 1928, died March 2002

Dame Dorothy Tutin, DBE
Actress
Born 1931, died August 2001

Professor William Thomas Tutte, FRS
Mathematician and codebreaker
Born 1917, died May 2002

Robert Kenneth Tyrrell (Ken)
Formula 1 team owner
Born 1924, died August 2001

Stanley Unwin
Comedian, 'master of glottal-stopped
gobbledegookian'
Born 1911, died January 2002

Norman Vaughan
Comedian
Born 1927, died May 2002

Elisabeth Vellacott
Painter
Born 1905, died May 2002

Rob (Robert Ramsay Campbell) **Walker**
Racing driver and Formula 1 team manager
Born 1917, died April 2002

**General Sir Walter Walker, KCB, CBE, DSO and
2 Bars**
Former Gurkha commander and director of
operations in Borneo
Born 1911, died August 2001

Professor Patrick Wall
Neuroscientist
Born 1925, died August 2001

Sidney Weighell
General Secretary, National Union of Railwaymen,
1975–83
Born 1922, died February 2002

Lord Weinstock (Arnold)
Industrialist and Managing Director of GEC,
1963–96
Born 1924, died July 2002

Garry (Garfield Howard) Weston
Food manufacturer and philanthropist
Born 1927, died February 2002

Sir Gerald Whent, CBE
Founder of Vodafone
Born 1927, died May 2002

Mary Whitehouse
Television campaigner
Born 1910, died November 2001

Harry Wingfield
Illustrator
Born 1910, died March 2002

Sir Walter Winterbottom
England football manager, 1946–62
Born 1913, died February 2002

Audrey Withers
Editor of *Vogue*, 1940–60
Born 1905, died October 2001

Kenneth Wolstenholme, DFC and Bar
Sports commentator
Born 1920, died March 2002

Irene Worth (Hon. CBE)
Actress
Born 1916, died March 2002

Lord Young of Dartington (Michael)
Sociologist
Born 1915, died January 2002

Appendix D Principal abbreviations

ACAS Advisory, Conciliation and Arbitration Service

AIDS Acquired Immune Deficiency Syndrome

AONB Area of Outstanding Natural Beauty

APACS Association for Payment Clearing Services

ASA Advertising Standards Authority

ASEM Asia-Europe Meeting

ASSI Area of Special Scientific Interest

ATMs Automated teller machines

BAFTA British Academy of Film and Television Arts

BBC British Broadcasting Corporation

BBSRC Biotechnology and Biological Sciences Research Council

BCC British Chambers of Commerce

BCS British Crime Survey

bfi British Film Institute

BL British Library

BNFL British Nuclear Fuels

BOA British Olympic Association

BSC Broadcasting Standards Commission

BSE Bovine spongiform encephalopathy

BTI British Trade International

CA Countryside Agency

CAA Civil Aviation Authority

CAF Charities Aid Foundation

CAP Common Agricultural Policy

CBI Confederation of British Industry

CCGT Combined cycle gas turbine

CCL Climate change levy

CCLRC Council for the Central Laboratory of the Research Councils

CCPR Central Council for Physical Recreation

CCW Countryside Council for Wales

CFCs Chlorofluorocarbons

CFP Common Fisheries Policy

CFSP Common Foreign and Security Policy

CGT Capital gains tax

CHAI Commission for Healthcare Audit and Inspection

CHD Coronary heart disease

CHP Combined heat and power

CITES Convention on International Trade in Endangered Species of Wild Fauna and Flora

CO Carbon monoxide

CO$_2$ Carbon dioxide

CoVEs Centres of Vocational Excellence

CPS Crown Prosecution Service

CRE Commission for Racial Equality

CSA Child Support Agency

DARD Department of Agriculture and Rural Development (Northern Ireland)

DCAL Department of Culture, Arts and Leisure (Northern Ireland)

DCMS Department for Culture, Media and Sport

DEFRA Department for Environment, Food & Rural Affairs

DEL Department for Employment and Learning (Northern Ireland)

DETI Department of Enterprise, Trade and Investment (Northern Ireland)

DfES Department for Education and Skills

DFID Department for International Development

DfT Department for Transport

DH Department of Health

DMO Debt Management Office

DNA Deoxyribonucleic acid

DOE Department of the Environment (Northern Ireland)

DPP Director of Public Prosecutions

DRC Disability Rights Commission

DRD Department for Regional Development (Northern Ireland)

DSD Department for Social Development (Northern Ireland)

DTI Department of Trade and Industry

DWP Department for Work and Pensions

EC European Community

ECGD Export Credits Guarantee Department

EEA European Economic Area

EEBPP Energy Efficiency Best Practice Programme

EHS Environment and Heritage Service (Northern Ireland)

ELWa Education and Learning Wales

EMU Economic and monetary union

EOC Equal Opportunities Commission

EP English Partnerships

EPSRC Engineering and Physical Sciences Research Council

ERDF European Regional Development Fund

ERDP England Rural Development Programme

ESA Environmentally sensitive area; European Space Agency

ESRC Economic and Social Research Council

EU European Union

EUROPOL European Police Office

FA Football Association

FCO Foreign & Commonwealth Office

FSA Financial Services Authority; Food Standards Agency

G7 Group of seven leading industrial countries

G8 Group of eight leading industrial countries (the G7 members plus Russia)

GCE General Certificate of Education

GCSE General Certificate of Secondary Education

GDP Gross domestic product

GLA Greater London Authority

GM Genetically modified

GNVQ General National Vocational Qualification

GOs Government Offices (for the Regions)

GP General practitioner

GVA Gross value added

HIMPs Health Improvement and Modernisation Plans

HIV Human Immuno-deficiency Virus

HSC Health and Safety Commission

HSE Health and Safety Executive

ICT Information and communications technology

IEA International Energy Agency

IiP Investors in People

ILO International Labour Organisation

IMF International Monetary Fund

IoD Institute of Directors

IPC Integrated Pollution Control

IPPC Integrated Pollution Prevention and Control

ISA Individual Savings Account

ISO International Organisation for Standardisation

ISP Internet Service Provider

IT Information technology

ITC Independent Television Commission

JNCC Joint Nature Conservation Committee

JSA Jobseeker's Allowance

km/h Kilometres per hour

kW Kilowatt

LEA Local education authority

LEC Local enterprise company

LFS Labour Force Survey

LIFFE London International Financial Futures and Options Exchange

LSC Learning and Skills Council

LTPs Local Transport Plans

LUL London Underground Ltd

m (mm, km) Metre (millimetre, kilometre)

MAs Modern Apprenticeships

MEP Member of the European Parliament

Ml Megalitre

MMR Measles, mumps and rubella

MoD Ministry of Defence

MP Member of Parliament

mph Miles per hour

MRC Medical Research Council

MSP Member of the Scottish Parliament

MW Megawatt

NATO North Atlantic Treaty Organisation

NATS National Air Traffic Services Ltd

NAW National Assembly for Wales

NCIS National Criminal Intelligence Service

NCSC National Care Standards Commission

NCSL National College for School Leadership

NDPBs Non-departmental public bodies

NERC Natural Environment Research Council

NETA New electricity trading arrangements

NFFO Non-fossil fuel obligation

NGLs Natural gas liquids

NHS National Health Service

NI Northern Ireland; National Insurance

NICE National Institute for Clinical Excellence

NICS Northern Ireland Civil Service

NIE Northern Ireland Electricity

NIHE Northern Ireland Housing Executive

NITHC Northern Ireland Transport Holding Company

NMW National minimum wage

NO$_x$ Oxides of nitrogen

NPQH National Professional Qualification for Headship

NQ National Qualification

NRU Neighbourhood Renewal Unit

NSF National Service Framework

NVQ National Vocational Qualification

NVZ Nitrate Vulnerable Zone

ODPM Office of the Deputy Prime Minister

OECD Organisation for Economic Co-operation and Development

OEICs Open-ended investment companies

OFSTED Office for Standards in Education

ONS Office for National Statistics

ORR Office of the Rail Regulator

OSCE Organisation for Security and Co-operation in Europe

OSPAR Oslo and Paris Convention on the Protection of the Marine Environment of the North East Atlantic

OST Office of Science and Technology

OTs Overseas Territories

OU Open University

PEP Personal Equity Plan

PFI Private finance initiative

PGCE Post Graduate Certificate in Education

plc Public limited company

PM$_{10}$ Particulate matter

PPARC Particle Physics and Astronomy Research Council

PPC Pollution Prevention and Control

PPG Planning Policy Guidance

PPP Public-private partnership

PSA Public Service Agreement

PSNI Police Service of Northern Ireland

R&D Research and development

R&T Research and technology

RAF Royal Air Force

RCUK Research Councils UK

RDAs Regional Development Agencies

RDPs Rural Development Programmes

RECs Regional electricity companies

RPG Regional Planning Guidance

RPI Retail Prices Index

RPIX Retail Prices Index (*ex*cluding mortgage interest payments)

RSL Registered social landlord

RSPB Royal Society for the Protection of Birds

SAC Scottish Agricultural College; Special Area of Conservation

SBS Small Business Service

SE Scottish Executive

SEERAD Scottish Executive Environment and Rural Affairs Department

SEN Special educational needs

SEPA Scottish Environment Protection Agency

SERPS State earnings-related pension scheme

SET Science, engineering and technology

SEU Social Exclusion Unit

SIC Standard Industrial Classification

SIP Social Inclusion Partnership

SMEs Small and medium-sized enterprises

SNH Scottish Natural Heritage

SO$_2$ Sulphur dioxide

sq km Square kilometre

SRA Strategic Rail Authority

SSSI Site of Special Scientific Interest

StHAs Strategic Health Authorities

SVQ Scottish Vocational Qualification

TA Territorial Army

TAC Total allowable catch

TOCs Train Operating Companies

TUC Trades Union Congress

UDG Urban Development Grant

UDP Unitary development plan

UK United Kingdom of Great Britain and Northern Ireland

UKCS United Kingdom Continental Shelf

UKSI United Kingdom Sports Institute

UN United Nations

URCs Urban Regeneration Companies

US United States

VAT Value added tax

VED Vehicle excise duty

VOCs Volatile organic compounds

WDA Welsh Development Agency

WFTC Working Families' Tax Credit

WTO World Trade Organisation

Appendix E Public holidays in 2003

Wednesday 1 January	New Year's Day	UK
Thursday 2 January	Bank Holiday	Scotland only
Monday 17 March	St Patrick's Day	Northern Ireland only
Friday 18 April	Good Friday	UK
Monday 21 April	Easter Monday	England, Wales and Northern Ireland
Monday 5 May	Early May Bank Holiday	UK
Monday 26 May	Spring Bank Holiday	UK
Monday 14 July	Orangemen's Day	Northern Ireland only
Monday 4 August	Summer Bank Holiday	Scotland only
Monday 25 August	Summer Bank Holiday	England, Wales and Northern Ireland
Thursday 25 December	Christmas Day	UK
Friday 26 December	Boxing Day	UK

Note: In addition, there are various traditional local holidays in Scotland which are determined by the local authorities there.

Index

F